Valuation Using Financial Statements

Second Edition

GREGORY A. SOMMERS
Southern Methodist University

PETER D. EASTON
University of Notre Dame

PHILIP D. DRAKE
Arizona State University

Cambridge
BUSINESS PUBLISHERS

Dedication

To my wife Susan, and my children Christian, Peter, and Philip
—GAS
To my daughters, Joanne and Stacey
—PDE
To my wife Laurna, and our children Alex, Mitchell, Elaine, Casey, and Andy
—PDD

VALUATION USING FINANCIAL STATEMENTS, Second Edition, by Gregory A. Sommers, Peter D. Easton, and Philip D. Drake

ISBN: 978-1-61853-363-0

Bookstores & Faculty: to order this book, contact the company via email **customerservice@cambridgepub.com** or call 800-619-6473.

Retail Customers & Students: to order this book, please visit the book's website and order directly online.

For permission to use material from this text, contact the company via email **permissions@cambridgepub.com**.

Printed in the United States of America.
10 9 8 7 6 5 4 3 2 1

ABOUT THE AUTHORS

GREGORY A. SOMMERS is Director of the Master of Science in Accounting program and Professor of Practice in Accounting in the Edwin L. Cox School of Business at Southern Methodist University. He holds an undergraduate degree in accounting from Fresno Pacific University and a PhD in Accounting and Management Information Systems from The Ohio State University. Professor Sommers is a Certified Public Accountant who practiced in and continues to be licensed in California. Professor Sommers' research focuses on market-based empirical studies of the relations between currently available accounting data, expectations of future accounting data, expected cost of capital and valuation. His research has been published in *Journal of Accounting Research*, *Journal of Business, Finance, and Accounting*, and *Journal of Applied Corporate Finance*. Professor Sommers serves on the editorial board of *Review of Accounting Studies*. Professor Sommers teaches financial accounting in the undergraduate and graduate programs as well as in executive education at Southern Methodist University. He has taught financial statement analysis and valuation for over fifteen years at the graduate level. In addition to being an author on another textbook in Financial Statement Analysis, his teaching materials were previously utilized as resources for another author's textbook in this area. Professor Sommers' teaching has earned him numerous awards including Outstanding MBA Teaching as well as recognition from student organizations. Professor Sommers is an active member of the American Accounting Association and its Financial Accounting and Reporting and Accounting Program Leaders Group Sections. He has served as chairman of the Trueblood Seminar for Professors sponsored by Deloitte. Professor Sommers is recognized as an expert in the areas of financial reporting, financial analysis, estimation of cost of capital, and business valuation.

PETER D. EASTON is an expert in accounting and valuation and holds the Notre Dame Alumni Chair in Accountancy in the Mendoza College of Business where he is the Director of the Center for Accounting Research and Education. Professor Easton's expertise is widely recognized by the academic research community and by the legal community. Professor Easton frequently serves as a consultant on accounting and valuation issues in federal and state courts. Professor Easton holds undergraduate degrees from the University of Adelaide and the University of South Australia. He holds a graduate degree from the University of New England and a PhD in Business Administration (majoring in accounting and finance) from the University of California, Berkeley. Professor Easton's research on corporate valuation has been widely published in academic journals including the *Journal of Accounting and Economics, Journal of Accounting Research, The Accounting Review, Contemporary Accounting Research, Review of Accounting Studies,* and *Journal of Business Finance and Accounting*. Professor Easton has served as an associate editor for 11 leading accounting journals and he is currently an associate editor for the *Journal of Business Finance and Accounting* and *Journal of Accounting, Auditing, and Finance*. He is an editor of the *Review of Accounting Studies* for the past 25 years. Professor Easton has held appointments at the University of Chicago, the University of California at Berkeley, Ohio State University, Macquarie University, the Australian Graduate School of Management, the University of Melbourne, Tilburg University, National University of Singapore, Seoul National University, and Nyenrode University. He is the recipient of numerous awards for excellence in teaching and in research. Professor Easton regularly teaches accounting analysis and security valuation to MBAs.

PHILIP D. DRAKE is a Clinical Professor of Accountancy at the W. P Carey School of Business at Arizona State University where he is the Faculty Director for the Master of Accountancy and the Master of Taxation programs. He holds an undergraduate degree in Accounting from the University of Alabama and a PhD in Accounting and Management Information Systems from The Ohio State University. Professor Drake is a Certified Public Accounting (Texas) and a Certified Financial Planner, CFP®. Professor Drake has held appointments at Southern Methodist University, the University of Illinois (visiting), and Thunderbird. His past professional experiences include being the Chief Financial Officer of Nature's One, Inc, a specialty medical foods company, and the Chief Investment Officer of Inspired Capitalworks, a boutique wealth management firm. Professor Drake has published in *Financial Management*, *The Journal of Portfolio Management*, and the *Journal of Risk Management in Financial Institutions* along with several case studies and book chapters. With nearly twenty years teaching financial statement analysis at the graduate level, Professor Drake has won numerous teaching and curriculum development awards including the prestigious John W. Teets Award for Outstanding Graduate Teaching Award.

PREFACE

Welcome to the Second Edition of *Valuation Using Financial Statements*. Our focus in writing this book is to provide the most complete, engaging, and user-oriented textbook for instructors and students who wish to learn and implement valuation methods based on accounting and/or cash flow information gathered from financial statements. This book is the result of many years of experience teaching valuation and guiding students through the process of valuing companies using financial statement information. We are grateful to students and colleagues whose insights, suggestions, and feedback were invaluable as we developed our book. We hope that you will enjoy the journey that is *Valuation Using Financial Statements* and, of course, we welcome your comments.

PRACTICAL GUIDANCE AT EVERY STEP

We walk the reader through a detailed analysis of the financial statements including the information reported in the footnotes as she/he creates expanded financial statements capturing all of the obtainable information about the operations of the firm. Armed with a detailed understanding of the components of operating income and the operating assets used to generate that income, the reader sees a demonstration of DuPont ratio analysis and the essential steps in forecasting future payoffs (cash flow and earnings). Next, we detail the estimation of the cost of capital, which is used to discount the expected payoffs to estimate firm value. Finally, we derive and demonstrate the use of cash-flow-based and earnings-based valuation models.

We hope that the textbook will be used as a guidebook. Where possible, we demonstrate each of the steps of financial statement analysis and valuation via an example, General Mills. We encourage readers to undertake a valuation based on financial statements of another firm as they read to enhance their understanding of each of the steps in financial statement analyses and valuation. We provide a detailed spreadsheet analysis of the financial statements and valuation of General Mills, which we expect will serve as a guide to the reader undertaking the valuation of the company they select. As an alternative, readers might choose to follow the spreadsheets that show the financial statement analysis and valuation of Kellogg, Thor Industries, or Winnebago, also provided with the text.

TARGET AUDIENCE

Valuation Using Financial Statements is intended for use in a valuation and/or financial statement analysis course in which a structured approach to company valuation via financial statement reformulation, profitability analysis, and forecasting is emphasized. With a clear (yet detailed) focus on each of the key steps in valuation, the book provides a template for students to follow as they complete a valuation using cash flow- and/or accounting-based models. This book accommodates graduate and advanced undergraduate courses ranging from a partial semester to a full semester in length. Some knowledge of accounting is assumed.

READABILITY

This textbook is written in a clear and succinct manner, allowing students and instructors to absorb complex concepts quickly and without being distracted by unnecessary materials. Additionally, there is a strong emphasis on covering the practical situations that will be encountered by students and instructors in applications of each of the steps in the process of financial statement analysis and valuation.

DEMONSTRATED IMPLEMENTATION

Students learn from seeing a demonstration of the concepts. The book illustrates every aspect of the valuation process by using General Mills throughout, literally starting with their Form 10-K and ending with an estimation of the equity value. Additionally, in the end of chapter materials, Kellogg's (a close competitor of General Mills) as well as recreational vehicle manufacturers—Thor Industries and Winnebago are also analyzed, providing further reinforcement of the valuation processes. Every step can be followed directly in the valuation spreadsheets for General Mills, Kellogg's, Thor Industries, and Winnebago provided with the textbook. These spreadsheets, which cover the entire financial statement analysis and valuation process, further reinforce the flow of the steps along the path to valuation. These spreadsheets and the practical spreadsheet tips in the modules serve as a critical guide to students undertaking independent or group valuation projects. For example:

ORDER OF YEARS AND SIGNS OF ITEMS

In a valuation spreadsheet, it is helpful to have the most recent information on the right. This is despite GIS having the current year on the left in its published financials. Having the most recent years on the right in the spreadsheet will prove particularly helpful when we move to forecasting in Chapter 7. This way, the historical years (2017, 2018) will flow smoothly into the forecasted years (2019, 2020, etc.) as you move from left to right.

MULTIPLE METHODOLOGIES, ONE FOCUSED TASK

Often, valuation textbooks brush past items or provide a rough approximation rather than tackling issues. *Valuation Using Financial Statements* provides full explanations and demonstrations of market multiples and discounted cash flows models clearly discussing the costs and benefits and implementation issues of each. Additionally, the relation to accounting models is shown with the residual operating income and abnormal operating income growth models being covered in detail. Requirements for model equivalence and how forecasting relates to the various valuation approaches are clearly presented. Throughout the text, each approach focuses on valuation of the company's operating activities (i.e., valuation of enterprise operations), rather than equity. Not only is this necessary to avoid having to forecast future leverage, but also provides the benefit of a more focused task.

NEW TO THE SECOND EDITION

The focus company has changed from Procter & Gamble to General Mills. Using General Mills' financial statements from May 2018, a value is calculated at May 1, 2019. Additionally, in each chapter, the data is updated to reflect recent information.

- **Chapter 1:** A discussion of issues around identifying material risks and companies with multiple business environments has been added. Also, an example of a SWOT analysis of General Mills produced by MarketLine is now included.
- **Chapter 2:** Figures showing the relations between the company, its product / input markets, and suppliers of capital are now included. These figures also demonstrate the relations of operating profits, operating assets, financial items, and cash flows. Additionally, a clearer description is now provided of the operating and financial aspects of the company and accounting's articulation over time.
- **Chapter 3:** A discussion of issues to be watched when downloading data from sources such as Mergent Online has been added. The discussion of classification of deferred tax assets and liabilities has been adjusted to reflect changes to accounting standards.
- **Chapter 4:** Effects of beginning with downloaded financial statements are discussed. Additionally, the changes in accounting for pension and other postemployment benefit costs are incorporated. Finally, the effects of changing the statutory tax rate (and its effect in each fiscal year) is addressed.
- **Chapter 5:** The discussion of operating leases has been completely revised to cover both the old standards and the new standards that require recording of an asset and liability related to operating leases on the balance sheet. Similarly, the discussion of share-based compensation and the calculations in the related spreadsheets have been completely revised to streamline and clarify the issues and steps required.

- **Chapter 6:** Complete coverage of effects related to 52-53 week years on DuPont analysis is illustrated using General Mills. Discussion of further analyses that may be performed has been expanded throughout the chapter. Finally, the effects of equity deficits on financial analysis are covered.
- **Chapter 7:** More direct coverage of the effects of an acquisition is added through examination of General Mills' acquisition of Blue Buffalo. Additionally, the adjustments to both the revenue and the operating efficiency forecasting procedures resulting from the 52-53 week year issue are addressed.
- **Chapter 8:** Discussion on situations in which the use of the market multiples has been expanded. Quotes from Warren Buffet and Charlie Munger related to the merits of using EBITDA in analysis have been added.
- **Chapter 9:** A discussion of the effects of interest capitalization on estimates of the pretax borrowing rate has been added. Also, additional guidance is provided on how to determine whether a cost of capital estimate is reasonable and steps that can be taken if they are not.
- **Chapters 10-12:** In the valuation models, the forecasted payoffs from Chapter 7 and the cost of capital for operations from Chapter 9 are used to show the value calculated from both cash- and earnings-based models is identical.
- **Chapter 13:** The order of the last two chapters has been reversed to allow students to get to equity value sooner. Additionally, a detailed discussion of how the models presented in the text relate to the Discounted Cash Flow and Adjusted Present Value Models presented in finance texts is included. Finally, detailed instruction on performing sensitivity analysis in Excel is shown.
- **Chapter 14:** Guidance drawn from the Delaware Court of Chancery on acceptable terminal growth rates is shown. This provides concrete evidence of the applicability of the material and justification to the approaches shown in the text.
- **End of Chapter Materials:** In each chapter, the questions, exercises, and continuing examples have been increased to provide additional items for faculty to draw from and students to practice. This includes coverage of three companies in the continuing examples.
- **Test Bank:** A test bank has been created that incorporates continuing examples of Procter & Gamble, Kimberly-Clark, Federal Express, and United Parcel Service. Valuation spreadsheets for these companies are also included.

Supplements

Valuation Spreadsheets: Excel spreadsheets for General Mills, Kellogg's, Thor Industries, and Winnebago central to the textbook are provided, which show the flow of information and calculations when moving from financial statements to a value estimate. Two bonus spreadsheets for Cooper Tire & Rubber and Goodyear are also available that can be used in presenting the materials in classes.

Solutions Manual: Created by the authors, the Solutions Manual contains complete solutions to all assignments.

Test Bank: Created by the authors, the Test Bank contains a variety of questions, exercises, and problems related to each aspect of the text. The Test Bank utilizes Procter & Gamble, Kimberly-Clark, Federal Express, and United Parcel Service as continuing examples and complete Excel spreadsheets on these companies are also available.

PowerPoint: Created by the authors, the PowerPoint slides outline key elements of each chapter.

Acknowledgments

The development of this book benefited greatly from the valuable feedback of our students and colleagues. We are extremely grateful to them for their help in making this project a success. In particular, we would like thank:

Brian Bratten, *University of Kentucky*

Keji Chen, *California State University—Northridge*

Barry Hettler, *SUNY Brockport*

Marilyn Johnson, *Michigan State University*
Catherine Lau, *Carthage College*
Henock Louis, *Penn State University*
Lester Reid, *Lynn University*
Andrew Schmidt, *North Carolina State University*
Brent Solomon, *University of Maryland*
Senyo Tse, *Texas A&M University*
Eric Weisbrod, *University of Miami*
John Wild, *University of Wisconsin—Madison*
Tracy Xu, *University of Denver*

In addition, we are extremely grateful to George Werthman, Jill Sternard, Debbie McQuade, Terry McQuade, and the entire team at Cambridge Business Publishers for their encouragement, enthusiasm, and guidance.

Finally, we would like to thank Stephen Penman and Jim Ohlson for their influence on our understanding of valuation methodologies and principles underlying this textbook.

Greg Peter Philip

TABLE OF CONTENTS

Chapter One
The Link between Valuation and Financial Statement Analysis 1.1

Chapter Two
Role of Accounting 2.1

Chapter Three
Reformulation to Identify Operating Activities 3.1

Chapter Four
Use of Additional Information to Enhance Reformulation 4.1

Chapter Five
Adjusting Accounting Information 5.1

Chapter Six
Analysis of Enterprise Operations 6.1

Chapter Seven
Full-Information Forecasting for Valuation 7.1

Chapter Eight
Market Multiple Valuation 8.1

Chapter Nine
Cost of Capital for Operations and Equity 9.1

Chapter Ten
Valuation using Forecasts of Cash Flows 10.1

Chapter Eleven
Valuation using the Residual Operating Income Valuation Model 11.1

Chapter Twelve
Valuation using the Abnormal Operating Income Growth Model 12.1

Chapter One

The Link between Valuation and Financial Statement Analysis

TAKEAWAYS

When you complete this chapter, you should be able to:

1. Explain why accounting-based valuation models may supplement other models.
2. Understand the importance of focusing on operations when valuing equity.
3. Know the steps to valuing a company.
4. Explain the importance of understanding the business environment when undertaking valuation.
5. Perform Porter's and SWOT analyses of a company.

WHY VALUATION?

Valuation is a critical input to many business decisions. Inside the company, business decisions are often anchored on the goal "maximize shareholder value." Being able to quantify (i.e., value) the potential effects of a business decision allows us to determine whether a particular decision will help or hinder the maximization of shareholder value. Valuation quantifies the anticipated outcomes (i.e., the forecasted payoffs) of different options and computes the associated effects on value.

Many have watched the popular television series *Shark Tank*, where budding entrepreneurs pitch their ideas to a panel of "shark" investors who then choose whether or not to invest. What factors do these sharks consider? How would you value a potential idea? A willingness to work hard and a good idea are necessary, but it appears more is involved in determining the value that might exist. Similarly, when a friend says he or she has a "great opportunity," a framework for determining value is necessary before making an investment of time, energy, or money.

The focus of this text is on practical methods for estimating value based on expected future payoffs. We will demonstrate a path from financial statements to expectations of future payoffs to the computation of value. The process of arriving at expectations of future payoffs requires an understanding of currently available information. Throughout the text, you will be provided with the tools necessary to (1) gather and understand currently available financial information (often contained in financial statements), (2) apply the understanding of current information to arrive at forecasts of future financial information, and (3) compute an estimate of value based on that available information.

The primary goal of this text is to develop an understanding of the use of accounting information in forecasting and valuation. Knowing how to calculate value is important, but, without being able to see every step of the connection between accounting information and the eventual value estimate, you do not have something you can apply. Although we do not cover the details of the accounting methods and rules necessary to prepare financial statements, an understanding of the role and effects of accounting is required.

CHAPTER OUTLINE

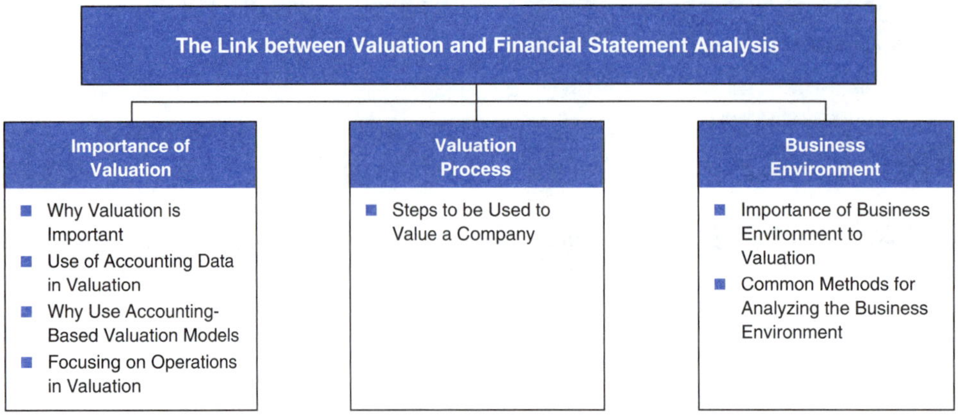

We will begin with valuation based on forecasts of cash flows. This is the valuation method that is familiar to most business students. Reported historical accounting information is usually the source used in creating the forecasts used by these models. We will discuss this valuation method, emphasizing the role of accounting information in its implementation. Then, we will consider accounting-based valuation methods.

Our framework aims to provide a step-by-step pass through the valuation process. Thus, we begin with reformulation and analysis of the financial statements. Reformulation is a process where we rearrange reported information to uncover and highlight the numbers that will be helpful in analysis and valuation. From this base, we then form forecasts, which we will use in valuation. Next, we consider methods for obtaining estimates of the cost of capital. By this stage, we are ready to carry out valuation based on cash flows as well as accounting-based valuation models.

When capturing expectations of payoffs, risks related to the future must be considered. Some of these may be readily apparent and others less so. A *Wall Street Journal* article dated March 4, 2015, for example, discusses how driverless cars are a risk for some companies because they may affect future payoffs: "**Cincinnati Financial Corp.**, an Ohio-based insurer generating nearly a quarter of its premiums from commercial and consumer auto policies, warned in the annual report it filed Friday that its forecasts could be flawed because of, among other things, 'Disruption of the insurance market caused by technology innovations such as driverless cars that could decrease consumer demand for insurance products.'"[1] Additionally, the article highlighted that "insurers aren't the only companies fretting. **LKQ Corp.**, a Chicago auto-parts maker, cited risks from the safety technologies that many see as leading the way to driverless cars. 'If the number of vehicles involved in accidents declines or the number of cars being repaired declines, our business could suffer,' reads a heading in the annual report LKQ filed on Monday." Because these risks could affect payoffs, they would affect value. As a result, risks must be explicitly considered, quantified, and incorporated into value calculations.

Further, our understanding of currently available information may affect our expectations. Changes in accounting rules, tax law revisions, and uncertain economic futures lead to data that may or may not be useful in predicting future payoffs. When discussing the effect of the new leasing standards, a *Wall Street Journal* article from July 11, 2019, cited a Credit Suisse Group report: "New lease accounting rules have resulted in potentially misleading data feeds, inconsistent financial reporting and other discrepancies that could confuse and misinform investors."[2] The article went on to say, "At issue is whether operating leases are automatically included in key financial metrics by data providers, and whether investors are aware that their data feeds have made these adjustments." American Airlines Inc., the Cheesecake Factory Inc., and Deutsche Post AG are given as examples where the new lease accounting could confuse or surprise investors. Failing to

---

[1] Francis, T., "The Driverless Car, Officially, Is a Risk: How to Set Prices for Casualty losses When the Driver's Age and Experience Doesn't Matter?" *Wall Street Journal (Online)* (March 4, 2015). Retrieved from http://search.proquest.com/docview/1660199519?accountid=6667

[2] Maurer, M., "New Lease Accounting Standard May Mislead Investors, Credit Suisse Says," *Wall Street Journal (Online)* (July 11, 2019). Retrieved from https://global.factiva.com/redir/default.aspx?P=sa&an=WSJO000020190710ef7a008px&cat=a&ep=ASE

understand how currently available information will relate to future payoffs will affect our ability to make an accurate estimate of value.

Thus, valuation has both a theoretical and a practical side. We can (and will) begin with widely accepted and widely used theoretical models that show how the future payoffs are related to the current value. These models are important because they help us focus on what information is needed and how our expectations affect the value calculation. The practical side enters the picture as we attempt to gather the information used in these calculations. What information is available, when is it available, and how confident are we in that information? This is where the role of accounting and its relation to cash flows will become apparent.

If we do not understand the theoretical models, we may misuse them. If we do not understand the information we are using in our estimations, we may misuse this information when forming our expectations of future payoffs. This text provides a set of implementable procedures for utilizing the theoretical models as a basis for settling on a set of practical processes for estimating value.

GETTING IT RIGHT: ANALYSTS' USE OF DISCOUNTED CASH FLOWS MODELS

A 2016 study by Green, Hand, and Zhang (June 2016 *Review of Accounting Studies*) examined analysts' discounted cash flow (DCF) models detailed in reports issued by U.S. brokerages. For a sample of 120 DCF models from 2012 and 2013, they "estimate that analysts make a median of three theory-related and/or execution errors and four questionable economic judgments per DCF." (p. 596)

Use of Accounting Data for Valuation

LO1: Explain why accounting-based valuation models may supplement other models.

Much of this text is based on the valuation of a company from the viewpoint of a current or potential investor. We will demonstrate the valuation of General Mills (NYSE ticker symbol: GIS). We focus on the annual report for the year ended May 2018 and assume a valuation date of May 1, 2019, throughout the text. In doing so, we calculate an estimate of what a share of GIS stock was worth on May 1, 2019. We suggest that readers choose a company in which they have an interest, choose a valuation date after the release of the most recent annual report, and follow the steps (the path) that we demonstrate via GIS. Throughout the text, we include practical tips to building our own spreadsheet for the careful and structured estimation of value.

Although we focus on the valuation of an exchange-listed company, the valuation tools covered in this text are widely applicable in a variety of settings, including estimation of value of equity securities, assessment of the value of potential merger and/or acquisition targets, evaluation of divisions and/or segments, as the key input to buy/sell decisions, determination of goodwill impairment, and implementation of accounting standards that require fair value estimation. Both finance and accounting professionals must seek to understand valuation to provide guidance to company decision makers or to investments.

In today's world, every financial and accounting professional must have a thorough understanding of the concepts underlying valuation. The strength of their understanding of valuation will determine the extent to which they can form meaningful expectations of future payoffs and translate them into value estimates. Just as a chain is only as strong as its weakest link, a professional's value estimate reflects an understanding of each step undertaken and will only be as strong as the weakest element. Each decision that these professionals make should be, at least in part, guided by the effect it will have on the value of their company.

Financial professionals are often trained to focus on the cash flows of a company because they are deemed to be "real." Accounting professionals bring their understanding of the relations between cash flows and accounting information to their decision making. This text will strengthen and refine your understanding of the roles of both the accounting and cash flow data in order to give you the necessary skills and tools to use valuation to inform decision making. Whether you will serve as a financial or accounting professional, having a clear understanding of the relations between cash flows, accounting information, future payoffs, and valuation will be essential to your future and your success as a financial decision maker.

A goal of accounting is to provide information about the amount, timing, and uncertainty of future payoffs. This is exactly the information we need to estimate value! It follows that a thorough understanding of currently available accounting information (usually in the form of financial statements) is necessary for the formation of future forecasts. The quality of those future forecasts is the primary driver of the quality of the estimate of value. There are many approaches to valuation in use today. Some models are based on theory, and some are ad hoc, having arisen from practice. By beginning with an understanding of accounting and a reliance on theoretical models, this text seeks to guide the choice of model to ensure accurate forecasts and to avoid common valuation fallacies. You will emerge with the tools necessary for practical valuation. We also recognize the increasing use of accounting-based valuation models in practice, which provides an opportunity to focus and improve valuation efforts.

In recent years, accounting standard setters have issued new standards that often incorporate elements reported at fair value. Additionally, there are new standards for revenue recognition and leasing, tax law revisions, and changes to reporting for pensions. These changes to accounting also reinforce the need to understand valuation (where do the numbers come from?) and change our understanding of the information available (what do the numbers imply about future payoffs?). The implications for preparers and for users of financial statements are clear. These ever-changing accounting standards require both preparers and users of financial statements to have an increasingly sophisticated understanding of accounting, finance, and the relation between these two fields.

We should not be surprised that the issuance of standards incorporating fair value elements has coincided with the adoption of an asset/liability approach by standard setters. The asset/liability approach has as its primary focus determination of what amounts should be reflected on the balance sheet for assets or liabilities. The revenues and expenses then arise due to changes in the amounts of the assets and liabilities. This emphasis on determining assets and liabilities at the time of the transaction and their subsequent remeasurement is, by its very nature, a valuation exercise that should be based on the same concepts, methods, and tools used to value a share of stock.

Measurement of the assets and/or liabilities requires a clear understanding of valuation. It follows that today's accounting professionals must understand valuation in order to prepare (and/or audit) the financial statements.

We will show in subsequent chapters that expected future payoffs can be stated in terms of cash flows or, alternatively, in terms of accounting numbers (e.g., earnings or net operating profit after tax). This is extremely important because accounting reports are readily available and provide much information that is helpful in forming expectations of future payoffs. One objective of accounting, according to the Financial Accounting Standards Board (FASB) Conceptual Framework, is to provide information that "may help those who desire to estimate the value of a business enterprise, but financial accounting is not designed to measure directly the value of an enterprise."[3] Stated in a different way, accounting will not tell you how much something is worth, but, rather, it provides information that may be very helpful in forming our estimate of value. Indeed, the conceptual framework for accounting issued by the FASB states, "Potential users of financial information most directly concerned with a particular business enterprise are generally interested in its ability to generate favorable cash flows because their decisions relate to amounts, timing, and uncertainties of expected cash flows."[4]

In summary, we study valuation because it is the driver of business decisions, and we study financial statement analysis because it provides decision-relevant financial information useful in assessing value. Our approach in this text, and accounting in general, recognizes the notion that investors are seeking future payoffs based on the operating activities and that they need information to help them project those payoffs.

Why Use Accounting-Based Valuation Models?

The reintroduction of accounting-based valuation models by Ohlson (1995) and the subsequent advancements by Ohlson and Juettner-Nauroth (2005) have changed the way accounting information is used in valuation. Both cash flow- and accounting-based valuation models should be among the tools available to you because they each provide advantages. Many trained in old-school finance may have, at best, only a passing awareness of the accounting-based valuation models. Often, misunderstandings about these models cause their dismissal as a viable option for valuation. They are, however, becoming more and more widely accepted; the Chartered Financial

[3] SFAC 1: Paragraph 41.

[4] SFAC 1: Paragraph 25.

Analyst (CFA) exam, for example, now covers the residual operating income valuation model, which is one of the accounting-based models covered in detail in this text.

The practical appeal of accounting-based valuation models is that they focus on reported information that is readily available. Earnings, which is the financial statement variable most used by participants in our financial markets, is at the core of these models.

WARREN BUFFETT'S COMMENTS ON USING ACCOUNTING INFORMATION

"When Charlie and I read reports, we have no interest in pictures of personnel, plants or products. References to EBITDA [earnings before interest, taxes, depreciation and amortization] make us shudder—does management think the tooth fairy pays for capital expenditures? We're very suspicious of accounting methodology that is vague or unclear, since too often that means management wishes to hide something. And we don't want to read messages that a public relations department or consultant has turned out. Instead, we expect a company's CEO to explain in his or her own words what's happening."

—Berkshire Hathaway Annual Report

The appeal of cash flow-based models stems from their use in valuing finite-lived projects and a reluctance to rely on accounting numbers, which some argue are easy to manipulate and possibly seriously affected by the arbitrary application of accounting rules and procedures. (We will show that, despite these possible concerns, accounting-based valuation remains very sound.)

Analysts forecast earnings (generally, earnings per share) for the coming years. Within companies, budgets and compensation plans generally rely on measures of earnings as well. However, valuation was traditionally done using forecasts of cash flows. These forecasts of cash flows were usually formed by making adjustments to the earnings forecasts to arrive at the forecasts of cash flows. These adjustments were attempts to remove the accruals and the effects of other "accounting estimates" to estimate future expected cash flows. We demonstrate in this book how the numbers forecast by analysts and also utilized for budgeting and compensation may be used for valuation without the need to estimate and undo future accruals.

Depending on your background, you may be very comfortable with the use of/reliance on accounting information, or you may view it as suspect. Both of these positions are warranted. Within this text, we will rely on accounting information to analyze the current status of the entity we are valuing. However, in doing so, we also recognize the implications of different choices of accounting methods and their application. We will suggest and consider potential adjustments to the reported information to better reflect the financial position of the firm and to enhance the usefulness of this information in forecasting future payoffs. Further, we will explore the use of cash flows in addition to the accounting information in forecasting and valuation. We will develop a thorough understanding of both cash flow-based and accounting-based valuation models; we will show their theoretical equivalence. And we will see the implementation issues we may encounter, which may lead us to choose one valuation model over another when undertaking a valuation.

DIFFERENT METHODS, ONE GOAL

If we completely understand the differing valuation models and the appropriate implementation, we will obtain the same estimate of value from each of these models. If not, we may obtain different estimates. The *SchweserNotes for the CFA Exam Level II, Book 3* states,

> "Theoretically, the intrinsic value derived using expected dividends, expected free cash flows to equity, or book value plus residual income should be identical if the underlying assumptions used to make the necessary forecasts are the same. In reality, however, it is rarely possible to forecast all of the common inputs with the same degree of accuracy, and the different models yield different results. . . . If the different models provide dramatically different estimates, the inconsistencies may result from the models' underlying assumptions." (Kaplan, 2012 p. 209)

Knowing multiple models allows us to verify that we have succeeded in correct implementation. Also, differences in the timing of capture of value (i.e., earlier or later in the forecast period) may yield differing levels of confidence in the output of the different models.

With a thorough understanding of cash flow and accounting-based valuation models, we can ensure consistent assumptions and proper implementation. However, the question of what we choose to forecast based on the anticipated degree of accuracy and how soon value is captured remains as a critical factor in choice of model, and this, in turn, affects the confidence we will have in the resulting estimate of value.

Focusing on Operations

LO2: Understand the importance of focusing on operations when valuing equity.

A feature of this text is that we keep the focus on enterprise operations. That is, we focus on the portion of a company: its operating activities, where value is created. To illustrate this feature, consider a simple example. Suppose you go to the bank and borrow money; to this stage, you have not created value, and there are no operating activities—there is only a financial activity. Subsequently, when you use that money to fund an operating activity, you have established the opportunity to create value via the operations of that enterprise. This distinction between the enterprise operating activities and the financial activities of the company is central to the valuation process and has far-reaching implications.

THE RELATION BETWEEN OPERATING ACTIVITIES, FINANCIAL ACTIVITIES, AND EQUITY

Our ultimate goal (generally) is to estimate the value of equity. This is because equity ownership is what we buy when we purchase either a company or a share of a company.

From our accounting background, we are familiar with the following relation:

$$\text{Assets} = \text{Liabilities} + \text{Equity}$$

Both the assets and the liabilities can arise from either operating or financial activities. If we separate the assets and liabilities based on whether they relate to enterprise operations or financial activities (a process called *reformulation* that will be introduced in Chapter 3), we can arrive at the net operating assets (*NOA*) and the net financial liabilities (*NFL*) of the company. Note that most companies are net borrowers from creditors, so we think of *NFL* despite the fact that some companies may be net lenders with excess cash and investments.

The reformulated balance sheet has the following relation:

$$NOA = NFL + \text{Common shareholders' equity } (CSE)$$

This reformulated balance sheet assists in the task of determining the value of *CSE*, which is our goal. If we are able to determine the value of *NOA* and *NFL*, the difference between them would be the value of *CSE* that we seek.[5]

While valuing *NOA* and *NFL* may be thought to entail extra effort, it actually simplifies the process. The reason is that valuing *NFL* is generally quite straightforward. Most items included in *NFL* are already reported at fair value in the balance sheet. An easy example is a loan from the bank where when we report a liability of $100,000, we probably owe the bank $100,000. Importantly, when items in *NFL* are not at fair value, accounting requires that their fair value be disclosed in the footnotes because they qualify as financial instruments.

Because the fair value of *NFL* is straightforward to determine, the question is whether it is easier to value *CSE* or to value *NOA*, and then subtract *NFL* to arrive at *CSE*. The answer in both traditional finance-oriented and in accounting-based valuation is to focus on the valuation of operations. One of the reasons is that we avoid having to anticipate future management choices related to leverage. Leverage is a measure of the portion of operations funded by debt (*NFL*) as compared to equity (*CSE*).

$$\text{Value of } NOA - \text{Value of } NFL = \text{Value of } CSE$$

As we move forward, we will see that valuing operations allows us to ignore potential future changes in leverage (funding) that management may make. This greatly simplifies the valuation process!

In the text, we will demonstrate that financial activities do not, in and of themselves, create value. Once we understand this fact, focusing on operating activities seems obvious. This is where a thorough grounding in valuation from the theoretical side will guide our practical implementation. For example, if we want to value the enterprise operations, we will need a measure of its risk. In Chapter 9, we will consider the relation between the riskiness of operations, riskiness of

[5] This focus on operating activities is consistent with the methods traditionally taught in finance. There they seek to value the operating activities then adjust for the value of the financial activities to arrive at the value of equity.

equity, and riskiness of debt. Additionally, we will see how the estimation of these risks affects our calculations. The implications of differences between use of cost of equity capital and weighted average cost of capital for operations in evaluating future payoffs are often ignored. In Chapter 13, we will see that assuming constant cost of capital is logical for operating activities but would usually be untenable for equity.

We will show that understanding the connections between the reported accounting information, the operating/financial activity distinction, and future payoffs is critical to valuation.

ORGANIZATION

LO3: Know the steps to valuing a company.

Next, we proceed with an overview of the steps we will take to learn valuation based on financial statement analysis. This will include explanations of some critical terminology. The end result will be a set of practical tools useful for valuation in a wide variety of contexts. This practical understanding will be built on the foundation of theoretical models.

This textbook is structured around a five-step process or pathway:

1. How to know a company's environment—Understanding the Business Environment
2. How to isolate a company's enterprise operations—Reformulation of the Financial Statements
3. How to determine the current status of a company—Financial Statement Analysis
4. How to formalize expectations of where the company is going—Forecasting Future Payoffs
5. How to calculate what the company is worth—Valuation

You may have had exposure to some or even all of these topics in prior courses or other disciplines. Alternatively, you may have little or no exposure to some of these topics. Either way, this text will enhance your knowledge of and provide linkages between each of these topics. You will gain a familiarity with the practical tools necessary to perform valuation, including how to build a valuation spreadsheet. The main differences evident in this text's approach as compared to traditional financial statement analysis and/or valuation texts are

- explicit linking of these steps,
- focus on valuation of the company's operating activities (i.e., valuation of enterprise operations), and
- full coverage of both cash flow- and accounting-based methods of valuation.

This text will focus on the interrelated aspects of the valuation task in providing an implementable approach.

A full understanding of valuing the operations of the company valuation using the discounted cash flow model, the residual operating income model, and the abnormal operating income growth model will be provided. Additionally, the process of multiples-based valuation commonly observed in practice will be demonstrated and its benefits/deficiencies will be examined. Valuation of equity using the discounted dividend model, the residual income model, and the abnormal income growth model will also be covered. To accomplish all this, cost of capital and forecasting will be covered in depth. In short, you will leave with the tools and a path (an understanding of their use) that is sufficient to allow you to perform competent valuations.

1. *Understanding the Business Environment*

   The foundation we will first lay is that of understanding the company's business/operating environment. In an absence of a thorough understanding, we may easily misinterpret the information we analyze or fail to recognize risks. An organized analysis will help ensure that important factors affecting our understanding of where the company is currently and/or where it is going are not overlooked. As an example, understanding potential effects on future sales of changes in the dynamics of the company's customer base or the potential for a technological innovation is critical to ensuring a meaningful valuation.

   Reported financial statements contain a large quantity of information on the performance of the company and the risks it faces. However, this information is not necessarily presented in a way that highlights the company's focus. Valuation efforts need to emphasize the main income-generating activities of the company; that is, the business's enterprise operating activities.

2. *Reformulation of the Financial Statements*

   The second step in laying the foundation for valuation is clearly identifying information about a company's operating activities. As we will discuss, financial activities do not directly create value. Enterprise operating activities do create value. We will reformulate the financial statements in such a way as to facilitate a focus on operating activities, thereby separating these activities from the activity of financing these operations. We will also consider adjustments to reported financial information, which may enhance the usefulness of the information for analysis and forecasting. Reformulation separates the information reported for operating and financial activities.

3. *Financial Statement Analysis*

   After reformulating and identifying the operating activities, we proceed to our analysis. Understanding the results of current operating activities likely will help in forming expectations (forecasts) of future results. That is, analyzing current financial statements helps in forecasting. The tools we will cover are commonly included in financial statement analysis texts and generally draw from DuPont analysis. This method, introduced by the **DuPont Company** almost a century ago, focuses on operating profit margins and asset turnovers as the drivers of profitability. Our reformulation provides the inputs to the analysis of the company's operating activities. By comparing the current information to information about what has occurred in prior years as well as with information about competitors, we can gain additional information that will yield benefits in the next step, where we forecast future financial information.

4. *Forecasting Future Payoffs*

   Valuation is a forward-looking exercise. Estimates of expected future payoffs are a key input to valuation. Without having taken the first three steps outlined above, our expectations of future payoffs are akin to random guesses. Our goal is to estimate the amount, timing, and uncertainty of future payoffs. Achieving this goal builds on the foundation of understanding the company's business environment and its current financial state.

   An important part of the forecasting process is ensuring that our forecasting will not be ad hoc but based on a firm understanding of assets required to generate future sales and the profit that we expect from those sales. Forecasting based on the financial statements is very helpful in this regard.

NEGATIVE CURRENT FREE CASH FLOWS

One *must* understand accounting-based valuation models in order to have alternatives available in situations where current free cash flows from operations are negative. Given the notion that current results are expected to forecast future results, starting from negative current free cash flow is highly problematic. Negative free cash flows are not unusual. Capital IQ's Compustat data, covering the largest publicly traded stocks, in the years 2011 to 2014, shows that almost 20 percent of firms had negative free cash flow. For these firms, we need to look beyond cash to find a measure for valuation. The accounting-based valuation models often provide an alternative where forecasting is easier, more meaningful, and more reliable.

5. *Valuation*

   After we have completed steps one through four, we will finally arrive at the goal: calculating what the company is worth. This is where the results of our structured pathway and systematic efforts to gather information reap benefits for us. By gathering the information using the prior steps, we can utilize either cash flow- or accounting-based valuation methods. Understanding the details of a valuation, both from a practical and theoretical side, provides awareness of the sensitivity of our model and value estimate. We will have the assurance that we have appropriately used information and relied on supportable assumptions.

   When undertaking the valuation, we will focus on valuation models that estimate the value of the operating activities. We will discuss how this estimate of the value of operating activities can be converted to an estimate of equity value, and we will provide reasons why equity value is not estimated directly.

A key element of the valuation process is the estimation of the cost of capital. Our approach highlights the sources of risk, which must be captured in the estimate of the cost of capital. Here again, we consider the theoretical and practical aspects of risk estimation and their effects on our choices. Understanding the differences in cost of capital for operations, for debt, and for equity and understanding the relations among these costs is particularly important.

Practical implementation of the cash flow- and accounting-based valuation methods will be demonstrated throughout the text, first by introducing key concepts via an example of a generic limited-life project, followed by application of these concepts to General Mills (GIS), a large publicly traded company. In both of these demonstrations, we will show how to understand the financial activities of the company in a manner that focuses on the profit-generating (and value-generating) operating activities of the company.

UNDERSTANDING THE BUSINESS AND THE BUSINESS ENVIRONMENT

LO4: Explain the importance of understanding the business environment when undertaking valuation.

We now proceed to our exploration of the steps necessary to estimate value. We will explore the first step in the remainder of this chapter: We must understand the business and the environment in which the business operates. This is essential. Deciding to open an ice cream shop may be a great idea, but perhaps not in Fairbanks, Alaska. Buying a franchise for tanning salons in South Florida also may not work out too well. The environment in which a company operates will drive the success of the business. Our valuation needs to reflect an understanding of that environment.

First, we must "know the business." Often, a goal in knowing the business is to understand the risks of the business.[6] The U.S. Army's separation of the concepts of risk and uncertainty is an interesting place to start. The analogy to the analysis of business operations is apparent. The U.S. Army defines risks as known hazards: "All hazards, tactical or accidental, that have the potential to injure or kill personnel, damage or destroy equipment, or otherwise impact mission effectiveness."[7] It defines uncertainties as unknown or ambiguous hazards: Unpredictability and ambiguity stemming from the complex and highly interactive nature of military operations, further complicated by inherent human interaction and a thinking enemy.[8] This distinction highlights that not all potential issues can be anticipated, but we must consider any known risks in computing value.

The understanding of the business includes determining the potential risks and rewards that may be expected in the future. While we introduce this step here, we do not dwell on it because there are entire business courses on this subject. Rather, we will mention some of the steps that may be taken as a way to formalize and document efforts directed toward gaining an understanding of the business environment of a company. Keep in mind that the brevity of our discussion should in no way be interpreted as a statement about the importance of this step! As we undertake each of the steps in the valuation, we will continually seek a better understanding of the business and the business environment.

IDENTIFYING MATERIAL RISKS

In a company's Form 10-K, section 1A is labeled and directly identifies "Risk Factors." While this seems like it would be incredibly helpful for our valuation efforts, it often is overloaded with information to the point of obscuring the important items. For various reasons, including potential litigation, firms will often discuss so many different factors that it is unclear which are the most crucial. For example, we would really like to know what the issues and/or risks are that most worry management. In the 2018 GIS Form 10-K, the company identified 22 different items as risks that "could materially, adversely affect our business, financial condition, and results of operations." (p. 8) While the list is accurate, providing us with such a large quantity makes determining which are most critical very difficult.

---

[6] Chapter 9 will directly address cost of capital issues, which are measures of risk related to forecasted payoffs.

[7] U.S. Army FM 5-19: Composite Risk Management. p. 1-1.

[8] Composite definition based on U.S. Army FM 6-0: Mission Command. p. 1-10.

LO5: Perform Porter's and SWOT analyses of a company.

One way to structure an understanding of the operations is through use of Porter's value-chain model (see Porter, *Competitive Advantage: Creating and Sustaining Superior Performance*, 1985, and the graphic below). Analysis using the value-chain model seeks to identify and understand the activities that create a company's profit margin. These are the primary activities:

- Inbound logistics
- Operations
- Outbound logistics
- Marketing and sales
- Servicing

These are the support activities:

- Firm infrastructure
- Human resource management
- Technology/product development
- Procurement

The results of these activities manifest themselves in a company's financial statements and supporting documents. The organization of these activities is depicted in **Exhibit 1.1**.

EXHIBIT 1.1 Porter's Value-Chain Model

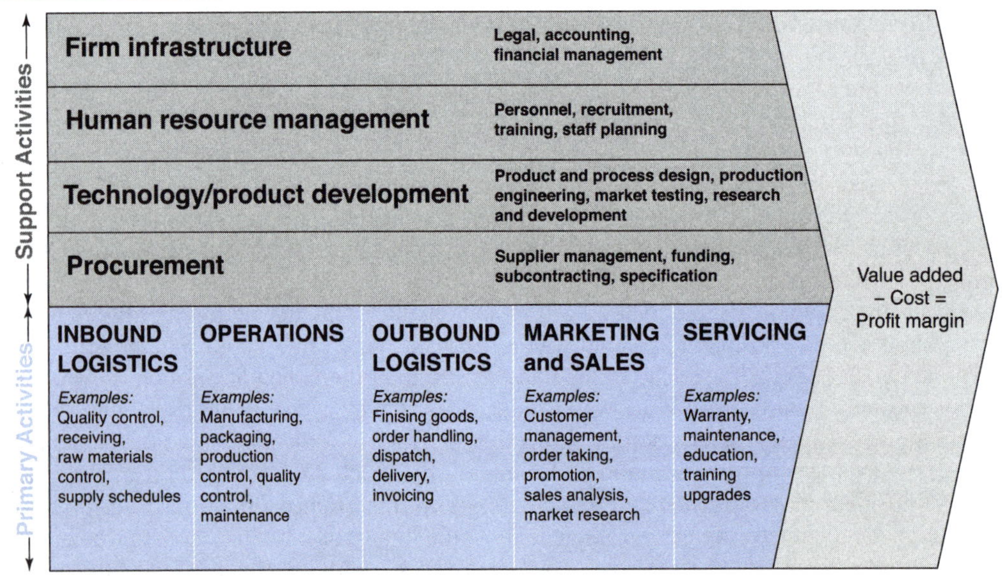

A company's primary and support activities are not carried out in isolation. They're influenced by five important forces that determine the company's competitive intensity:

- **Industry competition:** "Competition" and "rivalry" are synonyms raises the cost of doing business as companies must hire and train competitive workers, advertise products, research and develop products, and engage in other related activities.
- **Bargaining power of buyers:** Buyers with strong bargaining power can extract price concessions and demand a higher level of service and delayed payment terms, which reduces both profits from sales and the operating cash flows to sellers.
- **Bargaining power of suppliers:** Suppliers with strong bargaining power can demand higher prices and earlier payments, yielding adverse effects on profits and cash flows to buyers.
- **Threat of substitution:** As the number of product substitutes increases, sellers have less power to raise prices and/or pass on costs to buyers; accordingly, threat of substitution places downward pressure on sellers' profits.

- **Threat of entry:** New market entrants increase competition, and to mitigate that threat, companies spend money on activities such as new technologies, promotion, and human development to erect barriers to entry and to create economies of scale.

These five forces are key determinants of profitability (for further discussion, see Porter, *Competitive Strategy: Techniques for Analyzing Industries and Competitors*, 1980 and 1998).

Ignoring these competitive aspects could lead to forecasts that are inaccurate or unattainable. For example, as alternative tablet computers become available, Apple may begin to have trouble maintaining both its sales of and high margins on the iPad. This potential change in the threat of substitution must be considered as a part of the expected future sales growth and as a part of the future profit margin on sales. Taking the time to know the business and its environment may help us see what aspects of the current situation would be expected to improve or decline as the company moves forward.

MULTIPLE BUSINESS ENVIRONMENTS

Some companies operate across multiple industries. An example is PepsiCo which operates both in the snack and the beverage industries. While these areas may seem similar at first glance, each industry can carry different opportunities and threats. For example, while both of PepsiCo's industries may be affected by shifting global consumer health attitudes, they may experience differing impacts. Further, the rise of water resource availability constraints in some parts of the world would more directly affect the beverage portion of PepsiCo's operations. The more we understand a company's operations, the more accurate our valuation will be.

As an alternative to the Porter-based competitive analysis, some prefer a SWOT analysis of a company. SWOT is an acronym that stands for strength, weakness, opportunities, and threats. SWOT can be applied to almost any organization or activity. This approach is universally applicable and easy to apply, and it can be graphically portrayed, as shown in **Exhibit 1.2**.

EXHIBIT 1.2 Framework for Analysis of Strengths, Weaknesses, Opportunities, and Threats

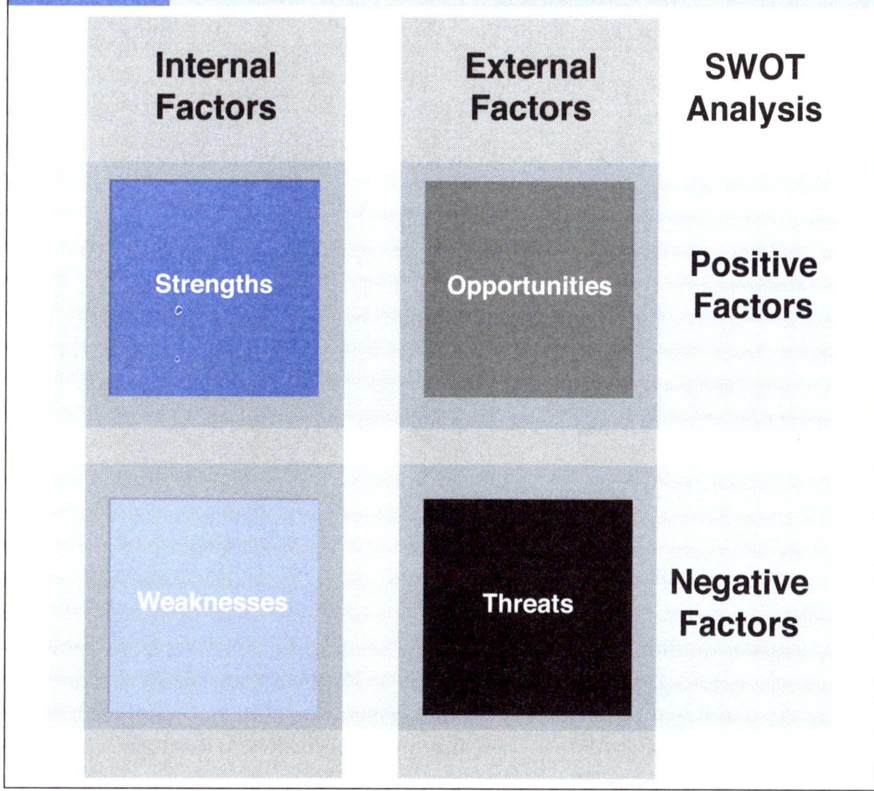

SWOT analysis has two parts. Looking internally, we review the strengths and weaknesses of a company, while externally, we review the opportunities of and threats to the company. SWOT analysis then tries to understand particular strengths and weaknesses that give rise to specific opportunities (to exploit the strengths) and threats (caused by the weaknesses). When used as part of an overall strategic analysis, SWOT can provide a good review of strategic options. It can be a useful guide in understanding the changes, both positive and negative, that may be expected going forward.

As an example, below is a SWOT analysis prepared by MarketLine dated November 16, 2018.

SWOT ANALYSIS

General Mills, Inc. (General Mills) is manufacturer and marketer of branded consumer food. Geographic presence, customer base and focus on R&D activities are the company's major strengths, whereas liquidity position and product recall remains the cause for concern. Launch of new products, acquisition of Blue Buffalo, growing concentration on natural and organic line and positive outlook for the US savory snacks market are likely to provide growth opportunities to the company. However, foreign currency fluctuations, expansion by competitors and stringent regulations could affect its business operations.

Strength	**Weakness**
Customer Base Geographic Footprint Research and Development	Product Recalls Liquidity Position
Opportunity Concentration of Natural and Organic Line Positive Outlook for the US Savory Snacks Market Launch of New Products Acquisition of Blue Buffalo	**Threat** Expansion by Competitors Foreign Currency Fluctuations Stringent Regulations

MarketLine Company Profile: General Mills Inc. (p. 4)

From this, you can see the types of issues that must be considered in understanding the financials, evaluating risks, and forecasting payoffs from GIS going forward. The better you understand the issues, both positive and negative, related to the company, the better valuation you will achieve.

There are potential drawbacks to using the SWOT analysis. SWOT is sometimes criticized as too subjective. Two individuals can identify entirely different factors from a SWOT analysis of the same company. This is partly because SWOT is intuitive and allows varying opinions on the relevant factors.

Another factor to be considered in an analysis of the company is its life cycle stage. Over time, companies pass through a number of distinct life cycle stages. While these do not have to occur in a set order, an understanding of the stage a company is in may help with analysis of its current profitability and provide insights useful in the forecasting exercise. Dickinson (2011) shows that a good proxy for the life cycle stage can be formed by looking at the signs of the cash flows reported in the financial statements. Her research finds the relations between life cycle stages and the signs of the cash flow types reported on the statement of cash flows shown in **Exhibit 1.3**.

EXHIBIT 1.3 Relation between Life Cycle Stages and Signs of Cash Flows (Dickinson, 2011)

Cash Flow Type	Introduction	Growth	Mature	Shake-Out	Decline
Operating	Negative	Positive	Positive	Either	Negative
Investing	Negative	Negative	Negative	Either	Positive
Financing	Positive	Positive	Negative	Either	Either

When forecasting the future of a company, consideration of whether the company is in the growth, mature, or decline stage may be quite important. Is the company in a decline stage, where it may be necessary to begin selling off operating assets to continue meeting obligations? If so, what affect will this have on the company's operating asset turnovers or profit margins going forward? Consideration of these questions shapes our expectations and how we predict the relation between current information and future realizations.

Another scenario to consider is a growth company. Forecasting payoffs for companies in the growth stage can be most difficult because their operations will not yet have reached a steady state. The company may be trying to increase their assets to maintain or achieve a desired level of sales growth. Also, the possibility of entrants to the market, as well as other forces, may mean that recent sales growth cannot continue indefinitely. The implications of achieving, steady state for forecasting and valuation will become apparent in subsequent chapters.

SUMMARY

Every business decision has valuation effects, and failing to understand these effects can lead to nonoptimal decisions. Thus, an understanding of the factors that shape value is critical for every accounting or financial professional. As we will see, accounting plays a central role in valuation because it provides and/or captures much of the information necessary to calculate value.

Valuation is a multi-step process. This text will outline these steps, providing you with the tools necessary for practical implementation. This will be beneficial as you begin a career in finance and/or accounting. With a strong understanding of the theoretical models and the practical issues that arise in implementation, you will have the tools necessary to understand valuation and apply that knowledge to sound decision making.

As the first step, a company's current business environment must be assessed and considered as the foundation for all the steps of valuation. This assessment and understanding will yield critical insights, which will assist in relating the current state of the company to forecasts of its future payoffs and risk.

We now proceed, in the next chapter, with a discussion of the role of accounting in valuation. We will illustrate the steps (the path) you need to know to isolate the operations of a company, to determine where a company is currently, to formalize expectations of where the company is going, and to calculate the value of the company. In the next chapter, we examine the role of accounting and its relation to cash flows. Following that, we will begin to look at the financial statements as we try to unlock the operating activities. Reformulation will allow us to split the company into its operating and financial activities. Separation of these activities recognizes that enterprise operating activities yield value and financial activities generally do not. This distinction becomes crucial as we move toward valuation because it allows us to focus our efforts where they will be most beneficial.

QUESTIONS

Q1.1 What are the five steps to valuation?

Q1.2 Why is understanding valuation necessary in business decision making?

Q1.3 What processes might be helpful in structuring our efforts to understand the business?

Q1.4 In which of the five steps in valuation is understanding the business environment most critical?

Q1.5 What is the meaning of the term *reformulation* of financial statements? What is the goal of reformulation?

Q1.6 Why use accounting-based valuation models?

Q1.7 Is value created through operating activities or through financing activities?

Q1.8 Valuation models use expected future payoffs to estimate value. What are possible measures of future payoffs?

Q1.9 Over a firm's life cycle, how does its expected profitability and growth impact the valuation process?

Q1.10. How does an accounting-based valuation method provide an alternative to a cash-flow valuation model for a firm with negative free cash flows?

EXERCISES

E1.11 Calculation of estimates of value requires knowledge of the business and the industry in which the business operates. Describe the industry in which Chipotle (CMG) and Del Taco (TACO) operate.

E1.12 What factors would appear to be most important in an industry analysis for Chipotle (CMG) and Del Taco (TACO)?

E1.13 List some differences in the business environments of Chipotle (CMG) and Del Taco (TACO), which may be expected to lead to differences in their valuation.

E1.14 Gildan Activewear (GIL) and lululemon athletica (LULU) both sell athletic apparel. For fiscal 2018, lululemon athletica had a gross margin percentage of 55.2 percent on sales of $3.3 billion while Gildan Activewear had a gross margin of 27.7 percent on sales of $2.9 billion. What are some possible reasons as to why lululemon has a higher gross profit margin than Gildan?

E1.15 Review Gildan's (GIL) and lululemon's (LULU) most recent annual report, calculate the current year's gross margin percent. Provide possible explanations for the changes in the gross margin.

CONTINUING EXAMPLES

Throughout the text, we will analyze General Mills (GIS) and move toward valuation of the company. Within the end-of-chapter materials, we will repeat the process illustrated within the text by following Kellogg's (K) which is a close competitor of General Mills as well as recreational vehicle manufacturers—Thor Industries (THO) and Winnebago (WGO). This will facilitate the application of the valuation steps to a similar real-life firm. In this chapter, the analysis of General Mills' business environment was not illustrated; this analysis will be conducted for both General Mills and Kellogg in these end-of-chapter exercises.

CE1.16 Calculation of estimates of value requires knowledge of the business and the industry in which the business operates. Describe the industry in which General Mills (GIS) and Kellogg (K) operate.

CE1.17 In performing an analysis using Porter's Five Forces of the industry of General Mills (GIS) and Kellogg (K), what assessments would you make for the different factors?

CE1.18 List some differences in the business environments of General Mills (GIS) and Kellogg (K), which may be expected to lead to differences in their valuation.

CE1.19 Use Dickinson's (2011) cash flow matrix to evaluate the life cycle stage classification of General Mills (GIS) and Kellogg (K).

CE1.20 Calculation of estimates of value requires knowledge of the business and the industry in which the business operates. Describe the industry in which Thor Industries (THO) and Winnebago (WGO) operate.

CE1.21 Perform a Porter's Five Forces analysis of the industry of which Thor Industries (THO) and Winnebago (WGO) are members.

CE1.22 What factors would appear to be most important in an industry analysis for Thor Industries (THO) and Winnebago (WGO)?

CE1.23 Based on the most recent financial statements for Thor Industries (THO) and Winnebago (WGO), determine the life cycle stage based on the classification system of Dickinson (2011)? What is a potential implication for the valuation process?

NOTES

Chapter Two

Role of Accounting

TAKEAWAYS

When you complete this chapter, you should be able to:

1. Explain the relation between accounting earnings and free cash flows.
2. Distinguish operating and financing activities of companies.
3. Demonstrate how free cash flows can be stated in terms of operating accounting information.
4. Discuss issues that prevent reliance on the statement of cash flows in calculating free cash flow.

The focus of this book is on understanding models for and methods of valuing the enterprise operating activities of a company. Identifying of information regarding the operating activities of the company is the necessary first step toward analysis, forecasting, and valuation of the company's operations. And, of course, accounting data provide a very important part of the required information. In this chapter, we begin with a discussion of the role of accounting, and then we define and explain the relation between accounting information (particularly earnings and book values) and cash flows. The next chapter begins a presentation and discussion of practical reformulation of the financial statements with the goal of identifying the net assets and the net earnings related to the operating activities.

UNDERSTANDING THE RELATION BETWEEN ACCOUNTING EARNINGS AND FREE CASH FLOWS

LO1: Explain the relation between accounting earnings and free cash flows.

The traditional approach to valuation focuses on cash flows. The specific emphasis is on *free* cash flows, which are the amounts available (i.e., free) for distribution from operations to the creditors and equity holders of the company after funding the operating activities. The discounted cash flow valuation model, which uses forecasts of free cash flows from operations, is familiar to most people who have an interest in or prior exposure to finance and/or valuation.

While free cash flows may be used as a basis for valuation, it is important to ask whether use of free cash flows is the best choice. A seemingly very reasonable alternative may be the payoffs on which management and outsiders focus for performance evaluation and decision making. A widely-cited study asked a large number of top finance executives of publicly traded companies to *rank the three most important measures to report to outsiders.*[1] The study reported,

[1] Graham, et al., *Journal of Accounting and Economics,* 2005.

CHAPTER OUTLINE

Role of Accounting

Accounting and Cash Flows
- Cash Flows are Important, but so are Earnings
- Role of Accruals

Operating/Financing Distinction
- Concept of Separating Operating versus Financing Activities
- Terms *NOA* and *NOPAT*

Relation of Accounting and Cash Flows
- Identity Relating Free Cash Flows to Operating Earnings and Net Assets
- Examples of Relation

Statement of Cash Flows
- Concerns about Calculating Free Cash Flow from Statement of Cash Flows

> [More than 50% of] CFOs state that earnings are the most important financial metric to external constituents . . . this finding could reflect superior informational content in earnings over the other metrics. Alternatively, it could reflect myopic managerial concern about earnings. The emphasis on earnings is noteworthy because cash flows continue to be the measure emphasized in the academic finance literature.

The study also noted that CFOs view year-over-year change in earnings to be of critical importance to outsiders. Why is that? The study provided the following insights.

> CFOs note that the first item in a press release is often a comparison of current quarter earnings with four quarters lagged quarterly earnings . . . CFOs also mention that while analysts' forecasts can be guided by management, last year's quarterly earnings number is a benchmark that is harder, if not impossible, to manage after the 10-Q has been filed with the SEC . . . Several executives mention that comparison to seasonally lagged earnings numbers provides a measure of earnings momentum and growth, and therefore is a useful gauge of corporate performance. Ditto.

So, are earnings important? To the majority of finance chiefs surveyed, the answer is a resounding yes.

These comments begin to call into question the myopic focus on cash flows often seen in finance valuation textbooks. We must ask, what can be learned from the accounting reports of the company, and why would executives focus on earnings? A good starting point for understanding this question is to analyze the difference between earnings and cash flows and then define the relation between them. We will discuss the two main differences between earnings and free cash flows in a general manner before explicitly defining the relation.

Accounting accruals (e.g., depreciation and accounts receivable) are the key difference between earnings, which include accruals, and cash flows, which do not include accruals. Accounting uses accruals to adjust the timing of revenues and expenses in an attempt to match them to the timing of the underlying economic event. Consider a firm whose policy is to pay monthly wages earned on the first Friday of the following month. If 4,000 hours were worked by employees during December at an average salary of $25 per hour, when should this affect the value of the company? In December, when the employees worked to earn their wages, or in January, when the wages are paid? The important question is this: Did the consumption of this resource (the employees' time and talents) by the company occur during December, when the employees worked, or during January, when wages were paid? December would seem to be the logical choice because that is when the company received the benefits of the employees' efforts. Accounting earnings would be reduced in December, when the $100,000 in wage expense and related wages payable are recorded. The cash outflow would not be seen until the payment of $100,000 is made in January. In this transaction, the accrual of the expense in December accelerates the timing so that the profitability effect in the accounting occurs at the time of the events that change value. There is no change in the value of shareholders' equity when the payment is made because the company offsets the reduction in an asset (cash) with a reduction in a liability (wages payable).

Another, more concrete, example would be, say, Southwest Airlines selling a ticket for $400 in November for a flight that will occur the following March. The cash flow occurs during November, when the ticket is sold. However, has Southwest really seen an economic event that would change its value? At this point, Southwest has cash (an asset) and an obligation to provide a service in the future (a liability shown as unearned revenue). At the time the flight is taken, Southwest will remove the liability from its books and show revenue from the sale, which increases income. Here, the cash flow happens first, but the change in economic value occurs later, when the company earns the $400. Had Southwest not provided the service, the $400 would be refunded. Again, the accrual serves to match the timing of the reported earnings to when the change in economic value occurs. Note also that the existence of the unearned revenue in this example and the wages payable in the prior example provide useful information about the amount and timing of cash flows that have occurred or will occur.

ACCRUALS: GOOD OR BAD?

Researchers use accounting accruals to study the effects of earnings management on financial accounting. Earnings management is broadly defined as the use of accounting discretion to distort reported earnings. Managers may have incentives to manage earnings in many situations. For example, academic research shows that managers have tendencies to accelerate revenue recognition to increase stock prices prior to equity offerings. In contrast, other research shows that managers decelerate revenue recognition to depress stock prices prior to a management buyout (where management repurchases common stock and takes the company "private"). Research also shows that managers use discretion when reporting special items to either meet or beat analysts' forecasts of earnings and/or to avoid reporting a loss. Not all earnings management occurs for opportunistic reasons. Research shows that managers use accruals to communicate private information about future profitability to outsiders. For example, management might signal future profitability through income-decreasing accruals to show investors that it can afford to apply conservative accounting. This "signaling" through accruals is found to precede stock splits and dividend increases. In sum, we must look at reported earnings in conjunction with other earnings quality signals (e.g., levels of disclosure, quality of corporate governance, and industry performance) to interpret information in accruals.

Both of these examples reflect the kinds of accruals that accounting seeks to make on a recurring basis. One more example further highlights the fundamental difference between accounting earnings and cash flows. Consider the purchase of a building for $2,000,000 in cash. The building is expected to be used for 5 years and then sold for $500,000. Notice that, during the time the building is owned, its economic value will decrease by $1,500,000. The cash flows are very straightforward: $2,000,000 as an outflow today and $500,000 expected as an inflow in 5 years. Accounting would record the purchase as an exchange of one asset for another asset (cash for building). At the time of the purchase, there would be no effect on income as no revenue or expense is recorded. Then, over the next 5 years, assuming straight-line depreciation, $300,000 in expense would be shown each year. At the time of the sale, if the building is sold for $500,000 as expected, there would be no gain or loss recognized in the accounting. **Exhibit 2.1** summarizes these accounting and cash flow effects.

EXHIBIT 2.1 Earnings and Cash Flow Effects

	Accounting Earnings	Cash Flows
Today	$ 0	–$2,000,000
Year 1	–300,000	0
Year 2	–300,000	0
Year 3	–300,000	0
Year 4	–300,000	0
Year 5	–300,000	500,000
Total	–$1,500,000	–$1,500,000

Exhibit 2.1 reveals several important insights. First, the total accounting earnings and the total cash flows are the same over the life of the building. That is, the difference is in the timing of the reporting rather than in the total amount reported. Second, it is likely that neither stream perfectly matches the economic change in value occurring each year. That is, the value of the company is probably not decreasing by exactly $300,000 every year.[2] We must also note, however, that the company does not decrease in value by $2,000,000 immediately upon purchase of the building, value is not unchanged in years 1 to 4, and the value of $500,000 is not created in year 5. This raises an interesting question. Because neither the accounting earnings nor the cash flows "get it right," which is closer to economic reality in capturing the timing of the change in value? Clearly, the accounting earnings would be expected to be closer. At the time of purchase, accounting recognizes that the asset, the building, exists, so no value change is recognized! It also recognizes that value is changing each year while the asset is utilized. Most important, consider using these two streams of information in a forecasting exercise (which we will be doing as a part of valuation). Which one seems to be more predictable? Accounting earnings are definitely more predictable from year to year than the cash flows.

These examinations of the accruals and the accounting for a fixed asset purchase highlight some of the major differences between accounting earnings and cash flows. Again, accounting may not be perfect in its timing, but it does attempt to match the timing of earnings to the timing of the underlying changes in value. The question then becomes this: Can we use the accounting earnings for valuation, eschewing the need to continue to use cash flows as the basis of our valuations? The answer is a resounding yes. We will show that the approach of "undoing" or "reversing-out" the accounting accruals to obtain an estimate of the "cash flows" from forecasts of earnings, which is often taught in finance classes, is unnecessary. We also see that accounting-based valuation models, which do not require the forecast of cash flows, are based on accounting numbers, which may be taken at face value; accruals do not have to be separately forecasted and then "reversed out." Stay tuned!

OPERATING VERSUS FINANCIAL ACTIVITIES

LO2: Distinguish operating and financing activities of companies.

Before proceeding to the formalization of the relation of free cash flows and accounting information, we take a moment to clarify the notion of operating and financial activities and the related notations. The concept of operating (used interchangeably with enterprise operations) is at the core of this text. A company's operations are the business/production activities undertaken by the company. **Hewlett-Packard** (HPQ), for example, makes printers and hardware, **Target** (TGT) is a retail chain, and **Walt Disney** (DIS)provides entertainment as a service. Each of these companies also engages in borrowing or lending (i.e., financial) activities, but those are tangential to their core business purpose, which is their "operations." **General Mills** (GIS), our focus company throughout the text, is a manufacturer of human and pet food sold through retail stores.[3]

The distinction between the operating and the financial aspects of a company is well recognized in finance courses where the traditional focus in valuation is on cash flow from *operations*. For external reporting purposes, accounting does not, however, emphasize this distinction. In financial statements prepared under generally accepted accounting principles, operating and financial items are intermingled. (Even in the statement of cash flows, the distinction between operating and financial activities is not immediately apparent despite sections labeled "Operating" and "Financing!")

Further confusion arises from the generic use of the term "free cash flows." There are actually two ways we can measure free cash flows, with the difference between them being the income tax shield. For now, we loosely refer to cash flows or free cash flows, but we will soon get very specific on how we identify free cash flows from operations.

[2] Accounting depreciation being subject to assumptions and not recognizing accurately the change in economic value is a commonly voiced criticism when arguing for the use of cash flows. We will show in Chapters 10 to 12 that this criticism is unfounded because the accounting-based valuation models are generally unaffected by these issues.

[3] As we move through the text, we will consider the implications of classification of income statement and balance sheet items as operating versus financial activities. The classification of these items has important implications on the forecasting task and cost of capital estimation. A direct examination of this issue is provided in Chapter 3, Appendix A.

Not too many years ago, the Financial Accounting Standards Board (FASB) and the International Accounting Standards Board (IASB) considered moving toward a separation of the operating and financial aspects of the company, which would be very similar to what we will do in this text. The FASB's Financial Statement Presentation Project resulted in issuance in 2008 of the discussion paper "Preliminary Views on Financial Statement Presentation." This project proposes a distinction in the reporting between business (which we refer to as operating) and financial activities. Paragraph 2.19 of the discussion paper stated "An entity should present information about the way it creates value (its business activities) separately from information about the way it funds or finances those business activities (its financing activities)" (2008, p. 12). This project is currently on hold, but it has not been abandoned.

To help illustrate the relation between operating and financial activities, we now introduce a diagram of a firm (**Figure 2.1**) from which we will gather insights throughout the chapter. Going forward, building out this model will help us understand the relation between operating profits and free cash flows.

FIGURE 2.1

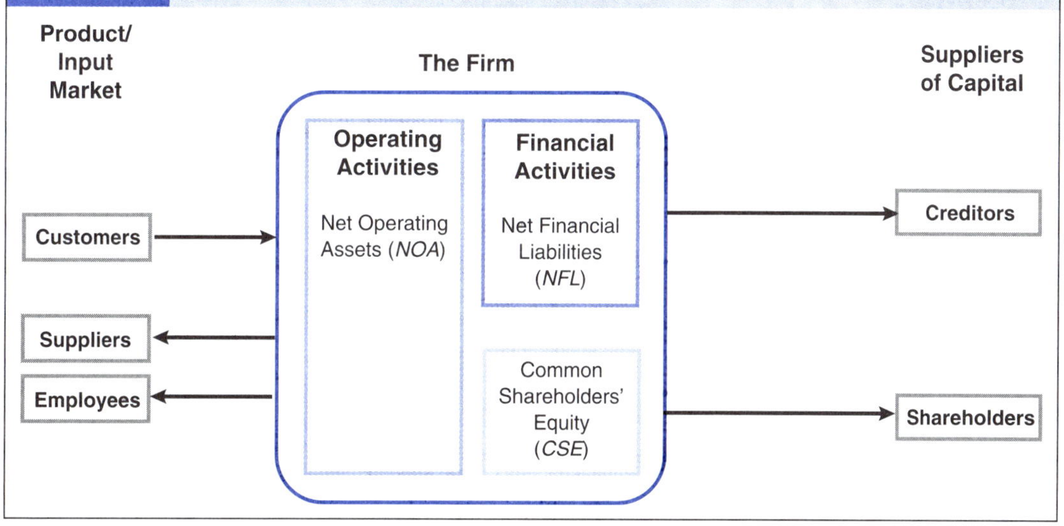

The firm is made up of the operating and financial activities. In the operating activities, the Net Operating Assets (*NOA*) includes both operating assets (accounts receivable, inventory, PP&E, intangibles) and operating liabilities (accounts payable, utilities payable, warranty liability). In the financing activities, the Net Financial Liabilities (*NFL*) includes both financial assets (excess cash and financial investments) and financial liabilities (debt obligations).[4] Common Shareholders' Equity (*CSE*) represents the ownership of both the operating activities and financial activities of the firm.

Interacting with the firm are the members of the product/input markets and the suppliers of capital. The product and input markets are those who supply the company and those who consume its goods or services, respectively. The capital of the firm is supplied by either creditors or shareholders.

Figure 2.2 shows further development. On the left side, we see that the interactions with product and input markets are operating in nature and cause changes in the firm's *NOA*. On the right side, we see that the interactions with capital suppliers are financial in nature and cause changes in either the firm's *NFL* or *CSE*.

[4] Most companies are net borrowers, so the common notation refers to financial activities as resulting in an obligation. However, firms could be net lenders that have Net Financial Assets (*NFA*).

FIGURE 2.2

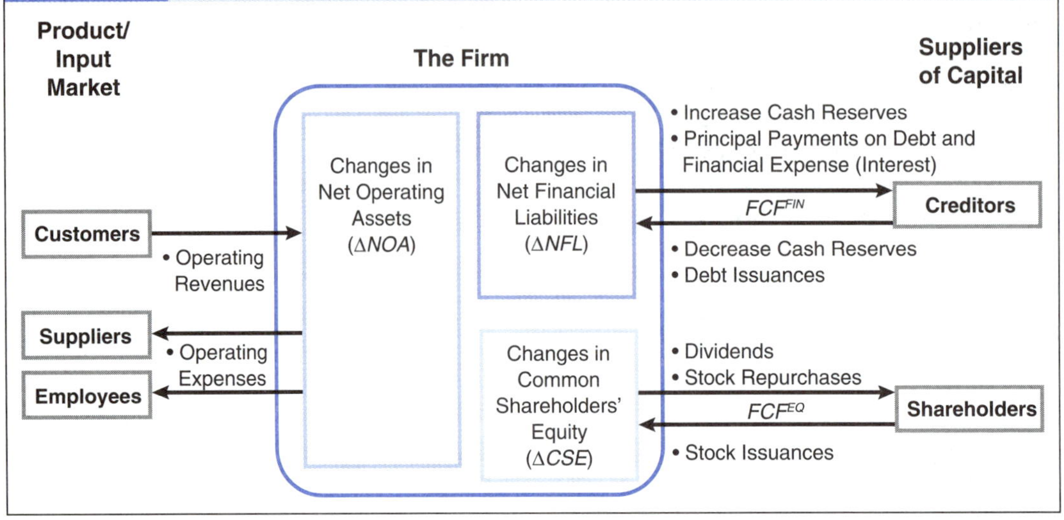

Operating activities result in Operating Revenues and Operating Expenses. Net Operating Profit After Tax (*NOPAT*) is defined as Operating Revenues less Operating Expenses. Other increases in *NOA* occur due to investments in operations (coming from funds received from creditors or shareholders). Other decreases occur due to transfers to owners of funds generated that are not being retained in operations.

Financial activities result in increases/decreases in cash reserves, principal payments/borrowings, and Financial Expenses and Financial Revenues. Financial Expense After Tax (*FEAT*) is defined as Financial Expenses less Financial Revenues. Note that if a firm is a net lender (has *NFAssets*), it likely will show income from financial activities (negative *FEAT*).

Shareholder activities result in stock issuances and repurchases as well as dividend payments. They do not result in any revenues or expenses. Effectively, the operating activities are owned by the creditors and shareholders who supplied capital and have the rights to the results of the operations.

From Figure 2.2, we can see and define free cash flows. Financial transfers going to creditors, a type of free cash flow (FCF^{FIN}), is composed of *FEAT* and any net borrowings/repayments (or lendings/collections if *NFA*). Shareholder transfers, also free cash flows, are referred to as Free Cash Flow to Equity (FCF^{EQ}). Total free cash flows are all amounts going to/from capital suppliers. As they are amounts not retained in operations, they are referred to as Free Cash Flow from Operating Activities (*FCF*). Because most companies are net lenders and regularly paying on debt or making dividend payments, the payments to capital markets are shown as positive *FCF*s. Transfers from the capital markets to operations are negative *FCF*s. In equation form:

$$FCF = FCF^{FIN} + FCF^{EQ} \tag{2.1}$$

Shortly, we will revisit this diagram to see how an accounting equivalent of *FCF* naturally can be found.

While current financial reporting does not directly offer the separation of the operating and financial activities of the company, we will, in the next chapter, reformulate the financial statements to capture this information. The process of reformulation separates the revenues/expenses and the assets/liabilities associated with these two activities. This separation permits a focus on the enterprise operating activities in our forecasting and valuation. (The valuation implications of financial activities will be discussed in a later chapter.) This process of separation of operating activities and financial activities examines each element of the balance sheet and each element of the income statement, asking this question: Is this element a part of the operating or the financial activities of the particular company?

The information reported in financial statements (particularly on the balance sheet) can be used in the identification of the net assets used in operating activities (*NOA*). Net operating assets will be defined more precisely later, but think of things like accounts receivable, inventories, equipment, and accounts payable as components of *NOA*. We also can identify income from operating activities (*NOPAT*) primarily from the income statement. Key components of *NOPAT* are sales revenue less expenditures like cost of goods sold and salaries expense. The operating assets reported on the balance sheet as components of *NOA* generate the components of *NOPAT* reported on the income statement. As an initial step in valuation, we identify current and past Net Operating Profit After Tax (*NOPAT*) and Net Operating Assets (*NOA*) as a prelude to forecasting future *NOPAT* and future *NOA*.

FORMALIZING THE RELATION BETWEEN FREE CASH FLOWS AND ACCOUNTING NUMBERS

LO3: Demonstrate how free cash flows can be stated in terms of operating accounting information.

We now formalize our understanding of the relation between free cash flows and accounting numbers; specifically, the relation between free cash flows from operations (*FCF*), *NOA*, and *NOPAT*. To do so, let us consider a finite-life project and examine the way the project would appear in the accounting reports.

Suppose you are offered the opportunity to invest in a project with the anticipated cash flows at the end of each year shown in **Exhibit 2.2**.

EXHIBIT 2.2 Anticipated Cash Flows of Finite-Life Project

Purchase price		\$1,000
Payoffs		
Year 1 cash flow (CF_1)		250
Year 2 cash flow (CF_2)		350
Year 3 cash flow (CF_3)		320
Year 4 cash flows (CF_4)		
Proceeds from sales	\$280	
Proceeds from disposition	200	
Year 4 Total		\$ 480

If we were to create accounting records for the project, the first economic transaction would be to exchange \$1,000 cash for the equity interest in the project. Thus, we would begin the project with the balance sheet shown in **Exhibit 2.3**.

EXHIBIT 2.3 Initial Balance Sheet of Finite-Life Project

Time period	\$ 0
Balance Sheet	
Project	1,000
Total assets	1,000
Equity	\$1,000

What happens to the cash flows from the project each period? During the first period, the project yields net cash from sales of \$250. This cash is not retained by the project but, rather, is given back to the equity holder. Thus, at the end of period 1, we would not list cash as an asset of the project because it would have been distributed to the equity holder rather than retained (it is a free cash flow coming out of the operations and being given to the project's owner). Similarly, in each future year, the net cash from sales (the payoffs) will be distributed to the equity holder. Further, the proceeds from disposition (the cash received upon sale at the end of the project) will also be distributed to the equity holder. From the viewpoint of the equity holder, these distributions are their payoffs from the project; they are the free cash flows from operations.

PROJECT DISTRIBUTIONS

Imagine purchasing a vending machine as your project. The vending machine would not keep the proceeds from sales each period. Rather, they are taken by you, the owner. In a similar way, a project seldom needs to retain the profits generated in any period. Those cash profits are distributed to the owners on an ongoing basis. If any taxes are due on those profits, we can consider the net distribution received by the owner after the payment of those taxes. Finally, in the last year of the project, any proceeds from selling the machine (perhaps as scrap metal) go to the owner. Note again that the project does not keep the cash from the final disposal. Rather, it is included in that year's distribution to the owner.

To add an accounting flavor to this analysis, let us assume that we choose to record depreciation on the project asset using the straight-line method.[5] Over the 4 years of the project, we would depreciate the asset from the original cost of $1,000 down to the salvage value (the expected proceeds from disposition) of $200. This would result in an annual depreciation charge of $200. In the final year of the project, the book value of the asset will be reduced to $200 ($1,000 less 4 years of depreciation at $200 per year) prior to the disposition. Therefore, when the project asset is sold for $200 at the end of year 4, there will be no gain or loss to recognize on the sale. If we capture this information in a format mirroring accounting financial statements, it would look like **Exhibit 2.4**.

EXHIBIT 2.4 Financial Statements of Finite-Life Project

	Time period	0	1	2	3	4
	Income Statement					
	Revenues		$250	$350	$320	$280
–	Depreciation		(200)	(200)	(200)	(200)
+	Gain on sale (proceeds less book value)					0
=	Net income		50	150	120	80
	Statement of Cash Flows					
	Contribution to fund purchase price	$(1,000)				
+	Revenues		250	350	320	280
+	Proceeds from disposition					200
=	Distributions to (received from) equity holder	(1,000)	250	350	320	480
	Statement of Changes in Equity					
	Beginning book value of project	0	1,000	800	600	400
+	Plus net income	0	50	150	120	80
+	Contributions by (distributions to) equity holder	1,000	(250)	(350)	(320)	(480)
=	Ending book value of project	$ 1,000	$ 800	$600	$400	$ 0

From **Exhibit 2.4**, we can track the cash flows of the project as well as the accounting income and accounting book value. At the beginning of the project, the equity holder would contribute $1,000 to purchase the project asset and then receive in the subsequent periods the periodic cash flows of $250, $350, $320, and $480. The distribution in year 4 of $480 represents the $280 in revenues from the project in that period plus the $200 in proceeds from disposal. The initial book value of the project asset is $1,000 based on the purchase price. The book value declines throughout the life of the project as it is depreciated and ends at $0 when the project is liquidated.

We can see in these financial statements that the cash distributed to the equity holder is the "free cash flow" or "payoffs" from this project. We could value the project based on these

[5] We will return to this example in Chapters 11 and 12, where we will examine the effect of alternative "accounting choices" on calculations of value. Of course, we will show that these choices do not affect the estimated value.

distributions using the discounted cash flow valuation model. Similarly, the operating activities of a firm may be valued based on the free cash flows from operations or distributions that it produces. An often overlooked point is that these distributions can be restated using equivalent accounting data drawn from the financial statements shown above. The key point here is this: There is a clear and unequivocal relation between accounting numbers and free cash flows.

Returning to **Figure 2.2**, what happens when the operations of the company make money? That is, what happens to *NOPAT*? The company has two options: (a) retain the profits for the year in operations, causing an increase in *NOA* or (b) transfer the profits to capital suppliers. That is,

$$NOPAT_t = \Delta NOA_t + FCF_t$$

where ΔNOA_t is the change in net operating assets during the period ended at t. From the relation above, we usually focus on understanding *FCF* by rearranging it as[6]

$$FCF_t \equiv NOPAT_t - \Delta NOA_t \tag{2.2}$$

Free cash flow is "operating profits not retained to fund future operations." These amounts are sent to creditors or distributed to shareholders. Note that some cash may be retained for use in operations, causing an increase in *NOA*. Any amount not needed in operations (i.e., excess cash), is available to distribute. When we examine a finite-life project shortly, none of the cash will be required by future operations and, therefore, all will be available for distribution.

Notice that the value creation (operational) perspective, which focuses on estimating free cash flow based on operations (*NOPAT* and ΔNOA), proves advantages because we no longer have to make assumptions on whether the firm will utilize debt or equity to fund the operations (FCF^{FIN} versus FCF^{EQ}).

The identity shown in Equation 2.2 defines free cash flow from operations in terms of accounting information. To understand the fact that Equation 2.2 is an identity, note that (1) *NOPAT* is the cash flow provided by (and to) operating activities less change in accruals, (2) change in *NOA* is the net capital (cash) investment in the operating activities less the change in accruals, and (3) the change in accruals in the two accounting variables used to identify *FCF* cancel each other out, leaving the cash flow provided by operating activities less the net capital expenditures. This *FCF* is the amount of cash flow from the operating activities to the owners of the operations (i.e., the debt and equity holders).

To begin tying it all together, let's look at how *NOA* and *NFL* change over time. This process mirrors what we see in accounting for retained earnings. In introductory financial accounting, you learned that

$$RE_{t-1} + NI_t - div_t = RE_t$$

The beginning retained earnings (RE_{t-1}) will be increased by current net income (NI_t) and decreased by any dividends (div_t) to arrive at ending retained earnings (RE_t). This process for operating activities is beginning operating assets plus operating profitability less distributions equals ending operating assets. That is:

$$NOA_{t-1} + NOPAT_t - FCF_t = NOA_t$$

This process for financing activities is beginning financial liabilities plus financial expenses less distributions to creditors equals ending financial liabilities. That is,

$$NFL_{t-1} + FEAT_t - FCF_t^{FIN} = NFL_t$$

[6] In this equation, an identity sign (≡) is used rather than an equal sign (=). This is done to emphasize the fact that free cash flow from operations, as we have defined it, is identically and unequivocally equal to net operating profit after taxes less change in net operating assets. An identity is a relation such that it is true no matter what numbers you plug into the equation; it will always be equal. This identity will be the foundation for our analysis of free cash flow and the relation between cash flows and financial statement information.

Combining operating and financial activities, we see that if we subtract the equations, we can see how operating and financial activities combine at the company level:

$$\begin{array}{cccc} NOA_{t-1} & NOPAT_t & FCF_t & NOA_t \\ -NFL_{t-1} & -FEAT_t & -FCF_t^{FIN} & -NFL_t \\ \hline CSE_{t-1} + & CI_t - & FCF_t^{EQ} = & CSE_t \\ \hline\hline \end{array}$$

We see that *NOA* less *NFL* equals *CSE* (since the obligations to creditors are shown as a positive number) and *NOPAT* less *FEAT* equals Comprehensive Income (*CI*). Also, beginning shareholders' equity (CSE_{t-1}) plus comprehensive income (CI_t) less net distributions to shareholders (FCF^{EQ}_t) equals ending shareholders' equity (CSE_t). The fundamental breakdown of the firm into the two pieces of operating and financial activities will prove advantageous in allowing a focus on either *FCF* or accounting measures of operations.

A further discussion of how financial statements articulate and the connection to free cash flow can be found in Appendix 2A.

Demonstrations of the Relation between Free Cash Flows and Accounting Numbers

The relation shown in Equation 2.2 may appear surprising to some; however, the key notion that we can state free cash flows using an equivalence written in terms of accounting numbers is a fact. Equation 2.2 shows that the distributions (*FCF*) from the enterprise operations are equal to the operating earnings (*NOPAT*) less the change in operating assets (ΔNOA). To strengthen the understanding of this critical relation, let us examine two illustrative scenarios.

Example 1

For the first example, consider the accounting of a service organization, which makes a sale of \$1,000 on account, collects the \$1,000 from the customer, and then subsequently distributes this cash to the equity holders. The first economic event occurs when the service organization, as a part of its operations, makes a sale of \$1,000 on account. Accounting would record that the asset, accounts receivable, has increased by \$1,000, and revenue has also increased by \$1,000. At this point in time, there has been no cash involved and no distribution to debt or equity holders. Net Operating Profit After Tax (*NOPAT*) has increased by \$1,000 due to the revenue, and the firm's Net Operating Assets (*NOA*) has increased by \$1,000 as well due to the increase in accounts receivable. Equation 2.2 would reflect this as

$$FCF_t \equiv NOPAT_t - \Delta NOA_t$$
$$0 = 1{,}000 - (+1{,}000)$$

The second economic event is the collection of the \$1,000 in cash from the customer. This would increase cash held in the operations by \$1,000 and reduce the account receivable from the customer by \$1,000. That is, we would substitute one operating asset for another, and there would be no effect on *FCF*, *NOPAT*, or the balance in *NOA*. Since we have no change in *FCF*, *NOPAT*, or *NOA*, we have

$$FCF_t \equiv NOPAT_t - \Delta NOA_t$$
$$0 = 0 - (0)$$

The third economic event is the distribution of the cash from the operations to the equity holders. This would decrease cash in the operating activities by \$1,000, reducing *NOA*. The cash distribution to the equity holders would be a free cash flow from operations. Thus, we have

$$FCF_t \equiv NOPAT_t - \Delta NOA_t$$
$$1{,}000 = 0 - (-1{,}000)$$

Note that the free cash flow did not occur until cash was removed from operating activities and transferred to a debt or an equity holder.

Example 2

For the second example, consider the accounting related to a service company buying a new office building financed by a bank loan. The company records depreciation on the building, makes principal and interest payments on the loan, and finally sells the building at the end of its useful life. Our discussion of this transaction will examine the following elements and assumed dollar values: first, borrowing \$1,000,000 from the bank; second, buying the building for \$1,000,000; third, depreciating the building \$80,000 each year (straight-line depreciation for simplicity); fourth, making the principal and interest payments on the debt totaling \$120,000 per year; and, fifth, selling the building at the end of its 10-year useful life for \$150,000.[7]

The first economic event is borrowing the money from the bank. Borrowing money is in and of itself a financing transaction. The funds could be subsequently used by the company for either a financial activity (e.g., investing in bonds of another company or even paying a dividend) or for an operating activity (e.g., buying a building, as we are considering). In the current case, this money is borrowed from the bank and then immediately transferred to the operations to allow for the purchase of the building. From the perspective of the operations, this results in an increase of operating cash of \$1,000,000 due to an inflow from a debt holder. This inflow is equivalent to a negative distribution because it goes *to* the enterprise operations rather than arising *from* it. That is, it is a negative free cash flow. Equation 2.2 would reflect this as

$$FCF_t \equiv NOPAT_t - \Delta NOA_t$$
$$-1{,}000{,}000 = 0 - (+1{,}000{,}000)$$

The second economic event is the purchase of the office building to be used as a part of operating activities. This will decrease the operating asset, cash, while also increasing the operating asset, building, by \$1,000,000. Again, we are substituting one operating asset for another, and there would be no effect on either *FCF* or *NOPAT*. Because we have no change in *FCF*, *NOPAT*, or total *NOA*, we have

$$FCF_t \equiv NOPAT_t - \Delta NOA_t$$
$$0 = 0 - (0)$$

The third economic event is the recording of depreciation each year. When depreciation is recorded, there is no cash involved; depreciation is a noncash expense. The firm records an expense of \$80,000 and a decrease in the operating asset (due to an increase in the accumulated depreciation account) of \$80,000. Because there is no cash involved in this expense, there is no *FCF*. Thus, we have

$$FCF_t \equiv NOPAT_t - \Delta NOA_t$$
$$0 = -80{,}000 - (-80{,}000)$$

The payment of the principal and interest on the bank loan is the fourth economic event. Although the allocation between principal and interest changes each year, we assume the total payment of \$120,000 does not. In general, accounting would record this transaction as interest expense together with a decrease in the loan payable and also a decrease in cash. The increase in interest expense and the decrease in the loan payable are related to financial activities and, therefore, are not a part of the operating activities. If the cash used to make the payment comes from the operating activities, it decreases *NOA*; both the principal and the interest are distributions from the operations to the debt holders and, therefore, constitute an *FCF* of \$120,000. Recognize that *NOPAT* does not include the interest expense because it measures the profitability of the operating activities, not profit related to financial activities. Therefore, based on Equation 2.2, if this payment is made with operating cash, it would result in

$$FCF_t \equiv NOPAT_t - \Delta NOA_t$$
$$120{,}000 = 0 - (-120{,}000)$$

[7] At this point, we do not consider the effects of taxes. The effects of taxes and the interest tax shield will be addressed later in the text. For now, the focus is on distinguishing between operating and financial activities.

The final economic event is selling the building at the end of its useful life for $150,000. From an accounting standpoint, this is perhaps the most complicated event. The building was originally purchased for $1,000,000 and has been depreciated at a rate of $80,000 per year for 10 years. So, its book value would be $200,000 ($1,000,000 – $80,000 * 10) at the time of sale. Thus, the accounting would remove the $200,000 from *NOA*, record the receipt of $150,000 proceeds from the sale, and show a $50,000 loss for the difference. The $50,000 loss would be a part of *NOPAT* (remember that we are ignoring the tax effect in this example). The proceeds of $150,000 could either be retained as a part of operating activities and reinvested in the business or distributed to debt or equity holders. If the $150,000 is retained in the operating activities, there is a net $50,000 decrease in *NOA* comprised of the $200,000 decrease in building and the $150,000 increase in operating cash. Using Equation 2.2, this would appear as

$$FCF_t \equiv NOPAT_t - \Delta NOA_t$$

$$0 = -50{,}000 - (-50{,}000)$$

Alternatively, if the $150,000 is distributed out of the operations to either debt or equity holders, it is a free cash flow from operations and Equation 2.2 would appear as:

$$FCF_t \equiv NOPAT_t - \Delta NOA_t$$

$$150{,}000 = -50{,}000 - (-200{,}000)$$

Examination of these two scenarios (sets of transactions) related to a sale of services and ownership of the building reinforces our understanding of the relation between free cash flow and the accounting numbers of the enterprise operations. Equation 2.2 demonstrates that the free cash flows from a firm's operations, like the distributions from the project, can be calculated using accounting numbers.

THE STATEMENT OF CASH FLOWS

LO4: Discuss issues that prevent reliance on the statement of cash flows in calculating free cash flow.

If we sought a focus on *FCF* rather than *NOA* and *NOPAT*, we might consider beginning with the statement of cash flows, as is done in some textbooks. As we grow more comfortable with *NOA* and *NOPAT*, we will find ourselves getting more uncomfortable with the statement of cash flows. Both the operating and investing cash flows sections of the statement of cash flows are not purely related to operating activities. Note that under U.S. GAAP, the operating cash flow section contains elements of *NOPAT*, but it also contains investment income and interest expense while failing to consider the allocation of taxes to operating and financial activities. The investing section contains the investment in operating plant assets, which are changes in *NOA*, but it also contains the company's investment in securities, most of which are financial in nature. Thus, the split between operating and financial activities is not readily apparent from the statement of cash flows, and we will get a rough approximation of free cash flows from operations at best.

Another very important issue is that there can be significant transactions omitted from the statement of cash flows if they do not involve cash. An illustrative example is the 2006 acquisition of **Gillette** by **Proctor & Gamble** (PG). During that year, PG acquired Gillette via a $53 billion stock issuance. That is, the currency for the transaction was PG shares rather than cash in the form of greenbacks. And, for this reason, this transaction is not included in the operating, investing, or financing sections of the statement of cash flows. However, if you look at the balance sheet and income statement, the transaction is very obvious. Total assets more than doubled to $136 billion from the reported $61 billion in 2005. When we calculate the change in *NOA* in Equation 2.2, the free cash flow from the equity holders to the firm is readily evident. This reinforces the superiority of an approach based in the reformulation of financial statements for identification of operating activities for valuation.

SUMMARY

This chapter has provided insight into the role of accounting in valuation. In doing so, we have formalized the link between the book value of net operating assets, net operating profit after tax, and free cash flows from operations. By understanding the role of accounting, we can come to see that the accruals process and various allocations, such as depreciation, allow the reported information to more closely mirror the economic events. Rather than creating problems, accruals are helpful. Of course, we do not ignore that accruals (and cash flows for that matter!) may be influenced by managerial incentives and are potentially subject to manipulation. The issues this can cause will be addressed in subsequent chapters. Still, the accounting accruals and allocations provide information that will be shown to be more useful in forecasting and, therefore, in valuation than relying on cash flows alone.

In the next chapter, we will implement the second step in the valuation process. We will reformulate the financial statements of GIS in order to isolate the company's operating activities. This reformulation will provide *NOA* and *NOPAT*, which we will use for analysis of the company, for forecasting future operating activities, and for the valuation of GIS.

APPENDIX 2A: Financial Statement Articulation and Free Cash Flows

A review of the articulation of financial statements and effects of reformulation verifies why computing free cash flows from operations from balance sheets and income statements is appropriate. We begin with a reminder of how financial statements connect (articulate) and then examine how operations provide measures of free cash flows via reformulation. From this exercise, we will see that thinking of free cash flow as the net operating profit adjusted for the change in operating resources ($FCF = NOPAT - \Delta NOA$) is natural and appropriate because it fully captures the payments made from operations to capital providers.

Articulation of Financial Statements

The ties between financial statements are well known, though sometimes underappreciated. Balance sheets measure the status of a company at a point in time. The income statement, statement of comprehensive income, cash flows statement, and statement of stockholders' equity all measure changes that occur during a period of time. When we look at two consecutive annual balance sheets, the other financial statements report on the changes that occurred between the start and end of the year.

Specifically, the following connections hold in accounting:

- The statement of stockholders' equity shows the elements that comprise the changes in equity accounts between balance sheet dates.
- The statement of cash flows shows the sources and uses of cash as it changed between balance sheet dates.
- The income statement and statement of comprehensive income measure the portion of the change in equity that is related to the activities of the company, both operating and financial, during the year. This amount feeds into the statement of stockholders' equity as a portion of the change in equity between balance sheet dates.

On the statement of stockholders' equity, the changes in equity can be segregated into two parts: the comprehensive income and the net amount of transfers to/from the equity holders. This second part is the net shareholder transactions of which the most common are stock issuances, purchases of treasury stock, and the payment of dividends.

EXHIBIT 2A.1 Relation between Financial Statements

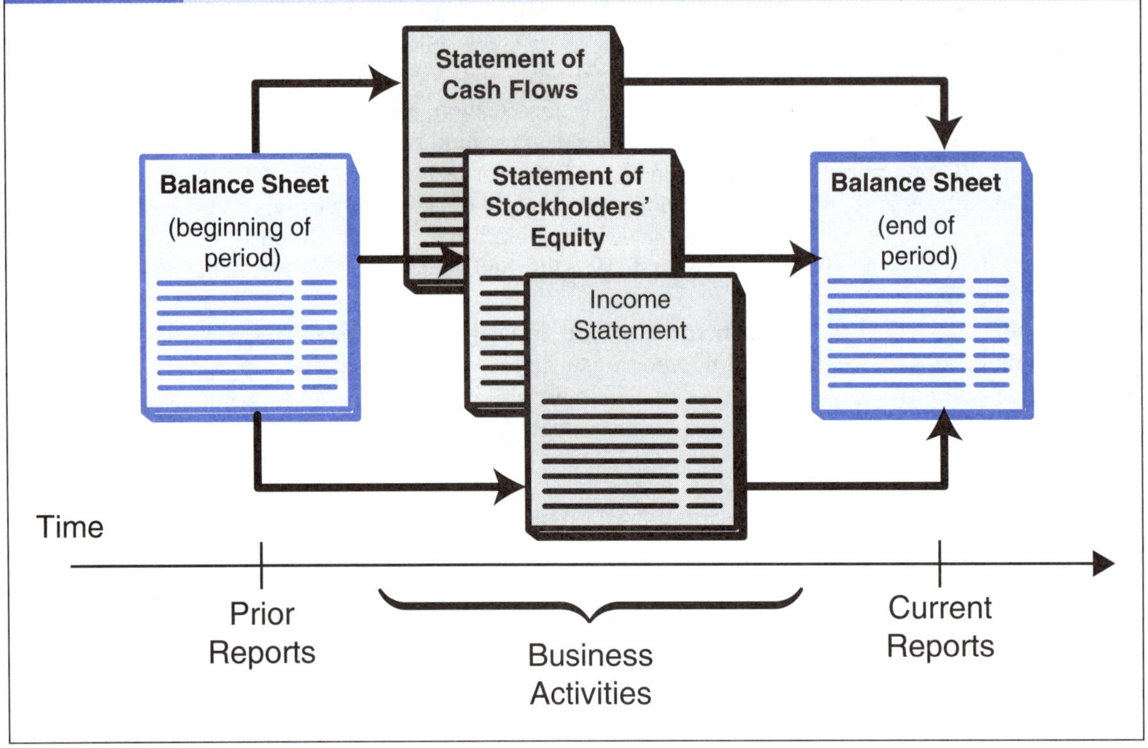

Connection to Free Cash Flows via Reformulation

When we reformulate the balance sheet, we separate the operating and financial activities of the company. That is

$$\text{Assets} = \text{Liabilities} + \text{Equity}$$

becomes

$$\text{Operating Assets} + \text{Financial Assets} = \text{Operating Liabilities} + \text{Financial Liabilities} + \text{Equity}$$

which may be rearranged to

$$\text{Operating Assets} - \text{Operating Liabilities} = \text{Financial Liabilities} - \text{Financial Assets} + \text{Equity}$$

$$NOA = NFL + CSE$$

$$NOA - NFL = CSE$$

Concentrating on the second to last line of the derivation above, notice that the right side, $NFL + CSE$, is the accounting measure of the amount owed to creditors and equity holders. These parties are the capital providers that finance the firm's operating activities. As such, funds going to/from them as a result of operations are free cash flows from operations. To show this, we revisit the relations described above.

In the prior section, we noted that the change in equity is composed of comprehensive income and the net shareholder transactions. Remembering that we notate the net shareholder transactions as FCF^{EQ}, where payments to shareholders are shown as positive, we arrive at[8]

$$CSE_{t-1} + CI_t - FCF^{EQ}_t = CSE_t$$

[8] Payments made to shareholders are shown as positive, and payments received from shareholders are negative. Therefore, a purchase of treasury stock is money paid out, so it would be shown as a positive number, while a new stock issuance is money received by the company, so it would be shown as a negative number.

Substituting the reformulations discussed in this chapter, we recognize that this can be rewritten and then rearranged to isolate enterprise operations as follows:

$$(NOA_{t-1} - NFL_{t-1}) + (NOPAT_t - FEAT_t) - FCF_t^{EQ} = (NOA_t - NFL_t)$$

$$NOA_{t-1} - NFL_{t-1} + NOPAT_t - FEAT_t - FCF_t^{EQ} = NOA_t - NFL_t$$

$$NOPAT_t + NOA_{t-1} - NOA_t = FEAT_t + NFL_{t-1} - NFL_t + FCF_t^{EQ}$$

$$NOPAT_t - \Delta NOA_t = FEAT_t - \Delta NFL_t + FCF_t^{EQ}$$

In this equation, we see that the left side is what we defined as free cash flows from operations in Equation 2.2. Now, consider the terms found on the right side. If the items on the right side are the amounts being distributed from operations to the capital providers (the creditors and equity holders) of the company, we have captured the free cash flows. The first term, *FEAT*, is primarily the interest expense that would have been paid to creditors during the year. The second term is the decrease in *NFL* during the period. Remember that a decrease in *NFL* is the result of principal payments made to creditors. The last term on the right side, FCF^{EQ}, is the net distributions to shareholders during the period. Together, these three items comprise the *FCF*s paid to capital providers; the principal and interest paid to creditors and the distributions made to equity holders.

If the firm were a net lender (negative *NFL*), the relation above would still hold as the amount received as interest income would be an inflow to the operations; a negative *FCF*. Additionally, if the firm lends money to the capital market, buys investments, or borrows money from creditors, these would result in an increase in *NFL*; negative free cash flows from operations. Remember that funds flowing to capital providers from the operations are positive *FCF*s and funds flowing from capital providers they are negative *FCF*s.

Focusing on the operations is a very clear way to capture the free cash flows of the period. It allows us to use the relations found in accounting to directly calculate the payoffs made to capital providers.

QUESTIONS

Q2.1 What is the most important measure of firm performance reported to outsiders? What is the most commonly used measure for valuation?

Q2.2 What is the difference between cash flows and earnings? What is the role of this item?

Q2.3 Are efforts to undo accounting as a step for valuation necessary?

Q2.4 Do the income statement and balance sheet prepared under U.S. GAAP report information for operating activities, financial activities, or both?

Q2.5 What is *FCF* equal to in accounting terms (i.e., provide the equation)?

Q2.6 Why is calculation of *FCF* from *NOPAT* and ΔNOA superior to calculating it from the statement of cash flows?

Q2.7 What are free cash flows (*FCF*)?

Q2.8 How is net operating profit after tax (*NOPAT*) different from cash flows provided by (and to) operating activities (*CFO*)?

Q2.9 How is the change in net operating assets (ΔNOA) different from net cash investments in operating activities?

Q2.10 What is $NOPAT - \Delta NOA$ in cash flows terms?

Q2.11 What is the benefit of reformulating GAAP financial statements between operating and financing activities?

Q2.12 Do accounting earnings or cash flows better reflects economic reality? Why?

EXERCISES

E2.13 Demonstrate that the total earnings and the cash flows are the same (similar to **Exhibit 2.1**) for the following scenarios:

a. Purchase of a 3-year insurance policy at the beginning of 2020 at a total cost of $240,000.

b. Sale of a round-trip ticket for $600 by an airline in November 2020. The first leg of the trip will occur in December 2020 and the return leg will occur in January 2021.

E2.14 Demonstrate that the relation shown in **Equation 2.2**, $FCF_t \equiv NOPAT_t - \Delta NOA_t$, holds for the following transactions:

a. Purchase of inventory on account for $700.
b. Sale of that inventory for $1,900 in cash (assume the cash is considered necessary for the operating activities).
c. Alternatively, assume the sale of the inventory in part *a.* for $1,900 on account.
d. Collection of the $1,900 receivable from part *c.* (assume the cash is considered necessary for the operating activities).

E2.15 Demonstrate that the relation shown in **Equation 2.2**, $FCF_t \equiv NOPAT_t - \Delta NOA_t$, holds for the following transactions:

a. Declaration of quarterly cash dividend of $450.
b. Payment of quarterly cash dividend of $450.
c. Payment of a 3-year insurance premium $675. The company records 1 year as expense and 2 years as a prepaid expense.
d. In the subsequent year, recording the "using up" of 1 year of the prepaid insurance in part *c.*

E2.16 For 2020, Montgomery, Inc. had net operating profit after tax (*NOPAT*) of $3,150. Montgomery's balance sheet for 2019 and 2020 is:

	2019	2020
Cash	$ 3,590	$ 4,260
Accounts receivable	5,650	8,340
Inventory	10,240	11,460
Property and equipment, net	21,840	26,110
Goodwill	13,160	14,310
Other operating assets	3,450	4,720
Accounts payable	10,400	13,310
Accrued expenses and other	10,350	13,740
Unearned revenues	3,120	4,770
Long-term debt	7,680	8,350
Common stock	18,840	18,930
Retained earnings	7,540	10,100

a. Calculate Montgomery's net operating assets (*NOA*) for 2019 and 2020.
b. Calculate Montgomery's 2020 free cash flow (*FCF*).

E2.17 Broad Company reported the following selected financial results for 2019 and 2020.

	2019	2020
Operating assets	$48,700	$57,300
Financial assets	11,600	13,500
Operating liabilities	27,900	31,300
Financial liabilities	19,400	25,400

NOPAT	$2,550
FEAT	1,050
Comprehensive Income (*CI*)	1,500

a. Calculate Broad's *NOA*, *NFL* and *CSE* for 2019 and 2020.
b. Calculate Broad's *FCF*, FCF^{FIN} and FCF^{EQ} for 2020.

E2.18 Cooper Corp. had another good year earning $25 million in comprehensive income that generated positive free cash flows of $18 million. The free cash flows supported Cooper's share repurchase program, which bought back $10 million of common stock, and its dividends, which were $7 million during the year. The shares repurchased are held in treasury for its equity compensation plan. During the year, employee stock options were exercised resulting in the issuance of stock for $3 million based on the options' exercise price.

a. What is Cooper's free cash flow from/to equity holders (FCF^{EQ}) for the year?

b. What is Cooper's free cash flows from/to its creditors/debtors for the year?

E2.19 Demski Co's income statement reported $45 million in comprehensive income during the year of which $50 million was *NOPAT*. From the statement of cash flows, Demski purchased $38 million in marketable securities and sold $16 million in marketable securities. Additionally, the statement of cash flow reported additional short-term borrowing of $30 million and repayment of long-term debt of $90 million.

What is Demski's free cash flows from/to creditor/debtors (FCF^{FIN}) for the year?

CONTINUING EXAMPLES

As stated in the prior chapter, at each point that we move along the five steps of valuation for **General Mills** (GIS), we will also analyze **Kellogg** (K) here. In this chapter, there is not a specific reference to GIS as we were establishing a conceptual understanding of the role of accounting. Wherever appropriate, we will also provide in the end-of-chapter materials a continuing example of a finite-life project similar to the one shown in **Exhibit 2.2**. This will provide the opportunity to practice these steps also as we move toward valuation.

CE2.20 The company has been offered the opportunity to invest a project expected to yield the following cash flows:

Anticipated Cash Flows of Finite-Life Project	
Purchase price	$2,300
Payoffs:	
Year 1	$600
Year 2	700
Year 3	750
Year 4	625
Year 5	500

In addition, at the end of the 5 years it is anticipated the remaining materials from the project can be sold for $240. The project is expected to be depreciated using the straight-line method over the 5-year period.

a. Prepare the income statement for the 5 years of the project.

b. Prepare the "statement of cash flows" as illustrated in **Exhibit 2.4** for the period of acquisition and the 5 years of operation of the project.

c. Prepare the statement of changes in equity for the period of acquisition and the 5 years of operation of the project.

CE2.21 A company is considering an investment in a project expected to yield the following cash flows:

Anticipated Cash Flows of Finite-Life Project	
Purchase price	$7,000
Payoffs:	
Year 1	$2,100
Year 2	2,500
Year 3	2,400

In addition, at the end of the three years it is anticipated the remaining assets from the project can be sold for $400. The project is expected to be depreciated using the straight-line method over the three-year period.

a. Prepare the income statement for the three years of the project.

b. Prepare the "statement of cash flows" as illustrated in **Exhibit 2.4** for the period of acquisition and the three years of operation of the project.

c. Prepare the statement of changes in equity for the period of acquisition and the three years of operation of the project.

Chapter Three

Reformulation to Identify Operating Activities

TAKEAWAYS

When you complete this chapter, you should be able to:

1. Separately identify the operating income and assets of the company.
2. Reformulate to calculate net operating assets.
3. Adjust for equity items that are liabilities from the viewpoint of a common shareholder.
4. Reformulate the financial statements to determine operating income and net operating profit after taxes.

In this chapter, we move to the second step of the valuation process, where we isolate the accounting information about the operating activities of a company. Identification of information regarding the operating activities of the company is necessary to allow for analysis, forecasting, and valuation of the company's operations. We will demonstrate, using General Mills (GIS) as an example, how the information contained in the balance sheet and the income statement may be split between the operating and the financial activities of the company. From this, we will be able to compute the net operating assets (*NOA*) and the net operating profit after tax (*NOPAT*) as a prelude to analysis, forecasting, and valuation.

SEPARATION OF OPERATING AND FINANCIAL ACTIVITIES

LO1: Separately identify the operating income and assets of the company.

The operating activities are the business/production activities undertaken by the company (i.e., what the company does). The financial activities are the borrowing/lending activities undertaken by the company (i.e., where the company gets the money). These are distinct activities, and each plays an important role in the valuation process.

As mentioned in Chapter 1, we seek to estimate the value of the operating activities of GIS. From that, we will be able to subtract the value of the financial activities to arrive at the value of the equity; that is, the value of the shares of stock in the company, which we purchase. The reasons for the separation of these are twofold.

First, financial activities are generally reported on the financial statements at fair value (or their value is disclosed), enabling a straightforward calculation of their value. This leaves the focus on the items that are harder to value, the operating activities.

Second, by calculating value for operating activities, we avoid having to consider the financial choices management may make in the future. That is, will they finance a new project by borrowing from the bank or by issuing more shares of stock? This choice does not affect the value or riskiness of the new project. Chapter 9 will provide additional insight as to the interplay of these decisions and the calculation of cost of capital.

CHAPTER OUTLINE

Reformulation to Identify Operating Activities

Separation of Operating and Financing Activities
- Identifying Operating Income and Assets

Separating Assets and Liabilities
- Elements of *NOA*
- Classification of Specific Balance Sheet Accounts as Operating or Financial

Equity
- Equity Items Considered as Liabilities in Reformulation

Separating Income and Expenses
- Elements of *NOPAT*
- Classification of Specific Income Statement Accounts as Operating or Financial
- Allocation of Income Taxes

EFFECTS OF DEBT VERSUS EQUITY FUNDING

To illustrate that the source of funding—debt versus equity—is irrelevant when valuing the operations, consider the following two scenarios:

- A company is considering investing in a project that will clearly yield a positive net present value even at a high hurdle rate. To fund the project, the company needs $10 million. What effect would getting the $10 million from creditors versus equity holders have on the project?

  None! Whether the project is funded with debt or equity has no effect on the anticipated payoffs or the riskiness of the payoffs from the project.
- Assume that the enterprise operations have generated $2 million in cash that will either be used to pay off debt or distributed to shareholders. Does this choice affect the risk or the future profitability of operating activities?

  No! After the cash has been distributed (it is a free cash flow from operations), it is no longer available to use in operations. Where it went has no impact on the anticipated payoffs or the riskiness of the payoffs from the operations. It can be either FCF^{FIN} or FCF^{EQ}.

The common methodology used in both cash flow- and accounting-based valuation is to focus on the enterprise operations without being concerned about their funding source, whether it be debt or equity.

The Starting Point: Identifying Operating Income and Assets, *NOPAT* and *NOA*

A goal in financial statement analysis is to gather information from the financial statements, which is useful in forecasting the future payoffs from investment in the operations. To arrive at estimates of future payoffs, we need to form expectations, and a key source of information for this process is what has previously occurred. Often, the past few years of financial statements are analyzed.

CREATING A SPREADSHEET FOR PRACTICAL IMPLEMENTATION

Throughout the text, we will provide practical tips and techniques for creating a valuation spreadsheet such as the ones used in gathering the data and computing the value for **General Mills** (GIS) and **Kellogg** (K) in the end-of-chapter materials. This first practical application box involves gathering the financial statement information from the recent Form 10-Ks. While that sounds straightforward, it can be complicated by issues arising from restatements.

Companies will have restatements due to changes in accounting methods, changes in the reporting entities (i.e., the subsidaries included/excluded), and corrections of errors in prior statements. Two questions arise: Should we use the originally reported information or the revised information? How do we make sure we are gathering the numbers we want?

Suppose we seek the last 5 years of financial statement information for GIS from its Consolidated Statement of Earnings, Statements of Comprehensive Income, Balance Sheets, and Statements of Shareholders' Equity. The 2018 10-K includes balance sheet data for 2 years and 3 years of data for the Statement of Comprehensive Income, Statement of Cash Flows, and Statement of Changes in Shareholders' Equity. Therefore, when looking at the 2018 financial statements, we can find the following information:

continued

General Mills' Financial Information

	Information for		
	2016	**2017**	**2018**
Statement of earnings	Yes	Yes	Yes
Statement of comprehensive income	Yes	Yes	Yes
Balance sheet	No	Yes	Yes
Statement of shareholders' equity	Yes	Yes	Yes

When we move backward in time to the 2017 financial statements, we see the income statement for 2017 and 2016 reported again, as well as the addition of 2015 information.

Sometimes, there is a difference between the two sets of data for 2017 and 2016. Which data should we use? We will use the 2016 information as gathered from the 2018 financials because these restated numbers will align with the subsequent reporting. In other words, rather than the information as originally reported, we desire the information as updated/corrected/revised/restated. This restated information is comparable to the current information.

The result is that, when building a valuation spreadsheet for a company, we start with the most recent financial statements and then move back a year at a time, adding the information we find. The 2017 financials are the most recent reporting of the 2015 statement of earnings, so they will be the source of that information. Similarly, the 2016 financials are the most recent reporting of the 2014 statement of earnings, so they will be the source of that information. The resulting 5-year information sources are as follows:

General Mills' Financial Information

	Information for				
	2014	**2015**	**2016**	**2017**	**2018**
Gathered from financials:					
Statements of earnings	2016	2017	2018	2018	2018
Statements of comprehensive income	2016	2017	2018	2018	2018
Balance sheets	2015	2016	2017	2018	2018
Statements of shareholders' equity	2016	2017	2018	2018	2018

Generally, further refinements to these past data are unnecessary because we are primarily using them to identify past trends, which we then use as a basis for forecasts of the future. Sometimes, however, adjustments may be necessary. Suppose, for example, there was a spin-off of a major subsidiary in 2017. This would be reflected in our earnings data for 2016, 2017, and 2018, but it would not be reflected in the data for 2014 and 2015. If we are able to form a reasonably reliable restatement of the earlier data (e.g., the company may have reported segment data for the segment that has been spun off), we will do so; if not, we may find ourselves choosing to rely on just the later data.

Another issue, which affects our use of historical information, is acquisition of another company. We would love to have a set of financial statements that show what would have been reported historically had the acquired company already been a part of the operations, but that information does not exist. While a company may provide some pro-forma information, it is not enough to let us reconstruct the past. Thus, all parties attempting a valuation face this same dilemma of determining the effects. The most direct effects of acquisitions on our valuation efforts will be seen in Chapter 7, when we begin forecasting.

One more issue that can arise is a change in the month of the year-end. While this is seldom seen, companies can change their year-end for tax or reporting reasons or as the result of a merger. In that case, we may end up with a historical "year" of information that is less than 12 months. With this data, we can still perform the analyses shown later in this chapter. However, as a preview to Chapter 6, we will need to recognize that operating asset turnover (*ATO*) will be problematic because we will be comparing a partial year of sales to *NOA*. In contrast, for operating profit margin (*PM*), both the expenses and the sales are partial year, so the ratio may be unaffected unless there is seasonality. Still, the notion that 1 "year" of historical data may not be representative must be borne in mind when we use the historical information as a starting point in our forecasting.

The components of *NOA* reported on the balance sheet generate the components of *NOPAT* reported on the income statement. As an initial step in valuation, we identify current and past net operating profit after tax (*NOPAT*) and net operating assets (*NOA*) and the inclusion of additional information beyond that in the financial statements as a prelude to forecasting future *NOPAT* and future *NOA*. In subsequent chapters, we will return to the issue of forecasting *NOPAT* and *NOA*, and we will also discuss adjustments to financial information, which may increase our confidence in our forecasts of *NOPAT* and *NOA*.

SOURCES OF FINANCIAL STATEMENT DATA AND SPREADSHEET PROGRAM CHOICE

When you seek to gather financial statement data, one option is the Form 10-K filed by the company with the Securities and Exchange Commission, which is available via the company website and other places, such as the EDGAR database. Another option is to avoid the initial manual entry of data by downloading a spreadsheet of financial statement data from a source such as Mergent Online. Any of these options is fine provided that you ensure you know what data you have.

Data downloaded from a source such as Mergent Online will often differ from those shown on the Form 10-K. This is due to the inclusion in the spreadsheet of details gathered from the footnotes. We will do a similar task in Chapter 4, where we expand items by including additional information. If you choose to start the process with a source other than the Form 10-K, make sure you reconcile it back to the Form 10-K and understand what items have been added. In doing so, you will likely find many places where the additional data duplicate items shown in the Form 10-K. Failure to catch these duplications and form appropriate subtotals/totals in your spreadsheet will result in unusable data. And, again, make sure all summations and totals are calculated by the spreadsheet and not hard-coded amounts. Taking these steps can help you avoid a lot of problems later.

Related to the initial setup is the choice of software program used in creating your spreadsheet. Because class projects are often completed in groups, there is a tendency to consider using Google Sheets or Excel Online to enable collaboration. From the feedback of prior students, we suggest, in order of highest to lowest preference, Excel, Excel Online, and Google Sheets. The students' experiences have shown that the capabilities of Excel far outweigh benefits created by the collaborative nature of Excel Online and Google Sheets.

When we reformulate the GIS balance sheet, we will classify each item other than common equity items as relating to the operating or the financial activities. In essence, we are segregating each item based on our understanding of the company (step 1 in the valuation process). Reformulation is not an exact science but, rather, an application of our knowledge of the company's structure and goals. The implications of our choices will be seen in effects on forecasting and cost of capital estimation. Note that, while we may "make the job harder" by our choices, our choices should not cause a change in the estimation of the value of common equity if done properly. Appendix 3A provides a discussion and detailed numerical example elaborating on this issue further.[1]

The overriding factor in our decision regarding whether items are part of operating or financing activities is the implications for the future steps we will take. Remember that we will be valuing operations while relying on the value of financial activities already available to us. (Note, this analysis was also implicitly done, although not always verbalized, in the discounted cash flow valuation exercises you may have seen previously.) Thus, when there is an element of our balance sheet where we are unsure of its purpose (i.e., operating or financial), we will focus on whether we are comfortable assuming it is already at fair value. Often, this leads us to classify the item as operating and include it in our analysis because we do not have confidence in the estimate of its value in the financial statements. An example would be "other assets" where we are not sure of the makeup nor of the value.

[1] For those with a background in and familiarity with utilizing free cash flows from operations in valuation, we suggest review of Appendix 3A in conjunction with this chapter. This would also be suggested for those for whom this text's approach appears to conflict with information from prior classes. Others may find it best to revisit Appendix 3A after coverage of cost of capital estimation in Chapter 9.

OFFERING FINANCING TO SUPPORT SALES

Some companies, such as Ford, General Electric, and Caterpillar, which sell large items, have operated "financing" divisions, which support the company's sales efforts by offering credit to customers who purchase those items. As mentioned in Caterpillar's 2018 10-K, "The Financial Products line of business also conducts operations under highly competitive conditions. Financing for users of Caterpillar products is available through a variety of competitive sources, principally commercial banks and finance and leasing companies. We offer various financing plans designed to increase the opportunity for sales of our products and generate financing income for our company." (p. 56)

The question arises as to whether these services (and the related assets/liabilities and revenues/expenses) should be considered as a part of the operating or financial activities of Caterpillar. It appears that this segment is primarily something the company does to facilitate the sale of equipment. Remember that the company could have contracted with banks to facilitate the financing process for Caterpillar's customers. As such, the effects of the Financial Products division will be felt on sales of machinery, energy, and transportation and included in our forecasts of revenues. Further, there is no evidence that the assets/liabilities related to the division are not reported in the financial statements at fair value. Therefore, although Caterpillar specifically designates Financial Products as one of its operating segments and also made $2.9 billion in revenue from the segment in 2018, we will choose to conclude that the Financial Products segment represents a financial activity for Caterpillar.

If we are examining Caterpillar competitor Deere, we arrive at a different conclusion. For Deere, footnote 16 of the 2018 Form 10-K reveals land, buildings, equipment, and other fixed assets related to its Financial Services division. Given that these items would not be shown on the balance sheet at fair value, we must include them in our valuation efforts. For Deere, the Financial Services division would be treated as a part of operations.

Whether we classify a "financing" segment as operating or financial will affect our valuation because it impacts the scope of what we are valuing and its risk. If financial services assets/liabilities are deemed to be financial activities, we are asserting that they are carried on the financial statements at fair value. Additionally, our measure of the risk of the operations will differ depending on the inclusion/exclusion of these items. This is similar to the effect seen in Appendix 3A.

ORDER OF YEARS AND SIGNS OF ITEMS

In a valuation spreadsheet, it is helpful to have the most recent information on the right. This is despite GIS having the current year on the left in its published financials. Having the most recent years on the right in the spreadsheet will prove particularly helpful when we move to forecasting in Chapter 7. This way, the historical years (2017, 2018) will flow smoothly into the forecasted years (2019, 2020, etc.) as you move from left to right.

Also, in setting up a valuation spreadsheet, on your balance sheets, and in your calculations of *NOA* and *NFL*, you should show assets as positive numbers and liabilities and equity as negative numbers. This will simplify netting of *NOA* and *NFL* as well as other calculations. On the income statement and calculations of *NOPAT* and *FEAT*, you should show income as positive numbers and expenses as negative numbers to facilitate calculations. Note, however, that when carrying numbers between income statements and balance sheets, net income (a positive number) will increase equity (a negative number). Pay close attention to the signs!

One more caveat on spreadsheet setup: Make sure to add things using calculations rather than inputting the totals. For example, use the SUM formula in Excel to calculate total current assets rather typing the total amount. This will allow you to find errors much faster.

Be aware of signs, and be sure to have all information arranged optimally. This will save much time and frustration later!

IDENTIFYING NET OPERATING ASSETS, *NOA*

LO2: Reformulate to calculate net operating assets.

We begin our reformulation with identification of the operating assets and liabilities (*NOA*). Essentially, this entails going through the company's balance sheet item by item to determine which items would be associated with operating activities. For some items, the classifications seem obvious: Inventory is related to operating activities, and a bond payable is financial (at least this is so except for financial institutions like banks). For other items, the distinction may not be quite as clear. At each step, we are asking whether the item is a necessary part of the operating activities of the company.

Exhibit 3.1 shows the reported balance sheet for GIS as of May 2018 and 2017.[2]

EXHIBIT 3.1 GIS Consolidated Balance Sheets

Amounts in millions	May 27, 2018	May 28, 2017
Assets		
Current assets:		
Cash and cash equivalents	**$ 399.0**	$ 766.1
Receivables	**1,684.2**	1,430.1
Inventories	**1,642.2**	1,483.6
Prepaid expenses and other current assets	**398.3**	381.6
Total current assets	**4,123.7**	4,061.4
Land, buildings, and equipment	**4,047.2**	3,687.7
Goodwill	**14,065.0**	8,747.2
Other intangible assets	**7,445.1**	4,530.4
Other assets	**943.0**	785.9
Total assets	**$30,624.0**	$21,812.6
Liabilities and Equity		
Current liabilities:		
Accounts payable	**$ 2,746.2**	$ 2,119.8
Current portion of long-term debt	**1,600.1**	604.7
Notes payable	**1,549.8**	1,234.1
Other current liabilities	**1,445.8**	1,372.2
Total current liabilities	**7,341.9**	5,330.8
Long-term debt	**12,668.7**	7,642.9
Deferred income taxes	**2,003.8**	1,719.4
Other liabilities	**1,341.0**	1,523.1
Total liabilities	**23,355.4**	16,216.2
Redeemable interest	**776.2**	910.9
Stockholders' equity:		
Common stock, 754.6 shares issued, $0.10 par value	**75.5**	75.5
Additional paid-in capital	**1,202.5**	1,120.9
Retained earnings	**14,459.6**	13,138.9
Common stock in treasury, at cost, shares of 161.5 and 177.7	**(7,167.5)**	(7,762.9)
Accumulated other comprehensive loss	**(2,429.0)**	(2,244.5)
Total stockholders' equity	**6,141.1**	4,327.9
Noncontrolling interests	**351.3**	357.6
Total equity	**6,492.4**	4,685.5
Total liabilities and equity	**$30,624.0**	$21,812.6

In **Exhibit 3.2**, we show the results of our initial reformulation of the amounts taken from the balance sheet of GIS into *NOA* and *NFL*. After presenting the results of reformulating the balance sheet, discussion of the more complex or unexpected classifications follows.

[2] Note that we use the most recently released annual financial information for GIS. Further, when we compare to prior years, we would use restated information if any adjustments have been made to previously reported information.

EXHIBIT 3.2 GIS Reformulation into *NOA* and *NFL*

	2018	*NOA*	*NFL*
Assets			
Cash and cash equivalents	$ 399.0	$ 314.8	$ 84.2
Receivables	1,684.2	1,684.2	
Inventories	1,642.2	1,642.2	
Prepaid expenses and other current assets	398.3	398.3	
Land, buildings, and equipment	4,047.2	4,047.2	
Goodwill	14,065.0	14,065.0	
Other intangible assets	7,445.1	7,445.1	
Other assets	943.0	943.0	
Total assets	$ 30,624.0	$ 30,539.8	84.2
Liabilities and Shareholders' Equity			
Accounts payable	$ (2,746.2)	(2,746.2)	
Current portion of long-term debt	(1,600.1)		(1,600.1)
Notes payable	(1,549.8)		(1,549.8)
Other current liabilities	(1,445.8)	(1,445.8)	
Long-term debt	(12,668.7)		(12,668.7)
Deferred income taxes	(2,003.8)	(2,003.8)	
Other liabilities	(1,341.0)	(1,341.0)	
Redeemable interest	(776.2)		(776.2)
Noncontrolling interest	(351.3)		(351.3)
Total liabilities	(24,482.9)	(7,536.8)	(16,946.1)
Net	$ 6,141.1	$23,003.0	$(16,861.9)

REQUIRED ELEMENTS OF SPREADSHEET ANALYSIS

In the valuation spreadsheet for GIS, there are worksheets whose names begin with "~." These are pages related to information shown in the text that is not necessary for your analysis. For example, the worksheet labeled "~3 Split" calculates the information shown above in Exhibit 3.2. Breaking down this information in this manner is not a required step in the completion of your valuation project.

A closer approximation to the analysis you would do in a valuation project is the analysis for K as described at the end of the chapter. However, remember that one size does not fit all. Not every company has exactly the same accounts or requires the same analysis. The better you understand the processes covered in this text and the company you are valuing, the better your ability to conduct a valuation analysis.

Classifying Balance Sheet Items as Operating or Financial

Working our way through the balance sheet means we start with *Cash and cash equivalents* and then take each item in order. Many of the classification decisions are straightforward and need little to no discussion (e.g., *Accounts receivable* as operating or *Long-term debt* as financial). Let us look closely at each of the balance sheet items.

- *Cash and cash equivalents* is interesting because some cash is necessary for the success of the enterprise operations, but a company may have more cash available than is required to fund its operating activities.[3] The operating activities need sufficient cash to ensure that they are able to continue uninterrupted by a shortage of cash. So, we estimate the amount of cash required to fund normal operating activities, such as collecting from customers, paying bills and employees, and buying inventory. Because operating cash is required to ensure

[3] Note that, depending on a company's cash management policies, its short-term investments may also serve the same role as cash. As a result, it may be appropriate to think of the necessary amount of cash and short-term investments required by operating activities when reformulating.

sales will be uninterrupted by an inability to pay for inputs as needed, sales revenue is often considered as a basis for determining the needed amount of cash. A common threshold for necessary cash is one week of sales (1/52 times sales) rounded up to 2 percent. For GIS, this would mean necessary cash, an operating asset, is estimated at $314.8 (sales of $15,740.4 times 2 percent). The excess cash of $84.2 ($399.0 – $314.8) is not considered a part of operating activities because it is assumed available for investing or could be distributed to debt or equity holders. It is important to note that 2 percent of sales is just a rule of thumb and there may be good reason to stray from this rule. For example, if an apparently healthy firm has, for some years, held cash that is less than 2 percent of sales, we may argue that the observed cash amount is sufficient for funding operating activities.

ALTERNATIVE VIEW OF CASH AS ENTIRELY FINANCIAL

In a study of analysts' discounted cash flow valuation models, Hand, Green, and Zhang (June 2016 *Review of Accounting Studies*) found that 95 percent of the reports treated all cash as a financial asset. This is consistent with the methodology used by Capital IQ and other financial websites. While a firm may manage its cash similarly to its short-term investments, this does not mean that no cash is needed to operate the enterprise. Assuming all cash is financial and therefore none is needed to support the operating activities will understate the resources necessary to generate sales. This will lead to underestimation of the operating asset turnover (discussed in Chapter 6). This assumption would also affect our forecasts formed in Chapter 7 and our estimate of cost of capital for operations in Chapter 9.

- *Prepaid expenses and other current assets* and *Other current liabilities* are examples of headings expected to be an aggregation of several things, which may be due to operating activities or financial activities. The most prominent in *Prepaid expenses and other current assets* is likely to be prepaid expenses, which, in almost all cases, would be part of operating assets. Given that the magnitude of each item included in these classes is unknown, for items like this, we will err on the side of including the entire amount in *NOA*. This reflects that we are unwilling to automatically assume they are at fair value.
- *Long-term investments* are not found on GIS' balance sheet but may be commonly found in the financial statements of publicly traded companies. When considering whether reported investments in other companies should be considered as a portion of *NOA*, the determination generally rests on the nature and level of control over actions of the company represented by the investment. Stock or debt instruments issued by another corporation would generally be considered as financial rather than operating assets unless they represent something used in the company's operating activities. An example where an investment would be included as an operating asset would be an investment in a joint venture or subsidiary. For example, **Coca-Cola** lists on its balance sheet Equity Method Investments, which represent, its interests in bottlers. This investment is obviously intricately related to Coca-Cola's enterprise operations. On the other hand, if GIS purchased a few shares of stock or bonds issued by, say, **General Motors**, this investment is not in the operations of GIS and, therefore would be included as part of financial assets.

  Viewing investments made as an investor through the lens of accounting classifications, those classified as trading and available for sale are reported at fair value, and the investor company does not have significant influence over the investee company. Thus, these items would generally be considered financial in nature. Because they are already reported at fair value, no further effort will be necessary as we move forward. Contrast this with an investment where there is significant influence and the amount shown is computed using the equity method. Here, we would want to show the investment as part of the operations and include it in our valuation exercise. Where the investor has control, the investee would be consolidated, and no further steps are required.
- *Current portion of long-term debt* and *Long-term debt* both represent claims on the operations by debt holders. As such, they are obviously financial items. They have not arisen directly due to the operations of the enterprise, but they have arisen because of

management's choice to fund the operating activities of the company via a combination of debt and equity rather than using only equity. Thus, they are not included as operating liabilities, but they will be treated as part of financial liabilities, and (later) their value will be subtracted from the estimate of operating value in order to calculate equity value. This choice to fund operating activities in part with debt rather than solely with equity is called leverage and will play a large role in cost of capital discussions and calculations later.

Similarly, within the liabilities section of the balance sheet, an amount shown as an obligation related to a capital lease is a financial obligation. Although the lease obligation arose in conjunction with the acquisition of an operating asset, the lease obligation itself is merely the financing of this transaction. It represents a creditor's claim upon the operating activities. This is more clearly seen if we consider that the company could have made a cash purchase or financed the acquisition in alternative ways, such as via a stock issuance.

- *Deferred income taxes* arise due to differences in timing between financial reporting and taxation. Recall that GIS prepares financial statements for shareholders using U.S. GAAP. When the company files its federal income tax return, it is prepared using the rules in the Internal Revenue Code (IRC). These two different sets of rules (U.S. GAAP and the IRC) may recognize revenues and expenses differently. As a result, they may yield markedly different levels of income in a particular year.[4] In general, companies prefer to report lower income to taxing authorities than to their shareholders so that they can reduce their tax liability and increase after-tax cash flow while maximizing perceived profitability. This practice is acceptable as long as the financial statements are prepared in conformity with U.S. GAAP and federal tax returns are filed in accordance with the IRC.

  Deferred taxes arise due to the timing differences between income tax expense calculated for financial reporting and income tax expense for tax payment purposes. A deferred tax asset represents a future tax expense that will be higher on the financial statements due to this timing difference. The deferred tax liability represents a future tax expense that will be lower on the future financial statements due to this timing difference. Under current U.S. accounting standards, it is possible to have deferred income taxes reported as a noncurrent asset or a noncurrent liability.[5] Regardless of where it appears, we must address whether it should be considered as part of operating activities. Deferred taxes are often a combination of items resulting from both operating and financial activities. Given our current limited focus on the information reported in the balance sheet, we will initially assume that deferred taxes should be included in operations. Consideration of additional information contained in footnotes (Chapter 4) and any required adjustments (Chapter 5) may alter the segregation into operating and financial aspects of deferred tax assets and liabilities.

- Any other assets/liabilities that may be encountered must be evaluated in light of the business purpose of the entity. That is, the classification of items must be decided within the context of an individual company. Classifications will, at times, differ across companies depending on the industry and purpose. This reinforces the need to "know the business" discussed in Chapter 1. As an example, UPS, in recent years, has reported on its balance sheet the item *Hedge margin liabilities*. Investigation of the footnotes reveals that the hedging activities of UPS primarily relate to foreign currencies. Because UPS foreign currency exposures arise from the company's international operations rather than foreign borrowings, we classify the hedge margin liabilities as arising from operating rather than financial activities.

  Another item shown on the UPS balance sheet is the liability *Self-insurance reserves*. This is described as "estimates of the loss that we will ultimately incur on reported claims,

[4] Similar differences in the level and timing of income will also arise from other tax filings at the international, state, or local levels.

[5] On November 20, 2015, the FASB issued ASU 2015-17, which requires entities to present deferred tax assets and deferred tax liabilities as noncurrent in a classified balance sheet beginning in 2017. Previously, it was possible to have deferred income taxes reported as a current asset, a current liability, a noncurrent asset, or a noncurrent liability. While this changed where the deferred taxes are shown on the balance sheet, it did not alter the method for their consideration in valuation.

as well as estimates of claims that have been incurred but not yet reported." They arise from items "associated with workers' compensation claims, automotive liability, health and welfare, and general business liabilities, up to certain limits" (2018 Form 10-K, footnote 1). Given this description, the liability clearly is a direct result of the company's operations rather than a financial choice. UPS's self-insurance reserves would be shown as a part of *NOA* rather than *NFL*.

CURRENT/NONCURRENT DISTINCTION

Within reformulation, there is no need to maintain a distinction between current and noncurrent assets or liabilities. Our analysis of current operations (step 3) and forecasting (step 4) will not utilize this classification. The place where the distinction could affect our analysis, and, therefore, our valuation, is in the estimation of cost of capital in Chapter 9. Because measures such as current ratio measure a firm's liquidity, the distinction could affect our assessment of the riskiness of the firm's operations as perceived by the debt and equity holders.

GATHERING INFORMATION FOR SPREADSHEET ANALYSIS

When gathering information from financial statements, make sure to verify whether items are shown in your spreadsheet as positive or negative. Do not assume brackets mean a negative. Brackets only mean that a person has chosen to use brackets! A financial statement could be prepared with absolutely no brackets. GIS has chosen to report Treasury stock with brackets to indicate this is a reduction of equity, but the company also could have chosen not to use brackets.

Another issue to be aware of is whether the financial statements are presented in millions or thousands. This is usually determined by the scale of the company. While the choice may be consistent across the financials, later, when we gather information from footnotes, it can differ. It is not unusual to see the financial statements presented with amounts in millions while the share-based compensation information in the footnotes is in thousands. Catching the details and understanding the information you are gathering will save much aggravation and avoid problems as you move forward with your spreadsheets.

THE EQUITY SECTION OF THE BALANCE SHEET

LO3: Adjust for equity items that are liabilities from the viewpoint of a common shareholder.

The equity section of the balance sheet identifies forms of equity ownership: common equity, preferred equity, and noncontrolling interests. If, as is often the case, our goal is to value the common equity of the company, we treat preferred equity and noncontrolling interests as additional financial liabilities, based on the logic that, from the common shareholder's viewpoint, they represent claims on the firm's net assets by another party.

- *Preferred stock* generally has constant payouts to the owners of the preferred shares expressed as a percentage of the face value of the shares. These shares are valued by the market based on the expectation of receiving these fixed payments in the future. In most cases, the market value of preferred stock does not greatly differ from the book value shown on the balance sheet. Because the preferred stock represents a claim on future cash outflows, when the focus is on valuing common equity, preferred stock is generally treated as a financial claim on the company's operations just like the claims of debt holders. For this reason, if GIS had preferred stock, it would be shown as a financial obligation rather than as a part of equity.
- *Noncontrolling interests* also represent a claim on a portion of the operating activities. Normally, the noncontrolling interest arises when a subsidiary has been acquired and the purchasing company (in our case, GIS) was unable to acquire 100 percent of the new subsidiary's stock. Noncontrolling interest represents the equity of noncontrolling (minority) shareholders who only have a claim on a portion of the net assets of one or more of the subsidiaries in the consolidated entity.

  If a company acquires a controlling interest in a subsidiary, it must consolidate that subsidiary when preparing its financial statements, thus reporting all of the subsidiary's assets and liabilities on the consolidated balance sheet and reporting all of the subsidiary's revenues and expenses in the consolidated income statement. If the company acquires less than 100 percent of the subsidiary, it must still include 100 percent of the subsidiary's assets, liabilities, revenues, and expenses in its consolidated balance sheet and income statement, but now there are two groups of shareholders that have a claim on the net assets and earnings of the subsidiary: the shareholders of the parent company and the noncontrolling shareholders (those shareholders who continue to own shares of the subsidiary).

GIS shows a *Noncontrolling interest* within the equity section of its 2018 financial statements. Those owning the noncontrolling interest are equity holders of a portion of the operating activities but are not equity holders of GIS. Akin to debt, these noncontrolling interests are no more than another form of ownership of the operations (for GIS, there are majority shareholders, noncontrolling interests, and debt holders). Thus, the noncontrolling interests are not *per se* part of the equity of GIS available to common shareholders. Rather, they represent a financial liability; hence, they will be treated in the same manner as debt owed to other debt holders when computing equity value.

MULTIPLE CLASSES OF COMMON STOCK

Some companies have multiple classes of common stock, which may have different voting rights, and liquidation rights, and they may receive different levels of dividends. UPS, for example, has Class A and B common shares, described in note 10 of the annual report as follows:

> We maintain two classes of common stock, which are distinguished from each other by their respective voting rights. Class A shares of UPS are entitled to 10 votes per share, whereas Class B shares are entitled to one vote per share. Class A shares are primarily held by UPS employees and retirees, as well as trusts and descendants of the Company's founders, and these shares are fully convertible into Class B shares at any time.

Because these shares have equal distribution and liquidation rights, we would use the total of the two classes (in amount and number of shares) in our valuation. If the rights to payoffs differed, we would calculate the value of the enterprise operations for all common stock and then allocate to the different classes based on distribution and liquidation rights.

CHECKING OUR WORK

If we have correctly reformulated the balance sheet to separate the reported information on operating and financial activities, we will not have changed the amount of common shareholders' equity (of course!). In **Exhibit 3.2**, the common shareholders' equity for GIS was shown as $6,141.1, which ties in to the balance sheet from **Exhibit 3.1** as follows:

Common stock	$ 75.5
Additional paid-in capital	1,202.5
Retained earnings	14,459.6
Common stock in treasury, at cost	(7,167.5)
Accumulated other comprehensive income/(loss)	(2,429.0)
Common shareholders' equity (*CSE*)	$ 6,141.1

After reformulation, we show this:

Net operating assets (*NOA*)	$23,003.0
Net financial liabilities (*NFL*)	16,861.9
Common shareholders' equity (*CSE*)	$ 6,141.1

This demonstrates that our initial reformulation splits the reported information based on whether the assets/liabilities arise from operating or financial activities without changing the amounts reported in the financial statements.

IDENTIFYING NET OPERATING PROFITABILITY AFTER TAX, *NOPAT*

LO4: Reformulate the financial statements to determine operating income and net operating profit after taxes.

We now continue by identifying the net operating profit after tax (*NOPAT*). Similar to the process for reformulating the balance sheet, this essentially entails going through the company's income statement item by item to determine which items would be associated with the operating activities. While the income statement ends with firm's net income, we want all earnings, so we also include the other comprehensive income items as shown on the statement of comprehensive income because these items may be an important part of the profitability of the enterprise operations. The result is an analysis that will be complete and tie the balance sheet to the income statement.

For some items, this identification process is very clear-cut; sales, for example, are related to operating activities while (for nonfinancial institutions) interest expense is not. For other items, the distinction may not be quite as clear. **Exhibit 3.3** shows the income statement and statement of comprehensive income for GIS.

EXHIBIT 3.3 GIS Consolidated Statements of Earnings and Comprehensive Income

	Fiscal Year		
Consolidated Statements of Earnings	**2018**	**2017**	**2016**
Net sales	**$15,740.4**	$15,619.8	$16,563.1
Cost of sales	**10,312.9**	10,056.0	10,733.6
Selling, general, and administrative expense	**2,752.6**	2,801.3	3,118.9
Divestitures loss (gain)	—	13.5	(148.2)
Restructuring, impairment, and other exit costs	**165.6**	182.6	151.4
Operating profit	**2,509.3**	2,566.4	2,707.4
Interest, net	**373.7**	295.1	303.8
Earnings before income taxes and after-tax earnings from joint ventures	**2,135.6**	2,271.3	2,403.6
Income taxes	**57.3**	655.2	755.2
After-tax earnings from joint ventures	**84.7**	85.0	88.4
Net earnings, including earnings attributable to redeemable and noncontrolling interests	**2,163.0**	1,701.1	1,736.8
Net earnings attributable to redeemable and noncontrolling interests	**32.0**	43.6	39.4
Net earnings attributable to General Mills	**$ 2,131.0**	$ 1,657.5	$ 1,697.4

Consolidated Statements of Comprehensive Income	**2018**	**2017**	**2016**
Net earnings, including earnings attributable to redeemable and noncontrolling interests	**$2,163.0**	$1,701.1	$1,736.8
Other comprehensive income/(loss), net of tax:			
Foreign currency translation	**(37.0)**	6.3	(108.7)
Net actuarial income (loss)	**140.1**	197.9	(325.9)
Other fair value changes:			
Securities	**1.2**	0.8	0.1
Hedge derivatives	**(50.8)**	53.3	16.0
Reclassification to earnings:			
Securities	**(5.1)**	—	—
Hedge derivatives	**17.4**	(25.7)	(9.5)
Amortization of losses and prior service costs	**117.6**	122.5	128.6
Other comprehensive income (loss), net of tax	**183.4**	355.1	(299.4)
Total comprehensive income	**2,346.4**	2,056.2	1,437.4
Comprehensive income attributable to redeemable and noncontrolling interests	**70.5**	31.0	41.5
Comprehensive income attributable to General Mills	**$2,275.9**	$2,025.2	$1,395.9

In **Exhibit 3.4**, we show the results of our initial reformulation of the comprehensive income of GIS into net operating profit after tax, *NOPAT*, and financial expense after tax, *FEAT*. After presenting the results of reformulating, discussion of the more complex or unexpected classifications follows.

EXHIBIT 3.4 GIS Reformulation into *NOPAT* and *FEAT*

Year Ending	5/27/2018	*NOPAT*	*FEAT*
Net sales	$15,740.4	$15,740.4	
Cost of sales	(10,312.9)	(10,312.9)	
Selling, general, and administrative expenses	(2,752.6)	(2,752.6)	
Restructuring, impairment, and other exit costs	(165.6)	(165.6)	
Interest expense	(373.7)		$(373.7)
Income taxes	(57.3)	(167.2)	109.9
After-tax earnings from joint ventures	84.7	84.7	
Net earnings attributable to redeemable and noncontrolling interests	(32.0)		(32.0)
Foreign currency translation	(37.0)	(37.0)	
Net actuarial income (loss)	140.1		140.1
Other fair value changes: Securities	1.2		1.2
Other fair value changes: Hedge derivatives	(50.8)	(50.8)	
Reclassification to earnings: Securities	(5.1)		(5.1)
Reclassification to earnings: Hedge derivatives	17.4	17.4	
Reclassification to earnings: Amortization of losses and prior service costs	117.6		117.6
Other comprehensive income attributable to noncontrolling interests, net	(38.5)		(38.5)
Net	$ 2,275.9	$ 2,356.4	$ (80.5)

Deciding if Income Items are Operating or Financial

Working our way through the income statement and statement of comprehensive income means we start with *Net sales* and then take each item in order and classify as operating or financial.[6] The first few items combine to form the accounting measure of *Operating income*. However, we must understand that this accounting measure is not equivalent to *NOPAT*. While many of these classification decisions are straightforward and need little to no discussion, let's look at the harder items to classify.

CHANGES TO REVENUE RECOGNITION STANDARDS

In May 2014, the FASB issued revised standards for revenue recognition that provided a "one size fits all" approach to determining revenue amounts and timing. The standard replaced a vast literature describing methodologies that were largely industry based with a five-step procedure.

1. Identify the contact(s) with a customer.
2. Identify the performance obligations in the contract.
3. Determine the transaction price.
4. Allocate the transaction price to the performance obligations.
5. Recognize revenue when (or as) each performance is satisfied.

Changing the timing of revenue recognition does not alter the reformulation process shown in this chapter, but it may affect the time series of information considered in Chapter 6 when we analyze the company's recent performance.

One additional item to note is that, in 2018, when most public companies began reporting using the new standards, there may be some items changing from gross to net (or vice versa) reporting. To understand gross versus net reporting, consider a travel agent who collects for his or her services and also sells the airline tickets. Revenue could be reported net (only the portion for the agent's services as revenue) or gross (reporting both the ticket and services as revenue and the ticket cost as an expense). The amount of income is unchanged between net and gross, but the assets, liabilities, revenues, and expenses reported may differ.

As a result of the new standards, care must be taken to understand the business (step 1) and how its results are reported. This is especially important during periods of transition, such as the implementation of new accounting standards.

[6] U.S. GAAP requires the recognition of the other comprehensive income items directly into equity without being reported on the income statement as a part of the computation of net income. This does not, however, preclude their consideration as a part of profitability as we do our financial statement reformulation.

- *Interest expense* represents payments to debt holders. Notice, however, that, had the company issued stock in order to fund the operating activities rather than borrowing from debt holders, this interest expense would have been avoided. In other words, interest expense results from a financial choice rather than as a result of the operating activities of the enterprise. *Interest income* represents earnings presumably accruing from excess cash and investments in debt that are held by the company. Similar to interest expense, had the company instead used this cash to pay down debt owed to creditors or made a distribution to equity holders, there would not have been any interest income. In other words, the interest income also arises from a financial choice and is not operating income.

EFFECTS OF VENEZUELAN HYPERINFLATION

In 2014 and 2015, many multinational companies that had been operating in Venezuela reported a *Venezuela deconsolidation charge* related to changes in the accounting for their activities within Venezuela. Previously, they had included the results of Venezuelan operations using the consolidation method of accounting. However, the lack of exchangeability and evolving conditions resulted in a lack of control over the Venezuelan subsidiaries. This resulted in a need to deconsolidate the Venezuelan subsidiaries and the use of the cost method of accounting going forward. As Venezuela became a hyperinflationary economy, following U.S. GAAP (ASC 255-10), the financial statements were required to be reported in the measuring unit of the consolidated balance sheet and remeasured using a general price index. These effects arose due to operating activities within Venezuela rather than financial transactions originating there. As a result, the charges would be considered as operating in nature. For forecasting, they would not be expected to repeat in the future and would not be foreseeable until such time as the issue arose.

- *Income taxes on continuing operations* relates to all items shown above this item on the income statement of GIS; that is, it represents the taxes on the $2,135.6 of *Earnings from continuing operations before income taxes*. **Exhibit 3.5** shows the split thus far between operating and financial activities of the prior items.

EXHIBIT 3.5 GIS Earnings from Continuing Operations before Income Taxes

Amounts in millions	Reported	Operating	Financial
Net sales	$15,740.4	$15,740.4	
Cost of sales	(10,312.9)	(10,312.9)	
Selling, general, and administrative expense	(2,752.6)	(2,752.6)	
Restructuring, impairment, and other exit costs	(165.6)	(165.6)	
Interest expense	(373.7)		$(373.7)
Earnings from continuing operations before income taxes	$ 2,135.6	$ 2,509.3	$(373.7)

We have classified most of the items shown above *Income taxes on continuing operations* as relating to the operating activities yielding a $2,509.3 profit, but *Interest expense* and *Interest income* were classified as associated with financial activities yielding $(373.7) in net expense. As a result, because the tax amount reported on the income statement relates to all of these items, we need to determine the portion of *Income taxes on continuing operations* that should be allocated to the operating activities. Ideally, we want the income tax expense that would have been incurred had the company had no interest expense or interest income.

Note a very important detail related to how accounting reports items on the financial statements: The tax shown on the income statement of $57.3 relates to what is referred to as continuing operations. All items subsequent to income from continuing operations, such as discontinued operations, extraordinary items, and items of other comprehensive income, will have their tax calculated separately and be reported net of the tax effect. We will return to this item after discussing the splitting of tax on continuing operations.

We estimate the income tax expense for the portion of *Earnings from continuing operations before income taxes* that is related to operating activities via the following steps. First, we would like to know GIS' marginal tax rate on financial activities to allow us to determine the extent to which taxes are reduced due to the deduction of the net interest expense for tax purposes (this amount is called the interest tax shield). We assume, for the sake of simplicity, a tax rate of 29.4 percent for this calculation based upon 29.4 percent federal statutory rate.[7] In doing so, we assume state and other taxes will be near zero. Had GIS not had the *Interest expense*, *Earnings from continuing operations before income taxes* would have been $373.7 higher. Had we shown an additional $373.7 of earnings (as a result of just reporting on the operating activities), we estimate that this income would have been taxed at 29.4 percent for an additional amount of tax of $109.9.

The firm's decision to be financed partially through debt rather than purely through equity resulted in a reduced income due to the deduction of *Interest expense*. The reduction in taxable income reduced the income tax expense by an estimated $109.9. Again, this amount is referred to as the interest tax shield; it protected us from paying that additional tax. To arrive at the amount of tax allocable to operating activities, we add the interest tax shield to the amount reported as *Income taxes on continuing operations* of $57.3. This gives an estimated income tax on the operations of $167.2.[8] This can be seen in **Exhibit 3.6**.

EXHIBIT 3.6

	Earnings from Continuing Operations before Tax	Income Taxes on Continuing Operations	Earnings from Continuing Operations after Tax
Operating	$2,509.3	$(167.2)	$2,342.1
Financial	(373.7)	109.9	(263.8)
Total reported	$2,135.6	$ (57.3)	$2,078.3

TAX EFFECTS OF OTHER INCOME ITEMS

Having computed the allocation of *Income taxes on continuing operations*, all remaining items on the income statement and the items contained in other comprehensive income are shown net of tax. Before we work with the specific items reported by GIS, let us consider, in general, the effect of these items on our calculation of *NOPAT*. Consider first an item of other comprehensive income that will be included in *NOPAT*. We will refer to this as item A and assume it has a positive effect on income of $1,000. Also consider an item that will be excluded from *NOPAT* as it relates to financial activities. We will refer to this as item B and assume it is reported as an expense of $600.

For item A, which will be included in *NOPAT*, the $1,000 listed in the financial reports as income is reported net of tax. This means that the income from this item has been reduced by the appropriate tax to arrive at $1,000. If we assume a 35 percent rate, we could gross up the reported amount to $1,538 [$1,000/(1 – 0.35)]. For this item, we could then show, as a part of *NOPAT*, the $1,538 revenue and also, as a part of *NOPAT*, the related tax of $538 ($1,538 × 0.35). We could even add the $538 to the tax after the allocation above to arrive at a total tax on operating activities. However, this may not be necessary, and we may introduce errors. First, in the calculation where we grossed up the amount by using an assumption for the tax rate, we do not know the correct rate to use, so the amount of $1,538 and related tax of $538 are, at best, estimates. Second, in Chapter 7, we will be forecasting tax on operating activities directly, so knowing the current amount of tax on operating activities will not be helpful. Instead, we will be applying an assumed tax rate to the forecasted amount of income before tax. Finally, when we are making our forecasts in Chapter 7, we will see that these items that appear net of tax generally have expected forecasts of zero; thus, the grossing up is at best an estimate and, more important, unnecessary.

continued

[7] The U.S. statutory tax rate changed from 35 percent to 21 percent beginning January 2018. As a result, for GIS, the first 7 months of the year ended May 2018 had the old rate, and the last 5 months had the new rate. This resulted in an average tax rate for that year of 29.4 percent. Future years will be expected to have a federal statutory tax rate of 21 percent.

[8] Notice that the tax on the operations of $167.2 is not 29.4 percent times the $2,509.3. Rather, it is the reported amount $57.3 increased by the interest tax shield of $109.9 ($373.7 × 0.294).

continued from previous page

Our handling of item B, which relates to financial activities, is more straightforward but also comes with a twist. Because we are valuing the operating activities, trying to "clean up" *FEAT* is not necessary. For item B, we see it listed as $600 of expense, which is reported net of tax. Again, assuming a tax rate of 35 percent, this would imply an underlying expense of $923 [$600/(1 – 0.35)] has been netted with a $323 interest tax shield ($923 × 0.35). That is, without this $923 in expense, the company would have paid an additional $323 in tax. Still, we do not need to make an adjustment for this item because that $323 in tax has already been excluded from the *Income taxes on continuing operations* when item B is reported net of tax. The twist on item B is that if we expect it to be non-zero in future periods, we will need to consider the $323 in determining the valuation of the interest tax shield in both Chapter 9 and 13. In most cases, item B would have an expectation of zero going forward, rendering this a nonissue.

- *Net earnings/(loss) from discontinued operations* are the result of subsidiaries or business segments that the board of directors has formally decided to divest. While GIS does not report discontinued operations, this entry will be seen in the financial statements of many companies. Companies must report discontinued operations as separate information, below income from continuing operations. The separate line item, discontinued operations, includes both the net income from discontinued operations (during the period of winding down) and any gains or losses on the disposal of the related net assets. Although not required, many companies disclose the net assets of discontinued operations separately on the balance sheet to distinguish them from continuing net assets if they have not yet been disposed of by the balance sheet date. The amount reported as *Net earnings/(loss) from discontinued operations* is part of current operating activities and needs to be included as we compute current *NOPAT*. Although we will cover forecasting later, we note that discontinued operations clearly would not be included in future expected *NOPAT* because these items are discontinued!
- *Net earnings attributable to noncontrolling interests* are the income statement equivalent to the items discussed when determining *NOA*. Note that there are two items with this title in **Exhibits 3.3** and **3.4**, which show the amounts from net earnings reported on the income statement and from other comprehensive income. Just as for the split of the balance sheet, we will treat these items as though they are from financial activities because the revenues/expenses are viewed as following the allocation made on the balance sheet. Later, we will discuss that one of the implications of classifying noncontrolling interest as financial is an assumption that the amounts shown on the balance sheet are at fair value. In situations where there is a very large number related to noncontrolling interest, this assumption may need to be reconsidered. For GIS, the amounts are not significant, and we will treat it in the same manner as debt owed to debt holders when computing equity value.

REPORTING OF NONCONTROLLING INTERESTS ON THE STATEMENT OF COMPREHENSIVE INCOME

The reporting of noncontrolling interests across the income statement and statement of comprehensive income can be tricky. For 2018, GIS' income statement showed $32.0 being allocated to noncontrolling interest, but then the statement of comprehensive earnings begins with the $2,163.0 "Net earnings, including earnings attributable to redeemable and noncontrolling interests," shown before this allocation! When $70.5 is subtracted on the statement of comprehensive earnings, this is really an additional $38.5 beyond that already seen on the income statement. Our spreadsheet needs to reflect an item of other comprehensive income in the amount beyond that already shown on the income statement.

Make sure that the comprehensive income on your spreadsheet matches what the company reported. Also, remember to let the spreadsheet sum items rather than hard coding the totals.

- *Foreign currency translation.*[9] For GIS, the foreign currency translation stems from its global operations. As it operates in many countries, GIS has international transactions

[9] Remember that all items after income taxes on continuing operations are shown net of tax. Therefore, even though *Foreign currency translation* is not labeled "net of tax," it will already have been adjusted for related taxes.

denominated in foreign currencies. GIS, at times, purchases assets in foreign currencies, borrows money in foreign currencies, and transacts business with its customers and suppliers in foreign currencies. It may also have subsidiaries whose entire balance sheets and income statements are maintained in foreign currencies. GIS financial statements prepared in accordance with U.S. GAAP are reported in $US. This means that financial statements of foreign subsidiaries must be translated into $US before they are consolidated with those of the U.S. parent company. These effects result in foreign currency translation. Note that, if the foreign currency translation resulted primarily from passive investments in stocks, bonds, or other securities or from borrowings in other countries, we would exclude it from the calculation of *NOPAT* because it would be considered to be a financial activity. For GIS, however, *Foreign currency translation* is primarily an operating item given its global presence, global production, and other global operating activities.

- *Other fair value changes* and *Reclassification to earnings from Securities* result from changes in values of available-for-sale investment debt securities. For GIS, its debt investment securities should be classified as financial activities because they are not a part of its operations. The fair value changes for these securities, which are unrealized gains/ (losses), and the reclassifications related to disposal of these investments will be classified similarly. Thus, they are not the result of operating activities but are financial in nature.
- *Other fair value changes* and *Reclassification to earnings from Hedge derivatives* is the result of GIS' activities related to efforts to reduce market, interest rate, currency exchange, and commodity price risks related to cash flows. For the purposes of computing *NOPAT*, we consider these items as arising from operating activities. Note that even though this item is treated as part of operating activities, it would have an expected future value that is, on average, zero because GIS' anticipated success in these efforts going forward is likely to have a net zero effect on average.
- *Net actuarial income (loss)* and *Reclassification to earnings from Amortization of losses and prior service costs* are the other items shown by GIS as an element of other comprehensive income. These amounts will arise from increases or decreases in the pension liability due to changes in pension plan assumptions. While the pension-related costs of GIS' current workforce working during this year arise as a result of its operations, it is doubtful that changes in assumptions directly result in incremental effort by the workforce on a continuing basis. As a result, they are considered as a part of its financial rather than operating activities.

CHECKING OUR WORK

If we have correctly reformulated the income statement and items of other comprehensive income to separate the reported information on operating and financial activities, we will not have changed the amount of comprehensive income (of course!). From **Exhibit 3.3**, the comprehensive income attributable to GIS was $2,275.9.

After reformulation, we show this:

Net operating profit after tax (*NOPAT*)	$2,356.4
Financial expense after tax (*FEAT*)	(80.5)
Comprehensive income	$2,275.9

This demonstrates that reformulation has split the reported information based on whether the income/expenses arise from operating or financial activities without changing the amounts reported in the financial statements.

FINANCIAL STATEMENT LINKAGES

The financial statements of a company are linked to one another and across time. We generally think of the balance sheets at the beginning and end of a year being linked by the income statement in that net income flows to retained earnings. That is, absent transactions with shareholders (items such as stock issuances, repurchases, or dividends), the change in retained earnings equals the net income for the period.

A more general equation can be written that recognizes that common shareholders' equity (*CSE*) changes during the year due to the comprehensive income (*CI*) attributable to the company and net shareholder transactions (FCF^{Eq}). We label the net shareholder transactions, the free cash flows to equity holders, as "dividends" because they will be positive when comprised primarily of dividends. Thus, stock issuances are "negative" FCF^{Eq} because funds flow to the company, and share repurchases are "positive" FCF^{Eq} because funds flow from the company to those who had been shareholders. This leads to the following equation, which is referred to as the clean surplus relation:

$$CSE_{t-1} + CI_t - FCF_t^{Eq} = CSE_t$$

The amount of shareholders' equity at the end of the year is the sum of the equity at the beginning of the year plus the comprehensive income for the year less the the free cash flows to equity holders for the year.

To ensure we are correctly presenting the required net assets and profitability they will generate from sales, it is very important that we ensure that this relation is present. As we proceed to focus on enterprise operations, we will see an analogous relation exists.

CHECKING OUR WORK

To allow us to verify the financial statement linkages (clean surplus), we require one more item. We must compute the amount of the free cash flows to equity holders for GIS. This information is gathered from the statement of shareholders' equity. We are looking for any items that caused changes in common shareholders' equity, but were not part of comprehensive income attributable to GIS; that is, the free cash flows to equity holders. When looking at GIS' consolidated statements of total equity and the entry *Redeemable interest*, every item that caused a change in the equity accounts is shown. As we evaluate every line to determine if the item was included in *CI*, those that were not included in *CI* must be a part of FCF^{Eq}. For GIS, in 2018, the items composing FCF^{Eq} were

Free cash flows to equity holders	
Cash dividends declared	$1,139.7
Shares purchased	601.6
Shares issued	(969.9)
Stock compensation plans	(130.1)
Unearned compensation related to stock unit awards	58.1
Earned compensation	(77.0)
Increase (decrease) in redemption value of redeemable interest	(159.7)
	$ 462.7

Having completed this analysis, we can now verify that the equation showing the linkage between beginning and ending equity (i.e., the clean surplus relation) holds:

$$CSE_{t-1} + CI_t - FCF_t^{Eq} = CSE_t$$

$$4{,}327.9 + 2{,}275.9 - 462.7 = 6{,}141.1$$

We note that repeating this check in our spreadsheet will verify that the financial statements continue to articulate after we add the additional information in Chapter 4 and after we make the adjustments in Chapter 5. You should be identifying FCF^{Eq} and also showing that clean surplus holds in the financial statements, as shown on worksheet "3 BS Reported." This is one of the best tools for finding any errors in your valuation spreadsheet as you move through the valuation exercise.

WATCH FOR DIFFERENT COMPREHENSIVE INCOME ACROSS FINANCIAL STATEMENTS

In trying to reconcile changes in *CSE* during the year with the *CI* attributable to GIS, we need to ensure the amount of *CI* agrees between the statement of comprehensive income and the statement of stockholders' equity. At times, there may be differences that arise. For **Procter & Gamble** (PG) in 2014, the amount of net earnings going to retained earnings of $11,643 plus the amount of other comprehensive income going to accumulated other comprehensive income of –$163 from the statement of stockholders' equity total $11,480. This amount does not match the total comprehensive income attributable to PG per the statement of comprehensive income in 2014 of $11,472! To deal with this $8 difference, we would add a line to the computation of the free cash flows to equity holders labeled "Difference in CI attrib to PG on statements of CI and SE."

Exercise a high level of care in making sure the linkages are clear between financials. This will save a large amount of time later.

SUMMARY

In this chapter, we have demonstrated the process by which we identify *NOPAT* and *NOA*, the measures of profitability and resources related to operating activities. We also, as a by-product of the process, identified *FEAT* (or *FIAT* if there is a net financial income) and *NFL*. In doing so, we must make judgments based on our knowledge of the business and understanding of accounting.

Quite often, when reformulating financial statements, you may run across an item not discussed above. When this happens, your goal is to determine the best classification as part of either operating or financial activities. To help with this, consider the following points:

1. Begin reformulation with a focus on the balance sheet. The goal is to determine what *NOA*s are available/required in operating activities.
2. Classification of an item as financial will exclude it from the calculation of cost of operating capital and the valuation of enterprise operations. It also assumes that either the amount shown is at fair value or that the fair value is readily available/determinable through other sources.
3. When moving to the elements of comprehensive income, think about what assets/liabilities would be related to these elements. Whenever possible, the classification of an item of revenue/expense as either operating or financial in nature should mirror the classification of the related assets/liabilities.
4. Most important, know the underlying business! Interest income would arise from operating activities for a bank but would be excluded as resulting from a financial choice for most other companies.

At all times during this process, one must consider the context of the company being evaluated. For a manufacturing company, such as GIS, we will classify items very differently than a financial services company, such as **J.P. Morgan Chase**, because its operations require different resources and achieve profitability through differing undertakings. Further, if you were determining *NOPAT* and *NOA* for a company of which you were a member of management, you would have much more information available and could perform a more detailed analysis than can be performed based on publicly available information.

In the next chapter, we will add information generally from footnotes that allows a more detailed examination of the elements of assets/liabilities and revenues/expenses.

APPENDIX 3A: A Detailed Example of Effects of Classification as Operating versus Financial Activities[10]

As some students have a more advanced understanding of free cash flow (*FCF*) from operations and cost of capital issues, we provide the following discussion and numerical example to show the effects of classifying of an item as operating versus financial activities on the calculation of free

[10] This appendix mirrors, and was the source of, a teaching note published by Easton and Sommers in the *Journal of Applied Corporate Finance*, Summer 2017, pp. 71–79.

cash flow and cost of capital measures. We provide this example at this early stage so that those who already have some understanding of free cash flow and calculation of cost of capital will be able to reconcile what they have learned in other classes with what they will learn in this class. Those who are less familiar with these concepts should plan to revisit this example after Chapter 9, which covers the estimation of the cost of capital.

Introduction

The computation of free cash flows is straightforward conceptually. Free cash flows, or *FCF,* are the distributions of the operating cash flow of the enterprise to its owners, debt holders as well as equity holders. The method for calculating this free cash flow that is presented in textbooks on financial statement analysis and valuation appears to differ from the method presented in corporate finance texts. This leads to confusion for students (and educators) and a number of questions: What is the correct method? Why are these *FCF*s different? And what are the implications of these differences for calculations of value? A related question that is critical to valuation is often overlooked: What effect does the choice of method have on calculations of the cost of capital?

To answer these questions, we begin by discussing the issue that gives rise to different calculations of *FCF*. The answers lie in differences in classification of items as part of enterprise operations as distinguished from purely financial activities. We describe and illustrate these differences. Then, we show the implications for valuation calculations; in particular, for estimating the cost of capital used to discount forecasted *FCF*s to a present value. We first illustrate the classification issue using **Starbucks** as an example and then show the effects on valuation and estimation of the cost of capital with a detailed numerical example. This illustration shows that the classification used in the financial statement analysis and valuation textbooks is both more intuitively appealing and easier to implement, and it does not change the reliability of the analysis.

Our aim in this appendix, then, is to clarify that the primary difference between the method for calculating free cash flow presented in texts about financial statement analysis and valuation and the method presented in corporate finance texts is rooted in classification decisions that are made when separating enterprise operations from financial activities. We will show that this difference in classification does not affect the resulting valuations, provided the proper discount rate is used and the proper adjustments for the value of the financial activities are made.

Classification as Enterprise Operations versus Financial Activities

We begin by considering the different approaches to calculating free cash flow from enterprise operations, which are driven by this key question: How should items like excess cash and investments be considered when reformulating financial statements for analysis and valuation? There are two common approaches to answering this question. One appears consistently in texts about financial statement analysis and valuation. The other appears in all corporate finance texts with which we are familiar. The key difference between these two methods is that financial statement analysis and valuation texts tend to separate enterprise operating activities from financial activities, while the corporate finance texts tend to commingle and treat them as one. Therefore, for convenience in our exposition, we will refer to these approaches as "separated" and "mingled", respectively.

To illustrate the difference, consider this question: What does Starbucks do? When asked this question, students will say, "They sell coffee." When pressed further, they will add selling coffee accessories, breakfast foods, and similar items. Will you hear the answer "offer a fund of marketable securities"? Probably not. Nevertheless, a review of its recent financial statements will show that Starbucks holds large quantities of cash and marketable securities. Without a closer look, such a large amount appears to make a significant part of Starbucks look a lot like a securities investment fund.

In the fiscal year ended September 2013, Starbucks reported total sales of almost $14.9 billion. At that time, the company also reported a total of cash and short- and long-term investments of almost $3.3 billion. Of course, some of this "cash" can be justified as providing its operations with a cushion against downturns, or as "dry powder" for acquisitions or other investment opportunities that could materialize.[11] But, given that this amount represents more than 80 days' worth of Starbucks' sales, it seems clear that not all the cash and investments are required for the company to run the day-to-day enterprise operations. And, in this sense, outside investors are likely to view part of the company's cash and investments as the equivalent of a securities investment fund.[12]

Another way to view the excess cash and investments of Starbucks is as a form of "negative debt," or as a form of lending rather than borrowing. **Ford**, for example, in its 2014 management discussion and analysis described a concept called "managed leverage" as "useful to its investors because it reflects the way Ford Credit manages its business."[13] As explained in Ford's account, managed leverage involves calculating "adjusted debt" by deducting from the company's total debt its holdings of cash, cash equivalents, and marketable securities.[14]

In the 2014 edition of the biggest-selling corporate finance text of all time, Richard Brealey, Stewart Myers, and Franklin Allen defined *FCF* as "the amount of cash that a firm can pay out to investors after paying for all investments necessary for growth."[15] Defined in this way, *FCF* can be estimated as the net payments that can be made to both debt and equity holders without hurting the company's ability to execute its strategy. If we decide that Starbucks' business is to sell coffee, then we have to ask ourselves the following question: What part of Starbucks' cash and investments could it pay out to its debt or equity holders without affecting its ability to sell coffee?

If the answer is a positive number, then that amount should be viewed as negative debt rather than as part of the capital base necessary to support its enterprise operations, and, as such, it should be classified as a financial activity. And that brings us to the next question: How do the two approaches, one separated and the other mingled, treat negative debt?

Calculation of Enterprise Operating Free Cash Flow (*FCF*)

The methods for determining *FCF* presented in most corporate finance texts include cash and investments in marketable securities as part of enterprise operations. This approach assumes that debt borrowings are financial activities and that all other activities of the company constitute the business, or enterprise, operations. This reasoning leads to a determination that Starbucks' business is both selling coffee *and* offering investments in cash and marketable securities.

To illustrate this corporate finance calculation of *FCF*, let's look at an example as a starting point. In another well-known and widely used corporate finance textbook, Steve Ross, Randy Westerfield, and Brad Jordan point out that, "in practice, there is some variation in exactly how free cash flow is computed; different users calculate it in different ways."[16] Then, they present the following formula for calculating what they call "cash flow from assets"—that is, *FCF*:

	Operating cash flow
−	Net capital spending
−	Change in net working capital (ΔNWC)
=	Free cash flow

[11] Amy Dittmar (2008) provides a detailed explanation of reasons some cash may be retained for enterprise operating activities.

[12] Another example is **Microsoft**, whose annual sales revenue from software and related products in 2014 was $87 billion, and it had cash, cash equivalents, and short-term investments of almost as much ($86 billion); in other words, it had enough cash to cover a whole year of sales!

[13] 2014 Ford annual report, p. 74.

[14] The treatment of cash as negative debt is clearly seen in the calculation of enterprise value by S&P Capital IQ, which is a well-known multi-national information provider headquartered in New York City. The *Capital IQ Stock Report Guide* describes the company's process as follows: "Enterprise value may be calculated by adding the market value of the company's stock, the balance sheet values of the company's debt, preferred stock and minority equity interests, and then subtracting the amount of cash equivalents that a company has."

[15] Brealey, Myers, and Allen (2014), p. 93. Full citations are provided in the References at the end of the article.

[16] Ross, Westerfield, and Jordan (2016), p. 34.

In this calculation, operating cash flow and net capital spending are defined as follows:

	Earnings before interest and taxes (*EBIT*)
+	Depreciation
−	Taxes
=	Operating cash flow

	Ending net fixed assets
−	Beginning net fixed assets
+	Depreciation
=	Net capital spending

	Ending *NWC*
−	Beginning *NWC*
=	Change in *NWC*

	Current assets
−	Current liabilities
=	*NWC*

When we combine these formulas, we are left with the following:

	Earnings before interest and taxes (*EBIT*)
+	~~Depreciation~~
−	Taxes
−	Ending net fixed assets
+	Beginning net fixed assets
−	~~Depreciation~~
−	Ending current assets
+	Ending current liabilities
+	Beginning current assets
−	Beginning current liabilities
=	Free cash flow

This computation of *FCF* effectively assumes that *all* fixed assets, current assets, and current liabilities are part of enterprise operations and that all other items—namely, longer-term liabilities and equity—are related to financial activities.

In contrast, the approach used in the financial statement analysis texts begins by classifying each item on the balance sheet into one of five categories: enterprise operating asset, enterprise operating liability, financial asset, financial liability, or part of common shareholders' equity.[17] Using this approach, the combination of enterprise operating assets and enterprise operating liabilities yields a quantity called enterprise net operating assets (*NOA*). Critical to this process is that each item is considered individually rather than in broad groupings, as in the corporate finance approach.

Under this separated approach, only the cash required to fund and support the operations is viewed as an enterprise operating asset, while the remainder of the cash and the short- and long-term financial investments are classified as assets arising from financial activities. This approach is based on the recognition that, to the extent such cash exceeds the amount required to support day-to-day operations and fund maintenance programs and current or foreseeable capital investment projects, it could be used to pay down debt or returned to shareholders. Should new growth opportunities later arise that require funding, such excess cash could then be "re-borrowed" or additional shares issued. (As an aside, a review of Starbucks' 2014 financial statements makes it clear that the company's cash and short- and long-term investments held at the end of 2013 were not being held to fund imminent growth.)

---

[17] See Easton et al. (2018), Chapter 3; Palepu and Healy (2013), Chapter 5; Penman (2012), Chapters 7 to 10; and Wahlen et al. (2015), Chapters 4 and 8.

Which classification of the Starbucks' cash and marketable securities is more representative of the underlying construct, *FCF*, as presented by Brealey, Myers, and Allen? As described above, the main difference between the approaches is in the determination of what items are included in enterprise operations. In essence, the mingled approach would include all of Starbucks' cash and marketable securities as part of the business (enterprise operations) because only long-term borrowings are viewed as financial activities. The separated approach would instead exclude much of Starbucks' cash and marketable securities from enterprise operations by classifying then as a negative debt arising from financial activities. If the assumption in the separated approach that the firm could re-borrow or issue shares is appropriate, then the excess cash and investments are available for distribution to debt or equity holders and should not be considered as part of the enterprise operations.

To sum up, then, the key difference between the two approaches is the identification of the enterprise net operating profit after tax (*NOPAT*) and the capital base (*NOA*). In the case of Starbucks, *NOPAT* and *NOA* are either identified as the separated earnings and assets associated with the coffee-selling business or mingled as the sum of the earnings and assets of two distinct businesses, a coffee-selling business *and* an investment in cash and marketable securities. In this latter case, the earnings and assets associated with *both* activities are identified as the *NOPAT* and *NOA*. And this means that both *NOPAT* and *NOA* will differ across the different classifications of enterprise operations versus financial activities. But when using either approach, the relation $FCF = NOPAT - \Delta NOA$ will continue to hold.[18]

This raises the natural next question: How do we reconcile the differing amounts of *FCF* when we undertake our valuation? We provide a detailed numerical example to illustrate this reconciliation.

Detailed Numerical Example of Effects of Classification of Financial Assets as Enterprise Operations vs. Financial Activities

The following example shows the effects of classifying a company's activity as enterprise operations versus financial activities on the calculation of its *FCF*, cost of capital, and valuation. As the example is meant to demonstrate, the estimation of the value of the equity, if done properly, is the same using either method. We examine a case that involves a capital project, an investment fund, and a loan. The alternative assumptions that lead to classification of the investment fund (say, Starbucks' cash and marketable securities) as part of enterprise operations or as a financial activity are examined more closely.

Setup[19]

- Project: The investment involves a $1,000 operating project, which is expected to provide cash flows of $600 in the first period and $800 in the second period. The expected rate of return on this investment is 10%.
- Investment fund: There is also a $400 investment in an investment fund, which is expected to earn 1%.
- Loan: These investments are partially funded by borrowing $300 at an interest rate of 2%.
- Equity: The equity holders are assumed to make an initial contribution of $1,100 to fund the excess cost of the project and the investment fund over the amount of the loan.
- Taxes: A zero tax rate is assumed. Including taxes would not further any of the illustrations or issues shown.[20]

Benchmark Valuations

To show the effects of differing assumptions, we form separate benchmark valuations of each component of the investment:

[18] This relation recognizes that enterprise profits (*NOPAT*) are either reinvested (increasing *NOA*) or distributed to debt or equity holders (*FCF*s).

[19] The setup includes an investment fund that is expected to yield a rate of return that is greater than the interest rate paid on a loan, which is used to fund the project. This may, at first glance, seem odd, but the setup reflects the large amounts of cash held by many U.S. corporations. For example, at the end of its 2015 fiscal year, **Apple Inc.** had $206 billion in cash and marketable securities, which yielded a return of 1.49% and long-term debt of $55,701 on which the interest rate ranged from 0.28% to 4.4%.

[20] Alternatively, the amounts shown could be thought of as after-tax amounts.

- Project: The discounted present value of the expected future cash flows for the project was estimated as follows: $600/1.10 + $800/1.10^2 = $1,206.61
- Investment fund: The $400 investment in this fund is its initial fair value.[21]
- Loan: The amount borrowed of $300 is its fair value.
- Equity: The value of the equity is $1,206.61 + $400.00 – $300.00 = $1,306.61.

Accounting for the Two Periods

Additional assumptions are necessary to prepare the accounting for this firm. Assume that the project will be depreciated using the straight-line method at a rate of $500 per period, with the project expected to be worthless and abandoned at the end of the second period. The investment fund's earnings each period will be received by the firm rather than reinvested. The required interest on the loan will be paid each period. Any additional cash that is available will be distributed to the equity holder. The resulting financial statements are as follows:

Financial Statements in Period	0	1	2
Balance Sheet			
Assets			
Project	$1,000	$ 500	$ —
Investment fund	400	400	400
Total assets	$1,400	$ 900	$400
Liabilities and equity:			
Loan	$ 300	$ 300	$300
Equity	1,100	600	100
Total liabilities and equity	$1,400	$ 900	$400
Income Statement			
Project income		$ 600	$800
Investment fund income		4	4
Total revenue		604	804
Depreciation		(500)	(500)
Interest expense		(6)	(6)
Net income		$ 98	$298
Cash Flows			
Amount distributed to equity holders:			
Project income		$ 600	$800
Investment fund income		4	4
Interest paid		(6)	(6)
Total distribution		$ 598	$798
Reconciliation of Equity			
Beginning of period	$ —	$1,100	$600
Net income		98	298
Contributions by/(distributions to) equity holders	1,100	(598)	(798)
End of period	$1,100	$ 600	$100

[21] The investment fund in this hypothetical example may represent cash and marketable securities, which we see on many corporate balance sheets. Amy Dittmar (2008) points out many reasons why this cash may not be recorded on the balance sheet at fair market value. A contemporary reason is that the cash may be held in foreign jurisdictions in order to avoid the tax that would be paid on that cash if it were repatriated to the U.S. For example, in a *60 Minutes* interview, the CEO of Apple Inc., Tim Cook, said in response to Charlie Rose's question "Why don't you bring the cash home?" "It would cost [Apple] 40% to bring it home and I don't think this is a reasonable thing to do." See http://www.cbsnews.com/news/apple-60-minutes-ceo-tim-cook/ (last accessed 9/19/2016). The possibility that some tax may eventually be paid on the cash is one of the reasons why a dollar of cash on Apple's balance sheet may be worth less than a dollar. The point of the hypothetical example would, however, be unchanged if the fair value was less than the book value.

Reformulation of Financial Statements

The financial statement reformulation process splits the assets/liabilities and revenues/expenses between enterprise operations and financial activities. In this example, we view the project as an enterprise operating activity and the loan as a financial activity. We show the results of reformulation under two alternative assumptions. In alternative A, the separated approach, the investment fund is assumed to be a financial asset, and in alternative B, the mingled approach, the investment fund is assumed to be an enterprise operating asset.

Period	0	1	2
Alternative A			
Enterprise net operating assets			
Project	$1,000	$500	$ —
NOA	1,000	500	—
Net financial assets (liabilities):			
Investment fund	400	400	400
Loan	(300)	(300)	(300)
NFA	100	100	100
Equity	$1,100	$600	$100
Enterprise net operating profit after tax			
Project income		$600	$800
Depreciation		(500)	(500)
NOPAT		100	300
Financial income (expense) after tax:			
Investment fund income		4	4
Interest expense		(6)	(6)
FEAT		(2)	(2)
Net income		$ 98	$298

	0	1	2
Alternative B			
Enterprise net operating assets			
Project	$1,000	$500	$ —
Investment fund	400	400	400
NOA	1,400	900	400
Net financial assets (liabilities):			
Loan	(300)	(300)	(300)
NFL	(300)	(300)	(300)
Equity	$1,100	$600	$100
Enterprise net operating profit after tax			
Project income		$600	$800
Investment fund income		4	4
Depreciation		(500)	(500)
NOPAT		104	304
Financial income (expense) after tax:			
Interest expense		(6)	(6)
FEAT		(6)	(6)
Net income		$ 98	$298

Computation of Enterprise Operating Free Cash Flow

The computations of *FCF* under these two treatments of the investment fund are as follows:

	1	2	1	2
Period	**Alternative A**		**Alternative B**	
Ending *NOA*	$ 500	$ —	$ 900	$ 400
Beginning *NOA*	1,000	500	1,400	900
Change in *NOA*	$ (500)	$(500)	(500)	$(500)
NOPAT	$ 100	$ 300	$ 104	$ 304
Less change in *NOA*	500	500	500	500
FCF	$ 600	$ 800	$ 604	$ 804

Clearly, the separated approach (alternative A) and the mingled approach (alternative B) yield different amounts of *FCF*, which is expected because they have different definitions of what is included in enterprise operations. If we have a different definition of financial activities, then we will have a different *FCF* because we are classifying debt differently (net debt in alternative A and gross debt in alternative B).

Now, we discuss implications of these differing calculations of *FCF*. We know that we are looking at the same company and that the equity value, as estimated above, is $1,306.61. Do both of these *FCF* numbers yield the same estimate of value? The key to obtaining the same valuation is appropriate calculations of the cost of capital for discounting these *FCF*s.

Effects of Classification on Cost of Capital

The key ingredients in valuation are the anticipated payoffs (net cash flows) and the associated risk; that is, the *FCF*s and the cost of capital. We can write the weighted average cost of capital (*WACC*) formula as follows:

$$r_{WACC} = \left(r_D \cdot \frac{V^{NFL}}{V^{Oper}} \right) + \left(r_{Eq} \cdot \frac{V^{Eq}}{V^{Oper}} \right)$$

where r_{WACC}, r_D, and r_{Eq} are the cost of capital for enterprise operations, the cost of debt capital, and the cost of equity capital, respectively, and where V^{Oper}, V^{NFL}, and V^{Eq} are the market value of enterprise operations, the market value of debt, and the market value of equity, respectively.

Consider each of the elements of this calculation under alternatives A and B. Under alternative A, the only component included as enterprise operations is the project, so r_{WACC} is 10 percent, and the value of the project, V^{Oper}, is $1,206.61, as calculated earlier. Financial activities contain two items: an investment fund asset and a loan, both of which are assumed to retain their initial market values throughout, which results in a market value of net debt, V^{NFL}, of –$100.00 (i.e., –$400.00 + $300.00). For these two items, we can calculate the weighted average cost of debt capital as follows:

$$\begin{aligned} r_D &= \left(r_{Investment\ Fund} \cdot \frac{V^{Investment\ Fund}}{V^{Financing}} \right) + \left(r_{Loan} \cdot \frac{V^{Loan}}{V^{Financing}} \right) \\ &= \left(1\% \cdot \frac{-400}{-100} \right) + \left(2\% \cdot \frac{300}{-100} \right) \\ &= -2\% \end{aligned}$$

At first glance, the fact that the calculated r_D is negative 2 percent may seem surprising, but further analysis shows the combined effect of the financial asset ($400), which yields a rate of return (1%) that is less than the interest rate paid on the $100 of debt (2%). Thus, we earned a net loss of $2.00 ($4.00 – $6.00) on the net financial asset value of $100.00 ($400.00 – $300.00), which is a negative 2 percent return. In other words, we are earning negative 2 percent on our net financial assets.

Finally, we previously showed V^{Eq} is $1,306.61. Now we can solve for the appropriate expected cost of capital for equity. In doing so, we note that a net financial asset enters the formula in a manner that amounts to a negative debt because the formulas are usually written expecting a net borrower rather than net lender.

$$\begin{aligned} r_{WACC} &= \left(r_D \cdot \frac{V^{NFL}}{V^{Oper}} \right) + \left(r_{Eq} \cdot \frac{V^{Eq}}{V^{Oper}} \right) \\ 10\% &= \left(-2\% \cdot \frac{-100.00}{1{,}206.61} \right) + \left(r_{Eq} \cdot \frac{1{,}306.61}{1{,}206.61} \right) \end{aligned}$$

Again, note that, in this calculation, there is an expected return of negative 2 percent on net financial *assets* of $100 (hence, the negative sign on V^{NFL}).

Thus, the expected return on equity is

$$r_{Eq} = \left[10\% - \left(-2\% \cdot \frac{-100.00}{1{,}206.61} \right) \right] \cdot \frac{1{,}206.61}{1{,}306.61} = 9.082\%$$

under alternative A.

Next, let us do the calculation for alternative B, which classifies the investment fund as a part of enterprise operations. Under this approach, V^{Oper} is the sum of the value of the two enterprise operating components (i.e., \$1,606.61 = \$1,206.61 project + \$400.00 investment fund). The calculation of the cost of capital for enterprise operations encompasses the project and the investment fund as follows:

$$\begin{aligned} r_{WACC} &= \left(r_{Project} \cdot \frac{V^{Project}}{V^{Oper}} \right) + \left(r_{Mutual\ Fund} \cdot \frac{V^{Mutual\ Fund}}{V^{Oper}} \right) \\ &= \left(10\% \cdot \frac{1{,}206.61}{1{,}606.61} \right) + \left(1\% \cdot \frac{400.00}{1{,}606.61} \right) \\ &= 7.759\% \end{aligned}$$

Then, we can solve for the appropriate expected cost of capital for equity under alternative B as follows:

$$r_{WACC} = \left(r_D \cdot \frac{V^{NFL}}{V^{Oper}} \right) + \left(r_{Eq} \cdot \frac{V^{Eq}}{V^{Oper}} \right)$$

$$7.759\% = \left(2\% \cdot \frac{300.00}{1{,}606.61} \right) + \left(r_{Eq} \cdot \frac{1{,}306.61}{1{,}606.61} \right)$$

$$r_{Eq} = \left[7.759\% - \left(2\% \cdot \frac{300.00}{1{,}606.61} \right) \right] \cdot \frac{1{,}606.61}{1{,}306.61} = 9.082\%$$

under alternative B.

And, of course, the cost of equity capital turns out to be exactly the same for each of the two alternatives, as it should be. Only the details of the calculation have changed.

To summarize:

	Alternative A (with net financial assets)	Alternative B (with net financial liabilities)
Cost of enterprise capital (*WACC*)	10%	7.759%
Cost of debt capital.	–2%	2%
Cost of equity capital	9.082%	9.082%

Discounted Cash Flow Valuation

If we were starting from scratch in implementing these two approaches, we would have first, for both alternatives, estimated the cost of equity capital of 9.082 percent as calculated using the capital asset pricing model (*CAPM*) or a similar method. Then, under alternative A, we would use the appropriate cost of debt with our negative debt (because we are a net lender) and arrive at a *WACC* estimate of 10 percent. When we use *WACC* to discount alternative A's *FCF*s above, we get the following estimate of enterprise value:

$$\begin{aligned} V_{Ent} &= \frac{600}{(1+0.10)} + \frac{800}{(1+0.10)^2} \\ &= 1{,}206.61 \end{aligned}$$

The general approach at this point in the valuation is to subtract the value of the financial activity (debt) from the value of the enterprise operations to arrive at the value of equity. Because we are assuming a net lender, we add in the negative debt (the investment fund and loan) of \$100.00 and arrive at the equity value of \$1,306.61, which is what was expected based on our benchmark calculations.

The analysis becomes more complicated under alternative B. The issue is the change in relative values of the project and investment fund in the enterprise operations in period 2; an important implication is that the estimate of *WACC*, at 7.759 percent, is not appropriate in the second period! We instead would need to recompute *WACC* for period 2 in order to take into account the new expected investment in the project and in the investment fund. We next show how this could be done.

At the beginning of period 2, there is only the remaining $800.00 cash flow to be received on the project. As a result, the value of the project is $727.27 = $800.00/1.10. Additionally, because the investment fund is being shown as an enterprise operating item, we must also consider its continuing value. We need to value the indefinite expected future income of $4.00 per period from the investment fund. Capitalizing this stream yields a value of $400.00 (i.e., $4.00/0.01), which must be added to the period 2 cash flows to yield $1,204.00. Because the value of the investment fund remains at $400.00, the value of the enterprise operations at the end of period 1 is $1,127.27 ($727.27 project + $400.00 investment fund). Using this information, we can compute the appropriate *WACC* to be used in period 2:

$$r_{WACC} = \left(r_{Project} \cdot \frac{V^{Project}}{V^{Oper}}\right) + \left(r_{Mutual\ Fund} \cdot \frac{V^{Mutual\ Fund}}{V^{Oper}}\right)$$
$$= \left(10\% \cdot \frac{727.27}{1{,}127.27}\right) + \left(1\% \cdot \frac{400.00}{1{,}127.27}\right)$$
$$= 6.806\%$$

Note that the *WACC* has changed from 7.759% to 6.806% for period 2. Using these *WACC* estimates of 7.759% for period 1 and 6.806% for period 2, we can discount expected free cash flows from enterprise operations as follows:

$$V^{Oper} = \frac{604}{(1+0.07759)} + \frac{1{,}204}{(1+0.07759)\cdot(1+0.06806)}$$
$$= 1{,}606.61$$

Subtracting the $300.00 value of the loan from this amount yields the expected (and correct) value of equity of $1,306.61.[22]

Valuation Implications Demonstrated by Numerical Example

While this was a long, detailed exercise, the consideration of the separated (alternative A) approach above, where the investment fund is considered a financial asset, and the mingled (alternative B) approach, in which the investment fund is considered an enterprise operating asset, illustrates three very important points:

1. The *FCF* in each period will differ based on classification.

Free Cash Flows	Separated Approach	Mingled Approach
Period 1	$600	$604
Period 2	$800	$804

[22] What would have occurred had we not adjusted our *WACC* estimate due to the changing values of the project and investment fund? Under alternative B, when we utilize the cost of equity capital of 9.082 percent along with the appropriate cost of debt (this time, as a net borrower), we arrive at a *WACC* estimate of 7.759 percent. This *WACC* would then be applied to the future *FCF*, which were shown above to be $604.00 in period 1 and $804.00 in period 2. Additionally, the investment fund's value of $400.00 ($4.00/0.01) would be added to the period 2 cash flows to yield $1,204.00. When we use the alternative B *WACC* estimate of 7.759 percent to discount these alternative B *FCF*s from enterprise operations above, we get the following estimate of enterprise value:

$$V^{Oper} = \frac{604}{(1+0.07759)} + \frac{1{,}204}{(1+0.7759)^2}$$
$$= 1{,}597.37$$

Next, we would subtract the debt (the loan) of $300.00 and arrive at an estimate of the equity value of $1,297.37. This is wrong! We should have continued to arrive at the known benchmark equity value of $1,306.61. Thus, failure to consider the changes in *WACC* due to the changes in relative value of the project and investment fund would have resulted in an incorrect valuation.

2. The cost of capital for debt and the *WACC* (i.e., the cost of capital for enterprise operations) will differ, but the cost of capital for equity is unaffected by classification. Additionally, the required *WACC* under the mingled approach cannot be assumed to be constant because of changes in the relative values of the project and the investment fund.

Cost of Capital	Separated Approach		Mingled Approach
Enterprise (*WACC*)	10%	Period 1	7.759%
		Period 2	6.806%
Debt	–2%		2%
Equity	9.082%		9.082%

3. The calculated value of equity is unaffected by the choice between the accounting and mingled approaches if both are properly implemented.

Value of Equity	Separated Approach	Mingled Approach
Enterprise value	$1,206.61	$1,606.61
Debt value	(100.00)	300.00
Equity value	$1,306.61	$1,306.61

Deciding between the Mingled and Separated Approaches to Classification

Valuations can be done using either the approach used in corporate finance texts or the approach used in texts on financial statement analysis and valuation. Either way, we should arrive at the same estimate of equity value. There are, however, very important differences in the tasks that arise due to the classification. The two main implications of our choice to include or exclude the investment fund in enterprise operations in our example are that it affects the scope of the valuation exercise and the calculation of the discount rate.

One reason to classify excess cash and investments as a financial asset is that accounting generally records these items, as a reasonable approximation, at market value. Cash is presumably at fair value, and the investments are often shown at fair value as well.[23] Note 1 of Starbucks' financial statements says, "Our short-term and long-term investments consist primarily of investment-grade debt securities, all of which are classified as available-for-sale. Available-for-sale securities are recorded at fair value, and unrealized holding gains and losses are recorded, net of tax, as a component of accumulated other comprehensive income."

Given this assumption, why would we complicate our task by including these items in the valuation exercise? The company has already provided us with a reliable (and audited) estimate of fair value. If, for example, the final goal is the estimation of the value of equity ownership, we can simply add their reported fair (market) value to the estimated value of enterprise operations (analogous to a way we subtract debt) to obtain our estimate of equity value.

The second, and more compelling, implication of classification of the investment fund as a financial asset is the effect on our choice of discount rate for valuing enterprise operations. The inclusion of the excess cash and investments in enterprise operations adds nothing to our valuation exercise. Instead, it actually makes it harder. Now, we will also have to forecast future returns to the excess cash and investments, and their risk would need to be considered in calculating the appropriate discount rate for enterprise operations in each future period. That is, returning to Starbucks, we would need to determine a cost of capital for enterprise operations (*WACC*) for a combined coffee *and* investment fund company rather than simply for a coffee company. This mixed discount rate covering both coffee and investment fund operations should be estimated by determining the risk of each endeavor. These risk estimates would then be weighted by their

[23] If the investments are not reported on the financial statements at fair value, then, as financial instruments, their fair values must be disclosed in the footnotes. Of course, exceptions may occur, as suggested in the Apple Inc. example discussed earlier.

relative market values in order to compute an appropriate weighted average of the two activities. Though this can be done, it is a much more complicated endeavor. Further, note that one of the inputs to the process is the value of the coffee operations, which is what we are trying to determine!

Much more important to the valuation task, the discount rate to be used for future payoffs from a coffee *and* investment fund combination changes over time. The changing proportion of activities in coffee and investment fund would require that a different discount rate be considered for each future period because we must consider the balance of their different risk levels. A primary reason for focusing a valuation exercise on enterprise operations is the avoidance of effects relating to changing leverage that must be considered if we try to value equity directly. If we combine the coffee and investment fund, we are back to estimating changing levels of these activities that have different levels of risk. We would effectively be reintroducing the issue of leverage that we were seeking to avoid.

Given that the investment fund is already at fair value and given our desire to use a constant discount rate, we conclude that classifying the investment fund as a financial asset will generally be the most sensible way to approach such valuations.

APPENDIX SUMMARY

The calculations of *FCF* in the financial statement analysis and valuation texts and in the corporate finance texts reflect different views of the assets that should be considered part of a company's operating (as distinguished from its financing) activities. But if such differences yield different values for its enterprise operations, they will not affect the valuation of the company's equity provided the following two conditions are met:

1. The discount rate used to calculate the value of enterprise operations correctly reflects the risk of what has been defined as enterprise operations. (Note that, if there are different parts in the enterprise operations with different levels of risk, we must calculate a weighted interest rate that reflects the changing balance between the activities in each time period. For example, if we view Starbucks as combining the sale of coffee with an investment in cash and marketable securities, use of a constant discount rate in future periods would be inappropriate.)
2. The estimated market value of the enterprise operations is adjusted for the fair value of the items being classified as a financial activity (whether financial assets or liabilities).

When valuing a company, a decision must be made as to what constitutes enterprise operations. Separating items that are already at market value (or have market value disclosed) eliminates a portion of the forecasting exercise. We do not need to forecast the returns of Starbucks' cash and marketable securities, determine their riskiness, or determine the changing quantity of cash and marketable securities that management will choose to maintain in future periods. Use of a definition of enterprise operations that excludes these components from the analysis is easier to implement and does not diminish the reliability of the analysis.

In sum, the main point of our article, then, is that the critical difference in the calculation of *FCF* and valuations based on the financial statement analysis and the corporate finance methods arises from their difference in how they classify assets as a part of enterprise net operating assets or financial activities. But although that choice changes the calculated *FCF*s, our estimates of the value of the company's equity should be unaffected provided the cost of capital is correctly computed. And because valuation is much more straightforward if we can assume a constant discount rate, we argue that attempting to estimate the expected relative values of the combined project and cash and marketable securities in each future period is likely to introduce needless complications (even when it proves to be possible).

Perhaps most important, separating operating and financial activities enables managers to avoid estimation of different discount rates for each of the forecast years. By treating the cash and marketable securities (which are conveniently accounted for at market value) as a financial asset, the *WACC* estimate does not have to be forecast separately for each future period. And for that reason alone, the exclusion of (some if not most) financial assets from the definition of enterprise operations should generally be significantly easier to implement and does not change the reliability of the analysis.

APPENDIX REFERENCES

Apple Inc. Fiscal 2015 Annual Report.

Brealey, R., S. Myers, and F. Allen. (2014). *Principles of corporate finance* (11th ed.). McGraw-Hill Irwin.

Dittmar, A. (2008). Corporate cash policy and how to manage it with stock repurchases. *Journal of Applied Corporate Finance*, 20(3), 22–34.

Easton, P., M. McAnally, G. Sommers, and X. Zhang. (2018). *Financial statement analysis and valuation* (5th ed.). Cambridge Business Publishers.

Ford Motor Company. Fiscal 2014 Annual Report.

Palepu, K., and P. Healy. (2013). *Business analysis and valuation using financial statements* (5th ed.). South-Western Cengage Learning.

Penman, S. (2012). *Financial statement analysis and security valuation* (5th ed.). McGraw-Hill Irwin.

Ross, S., R. Westerfield, and B. Jordan. (2016). *Fundamentals of corporate finance* (11th ed.). McGraw-Hill.

S&P Capital IQ. (2015). "Your Guide to S&P Capital IQ™ Stock Reports."

Starbucks. Fiscal 2014 Annual Report.

Wahlen, J., S. Baginski, and M. Bradshaw. (2015). *Financial reporting, financial statement analysis, and valuation* (8th ed.). Cengage Learning.

QUESTIONS

Q3.1 What is the goal of reformulation?

Q3.2 Why focus on the operating activities, not the financing activities, when determining a firm's value?

Q3.3 In what order do you consider financial statements in reformulating?

Q3.4 When reformulating the balance sheet, what question are we asking about each reported item?

Q3.5 What is the argument for potentially splitting cash when reformulating rather than showing the entire amount as part of operating activities?

Q3.6 When questions arise about the classification of an item as related to operating or financial activities, which classification do we choose by default? What is a common cause for needing to do this?

Q3.7 What is the rationale behind classifying preferred stock as a part of *NFL*?

Q3.8 What is the rationale behind classifying noncontrolling interest as a part of *NFL*?

Q3.9 When reformulating the income statement, what question are we asking about each reported item?

Q3.10 How are reported taxes handled in the reformulation process?

Q3.11 When allocating the reported income tax expense between operating and financing activities, why does the allocation begin with tax impact for financing activities?

Q3.12 In identifying the components of net operating profit after tax (*NOPAT*), why is comprehensive income used and not net income?

Q3.13 What factors need to be considered when reformulating industrial companies that have support financing divisions?

EXERCISES

E3.14 Below is a recent balance sheet for Chipotle (CMG). For each item listed, determine the classification that would be used in reformulation from the following list:

- O – Operating activities
- F – Financial activities
- S – Split between operating and financial activities
- ? – Desire more detailed information but will initially classify as related to operating activities
- CSE – Common shareholders' equity

CHIPOTLE MEXICAN GRILL INC.
CONSOLIDATED BALANCE SHEET
(in thousands, except per-share data)

	Year Ended December 31,	
	2018	2017
Assets		
Current assets:		
Cash and cash equivalents	$ 249,953	$ 184,569
Accounts receivable	62,312	40,453
Inventory	21,555	19,860
Prepaid expenses and other current assets	54,129	50,918
Income tax receivable	—	9,353
Investments	426,845	324,382
Total current assets	814,794	629,535
Leasehold improvements, property and equipment, net	1,379,254	1,338,366
Restricted cash	30,199	29,601
Other assets	19,332	26,251
Goodwill	21,939	21,939
Total assets	$2,265,518	$2,045,692
Liabilities and Shareholders' Equity		
Current liabilities:		
Accounts payable	$ 113,071	$ 82,028
Accrued payroll and benefits	113,467	82,541
Accrued liabilities	145,849	95,679
Unearned revenue	70,474	63,645
Income tax payable	5,129	—
Total current liabilities	449,990	323,893
Commitments and contingencies (Note 13)		
Deferred rent	330,985	316,498
Deferred income tax liability	11,566	814
Other liabilities	31,638	40,042
Total liabilities	824,179	681,247
Shareholders' equity:		
Preferred stock, $0.01 par value, 600,000 shares authorized, no shares issued as of December 31, 2018 and 2017, respectively	—	—
Common stock $0.01 par value, 230,000 shares authorized, and 35,973 and 35,852 shares issued as of December 31, 2018 and 2017, respectively	360	359
Additional paid-in capital	1,374,154	1,305,090
Treasury stock, at cost, 8,276 and 7,826 common shares at December 31, 2018 and 2017, respectively	(2,500,556)	(2,334,409)
Accumulated other comprehensive income (loss)	(6,236)	(3,659)
Retained earnings	2,573,617	2,397,064
Total shareholders' equity	1,441,339	1,364,445
Total liabilities and shareholders' equity	$2,265,518	$2,045,692

E3.15 Below is a recent balance sheet for Amazon (AMZN). For each item listed, determine the classification that would be used in reformulation from the following list:

- O – Operating activities
- F – Financial activities
- S – Split between operating and financial activities
- ? – Desire more detailed information but will initially classify as related to operating activities
- CSE – Common shareholders' equity

AMAZON.COM INC.
CONSOLIDATED BALANCE SHEETS
(in millions, except per-share data)

	Year Ended December 31,	
	2017	**2018**
Assets		
Current assets:		
Cash and cash equivalents	$ 20,522	$ 31,750
Marketable securities	10,464	9,500
Inventories	16,047	17,174
Accounts receivable, net and other	13,164	16,677
Total current assets	60,197	75,101
Property and equipment, net	48,866	61,797
Goodwill	13,350	14,548
Other assets	8,897	11,202
Total assets	$131,310	$162,648
Liabilities and Stockholders' Equity		
Current liabilities:		
Accounts payable	$ 34,616	$ 38,192
Accrued expenses and other	18,170	23,663
Unearned revenue	5,097	6,536
Total current liabilities	57,883	68,391
Long-term debt	24,743	23,495
Other long-term liabilities	20,975	27,213
Commitments and contingencies (Note 7)		
Stockholders' equity		
Preferred stock, $0.01 par value:		
Authorized shares—500		
Issued and outstanding shares—none	—	—
Common stock, $0.01 par value:		
Authorized shares—5,000		
Issued shares—507 and 514		
Outstanding shares—484 and 491	5	5
Treasury stock, at cost	(1,837)	(1,837)
Additional paid-in capital	21,389	26,791
Accumulated other comprehensive loss	(484)	(1,035)
Retained earnings	8,636	19,625
Total stockholders' equity	27,709	43,549
Total liabilities and stockholders' equity	$131,310	$162,648

E3.16 Below is a recent balance sheet for Marriott (MAR). For each item listed, determine the classification that would be used in reformulation from the following list:

- O – Operating activities
- F – Financial activities
- S – Split between operating and financial activities
- ? – Desire more detailed information but will initially classify as related to operating activities
- CSE – Common shareholders' equity

MARRIOTT INTERNATIONAL INC.
CONSOLIDATED BALANCE SHEETS
Fiscal Years Ended 2018 and 2017
($ in millions)

	Year Ended December 31,	
	2018	2017
Assets		
Current assets		
Cash and equivalents	$ 316	$ 383
Accounts and notes receivable, net	2,133	1,973
Prepaid expenses and other	249	235
Assets held for sale	8	149
	2,706	2,740
Property and equipment, net	1,956	1,793
Intangible assets		
Brands	5,700	5,922
Contract acquisition costs and other	2,590	2,622
Goodwill	9,036	9,207
	17,419	17,751
Equity method investments	732	734
Notes receivable, net	125	142
Deferred taxes assets	171	93
Other noncurrent assets	587	593
	$23,696	$23,846
Liabilities and Shareholders' Deficit		
Current liabilities		
Current portion of long-term debt	$ 833	$ 398
Accounts payable	767	783
Accrued payroll and benefits	1,345	1,214
Liability for guest loyalty programs	2,529	2,121
Accrued expenses and other	963	1,291
	6,437	5,807
Long-term debt	8,514	7,840
Liability for guest loyalty programs	2,932	2,819
Deferred tax liabilities	485	605
Deferred revenue	731	583
Other noncurrent liabilities	2,372	2,610
Shareholders' equity		
Class A common stock	5	5
Additional paid-in capital	5,814	5,770
Retained earnings	8,982	7,242
Treasury stock, at cost	(12,185)	(9,418)
Accumulated other comprehensive loss	(391)	(17)
	2,225	3,582
	$23,696	$23,846

E3.17 Below is a recent income statement for Chipotle (CMG). For each item listed, determine the classification that would be used in reformulation from the following list:

- O – Operating activities
- F – Financial activities
- S – Split between operating and financial activities
- ? – Desire more detailed information but will initially classify as related to operating activities

CHIPOTLE MEXICAN GRILL INC.
CONSOLIDATED STATEMENT OF INCOME
(in thousands, except per-share data)

	Years Ended December 31,		
	2018	2017	2016
Revenue	$4,864,985	$4,476,412	$3,904,384
Restaurant operating costs (exclusive of depreciation and amortization shown separately below):			
Food, beverage, and packaging	1,600,760	1,535,428	1,365,580
Labor	1,326,079	1,205,992	1,105,001
Occupancy	347,123	327,132	293,636
Other operating costs	680,031	651,644	641.953
General and administrative expenses	375,460	296,388	276,240
Depreciation and amortization	201,979	163,348	146,368
Pre-opening costs	8,546	12,341	17,162
Loss on disposal of assets	66,639	13,345	23,877
Total operating expenses	4,606,617	4,205,618	3,869,817
Income from operations	258,268	270,794	34,567
Interest and other income, net	10,068	4,949	4,172
Income before income taxes	268,436	275,743	38,739
Provision for income taxes	(91,883)	(99,490)	(15,801)
Net income	$ 176,553	$ 176,253	$ 22,938
Earnings per share:			
Basic	$ 6.35	$ 6.19	$ 0.78
Diluted	$ 6.31	$ 6.17	$ 0.77
Weighted-average common shares outstanding:			
Basic	27,823	28,491	29,265
Diluted	27,962	28,561	29,770

CONSOLIDATED STATEMENT OF COMPREHENSIVE INCOME
(in thousands)

	Years Ended December 31,		
	2018	2017	2016
Net income	$176,553	$176,253	$ 22,938
Other comprehensive income (loss), net of income taxes:			
Foreign currency translation adjustments	(,2736)	4,689	(1,291)
Unrealized gain (loss) on available-for-sale securities	291	(274)	2,251
Tax benefit (expense)	(132)	88	(849)
Other comprehensive income (loss), net of income taxes	(2,577)	4,503	111
Comprehensive income	$173,976	$180,756	$ 23,049

E3.18 Below are a recent Income Statement and Statement of Comprehensive Income for Amazon (AMZN). For each item listed, determine the classification that would be used in reformulation from the following list:

- O – Operating activities
- F – Financial activities
- S – Split between operating and financial activities
- ? – Desire more detailed information but will initially classify as related to operating activities

AMAZON.COM INC.
CONSOLIDATED INCOME STATEMENT
(in millions, except per share)

	Year Ended December 31,		
	2016	**2017**	**2018**
Net product sales	$ 94,665	$118,573	$141,915
Net services sales	41,322	59,293	90,972
Total net sales	135,987	177,866	232,887
Operating expenses:			
Cost of sales	88,265	111,934	139,156
Fulfillment	17,619	25,249	34,027
Marketing	7,233	10,069	13,814
Technology and content	16,085	22,620	28,837
General and administrative	2,432	3,674	4,336
Other operating expense, net	167	214	296
Total operating expenses	131,801	173,760	220,466
Operating income	4,186	4,106	12,421
Interest income	100	202	440
Interest expense	(484)	(848)	(1,417)
Other income (expense), net	90	346	(183)
Total nonoperating income (expense)	(294)	(300)	(1,160)
Income before income taxes	3,892	3,806	11,261
Provision for income taxes	(1,425)	(769)	(1,197)
Equity-method investment activity, net of tax	(96)	(4)	9
Net income (loss)	$ 2,371	$ 3,033	$ 10,073

AMAZON.COM INC.
CONSOLIDATED STATEMENTS OF COMPREHENSIVE INCOME
(in million)

	Year Ended December 31,		
	2016	**2017**	**2018**
Net income	$2,371	$3,033	$10,073
Other comprehensive income (loss):			
Foreign currency translation adjustments, net of tax of $(49), $5, and $6	(279)	533	(538)
Net change in unrealized gains (losses) on available-for-sale debt securities:			
Unrealized gains(losses), net of tax of $(12), $5, and $0	9	(39)	(17)
Reclassification adjustment for losses (gains) included in "Other income (expense), net," net of tax of $0, $0, and $0	8	7	8
Net unrealized gains (losses) on available-for-sale debt securities	17	(32)	(9)
Total other comprehensive income (loss)	(262)	501	(547)
Comprehensive income	$2,109	$3,534	$ 9,526

E3.19 Below are a recent income statement and statement of comprehensive income for Marriott (MAR). For each item listed, determine the classification that would be used in reformulation from the following list:

- O – Operating activities
- F – Financial activities
- S – Split between operating and financial activities
- ? – Desire more detailed information but will initially classify as related to operating activities

MARRIOTT INTERNATIONAL INC.
CONSOLIDATED STATEMENTS OF INCOME
Fiscal Years 2018, 2017, and 2016
($ in millions, except per-share amounts)

	Year Ended December 31,		
	2018	2017	2016
Revenues			
Base management fees	$ 1,140	$ 1,102	$ 806
Franchise fees	1,849	1,618	988
Incentive management fees	649	607	425
Gross fee revenues	3,638	3,295	2,388
Contract investment amortization	(58)	(50)	(40)
Net fee revenues	3,580	3,245	2,384
Owned, leased, and other revenue	1,635	1,752	1,125
Cost reimbursement revenue	15,543	15,455	11,934
	$20,758	$20,452	$15,407
Operating Costs and Expenses			
Owned, leased, and other—direct	1,306	1,411	901
Depreciation, amortization, and other	226	229	119
General, administrative, and other	927	921	743
Merger-related costs and charges	155	159	386
Reimbursed expenses	15,778	15,228	11,834
	18,392	17,948	13,983
Operating Income	2,366	2,504	1,424
Gains and other income, net	194	688	5
Interest expense	(340)	(288)	(234)
Interest income	22	38	35
Equity in earnings	103	40	9
Income before Income Taxes	2,345	2,982	1,239
Provision for income taxes	(438)	(1,523)	(431)
Net Income	$ 1,907	$ 1,459	$ 808

MARRIOTT INTERNATIONAL INC.
CONSOLIDATED STATEMENTS OF COMPREHENSIVE INCOME
Fiscal Years 2018, 2017, and 2016
($ in millions)

	Year Ended December 31,		
	2018	2017	2016
Net income	$1,907	$1,459	$ 808
Other comprehensive (loss) income:			
Foreign currency translation adjustments	(391)	478	(311)
Derivative instrument adjustments, net of tax	12	(14)	1
Unrealized (loss) gain on available-for-sale securities, net of tax	—	(2)	2
Pension and postretirement adjustments, net of tax	(8)	7	5
Reclassification of losses, net of tax	17	11	2
Total other comprehensive (loss) income, net of tax	(370)	480	(301)
Comprehensive income	$1,537	$1,939	$ 507

E3.20 Using the reformulations of Davidson Inc.'s income statement (in thousands), calculate net operating profit after tax (*NOPAT*). Assume Davidson has a marginal tax rate of 25 percent (federal and state).

Revenue	$10,000
Cost of goods sold	(5,000)
SG&A expenses	(2,800)
R&D expenses	(350)
Equity share in subsidiary income	275
Losses on debt retirement	(150)
Interest income	50
Interest expense	(400)
Income tax expense	(500)
Net income	$ 1,125

E3.21 For its fiscal year 2018, Home Depot reported income before taxes of $14,556 million, income tax expense of $3,435 million, and net income of $11,121 million. Home Depot's net operating profit before tax was $ 15,524 million and financial expense before tax of $958 million. Using a statutory tax rate of 21 percent, calculate Home Depot's income tax expense allocation between operating and financing activities.

E3.22 **Apple Inc.** reported the following income statements for fiscal 2019, 2018, and 2017.

APPLE INC.
CONSOLIDATED STATEMENT OF OPERATIONS
(in millions, except number of shares, which are reflected in thousands and per-share amounts)

	Year Ended		
	September 28, 2019	**September 29, 2018**	**September 30, 2017**
Net sales:			
Products	$213,883	$225,847	$196,534
Services	46,291	39,748	32,700
Total net sales	260,174	265,595	229,234
Cost of sales:			
Products	144,996	148,164	126,337
Services	16,786	15,592	14,711
Total cost of sales	161,782	163,756	141,048
Gross margin	98,392	101,839	88,186
Operating expenses:			
Research and development	16,217	14,236	11,581
Selling, general, and administrative	18,245	16,705	15,261
Total operating expenses	34,462	30,941	26,842
Operating income	63,930	70,898	61,344
Other income/(expense), net	1,807	2,005	2,745
Income before provision for income taxes	65,737	72,903	64,089
Provision for income taxes	10,481	13,372	15,738
Net income	$ 55,256	$ 59,531	$ 48,351

A footnote to the financial statements broke out the components within *Other income(expense), net*.

OTHER INCOME/(EXPENSE), NET
The following table shows the detail of OI&E for 2019, 2018, and 2017 (in millions):

	2019	2018	2017
Interest and dividend income	$4,961	$5,686	$5,201
Interest expense	(3,576)	(3,240)	(2,323)
Other income/(expense), net	422	(411)	(133)
Total other income/(expense), net	$1,807	$2,005	$2,745

Calculate Apple's income tax expense allocation between operating and financing activities. Apple reported that its statutory tax rate for 2019 was 21.0 percent.

CONTINUING EXAMPLES

CE3.23 From the company website, EDGAR database, or a similar source, obtain the 2018, 2017, and 2016 annual reports for **Kellogg** (K). Using this information, reformulate the balance sheet to calculate *NOA* and *NFL* for 2016–2018.

CE3.24 From the company website, EDGAR, or a similar source, obtain the 2018, 2017, and 2016 annual reports for **Kellogg** (K). Using this information, reformulate the income statement and statement of comprehensive income to calculate *NOPAT* and *FEAT* for 2016–2018.

CE3.25 From the company website, EDGAR, or a similar source, obtain the fiscal 2018, 2017, and 2016 annual reports for **Thor Industries** (THO). Using this information, reformulate the balance sheet to calculate *NOA* and *NFL* for 2015–2018.

CE3.26 From the company website, EDGAR, or a similar source, obtain the fiscal 2018, 2017, and 2016 annual reports for **Thor Industries** (THO). Using this information, reformulate the income statement to calculate *NOPAT* and *FEAT* for 2015–2018.

CE3.27 From the company website, EDGAR, or a similar source, obtain the fiscal 2018, 2017, and 2016 annual reports for **Winnebago** (WGO). Using this information, reformulate the balance sheet to calculate *NOA* and *NFL* for 2015–2018.

CE3.28 From the company website, EDGAR or a similar source, obtain the 2018, 2017, and 2016 annual reports for **Winnebago** (WGO). Using this information, reformulate the income statement to calculate *NOPAT* and *FEAT* for 2015–2018.

Chapter Four

Use of Additional Information to Enhance Reformulation

TAKEAWAYS

When you complete this chapter, you should be able to:

1. Explain the benefits of including additional information beyond the financial statements in reformulation.
2. Expand the balance sheet to incorporate additional detail information.
3. Gross up reported amounts, and address implied additional amounts while maintaining balanced numbers.
4. Expand the income statement to incorporate additional detail information.
5. Explain why a marginal tax rate is preferred to an effective tax rate in reformulation.

In the last chapter, our reformulation used a set of information drawn from the face of the financial statements despite our knowledge that additional information is available from footnotes and other sources. This was done in order to focus on the concept of reformulation and allow for an introduction to its implementation. Now, in this chapter, we see what additional information beyond that contained on the face of the financial statements may be useful in refining our estimates of *NOA* and *NOPAT* for forecasting and valuation. Keep in mind that the information available will be different for every company. Therefore, view this chapter as a guide when seeking and using additional information that may be available. This chapter presents an example and should not be viewed as just a checklist of what needs to be done.

LO1: Explain the benefits of including additional information beyond the financial statements in reformulation.

The footnotes and the management discussion and analysis (MD&A) provide additional detail for some of the items contained in the financial statements, as well as clues to whether items are related to the operating or financial activities of the company. Our goals when gathering additional information are (1) to focus more clearly on identification of operating activities and financial activities (e.g., finding the detail on the nature of items like *other assets*, some of which fall into each category) and (2) to use the data to facilitate improved forecasting (e.g., it could be that different items contained in a summary number reported by the company may have different expected future growth—sales for different segments may be growing at different rates or *property, plant, and equipment* may include equipment expected to grow with sales, but no changes in the land and buildings may be required in the foreseeable future).

During the initial reformulation, we saw several items, which we were unable to segregate into operating or financial activities (e.g., *Deferred income tax* assets). We now gather the additional information that is available from footnotes and the MD&A. If we are able to either segregate or refine the classification of whether these items arise from operating or financial activities, we will have updated and improved our estimates of *NOA* and *NOPAT*. If we improve the quality of the information we gather, we may change our segregation of operating and financial activities and our expectations of future payoffs, and, in turn, we may change our estimate of value.

CHAPTER OUTLINE

Use of Additional Information to Enhance Reformulation

Incorporating Additional Information
- Motivations for Expanding Reformulation
- Sources of Additional Information

Expanded Balance Sheet
- Deferred Taxes
- Pension and Other Postretirement Benefits
- Other Items

Expanded Income Statement
- Pension and Other Postretirement Benefits
- Other Items

Tax Rate for Operations
- Effective Tax Rate or Marginal Tax Rate

DOWNLOADED SPREADSHEETS OF FINANCIAL STATEMENT DATA

If financial statement data has been downloaded as a spreadsheet from a third-party source such as Mergent Online, a portion of the data gathering discussed in this chapter is likely already completed. Nevertheless, the concerns in the prior chapter about being aware of duplication of data remain. Care must be taken to ensure that the totals from the downloaded information match those in the Form 10-K. That is, you must ensure that you understand the source of the details gathered by the spreadsheet's provider. Additionally, perusal of the Form 10-K may yield information not included by a third-party data provider. Do not passively assume that their efforts were sufficient or in accordance with your analysis goals. Understanding the data, including their source and meaning, will be critical in maximizing their benefit to your valuation efforts.

Following the pattern from earlier, we first present in **Exhibits 4.1** and **4.2** the expanded reformulations of **General Mills** (GIS), and then we discuss the notable changes to the balance sheet, followed by notable changes to the income statement.

EXHIBIT 4.1 GIS Expanded Balance Sheet Reformulation

Amounts in Millions	May 27, 2018	*NOA*	*NFL*
Assets			
Cash and cash equivalents	$ 399.0	$ 314.8	$ 84.2
Receivables: Customers	1,712.6	1,712.6	
Receivables: Allowance for doubtful accounts	(28.4)	(28.4)	
Inventories: Raw materials and packaging	400.0	400.0	
Inventories: Finished goods	1,364.2	1,364.2	
Inventories: Grain	91.2	91.2	
Inventories: Excess of FIFO over LIFO cost	(213.2)	(213.2)	
Deferred tax assets: Accrued liabilities	47.2	47.2	
Deferred tax assets: Compensation and employee benefits	210.2	210.2	
Deferred tax assets: Pension	57.1		57.1
Deferred tax assets: Tax credit carryforwards	7.4	7.4	
Deferred tax assets: Stock, partnership, and miscellaneous investments	147.9		147.9
Deferred tax assets: Capital losses	12.9	12.9	
Deferred tax assets: Net operating losses	161.2	161.2	
Deferred tax assets: Other	52.9	52.9	
Deferred tax assets: Valuation allowance	(176.0)	(176.0)	
Prepaid expenses and other current assets: Other receivables	174.4		174.4
Prepaid expenses and other current assets: Prepaid expenses	165.6	165.6	
Prepaid expenses and other current assets: Derivative receivables, primarily commodity-related	40.5	40.5	
Prepaid expenses and other current assets: Grain contracts	7.1	7.1	
Prepaid expenses and other current assets: Miscellaneous	10.7	10.7	
Land, buildings, and equipment: Land	77.7	77.7	
Land, buildings, and equipment: Buildings	2,396.3	2,396.3	
Land, buildings, and equipment: Buildings under capital lease	0.3	0.3	

continued

continued from previous page

EXHIBIT 4.1 GIS Expanded Balance Sheet Reformulation

Amounts in Millions	May 27, 2018	*NOA*	*NFL*
Land, buildings, and equipment: Equipment	6,236.6	6,236.6	
Land, buildings, and equipment: Equipment under capital lease	5.8	5.8	
Land, buildings, and equipment: Capitalized software	593.6	593.6	
Land, buildings, and equipment: Construction in progress	692.9	692.9	
Land, buildings, and equipment: Accumulated depreciation	(5,956.0)	(5,956.0)	
Goodwill: North America retail	6,410.6	6,410.6	
Goodwill: Pet	5,294.9	5,294.9	
Goodwill: Convenience stores and food service	918.8	918.8	
Goodwill: Europe and Australia	729.9	729.9	
Goodwill: Asia and Latin America	285.0	285.0	
Goodwill: Joint Ventures	425.8	425.8	
Other intangible assets: Brands and other indefinite-lived intangibles	6,818.7	6,818.7	
Other intangible assets: Franchise agreements, customer relationships, and other	811.7	811.7	
Other intangible assets: Accumulated amortization	(185.3)	(185.3)	
Other assets: Investments in and advances to joint ventures	499.6	499.6	
Other assets: Life insurance	26.9	26.9	
Other assets: Miscellaneous	106.6	106.6	
Defined benefit pension plans: Plan assets	6,177.4		6,177.4
Other postretirement benefit plans: Plan assets	726.1		726.1
Total assets	37,738.4	30,371.3	7,367.1
Liabilities and Shareholders' Equity			
Accounts payable	(2,746.2)	(2,746.2)	
Current portion of long-term debt	(1,600.1)		(1,600.1)
Notes payable: U.S. commercial paper	(1,213.5)		(1,213.5)
Notes payable: Financial institutions	(336.3)		(336.3)
Other current liabilities: Accrued trade and consumer promotions	(499.6)	(499.6)	
Other current liabilities: Accrued payroll	(347.0)	(347.0)	
Other current liabilities: Dividend payable	(17.5)		(17.5)
Other current liabilities: Accrued taxes	(94.8)	(94.8)	
Other current liabilities: Accrued interest, including interest rate swaps	(107.7)		(107.7)
Other current liabilities: Grain contracts	(1.2)	(1.2)	
Other current liabilities: Restructuring and other exit costs reserve	(66.8)	(66.8)	
Other current liabilities: Derivative payable	(8.3)	(8.3)	
Other current liabilities: Miscellaneous	(302.9)	(302.9)	
Long-term debt	(12,668.7)		(12,668.7)
Deferred tax liabilities: Brands	(1,498.7)	(1,498.7)	
Deferred tax liabilities: Fixed assets	(329.5)	(329.5)	
Deferred tax liabilities: Intangible assets	(255.1)	(255.1)	
Deferred tax liabilities: Tax lease transactions	(26.0)	(26.0)	
Deferred tax liabilities: Inventories	(38.8)	(38.8)	
Deferred tax liabilities: Stock, partnership, and miscellaneous investments	(317.1)		(317.1)
Deferred tax liabilities: Unrealized hedges	(28.5)	(28.5)	
Deferred tax liabilities: Other	(30.9)	(30.9)	
Other noncurrent liabilities: Accrued compensation and benefits, including pensions	(178.5)		(178.5)
Other noncurrent liabilities: Accrued taxes	(265.3)	(265.3)	
Other noncurrent liabilities: Miscellaneous	(76.3)	(76.3)	
Defined benefit pension plans: Benefit obligation	(6,416.0)		(6,416.0)
Other postretirement benefit plans: Benefit obligation	(871.8)		(871.8)
Post-employment benefit plans: Benefit obligation	(126.7)		(126.7)
Redeemable interest	(776.2)		(776.2)
Noncontrolling interests	(351.3)		(351.3)
Total liabilities	(31,597.3)	(6,615.9)	(24,981.4)
Net	$ 6,141.1	$ 23,755.4	$(17,614.3)

As you can see, the most notable items of expansion for the balance sheet are the deferred taxes, intangibles, and accrued liabilities. We will discuss the classification of some of these items shortly.

EXHIBIT 4.2 GIS Expanded Income Statement Reformulation

Amounts in Millions	May 27, 2018	*NOPAT*	*FEAT*
Net sales: North America retail	$ 10,115.4	$ 10,115.4	
Net sales: Convenience stores and food service	1,930.2	1,930.2	
Net sales: Europe and Australia	1,984.6	1,984.6	
Net sales: Asia and Latin America	1,710.2	1,710.2	
Cost of sales	(10,312.9)	(10,312.9)	
Advertising expense	(575.9)	(575.9)	
Research expense	(219.1)	(219.1)	
Defined benefit pension plans: Service cost	(102.9)	(102.9)	
Defined benefit pension plans: Interest cost	(217.9)		$(217.9)
Defined benefit pension plans: Expected return on plan assets	480.2		480.2
Defined benefit pension plans: Amortization of losses	(177.0)		(177.0)
Defined benefit pension plans: Amortization of prior service cost	(1.9)		(1.9)
Other postretirement benefit plans: Service cost	(11.6)	(11.6)	
Other postretirement benefit plans: Interest cost	(30.1)		(30.1)
Other postretirement benefit plans: Expected return on plan assets	52.2		52.2
Other postretirement benefit plans: Amortization of losses	(0.8)		(0.8)
Other postretirement benefit plans: Amortization of prior service cost	5.4		5.4
Post-employment benefit plans: Service cost	(8.6)	(8.6)	
Post-employment benefit plans: Interest cost	(2.3)		(2.3)
Post-employment benefit plans: Amortization of losses	(0.8)		(0.8)
Post-employment benefit plans: Amortization of prior service cost	(0.6)		(0.6)
Post-employment benefit plans: Other adjustments	(6.7)		(6.7)
Other selling, general, and administrative expenses	(1,934.2)	(1,934.2)	
Restructuring, impairment, and other exit costs	(165.6)	(165.6)	
Interest expense	(389.5)		(389.5)
Capitalized interest	4.1		4.1
Interest income	11.7		11.7
Income taxes	(57.3)	(137.9)	80.6
After-tax earnings from joint ventures	84.7	84.7	
Net earnings attributable to redeemable and noncontrolling interests	(32.0)		(32.0)
Comprehensive income items:			
Foreign currency translation	(37.0)	(37.0)	
Net actuarial income (loss)	140.1		140.1
Other fair value changes: Securities	1.2		1.2
Other fair value changes: Hedge derivatives	(50.8)	(50.8)	
Reclassification to earnings: Securities	(5.1)		(5.1)
Reclassification to earnings: Hedge derivatives	17.4	17.4	
Reclassification to earnings: Amortization of losses and prior service costs	117.6		117.6
Other comprehensive income attributable to noncontrolling interests, net	(38.5)		(38.5)
Net	$ 2,275.9	$ 2,286.0	$ (10.1)

On the income statement, the most notable expansions are of sales and the pension and postretirement items. Additional expansions relate to research and development costs and advertising costs. We can see adjustments to both *NOA* and *NOPAT* as a result of the inclusion of additional information. Just as we did before, we will follow this same pattern by beginning our discussion with the balance sheet before proceeding to the income statement.

ADDITIONAL INFORMATION RELATED TO GENERAL MILLS' BALANCE SHEET

LO2: Expand the balance sheet to incorporate additional detail information.

Review of the '4 Add'l Info' worksheet in the GIS' spreadsheet shows the information gathered from the notes to the financial statements. From this, we can trace the information used to expand the balance sheet reformulation. For example, *Goodwill* of $14,065.0 million and $8,747.2 million were reported in the years ended May 2018 and 2017, respectively. Incorporating the breakdown from Note 6 shows the change is driven by the acquisition in the Pet segment (the Blue Buffalo addition) of $5,294.9 million. Substituting this more detailed information for what was reported on the balance sheet allows us to see that the small changes in other components of goodwill are driven by foreign currency translation. For each item where the company has provided a breakdown in the notes or MD&A, we follow a similar process to introduce the additional information to our analyses. Elaboration on a sample of the expansions follows with the details of the remainder of the items covered in Appendix 4A.

GIS' Note 6 In Millions	North America Retail	Pet	Convenience Stores & Foodservice	Europe & Australia	Asia & Latin America	Joint Ventures	Total
Balance as of May 28, 2017	$6,406.5	$ —	$918.8	$700.8	$312.4	$408.7	$ 8,747.2
Acquisition	—	5,294.9	—	—	—	—	5,294.9
Other activity, primarily foreign currency translation	4.1	—	—	29.1	(27.4)	17.1	22.9
Balance as of May 27, 2018	**$6,410.6**	**$5,294.9**	**$918.8**	**$729.9**	**$285.0**	**$425.8**	**$14,065.0**

Total on balance sheet (→ $ 8,747.2)

Total on balance sheet (→ $14,065.0)

- *Deferred income taxes* breakdown of the assets and the related liabilities was found in GIS' Note 14. Here, we are seeking additional information to refine our separation of operating and financial activities. The schedule in the footnotes gives details on the sources of the timing differences between financial reporting and tax reporting, which have given rise to these deferred income taxes. Because we are expanding this item, we can look at each individual item by the source of the *Deferred tax asset or liability* and make a determination as to whether each item arose due to operating or financial activities.

    Earlier, we treated the entire amount of reported deferred tax asset and liability as related to enterprise operating activities. Now, we see that the additional information facilitates refinement of the reformulation. It is clear that treating the deferred tax asset from *Compensation and employee benefits* as related to operating activities is appropriate. For other items or for other companies, with additional information, we may be able to refine our reformulation using the detailed information provided in the footnote, resulting in changes to the amount of *NOA*. An item for which the classification might be unanticipated is the deferred taxes related to *Pensions*. Detail of the reasoning behind our classification of pension and postretirement items will be fully discussed shortly. Also, the *Stock, partnership, and miscellaneous investments* deferred tax assets and liabilities are shown as financial. This is based on our understanding that these items are primarily arising from passive investments of GIS rather than active operating interests. As a result, because the underlying item is financial in nature, the related deferred taxes are treated similarly.

DETAILED INFORMATION ON DEFERRED TAXES

When considering the deferred taxes, it is essential to note that the amounts reported in the footnotes may not tie to the amounts reported on the face of the financial statements! This is driven by the method in which deferred taxes are calculated and reported. On the balance sheet, companies report deferred tax assets and liabilities based on the classification of the related asset or liability that led to the creation of the deferred tax. Previously, companies were able to report these items as current or noncurrent and could even have any combination of current assets, current liabilities, noncurrent assets, and noncurrent liabilities. When added to the possibility of combining deferred taxes with other accounts on the balance sheet, it may not be clear exactly how the amounts on the face of the financial statements and discussed in the notes are connected. Thus, for many companies, it is impossible to completely reconcile the tax footnote to the balance sheet.

continued

continued from previous page

The schedule below provides the reconciliation of the amounts from the footnotes and financial statements for **Procter & Gamble** (PG) in 2015. We see that the net amount reported on the balance sheet of deferred tax assets and liabilities was a liability of $8,175. This differs from the net amount disclosed in Note 10 of $6,945. This requires us to assume that there is a $1,230 deferred tax asset not labeled as such on the balance sheet.

Reported in footnotes:	
Deferred tax assets	$ 5,283
Deferred tax liabilities	(12,228)
Net	$ (6,945)
Reported on balance sheet:	
Deferred tax asset	$ 1,356
Deferred tax liability	(9,531)
	(8,175)
Implied additional asset	1,230
Total	$ (6,945)

This additional asset of $1,230 must be appearing with other assets or at some other place on the balance sheet; otherwise, the balance sheet would not balance! Thus, we would need to separate out a part of other assets as an additional deferred tax asset in our subsequent analysis.

Note that including this additional information leads to an increase in both assets and liabilities of PG in the amount of $2,697 (liabilities of $12,228 instead of $9,531). In short, $2.7 billion in assets and liabilities were omitted from the balance sheet due to the netting that occurs within deferred tax reporting.

As an aside, this highlights an issue that arises related to ratio analysis. In the next chapter, we will address the issue of accounting methods and their impact. Here, the omission of assets and liabilities due to netting would affect commonly used ratios such as return on assets and debt-to-equity. These effects are often overlooked by those without sufficient understanding of accounting.

MAINTAINING BALANCE WHEN ADDING INFORMATION

When dealing with items where the detailed information does not tie directly to financial statement reported amounts, caution must be used. Whenever adding information from sources beyond the balance sheet and income statement, you must ensure total balances are unchanged. It is best to think of this as substituting. For example, you may replace total inventories with amounts for raw materials, work in process, and finished goods. However, in doing so, the dollar amount of inventory originally reported and the dollar amount of the more detailed information replacing it must agree. Sometimes, this may require creating an additional "implied" asset or liability in order to maintain balance.

INCOME TAXES PAYABLE OR RECEIVABLE

Given our efforts to split the tax expense and also the deferred tax assets and liabilities between operating and financial activities, it would seem that we should similarly seek to split income taxes payable or receivable. Normally, this is not possible because it would require us to determine the items where taxes for financial reporting purposes differ from taxes paid. As this is not possible, we choose to show all the income taxes payable or receivable as part of net operating assets.

- The details of *Land, buildings, and equipment* are found in Note 17. Additionally, we find in Note 6 that GIS has provided a breakdown of *Other intangible assets, net* by type. While these items will all be classified as related to operating activities, we may choose to include additional information in our analysis because utilizing detailed information may improve our ability to forecast the amount of fixed assets necessary in GIS' operating activities. These assets are required to support anticipated future sales growth in differing segments, and there may be variation in how they change over time. For example, we may have differing expectations of the growth in intangibles in the North America retail and Asia and Latin America segments of GIS based on differences in expected sales growth in these segments. Thus, even when we do not change the operating/financial classification, additional information can yield improvements in our forecasts and valuation.

- *Current portion of long-term debt* and *Long-term debt* are clearly financial items and, as such, are not a focal point in our analysis. However, the breakdown provided in Note 8 may be helpful in understanding the company's cost of debt capital (discussed in Chapter 9) because it provides information on the sources of funds from debt holders. Although information on debt could be omitted from our current reformulation efforts, this information may affect our valuation process at other stages.

Information on Pension and Other Postretirement Benefits

LO3: Gross up reported amounts, and address implied additional amounts while maintaining balanced numbers.

While many of the items seen thus far in this chapter may have seemed quite straightforward, the reporting of pension and postretirement assets and liabilities is very convoluted in the financial statements. Two main issues are occurring: (1) reporting of pension and other postretirement benefit-related items across multiple places and (2) netting of items we may want to classify and/or forecast separately. This complexity is compounded by disclosures that often run three or more pages in length!

Before getting to the details, let us consider the big picture. The portion of the expense related to the employees' service to the company in the current year (service cost) will be considered as arising from the operating activities. Despite this, the related assets and liabilities will be treated as financial because they do not contribute to the profitability of the current operating activities. Rather, they arise due to the company's decisions on how to fund (or not currently fund) the obligations made to current and former employees.

It should be noted that on March 10, 2017, the FASB issued Accounting Standards Update No. 2017-07, *Compensation—Retirement Benefits (Topic 715): Improving the Presentation of Net Periodic Pension Cost and Net Periodic Postretirement Benefit Cost*, which altered the presentation of pension and other postretirement expense. This new standard requires all elements of expense other than service cost to be considered as nonoperating (using the income statement definition) effective for fiscal years beginning after December 15, 2017.[1] This reporting is in line with how we are reformulating. Service cost, the expense related to current employees' efforts, is shown in the reformulation as operating, while all the other elements, such as interest cost and other aspects of the funding mechanism, are shown as financial in nature.

The detailed information on pension and related assets and liabilities of GIS is provided in Note 13. For the balance sheet reformulation, the items to be considered are shown in **Exhibit 4.3**.

The issue is determining where the net liability of $511.0 was reported on GIS' balance sheet. Many companies will have information on the location of the items within their pension-related disclosures. This would allow for the substitution of the detailed information in **Exhibit 4.3** for the originally reported information. While GIS does not report within Note 13 where these items are included, we find some information in Note 17.

The breakdown of balance sheet items in Note 17 shows that *Other assets* includes pension assets of $309.9 and *Other noncurrent liabilities* has as the largest element $999.4 of *Accrued compensation and benefits, including obligations for underfunded other postretirement benefit and postemployment benefit plans*. The fact that these items are included was previously obscured by aggregation. In our reformulation, we assume that $511.0 of net liability are the items shown in **Exhibit 4.3**, and the excess of $178.5 ($999.4 liability net of $309.9 asset less the $511.0 in **Exhibit 4.3**) is the amount that is *Accrued compensation*.

Note that, in this process, we are not changing the amount of net assets but breaking out the information to provide more detail based on other non-balance sheet disclosures. In effect, by grossing up the numbers, we are undoing some of the netting of liabilities and assets allowed by the accounting standards. Clearly, this can trigger large changes in metrics used in ratio analysis, such

[1] GIS' most recent fiscal year, which ended in May 2018, does not reflect the new standard: the new standard will be adopted in the May 2019 financial statements.

EXHIBIT 4.3 GIS' Retirement Benefits and Post-Employment Benefit Disclosures—Note 13

Amounts in Millions, Year Ended May 2018	
Defined benefit pension plans:	
Fair value of plan assets at end of year	$6,177.4
Benefit obligation at end of year	(6,416.0)
Funded status	$ (238.6)
Other postretirement benefit plans:	
Fair value of plan assets at end of year	$ 726.1
Benefit obligation at end of year	(871.8)
Funded status	$ (145.7)
Post-employment benefit plans:	
Benefit obligation at end of year	$ (126.7)
Funded status	$ (126.7)
Total	$ (511.0)

as a return on assets. Remember that the outstanding net liability for pensions and other postretirement benefits arises from the delay in satisfying the obligation rather than being necessary for the current operations of the company, leading to a classification of these items as financial in nature. The company could have chosen to pay the employees cash today and avoided the future liability.

ADDITIONAL INFORMATION RELATED TO GENERAL MILLS' INCOME STATEMENT

LO4: Expand the income statement to incorporate additional detail information.

Having gathered information for expanding the balance sheet, we now move to the income statement (including items of other comprehensive income). GIS provides very little detail about its expenses on the income statement. In the year ended May 2018, only four line items provide detail of operating income! However, we can find information in the footnotes about some items we can reasonably assume are included in captions such as *Selling, general, and administrative expenses*.[2] This information will allow us to expand our analysis of this account, which will enhance our understanding of operating and financial activities and/or contribute to improved forecasts.

- *Net sales* are split into segments as detailed in Note 16. This breakdown of sales by segment, when combined with our knowledge of the business, will be crucial in improving our forecasting of future sales growth. When we examine forecasting in subsequent chapters, we will incorporate even more detailed information from the MD&A section that describes the year-by-year changes in sales arising from things such as changes in organic sales growth versus other items, such as acquisitions or foreign currency exchange.

GIS' Note 16	Fiscal Year		
In Millions	2018	2017	2016
Net sales:			
North America Retail	**$10,115.4**	$10,196.9	$10,936.6
Convenience Stores & Foodservice	**1,930.2**	1,870.0	1,923.8
Europe & Australia	**1,984.6**	1,824.5	1,998.0
Asia & Latin America	**1,710.2**	1,728.4	1,704.7
Total	**$15,740.4**	$15,619.8	$16,563.1

Total on income statement

[2] If we were an employee in the accounting or finance areas of GIS, we would have available much more detailed information concerning account balances. This would allow a much more exact reformulation and presumably lead to more accurate forecasting. As we are acting in the role of a (potential) investor, we rely on publicly available information and make some assumptions as to where the items under consideration would most likely be recorded. Of course, we may ask for more information from the investor relations people at the company we are valuing.

- *Selling, general, and administrative (SG&A) expenses* include research of $219.1 million and advertising expense of $575.9 million according to Note 16. Some would argue that we should make an attempt to record the intangible asset associated with research and development and/or advertising. We could do this if we had knowledge of the expected timing and duration of the associated increased future revenues. Then, we would match an expense each period to the expected future revenues. Note two issues that arise in attempting this capitalization and subsequent expensing. First, we generally do not know when the future revenues associated with these expenses will accrue. Second, if the number of periods over which these future revenues accrue and the expenses are somewhat consistent over time, the expense each period would be the same, as we see with expensing under U.S. GAAP! Additionally, in that scenario, there would not be a change in the amount of intangible assets between periods. Keep in mind that, to the extent that we break items such as research or advertising out of SG&A, we will have more detailed information, which will be helpful for forecasting because different items may evolve in different patterns over time.

MORE INFORMATION ON PENSION AND OTHER POSTRETIREMENT BENEFITS

A large amount of information regarding the pension and other retiree benefit-related income/expense items is available in Note 13. Here again, we are not told exactly where these items have been included in the income statement. Therefore, our presumption is that they have been primarily included in SG&A. The amounts that we learn from Note 13 about GIS' pension and other retiree benefit expense plus the information about research and advertising together lead to the breakdown of SG&A shown in **Exhibit 4.4**.

EXHIBIT 4.4 GIS Selling, General, and Administrative Expense

		Operating	Financial
Advertising expense	$ 575.9	X	
Research expense	219.1	X	
Defined benefit pension plans: Service cost	102.9	X	
Defined benefit pension plans: Interest cost	217.9		X
Defined benefit pension plans: Expected return-on-plan assets	(480.2)		X
Defined benefit pension plans: Amortization of losses	177.0		X
Defined benefit pension plans: Amortization of prior service cost	1.9		X
Other postretirement benefit plans: Service cost	11.6	X	
Other postretirement benefit plans: Interest cost	30.1		X
Other postretirement benefit plans: Expected return-on-plan assets	(52.2)		X
Other postretirement benefit plans: Amortization of losses	0.8		X
Other postretirement benefit plans: Amortization of prior service cost	(5.4)		X
Post-employment benefit plans: Service cost	8.6	X	
Post-employment benefit plans: Interest cost	2.3		X
Post-employment benefit plans: Amortization of losses	0.8		X
Post-employment benefit plans: Amortization of prior service cost	0.6		X
Post-employment benefit plans: Other adjustments	6.7		X
Defined contribution plan expense	49.2	X	
Other selling, general, and administrative expenses	1,885.0	X	
Total reported on income statement	$2,752.6		

The additional information, which we have included, has explained about 30 percent of the amount originally shown on the face of the financial statements as SG&A. Additionally, within the pension and other retiree benefit expense, we see both items that will be shown as relating to operating (i.e., *Service cost*) and financial (i.e., *Interest cost*) activities. Essentially, the items related to service cost are deemed to be related to services provided by employees toward operating activities, while the remaining items, which capture the implementation of pension accounting and funding and deferral of payment to later dates, are financial. This additional information will help us refine and improve our reformulation to focus on the operating activities.

In addition to providing details on pension and other retiree benefit expenses included in SG&A as a part of net income, Note 13 also provides detail on the amounts reported as elements of other comprehensive income. For GIS, on the consolidated statements of comprehensive income, there was an income item reported as amortization of losses and prior service costs, which, net of tax, is $117.6. The detail in Note 13 shows net actuarial loss of $1,723.6 and prior service credits of $26.3 for a net reduction in comprehensive income of $1,697.3. Clearly, the difference is not just the result of income taxes! As we are unable to sort out the effects of these items on comprehensive income and they are financial in nature, we do not add more detail to the GIS income statement.

APPROPRIATE TAX RATE ASSUMPTION FOR REFORMULATING GENERAL MILLS

LO5: Explain why a marginal tax rate is preferred to an effective tax rate in reformulation.

We previously assumed a statutory rate of 29.4 percent for GIS when computing the tax on financial expenses and the related adjustment to operating activities. Where did this come from, and why is it appropriate? Let's revisit that decision and consider the motives for choosing what tax rate should be used for reformulating the income statement of GIS. Note 10 disclosed the effective tax rate of GIS by year. While using an effective tax rate is an option, we first need to consider whether effective tax rates are what we need. Effective tax rates are approximations of average tax rates. Our ideal outcome in separating operating and financial profitability for valuation is to estimate the amount of tax that would have been paid had the firm not had any financial expense; that is, the tax rate for the interest tax shield. Stated a different way, we want to know what the tax would have been on the operating activities if the firm had been funded entirely by equity and, therefore, would have had no financial income or expense. The difference from the actual amount of tax reported is the interest tax shield.

Estimation of the interest tax shield requires the marginal rate related to an additional dollar more or less of *FEAT*. That is, the desired tax rate for our allocation is the current period's marginal tax rate on the financial expenses; however, this rate is unobservable. What would be a better proxy, an effective (average) rate or a statutory (maximum) rate? While the company has undertaken actions to reduce its taxes and has been affected by the tax law changes (as evidenced by the 2.7 percent effective tax rate for GIS in the year ended May 2018), it is not clear that the items comprising financial expenses are being taxed at the effective tax rate of 2.7 percent. More likely, the items of interest expense, interest income, and other financial items would have been taxed at the maximum rate applicable in the primary taxing jurisdiction. Thus, we use a statutory rate for the estimation of the adjustment to *NOPAT* related to taxes on the financial expenses.

The next concern is which period's and what jurisdiction's statutory tax rate. At the federal level, with the U.S. tax law changes passed in December 2017, we, for the first time in many years, saw that historical rates differed from future tax rates. For GIS, in years prior to the one ending in May 2018, the U.S. statutory rate was 35 percent, while future years are expected to have a U.S. statutory rate of 21 percent. In the year ended in May 2018, the GIS statutory rate was 29.4 percent due to 7 months at 35 percent and 5 months at 21 percent. Because we are looking at the income in the year ended May 2018, we use the federal statutory rate for that year: 29.4 percent.

Though we started with the federal statutory rate as the anchor (just as is done in effective rate reconciliations), we must consider whether adjustments should be done for state and local, international, or other items. Per Note 14, GIS has had state and local income taxes, net of federal tax benefits of 1.7, 0.8, and 0.7 percent in the most recent three years, respectively. Focusing on this item, the question is should we assume a current tax rate of 31.1 percent (29.4 percent plus 1.7 percent) or omit the state and local taxes yielding 29.4 percent? The answer is not clear cut and either approach is supportable. We choose in our analyses to omit the state and local tax in our historical tax rate assumption as we are focusing on a marginal tax and companies would be expected to make choices consistent with minimizing the impact of state and local taxes. Further, the extent to which the elements of the tax reconciliation beyond the statutory rate are driven by operations or financing aspects and the extent to which they will continue going forward is unclear. If desired, the spreadsheet underlying our valuation can be used to test the "what if" effect of this assumption on the value of GIS similar to any other assumption. It is expected that in most cases the effect of inclusion/exclusion of other tax elements on the estimate of value will be minimal.

If, instead of focusing on GIS, we had been looking at a company not taxed primarily in the United States, we would have sought to determine the statutory tax rate of the company's primary tax jurisdiction. For example, in Unilever's 2018 Note 6A, it disclosed a computed rate of tax of 25 percent, which it described as "the average of the standard rate of tax applicable in the countries in which Unilever operates." This rate of tax would then be used in determining the necessary adjustment to tax related to the exclusion of the financial expenses.

Everywhere we use a tax rate within our valuation, we need to think about whether the tax rate needed is for the current period or a future period. Thus far, we have been looking at the historical performance of GIS and the splitting of operating and financial activities. Because we are looking at a historical result, we need a historical rate. The rate used for this computation in reformulation is the historical statutory rate of 29.4 percent because that was the rate during the period we are considering. There will be times in upcoming computations where the future tax rate will be appropriate, and we will use the 21 percent future expected statutory rate.

The inclusion of this additional information in our analysis is done to allow us to refine our reformulation where we separate the operating and financial activities. Additionally, it will provide us more detail to consider as we forecast the future operations of GIS. This will allow us to improve our forecasts, leading to an improved, more meaningful estimate of value.

SUMMARY

This chapter demonstrated how our initial judgment regarding classification as operating or financial may be modified/improved when we examine disclosures included in the MD&A section of or notes to the financial statements. Our process is not limited to the use of financial statement notes. It can incorporate any available information. For a manager within a firm, this analysis could be done at the account or segment level. The benefits of these efforts will be seen in future chapters when we perform a full analysis and full-information forecasting. These efforts will be enhanced by the refinements of our reformulation that are possible due to this additional information.

The next step is to consider the effects of accounting methods and any adjustments to reported information that could be helpful in the analysis and forecasting process. This will be performed via a series of mini-analyses examining differing topics in Chapter 5. We will conclude the next chapter with the expanded and updated reformulations reflecting our efforts so far.

APPENDIX 4A: Detail on Incorporation of Additional Information

In Chapter 3, the reformulation of the balance sheet is shown in **Exhibit 3.2** and the income statement is shown in **Exhibit 3.4**. These reformulations are based solely on the information drawn from the face of the financial statements. In this chapter, we go through the MD&A and notes to the financial statements to cull the information need for the expanded reformulation. This results in the expanded reformulated financial statements shown in **Exhibits 4.1** and **4.2**. Our rationale for expanding the reformulation is to (1) better define *NOA*/*NFL* and *NOPAT*/*FEAT* and (2) provide greater detail to improve our forecasts. This appendix further develops the mapping between them. This will be presented step-by-step in the order and amounts in the most recent year of the items shown in **Exhibits 3.2** and **3.4** to facilitate investigation of any particular items of interest.

GIS' Balance sheet items at May 27, 2018 (in millions)

From Exhibit 3.2		Source for Change	From Exhibit 4.1	
Receivables	$ 1,684.2	Note 17: Supplemental information **In Millions** — **May 27, 2018** Receivables: Customers — $1,712.6 Less allowance for doubtful accounts — (28.4) Total — $1,684.2	Receivables: Customers	$ 1,712.6
			Receivables: Allowance for doubtful accounts	(28.4)
Inventories	1,642.2	Note 17: Supplemental information **In Millions** — **May 27, 2018** Inventories: Raw materials and packaging — $ 400.0 Finished goods — 1,364.2 Grain — 91.2 Excess of FIFO over LIFO cost — (213.2) Total — $1,642.2	Inventories: Raw materials and packaging	400.0
			Inventories: Finished goods	1,364.2
			Inventories: Grain	91.2
			Inventories: Excess of FIFO over LIFO cost	(213.2)
Prepaid expenses and other current assets	398.3	Note 17: Supplemental information **In Millions** — **May 27, 2018** Prepaid expenses and other current assets: Other receivables — $ 174.4 Prepaid expenses — 165.6 Derivative receivables, primarily commodity-related — 40.5 Grain contracts — 7.1 Miscellaneous — 10.7 Total — $ 398.3	Prepaid expenses and other current assets: Other receivables	174.4
			Prepaid expenses and other current assets: Prepaid expenses	165.6
			Prepaid expenses and other current assets: Derivative receivables, primarily commodity-related	40.5
			Prepaid expenses and other current assets: Grain contracts	7.1
			Prepaid expenses and other current assets: Miscellaneous	10.7

continued

continued from previous page

GIS' Balance sheet items at May 27, 2018 (in millions)

From Exhibit 3.2		Source for Change	From Exhibit 4.1	
Land, buildings, and equipment	4,047.2	Note 17: Supplemental information (see table below)	Land, buildings, and equipment: Land	77.7
			Land, buildings, and equipment: Buildings	2,396.3
			Land, buildings, and equipment: Buildings under capital lease	0.3
			Land, buildings, and equipment: Equipment	6,236.6
			Land, buildings, and equipment: Equipment under capital lease	5.8
			Land, buildings, and equipment: Capitalized software	593.6
			Land, buildings, and equipment: Construction in progress	692.9
			Land, buildings, and equipment: Accumulated depreciation	(5,956.0)
Goodwill	14,065.0	Note 6: Goodwill and other intangible assets (see table below)	Goodwill: North America Retail	6,410.6
			Goodwill: Pet	5,294.9
			Goodwill: Convenience Stores & Foodservice	918.8
			Goodwill: Europe & Australia	729.9
			Goodwill: Asia & Latin America	285.0
			Goodwill: Joint Ventures	425.8

Note 17: Supplemental information

In Millions	May 27, 2018
Land, buildings, and equipment:	
Land	$ 77.7
Buildings	2,396.3
Buildings under capital lease	0.3
Equipment	6,236.6
Equipment under capital lease	5.8
Capitalized software	593.6
Construction progress	692.9
Total land, buildings and equipment	10,003.2
Less accumulated depreciation	(5,956.0)
Total	$ 4,047.2

Note 6: Goodwill and other intangible assets

In Millions	North America Retail	Pet	Convenience Stores & Foodservice	Europe & Australia	Asia & Latin America	Joint Ventures	Total
Balance as of May 28, 2017	$6,406.5	$ —	$918.8	$700.8	$312.4	$408.7	$ 8,747.2
Acquisition	—	5,294.9	—	—	—	—	5,294.9
Other activity, primarily foreign currency translation	4.1	—	—	29.1	(27.4)	17.1	22.9
Balance as of May 27, 2018	**$6,410.6**	**$5,294.9**	**$918.8**	**$729.9**	**$285.0**	**$425.8**	**$14,065.0**

continued

continued from previous page

GIS' Balance sheet items at May 27, 2018 (in millions)

From Exhibit 3.2		Source for Change	From Exhibit 4.1	
Other intangible assets	7,445.1	Note 6: Goodwill and other intangible assets	Other intangible assets: Brands and other indefinite-lived intangibles	6,818.7
			Other intangible assets: Franchise agreements, customer relationships, and other	811.7
			Other intangible assets: Accumulated amortization	(185.3)

Note 6: Goodwill and other intangible assets

In Millions	May 27, 2018
Goodwill	$14,065.0
Other intangible assets:	
Intangible assets not subject to amortization:	
Brands and other indefinite-lived intangibles	6,818.7
Intangible assets subject to amortization:	
Franchise agreements, customer relationships, and other finite-lived intangibles	811.7
Less accumulated amortization	(185.3)
Intangible assets subject to amortization	626.4
Other Intangible assets	7,445.1
Total	$21,510.1

From Exhibit 3.2		Source for Change	From Exhibit 4.1	
Other assets	943.0	Note 17: Supplemental information	Other assets: Investments in and advances to joint ventures	499.6
			Other assets: Life insurance	26.9
			Other assets: Miscellaneous	106.6

Note 17: Supplemental information

In Millions	May 27, 2018
Other assets:	
Investment in and advances to joint ventures	$499.6
Pension assets	309.9
Life insurance	21.9
Miscellaneous	106.6
Total	$943.0

* Pension assets of $309.9 will be a part of the pension adjustment to Other liabilities shown shortly.

continued

continued from previous page

<table>
<tr><th colspan="3">GIS' Balance sheet items at May 27, 2018 (in millions)</th></tr>
<tr><th>From Exhibit 3.2</th><th>Source for Change</th><th>From Exhibit 4.1</th></tr>
<tr>
<td>Notes payable . . . . . (1,549.8)</td>
<td>Note 8: Debt
<table>
<tr><th></th><th colspan="2">May 27, 2018</th></tr>
<tr><th>In Millions</th><th>Notes Payable</th><th>Weighted-Average Interest Rate</th></tr>
<tr><td>U.S. commercial paper</td><td>$1,213.5</td><td>2.2%</td></tr>
<tr><td>Financial institutions</td><td>336.3</td><td>6.2</td></tr>
<tr><td>Total</td><td>$1,549.8</td><td>3.1%</td></tr>
</table>
</td>
<td>Notes payable: US commercial paper . . . . . (1,213.5)
Notes payable: Financial institutions . . . . . (336.3)</td>
</tr>
<tr>
<td>Other current liabilities . . . . . (1,445.8)</td>
<td>Note 17: Supplemental information
<table>
<tr><th>In Millions</th><th>May 27, 2018</th></tr>
<tr><td>Other current liabilities:</td><td></td></tr>
<tr><td>Accrued trade and consumer promotions</td><td>$ 499.6</td></tr>
<tr><td>Accrued payroll</td><td>347.0</td></tr>
<tr><td>Dividends payable</td><td>17.5</td></tr>
<tr><td>Accrued taxes</td><td>94.8</td></tr>
<tr><td>Accrued interest including interest rate swaps</td><td>107.7</td></tr>
<tr><td>Grain contracts</td><td>1.2</td></tr>
<tr><td>Restructuring and other exit costs reserve</td><td>66.8</td></tr>
<tr><td>Derivative payable</td><td>8.3</td></tr>
<tr><td>Miscellaneous</td><td>302.9</td></tr>
<tr><td>Total</td><td>$1,445.8</td></tr>
</table>
</td>
<td>Other current liabilities: Accrued trade and consumer promotions . . . . . (499.6)
Other current liabilities: Accrued payroll . . . . . (347.0)
Other current liabilities: Dividend payable . . . . . (17.5)
Other current liabilities: Accrued taxes . . . . . (94.8)
Other current liabilities: Accrued interest, including interest rate swaps . . . . . (107.7)
Other current liabilities: Grain contracts . . . . . (1.2)
Other current liabilities: Restructuring and other exit costs reserve . . . . . (66.8)
Other current liabilities: Derivative payable . . . . . (8.3)
Other current liabilities: Miscellaneous . . . . . (302.9)</td>
</tr>
</table>

continued

continued from previous page

GIS' Balance sheet items at May 27, 2018 (in millions)

From Exhibit 3.2		Source for Change	From Exhibit 4.1	
Deferred income taxes	(2,003.8)	Note 14: Income taxes	Deferred tax assets: Accrued liabilities	47.2
			Deferred tax assets: Compensation and employee benefits	210.2
			Deferred tax assets: Pension	57.1
			Deferred tax assets: Tax credit carryforwards	7.4
			Deferred tax assets: Stock, partnership, and miscellaneous investments	147.9
			Deferred tax assets: Capital losses	12.9
			Deferred tax assets: Net operating losses	161.2
			Deferred tax assets: Other	52.9
			Deferred tax assets: Valuation allowance	(176.0)
			Deferred tax liabilities: Brands	(1,498.7)
			Deferred tax liabilities: Fixed assets	(329.5)
			Deferred tax liabilities: Intangible assets	(255.1)
			Deferred tax liabilities: Tax lease transactions	(26.0)
			Deferred tax liabilities: Inventories	(38.8)
			Deferred tax liabilities: Stock, partnership, and miscellaneous investments	(317.1)
			Deferred tax liabilities: Unrealized hedges	(28.5)
			Deferred tax liabilities: Other	(30.9)

In Millions	May 27, 2018
Accrued liabilities	$ 47.2
Compensation and employee benefits	210.2
Pension	57.1
Tax credit carryforwards	7.4
Stock, partnership, and miscellaneous investments	147.9
Capital losses	12.9
Net operating losses	161.2
Other	52.9
Gross deferred tax assets	696.8
Valuation allowance	176.0
Net deferred tax assets	520.8
Brands	1,498.7
Fixed assets	329.5
Intangible assets	255.1
Tax lease transactions	26.0
Inventories	38.8
Stock, partnership, and miscellaneous investments	317.1
Unrealized hedges	28.5
Other	30.9
Gross deferred lax liabilities	2,524.6
Net deferred tax liability	$2,003.8

continued

continued from previous page

GIS' Balance sheet items at May 27, 2018 (in millions)

From Exhibit 3.2		Source for Change	From Exhibit 4.1	
Other liabilities	(1,341.0)	Note 17: Supplemental information	Defined benefit pension plans: Plan assets	6,177.4
			Other postretirement benefit plans: Plan assets	726.1
			Other noncurrent liabilities: Accrued compensation and benefits, including pensions	(178.5)
			Other noncurrent liabilities: Accrued taxes	(265.3)
			Other noncurrent liabilities: Miscellaneous	(76.3)
			Defined benefit pension plans: Benefit obligation	(6,416.0)
			Other postretirement benefit plans: Benefit obligation	(871.8)
		Note 13: Retirement benefits and postemployment benefits	Postemployment benefit plans: Benefit obligation	(126.7)

In Millions	May 27, 2018
Other noncurrent liabilities:	
Accrued compensation and benefits, including obligations for underfunded other postretirement benefit and postemployment benefit plans	$ 999.4
Accrued taxes	265.3
Miscellaneous	76.3
Total	$1,341.0

* Pension assets of $309.9 reported in Other assets less the Accrued compensation and benefits, including obligations for underfunded other postretirement benefit and postemployment benefit plans of $999.4 reported in Other liabilities is the basis for the $689.5 adjustment composed of the following:

continued

continued from previous page

GIS' Balance sheet items at May 27, 2018 (in millions)

From Exhibit 3.2	Source for Change	From Exhibit 4.1

In Millions	Defined Benefit Pension Plans Fiscal Year 2018	Defined Benefit Pension Plans Fiscal Year 2017	Other Postretirement Benefit Plans Fiscal Year 2018	Other Postretirement Benefit Plans Fiscal Year 2017	Postemployment Benefit Plans Fiscal Year 2018	Postemployment Benefit Plans Fiscal Year 2017
Change in Plan Assets:						
Fair value at beginning of year	**$5,925.2**	$5,539.9	**$ 694.8**	$ 602.4		
Actual return assets	**496.5**	645.6	**50.5**	75.2		
Employer contributions	**41.8**	25.4	**0.1**	20.1		
Plan participant contributions	**6.1**	8.8	**15.7**	15.2		
Benefits payments	**(298.0)**	(282.2)	**(35.0)**	(18.1)		
Foreign currency	**5.8**	(12.3)	**—**	—		
Fair value at end of year	**$6,177.4**	$5,925.2	**$ 726.1**	$ 694.8		
Change in Projected Benefit Obligation:						
Benefit obligation at beginning of year	**$6,458.6**	$6,448.5	**$ 951.4**	$1,028.9	**$ 134.5**	$ 164.1
Service cost	**102.9**	119.7	**11.6**	12.5	**8.6**	8.8
Interest cost	**217.9**	216.5	**30.1**	32.2	**2.3**	2.6
Plan amendment	**25.4**	(130.9)	**(0.7)**	—	**1.2**	—
Curtailment/other	**—**	1.9	**—**	(0.3)	**—**	1.3
Plan participant contributions	**6.1**	8.8	**15.7**	15.2	**—**	—
Medicare Part D reimbursements	**—**	—	**3.0**	3.4	**—**	—
Actuarial loss (gain)	**(102.0)**	88.5	**(73.9)**	(77.6)	**(7.0)**	(7.4)
Benefits payments	**(298.6)**	(282.6)	**(64.9)**	(63.3)	**(13.1)**	(34.7)
Foreign currency	**5.7**	(11.8)	**(0.5)**	0.4	**0.2**	(0.2)
Projected benefit obligation at end of year	**$6,416.0**	$6,458.6	**$ 871.8**	$ 951.4	**$ 126.7**	$ 134.5

This results in the following:

Defined benefit pension plan asset	$6,177.4
Other postretirement benefit plan asset	726.1
Defined benefit pension plan liability	(6,416.0)
Other postretirement benefit plan liability	(871.8)
Postemployment benefit plan liability	(126.7)
Remaining other remaining accrued compensation	(178.5)
Total	$ (689.5)

GIS' Income statement items for the year ended May 27, 2018 (in millions)

From Exhibit 3.4		Source for Change	From Exhibit 4.2	
Net sales	$15,740.4	Note 16: Business segment and geographic information **In Millions** — **2018** Net sales: North America Retail — **$10,115.4** Convenience Stores & Foodservice — **1,930.2** Europe & Australia — **1,984.6** Asia & Latin America — **1,710.2** Total — **$15,740.4**	Net sales—North America retail Net sales—Convenience stores & foodservice Net sales—Europe & Australia Net sales—Asia & Latin America	$10,115.4 1,930.2 1,984.6 1,710.2
Selling, general, and administrative expenses	(2,752.6)	Assumption is that advertising, R&D, and pension items are being reported in this caption. Thus, we expand using the following:	Advertising expense Research expense Defined benefit pension plans: Service cost	(575.9) (219.1) (102.9)

continued

continued from previous page

GIS' Income statement items for the year ended May 27, 2018 (in millions)

From Exhibit 3.4	Source for Change

Note 17: Supplemental information

In Millions	2018
Depreciation and amortization	**$618.8**
Research and development expense.	**219.1**
Advertising and media expense (including production and communication costs)	**$575.9**

*Depreciation and amortization would be included in both Cost of sales and Selling, general, and administrative expenses so it is not expanded.

Note 13: Retirement benefits and postemployment benefits

	Defined Benefit Pension Plans			Other Postretirement Benefit Plans			Postemployment Benefit Plans		
	Fiscal Year			Fiscal Year			Fiscal Year		
In Millions	**2018**	**2017**	**2016**	**2018**	**2017**	**2016**	**2018**	**2017**	**2016**
Service cost	**$102.9**	$119.7	$134.6	**$ 11.6**	$ 12.5	$ 19.0	**$ 8.6**	$ 8.8	$ 7.6
Interest cost	**217.9**	216.5	267.8	**30.1**	32.2	44.1	**2.3**	2.6	3.9
Expected return on plan assets	**(480.2)**	(486.7)	(496.9)	**(52.2)**	(48.5)	(46.2)	**—**	—	—
Amortization of losses	**177.0**	190.2	189.8	**0.8**	2.5	6.6	**0.8**	1.7	0.7
Amortization of prior service costs (credits) . . .	**1.9**	2.5	4.7	**(5.4)**	(5.4)	(5.4)	**0.6**	0.6	2.5
Other adjustments	**—**	3.1	5.0	**—**	1.3	2.3	**6.7**	1.3	10.7
Settlement or curtailment losses	**—**	3.8	13.1	**—**	(0.9)	(1.0)	**—**	(1.4)	—
Net expense	**$ 19.5**	$ 49.1	$118.1	**$(15.1)**	$ (6.3)	$ 19.4	**$19.0**	$13.6	$25.4

From Exhibit 4.2

Defined benefit pension plans: Interest cost	(217.9)
Defined benefit pension plans: Expected return on plan assets	480.2
Defined benefit pension plans: Amortization of losses	(177.0)
Defined benefit pension plans: Amortization of prior service cost.	(1.9)
Other postretirement benefit plans: Service cost	(11.6)
Other postretirement benefit plans: Interest cost	(30.1)
Other postretirement benefit plans: Expected return on plan assets	52.2
Other postretirement benefit plans: Amortization of losses.	(0.8)
Other postretirement benefit plans: Amortization of prior service cost	5.4
Postemployment benefit plans: Service cost	(8.6)

continued

continued from previous page

GIS' Income statement items for the year ended May 27, 2018 (in millions)

From Exhibit 3.4		Source for Change	From Exhibit 4.2	
		Also in Note 13, "Our total recognized expense related to defined contribution plans was $49.2 million in fiscal 2018, $54.1 million in fiscal 2017, and $61.2 million in fiscal 2016." This results in the following: Advertising: $ 575.9 Research: 219.1 Defined benefit pension plans: 19.5 Other postretirement benefit plans: (15.1) Postemployment benefit plans: 19.0 Defined contribution plans: 49.2 Remaining other selling, general, and administrative expenses: 1,885.0 Total: $2,752.6	Postemployment benefit plans: Interest cost Postemployment benefit plans: Amortization of losses Postemployment benefit plans: Amortization of prior service cost Postemployment benefit plans: Other adjustments Defined contribution plan expense Other selling, general, and administrative expenses	(2.3) (0.8) (0.6) (6.7) (49.2) (1,885.0)
Interest expense	(373.7)	Note 17: Supplemental information (see table below)	Interest expense Capitalized interest Interest income	(389.5) 4.1 11.7

Expense (Income), in Millions	2018
Interest expense	**$389.5**
Capitalized interest	**(4.1)**
Interest income	**(11.7)**
Interest, net	**$373.7**

QUESTIONS

Q4.1 What benefit would there be to gathering information beyond that contained on the face of the financial statements?

Q4.2 Where could we gather information to refine our reformulation beyond that contained on the face of the financial statements?

Q4.3 How would our role affect the availability of information?

Q4.4 Does the information contained in footnotes always tie directly to the amounts reported on the face of the financial statements?

Q4.5 What tax rate should be used in splitting the provision for income taxes into the enterprise operating and financial activities portions?

Q4.6 How does the marginal tax rate differ from the effective tax rate?

Q4.7 Which financial statement accounts typically have additional information in the footnotes?

Q4.8 Some accounts, such as deferred taxes, reported on the balance sheet may not tie directly to the detailed additional information in the related footnote. Explain why one may need to use an implied asset or implied liability in reconciling the reported number with the footnote detail.

Q4.9 For net periodic pension expense/benefit, explain which components are classified as operating and which components are financing.

EXERCISES

E4.10 On December 5, 2018, PepsiCo (PEP) acquired all the outstanding shares of SodaStream, a manufacturer and distributor of sparkling water makers, for $144.00 per share in cash, in a transaction valued at approximately $3.3 billion. As of the balance sheet date, $1,997 million of the consideration was held by the paying agent in connection with this acquisition and reports as restricted cash as of December 29, 2018.

The restricted cash associated with this acquisition is detailed in Note 13, and the corresponding payable is reported in Note 15.

Note 13—Restricted Cash

The following table provides a reconciliation of cash and cash equivalents and restricted cash as reported within the balance sheet to the same items as reported in the cash flow statement.

	2018	2017
Cash and cash equivalents	**$ 8,721**	$10,610
Restricted cash [(a)]	**1,997**	—
Restricted cash included in other assets [(b)]	**51**	47
Total cash and cash equivalents and restricted cash	**$10,769**	$10,657

[(a)] Represents consideration held by our paying agent in connection with our acquisition of SodaStream.
[(b)] Restricted cash included in other assets primarily relates to collateral posted against our derivative asset or liability positions.

Note 15—Supplemental Financial Information
Balance Sheet

	2018	2017
Accounts payable and other current liabilities		
Accounts payable	**$ 7,213**	$ 6,727
Accrued marketplace spending	**2,541**	2,390
Accrued compensation and benefits	**1,755**	1,785
Dividends payable	**1,329**	1,161
SodaStream consideration payable	**1,997**	—
Other current liabilities	**3,277**	2,954
	$18,112	$15,017

For each item in the two notes, identify whether the item would be used in calculating *NOA*, *NFL*, or be split.

E4.11 **Amazon's** (AMZN) 2018 financial statements report a liability, "Accrued expenses and other," in the amount of $23,663 million. In the prior chapter, the accrued expenses balance is considered as part of *NOA* because we lacked further breakdown to determine if any part of it was financial. After reviewing AMZN's footnotes (e.g., search for "accrued expenses"), which elements would be used in calculating *NOA* and *NFL*?

E4.12 **Amazon's** (AMZN) reported no deferred tax account in its 2018 balance sheet. However, Note 9, reports the components for the deferred tax assets and liabilities. In the prior chapter, the deferred income taxes were considered part of *NOA* because we lacked further breakdown to determine if any part of it was financial. Given this additional information from the footnote, which elements would be used in calculating *NOA*, and which would be a part of *NFL*? Is there an additional asset or liability implied by this disclosure that was not readily apparent from the information on the face of the financial statements?

Note 9—INCOME TAXES

Deferred income tax assets and liabilities are as follows (in millions):

	December 31,	
	2017	**2018**
Deferred tax assets[(1)]:		
Loss carryforwards U.S.—Federal/States	$ 211	$ 222
Loss carryforwards—Foreign	2,149	2,551
Accrued liabilities, reserves, and other expenses	901	1,064
Stock-based compensation	1,026	1,293
Deferred revenue	349	321
Assets held for investment	35	69
Depreciation and amortization	279	2,386
Other items	167	94
Tax credits	381	734
Total gross deferred tax assets	5,498	8,734
Less valuation allowance[(2)]	(2,538)	(4,950)
Deferred tax assets, net of valuation allowance	2,960	3,784
Deferred tax liabilities:		
Depreciation and amortization	(2,568)	(3,579)
Acquisition related intangible assets	(531)	(682)
Other items	(58)	(67)
Net deferred tax assets (liabilities), net of valuation allowance	$ (197)	$ (544)

[(1)] Deferred tax assets are presented net of tax contingencies.

[(2)] Relates primarily to deferred tax assets that would only be realizable upon the generation of net income in certain foreign taxing jurisdictions and future capital gains.

E4.13 **PepsiCo** (PEP) provides pension as well as retiree medical plans to certain employees. In the footnotes to its 2018 financial statements, PEP reported the funding status of its plans along with its classification in the financial statements.

Note 7—Pension, Retiree Medical and Savings Plans

	Pension				Retiree Medical	
	U.S.		International			
	2018	**2017**	**2018**	**2017**	**2018**	**2017**
Funded status	**$(1,549)**	$(2,195)	**$ (8)**	$ (30)	**$ (711)**	$ (866)
Amounts recognized						
Other assets	**$ 185**	$ 286	**$ 81**	$ 85	**$ —**	$ —
Other current liabilities	**(107)**	(74)	**(1)**	(1)	**(41)**	(75)
Other liabilities	**(1,627)**	(2,407)	**(88)**	(114)	**(670)**	(791)
Net amount recognized	**$(1,549)**	$(2,195)	**$ (8)**	$ (30)	**$ (711)**	$ (866)

In the prior chapter, the other asset/liability balances are considered part of *NOA* because we lacked further breakdown to determine if any part of it was financial. What adjustments are needed from the initial assignment of the balance sheet items for *NOA* and *NFL*?

E4.14 PepsiCo (PEP) reported in its 2018 footnotes, that it changed the presentation of net periodic benefit cost for its pension and retiree medical plans. The guidance requires the service cost component of the net periodic benefit cost to be included in operating profit, while the other components are presented separately below operating profit in the income statement.

> ***Recently Issued Accounting Pronouncements—Adopted***
> In 2017 , the Financial Accounting Standards Board (FASB) issued guidance to retrospectively present the service cost component of net periodic benefit cost for pension and retiree medical plans along with other compensation costs in operating profit and present the other components of net periodic benefit cost separately below operating profit in the income statement. The guidance also allows only the service cost component of net periodic benefit cost to be eligible for capitalization within inventory or fixed assets on a prospective basis. We adopted the provisions of this guidance retrospectively in the first quarter of 2018, using historical information previously disclosed in our pension and retiree medical benefits footnote as the estimation basis. We also updated our allocation of service costs to our divisions to better approximate actual service cost.

Consolidated Statement of Income
PepsiCo, Inc. and Subsidiaries
Fiscal years ended December 29, 2018, December 30, 2017 and December 31, 2016
(in millions except per share amounts)

	2018	2017	2016
Net Revenue	**$64,661**	$63,525	$62,799
Cost of sales	**29,381**	28,796	28,222
Gross profit	**35,280**	34,729	34,577
Selling, general and administrative expenses	**25,170**	24,453	24,773
Operating Profit	**10,110**	10,276	9,804
Other pension and retiree medical benefits income/(expense)	**298**	233	(19)
Interest expense	**(1,525)**	(1,151)	(1,342)
Interest income and other	**306**	244	110
Income before income taxes	**9,189**	9,602	8,553
(Benefit from)/provision for income taxes (See Note 5)	**(3,370)**	4,694	2,174
Net income	**12,559**	4,908	6,379
Less: Net income attributable to noncontrolling interests	**44**	51	50
Net Income Attributable to PepsiCo	**$12,515**	$ 4,857	$ 6,329

Given the additional information, what adjustments to the initial assignment of items to *NOPAT* and *FEAT* from PEP's income statement above are needed?

E4.15 Below is the information about the deferred income taxes for Hyatt (H) taken from Note 14, *Income Taxes*, of the financial statements. In the prior chapter, the deferred income taxes were considered part of *NOA* because we lacked further breakdown to determine if any part of it was financial. Given this additional information from the footnote, which elements would be used in calculating *NOA*, and which would be a part of *NFL*?

	December 31, 2018	December 31, 2017
Deferred tax assets related to:		
Employee benefits	$ 133	$ 128
Foreign and state net operating losses and credit carryforwards	57	65
Investments	37	30
Allowance for uncollectible assets	31	31
Loyalty program	99	89
Interest and slate benefits	3	1
Unrealized losses	3	2
Other	41	46
Valuation allowance	(41)	(51)
Total deferred tax asset	$ 363	$ 341

continued

continued from previous page

	December 31, 2018	December 31, 2017
Deferred tax liabilities related to:		
Property and equipment	$(131)	$(157)
Investments	(16)	(19)
Intangibles	(49)	(32)
Unrealized gains	(24)	(35)
Prepaid expenses	(7)	(8)
Other	(10)	(11)
Total deferred tax liabilities	$(237)	$(262)
Net deferred tax assets	$ 126	$ 79
Recognized in the balance sheet as:		
Deferred tax assets—noncurrent	$180	$141
Deferred tax liabilities—noncurrent	(54)	(62)
Total	$ 126	$ 79

CONTINUING EXAMPLES

CE4.16 Using the 2018, 2017, and 2016 annual reports for Kellogg (K) gathered in the prior chapter, collect additional information from the footnotes about the balances reported as goodwill and other intangible, net in the balance sheet. Being able to have a more detailed breakdown of these numbers can be helpful in subsequent forecasting exercises.

CE4.17 Using the 2018, 2017, and 2016 annual reports for Kellogg (K) gathered in the prior chapter, collect additional information from the footnotes to break down the amounts reported as notes payable within the balance sheet.

CE4.18. Using the 2018, 2017, and 2016 annual reports for Kellogg (K) gathered in the prior chapter, collect additional information from the footnotes related to pensions, postretirement, and postemployment benefits.

a. What is the funded status of the pensions, postretirement, and postemployment benefits for K for 2015–2018?

b. What are the amounts included as assets and liabilities within the balance sheet for 2015–2018?

c. What are the components for the net benefits cost for pensions, postretirement, and postemployment benefits for K for 2015–2018?

d. In addition to the pension, postretirement, and postemployment benefits, K sponsors 401(k) or similar savings plans. What is the expense for these benefits for 2015–2018?

CE4.19 Using the 2018, 2017, and 2016 annual reports for Kellogg (K) gathered in the prior chapter, collect additional information from the footnotes related to income taxes, deferred tax assets, and liabilities.

a. Gather information from Note 13 on the underlying deferred tax assets, and liabilities of K for 2015–2018.

b. What amounts are included as assets and liabilities within the balance sheet for 2015–2018?

CE4.20 Using the 2018, 2017, and 2016 annual reports for Kellogg (K) gathered in the prior chapter, collect the sales data by segment. This information will be useful in Chapter 7, where we will forecast sales by segment.

CE4.21 Using the 2018, 2017, and 2016 annual reports for Kellogg (K) gathered in the prior chapter, collect additional data to break down the following items:

a. Research and development

b. Advertising expense

c. Accounts receivable

d. Inventories

e. Other assets

f. Property, plant, and equipment
g. Other current assets
h. Other current liabilities
i. Other liabilities
j. Bad debt expense (additions to allowance for doubtful accounts)

With the additional information added into the balance sheet and income statement of K for 2015–2018, we arrive at the following expanded statements:

Balance Sheet	2015	2016	2017	2018
Assets				
Cash and cash equivalents	$ 251	$ 280	$ 28	$ 321
Accounts receivable: Trade	1,169	1,106	1,250	1,163
Accounts receivable: Allowance for doubtful accounts	(8)	(8)	(10)	(10)
Accounts receivable: Refundable income taxes	27	24	23	28
Accounts receivable: Other receivables	156	109	126	194
Inventories: Raw materials and supplies	315	315	333	339
Inventories: Finished goods and materials in progress	935	923	884	991
Other current assets	164	191	149	131
Property, net: Land	142	131	111	120
Property, net: Buildings	2,076	2,020	2,200	2,061
Property, net: Machinery and equipment	5,617	5,646	6,018	5,971
Property, net: Capitalized software	328	366	403	438
Property, net: Construction in progress	694	686	634	583
Property, net: Accumulated depreciation	(5,236)	(5,280)	(5,650)	(5,442)
Goodwill: U.S. morning Foods	131	131	131	131
Goodwill: U.S. snacks	3,568	3,568	3,568	3,568
Goodwill: U.S. specialty	82	82	82	82
Goodwill: North America other	456	457	836	830
Goodwill: Europe	431	376	414	392
Goodwill: Latin America	76	328	244	218
Goodwill: Asia Pacific	224	224	229	829
Intangible assets subject to amortization: U.S. morning Foods	8	8	8	8
Intangible assets subject to amortization: U.S. snacks	42	42	42	42
Intangible assets subject to amortization: North America other	5	5	22	24
Intangible assets subject to amortization: Europe	45	40	45	43
Intangible assets subject to amortization: Latin America	6	36	74	63
Intangible assets subject to amortization: Asia Pacific	10	10	10	428
Intangible assets accumulated amortization: U.S. morning Foods	(8)	(8)	(8)	(8)
Intangible assets accumulated amortization: U.S. snacks	(16)	(19)	(22)	(25)
Intangible assets accumulated amortization: North America other	(4)	(4)	(5)	(6)
Intangible assets accumulated amortization: Europe	(11)	(14)	(18)	(20)
Intangible assets accumulated amortization: Latin America	(6)	(6)	(10)	(12)
Intangible assets accumulated amortization: Asia Pacific	(2)	(3)	(4)	(16)
Intangible assets not subject to amortization: U.S. snacks	1,625	1,625	1,625	1,625
Intangible assets not subject to amortization: North America other	158	176	360	360
Intangible assets not subject to amortization: Europe	416	383	434	415
Intangible assets not subject to amortization: Latin America	—	98	86	73
Intangible assets not subject to amortization: Asia Pacific	—	—	—	367
Investments in unconsolidated entities	456	438	429	413
Deferred tax assets: U.S. state income taxes	13	—	—	—
Deferred tax assets: Advertising and promotion related	15	17	22	11
Deferred tax assets: Wages and payroll taxes	21	42	26	20
Deferred tax assets: Inventory valuation	31	28	20	14
Deferred tax assets: Employee benefits	366	403	154	132
Deferred tax assets: Operating loss, credit, and other carryforwards	55	181	239	270
Deferred tax assets: Hedging transactions	43	—	42	10
Deferred tax assets: Deferred compensation	35	38	25	20

continued

continued from previous page

Balance Sheet	2015	2016	2017	2018
Deferred tax assets: Stock options	42	41	33	31
Deferred tax assets: Other	86	31	71	26
Deferred tax assets: Valuation allowance	(63)	(131)	(153)	(166)
Pension: Plan assets	4,584	4,544	5,043	4,677
Postretirement: Plan assets	1,084	1,136	1,292	1,140
Other assets	338	376	385	487
Total assets	$20,972	$21,188	$22,523	$23,384

	2015	2016	2017	2018
Liabilities and Shareholders' Equity				
Current maturities of long-term debt	$ (1,266)	$ (631)	$ (409)	$ (510)
Notes payable: U.S. commercial paper	(899)	(80)	(196)	(15)
Notes payable: Europe commercial paper	(261)	(306)	(96)	—
Notes payable: Bank borrowings	(44)	(52)	(78)	(161)
Accounts payable	(1,907)	(2,014)	(2,269)	(2,427)
Other current liabilities: Accrued income taxes	(42)	(47)	(30)	(48)
Other current liabilities: Accrued salaries and wages	(325)	(318)	(311)	(309)
Other current liabilities: Accured advertising and promotion	(447)	(436)	(582)	(557)
Other current liabilities: Other	(512)	(569)	(526)	(478)
Long-term debt	(5,289)	(6,698)	(7,836)	(8,207)
Deferred tax liabilities: U.S. state income taxes	(43)	(34)	(48)	(19)
Deferred tax liabilities: Hedging transactions	—	(51)	—	—
Deferred tax liabilities: Depreciation and asset disposals	(345)	(318)	(208)	(220)
Deferred tax liabilities: Trademarks and other intangibles	(576)	(602)	(332)	(613)
Pension: Benefit obligation	(5,316)	(5,510)	(5,648)	(5,117)
Postretirement: Benefit obligation	(1,163)	(1,161)	(1,190)	(1,069)
Postemployment: Benefit obligation	(108)	(87)	(43)	(42)
Other liabilities: Income taxes payable	—	(48)	(192)	(115)
Other liabilities: Nonpension postretirement benefits	(77)	(40)	(40)	(34)
Other liabilities: Pension	(214)	(260)	(295)	(284)
Total liabilities	(18,834)	(19,262)	(20,329)	(20,225)
Shareholders' equity				
Common stock—$0.25 par value	(105)	(105)	(105)	(105)
Capital in excess of par value	(745)	(806)	(878)	(895)
Retained earnings	(6,597)	(6,571)	(7,069)	(7,652)
Treasury stock, at cost	3,943	3,997	4,417	4,551
Accumulated other comprehensive (income)/loss	1,376	1,575	1,457	1,500
Noncontrolling interests	(10)	(16)	(16)	(558)
Total shareholders' equity	(2,138)	(1,926)	(2,194)	(3,159)
Total liabilities and shareholders' equity	$(20,972)	$(21,188)	$(22,523)	$(23,384)

Income Statement	2015	2016	2017	2018
Net sales: U.S. morning Foods	$ 2,992	$2,917	$2,709	$2,643
Net sales: U.S. snacks	3,234	3,197	3,110	2,957
Net sales: U.S. specialty channels	1,181	1,207	1,242	1,235
Net sales: North America other	1,687	1,593	1,612	1,853
Net sales: Europe	2,497	2,383	2,291	2,395
Net sales: Latin America	1,015	772	944	947
Net sales: Asia Pacific	919	896	946	1,517
Cost of goods sold	—	(8,131)	(8,155)	(8,821)
Gross profit	$13,525	$4,834	$4,699	$4,726
401k plan expense		(39)	(41)	(38)
Pension: Service cost		(98)	(96)	(87)
Pension: Interest cost		(174)	(164)	(165)
Pension: Expected return on plan assets		352	371	361
Pension: Amortization of unrecognized prior service cost		(13)	(9)	(8)
Pension: Recognized net actuarial loss		(323)	36	(269)
Pension: Curtailment and special termination benefits		(1)	151	30
Pension: Defined contribution plans		(36)	(34)	(27)
Postretirement: Service cost		(21)	(18)	(18)
Postretirement: Interest cost		(39)	(37)	(36)
Postretirement: Expected return on plan assets		90	98	94
Postretirement: Amortization of unrecognized prior service cost		9	9	9
Postretirement: Recognized net (gain) loss		19	90	(81)
Postretirement: Curtailment		—	(3)	—
Postretirement: Defined contribution plans		(17)	(16)	(11)
Postemployment: Service cost		(7)	(6)	(3)
Postemployment: Interest cost		(3)	(3)	(1)
Postemployment: Amortization of unrecognized prior service cost		(1)	(1)	(1)
Postemployment: Recognized net (gain) loss		(3)	—	5
Research and development expense		(182)	(148)	(154)
Advertising expense		(735)	(732)	(752)
Bad debt expense		(9)	(14)	(4)
Other selling, general, and administrative expense		(2,120)	(2,745)	(1,864)
Operating profit		1,483	1,387	1,706
Interest expense		(406)	(256)	(287)
Other income (expense), net		(143)	526	(90)
Income before income taxes, equity interests and extraordinary loss		934	1,657	1,329
Income taxes		(235)	(410)	(181)
Earnings from unconsolidated entities		1	7	196
Net income		700	1,254	1,344
Net income attributable to noncontrolling interests		(1)	—	(8)
Net income attributable to Kellogg Company		699	1,254	1,336
Comprehensive income items:				
Foreign currency translation adjustments, net of tax		(254)	79	(48)
Cash flow hedges, net of tax		(28)	6	8
Postretirement and postemployment benefits, net of tax:				
Net experience gain		18	32	(11)
Prior service credit		2	1	1
Venezuela deconsolidation loss		63	—	—
Other comprehensive income attributable to noncontrolling interests, net		—	—	7
Comprehensive income attributable to Kellogg		$ 500	$1,372	$1,293

CE4.22 Using the 2018, 2017, and 2016 annual reports for **Thor Industries** (THO) gathered in the prior chapter, collect additional information from the consolidated statement of cash flows and footnotes about the balances reported as depreciation expense, allowance for bad debts, and advertising costs. Being able to have a more detailed breakdown of these numbers can be helpful in subsequent forecasting exercises.

a. What is the depreciation expense reported in the consolidated statement of cash flows from fiscal 2015–2018?

b. Per Note 1, what is the deprecation expense reported in cost of products sold and selling, general, and administrative expenses?

c. Per Note 1, what is THO's allowance for bad debts for fiscal years 2015–2018?

d. Per Note 1, what are THO's advertising costs for fiscal years 2015–2018?

e. Per Note 11, what are THO's product warranty expenses for fiscal years 2015–2018? Also, in which income statement account is this expense reported?

f. Per Note 16, what are THO's 401(k) plan expense for fiscal years 2015–2018?

g. Per Note 16, what is THO's deferred compensation asset and liability for fiscal years 2015–2018?

CE4.23 Using the 2018, 2017, and 2016 annual reports for **Thor Industries** (THO) gathered in the prior chapter, collect the sales data by segment in Note 4. This information will be useful in Chapter 7, where we will forecast sales by segment.

CE4.24 Using the 2018, 2017, and 2016 annual reports for **Thor Industries** (THO) gathered in the prior chapter, collect the inventory components in Note 5.

CE4.25 Using the 2018, 2017, and 2016 annual reports for **Thor Industries** (THO) gathered in the prior chapter, collect the property, plant, and equipment components in Note 6. Also, identify the amount and the financial statement location for THO's fiscal year 2017 gain on sale of land, buildings, and improvements related to a towable RV facility.

CE4.26 Using the 2018, 2017, and 2016 annual reports for **Thor Industries** (THO) gathered in the prior chapter, collect additional information from Note 7, about the balances reported as amortizable intangible assets and goodwill. Being able to have a more detailed breakdown of these numbers can be helpful in subsequent forecasting exercises.

CE4.27 Using the 2018, 2017, and 2016 annual reports for **Thor Industries** (THO) gathered in the prior chapter, collect additional information from Note 13, regarding THO's income tax expense, deferred tax assets, and liabilities.

From Note 13, gather information on THO's underlying deferred tax assets and liabilities for 2015–2018.

With the additional information added into the balance sheet and income statement of Thor Industries for 2015–2018, we arrive at the following expanded statements:

Balance Sheet	2015	2016	2017	2018
Assets				
Cash and cash equivalents	$ 183,478	$ 209,902	$ 223,258	$ 275,249
Accounts receivable, trade	245,335	370,710	454,446	467,488
Accounts receivable, other	25,642	22,454	31,090	19,747
Allowance for doubtful accounts	(1,283)	(625)	(692)	—
Inventory: Finished products—RV	35,693	39,943	24,904	44,998
Inventory: Finished products—other	18,045	20,141	27,862	35,320
Inventory: Work in progress	51,556	97,872	117,319	124,703
Inventory: Raw materials	133,482	173,362	214,518	258,429
Inventory: Chassis	37,739	102,686	109,555	116,308
Inventory: Excess of FIFO costs over LIFO costs	(30,400)	(30,135)	(33,670)	(41,849)
Prepaid expenses and other	8,323	10,548	11,577	11,281
Notes receivable	8,367	—	—	—
Property, plant and equipment: Land	27,447	46,422	48,812	57,413
Property, plant and equipment: Buildings and improvements	214,462	300,902	380,139	468,824
Property, plant and equipment: Machinery and equipment	106,959	133,112	161,724	197,294
Property, plant and equipment: Accumulated depreciation	(114,823)	(136,169)	(165,437)	(201,477)

continued

continued from previous page

Balance Sheet	2015	2016	2017	2018
Goodwill: Towables	269,751	334,822	334,822	334,822
Goodwill: Other	42,871	42,871	42,871	42,871
Amortizable intangible assets: Dealer networks/customer relationships	143,860	404,960	404,960	404,960
Amortizable intangible assets: Dealer networks/customer relationships—accum amort	(37,194)	(55,191)	(101,795)	(147,077)
Amortizable intangible assets: Trademarks	55,282	148,117	147,617	146,117
Amortizable intangible assets: Trademark—accum amort	(7,608)	(10,539)	(17,570)	(24,364)
Amortizable intangible assets: Design technology and other intangibles	22,400	22,400	19,300	18,200
Amortizable intangible assets: Design technology and other intangibles—accum amort	(8,168)	(10,870)	(9,203)	(9,555)
Amortizable intangible assets: Non-compete agreements	4,710	450	450	450
Amortizable intangible assets: Non-compete agreements—accum amort	(4,264)	(203)	(293)	(383)
Amortizable intangible assets: Backlog	—	12,400	—	—
Amortizable intangible assets: Backlog—accum amort	—	(4,133)	—	—
Deferred tax assets: Inventory basis	467	1,196	1,460	922
Deferred tax assets: Employee benefits	3,625	4,587	6,471	3,427
Deferred tax assets: Self-insurance reserves	10,411	10,504	9,940	6,368
Deferred tax assets: Accrued product warranties	39,486	43,388	73,393	62,332
Deferred tax assets: Accrued incentives	3,959	5,154	6,175	5,235
Deferred tax assets: Sales returns and allowances	1,520	1,642	2,340	1,741
Deferred tax assets: Accrued expenses	2,067	2,607	3,399	1,905
Deferred tax assets: Property, plant and equipment	(340)	(4,164)	(8,151)	(9,060)
Deferred tax assets: Deferred compensation	6,367	9,145	14,556	12,864
Deferred tax assets: Tax credit carry forward	110	—	—	—
Deferred tax assets: Intangibles	(30,246)	(22,308)	(17,184)	(9,151)
Deferred tax assets: Unrecognized tax benefits	3,913	4,105	3,925	2,581
Deferred tax assets: Other	(2,038)	(2,439)	(3,355)	(720)
Equity investment in joint venture	—	—	—	48,463
Other assets	11,722	25,838	38,398	51,989
Total assets	$1,482,685	$2,325,464	$2,557,931	$2,778,665

	2015	2016	2017	2018
Liabilities and Shareholders' Equity				
Accounts payable	$ (162,587)	$ (263,774)	$ (328,601)	$ (286,974)
Accrued liabilities:				
Compensation and related items	(51,984)	(81,159)	(100,114)	(97,122)
Product warranties	(108,206)	(201,840)	(216,781)	(264,928)
Income and other taxes	(11,000)	(25,531)	(51,211)	(19,345)
Promotion and rebates	(19,817)	(40,452)	(46,459)	(59,133)
Product, property and related liabilities	(10,892)	(15,969)	(16,521)	(17,815)
Other	(13,849)	(22,927)	(21,359)	(24,013)
Long-term debt	—	(360,000)	(145,000)	—
Unrecognized tax benefits	(11,945)	(9,975)	(10,263)	(12,446)
Other liabilities	(27,218)	(38,615)	(45,082)	(59,148)
Total liabilities	(417,498)	(1,060,242)	(981,391)	(840,924)
Shareholders' equity				
Common stock	(6,231)	(6,244)	(6,260)	(6,277)
Additional paid-in capital	(215,539)	(224,496)	(235,525)	(252,204)
Retained earnings	(1,172,432)	(1,365,981)	(1,670,826)	(2,022,988)
Treasury shares	329,015	331,499	336,071	343,728
Total shareholders' equity	(1,065,187)	(1,265,222)	(1,576,540)	(1,937,741)
Total liabilities and shareholders' equity	$(1,482,685)	$(2,325,464)	$(2,557,931)	$(2,778,665)

Income Statement	2015	2016	2017	2018
Net sales: Recreational vehicles—towables	$3,096,405	$3,338,659	$5,127,491	$6,008,700
Net sales: Recreational vehicles—motorized	870,799	1,094,250	1,971,466	2,146,315
Net sales: Other	56,594	218,673	253,557	305,947
Net sales: Intercompany eliminations	(16,979)	(69,470)	(105,562)	(132,053)
Cost of products sold		(3,720,867)	(5,978,947)	(6,871,328)
Depreciation expense		(24,613)	(34,333)	(38,105)
Product warranty expense		(114,119)	(195,799)	(259,845)
Selling, general, and administrative expenses		(287,068)	(387,343)	(442,846)
Advertising costs		(14,472)	(24,997)	(26,874)
401(k) plan expense		(917)	(1,797)	(2,689)
Impairment charges		(9,113)	—	—
Amortization of intangible assets		(27,962)	(63,925)	(55,118)
Interest income		743	923	2,148
Interest expense		(1,592)	(9,730)	(5,187)
Gain on sale of facility		—	2,165	—
Other (income) and expense, net		1,181	3,217	3,964
Income from continuing operations before income taxes		383,313	556,386	633,029
Income taxes		(125,291)	(182,132)	(202,878)
Net income from continuing operations		258,022	374,254	430,151
Loss from discontinued operations, net of taxes		(1,503)	—	—
Net income and comprehensive income		$ 256,519	$ 374,254	$ 430,151

CE4.28 Using the 2018, 2017 and 2016 annual reports for Winnebago (WGO) gathered in the prior chapter, gather additional information from the management discussion and analysis (MD&A) and the footnotes about the balances reported as advertising expense, warranty expense and segment revenues. Being able to have a more detailed breakdown of these numbers can be helpful in subsequent forecasting exercises.

a. Per Note 1, what are Winnebago's advertising costs for fiscal 2015–2018?

b. Per Note 8, what are Winnebago's advertising costs for fiscal 2015–2018?

c. In Winnebago's 10-K, the management discussion and analysis (MD&A) provides an analysis of the firm's financial condition and results of operations. In the Segment Results of Operations, the net revenues for motorized vehicles (i.e., motorhome) and towable vehicles (i.e., towable) are provided. Identify the net revenues for motorized and towable vehicles with remaining net revenues being classified as Other for fiscal 2015–2018.

CE4.29 Using the 2018, 2017 and 2016 annual reports for Winnebago (WGO) gathered in the prior chapter, gather the inventory components in Note 5.

CE4.30 Using the 2018, 2017 and 2016 annual reports for Winnebago (WGO) gathered in the prior chapter, gather the property, plant and equipment components in Note 6.

CE4.31 Using the 2018, 2017 and 2016 annual reports for Winnebago (WGO) gathered in the prior chapter, gather additional information from Note 7 about the balances reported as goodwill and amortizable intangible assets.

CE4.32. Using the 2018, 2017 and 2016 annual reports for Winnebago (WGO) gathered in the prior chapter, gather additional information from Note 13 regarding WGO's income tax expense, deferred tax assets and liabilities.

CE4.33 Using the 2018, 2017 and 2016 annual reports for Winnebago (WGO) gathered in the prior chapter, gather additional information from Note 10 related to deferred compensation benefits and postretirement health care benefits.

a. What is the composition of the deferred compensation benefits for each of the fiscal years 2015–2018?

b. Winnebago provided health care and other benefits for its retired employees until the postretirement health care benefits were discontinued as of January 1, 2017. Identify the components of net periods postretirement benefit income for fiscal 2015–2018?

CE4.34 Using the 2018, 2017 and 2016 annual reports for Winnebago (WGO) gathered in the prior chapter, gather additional information from Note 13 regarding Winnebago's income tax expense, deferred tax assets and liabilities.

From Note 13 gather information on the underlying deferred tax assets and liabilities of Winnebago for 2015–2018.

With the additional information added into the balance sheet and income statement of Winnebago for 2015–2018, we arrive at the following expanded statements:

Balance Sheet	2015	2016	2017	2018
Assets				
Cash and cash equivalents	$ 70,239	$ 85,583	$ 35,945	$ 2,342
Receivables, net	66,936	66,184	124,539	164,585
Inventories: Finished goods	12,179	19,129	16,947	26,513
Inventories: Work-in-process	66,602	76,350	60,818	68,339
Inventories: Raw materials	65,928	60,740	99,919	139,039
Inventories: LIFO reserve	(32,544)	(33,697)	(35,419)	(38,763)
Prepaid expenses and other assets	6,882	6,300	11,388	9,883
Property, plant and equipment: Land	1,874	3,864	3,914	6,747
Property, plant and equipment: Buildings and building improvements	53,388	62,073	73,831	94,622
Property, plant and equipment: Machinery and equipment	94,034	95,087	99,952	105,663
Property, plant and equipment: Software	8,033	15,878	17,844	23,388
Property, plant and equipment: Transportation	8,913	8,956	8,993	8,837
Property, plant and equipment: Accumulated depreciation	(128,992)	(129,927)	(132,974)	(138,064)
Goodwill: Towable	1,228	1,228	242,728	244,684
Goodwill: Corporate/All Other	—	—	—	29,686
Intangibles: Trade name	—	—	148,000	177,250
Intangibles: Dealer network	—	—	80,500	95,581
Intangibles: Backlog	—	—	18,000	19,527
Intangibles: Non-compete agreements	—	—	4,600	5,347
Intangibles: Leasehold interest-favorable	—	—	2,000	2,000
Intangibles—Accum Amortization: Dealer network	—	—	(5,348)	(12,328)
Intangibles—Accum Amortization: Backlog	—	—	(18,000)	(19,135)
Intangibles—Accum Amortization: Non-compete agreements	—	—	(1,116)	(2,084)
Intangibles—Accum Amortization: Leasehold interest-favorable	—	—	(196)	(441)
Investment in life insurance	26,172	26,492	27,418	28,297
Deferred tax assets: Deferred compensation	10,757	9,609	9,135	4,730
Deferred tax assets: Warranty reserves	4,288	4,729	11,675	9,842
Deferred tax assets: Postretirement health care benefits	12,792	2,262	—	—
Deferred tax assets: Self-insurance reserve	2,378	2,214	1,967	2,601
Deferred tax assets: Accrued vacation	1,938	2,006	2,142	1,298
Deferred tax assets: Stock based compensation	1,239	1,030	943	1,277
Deferred tax assets: Inventory	—	—	—	615
Deferred tax assets: Unrecognized tax benefit	726	698	437	584
Deferred tax assets: Other	1,592	1,785	2,072	1,797
Other assets	9,313	7,725	5,493	10,290
Total assets	$365,895	$396,298	$918,147	$1,074,549

	2015	2016	2017	2018
Liabilities and Shareholders' Equity				
Accounts payable	$ (33,158)	$ (44,134)	$ (79,194)	$ (81,039)
Current maturities of long-term debt	—	—	(2,850)	—
Income taxes payable	(2,314)	(19)	(7,450)	(15,655)
Accrued expenses: Accrued compensation	(13,415)	(15,125)	(21,197)	(24,608)
Accrued expenses: Product warranties	(11,254)	(12,412)	(30,805)	(40,498)
Accrued expenses: Self-insurance	(6,242)	(5,812)	(6,122)	(12,262)
Accrued expenses: Accrued loss on repurchases	(1,329)	(881)	—	—
Accrued expenses: Promotional	(3,149)	(4,756)	(6,560)	(11,017)
Accrued expenses: Accrued interest	—	—	(3,128)	(3,095)
Accrued expenses: Other	(5,818)	(5,236)	(6,503)	(11,269)
Long-term debt, less current maturities	—	—	(271,726)	(291,441)
Unrecognized tax benefits	(2,511)	(2,461)	(1,606)	(1,745)

continued

continued from previous page

	2015	2016	2017	2018
Deferred tax liabilities: Inventory	(2,383)	(1,930)	(1,919)	—
Deferred tax liabilities: Intangibles	—	—	(7,455)	(21,292)
Deferred tax liabilities: Depreciation	(1,338)	(3,650)	(6,261)	(5,909)
Postretirement health care benefit cost	(34,535)	(6,346)	—	—
Non-qualified deferred compensation	(19,508)	(18,003)	(16,476)	(14,831)
Executive share option plan liability	(4,788)	(3,341)	(1,498)	(935)
SERP benefit liability	(2,649)	(2,681)	(2,534)	(2,309)
Executive deferred compensation	(299)	(389)	(447)	(421)
Officer stock-based compensation	(242)	(763)	(1,664)	(1,528)
Other liabilities	—	—	(1,078)	(250)
Total liabilities	(144,932)	(127,939)	(476,473)	(540,104)
Shareholders' equity				
Common stock—$0.50 par value	(25,888)	(25,888)	(25,888)	(25,888)
Additional paid-in capital	(32,018)	(32,717)	(80,401)	(86,223)
Retained earnings	(585,941)	(620,546)	(679,138)	(768,816)
Accumulated other comprehensive (income)/loss	2,274	(10,975)	1,023	(892)
Treasury stock, at cost	420,610	421,767	342,730	347,374
Total shareholders' equity	(220,963)	(268,359)	(441,674)	(534,445)
Total liabilities and shareholders' equity	$(365,895)	$(396,298)	$(918,147)	$(1,074,549)

Income Statement

	2015	2016	2017	2018
Net sales: motorized	$ 904,821	$ 881,363	$ 853,360	$ 860,675
Net sales: towable	71,684	89,412	685,197	1,127,723
Net sales: Other	—	4,451	8,562	28,431
Cost of products sold		(846,074)	(1,292,911)	(1,674,616)
Warranty expense		(16,503)	(31,631)	(42,377)
Gross profit		112,649	222,577	299,836
Advertising expense		(4,900)	(5,700)	(7,400)
SG&A: Selling		(14,923)	(29,968)	(42,450)
Net periodic postretirement benefit income: Interest cost		(327)	(29)	—
Net periodic postretirement benefit income: Service cost		(108)	(16)	—
Profit sharing plan and 401(k) plan expense		(1,500)	(1,600)	(2,300)
SG&A: General and administrative		(31,274)	(53,702)	(75,789)
Net periodic postretirement benefit income: Amortization of prior service benefit		7,736	40,444	—
Net periodic postretirement benefit income: Amortization of net actuarial loss		(1,612)	(15,648)	—
SG&A: Transaction costs		—	(6,592)	(2,177)
SG&A: Amortization of intangible assets		—	(24,660)	(9,328)
Interest expense		—	(16,837)	(18,246)
Non-operating income		457	330	494
Income before taxes		66,198	108,599	142,640
Provision for income taxes		(20,702)	(37,269)	(40,283)
Net income		45,496	71,330	102,357
Comprehensive income items:				
Amortization of prior service credit		(4,788)	(25,035)	—
Amortization of net actuarial loss		1,010	9,705	27
Increase in actuarial loss		(674)	(57)	—
Plan amendment		17,701	3,903	—
Change in fair value of interest rate swap		—	(514)	1,947
Comprehensive income attributable to WGO		$ 58,745	$ 59,332	$ 104,331

Chapter Five

Adjusting Accounting Information

TAKEAWAYS

When you complete this chapter, you should be able to:

1. Explain the effects of accounting method choices on valuation and when adjustments are helpful.
2. Adjust from LIFO to FIFO inventory to facilitate comparison.
3. Analyze the effects of leasing transactions both before and after the new leasing standard.
4. Discuss the potential impacts of special-purpose entities on valuation.
5. Capture the economic effects of share-based compensation in the adjusted financial statements.

In the prior chapters, we reformulated the financial statements and included information from additional sources, such as that in the footnotes and the MD&A. This will allow us to revise and improve our identification of *NOA* and *NOPAT* and our forecasts. Now, we consider, effects of accounting method choices. From our understanding of accounting, we know that the reported numbers are the result of a set of accounting methods that management chose. Had management employed an alternative set of accounting methods, different numbers would have been reported. To understand the effects of the accounting choices and whether adjustments are necessary, we need to separately address the effects on calculations of value and on forecasting. This chapter includes a general discussion about the effects of accounting methods followed by a series of mini-chapters covering potential adjustments to address particular accounting methods and valuation-relevant issues regarding these methods. The chapter then concludes with an update to the calculations of *NOA*, *NFL*, *NOPAT*, and *FEAT* for **General Mills** (GIS) based on these efforts.

THE EFFECT OF ACCOUNTING METHOD CHOICES ON VALUATION MODELS

LO1: Explain the effects of accounting method choices on valuation and when adjustments are helpful.

Many users of financial information express concern that the possibility of choice among accounting methods (i.e., accounting discretion) provides a tool for manipulation of reported information. We address this issue and its possible effects. The essence of our arguments is as follows: Most choices among accounting methods result in the shifting of reported income across periods. The choice of accounting method usually does not change total income over the life of a project or a company. The issue is simply one of determining the period in which the revenues/expenses are reported.[1] This should not affect valuation but will have an effect on forecasting because we are attempting to determine what will be reported in future periods.

[1] Arguments that cash flows are superior to accounting numbers due to potential timing issues fail to acknowledge that cash flows can be shifted between periods. A company can choose to pay a bill from a supplier in December or wait until January, causing the cash flow to occur in a different year.

CHAPTER OUTLINE

Adjusting Accounting Information

Effects of Accounting Method Choices

- Value Should Not Change
- Why Adjustments Are Helpful

Illustrative Scenarios

- LIFO Inventory
- Operating Leases
- Special Purpose Entities
- Share-Based Compensation

Accounting issues, which may lead to hesitant use of financial statements, may be divided into four categories:

1. accounting method choice,
2. accrual management,
3. real earnings management, and
4. flat out lying!

Often, those who raise these issues are fuzzy about their reasons for hesitation and may tend to blend the issues. Clearly seeing the different issues may help us understand the concerns and allow us to address the question of whether the issues affect our valuation process.

Accounting methods allow discretion to choose among differing allowable methods to account for the same transaction. A straightforward example is the choice between using LIFO or FIFO to account for inventory. We must understand the effects of this choice on reported information because it affects our financial statement analysis (step 3). We also must understand the effects it may have on our forecasts (step 4) because they will form the basis of the valuation (step 5). This chapter will address accounting method choice directly, while the other three categories will be addressed in subsequent chapters as part of our financial statement analysis and valuation.

Accrual management is the adjustment upward or downward of accounts such as prepaid expenses and/or unearned revenues in an attempt to affect the timing of income. Adjusting the timing of the point when it is assumed that a gift card will never be redeemed is an example. This revenue, called breakage, could be accelerated by assuming an earlier date, causing increased current income. Accelerating the revenue now means it will not be reported in the future, leading to a reduction in forecasted future revenue.

Real earnings management involves steps taken by management to alter income by changing operating activities. Reducing fourth quarter expenditures on advertising (a current expense) to show higher current income is an example. A concern with respect to real earnings management is the possible negative effect on future sales, which we would want to anticipate in our forecasts.

Before proceeding to the mini-chapters, we clarify one point related to income shifting: We will see an example of income shifting in a later chapter where we adjust the depreciation on the project that was introduced in Chapter 2. The total amount of net income over the life of the project will remain unchanged even though periodic earnings change. As a preview, in **Exhibit 5.1**, we provide the depreciation and net income amounts for the project previously introduced. The income in period 4 is increased by $200 under assumption 2 because a greater amount of prior depreciation has lowered the book value of the project, resulting in a gain of $200 upon completion of the project.

Most important, in a subsequent chapter we will demonstrate that the accounting method does not affect the computed value for the project. That is, what we report in the company's books and records does not change the underlying economic value of the activities undertaken.[2]

From this fact, it may appear that accounting method choice has no effect whatsoever on the valuation exercise. But, this is not so. The project used as an example has known payoffs and a

[2] There can be a change in value if a different amount of tax will have to be paid or the timing of the payment of tax changes. However, absent tax-related effects, the movement of income between periods will have no effect on value.

EXHIBIT 5.1 Financial Information for Finite-Life Project

	Assumption #1		Assumption #2	
Period	**Depreciation**	**Net Income**	**Depreciation**	**Net Income**
0	$ 0	$ 0	$200	$(200)
1	200	50	200	50
2	200	150	200	150
3	200	120	200	120
4	200	80	200	280
Total		$400		$ 400

finite life; it exists for 4 years, and then the assets are sold. If, however, past accounting data are used as the basis for forecasting, income shifting or differing accounting method choices may lead to less comparability or create an appearance of comparability where it does not actually exist. Appropriate assumptions for forecasted sales growth, profit margins, and asset turnovers may depend, to some extent, on observed values of past sales growth, *NOPAT*, *NOA*, and their components for the company as well as for comparable companies.

We now explore several ways in which accounting method choices may affect realized *NOPAT* and *NOA*, thus, altering comparability and influencing forecasts to the extent that we rely on past realizations or analysis of competitors/comparables in determining inputs to our forecasts.

ADJUSTMENT A: INVENTORY METHOD

LO2: Adjust from LIFO to FIFO inventory to facilitate comparison.

The financial statements of companies that use different inventory costing methods may not be comparable—particularly due to the use of LIFO. This lack of comparability is likely most serious when companies hold large amounts of inventory and when prices markedly rise or fall. To compare companies using different inventory costing methods, say LIFO and FIFO, we adjust the LIFO numbers to their FIFO equivalents.[3] This is not difficult because, if companies choose to disclose an inventory balance under LIFO, they must also, as required by U.S. GAAP, provide the amount of the LIFO adjustment, which enables us to calculate the value of the inventory and cost of goods sold that would have been reported if they had chosen to use the FIFO method.

Before proceeding with our example it is important to note that this is an adjustment that should be considered even if all companies being compared use LIFO. This is because the magnitude of the LIFO adjustment is often a function of how long the company has utilized LIFO. Consider, for example, two energy companies using LIFO, one of which has been a long-time user. This long-time user of LIFO could have barrels of oil in inventory with a much lower cost when compared with a more recent adopter of LIFO. Valuation of the inventory of both companies using FIFO would be necessary to ensure comparability.

We will begin by demonstrating the adjustment for inventory method with two energy companies who both use LIFO. In doing so, we will see that the adjustment reveals that using a LIFO-to-LIFO comparison is not necessarily apples to apples. Then, we will revisit GIS and a competitor, Kellogg (K). Although K does not use LIFO, we find that GIS has a portion of its inventory reported under LIFO, and we will demonstrate the adjustment of this inventory to FIFO to enhance comparability.

Example 1: ConocoPhillips and HollyFrontier

To demonstrate the adjustment of *NOPAT* and *NOA* resulting from a change in inventory valuation method from LIFO to FIFO when both companies use LIFO, consider ConocoPhillips

[3] Note that methods other than LIFO (e.g., the weighted average inventory method) generally do not result in amounts that differ drastically from FIFO. The reason for LIFO needing special consideration is that very old inventory with drastically outdated prices may continue to be shown on the balance sheet for many years, causing an understatement of the resources necessary to support sales.

Corporation (COP) and HollyFrontier (HFC).[4] We will walk through the adjustment for COP and provide the resulting numbers for HFC as well. Based on their 2012 financial statements, we can compute each company's *NOPAT* and *NOA* following the process outlined in the prior chapters. Then, using each company's disclosures of their LIFO reserve (the difference between reported LIFO and "as if" FIFO), we can adjust the balance sheet and income statement. This adjustment should be "net of tax" because, if the company had used FIFO inventory valuation for financial reporting purposes, the IRS would have required that tax reporting also be based on FIFO.

COP's *NOA* at December 31, 2012, was $66,945 (all numbers in millions) based on the information using LIFO that was reported on the face of the financial statements. To compare COP with HFC, which is also being converted to "as-if" FIFO inventory valuation, we add COP's LIFO reserve (of $200) to its LIFO inventory. This $200 increase in 2012 inventories would have increased its cumulative pretax profits by $200 and taxes by $70 based on a 35 percent statutory tax rate ($200 × 0.35 = $70).[5] Thus, to adjust the 2012 balance sheet, we increase inventories by $200, increase tax liabilities by $70 (the extra taxes COP would have had to pay under FIFO), and increase equity by the difference of $130. Therefore, *NOA* for COP would increase by the net amount of $130 to $67,075.

COP's *NOPAT* for 2012 was $9,537 based on the information, using the LIFO inventory method, that was reported in the financial statements. To adjust COP's 2012 income statement from LIFO to as-if FIFO, we use the (footnoted) change in LIFO reserve. COP's LIFO reserve decreased by $8,200 during 2012, from $8,400 at the end of 2011 to $200 at the end of 2012. This means that, had COP been using FIFO, its cost of goods sold would have been $8,200 higher, and its 2012 gross profit and pretax income would have been $8,200 lower. In 2012, COP would have paid $2,870 less in taxes had it used FIFO for inventory valuation ($8,200 × 0.35). Therefore, *NOPAT* for COP would decrease by the net amount of $5,330 to $4,207.

Similar steps can be taken to determine as-if FIFO numbers for HFC.[6] These adjusted *NOA*, *NOPAT*, profit margin (*PM* = *NOPAT*/Sales), and asset turnover (*ATO* = Sales/*NOA*) for COP and HFC (again, dollar amounts in millions) are shown in **Exhibit 5.2**.

EXHIBIT 5.2 Effects of LIFO Inventory Method on Two Energy Companies

	ConocoPhillips		HollyFrontier	
	As Reported under LIFO	**As if under FIFO**	**As Reported under LIFO**	**As if under FIFO**
Average *NOA*	$75,120	$79,385	$ 5,753	$ 5,986
NOPAT	$ 9,537	$ 4,207	$ 1,739	$ 1,581
Sales	$57,967	$57,967	$20,091	$20,091
PM (*NOPAT*/Sales)	16.45%	7.26%	8.66%	7.87%
ATO (Sales/Average *NOA*)	0.77	0.73	3.49	3.36

Clearly the conversion from "as reported under LIFO" to "as-if" reported under FIFO can affect our understanding of reported results. Changing from LIFO to FIFO makes the *PM* of COP and HFC change from vastly different, to quite comparable. We would expect these similar companies to have comparable *PM*s, but LIFO makes COP look much more profitable. It is only after the adjustment that the effects of accounting choice are stripped away to reveal the expected similar levels of profitability. If, for example, the FIFO-based *PM* of 7.26 percent and/or *ATO* of 0.73 for

[4] We choose to demonstrate the effects of LIFO using the 2012 financial statements of COP and HFC because the effects of the adjustment are so stark. The profit margin of two companies that we would expect to be comparable are quite different before the LIFO adjustment and quite similar after the adjustment.

[5] For all adjustments to enterprise operations demonstrated in this chapter, we use the assumed future statutory tax rate. COP disclosed in Note 20 that foreign taxes in excess of federal statutory rate adds 18.6 percent to the effective tax rate. Because LIFO is a U.S. tax issue related to the IRC, this should not apply in the computation of the adjustment from LIFO to FIFO. As a result, for the inventory adjustment, we use the 35 percent assumed tax rate rather than COP's disclosed effective tax rate of 51.5 percent.

[6] For HFC, the assumed statutory rate of 35 percent is, for the purposes of our illustration, also used in lieu of its disclosed effective tax rate of 36.9 percent.

COP lead to improved forecasts, we will be more confident in our valuation. Clearly, a large part of the current profitability of COP was caused by the LIFO liquidation (reduction in LIFO reserve from $8,400 to $200) during 2012.

If we had used the reported LIFO numbers for both COP and HFC, it would have seemed that COP had a much higher *PM* at 16.45 percent as compared to HFC's *PM* of 8.66 percent. But comparing LIFO to LIFO may not be appropriate. We find that when both companies are adjusted to FIFO, which is an apples-to-apples comparison, HFC has a higher *PM* of 7.87 percent as compared to COP's *PM* of 7.26 percent. Further, these as-if FIFO inventory values are generally more meaningful when comparing to similarly adjusted numbers of other companies and when forecasting.

Example 2: General Mills

Next, we return to our focus companies in this text—GIS and its main competitor, K. The difference due to adjusting for the inventory method is not as stark for GIS and K as it was for the two energy companies. K does not have any inventory, which is valued using LIFO. GIS, however, does. The *NOA* of GIS at May 27, 2018, was $23,755.4 (all numbers in millions) based on the information using LIFO that was reported in the financial statements.[7] In order to compare GIS to K, we add the LIFO reserve of GIS of $213.2 per Note 17 to its LIFO inventory. This $213.2 increase in May 2018 inventories would have increased cumulative pretax profits by $213.2 and taxes by $44.8 based on a 21 percent statutory tax rate ($13.2 × 0.21 = $44.8). Thus, to adjust the May 2018 balance sheet, we increase inventories by $213.2, increase tax liabilities by $44.8 (the extra taxes GIS would have had to pay under FIFO), and increase equity by the difference of $168.4. Therefore, *NOA* for GIS would increase by the net amount of $168.4 to $23,923.8.

The *NOPAT* of GIS for the year ended May 2018 was $2,286.0 based on the information in the statements and using the LIFO inventory method. To adjust the 2018 income statement of GIS from LIFO to as-if FIFO, we use the change in LIFO reserve. The LIFO reserve for GIS increased by $4.1 during 2018, from $209.1 at May 2017 to $213.2 at May 2018. This means that, had GIS been using FIFO, its cost of goods sold would have been $4.1 lower, and its gross profit and pretax income for the year ended May 2018 would have been $4.1 higher. In 2018, GIS would have paid

ACCOUNTING FOR THE ADJUSTMENT: INVENTORY METHOD

Within each adjustment mini-chapter, we will also present the accounting for the adjustment. For some with stronger accounting backgrounds, seeing the journal entries laid out may be helpful for processing the information and the effects of the adjustment.

For COP, HFC, and GIS, we could write the following journal entries to record these adjustments:

	COP 2012		HFC 2012		GIS 2018	
	Dr	Cr	Dr	Cr	Dr	Cr
Inventory	$ 200		$134		$213.2	
Taxes payable		$ 70		$ 47		$ 44.8
Cost of goods sold	8,200		244			4.1
Tax expense		2,870		85	0.9	
Retained earnings		5,460		246		165.2
	$8,400	$8,400	$378	$378	$214.1	$214.1

Note that the amount of adjustment needed to retained earnings is the prior period adjustment. That is, for COP, the opening LIFO reserve was $8,400, which, net of tax, yields an adjustment of $5,460 [$8,400 × (1 – 0.35)].

[7] We compare to K's financial statements from December 29, 2018, in this example because they are the most recent available at the time of writing this book. In Chapter 6, we will discuss in detail the issues (and potential approaches to addressing them) that arise with comparisons of companies with differing year-ends.

\$0.9 more in taxes had it used FIFO for inventory valuation (\$4.1 × 0.21). Therefore, *NOPAT* for GIS would increase by the net amount of \$3.2 to \$2,289.2.

Use of different methods of inventory valuation creates dissimilar information and affects the comparability of financial statements. In order to use GIS as a source of information to aid our understanding of the industry and the competitive environment in which it and K operate, it is important to ensure consistent (i.e., comparable) accounting methods are being used. For GIS, the necessary adjustment to its financial statements is minor in amount but, the process is nonetheless important.

ADJUSTMENT B: OPERATING LEASES

LO3: Analyze the effects of leasing transactions both before and after the new leasing standard.

Historically, operating leases have been the most common form of off-balance-sheet financing undertaken by companies.[8] The term "off-balance sheet financing" refers to a financing transaction that is not reported on the balance sheet. Note that neither the liability nor the related asset is recorded on the balance sheet. Even though U.S. GAAP has required detailed footnote disclosures, some managers believe that keeping such assets and liabilities off the balance sheet improves the market's perception of company performance and financial condition. U.S. GAAP defines criteria to be used when determining whether a lease is accounted for using the capital or operating approach. Managers, seeking off-balance-sheet financing, structure their leases around the U.S. GAAP rules. These efforts presume that the market is somewhat inefficient, a notion that persists despite empirical evidence suggesting that analysts and other informed investors adjust balance sheets to include these assets and liabilities, which managers have excluded.

Classification of Leases and the Financial Statement Effects

In the first quarter of 2016, the FASB issued ASU 2016-02 and the IASB issued IFRS 16, which changed lease reporting. Previously, U.S. GAAP identified two approaches for the reporting of leases by the lessee:[9]

- *Capital lease method*: This method required that both the lease asset (part of operating assets) and the lease liability (a financial liability) be reported on the balance sheet. The lease asset is depreciated as with any other long-term asset, thereby reducing *NOPAT*. The lease liability is amortized in the same manner as debt, where lease payments are separated into interest expense and principal repayment, both of which are part of free cash flows from operations to the lessor, who is a debt holder (FCF^{FIN}).
- *Operating lease method*: Under this method, neither the operating lease asset nor the financial lease liability were reported on the balance sheet. Lease payments were recorded as rent expense, often as part of selling, general, and administrative expenses, thereby reducing *NOPAT* of the lessee company.

Both the new U.S. GAAP and IFRS standards substantially changed the accounting by requiring the reporting of assets and liabilities for all leases with a term greater than 12 months. The new U.S. GAAP standard has two approaches:

- *Capital lease method:* This method did not change.
- *Operating lease method:* Now, the operating lease right-of-use asset and the financial lease liability are reported on the balance sheet. Lease payments are still recorded as rent (lease) expense and often included in selling, general, and administrative expenses, thereby reducing *NOPAT* of the lessee company.

Classifying leases as operating rather than capital has differing financial reporting consequences for the lessee under the old and new standards:

[8] This discussion of operating leases is about the accounting in the financial statements of the lessee. A discussion of accounting and operating leases for the lessor follows later in the chapter.

[9] The method of reporting leases does not affect our calculation of operating value, but it will affect the adjustment made to the value of operations when calculating the value of equity as discussed in a subsequent chapter.

Old Standard	New Standard
1. The lease asset is not reported on the balance sheet. Thus, operating asset turnover (*ATO*) is higher because reported *NOA* (the denominator in *ATO*) is lower.	1. The lease right-of-use asset is reported on the balance sheet, so there is very little difference in *NOA*. The yearly amortization (equivalent to depreciation) on the right-of-use asset will be equivalent to the reduction in the lease liability.
2. The lease liability is not reported on the balance sheet. This means that balance sheet measures of financial leverage (e.g., the total liabilities-to-equity ratio) are improved. Many managers believe the reduced financial leverage will result in a better credit rating and, consequently, a lower interest rate on borrowed funds. Without adjustment (i.e., capitalization of operating leases), the return on *NOA* (*RNOA* = *NOPAT*/Average *NOA*) appears higher, as is the return on equity.	2. The lease liability is reported on the balance sheet, so there is no effect on financial leverage.
3. During the early years of the lease term, rent expense reported for an operating lease is less than the depreciation and the interest expense that would be reported for a capital lease.[10] This means that net income associated with operating leases is higher in those early years. Note that, if the company is growing and continually adding assets financed with operating leases, the level of net income may continue to remain higher during the growth period. Generally, *NOPAT* is lower for an operating lease in all years because all of the rent expense is an operating expense whereas only depreciation expense (and not interest expense) is an operating expense for a capital lease.	3. Reporting of income statement is essentially unchanged under the new standard.

The benefits of applying the operating method for leases under the old standard were obvious to managers, thus leading some to avoid lease capitalization. Furthermore, the lease accounting standards (both old and new) include rigid requirements relating to capitalization. Whenever accounting standards are rigidly defined, managers can structure transactions to meet the letter of the standard to achieve a desired accounting result even when the essence and economics of the transaction would suggest a different accounting treatment. At this point, whether the new standards will alter the efforts of managers to achieve particular reporting outcomes is still unclear.

The Economics of Leases

The underlying economic issue when considering leases is whether the company is making payments to the lessor that are operating or financial in nature. The reporting model for operating leases assumes that the lease payments are rentals paid to a creditor for the operations of the firm (they arise in a manner similar to renting an apartment). The capital lease assumes that the lease payments are composed of principal and interest paid throughout the lease term similar to the payments associated with long-term debt.

Despite the financial reporting differences, choosing to account for a lease as capital or operating does not change the fact that the company has acquired the use of an asset and has agreed to make payments as a result. For this reason, analysts and users of financial information often adjust the accounting in a process called constructive capitalization, which attempts to reconstruct the financial ratios to what they would have been had the operating leases been capital leases. This process not only allows us to see the full amount of resources (the operating asset) and the related obligation (the financial liability), it also recognizes that a portion of the payment is financial in nature (effectively interest expense). In doing so, we will increase comparability, better capture all elements of operating activities, and improve our estimates of value.

[10] This is true even if the company employs straight-line depreciation for the lease asset because interest expense accrues on the outstanding balance of the lease liability, which is higher in the early years of the lease life. Note that a company that routinely acquires assets through capital leases is likely to have leases at every stage, and the net income in the current year is unchanged by whether the leases are operating or capital in nature. Further exploration of the effect on income will follow later in this section.

The extent to which operating leases are used varies by industry. The airline industry tends to acquire most of its fleets of airplanes using operating leases and, therefore, these operating assets are not recorded as operating assets. Sir David Tweedie, then chairman of the International Accounting Standards Board, famously said, "One of my great ambitions before I die is to fly in an aircraft that is on an airline's balance sheet."[11] With the new leasing standards, his dream is finally realized!

Determining the Lease Standard Used

The first step to adjusting the financial statements is to understand whether the company is reporting under the old or new accounting standards. Even more, you must understand that the reporting may differ between years in the same financial statement! For most companies, the new standards will be implemented in the first year beginning after December 15, 2018; that is, calendar year 2019 and later. Delta Air Lines (DAL) disclosed on page 45 of its Form 10-K for December 31, 2018, the following (emphasis added):

> In 2016, the FASB issued ASU No. 2016-02, "Leases (Topic 842)." This ASU and subsequently issued amendments require leases with durations greater than 12 months to be recognized on the balance sheet. The standard is effective for interim and annual reporting periods beginning after December 15, 2018, and early adoption is permitted.
>
> In July 2018, the FASB issued ASU No. 2018-11, "Targeted Improvements—Leases (Topic 842)." This update provides an optional transition method that allows entities to elect to apply the standard using the modified retrospective approach at its effective date, versus recasting the prior years presented. If elected, an entity would recognize a cumulative-effect adjustment to the opening balance of retained earnings in the year of adoption. We adopted the new standard as of January 1, 2018 during the December quarter using the transition method that provides for a cumulative-effect adjustment to retained earnings upon adoption and have recast our 2018 quarterly results. ***The Consolidated Financial Statements for the fiscal year ended December 31, 2018 are presented under the new standard, while comparative years presented are not adjusted and continue to be reported in accordance with our historical accounting policy.***

DAL reported 2018 leases under the new standard; this means that for the operating leases, there is a right-of-use asset and lease liability computed and shown. However, the 2017 and 2016 information remained computed under the old standard. Clearly, we have issues with comparability within these financial statements, and forecasting is nearly impossible with data that is not consistent. Thus, we need to determine what adjustments are needed to operating leases under the new (2018 for DAL) and old (2017 and 2016 for DAL) standards.

Understanding when standards are implemented will be critical to our analyses. Companies have some latitude as to when the standards are implemented due to the possibility of early adoption. GIS disclosed the following in its May 2018 10-K (emphasis added):

> In February 2016, the FASB issued new accounting requirements for accounting, presentation and classification of leases. This will result in most leases being capitalized as a right of use asset with a related liability on our Consolidated Balance Sheets. ***The requirements of the new standard are effective for annual reporting periods beginning after December 15, 2018, and interim periods within those annual periods, which for us is the first quarter of fiscal 2020.*** We are in the process of implementing lease accounting software and analyzing the impact of this standard on our results of operations and financial position. Based on our assessment to date, we expect this guidance will have a material impact on our Consolidated Balance Sheets due to the amount of our lease commitments but we are unable to quantify the impact at this time.

Thus, the adjustments for GIS in each of the years examined will follow the methods related to the old standard. It also should be noted that, despite GIS being "unable to quantify the impact at this time," our constructive capitalization at least gets us in the ballpark.

[11] Excerpt taken from a speech at Empire Club of Canada in Toronto on April 25, 2008.

PAY CLOSE ATTENTION TO COMPANY'S ADOPTION DATES

You must know the standards employed by a company in preparing each year of the financial statements to determine the required adjustments. As companies transition to the new standards, look for disclosures such as those for DAL and GIS to aid in determining adoption status. Potential differences in the adoption timing reinforce the need to ensure understanding of the information and adjustment to achieve consistency. Once adjustments have been made, whether under the new or old standards, we will implicitly forecast adjusted data.

Example 1: Operating Lease Adjustments for Delta Air Lines (DAL)

Disclosures and resulting adjustments are very different under the old and new leasing standards. To demonstrate the required adjustments, we will work with DAL in 2018 (new standard) and also consider prior years (old standard). We can utilize these disclosures to form an estimate of *NOA* and *NOPAT* using constructive capitalization had the operating leases instead been capital leases. This capitalization process involves several steps.

	Old Standard	New Standard
1.	Determine the discount rate.	Same.
2.	Compute the present value of future lease payments this year and last.	Not required.
3.	Adjust the balance sheet to include the present value from step 2 as a lease liability, and include the related asset.	Not required because the right-of-use asset and related liability are already recognized.
4.	Adjust the income statement to include depreciation and interest in lieu of the rent (lease) expense.	Same.[12]

There are at least three approaches to determining the appropriate discount rate for our analysis: (1) If the company discloses capital leases in addition to the operating leases, we can impute (infer) an implicit rate of return on those capital leases—this is the rate that yields the present value computed by the company given the future capital lease payments; (2) use the rate that corresponds to the company's credit rating or the rate from any recent borrowings involving intermediate-term secured obligations; or (3) employ the cost of debt capital because the operating lease is essentially a borrowing from debt holders (which is a reason why we are making an adjustment). Whichever method is used, one must verify that the rate obtained is reasonable. Note also that the capitalization will be done using a pretax interest rate, and then the adjustment to *NOPAT* will be done on an after-tax basis.

For DAL in 2018, Note 8 provided the following useful information on the operating leases:

Weighted-average discount rate for operating leases		3.69%
Operating lease right-of-use assets		$5,994
Operating lease liability at year-end:		
Current maturities of operating leases	$ 955	
Noncurrent operating leases.	5,801	$6,756
Operating lease cost.		$ 994

Because the right-of-use asset of $5,994 and lease liability totaling $6,756 have already been computed and included in the balance sheet under the new standard, the only adjustment necessary

[12] Under the new leasing standards, the right-of-use asset is amortized. This is equivalent to the depreciation of the asset established under constructive capitalization. We will use the terms *amortization* and *depreciation* interchangeably in describing the yearly reduction in the lease-related asset.

is to the income statement. We will seek to reclassify the portion of the $994 operating lease cost that should be considered as a financial (interest) expense. For 2017 and before, we will need both the balance sheet and income statement adjustments. We now walk through how to compute the required calculations under both sets of rules using DAL.

Step 1: Determine Discount Rate. The discount rate for 2018 of 3.69 percent is provided in DAL's Note 8. For 2017, we can infer the year-end discount rate on the capital leases for DAL by utilizing DAL's disclosures of the future payments and the present value of the capital leases in the footnotes. These disclosures allow us to compute an internal rate of return, which equates the future payments to the disclosed present value of those payments. **Exhibit 5.3** shows the required payments by DAL under capital leases, as disclosed in 2017.

EXHIBIT 5.3 Delta Air Lines' 2017 Required Payments under Capital Leases—Note 8

2018	2019	2020	2021	2022	Thereafter	Total
$116	$92	$65	$41	$24	$126	$464

DAL also disclosed in the notes that the present value of these payments was $394. We will assume that the portion labeled *"Thereafter"* will be paid at the same amount per year as the payment in 2022. This means that, of the $126 labeled *"Thereafter,"* $24 will be paid in each subsequent year until the total has been paid. To estimate the inherent interest rate in the capital leases, we recognize that the payments listed in **Exhibit 5.3** will not all occur at the end of the year but, rather, throughout the year. Because payments happen throughout the year, we make the assumption that they will happen evenly. This is equivalent to assuming each payment for DAL will happen on June 30.[13] These payments and assumptions allow us to estimate an interest rate related to DAL's capital leases.

Thus, in **Exhibit 5.4**, utilizing the XIRR function (i.e., internal rate of return with dates specified) in Excel, we can use we use dates in column A and the values in column B to calculate the implied rate of return. The formula in cell C1, XIRR(B1:B12,A1:A12), yields an implied interest rate of return of 5.28 percent.

EXHIBIT 5.4 Calculation of 2017 Rate of Return Implied by DAL's Capital Leases

	A	B	C
1	12/31/2017	–394	5.280%
2	6/30/2018	116	
3	6/30/2019	92	
4	6/30/2020	65	
5	6/30/2021	41	
6	6/30/2022	24	
7	6/30/2023	24	
8	6/30/2024	24	
9	6/30/2025	24	
10	6/30/2026	24	
11	6/30/2027	24	
12	6/30/2028	6	

Remember that our discounting of the operating leases should use the discount rate that would relate to a leasing transaction. Still, it is important to evaluate the number we have calculated in

[13] The assumption that payments happen evenly throughout the year will be revisited in Chapter 13 when we make a mid-year adjustment as part of equity valuation.

light of the cost of debt capital for the company. In 2017's Note 6, DAL reported secured aircraft financings with interest rates ranging from 1.81 to 8.02 percent. Given that DAL reported in Note 7 that the items under lease (does not specify capital versus operating) were "aircraft, airport terminals, maintenance facilities, ticket offices and other property and equipment," it is reassuring that the riskiness of the leases is in line with that of its borrowings for aircraft.

Before proceeding with the use of 5.28 percent, it is prudent to consider another option. We could also compute as a proxy for the cost of debt capital the borrowing rate implied by interest expense and debt of DAL. In 2017, interest expense was $396 while average current and long-term debt and finance leases was $8,083. Together, these imply a cost of borrowing of 4.90 percent. This confirms that the estimated rate of 5.28 percent is reasonable. Had we computed an implied rate from the capital leases that was much higher than that observed in borrowings or implied by interest expense, we would not have been willing to use it. We expect an answer consistent with other borrowings!

Repeating this process for each of the prior 2 years yields estimated rates of 8.85 and 10.89 percent implied by the capital leases in 2016 and 2015, respectively. For the borrowing rate implied by interest expense and debt, the estimates of the rates are 4.95 and 5.78 percent in 2016 and 2015, respectively. While the 2017 implied rate of 5.28 percent looks reasonable and will be used going forward, for 2016 and 2015 the implied rates look high. For calculating adjustments in 2016 and 2015, we would instead use the cost of debt capital proxies of 4.95 and 5.78 percent.

Step 1 Summary

Year	Standards	Interest Rate	Source
2018	New	3.69%	Disclosed by DAL
2017	Old	5.28%	Implied by capital leases
2016	Old	4.95%	Cost-of-debt proxy

Step 2: Compute Liability. While we have been provided with the amount of the lease liability for 2018, under the old standard, this amount had to be estimated. The notes to the 2017 financial statements for DAL reported future required payments on operating leases, as shown in **Exhibit 5.5**.

EXHIBIT 5.5 Delta Air Lines' 2017 Required Payments under Operating Leases—Note 9

2018	2019	2020	2021	2022	Thereafter	Total
$1,735	$1,589	$1,430	$1,156	$1,036	$9,290	$16,236

We can use the amount and timing of these future payments existing at the end of 2017 and the 5.28 percent interest rate at the end of 2017 from step 1 to estimate the outstanding liability. Similar to what we assumed on the capital leases interest rate computation above, the *thereafter* years will have payments equal to the 2022 magnitude until the amount is satisfied, and payments are computed based on June 30 of the year listed. This yields the estimated present value of operating lease payments for DAL (all dollar amounts are in millions), as shown in **Exhibit 5.6** (on the next page).

Our estimate is that the present value of DAL's operating lease commitments is $11,959 as of December 31, 2017.

Step 2 Summary

Year	Standards	Present Value of Future Lease Payments	Source
2018	New	$ 6,756	Disclosed by DAL
2017	Old	$11,959	Computed using disclosed payments
2016	Old	$ 8,924	Computed using disclosed payments

Step 3: Adjust Balance Sheet. For 2018, no adjustment to DAL's balance sheet is needed because, under the new standard, the right-of-use asset and lease liability are already recognized.

EXHIBIT 5.6 DAL's Estimated Lease Liability

Date	Operating Lease Payment	Present Value
June 30, 2018.	1,735	1,691
June 30, 2019.	1,589	1,471
June 30, 2020.	1,430	1,257
June 30, 2021.	1,156	965
June 30, 2022.	1,036	822
June 30, 2023*	1,036	781
June 30, 2024.	1,036	742
June 30, 2025.	1,036	704
June 30, 2026.	1,036	669
June 30, 2027.	1,036	635
June 30, 2028.	1,036	604
June 30, 2029.	1,036	573
June 30, 2030.	1,036	545
June 30, 2031.	1,002	500
Total	$16,236	$11,959

*Assuming payments continue at 2022 amount.

We have computed the 2017 lease liability as $11,959. But what amount should be recorded as the 2017-related asset? Do we record an asset of the same amount or a different amount? Normally, we would expect that the asset and liability are the same amount only at the beginning and end of the lease. This is confirmed by the 2018 disclosure that at December 31, 2018, the right-of-use asset was $5,994 and the lease liability was $6,756. Determining an appropriate asset value would require knowing the original cost, useful life of the asset (which is not automatically the same as the lease period), estimated salvage value, and the depreciation method that would have been used.

Given all this uncertainty around computing a value for the asset, it is unclear that we would arrive at a better approximation under the old leasing standards than recording the asset at an amount equal to the computed liability. As such, we make the assumption that the right-of-use asset value is fairly approximated by the amount of the estimated lease liability. (At a minimum, this is a much better estimate than not having recorded an asset at all under the old operating lease standards!) Note that some textbooks and/or professionals attempt to refine the asset value estimate via assumed depreciable lives or rule of thumb, such as the asset equals 70 percent of the estimated liability. For DAL, we assume the asset is $11,959, equal to the computed liability.

Step 3 Summary

Year	Standards	Increase in Right-of-Use Asset	Increase in Lease Liability
2018	New	Not needed, already included	Not needed, already included
2017	Old	$11,959	$11,959
2016	Old	$ 8,924	$ 8,924

Step 4: Adjust Income Statement. Capitalizing operating leases affects *NOPAT* via the addition of depreciation related to the lease equipment and the removal of the operating lease payments, which had been reported as rent expense, typically included in selling, general, and administrative expenses. This adjustment was needed under the old standard and continues to be needed under the new standard. The amount of payments made under operating leases was a required disclosure for each income statement period under the old standard and is still required under the new standard. DAL disclosed that its rental expense under the operating basis totaled $994 in 2018 and was approximately $1,300 in 2017.

To determine the portion of these payments to be considered as interest, we utilize the borrowing rate for the year and the average of the lease liability at the beginning and end of the year. For 2018, the beginning lease liability was $11,959, and the ending lease liability was $6,756. The borrowing rate disclosed for operating leases was 3.69 percent, implying interest expense of $345. For 2017, the beginning and ending lease liabilities were calculated as $8,924 and $11,959, respectively. The interest rate computed from the capital lease disclosures in step 1 was 5.28 percent. This implies interest for 2017 of $551.

For calculating the reduction of the additional right-of-use asset (the new standard records amortization expense rather than depreciation), we are back to the problem discussed above of estimating the useful life of the asset, estimated salvage value, and the depreciation method that would have been used. One option would be to assume that the useful life is the same as the amount of years used in computing the liability. Then, we could apply straight-line depreciation using a zero salvage value. This, however, is just an estimate based on ad hoc assumptions. An alternate approach (that is also just the result of an assumption) is that the depreciation equals the principal payment; that is, the amount of the lease payments that were not interest expense.

Step 4 Summary

Year	Standards	Decrease in Lease Expense	Increase in Interest Expense	Increase in Amortization Expense
2018	New	$ 994	$345	$649
2017	Old	$1,300	$551	$749
2016	Old	$1,300	$433	$867

The adjustments under both the old and the new leasing standards increase *NOA* (lease liability is financial in nature). The adjustments also increase *NOPAT* due to reclassification of a portion of lease expense as interest expense.[14] For companies in industries that more heavily utilize operating leases, the increase in *NOA* and *NOPAT* can be almost 30 percent each! Clearly, capitalization of operating leases can alter our understanding of the operating activities of the company. We need to obtain comparable and reliable estimates of operating *PM* and *ATO*, as will be discussed in Chapter 6. Further, it will affect our forecasts of future operating activities in Chapter 7 and, therefore, the estimate of value for a company like DAL.

Example 2: General Mills

Now that we have estimated the effects of capitalizing operating leases for DAL, we return to our focus company, GIS. Two things differ from DAL: the new leasing standards have not been adopted in any of the years analyzed, and GIS has almost no capital leases and only a small amount of operating leases. Still, we can utilize GIS' disclosures to demonstrate the necessary operating lease adjustment. Note 15 of the May 2018 GIS financial statements reported future required payments on operating leases (dollar amounts in millions) as shown in **Exhibit 5.7**.

EXHIBIT 5.7 GIS' Required Payments under Operating Leases—Note 15

2019	2020	2021	2022	2023	Thereafter	Total
$137.4	$115.7	$92.3	$70.9	$51.8	$91.2	$559.3

Step 1: Determine Discount Rate. GIS does not have sufficient capital leasing activity to require provision of information that would allow us to estimate the implied interest rate. Thus, to illustrate the capitalization of operating leases, we consider the weighted-average interest rate on

[14] The adjustment to interest expense will result in reallocation of tax between operating and financial activities. As a result, classifying $345 as interest expense in 2018 will increase *NOPAT* by $273 [$345 × (1 − 0.21)].

GIS' debt as disclosed in Note 8 of the May 2018 financial statements. The weighted-average rates are 3.61 percent and 3.25 percent as of May 2018 and 2017, respectively. We also consider the borrowing rate implied by the interest expense and interest-bearing debt of 3.08 percent and 3.42 percent at May 2018 and 2017, respectively. Given that they appear reasonable, we choose to use the rates calculated based on the debt disclosures in Note 8. Note, again, that the capitalization is done using a pretax interest rate and then the adjustment to *NOPAT* will be done on an after-tax basis.

Step 1 Summary

Year	Standards	Interest Rate	Source
2018	Old	3.61%	GIS debt disclosures
2017	Old	3.25%	GIS debt disclosures
2016	Old	3.58%	GIS debt disclosures

Step 2: Compute Liability. After choosing a discount rate in step 1, we compute the present value of future operating lease payments. We assume that future years after 2023 will have payments equal to the fifth year until the amount labeled *"Thereafter"* is satisfied. This yields our estimate that the omitted liability related to recording a portion of the leases of GIS as operating rather than capital is $1,111.6 as of May 2018 (the estimated present value of operating lease payments for GIS assuming even payments throughout each year). If we repeat steps 1 and 2 for the prior year, we find the estimated unrecorded obligation at May 2017 was $1,013.2.

Step 2 Summary

Year	Standards	Present Value of Future Lease Payments	Source
2018	Old	$1,111.6	Computed using disclosed payments
2017	Old	$1,013.2	Computed using disclosed payments
2016	Old	$ 793.5	Computed using disclosed payments

Step 3: Adjust Balance Sheet. Having computed the present value of the future operating lease payments for GIS, we adjust *NOA* upward at May 2018 by $1,111.6 to include this additional operating right-of-use asset. The financial liabilities will be increased by the $1,111.6 to recognize this implied borrowing.

Step 3 Summary

Year	Standards	Increase in Right-of-Use Asset	Increase in Lease Liability
2018	Old	$1,111.6	$1,111.6
2017	Old	$1,013.2	$1,013.2
2016	Old	$ 793.5	$ 793.5

Step 4: Adjust Income Statement. Capitalizing operating leases affects *NOPAT* via the addition of amortization of the right-of-use asset as well as the removal of the operating lease payments, which had been reported as rent expense, typically included in selling, general, and administrative expenses. The amount of payments made under operating leases is a required disclosure for each income statement period, making this information readily available. GIS disclosed that the amount of operating lease payments in the year ended May 2018 was $189.4. We estimated an unrecorded obligation of $1,013.2 and $1,111.6 at the beginning and end of the period, respectively. The average amount of lease obligation and our estimated interest rate of 3.61 percent yield an interest expense in the current year of $38.3. Therefore, we will remove the payment of $189.4 from selling, general, and administrative expenses and reclassify it as $38.3 of interest expense and the remainder of $151.1 as amortization expense. Using an assumed current tax rate of 21 percent for GIS, the net increase to *NOPAT* is $30.3 ([remove $189.4 rent expense and add $151.5 depreciation expense] times [1 – 0.21]).

Step 4 Summary				
Year	Standards	Decrease in Lease Expense	Increase in Interest Expense	Increase in Amortization Expense
2018	Old	$189.4	$38.3	$151.1
2017	Old	$118.1	$29.3	$ 88.8
2016	Old	$189.1	$28.4	$160.7

For GIS, the adjustments in the year ended May 2018 (increasing *NOA* by $1,111.6 and increasing *NOPAT* by $30.3) are relatively minor, but they are calculated for completeness.

ACCOUNTING FOR THE ADJUSTMENT: CAPITALIZATION OF OPERATING LEASES

For DAL and GIS, we could write the following two journal entries to record these adjustments in their most recent years:

	DAL		GIS	
	Dr	Cr	Dr	Cr
Asset under capital lease	$ 0		$1,111.6	
Capitalized lease liability		$ 0		$1,111.6
Amortization expense	649		151.1	
Interest expense	345		38.3	
Selling, general and administrative expense		994		189.4
	$994	$994	$1,301.0	$1,301.0

Note that there is not an adjustment to the amount of tax expense or tax payable. The assumption is that the total expense in the period has remained the same; expenses are reclassified, but the amount is unchanged. This will not preclude our adjustments to *NOPAT* and *FEAT* where the allocation of tax will be affected by this adjustment during reformulation.

LESSORS' OPERATING LEASES

Generally, lessors prefer a direct financing or sales-type lease (equivalent to capital lease for lessee) because they result in income being recognized earlier during the lease. Historically, leases and lessors would structure leases, via judgments and estimates, in such a way that both parties achieved a classification that had income occur earlier in the lease term. It is not uncommon to see a lessor record a particular lease of an asset, such as machinery, as direct financing while the lessee recorded it as operating. Prior to the new accounting standards, the result was the physical machinery not appearing on either set of books!

Given that few lessors were inclined to use operating leases, detailing the process for adjustment akin to constructive capitalization is generally not explored. It should be noted that the new leasing standard left lessor accounting virtually unchanged because it was not seen as the area of concern that lessee accounting was. Still, we can consider what would occur if we wanted to also adjust the lessor from operating to capital lease treatment. We will first consider the balance sheet effect and then follow with the income statement.

For the balance sheet of the lessor, an operating lease would show the asset (machinery). The capital lease would instead show a different asset, a lease receivable. (Assume, for the sake of argument, they are the same dollar amount even though they may slightly differ.) If the operations of the lessor are leasing, the asset (the machinery or the lease receivable) would be an operating asset, and there is no change in *NOA*. If the operations of the lessor do not include leasing as a primary activity, the lease receivable would be a financial asset, and the move from operating to capital lease accounting would have caused a reduction in *NOA* while also changing the amount of *NFL*.

continued

continued from previous page

For the income statement of the lessor, an operating lease results in lease revenue as well as depreciation on the machinery, with the difference being the profit on the lease. The capital lease would instead result in interest revenue (the excess of the cash received would be a principal payment on the lease receivable). To the extent that the lease revenue less depreciation approximates the amount of interest revenue, there is no effect on net income. If the operations of the lessor do not include leasing as a primary activity, the interest revenue would be financial, and there is a reduction in *NOPAT* while also changing the amount of *FEAT*.

On both the balance sheet and the income statement, the leasing would need to be classified as a financing activity for there to be a substantial effect. That said, both the *NOA* and *NOPAT* are affected, as are measures of financial activities. This will result in adjustments to cost of capital and valuation calculations. Because most leases originate from leasing companies, there are not too many situations where adjustments parallel to those detailed in this section will be required for the lessor.

ADJUSTMENT C: SPECIAL-PURPOSE ENTITIES

LO4: Discuss the potential impacts of special-purpose entities on valuation.

Special-purpose entities (SPEs) allow companies to structure projects or transactions to achieve a number of financial advantages. SPEs have long been used in and are an integral part of corporate finance. Many SPEs have the following characteristics:

- A sponsoring company (e.g., **Ford Credit**, the finance subsidiary of **Ford Motor Company**) forms a subsidiary that is capitalized entirely with equity, which creates a bankruptcy remote structure so that, even if Ford Credit becomes bankrupt, neither it nor its creditors will be able to access the assets of the subsidiary. This reduces the risk for subsequent investors.
- The subsidiary purchases assets from the sponsoring company and sells them to a securitization (off-balance-sheet) trust (the SPE), which purchases the assets using borrowed funds (here, the SPE purchases receivables from Ford Credit's subsidiary using cash from investors).
- The SPE uses cash flows from the acquired assets to repay its debt (here, the SPE collects receivables and uses the funds to repay any borrowings).

The sponsoring company benefits in two ways. First, SPEs create direct economic benefits by speeding up receipt of the company's operating cash flows and by mitigating certain types of risk. Second, SPEs create indirect economic benefits by providing financial reporting benefits and alternatives. These indirect benefits derive from having assets and their related debt moved off the balance sheet. Also, the SPE owns the sponsoring company's former assets. Thus, the sponsoring company enjoys an improved asset-turnover ratio (i.e., assets are typically less in the denominator of the turnover ratio) and an improved financial leverage ratio (i.e., liabilities are less in the numerator of the debt-to-equity ratio).

Two common uses of SPEs as financing tools are asset securitization and project and/or real estate financing. In asset securitization, consumer finance companies, retailers, and financial subsidiaries of manufacturing companies commonly use SPEs to securitize (sell) their financial assets. As Ford Credit provides financing to customers who purchase autos from Ford Motor Company, it accumulates the receivables on its balance sheet. Periodically, through a subsidiary, Ford Credit packages certain receivables and sells them to its SPE, which funds the purchase by selling certificates entitling the holder to a portion of the cash receipts from eventual collection of receivables. Ford Credit does not provide any other form of protection to the outside certificate holders (its footnote indicates that the receivables are sold "without recourse," meaning without collection rights against Ford Credit or its parent, Ford Motor Company).

The credit ratings of Ford Motor Company have declined in recent years, thus increasing the cost of unsecured loans, as well as limiting Ford's ability to borrow funds. In response, Ford has increased its use of SPEs as a financing source. This funding mechanism is now an important source of liquidity for the company, as Ford Credit's cost of debt capital is substantially less, and exhibits less volatility, than that of Ford Motor Company. Thus, Ford's use of SPEs as a funding source provides necessary liquidity and capital at a substantially lower interest rate. Due to the SPE's limited scope of operations and its isolation from the general business risk of the parent company, the SPE's lenders face lower risk of default and can, therefore, charge a comparatively lower rate of interest on money they lend to the SPE.

In project and/or real estate financing, the SPE is used to finance construction projects. For example, a sponsoring company desires to construct a manufacturing plant. It establishes an SPE and executes a contract with the SPE to build the plant and to later purchase output from the plant. The SPE uses the contract, and the newly constructed manufacturing plant assets, to collateralize debt, which it issues to finance the plant's construction. The sponsoring company obtains the benefits of the plant but does not recognize either the SPE asset or the related liability on its balance sheet. The sponsoring company has commitments with the SPE, labeled "executory contracts," but U.S. GAAP currently does not require such contracts to be recognized on the balance sheet, nor does it even require footnote disclosure of these contracts.

A slight variation is to add leasing to this transaction. To illustrate, assume a company wants to construct an office building. It establishes an SPE to construct and finance the building and then leases the building from the SPE under an operating lease. As we explained earlier in this chapter, if the lease is structured as an operating lease, neither the lease asset nor the lease obligation is reported on the company's balance sheet. Thus, the company obtains the use and benefit of the building without recording either the building or the related debt on its balance sheet.

SPEs, such as those Ford uses to securitize its loan and lease assets, must be consolidated by whichever company has the power to direct the activities of the SPE and the right to receive its benefits (or absorb the losses). For companies that issue common stock, consolidation means that the balance sheet and income statement of the SPE are reported with those of the parent company. The consolidation of SPEs is no different, and their financial statements must be combined with those of the sponsoring company (Ford Credit in this case).

The effect of consolidating SPEs is to report both the loan and lease receivables on Ford's consolidated balance sheet as well as the liabilities of the SPE. Similarly, the loan and lease income are reported in Ford's income statement together with the SPE's expenses, including interest expense on borrowed funds. As a result, the securitization of consolidated SPEs is fully reflected in Ford's financial statements. Further, companies are required to provide extensive disclosures relating to the magnitude of the assets securitized and the effects (and risks) on their liquidity of reliable access to securitization credit markets.

Despite the fact that SPEs are consolidated in the financial statements of the sponsoring company, the securitization process continues to provide a lower-cost financing source to companies by reducing credit risk for the lenders due to the legal structure. Accordingly, SPEs will continue to be part of the business landscape. As such, there are at least two implications for analyses related to SPEs:

- *Cost of debt capital*: As discussed, SPEs reduce business risk and bankruptcy risk for their lenders. Consequently, the sponsoring company is able to obtain capital at a lower cost. Ford Motor Company (a manufacturer), for example, has witnessed a reduction in its credit ratings and a consequent increase in its cost of borrowed funds. Ordinarily, its poor credit rating would be ascribed to its subsidiaries as well, including its finance subsidiary. Using SPEs, however, the finance subsidiary, Ford Credit, is able to obtain financing at lower interest rates, which allows it to pass along that lower cost in the form of lower interest rates on auto and other loans to its customers. Without that financing source, Ford Credit would be less competitive in the marketplace than, financially stronger, financial institutions.
- *Liquidity*: Financial institutions, and finance subsidiaries of manufacturing companies, rely on a business model of generating a high volume of loans, each of which carries a relatively small profit (i.e., the spread of the interest rate over the cost of the funds is small). If they were forced to hold all of those loans on their own balance sheets, they would eventually need to raise costly equity capital to balance the increase in debt financing. This would also serve to reduce their competitiveness in the marketplace. These companies must, therefore, be able to package loans for sale (as SPEs), a crucial source of liquidity.

Given the importance of the cash flows contributed by the Ford Credit financing subsidiary to Ford Motor Company, analysts would be concerned about the welfare of the overall entity were there indications that its SPE financing sources would no longer be available (e.g., if further accounting standards limited Ford's ability to remove these loans from its consolidated balance sheet and record their transfer to the SPE as a sale). Analysts would also be concerned if the credit markets no longer favored this SPE structure as a financing mechanism (e.g., if the presumed bankruptcy protection of the SPEs was ultimately proven to be false following the bankruptcy of the sponsoring company and the consequent bankruptcy of an SPE that it sponsored). Neither of these events has occurred, and lenders rely on legal opinions that SPEs are "bankruptcy remote." Analysts must always assess these risks when assessing the financial strength of companies that rely on the SPE financial structure.

Given that the SPEs are consolidated into the parent company, our analyses of *NOPAT* and *NOA* are not affected by their existence. However, as noted, we must understand their effect on the cost of debt capital (discussed in a later chapter) and on the liquidity of the company. The transactions within the SPE may be of interest because something such as a sale of receivables *by the SPE* will alter the consolidated amount of receivables reducing *NOA*. If one company sells receivables and another does not, we see a reduction in comparability. Usually, because the quantity of receivables sold through the SPE is not disclosed, we are not able to directly adjust *NOA*. Still, understanding the use of SPEs helps shape our analysis of profitability and our forecasts of future operations in the next two chapters.

LO5: Capture the economic effects of share-based compensation in the adjusted financial statements.

ADJUSTMENT D: SHARE-BASED COMPENSATION

Companies use various forms of share-based compensation (SBC), such as employee stock options (ESOs), restricted stock, stock appreciation rights, and/or performance- or time-based share units as a means to compensate employees and to better align the interests of employees and shareholders.[15] While accounting recognizes (as an expense) the grant date value of SBC, the accounting does not fully capture the economics of the transaction. The differing degree to which companies utilize these forms of SBC creates a lack of comparability and omits an economic cost of the company unless we adjust the financial statements. At the extreme, one company could choose to pay all compensation in the form of SBC and show almost no wage expense! More important, accounting fails to recognize the liability existing due to outstanding prior commitments to employees arising from SBC. The implied transfer to employees as share price increases over time is also omitted from the financial statements.

The notion behind the use of SBC is that employees will work harder to increase the stock price of their company when they can benefit directly from future price increases. Because an employee with stock options can purchase stock at a fixed price and resell it at the prevailing (expectedly higher) market price, the SBC creates the possibility of a future gain. While an equivalent expected (present) value could currently be given in cash, unlike cash compensation, options can align the interests of employees with those of shareholders—both benefit from a future increase in stock price.

USE OF RESTRICTED STOCK OR STOCK UNITS

Companies may choose to compensate employees with restricted stock or stock units instead of with stock options. Increasingly, companies have moved away from stock options in favor of restricted stock, restricted stock units, or performance stock units as compensation for multiple reasons. First, stock options were seen as creating excess compensation during recent stock-market booms and have received a large amount of negative press. Second, stock options can create incentives for managers to take on excessive company risk because the value of an option increases with company

continued

[15] An interesting, often underappreciated, fact is that SBC expense pervades the income statement. Companies often allocate their SBC expense to various income statement items, including cost of sales, research and development, sales and marketing expenses, and general and administrative expenses similar to other items considered as salaries or overhead.

continued from previous page

risk. The stock units do not create such severe risk-taking incentives. Third, there are certain tax advantages to stock units versus stock options.

Under restricted stock and stock unit plans, the company transfers shares to the employee, but the shares are restricted in that they cannot be sold until the end of a vesting period. Restricted stock units differ from restricted stock in two key ways: First, the company does not distribute shares of stock to employees until certain conditions are met. Second, the number of shares ultimately given to employees is typically a function of their performance relative to specified targets. The accounting for these alternatives is similar to that which we describe for stock options. Specifically, compensation expense is recognized at an amount equal to the value of the shares given to employees at the time of grant, and the outstanding liability related to the SBC is not shown on the financial statements.

Under ASC 718-10-25-2 (originally issued as SFAS 123R), for SBC granted after 2005, companies must expense the fair value of SBC at the grant date and recognize an equivalent increase in stockholders' equity (recorded as an increase to the additional paid-in capital account). Note that the use of the grant date to measure this expense omits any changes in the value of the obligation related to stock options between the grant and exercise date, normally several years later. Subsequent changes in the obligation for the options that occur prior to exercise are an additional transfer to the employee in that period and should be considered. Measuring the outstanding obligation to the employee as well as the changes in the liability that is created over time are the goals of our adjustments because these liabilities and changes in the liability will affect our analysis, forecasting, and valuation. The questions that must be answered are the amounts involved and whether the fair value at the grant date and also the subsequent changes in the obligation to the employee should be treated as operating or financial activities.

Our analysis will discuss three types of SBC that are most easily distinguished based on the related disclosures. GIS provides all three. The first category is stock options, and they are distinguished by the disclosures that include information on both outstanding and exercisable options. **Exhibit 5.8** shows GIS' Note 11 disclosure in May 2018.

EXHIBIT 5.8 GIS' Stock Option Disclosures—Note 11

Information on stock option activity follows:

	Options Exercisable (Thousands)	Weighted-Average Exercise Price Per Share	Options Outstanding (Thousands)	Weighted-Average Exercise Price Per Share
Balance as of May 31, 2015	26,991.5	$30.44	39,077.2	$34.35
Granted			1,930.2	55.72
Exercised			(8,471.0)	28.49
Forfeited or expired			(134.8)	48.16
Balance as of May 29, 2016	22,385.1	$32.38	32,401.6	$37.09
Granted			2,446.0	66.52
Exercised			(4,904.9)	30.76
Forfeited or expired			(108.3)	57.52
Balance as of May 28, 2017	20,899.2	$33.83	29,834.4	$40.47
Granted			2,816.7	55.52
Exercised			(3,489.6)	31.46
Forfeited or expired			(197.7)	58.67
Balance as of May 27, 2018	**20,021.1**	**$36.15**	**28,963.8**	**$42.90**

The second and third categories are comprised of restricted stock, restricted stock units, and share units (often, either performance or time based), which may be classified as either equity or a liability. These two categories have a different set of disclosures. They will be referred to as equity-classified and liability-classified share-unit items going forward. The classification as either equity or liability based depends on the settlement mechanism or restrictions placed on the award.[16] **Exhibit 5.9** shows GIS' disclosures related to their restricted stock, restricted stock units, and performance share units.[17]

EXHIBIT 5.9 GIS' Share Unit Disclosures—Note 11

Information on restricted stock unit and performance share unit activity follows:

	Equity Classified		Liability Classified	
	Share-Settled Units (Thousands)	**Weighted-Average Grant-Date Fair Value**	**Share-Settled Units (Thousands)**	**Weighted-Average Grant-Date Fair Value**
Non-vested as of May 28, 2017	4,491.2	$56.08	123.3	$56.93
Granted	1,505.7	55.11	45.6	55.48
Vested	(1,798.8)	50.73	(34.8)	50.14
Forfeited, expired, or reclassified . . .	(466.3)	62.19	(12.8)	58.71
Non-vested as of May 27, 2018	**3,731.8**	**$57.50**	**121.3**	**$58.26**

Each item that a company separately discloses must have its impact addressed individually. Thus, for GIS, we will have three items to consider: stock options, equity-classified share units, and liability-classified share units. Some companies may have multiples of these items or not have them at all.[18] Thus, understanding exactly what we are considering is extremely important.

The Economics and Accounting of SBC

First, let us consider the economics of and the accounting for the fair value of SBC *at the grant date* (whether in the form of ESOs, equity-classified share units, or liability-classified share units). It seems a reasonable assumption that, were these amounts not transferred to the employee, additional salary payments would have been necessary. That is, this fair value can be presumed to be a cash equivalent to making a transfer to the employee. Note that this value is being promised in anticipation of efforts expected to occur during the vesting period. As such, the compensation for each type of SBC as measured at grant date is expensed over the vesting period under U.S. GAAP.

If we had compensated the employees using cash, there would not be any argument that the expense has arisen due to operating activities and therefore would reduce *NOPAT* across the vesting period. As the company has chosen to utilize SBC, the expense at grant date is related in a similar fashion to the operating activities and, as such, should be included in the calculation of *NOPAT*. This part of SBC is straightforward.

Several issues arise going forward after grant date that make understanding SBC challenging. We must dig into the details. Rest assured that at the end of the discussion, we will have clarified the steps necessary to properly performing the valuation of each SBC item.

The first issue that makes SBC interesting is that, under U.S. GAAP for stock options and equity-classified share units, the anticipated future transfers to the employee are initially recorded as an expense at fair value on grant date via an increase to equity (i.e., additional paid-in capital) rather than as a compensation payable. Thus, when the expense is closed (i.e., transferred) to equity at year-end, there is nothing left on the books as a liability. Equity is both increased at grant date and, subsequently, decreased at year-ends by the fair value expense of the award. This means that, unlike other expenses, we do not see a permanent equity reduction due to these items. They are not merely a timing difference but, rather, a permanent difference because they are never

[16] Companies may not specifically identify whether items are equity classified or liability classified. In these situations, the default assumption is that they are equity classified. The December 2018 financial statements of Kellogg contain share-unit disclosures but do not detail their classification. Our valuation considers these as equity-classified share units.

[17] GIS does not provide information about the quantities and values of its restricted stock activities in its financial statements.

[18] Procter & Gamble's (PG) June 2018 Note 7 states that they "grant stock option, restricted stock unit (RSU) and performance stock unit (PSU) awards to key managers and directors." Both the RSU and PSU awards are equity classified. Thus, an analysis of PG would have three separate items: one stock option item and two equity classified share-unit items.

shown as a reduction of equity. Liability-classified share units are recorded as a liability (hence, the name!), so they will be handled differently.

The second effect occurs upon exercise of the award when we transfer a share to the employee for an amount below current market value. As an example, assume an employee is offered an option to buy a share for $30 (the strike price) in the future and the value of the option using the Black-Scholes option-pricing model is $10. If, upon exercise, the shares are trading for $55, the company will receive $30 in cash and has already received services with a value of $10 from the employee. Giving up the share that is currently worth $55 and having received only $40 results in $15 less equity than if we had simply issued the share in a normal offering. This $15 is in addition to the amount measured at grant date and expensed during the vesting period for the stock option and equity-classified share unit. Adding this $15 in our example to the fair value that we knew at grant date is a necessary adjustment to expenses for these items. Liability-classified awards are adjusted to fair value each period, so the $15 would have been captured, and there should be very little additional compensation that has not previously been recorded at the time of exercise.

OMITTING SBC EXPENSE WILL RESULT IN OVERVALUATION

In a recent working paper, Mohanram, White, and Zhao found that analysts who include SBC in their models for deriving price targets are unbiased, while those who exclude SBC derive optimistically biased target prices. They noted that "anecdotal evidence suggests that market participants ignore SBC in valuation." Their study concluded, "Our evidence indicates that market participants' failure to account for stock-based compensation as an expense leads to the overvaluation of equity."[19] While not necessarily easy, adjustments for SBC are critical to achieving the best possible value estimate.

The next issue related to SBC results from how these awards are taxed. U.S. tax law does not allow the deduction of SBC expense until exercise. Additionally, at the time of the exercise, the deduction is not based on the fair value at grant date but, rather, the difference between market value and exercise price, (i.e., $10 expense at grant date plus the $15 extra in our example). The $15 additional expense allowed as a tax deduction but not recording it in the financial statements under U.S. GAAP creates an excess tax benefit. This excess tax benefit caused by the option being in the money was recorded by U.S. GAAP as an increase in additional paid-in-capital rather than on the income statement prior to ASU 2016-09 (effective beginning in 2017). More important, prior to this change, the excess tax benefit was separately stated in the statement of cash flows, statement of shareholders' equity, footnotes, or a combination of these places. Now, under the new standard, the excess tax benefit is included in the income statement as a component of taxes, so identifying the amount may not be possible.

If we are able to identify the amount of the excess tax benefit, we can infer the additional compensation transferred to the employee at exercise beyond what was estimated as fair value at grant date. We compute this by dividing the excess tax benefit by the assumed marginal tax rate to yield an estimate of the additional compensation. How we adjust for the implied additional compensation depends on whether the year being considered is before or after the adoption of ASU 2016-09. Before adoption, both the inferred compensation and its tax effects had to be adjusted for on the financial statements because the excess tax benefit was recorded directly to equity. After adoption, the tax effect is included on the income statement, so only the inferred compensation must be added.

DETERMINING THE AMOUNT OF EXCESS TAX BENEFIT

Because the amount of excess tax benefit can be disclosed in a number of locations throughout the financial statements, a practical way to find it is a search of the Form 10-K. Simply search for the phrase "excess tax" or "tax benefit" in the PDF version of the company's 10-K. You may have to wade through many results, especially for "tax benefit." Still conducting a search can save a lot of time gathering information for the required adjustment.

continued

[19] Mohanram, Partha S. and White, Brian J. and Zhao, Wuyang, Stock-based Compensation, Financial Analysts, and Equity Overvaluation (August 18, 2019). Available at SSRN: https://ssrn.com/abstract=3439089 or http://dx.doi.org/10.2139/ssrn.3439089

continued from previous page

For GIS, we found the following disclosure on page 68 of the May 2018 Form 10-K: "In the first quarter of fiscal 2018, we adopted new requirements for the accounting and presentation of stock-based payments. The adoption of this guidance resulted in the prospective recognition of realized windfall and shortfall tax benefits related to the exercise or vesting of stock-based awards in our Consolidated Statements of Earnings instead of additional paid-in capital within our Consolidated Balance Sheets. We recognized a windfall tax benefit in income tax expense in our Consolidated Statements of Earnings of $25.2 million in fiscal 2018." Thus, we see evidence that there has been an excess tax benefit, and we have been able to identify the amount included in earnings.

As an example of the disclosures before the new accounting standard, we look at the GIS Statement of Cash Flows for the year ended May 2016. There, GIS reported, "Tax benefit on exercised options $94.1" in their financing activities. With these disclosures, a determination of the implied compensation is possible.

As this additional compensation arises after the grant date due to the choice to utilize SBC rather than cash, we classify it as a financial expense. Compensation *after* the grant date rather than *at* the grant date means that the firm is, in effect, borrowing from the employees inasmuch as their compensation is deferred into the future. In other words, the employees are creditors, and the deferred compensation expense is similar to an interest payment.

The final issue is the outstanding liability and changes in the liability subsequent to grant date related to stock options and equity-classified share units. These items are not recorded in the financial statements, yet they can be substantial for many companies. To be clear, the grant date fair values of all SBC items are being expensed, but only liability-classified share units have the related liabilities shown. Additionally, subsequent changes to the liabilities for stock options and equity-classified share units over time are also not being shown. Ideally, we would seek to know each liability each period and then show changes from the prior year as additional expense. Our best proxy for the liabilities (and their changes) for stock options and equity-classified share units can be formed from the disclosures in the footnotes regarding numbers of options and share units outstanding and the related weighted average exercise prices. By comparing the ending market value of the firm's shares to the weighted average exercise prices, we can form proxies for the option and equity-classified share unit liabilities.[20]

The outstanding liability for SBC results from management's choice to incentivize the employee via SBCs rather than paying cash. For the most part, the amount of liability is driven by increases in share price rather than the fair value at grant date.[21] Based on our earlier arguments, we treat the liability as a financial liability; this is an amount owed to employees, who are, effectively, debtors—the awarding of stock options or share units represents a transfer of value to the employees, who are similar to a financial creditor in this case. The method of funding this transfer (delayed payment via SBC) affects the amounts available to other debt and equity holders. Once we have determined the value of the operating activities, the adjustment for obligations to debt holders should include this liability to allow us to arrive at the amount of value remaining for equity holders. Further, any future changes in the liability subsequent to the grant date are a financial item because they have arisen due to management's choice to use SBC rather than cash to pay employees. That is, the changes over time in SBC liabilities represent a financial expense to be included in the computation of *FEAT*.

[20] By construction, this process results in the computation of a minimum floor for the outstanding liabilities. Because there is the possibility of subsequent stock price increases, at any point, the fair value of the item will exceed market value less exercise price. However, because accounting does not record any liability, this estimate is a significant improvement. Refinements, such as the use of the Black-Scholes formula, to take account of possible increases (and decreases) in stock prices would generally result in a higher estimate of the value of the liability.

[21] In fact, if the options outstanding are also exercisable, the liability established at grant date will have been totally expensed because the vesting period for the option will have expired.

Summary of adjustments needed for SBC:

	Stock Options	Equity-Classified Share Units	Liability-Classified Share Units
Add beginning liability with offset to deferred tax and equity	Yes	Yes	No
Change in liability (and deferred tax) shown as expense and tax effect	Yes	Yes	No
Infer compensation from excess tax benefit disclosure if possible (done net of tax pre-change or gross post-change in accounting standards)	Yes	Yes	Yes

Calculating the Adjustments Necessary for SBC

The process for capturing the SBC effects begins with recording the liability and change in liability for any options and equity-classified share units. To determine this, we first adjust the opening balance and then record the change during the year to get to the ending balance. **Exhibit 5.8** and **5.9** provide the majority of information we'll use in our calculations. The other item we need is the closing price per share for GIS in the current and prior year. According to **finance.yahoo.com**, GIS' closing prices were $42.64 on May 27, 2018, and $57.32 on May 28, 2017. Now, we can perform the following calculations for stock options:

1. Compute the opening adjustment.
   - The value of stock option and equity-classified share-unit commitments outstanding at the beginning of the year are computed using beginning-of-year share price, number of options outstanding, and weighted average exercise price. For GIS at May 2017, 29,834.4 options were outstanding with an estimated value of $16.85 (price of $57.32 less average exercise price of $40.47) per option for a total value of $502.7.
   - The related deferred tax asset on the stock option liability is computed using the assumed future tax rate of 21 percent for $105.6 ($502.7 times 21 percent).
   - This yields an estimate of the beginning SBC liability overhang and deferred tax asset. The difference of $397.1 is an adjustment to equity; effectively, this is a prior period adjustment.

REASONABLENESS CHECKS ON SBC

In computing the adjustments due to SBC, it is very easy to make mistakes due to different presentations. It is not uncommon to have the financial statements presented with dollars in millions and the SBC data presented with units in thousands. For example, GIS presents its financial statements in millions, and the SBC disclosures show thousands of options. In Kellogg's 2018 financial statements, stock options are in millions, while restricted stock and restricted stock units are in thousands! This must be taken into account when calculating the SBC liability and other elements of the adjustment. Not stopping to ensure that the correct number of zeros are included and that data pass the "smell test" can lead to incorrect conclusions.

2. Compute the change during the year via the ending value of the SBC commitments in a manner similar to step 1.
   - The value of stock option commitments outstanding at the end of the year is computed using end-of-year share price, number of options outstanding, and weighted average exercise price. At May 2018, GIS had 28,963.8 options outstanding with an estimated value of $0 (the price of $42.64 is less than the average exercise price of $42.90) because the

options are out of the money at this point.[22] The change during the year is a reduction in the liability of $502.7.

- The related deferred tax asset on the stock option liability at year-end is computed (using the assumed future tax rate of 21 percent) as $0 because the options are out of the money. The change during the year is a reduction in the deferred tax asset of $105.6.
- The changes in the liability and the deferred tax asset yield the implied current compensation expense. For GIS in the year ended May 2018, there is a negative expense because the net liability decreased from $397.1 ($502.7 less $105.6) to $0. This reduction in compensation expense is an adjustment to *FEAT* because the change in the liability for stock options arises after grant date due to the choice to use SBC rather than cash compensation.

These calculations are now repeated for the equity-classified share units:

1. Compute the opening adjustment.
    - At May 2017, GIS had 4,491.2 equity-classified share units outstanding with an estimated value of $1.24 (price of $57.32 less the weighted-average grant-date fair value of $56.08) per unit for a total value of $5.6.
    - The related deferred tax asset on the equity-classified share unit liability is computed using the assumed future tax rate of 21 percent for $1.2 ($5.6 times 21 percent).
    - This yields estimates of the beginning stock overhang and deferred tax asset. The difference of $4.4 is an adjustment to equity; effectively, this is a prior period adjustment.
2. Compute the change during the year via the ending value of the equity-classified share unit commitments in a manner similar to step 1.
    - At May 2018, GIS had 3,731.8 equity-classified share units outstanding with an estimated value of $0 (the price of $42.64 is less than the weighted-average grant-date fair value of $57.50) because the equity-classified share units are out of the money at this point. The change during the year is a reduction in the liability of $5.6.
    - The related deferred tax asset on the equity-classified share unit liability at year-end is computed using the assumed future tax rate of 21 percent and is $0 because the options are out of the money. The change during the year is a reduction in the deferred tax asset of $1.2.
    - In the year ended May 2018, GIS had an implied negative expense because the net liability decreased from $4.4 ($5.6 less $1.2) to $0.

The remaining step is to compute the compensation implied by the excess tax benefit. Remember that this item will either be recorded net of tax if before or gross if after implementation of ASU 2016-09. Additionally, because we do not have access to a breakdown between stock options, equity-classified share units, and liability-classified share units, only one computation covers all SBC items.

3. Compute the amount of implied additional compensation from the excess tax benefit disclosure and our assumed current tax rate.
    - In the year ended May 2018, GIS had a tax benefit of $25.2. Using the current tax rate of 29.4 percent because this is compensation this year, additional compensation of $85.7 ($25.2 divided by 29.4 percent) is implied. As the new standard has been implemented for this year, our adjustment will be to record an additional compensation of $85.7 as a part of *FEAT*.
    - To demonstrate the adjustment net of tax, GIS had a disclosed excess tax benefit of $64.1 in the year ended May 2017. This suggests an implied compensation of $183.1 using the current tax rate for that year of 35 percent ($64.1 divided by 35.0 percent).

[22] Note that if the exercise price exceeds the market value, the liability is zero because there would be no reason for an employee to pay more than the current market price for the shares. In other words, the liability cannot be negative.

Because, the excess tax benefit was recorded directly to equity, we need to adjust *FEAT* for the net amount of $119.0 ($183.1 in compensation less the tax benefit of $64.1).

EFFECTS OF STOCK SPLITS ON SBC CALCULATIONS

Companies will, at times, choose to adjust the number of shares by engaging in a stock split or reverse stock split. For example, if a company has 2,000 shares of common stock and engages in a 3-for-1 stock split, there would subsequently be 6,000 shares. Given that there is no change to the activities of the company, if the shares were trading at $45 per share before the split, they would be expected to trade at $15 after the split.

When considering SBC, stock splits also adjust the number of options and the exercise price in a similar manner. If there were 150 options to buy shares at an exercise price of $24 per share before the 3-for-1 stock split, after the split, this would become 450 options to buy shares at an exercise price of $8 per share. If a stock split occurs, it is best to restate all prior data in the analysis retroactively. In doing so, we act as though the split happened at the beginning of the earliest period. That is, consider this as a retroactive adjustment to the data.

CHANGES TO REPORTING OF SHARE-BASED PAYMENT ARRANGEMENTS

Upcoming changes will simplify calculations related to SBC. Beginning in 2019, companies will be required to provide the aggregate intrinsic value for fully vested share options or share units and those expected to vest (ASC 718-10-65-11). This the SBC overhang we have been attempting to calculate! Further, the company's calculation should be more accurate than ours; particularly in situations where some options are underwater and some are above. Our calculation based on the average exercise price treats all items equally, whereas the company's intrinsic value calculation only considers the options that are in the money, since you cannot have negative intrinsic value.

In addition to the option overhang, a disclosure of the total intrinsic value of options exercised (or share units converted) will be required. This estimate is the unrecorded compensation cost we sought to calculate using the disclosure of the excess tax benefit.

If companies are early adopters of the additional disclosures, or once the transition date passes, these disclosures should be used in forming our SBC adjustments as they are based on much more detailed information possessed by the company rather than our inferences.

Summary of SBC Adjustments

By making these adjustments, we have been able to capture estimates of the compensation owed by and liability of GIS as a result of SBC. This process goes beyond the grant date effects picked up by U.S. GAAP, and we capture the economics of the SBC. These adjustments also recognize changes in the unrecognized SBC and liability over time. Adjusting the *NFL* and *FEAT* for the portion of SBC related to financial activities ensures inclusion of the full effects of this item. SBC must be adjusted to allow for comparability between companies that may have differing levels of usage and ensure a proper adjustment of calculated enterprise value to show what is available to equity holders.

The largest change in our adjustments for SBC is normally the recording of the overhang (SBC liability) as a part of *NFL*. While the adjustments made above do not directly affect our valuation of operations, they remain very important. This is because omitting this obligation to employees (acting in the role of a creditor) would cause an overstatement of the portion of operating value available to equity holders because *NFL* would be understated. Additionally, our estimate of cost of capital for operations would also be affected by omission of the financial liability for SBC.

Note, again, that the additional compensation we are recording is not merely shifting income between years (as for the inventory and leasing items discussed previously) but, rather, it is addressing an omission from the financial statements. Thus, the potential effect of recognition of these items should be considered because they will affect analysis, cost of capital estimation, and valuation.

ACCOUNTING FOR THE ADJUSTMENT: SBC

For GIS, we could write the following journal entry to record these adjustments:

	Dr	Cr
SBC liability, financial		$ 508.3
Deferred tax asset, financial	$ 106.7	
Retained earnings	401.5	
SBC liability, financial	508.3	
Deferred tax asset, financial		106.7
SBC expense, financial		315.8
Retained earnings		85.7
	$1,016.5	$1,016.5

The first entry records the opening balances of the liability for SBC (sum of stock option and equity-classified share unit adjustments for GIS) as a prior period adjustment. The next records the changes in the liability and related deferred tax asset during the year, which represent additional compensation as well as the implied additional compensation adjustment based on the excess tax benefit disclosed.

REFORMULATION UPDATED FOR ADDITIONAL INFORMATION AND ADJUSTMENTS

Having included a large amount of information drawn from the footnotes and MD&A in Chapter 4 and made the adjustments to achieve comparability across accounting methods in this chapter, we return to the task of reformulation presented in Chapters 3 and 4. Below are updated schedules of *NOA*, *NFL*, *NOPAT*, and *FIAT (FEAT)* for the last few years with our efforts to this stage incorporated. This information will serve as the basis for the analysis performed in the following chapter.

EXHIBIT 5.10 GIS' Computation of *NOA*

Amounts in Millions	5/31/2015	5/29/2016	5/28/2017	5/27/2018
Operating Assets (*OA*)				
Cash and cash equivalents	$ 334.2	$ 331.3	$ 312.4	$ 314.8
Receivables: Customers	1,412.0	1,390.4	1,454.4	1,712.6
Receivables: Allowance for doubtful accounts	(25.3)	(29.6)	(24.3)	(28.4)
Inventories: Raw materials and packaging	390.8	397.3	395.4	400.0
Inventories: Finished goods	1,268.6	1,163.1	1,224.3	1,364.2
Inventories: Grain	95.7	72.6	73.0	91.2
Deferred tax assets: Accrued liabilities	98.0	89.9	70.0	47.2
Deferred tax assets: Compensation and employee benefits	536.2	491.5	419.2	210.2
Deferred tax assets: Tax credit carryforwards	5.6	4.5	18.4	7.4
Deferred tax assets: Capital losses	6.1	14.5	29.8	12.9
Deferred tax assets: Net operating losses	89.3	97.9	109.5	161.2
Deferred tax assets: Other	74.5	84.1	85.6	52.9
Deferred tax assets: Valuation allowance	(215.4)	(227.0)	(231.8)	(176.0)
Prepaid expenses and other current assets: Prepaid expenses	169.3	177.9	168.9	165.6
Prepaid expenses and other current assets: Derivative receivables, primarily commodity related	80.9	44.6	35.0	40.5

continued

continued from previous page

EXHIBIT 5.10 GIS' Computation of *NOA*

Amounts in Millions	5/31/2015	5/29/2016	5/28/2017	5/27/2018
Prepaid expenses and other current assets: Grain contracts	3.3	1.8	2.7	7.1
Prepaid expenses and other current assets: Miscellaneous	21.5	15.4	11.3	10.7
Land, buildings, and equipment: Land	96.0	92.9	79.8	77.7
Land, buildings, and equipment: Buildings	2,272.7	2,236.0	2,249.2	2,396.3
Land, buildings, and equipment: Buildings under capital lease	0.3	0.3	0.3	0.3
Land, buildings, and equipment: Equipment	6,091.1	5,945.6	6,095.9	6,236.6
Land, buildings, and equipment: Equipment under capital lease	9.8	3.0	3.0	5.8
Land, buildings, and equipment: Capitalized software	499.0	523.0	545.4	593.6
Land, buildings, and equipment: Construction in progress	622.2	702.7	553.0	692.9
Land, buildings, and equipment: Accumulated depreciation	(5,807.8)	(5,759.9)	(5,838.9)	(5,956.0)
Capitalized lease asset	788.6	793.5	1,013.2	1,111.6
Goodwill: North America Retail	6,546.2	6,410.3	6,406.5	6,410.6
Goodwill: Pet	0.0	0.0	0.0	5,294.9
Goodwill: Convenience stores and food service	921.1	921.1	918.8	918.8
Goodwill: Europe and Australia	719.1	716.5	700.8	729.9
Goodwill: Asia and Latin America	287.0	287.1	312.4	285.0
Goodwill: Joint ventures	401.5	406.2	408.7	425.8
Other intangible assets: Brands and other indefinite-lived intangibles	4,262.1	4,147.5	4,161.1	6,818.7
Other intangible assets: Franchise agreements, customer relationships, and other	544.0	536.9	524.8	811.7
Other intangible assets: Accumulated amortization	(129.1)	(145.8)	(155.5)	(185.3)
Other assets: Investments in and advances to joint ventures	530.6	518.9	505.3	499.6
Other assets: Life insurance	26.6	26.3	25.6	26.9
Other assets: Miscellaneous	85.1	102.9	110.1	106.6
	23,112.2	22,585.2	22,773.3	31,696.1
Operating Liabilities (*OL*)				
Accounts payable	(1,684.0)	(2,046.5)	(2,119.8)	(2,746.2)
Other current liabilities: Accrued trade and consumer promotions	(564.7)	(563.7)	(482.6)	(499.6)
Other current liabilities: Accrued payroll	(361.8)	(386.4)	(326.6)	(347.0)
Other current liabilities: Accrued taxes	(95.7)	(187.3)	(101.9)	(139.6)
Other current liabilities: Grain contracts	(7.8)	(5.5)	(5.6)	(1.2)
Other current liabilities: Restructuring and other exit costs reserve	(120.8)	(76.6)	(85.0)	(66.8)
Other current liabilities: Derivative payable	(122.9)	(35.6)	(18.1)	(8.3)
Other current liabilities: Miscellaneous	(271.5)	(302.5)	(291.0)	(302.9)
Deferred tax liabilities: Brands	(1,346.3)	(1,311.7)	(1,310.1)	(1,498.7)
Deferred tax liabilities: Fixed assets	(446.5)	(476.3)	(484.5)	(329.5)
Deferred tax liabilities: Intangible assets	(208.4)	(221.8)	(238.6)	(255.1)
Deferred tax liabilities: Tax lease transactions	(50.8)	(48.0)	(45.8)	(26.0)
Deferred tax liabilities: Inventories	(59.7)	(53.0)	(60.0)	(38.8)
Deferred tax liabilities: Unrealized hedges	0.0	(22.6)	(45.4)	(28.5)
Deferred tax liabilities: Other	(14.2)	(21.2)	(29.0)	(30.9)
Other noncurrent liabilities: Accrued taxes	(202.5)	(204.0)	(162.3)	(265.3)
Other noncurrent liabilities: Miscellaneous	(90.9)	(128.6)	(111.1)	(76.3)
	(5,648.5)	(6,091.3)	(5,917.4)	(6,660.7)
NOA	$17,463.8	$16,493.9	$16,855.9	$25,035.4

EXHIBIT 5.11 GIS' Computation of *NFL*

Amounts in Millions	5/31/2015	5/29/2016	5/28/2017	5/27/2018
Financial Assets (*FA*)				
Cash and cash equivalents	$ 0.0	$ 432.4	$ 453.7	$ 84.2
Deferred tax assets: Pension	169.0	322.0	196.3	57.1
Deferred tax assets: Stock, partnership, and miscellaneous investments	384.1	353.6	276.4	147.9
Deferred tax assets: Stock-based compensation	319.4	317.8	106.7	0.0
Prepaid expenses and other current assets: Other receivables	148.8	159.3	163.7	174.4
Other assets: Exchangeable note with related party	30.7	12.7	0.0	0.0
Defined benefit pension plans: Plan assets	5,758.5	5,539.9	5,925.2	6,177.4
Other postretirement benefit plans: Plan assets	582.8	602.4	694.8	726.1
	7,393.3	7,740.2	7,816.8	7,367.1
Financial Liabilities (*FL*)				
Accounts payable				
Current portion of long-term debt	(1,000.4)	(1,103.4)	(604.7)	(1,600.1)
Notes payable: U.S. commercial paper	(432.0)	0.0	(954.7)	(1,213.5)
Notes payable: Financial institutions	(183.8)	(269.8)	(279.4)	(336.3)
Other current liabilities: Dividend payable	(27.9)	(23.8)	(21.5)	(17.5)
Other current liabilities: Accrued interest, including interest rate swaps	(91.8)	(90.4)	(83.8)	(107.7)
Long-term debt	(7,575.3)	(7,057.7)	(7,642.9)	(12,668.7)
Deferred tax liabilities: Stock, partnership, and miscellaneous investments	(472.5)	(476.0)	(479.4)	(317.1)
Other noncurrent liabilities: Accrued compensation and benefits, including pensions	(176.2)	(164.9)	(180.3)	(178.5)
Defined benefit pension plans: Benefit obligation	(6,252.1)	(6,448.5)	(6,458.6)	(6,416.0)
Other postretirement benefit plans: Benefit obligation	(1,079.6)	(1,028.9)	(951.4)	(871.8)
Postemployment benefit plans: Benefit obligation	(146.6)	(164.1)	(134.5)	(126.7)
Capitalized lease liability	(788.6)	(793.5)	(1,013.2)	(1,111.6)
Stock-based compensation liability (*NFL*)	(912.4)	(908.1)	(508.3)	0.0
Redeemable interest	(778.9)	(845.6)	(910.9)	(776.2)
Noncontrolling interests	(396.0)	(376.9)	(357.6)	(351.3)
	(20,314.2)	(19,751.6)	(20,581.2)	(26,093.0)
Net Financial Liabilities (*NFL*)	$(12,920.9)	$(12,011.4)	$(12,764.3)	$(18,725.9)

EXHIBIT 5.12 GIS' Computation of *NOPAT*

Amounts in Millions: Year Ended	5/29/2016	5/28/2017	5/27/2018
Net sales: North America retail	$10,936.6	$10,196.9	$10,115.4
Net sales: Convenience stores and food service	1,923.8	1,870.0	1,930.2
Net sales: Europe and Australia	1,998.0	1,824.5	1,984.6
Net sales: Asia and Latin America	1,704.7	1,728.4	1,710.2
Cost of sales	(10,728.5)	(10,066.2)	(10,308.8)
Advertising expense	(754.4)	(623.8)	(575.9)
Research expense	(222.1)	(218.2)	(219.1)
Depreciation on capitalized leases	(160.7)	(88.8)	(151.1)
Defined benefit pension plans: Service cost	(134.6)	(119.7)	(102.9)
Other postretirement benefit plans: Service cost	(19.0)	(12.5)	(11.6)
Postemployment benefit plans: Service cost	(7.6)	(8.8)	(8.6)
Defined contribution plan expense	(61.2)	(54.1)	(49.2)
Other selling, general, and administrative expenses	(1,729.2)	(1,730.7)	(1,695.6)
Divestitures (loss) gain	148.2	(13.5)	—

continued

continued from previous page

EXHIBIT 5.12 GIS' Computation of *NOPAT*

Amounts in Millions: Year Ended	5/29/2016	5/28/2017	5/27/2018
Restructuring, impairment, and other exit costs	(151.4)	(182.6)	(165.6)
Income taxes	(873.8)	(706.3)	(150.0)
After-tax earnings from joint ventures	88.4	85.0	84.7
Foreign currency translation	(108.7)	6.3	(37.0)
Other fair value changes: Hedge derivatives	16.0	53.3	(50.8)
Reclassification to earnings: Hedge derivatives	(9.5)	(25.7)	17.4
Net Operating Profit after Tax (*NOPAT*)	$ 1,854.9	$ 1,913.5	$ 2,316.4

EXHIBIT 5.13 GIS' Computation of *FIAT* (*FEAT*)

Amounts in Millions; Year Ended	5/29/2016	5/28/2017	5/27/2018
Defined benefit pension plans: Interest cost	$(267.8)	$(216.5)	$(217.9)
Defined benefit pension plans: Expected return on plan assets	496.9	486.7	480.2
Defined benefit pension plans: Amortization of losses	(189.8)	(190.2)	(177.0)
Defined benefit pension plans: Amortization of prior service cost	(4.7)	(2.5)	(1.9)
Defined benefit pension plans: Other adjustments	(5.0)	(3.1)	—
Defined benefit pension plans: Settlements or curtailment losses	(13.1)	(3.8)	—
Other postretirement benefit plans: Interest cost	(44.1)	(32.2)	(30.1)
Other postretirement benefit plans: Expected return on plan assets	46.2	48.5	52.2
Other postretirement benefit plans: Amortization of losses	(6.6)	(2.5)	(0.8)
Other postretirement benefit plans: Amortization of prior service cost	5.4	5.4	5.4
Other postretirement benefit plans: Other adjustments	(2.3)	(1.3)	—
Other postretirement benefit plans: Settlements or curtailment losses	1.0	0.9	—
Postemployment benefit plans: Interest cost	(3.9)	(2.6)	(2.3)
Postemployment benefit plans: Amortization of losses	(0.7)	(1.7)	(0.8)
Postemployment benefit plans: Amortization of prior service cost	(2.5)	(0.6)	(0.6)
Postemployment benefit plans: Other adjustments	(10.7)	(1.3)	(6.7)
Postemployment benefit plans: Settlements or curtailment losses	—	1.4	—
Interest expense	(348.0)	(336.0)	(427.8)
Capitalized interest	7.7	4.6	4.1
Interest income	8.1	7.0	11.7
Income taxes	116.8	83.9	91.8
Financial stock-based compensation expense, net of tax	2.8	188.7	401.5
Net earnings attributable to redeemable and noncontrolling interests	(39.4)	(43.6)	(32.0)
Net actuarial income (loss)	(325.9)	197.9	140.1
Other fair value changes: Securities	0.1	0.8	1.2
Reclassification to earnings: Securities	—	—	(5.1)
Reclassification to earnings: Amortization of losses and prior service costs	128.6	122.5	117.6
Other comprehensive income attributable to noncontrolling interests, net	(2.1)	12.6	(38.5)
Financial income (expense) after tax—*FIAT* (*FEAT*)	$(452.9)	$ 323.0	$ 364.3

ENSURING ARTICULATION OF FINANCIAL STATEMENTS AFTER ADJUSTMENTS

To ensure that financial statement adjustments were done correctly, verify that the amounts of *CI* and *CSE* make sense. GIS' adjusted balance sheet and income statement both contain reconciliation from the balances after Chapter 4 to the adjusted balances after addressing inventory, leases, and options.

Also, remember to make sure that all totals in your spreadsheet are calculated rather then entered (i.e., hard coded). Nothing is worse than not tying out your numbers and then having to hunt for issues later.

SUMMARY

Our evaluation of financial accounting method choices retains our focus on valuation of the operating activities of the company, a process that includes analysis and forecasting. It is important to understand that this process is aided by high-quality accounting information.

What is high-quality accounting information? Although there is not a single definition of high-quality information, there are factors that enhance information quality. Accounting information is more useful when it is reliable and relevant. Reliable denotes that the numbers reflect an economic reality and include all appropriate items in such a way that their true nature is not obscured. Relevant denotes that the observable earnings and cash flow numbers can be used to forecast the amount and timing of future earnings and cash flows. An adjustment such as was made for SBC yields information higher in both reliability and relevance.

While it will be shown that the accounting-based valuation models are not affected by income shifting if the company is in steady state, there is the possibility that we will be misled by what has been reported if adjustments are not made. Further, any lack of comparability across the financial statements of companies impedes our determination of forecasts of future operating *PM* and *ATO*. To that end, we must consider the accounting quality and whether adjustments are necessary. There is no tried-and-true formula for assessing accounting quality or for identifying earnings management. We also cannot address all issues that may need adjustment. However, the processes identified within the mini-chapters above address some common issues and give a framework to be used in considering whether adjustments are necessary. Remember that we can at least implement the following analysis and remediation techniques:

- Read both reports from the external auditor, taking special note of any deviation from boilerplate language.
- Peruse the footnote on accounting policies (typically Note 1), and compare the company's policies to its industry peers. Deviations from the norm can signal opportunism.
- Recast (adjust) financial statements as necessary to reflect an accounting policy that is more in line with competitors or that better reflects economically relevant numbers. And pay close attention to when new accounting standards have been implemented.

The next chapter will build on this topic by addressing how we analyze operating activities leading to full-information forecasting. Additionally, we will discuss the effects of accrual management, real earnings management, and financial fraud on our analysis. We will learn how to compute key ratios and then compare them over time and across companies. In doing so, we focus our efforts on following up on unexpected changes or a lack of change when one would be expected. These steps are necessary to allow us to identify appropriate assumptions to use when we forecast as well as to identify nonrecurring items and separately assess their impact on company performance and position.

QUESTIONS

Q5.1 Why would adjust the information shown on the face of the financial statements? In thinking of potential adjustments, what issue drives the need to make an adjustment?

Q5.2 What is the effect on earnings of accounting method choice?

Q5.3 Should the underlying value of something be changed by the accounting method used to report it? What implications does this have for the five steps in our valuation process?

Q5.4 When considering inventory methods, is it acceptable to compare a FIFO company to a LIFO company? Is it acceptable to compare two companies that use LIFO?

Q5.5 How do accruals management differ from earnings management?

Q5.6 For lease transactions, why are the leased assets classified as an operating activity and part of *NOA* and the lease obligation is classified as a financial activity and part of *NFL*?

Q5.7 When conducting a constructive capitalization of operating leases (old lease rules), how are the lease payments recharacterized between *NOPAT* and *FEAT*?

Q5.8 Explain how a special-purpose entity can affect a firm's cost of debt capital.

Q5.9 For firms that utilize special purpose entities (SPE), what adjustments are needed to the firm's *NOPAT* and *NOA*?

Q5.10 For stock options and equity-classified share units, how does current GAAP accounting for share-based compensation not capture the economics of the resulting wealth transfer from the firm to the option or equity-unit holder?

EXERCISES

E5.11 **Hershey** (HSY) values the majority of U.S. inventories under the LIFO method and its international business using the FIFO method. Using the information below from HSY's footnote, what adjustments are needed to convert the 2018 *NOA* and *NOPAT* from LIFO to as-if FIFO? Assume the statutory tax rate is 21 percent.

THE HERSHEY COMPANY
NOTES TO CONSOLIDATED FINANCIAL STATEMENTS-(Continued)
(amounts in thousands , except share data or if otherwise indicated)

17. SUPPLEMENTAL BALANCE SHEET INFORMATION

The components of certain consolidated balance sheet accounts are as follows:

December 31,	2018	2017
Inventories:		
Raw materials	$237,086	$224,940
Goods in process	107,139	93,627
Finished goods	618,798	614,945
Inventories at FIFO	963,023	933,512
Adjustment to LIFO	(178,144)	(180,676)
Total inventories	$784,879	$752,836

E5.12 In Note 11, of its 2018 financial statements, **Chipotle** (CMG) reported the following future operating lease information:

Contractually required future minimum cash lease payments under existing operating leases as of December 31, 2018, are as follows:	
2019	$ 294,191
2020	296,579
2021	294,941
2022	295,290
2023	290,980
Thereafter	2,478,397
Total minimum lease payments	$3,950,378

a. Assuming a discount rate of 5 percent, estimate the unrecognized asset and liability for assets acquired under operating leases for CMG at December 31, 2018.

b. Given the estimated unrecognized liability calculated in part a., what impact does including this amount have on the liabilities of CMG reported on the balance sheet?

E5.13 In Note 11, of its 2018 financial statements, **Costco** (COST) reported the following future operating lease information:

At the end of 2018, future minimum payments, net of sub-lease income of $105 for all years combined, under non-cancelable operating leases with terms of at least one year and capital leases were as follows:

	Operating Leases	Capital Leases
2019	$ 227	$ 34
2020	214	35
2021	193	36
2022	183	36
2023	175	36
Thereafter	2,215	647
Total	$3,207	824
Less amount representing interest		(427)
Net present value of minimum lease payments		397
Less current installments(2)		(7)
Long-term capital lease obligations less current installments(3)		$390

a. Assuming the capital lease payments after 2023 will be $36 per year, what is the implied discount rate on COST's capital leases?

b. Now assume a discount rate of 6 percent for COST's operating leases. Estimate the unrecognized asset and liability for assets acquired under operating leases for COST at December 31, 2018.

E5.14 Based on the fiscal 2018 footnote disclosure below for **lululemon** (LULU), calculate the share-based compensation liability (i.e., overhang) and the related deferred tax asset as of February 3, 2019. The closing share price for LULU was $146.12, and the statutory tax rate is 21 percent.

A summary of the balances of the Company's stock-based compensation plans as of February 3, 2019, January 28, 2018, and January 29, 2017, and changes during the fiscal years then ended is presented below:

	Stock Options		Performance-Based Restricted Stock Units		Restricted Shares		Restricted Stock Units		Restricted Stock Units (Liability Accounting)	
	Number	Weighted-Average Exercise Price	Number	Weighted-Average Grant Date Fair Value	Number	Weighted-Average Grant Date Fair Value	Number	Weighted-Average Grant Date Fair Value	Number	Weighted-Average Exercise Price
	(In thousands, except per share amounts)									
Balance at January 31, 2016	867	$49.54	395	$ 58.58	31	$ 57.67	333	$55.91	—	$ —
Granted	428	68.63	164	68.64	17	69.94	216	68.15	—	—
Exercised/vested	191	36.76	7	64.36	34	58.39	91	56.87	—	—
Forfeited/expired	186	58.87	162	62.54	—	—	98	55.95	—	—
Balance at January 29, 2017	918	$59.20	390	$ 61.05	14	$ 70.54	360	$62.99	—	$ —
Granted	619	52.34	192	52.38	24	52.38	336	52.83	—	—
Exercised/vested	109	51.62	—	—	14	70.29	135	60.64	—	—
Forfeited/expired	311	58.09	253	55.30	3	51.72	134	57.28	—	—
Balance at January 28, 2018	1,117	$56.44	329	$ 60.42	21	$ 52.45	427	$57.54	—	$ —
Granted	388	96.96	123	102.49	6	124.19	257	88.75	44	136.67
Exercised/vested	316	56.29	39	63.04	21	52.45	174	58.94	—	—
Forfeited/expired	319	59.76	133	61.71	—	—	70	66.90	—	—
Balance at February 3, 2019	870	$73.34	280	$ 78.01	6	$124.19	440	$73.73	44	$146.12

E5.15 **Salesforce** (CRM) is a global leader in customer relationship management technology and software. Based on CRM's tax footnote, identify the additional compensation expense provided by its SBC plans for the past three years.

A reconciliation of income taxes at the statutory federal income tax rate to the provision for (benefit from) income taxes included in the accompanying consolidated statements of operations is as follows (in millions):

	Fiscal Year Ended January 31,		
	2019	2018	2017
U.S. federal taxes at statutory rate[1]	$ 206	$ 142	$ 63
State, net of the federal benefit	79	(21)	7
Effects of non-U.S. operations	379	(35)	62
Tax credits	(132)	(107)	(50)
Non-deductible expenses	63	53	48
Excess tax benefits related to shared based compensation	(137)	(135)	(95)
Effect of U.S. tax law change	43	126	0
Change in valuation allowance	(612)	42	(179)
Other, net	(16)	(5)	0
Provision for (benefit from) income taxes	$(127)	$ 60	$(144)

(1) The Company's statutory rates were 21.0 percent and 33.8 percent for fiscal 2019 and fiscal 2018, respectively, which reflected the corporate tax rate reduction effective January 1, 2018 due to the Tax Act.

CONTINUING EXAMPLES

CE5.16 Using the 2018, 2017, 2016, and 2015 annual reports for **Kellogg's** (K), assume a discount rate equal to the weighted average interest rate on notes disclosed in the debt footnote each year.

a. Utilizing this discount rate for K's operating leases, estimate the unrecognized asset and liability for assets acquired under operating leases at year end for each of the last 4 years. Assume the payments after the fifth year will be equal to those in the fifth year.

b. For fiscal years 2016–2018, determine the assumed operating lease payments (last year's year 1 amount), the estimated interest and principal payments, and the related depreciation expense.

c. For 2015–2018, prepare the related journal entries to record the liability and asset for the effective capitalization of the operating lease.

d. For 2015–2018, prepare the related journal entries to record the amount of adjustment to SG&A, interest, and depreciation expense.

CE5.17 Using the 2018, 2017, 2016, and 2015 annual reports for **Kellogg's** (K) and stock price information found from a financial website, compute the adjustment needed for stock-based compensation for each of the years 2015–2018.

a. Compute the amount of adjustment for the stock options in each of the years from 2015 to 2018.

b. For 2015–2018, prepare the related journal entries to record the amount of adjustment to the stock option overhang, related deferred tax assets *DTA*s, and *FEAT*.

c. For 2015–2018, prepare the related journal entry(ies) to record the excess tax benefit associated with K's stock option plans.

d. Compute the amount of adjustment for the equity-based restricted stock units in each of the years from 2015 to 2018.

e. For 2015–2018, prepare the related journal entries to record the amount of adjustment to for the RSU overhang, related *DTA*s and *FEAT*.

f. For 2015–2018, prepare the adjustments to the opening balances for SBC liability, *DTA*s and to common stock equity (*CSE*).

g. For 2015–2018, prepare the combined journal entries for both stock options and RSU from above for SBC liability, *DTA*s, and *FEAT* and to *CSE*.

With the adjustments for the leases and stock-based compensation included in K's balance sheet and income statement for 2015–2018, we arrive at the following adjusted financial statements:

Balance Sheet Amounts in Millions	2015	2016	2017	2018
Assets				
Cash and cash equivalents	$ 251	$ 280	$ 281	$ 321
Accounts receivable: Trade	1,169	1,106	1,250	1,163
Accounts receivable: Allowance for doubtful accounts	(8)	(8)	(10)	(10)
Accounts receivable: Refundable income taxes	27	24	23	28
Accounts receivable: Other receivables	156	109	126	194
Inventories: Raw materials and supplies	315	315	333	339
Inventories: Finished goods and materials in progress	935	923	884	991
Other current assets	164	191	149	131
Property, net: Land	142	131	111	120
Property, net: Buildings	2,076	2,020	2,200	2,061
Property, net: Machinery and equipment	5,617	5,646	6,018	5,971
Property, net: Capitalized software	328	366	403	438
Property, net: Construction in progress	694	686	634	583
Property, net: Accumulated depreciation	(5,236)	(5,280)	(5,650)	(5,442)
Capitalized lease asset	497	555	420	478
Goodwill: U.S. morning foods	131	131	131	131
Goodwill: U.S. snacks	3,568	3,568	3,568	3,568
Goodwill: U.S. specialty	82	82	82	82
Goodwill: North America other	456	457	836	830
Goodwill: Europe	431	376	414	392
Goodwill: Latin America	76	328	244	218
Goodwill: Asia Pacific	224	224	229	829
Intangible assets subject to amortization: U.S. morning foods	8	8	8	8
Intangible assets subject to amortization: U.S. snacks	42	42	42	42
Intangible assets subject to amortization: North America other	5	5	22	24
Intangible assets subject to amortization: Europe	45	40	45	43
Intangible assets subject to amortization: Latin America	6	36	74	63
Intangible assets subject to amortization: Asia Pacific	10	10	10	428
Intangible assets accumulated amortization: U.S. morning foods	(8)	(8)	(8)	(8)
Intangible assets accumulated amortization: U.S. snacks	(16)	(19)	(22)	(25)
Intangible assets accumulated amortization: North America other	(4)	(4)	(5)	(6)
Intangible assets accumulated amortization: Europe	(11)	(14)	(18)	(20)
Intangible assets accumulated amortization: Latin America	(6)	(6)	(10)	(12)
Intangible assets accumulated amortization: Asia Pacific	(2)	(3)	(4)	(16)
Intangible assets not subject to amortization: U.S. snacks	1,625	1,625	1,625	1,625
Intangible assets not subject to amortization: North America other	158	176	360	360
Intangible assets not subject to amortization: Europe	416	383	434	415
Intangible assets not subject to amortization: Latin America	0	98	86	73
Intangible assets not subject to amortization: Asia Pacific	0	0	0	367
Investments in unconsolidated entities	456	438	429	413
Deferred tax assets: U.S. state income taxes	13	0	0	0
Deferred tax assets: Advertising and promotion related	15	17	22	11
Deferred tax assets: Wages and payroll taxes	21	42	26	20

continued

continued from previous page

Balance Sheet Amounts in Millions	2015	2016	2017	2018
Deferred tax assets: Inventory valuation	31	28	20	14
Deferred tax assets: Employee benefits	366	403	154	132
Deferred tax assets: Operating loss, credit, and other carryforwards	55	181	239	270
Deferred tax assets: Hedging transactions	43	0	42	10
Deferred tax assets: Deferred compensation	35	38	25	20
Deferred tax assets: Stock options	141	107	51	31
Deferred tax assets: Other	86	31	71	26
Deferred tax assets: Valuation allowance	(63)	(131)	(153)	(166)
Pension: Plan assets	4,584	4,544	5,043	4,677
Postretirement: Plan assets	1,084	1,136	1,292	1,140
Other assets	338	376	385	487
Total assets	$21,568	$21,809	$22,961	$23,862

Liabilities and Shareholders' Equity CURRENT LIABILITIES				
Current maturities of long-term debt	$ (1,266)	$ (631)	$ (409)	$ (510)
Notes payable: U.S. commercial paper	(899)	(80)	(196)	(15)
Notes payable: Europe commercial paper	(261)	(306)	(96)	0
Notes payable: Bank borrowings	(44)	(52)	(78)	(161)
Accounts payable	(1,907)	(2,014)	(2,269)	(2,427)
Other current liabilities: Accrued income taxes	(42)	(47)	(30)	(48)
Other current liabilities: Accrued salaries and wages	(325)	(318)	(311)	(309)
Other current liabilities: Accured advertising and promotion	(447)	(436)	(582)	(557)
Other current liabilities: Other	(512)	(569)	(526)	(478)
Long-term debt	(5,289)	(6,698)	(7,836)	(8,207)
Deferred tax liabilities: U.S. state income taxes	(43)	(34)	(48)	(19)
Deferred tax liabilities: Hedging transactions	0	(51)	0	0
Deferred tax liabilities: Depreciation and asset disposals	(345)	(318)	(208)	(220)
Deferred tax liabilities: Trademarks and other intangibles	(576)	(602)	(332)	(613)
Deferred tax liabilities: Unremitted foreign earnings	0	0	0	0
Pension: Benefit obligation	(5,316)	(5,510)	(5,648)	(5,117)
Postretirement: Benefit obligation	(1,163)	(1,161)	(1,190)	(1,069)
Postemployment: Benefit obligation	(108)	(87)	(43)	(42)
Capitalized lease liability	(497)	(555)	(420)	(239)
Stock-based compensation liability (*NFL*)	(283)	(188)	(85)	0
Other liabilities: Income taxes payable	—	(48)	(192)	(115)
Other liabilities: Nonpension postretirement benefits	(77)	(4)	(40)	(34)
Other liabilities: Pension	(214)	(260)	(295)	(284)
Total liabilities	(19,614)	(20,005)	(20,834)	(20,464)
Shareholders' equity				
Common stock—$0.25 par value	(105)	(105)	(105)	(105)
Capital in excess of par value	(745)	(806)	(878)	(895)
Retained earnings	(6,597)	(6,571)	(7,069)	(7,652)
Treasury stock, at cost	3,943	3,997	4,417	4,551
Accumulated other comprehensive (income)/loss	1,376	1,575	1,457	1,500
RE adjustment for stock-based compensation	184	122	67	0
Noncontrolling interests	(10)	(16)	(16)	(558)
Total shareholders' equity	(1,954)	(1,804)	(2,127)	(3,159)
Total liabilities and shareholders' equity	$(21,568)	$(21,809)	$(22,961)	$(23,623)

Income Statement Amounts in Millions; Year Ended December	2015	2016	2017	2018
Net sales: U.S. morning foods	$2,992	$2,917	$2,709	$2,643
Net sales: U.S. snacks	3,234	3,197	3,110	2,957
Net sales: U.S. specialty channels	1,181	1,207	1,242	1,235
Net sales: North America other	1,687	1,593	1,612	1,853
Net sales: Europe	2,497	2,383	2,291	2,395
Net sales: Latin America	1,015	772	944	947
Net sales: Asia Pacific	919	896	946	1,517
Cost of goods sold		(8,131)	(8,155)	(8,821)
Gross profit		4,834	4,699	4,726
401(k) plan expense		(39)	(41)	(38)
Pension: Service cost		(98)	(96)	(87)
Pension: Interest cost		(174)	(164)	(165)
Pension: Expected return on plan assets		352	371	361
Pension: Amortization of unrecognized prior service cost		(13)	(9)	(8)
Pension: Recognized net actuarial loss		(323)	36	(269)
Pension: Curtailment and special termination benefits		(1)	151	30
Pension: Defined contribution plans		(36)	(34)	(27)
Postretirement: Service cost		(21)	(18)	(18)
Postretirement: Interest cost		(39)	(37)	(36)
Postretirement: Expected return on plan assets		90	98	94
Postretirement: Amortization of unrecognized prior service cost		9	9	9
Postretirement: Recognized net gain (loss)		19	90	(81)
Postretirement: Curtailment		0	(3)	0
Postretirement: Defined contribution plans		(17)	(16)	(11)
Postemployment: Service cost		(7)	(6)	(3)
Postemployment: Interest cost		(3)	(3)	(1)
Postemployment: Amortization of unrecognized prior service cost		(1)	(1)	(1)
Postemployment: Recognized net gain (loss)		(3)	0	5
Research and development expense		(182)	(148)	(154)
Advertising expense		(735)	(732)	(752)
Bad debt expense		(9)	(14)	(4)
Depreciation on capitalized leases		(124)	(169)	(114)
Other selling, general, and administrative expense		(1,978)	(2,558)	(1,737)
Operating profit		1,501	1,405	1,719
Interest expense		(424)	(274)	(300)
Other income (expense), net		(143)	526	(90)
Income before income taxes, equity interests, and extraordinary loss		934	1,657	1,329
Income taxes		(235)	(410)	(181)
Financial stock-based compensation expense, net of tax		62	55	67
Earnings from unconsolidated entities		1	7	196
Net income		762	1,309	1,411
Net income attributable to noncontrolling interests		(1)	0	(8)
Net income attributable to Kellogg Company		$ 761	$1,309	$1,403
Comprehensive income items:				
Foreign currency translation adjustments, net of tax		$ (254)	$ 79	$ (48)
Cash flow hedges, net of tax		(28)	6	8
Postretirement and postemployment benefits, net of tax:				
Net experience gain		18	32	(11)
Prior service credit		2	1	1
Venezuela deconsolidation loss		63	0	0
Other comprehensive income attributable to noncontrolling interests, net		0	0	7
Comprehensive income attributable to Kellogg		$ 562	$1,427	$1,360

This leads to the following updated calculations of *NOA*, *NFL*, *NOPAT*, and *FEAT* after the additional information was included from Chapter 4 and the adjustments here in Chapter 5.

Amounts in Millions	2015	2016	2017	2018
Cash and cash equivalents	$ 251	$ 178	$ 173	$ 174
Accounts receivable: Trade	1,169	1,106	1,250	1,163
Accounts receivable: Allowance for doubtful accounts	(8)	(8)	(10)	(10)
Accounts receivable: Refundable income taxes	27	24	23	28
Accounts receivable: Other receivables	156	109	126	194
Inventories: Raw materials and supplies	315	315	333	339
Inventories: Finished goods and materials in progress	935	923	884	991
Other current assets	164	191	149	131
Property, net: Land	142	131	111	120
Property, net: Buildings	2,076	2,020	2,200	2,061
Property, net: Machinery and equipment	5,617	5,646	6,018	5,971
Property, net: Capitalized software	328	366	403	438
Property, net: Construction in progress	694	686	634	583
Property, net: Accumulated depreciation	(5,236)	(5,280)	(5,650)	(5,442)
Capitalized lease asset	497	555	420	513
Goodwill: U.S. morning foods	131	131	131	131
Goodwill: U.S. snacks	3,568	3,568	3,568	3,568
Goodwill: U.S. specialty	82	82	82	82
Goodwill: North America other	456	457	836	830
Goodwill: Europe	431	376	414	392
Goodwill: Latin America	76	328	244	218
Goodwill: Asia Pacific	224	224	229	829
Intangible assets subject to amortization: U.S. morning foods	8	8	8	8
Intangible assets subject to amortization: U.S. snacks	42	42	42	42
Intangible assets subject to amortization: North America other	5	5	22	24
Intangible assets subject to amortization: Europe	45	40	45	43
Intangible assets subject to amortization: Latin America	6	36	74	63
Intangible assets subject to amortization: Asia Pacific	10	10	10	428
Intangible assets accumulated amortization: U.S. morning foods	(8)	(8)	(8)	(8)
Intangible assets accumulated amortization: U.S. snacks	(16)	(19)	(22)	(25)
Intangible assets accumulated amortization: North America other	(4)	(4)	(5)	(6)
Intangible assets accumulated amortization: Europe	(11)	(14)	(18)	(20)
Intangible assets accumulated amortization: Latin America	(6)	(6)	(10)	(12)
Intangible assets accumulated amortization: Asia Pacific	(2)	(3)	(4)	(16)
Intangible assets not subject to amortization: U.S. snacks	1,625	1,625	1,625	1,625
Intangible assets not subject to amortization: North America other	158	176	360	360
Intangible assets not subject to amortization: Europe	416	383	434	415
Intangible assets not subject to amortization: Latin America	—	98	86	73
Intangible assets not subject to amortization: Asia Pacific	—	—	—	367
Investments in unconsolidated entities	456	438	429	413
Deferred tax assets: U.S. state income taxes	13	—	—	—
Deferred tax assets: Advertising and promotion related	15	17	22	11
Deferred tax assets: Wages and payroll taxes	21	42	26	20
Deferred tax assets: Inventory valuation	31	28	20	14
Deferred tax assets: Operating loss, credit, and other carryforwards	55	181	239	270
Deferred tax assets: Hedging transactions	43	—	42	10
Deferred tax assets: Deferred compensation	35	38	25	20
Deferred tax assets: Other	86	31	71	26
Deferred tax assets: Valuation allowance	(63)	(131)	(153)	(166)
Other assets	338	376	385	487
Total operating assets	15,393	15,517	16,313	17,770

continued

continued from previous page

Amounts in Millions	2015	2016	2017	2018
Accounts payable	$ (1,907)	$ (2,014)	$ (2,269)	$ (2,427)
Other current liabilities: Accrued income taxes	(42)	(47)	(30)	(48)
Other current liabilities: Accrued salaries and wages	(335)	(318)	(311)	(309)
Other current liabilities: Accrued advertising and promotion	(447)	(436)	(582)	(557)
Other current liabilities: Other	(512)	(569)	(526)	(478)
Deferred tax liabilities: U.S. state income taxes	(43)	(34)	(48)	(19)
Deferred tax liabilities: Hedging transactions	—	(51)	—	—
Deferred tax liabilities: Depreciation and asset disposals	(345)	(318)	(208)	(220)
Deferred tax liabilities: Trademarks and other intangibles	(576)	(602)	(332)	(613)
Deferred tax liabilities: Unremitted foreign earnings	—	—	—	—
Other liabilities: Income taxes payable	—	(48)	(192)	(115)
Total operating liabilities	(4,197)	(4,437)	(4,498)	(4,786)
NOA	$11,196	$11,080	$11,815	$12,949

Amounts in Millions	2015	2016	2017	2018
Deferred tax assets: Employee benefits	$ 366	$ 403	$ 154	$ 132
Deferred tax assets: Stock options	141	107	51	31
Pension: Plan assets	4,584	4,544	5,043	4,677
Postretirement: Plan assets	1,084	1,136	1,292	1,140
Total financial assets	6,175	6,292	6,648	6,127
Current maturities of long-term debt	(1,266)	(631)	(409)	(510)
Notes payable: U.S. commercial paper	(899)	(80)	(196)	(15)
Notes payable: Europe commercial paper	(261)	(306)	(96)	—
Notes payable: Bank borrowings	(44)	(52)	(78)	(161)
Long-term debt	(5,289)	(6,698)	(7,836)	(8,207)
Pension: Benefit obligation	(5,316)	(5,510)	(5,648)	(5,117)
Postretirement: Benefit obligation	(1,163)	(1,161)	(1,190)	(1,069)
Postemployment: Benefit obligation	(108)	(87)	(43)	(42)
Capitalized lease liability	(497)	(555)	(420)	(478)
Stock-based compensation liability (*NFL*)	(283)	(188)	(85)	—
Other liabilities: Nonpension postretirement benefits	(77)	(40)	(40)	(34)
Other liabilities: Pension	(214)	(260)	(295)	(284)
Noncontrolling interests	(10)	(16)	(16)	(558)
Total financial liabilities	(15,427)	(15,584)	(16,352)	(16,475)
NFL	$ (9,252)	$ (9,292)	$ (9,704)	$(10,348)

Amounts in Millions; Year Ended December	2015	2016	2017	2018
Net sales: U.S. morning foods	$2,992	$2,917	$2,709	$2,643
Net sales: U.S. snacks	3,234	3,197	3,110	2,957
Net sales: U.S. specialty channels	1,181	1,207	1,242	1,235
Net sales: North America other	1,687	1,593	1,612	1,853
Net sales: Europe	2,497	2,383	2,291	2,395
Net sales: Latin America	1,015	772	944	947
Net sales: Asia Pacific	919	896	946	1,517
Cost of goods sold		(8,131)	(8,155)	(8,821)
Gross profit		4,834	4,699	4,726
401(k) plan expense		(39)	(41)	(38)
Pension: service cost		(98)	(96)	(87)

continued

continued from previous page

Amounts in Millions; Year Ended December	2015	2016	2017	2018
Pension: Defined contribution plans		(36)	(34)	(27)
Postretirement: Service cost		(21)	(18)	(18)
Postretirement: Defined contribution plans		(17)	(16)	(11)
Postemployment: Service cost		(7)	(6)	(3)
Research and development expense		(182)	(148)	(154)
Advertising expense		(735)	(732)	(752)
Bad debt expense		(9)	(14)	(4)
Depreciation on capitalized leases		(124)	(169)	(114)
Other selling, general, and administrative expense		(1,978)	(2,558)	(1,737)
Other income (expense), net		(143)	526	(90)
Income taxes		(414)	(318)	(257)
Earnings from unconsolidated entities		1	7	196
Foreign currency translation adjustments, net of tax		(254)	79	(48)
Cash flow hedges, net of tax		(28)	6	8
Venezuela deconsolidation loss		63	—	—
NOPAT		$ 813	$1,167	$1,590

Amounts in Millions; Year Ended December	2015	2016	2017	2018
Pension: Interest cost		$(174)	$(164)	$(165)
Pension: Expected return on plan assets		352	371	361
Pension: Amortization of unrecognized prior service cost		(13)	(9)	(8)
Pension: Recognized net actuarial loss		(323)	36	(269)
Pension: Curtailment and special termination benefits		(1)	151	30
Postretirement: Interest cost		(39)	(37)	(36)
Postretirement: Expected return on plan assets		90	98	94
Postretirement: Amortization of unrecognized prior service cost		9	9	9
Postretirement: Recognized net (gain) loss		19	90	(81)
Postretirement: Curtailment		—	(3)	—
Postemployment: Interest cost		(3)	(3)	(1)
Postemployment: Amortization of unrecognized prior service cost		(1)	(1)	(1)
Postemployment: Recognized net (gain) loss		(3)	—	5
Interest expense		(424)	(274)	(300)
Income taxes		179	(92)	76
Financial stock-based compensation expense, net of tax		62	55	67
Net income attributable to noncontrolling interests		(1)	—	(8)
Net experience gain		18	32	(11)
Prior service credit		2	1	1
Venezuela deconsolidation loss				
Other comprehensive income attributable to noncontrolling interests, net		—	—	7
FEAT		$(251)	$ 260	$(230)

CE5.18 Review the 2018, 2017, 2016, and 2015 annual reports for Thor Industries (THO) to answer the following questions:

a. How does THO determine its inventory valuation?

b. What is the amount of the LIFO reserve and the future statutory tax rate for each of the fiscal years 2015–2018?

c. To convert THO's LIFO accounting to a FIFO basis, what adjustments are needed to inventory, taxes payable, cost of goods sold, tax expense, and retained earnings?

CE5.19 Using the 2018, 2017, 2016, and 2015 annual reports for Thor Industries (THO), assume a discount rate equal to the weighted average interest rate on notes disclosed in the debt footnote each year.

a. Utilizing this discount rate for THO's operating leases, estimate the unrecognized asset and liability for assets acquired under operating leases for THO at year-end for each of the last 4 years. Assume the payments after the fifth year will be equal to those in the fifth year.

b. For fiscal years 2016–2018, determine the assumed operating lease payments (last year's year 1 amount), the estimated interest and principal payments, and the related depreciation expense.

c. For fiscal years 2015–2018, prepare the related journal entries to record the liability and asset for the effective capitalization of the operating lease.

d. For fiscal years 2016–2018, prepare the related journal entries to record the amount of adjustment to SG&A, interest, and depreciation expense.

CE5.20 Using the 2018, 2017, 2016, and 2015 annual reports for **Thor Industries** (THO) and stock price information found from a financial website, compute the adjustment needed for stock-based compensation for each of the fiscal years 2015–2018.

a. Identify the stock-based compensation plans THO offers.

b. Compute the amount of adjustment for the restricted stock awards (RSAs) in each of the fiscal years from 2015 to 2018.

c. For fiscal years 2015–2018, prepare the related journal entries to record the amount of adjustment to the RSA overhang, related deferred tax assets (*DTA*s), and *FEAT*.

d. For fiscal years 2015–2018, prepare the related journal entries to record the liability and asset for the effective capitalization of the operating lease.

e. Compute the amount of adjustment for the equity-based restricted stock units (RSUs) in each of the fiscal years from 2015 to 2018.

f. For fiscal years 2015–2018, prepare the related journal entries to record the amount of adjustment to for the RSU overhang, related *DTA*s and *FEAT*.

g. For fiscal years 2015–2018, prepare the combined (RSA and RSU) adjustments to the opening balances for SBC liability and *DTA*s and to common stock equity (CSE).

h. For fiscal years 2015–2018, prepare the combined journal entries for both RSAs and RSUs from above for SBC liability, and *DTA*s, *FEAT* and to CSE via *FEAT*.

With the adjustments for the inventory, leases, and stock-based compensation included in THO's balance sheet and income statement for fiscal years 2015–2018, we arrive at the following adjusted financial statements:

Balance Sheet Amounts in Thousands	7/31/15	7/31/16	7/31/17	7/31/18
Assets				
Cash and cash equivalents	$ 183,478	$ 209,902	$ 223,258	$ 275,249
Accounts receivable, trade	245,335	370,710	454,446	467,488
Accounts receivable, other	25,642	22,454	31,090	19,747
Allowance for doubtful accounts	(1,283)	(625)	(692)	—
Inventory: Finished products—RV	35,693	39,943	24,904	44,998
Inventory: Finished products—other	18,045	20,141	27,862	35,320
Inventory: Work in progress	51,556	97,872	117,319	124,703
Inventory: Raw materials	133,482	173,362	214,518	258,429
Inventory: Chassis	37,739	102,686	109,555	116,308
Inventory: Excess of FIFO costs over LIFO costs	0	0	0	0
Prepaid expenses and other	8,323	10,548	11,577	11,281
Notes receivable	8,367	0	0	0
Property, plant, and equipment: Land	27,447	46,422	48,812	57,413
Property, plant, and equipment: Buildings and improvements	214,462	300,902	380,139	468,824
Property, plant, and equipment: Machinery and equipment	106,959	133,112	161,724	197,294
Property, plant, and equipment: Accumulated depreciation	(114,823)	(136,169)	(165,437)	(201,477)
Asset under capital lease	11,857	11,394	13,622	12,161
Goodwill: Towables	269,751	334,822	334,822	334,822
Goodwill: Other	42,871	42,871	42,871	42,871

continued

continued from previous page

Balance Sheet				
Amounts in Thousands	**7/31/15**	**7/31/16**	**7/31/17**	**7/31/18**
Amortizable intangible assets: Dealer networks/ customer relationships	143,860	404,960	404,960	404,960
Amortizable intangible assets: Dealer networks/ customer relationships—accum amort	(37,194)	(55,191)	(101,795)	(147,077)
Amortizable intangible assets: Trademarks	55,282	148,117	147,617	146,117
Amortizable intangible assets: Trademark—accum amort	(7,608)	(10,539)	(17,570)	(24,364)
Amortizable intangible assets: Design technology and other intangibles	22,400	22,400	19,300	18,200
Amortizable intangible assets: Design technology and other intangibles—accum amort	(8,168)	(10,870)	(9,203)	(9,555)
Amortizable intangible assets: Noncompete agreements	4,710	450	450	450
Amortizable intangible assets: Noncompete agreements—accum amort	(4,264)	(203)	(293)	(383)
Amortizable intangible assets: Backlog	0	12,400	0	0
Amortizable intangible assets: Backlog—accum amort	0	(4,133)	0	0
Deferred tax assets: Stock-based compensation	607	2,662	2,539	0
Deferred tax assets: Inventory basis	467	1,196	1,460	922
Deferred tax assets: Employee benefits	3,625	4,587	6,471	3,427
Deferred tax assets: Self-insurance reserves	10,411	10,504	9,940	6,368
Deferred tax assets: Accrued product warranties	39,486	43,388	73,393	62,332
Deferred tax assets: Accrued incentives	3,959	5,154	6,175	5,235
Deferred tax assets: Sales returns and allowances	1,520	1,642	2,340	1,741
Deferred tax assets: Accrued expenses	2,067	2,607	3,399	1,905
Deferred tax assets: Property, plant, and equipment	(340)	(4,164)	(8,151)	(9,060)
Deferred tax assets: Deferred compensation	6,367	9,145	14,556	12,864
Deferred tax assets: Tax credit carry-forward	110	0	0	0
Deferred tax assets: Intangibles	(30,246)	(22,308)	(17,184)	(9,151)
Deferred tax assets: Unrecognized tax benefits	3,913	4,105	3,925	2,581
Deferred tax assets: Other	(2,038)	(2,439)	(3,355)	(720)
Equity investment in joint venture	—	—	—	48,463
Other assets	11,722	25,838	38,398	51,989
Total assets	$1,525,549	$2,369,656	$2,607,762	$2,832,675

Amounts in Thousands	**7/31/15**	**7/31/16**	**7/31/17**	**7/31/18**
Liabilities				
Accounts payable	$ (162,587)	$ (263,774)	$ (328,601)	$ (286,974)
Accrued liabilities:				
Compensation and related items	(51,984)	(81,159)	(100,114)	(97,122)
Product warranties	(108,206)	(201,840)	(216,781)	(264,928)
Income and other taxes	(21,640)	(36,078)	(58,282)	(28,133)
Promotion and rebates	(19,817)	(40,452)	(46,459)	(59,133)
Product, property, and related liabilities	(10,892)	(15,969)	(16,521)	(17,815)
Other	(13,849)	(22,927)	(21,359)	(24,013)
Long-term debt	—	(360,000)	(145,000)	—
Unrecognized tax benefits	(11,945)	(9,975)	(10,263)	(12,446)
Capitalized lease liability	(11,857)	(11,394)	(13,622)	(12,161)
Stock-based compensation liability (*NFL*)	(1,734)	(7,607)	(12,091)	—
Other liabilities	(27,218)	(38,615)	(45,082)	(59,148)
Total liabilities	(441,729)	(1,089,791)	(1,014,175)	(861,873)

continued

continued from previous page

Amounts in Thousands	7/31/15	7/31/16	7/31/17	7/31/18
Shareholders' equity				
Preferred stock—no par value	—	—	—	—
Common stock	(6,231)	(6,244)	(6,260)	(6,277)
Additional paid-in capital	(215,539)	(224,496)	(235,525)	(252,204)
Retained earnings	(1,172,432)	(1,365,981)	(1,670,826)	(2,022,988)
RE adjustment for inventory	(19,760)	(19,588)	(26,599)	(33,061)
RE adjustment for stock-based compensation	1,127	4,945	9,552	0
Treasury shares	329,015	331,499	336,071	343,728
Total shareholders' equity	(1,083,820)	(1,279,865)	(1,593,587)	(1,970,802)
Total liabilities and shareholders' equity	$(1,525,549)	$(2,369,656)	$(2,607,762)	$(2,832,675)

Income Statement Amounts in Thousands; Year Ended	7/31/15	7/31/16	7/31/17	7/31/18
Net sales: Recreational vehicles—towables	$3,096,405	$3,338,659	$5,127,491	$6,008,700
Net sales: Recreational vehicles—motorized	870,799	1,094,250	1,971,466	2,146,315
Net sales: Other	56,594	218,673	253,557	305,947
Net sales: Intercompany eliminations	(16,979)	(69,470)	(105,562)	(132,053)
Cost of products sold		(3,721,132)	(5,975,412)	(6,863,149)
Depreciation expense		(24,613)	(34,333)	(38,105)
Product warranty expense		(114,119)	(195,799)	(259,845)
Selling, general, and administrative expenses		(284,578)	(384,826)	(440,299)
Depreciation on capitalized leases		(2,188)	(2,226)	(2,176)
Advertising costs		(14,472)	(24,997)	(26,874)
401(k) plan expense		(917)	(1,797)	(2,689)
Impairment charges		(9,113)	—	—
Amortization of intangible assets		(27,962)	(63,925)	(55,118)
Interest income		743	923	2,148
Interest expense		(1,894)	(10,021)	(5,558)
Gain on sale of facility		—	2,165	—
Other (income) and expense, net		1,181	3,217	3,964
Income from continuing operations before income taxes		383,048	559,921	641,208
Income taxes		(125,198)	(178,655)	(204,596)
Financial stock-based compensation expense, net of tax		(3,817)	(4,608)	9,552
Loss from discontinued operations, net of income taxes		(1,503)	—	—
Net income and comprehensive income		$ 252,529	$ 376,658	$ 446,165

This leads to the following updated calculations of *NOA*, *NFL*, *NOPAT*, and *FEAT* after the additional information was included from Chapter 4 and the adjustments here in Chapter 5.

	7/31/15	7/31/16	7/31/17	7/31/18
Cash and cash equivalents	$ 80,136	$ 91,642	$ 144,939	$ 166,578
Accounts receivable, trade	245,335	370,710	454,446	467,488
Accounts receivable, other	—	—	—	—
Allowance for doubtful accounts	(1,283)	(625)	(692)	—
Inventory: Finished products—RV	35,693	39,943	24,904	44,998
Inventory: Finished products—other	18,045	20,141	27,862	35,320
Inventory: Work in progress	51,556	97,872	117,319	124,703
Inventory: Raw materials	133,482	173,362	214,518	258,429
Inventory: Chassis	37,739	102,686	109,555	116,308

continued

continued from previous page

	7/31/15	7/31/16	7/31/17	7/31/18
Prepaid expenses and other	8,323	10,548	11,577	11,281
Property, plant, and equipment: Land	27,447	46,422	48,812	57,413
Property, plant, and equipment: Buildings and improvements	214,462	300,902	380,139	468,824
Property, plant, and equipment: Machinery and equipment	106,959	133,112	161,724	197,294
Property, plant, and equipment: Accumulated depreciation	(114,823)	(136,169)	(165,437)	(201,477)
Asset under capital lease	11,857	11,394	13,622	12,161
Goodwill: Towables	269,751	334,822	334,822	334,822
Goodwill: Other	42,871	42,871	42,871	42,871
Amortizable intangible assets: Dealer networks/customer relationships	143,860	404,960	404,960	404,960
Amotizable intangible assets: Dealer networks/customer relationships—accum amort	(37,194)	(55,191)	(101,795)	(147,077)
Amortizable intangible assets: Trademarks	55,282	148,117	147,617	146,117
Amortizable intangible assets: Trademark—accum amort	(7,608)	(10,539)	(17,570)	(24,364)
Amortizable intangible assets: Design technology and other intangibles	22,400	22,400	19,300	18,200
Amortizable intangible assets: Design technology and other intangibles—accum amort	(8,168)	(10,870)	(9,203)	(9,555)
Amortizable intangible assets: Noncompete agreements	4,710	450	450	450
Amortizable intangible assets: Noncompete agreements—accum amort	(4,264)	(203)	(293)	(383)
Amortizable intangible assets: Backlog	—	12,400	—	—
Amortizable intangible assets: Backlog—accum amort	—	(4,133)	—	—
Deferred tax assets: Inventory basis	467	1,196	1,460	922
Deferred tax assets: Employee benefits	3,625	4,587	6,471	3,427
Deferred tax assets: Self-insurance reserves	10,411	10,504	9,940	6,368
Deferred tax assets: Accrued product warranties	39,486	43,388	73,393	62,332
Deferred tax assets: Accrued incentives	3,959	5,154	6,175	5,235
Deferred tax assets: Sales returns and allowances	1,520	1,642	2,340	1,741
Deferred tax assets: Accrued expenses	2,067	2,607	3,399	1,905
Deferred tax assets: Property, plant, and equipment	(340)	(4,164)	(8,151)	(9,060)
Deferred tax assets: Deferred compensation	6,367	9,145	14,556	12,864
Deferred tax assets: Tax credit carry-forward	110	—	—	—
Deferred tax assets: Intangibles	(30,246)	(22,308)	(17,184)	(9,151)
Deferred tax assets: Unrecognized tax benefits	3,913	4,105	3,925	2,581
Deferred tax assets: Other	(2,038)	(2,439)	(3,355)	(720)
Equity investment in joint venture	—	—	—	48,463
Other assets	11,722	25,838	38,398	51,989
Total operating assets	1,387,591	2,226,280	2,495,814	2,704,257
Accounts payable	(162,587)	(263,774)	(328,601)	(286,974)
Accrued liabilities:				
Compensation and related items	(51,984)	(81,159)	(100,114)	(97,122)
Product warranties	(108,206)	(201,840)	(216,781)	(264,928)
Income and other taxes	(21,640)	(36,078)	(58,282)	(28,133)
Promotion and rebates	(19,817)	(40,452)	(46,459)	(59,133)
Product, property, and related liabilities	(10,892)	(15,969)	(16,521)	(17,815)
Other	(13,849)	(22,927)	(21,359)	(24,013)
Unrecognized tax benefits	(11,945)	(9,975)	(10,263)	(12,446)
Other liabilities	(27,218)	(38,615)	(45,082)	(59,148)
Total operating liabilities	(428,138)	(710,789)	(843,462)	(849,712)
NOA	$ 959,453	$1,515,490	1,652,352	$1,854,544

	7/31/15	7/31/16	7/31/17	7/31/18
Cash and cash equivalents	$ 103,342	$ 118,260	$ 78,319	$ 108,671
Accounts receivable, other	25,642	22,454	31,090	19,747
Notes receivable	8,367	—	—	—
Deferred tax assets: Stock-based compensation	607	2,662	2,539	—
Total financial assets	137,958	143,376	111,948	128,418
Long-term debt	—	(360,000)	(145,000)	—
Capitalized lease liability	(11,857)	(11,394)	(13,622)	(12,161)
Stock-based compensation liability (*NFL*)	(1,734)	(7,607)	(12,091)	—
Preferred stock—no par value	—	—	—	—
Total financial liabilities	(13,591)	(379,002)	(170,713)	(12,161)
NFL	$ 124,367	$(235,625)	$ (58,765)	$ 116,257

Amounts in Thousands; Year Ended	7/31/15	7/31/16	7/31/17	7/31/18
Net sales: Recreational vehicles—towables	$3,096,405	$3,338,659	$5,127,491	$6,008,700
Net sales: Recreational vehicles—motorized	870,799	1,094,250	1,971,466	2,146,315
Net sales: Other	56,594	218,673	253,557	305,947
Net sales: Intercompany eliminations	(16,979)	(69,470)	(105,562)	(132,053)
Cost of products sold		(3,721,132)	(5,975,412)	(6,863,149)
Depreciation expense		(24,613)	(34,333)	(38,105)
Product warranty expense		(114,119)	(195,799)	(259,845)
Selling, general, and administrative expenses		(284,578)	(384,826)	(440,299)
Depreciation on capitalized leases		(2,188)	(2,226)	(2,176)
Advertising costs		(14,472)	(24,997)	(26,874)
401(k) plan expense		(917)	(1,797)	(2,689)
Impairment charges		(9,113)	—	—
Amortization of intangible assets		(27,962)	(63,925)	(55,118)
Gain on sale of facility		—	2,165	—
Other (income) and expense, net		1,181	3,217	3,964
Income taxes		(125,601)	(181,840)	(205,513)
Loss from discontinued operations, net of income taxes		(1,503)	—	—
NOPAT		$ 257,095	$ 387,179	$ 439,105

Amounts in Thousands; Year Ended	7/31/15	7/31/16	7/31/17	7/31/18
Interest income		$ 743	$ 923	$ 2,148
Interest expense		(1,894)	(10,021)	(5,558)
Income taxes		403	3,184	917
Financial stock-based compensation expense, net of tax		(3,817)	(4,608)	9,552
FEAT		$(4,566)	$(10,521)	$ 7,060

CE5.21 Review the 2018, 2017, 2016, and 2015 annual reports for **Winnebago** (WGO) to answer the following questions:

a. How does WGO determine its inventory valuation?

b. What is the amount of the LIFO reserve and the future statutory tax rate for each of the fiscal years 2015–2018?

c. To convert WGO's LIFO accounting to a FIFO basis, what adjustments are needed to inventory, taxes payable, cost of goods sold, tax expense, and retained earnings?

CE5.22 Using the 2018, 2017, 2016, and 2015 annual reports for **Winnebago** (WGO), assume a discount rate equal to the weighted average interest rate on notes disclosed in the debt footnote each year.

a. Utilizing this discount rate for WGO's operating leases, estimate the unrecognized asset and liability for assets acquired under operating leases for WGO at year-end for each of the last 4 years. Assume the payments after the fifth year will be equal to those in the fifth year.

b. For fiscal years 2016–2018, determine the assumed operating lease payments (last year's year 1 amount), the estimated interest and principal payments, and the related depreciation expense.

c. For fiscal years 2015–2018, prepare the related journal entries to record the liability and asset for the effective capitalization of the operating lease.

d. For fiscal years 2016–2018, prepare the related journal entries to record the amount of adjustment to SG&A, interest, and depreciation expense.

CE5.23 Using the 2018, 2017, 2016, and 2015 annual reports for Winnebago (WGO) and stock price information found from a financial website, compute the adjustment needed for stock-based compensation for each of the fiscal years 2015–2018.

a. Identify the stock-based compensation plans WGO offers.

b. Compute the amount of adjustment for the stock options in each of the fiscal years from 2015 to 2018.

c. For fiscal years 2016–2018, prepare the related journal entries to record the amount of adjustment to the stock option overhang, related *DTA*s, and *FEAT*.

d. Compute the amount of adjustment for the stock rewards in each of the fiscal years from 2015 to 2018.

e. For fiscal years 2016–2018, prepare the related journal entries to record the amount of adjustment to for the stock award, related *DTA*s, and *FEAT*.

f. For fiscal years 2015–2018, prepare the combined (stock option and stock award) adjustments to the opening balances for SBC liability, and *DTA*s and to *CSE*.

g. For fiscal years 2015–2018, prepare the combined journal entries for both stock options and awards from above for SBC liability, *DTA*s, *FEAT* and to *CSE* via *FEAT*.

With the adjustments for the inventory, leases, and stock-based compensation included in WGO's balance sheet and income statement for fiscal years 2015–2018, we arrive at the following adjusted financial statements:

Balance Sheet				
Amounts in Thousands	**8/29/15**	**8/27/16**	**8/26/17**	**8/25/18**
Assets				
Cash and cash equivalents	$ 70,239	$ 85,583	$ 35,945	$ 2,342
Receivables, net	66,936	66,184	124,539	164,585
Inventories: Finished goods	12,179	19,129	16,947	26,513
Inventories: Work in process	66,602	76,350	60,818	68,339
Inventories: Raw materials	65,928	60,740	99,919	139,039
Prepaid expenses and other assets	6,882	6,300	11,388	9,883
Property, plant, and equipment: Land	1,874	3,864	3,914	6,747
Property, plant, and equipment: Buildings and building improvements	53,388	62,073	73,831	94,622
Property, plant, and equipment: Machinery and equipment	94,034	95,087	99,952	105,663
Property, plant, and equipment: Software	8,033	15,878	17,844	23,388
Property, plant, and equipment: Transportation	8,913	8,956	8,993	8,837
Property, plant, and equipment: Accumulated depreciation	(128,992)	(129,927)	(132,974)	(138,064)
Capitalized lease asset	293	256	15,474	14,011
Goodwill: Towable	1,228	1,228	242,728	244,684
Goodwill: Corporate/All other	—	—	—	29,686
Intangibles: Trade name	—	—	148,000	177,250
Intangibles: Dealer network	—	—	80,500	95,581
Intangibles: Backlog	—	—	18,000	19,527
Intangibles: Noncompete agreements	—	—	4,600	5,347
Intangibles: Leasehold interest-favorable	—	—	2,000	2,000
Intangibles—accum amortization: Dealer network	—	—	(5,348)	(12,328)
Intangibles—accum amortization: Backlog	—	—	(18,000)	(19,135)

continued

continued from previous page

Balance Sheet Amounts in Thousands	8/29/15	8/27/16	8/26/17	8/25/18
Intangibles—accum amortization: Noncompete agreements	—	—	(1,116)	(2,084)
Intangibles—accum amortization: Leasehold interest-favorable	—	—	(196)	(441)
Investment in life insurance	26,172	26,492	27,418	28,297
Deferred tax assets: Deferred compensation	10,757	9,609	9,135	4,730
Deferred tax assets: Warranty reserves	4,288	4,729	11,675	9,842
Deferred tax assets: Postretirement health-care benefits	12,792	2,262	—	—
Deferred tax assets: Self-insurance reserve	2,378	2,214	1,967	2,601
Deferred tax assets: Accrued vacation	1,938	2,006	2,142	1,298
Deferred tax assets: Stock-based compensation	1,239	1,399	1,591	1,488
Deferred tax assets: Inventory	—	—	—	615
Deferred tax assets: Unrecognized tax benefit	726	698	437	584
Deferred tax assets: Other	1,592	1,785	2,072	1,797
Other assets	9,313	7,725	5,493	10,290
Total assets	$398,732	$430,620	$969,689	$1,127,573

Amounts in Thousands	8/29/15	8/27/16	8/26/17	8/25/18
Liabilities				
Accounts payable	$ (33,158)	$ (44,134)	$ (79,194)	$ (81,039)
Current maturities of long-term debt	—	—	(2,850)	—
Income taxes payable	(13,704)	(11,813)	(14,888)	(23,795)
Accrued expenses: Accrued compensation	(13,415)	(15,125)	(21,197)	(24,608)
Accrued expenses: Product warranties	(11,254)	(12,412)	(30,805)	(40,498)
Accrued expenses: Self-insurance	(6,242)	(5,812)	(6,122)	(12,262)
Accrued expenses: Accrued loss on repurchases	(1,329)	(881)	—	—
Accrued expenses: Promotional	(3,149)	(4,756)	(6,560)	(11,017)
Accrued expenses: Accrued interest	—	—	(3,128)	(3,095)
Accrued expenses: Other	(5,818)	(5,236)	(6,503)	(11,269)
Long-term debt, less current maturities	—	—	(271,726)	(291,441)
Unrecognized tax benefits	(2,511)	(2,461)	(1,606)	(1,745)
Deferred tax liabilities: Inventory	(2,383)	(1,930)	(1,919)	—
Deferred tax liabilities: Intangibles	—	—	(7,455)	(21,292)
Deferred tax liabilities: Depreciation	(1,338)	(3,650)	(6,261)	(5,909)
Postretirement health-care benefit cost	(34,535)	(6,346)	—	—
Nonqualified deferred compensation	(19,508)	(18,003)	(16,476)	(14,831)
Executive share option plan liability	(4,788)	(3,341)	(1,498)	(935)
SERP benefit liability	(2,649)	(2,681)	(2,534)	(2,309)
Executive deferred compensation	(299)	(389)	(447)	(421)
Officer stock-based compensation	(242)	(763)	(1,664)	(1,528)
Capitalized lease liability	(293)	(256)	(15,474)	(14,011)
Stock-based compensation liability (*NFL*)	—	(1,055)	(3,088)	(1,188)
Other liabilities	—	—	(1,078)	(250)
Total liabilities	(156,615)	(141,043)	(502,473)	(563,443)

continued

continued from previous page

Amounts in Thousands	8/29/15	8/27/16	8/26/17	8/25/18
Shareholders' equity				
Common stock—$0.50 par value	(25,888)	(25,888)	(25,888)	(25,888)
Additional paid-in capital	(32,018)	(32,717)	(80,401)	(86,223)
Retained earnings	(585,941)	(620,546)	(679,138)	(768,816)
RE adjustment for inventory	(21,154)	(21,903)	(27,981)	(30,623)
RE adjustment for stock-based compensation	—	686	2,439	938
Accumulated other comprehensive (income)/loss	2,274	(10,975)	1,023	(892)
Treasury stock, at cost	420,610	421,767	342,730	347,374
Total shareholders' equity	(242,117)	(289,577)	(467,216)	(564,130)
Total liabilities and shareholders' equity	$(398,732)	$(430,620)	$(969,689)	$(1,127,573)

Income Statement				
Amounts in Thousands; Year Ended	**8/29/15**	**8/27/16**	**8/26/17**	**8/25/18**
Net sales: Motorized	$ 904,821	$ 881,363	$ 853,360	$ 860,675
Net sales: Towable	71,684	89,412	685,197	1,127,723
Net sales: Other	—	4,451	8,562	28,431
Cost of products sold		(844,921)	(1,291,189)	(1,671,272)
Warranty expense		(16,503)	(31,631)	(42,377)
Gross profit		113,802	224,299	303,180
Advertising expense		(4,900)	(5,700)	(7,400)
Depreciation on capitalized leases		(96)	(113)	(1,658)
SG&A: Selling		(14,923)	(29,968)	(42,450)
SG&A: General and administrative		(33,096)	(55,219)	(75,549)
Net periodic postretirement benefit income: Amortization of prior service benefit		7,736	40,444	—
Net periodic postretirement benefit income: Amortization of net actuarial loss		(1,612)	(15,648)	—
SG&A: Transaction costs		—	(6,592)	(2,177)
SG&A: Amortization of intangible assets		—	(24,660)	(9,328)
Interest expense		(17)	(16,852)	(19,128)
Nonoperating income		457	330	494
Income before taxes		67,351	110,321	145,984
Provision for income taxes		(21,106)	(32,913)	(40,985)
Financial stock-based compensation expense, net of tax		(686)	(1,754)	1,646
Net income		45,560	75,654	106,645
Comprehensive income items:				
Amortization of prior service credit		(4,788)	(25,035)	—
Amortization of net actuarial loss		1,010	9,705	27
Increase in actuarial loss		(674)	(57)	—
Plan amendment		17,701	3,903	—
Change in fair value of interest rate swap		—	(514)	1,947
Comprehensive income attributable to WGO		$ 58,809	$ 63,656	$ 108,619

This leads to the following updated calculations of *NOA*, *NFL*, *NOPAT*, and *FEAT* after the additional information was included from Chapter 4 and the adjustments here in Chapter 5.

Amounts in Thousands	8/29/15	8/27/16	8/26/17	8/25/18
Cash and cash equivalents	19,530	19,505	30,942	$ 2,342
Receivables, net	66,936	66,184	124,539	164,585
Inventories: Finished goods	12,179	19,129	16,947	26,513
Inventories: Work-in-process	66,602	76,350	60,818	68,339
Inventories: Raw materials	65,928	60,740	99,919	139,039
Prepaid expenses and other assets	6,882	6,300	11,388	9,883
Property, plant, and equipment: Land	1,874	3,864	3,914	6,747
Property, plant, and equipment: Buildings and building improvements	53,388	62,073	73,831	94,622
Property, plant, and equipment: Machinery and equipment	94,034	95,087	99,952	105,663
Property, plant, and equipment: Software	8,033	15,878	17,844	23,388
Property, plant, and equipment: Transportation	8,913	8,956	8,993	8,837
Property, plant, and equipment: Accumulated depreciation	(128,992)	(129,927)	(132,974)	(138,064)
Capitalized lease asset	293	256	15,474	14,011
Goodwill: Towable	1,228	1,228	242,728	244,684
Goodwill: Corporate/All other	—	—	—	29,686
Intangibles: Trade name	—	—	148,000	177,250
Intangibles: Dealer network	—	—	80,500	95,581
Intangibles: Backlog	—	—	18,000	19,527
Intangibles: Non-compete agreements	—	—	4,600	5,347
Intangibles: Leasehold interest-favorable	—	—	2,000	2,000
Intangibles—accum amortization: Dealer network	—	—	(5,348)	(12,328)
Intangibles—accum amortization: Backlog	—	—	(18,000)	(19,135)
Intangibles—accum amortization: Noncompete agreements	—	—	(1,116)	(2,084)
Intangibles—accum amortization: Leasehold interest—favorable	—	—	(196)	(441)
Deferred tax assets: Warranty reserves	4,288	4,729	11,675	9,842
Deferred tax assets: Accrued vacation	1,938	2,006	2,142	1,298
Deferred tax assets: Inventory	—	—	—	615
Deferred tax assets: Unrecognized tax benefit	726	698	437	584
Deferred tax assets: Other	1,592	1,785	2,072	1,797
Other assets	9,313	7,725	5,493	10,290
Total operating assets	294,685	322,565	924,574	1,090,418
Accounts payable	(33,158)	(44,134)	(79,194)	(81,039)
Income taxes payable	(13,704)	(11,813)	(14,888)	(23,795)
Accrued expenses: Accrued compensation	(13,415)	(15,125)	(21,197)	(24,608)
Accrued expenses: Product warranties	(11,254)	(12,412)	(30,805)	(40,498)
Accrued expenses: Promotional	(3,149)	(4,756)	(6,560)	(11,017)
Accrued expenses: Other	(5,818)	(5,236)	(6,503)	(11,269)
Unrecognized tax benefits	(2,511)	(2,461)	(1,606)	(1,745)
Other liabilities	—	—	(1,078)	(250)
Total operating liabilities	(83,009)	(95,937)	(161,831)	(194,221)
NOA	$ 211,675	$ 226,628	$ 762,743	$ 896,197

Amounts in Thousands	8/29/15	8/27/16	8/26/17	8/25/18
Investment in life insurance	$ 26,172	$ 26,492	$ 27,418	$ 28,297
Deferred tax assets: Deferred compensation	10,757	9,609	9,135	4,730
Deferred tax assets: Postretirement health-care benefits	12,792	2,262	—	—
Deferred tax assets: Self-insurance reserve	2,378	2,214	1,967	2,601
Deferred tax assets: Stock based compensation	1,239	1,399	1,591	1,488
Total financial assets	104,047	108,055	45,114	37,116

continued

continued from previous page

Amounts in Thousands	8/29/15	8/27/16	8/26/17	8/25/18
Current maturities of long-term debt	—	—	(2,850)	—
Accrued expenses: Self-insurance	(6,242)	(5,812)	(6,122)	(12,262)
Accrued expenses: Accrued loss on repurchases	(1,329)	(881)	—	—
Accrued expenses: Accrued interest	—	—	(3,128)	(3,095)
Long-term debt, less current maturities	—	—	(271,726)	(291,441)
Deferred tax liabilities: Inventory	(2,383)	(1,930)	(1,919)	—
Deferred tax liabilities: Intangibles	—	—	(7,455)	(21,292)
Deferred tax liabilities: Depreciation	(1,338)	(3,650)	(6,261)	(5,909)
Postretirement health-care benefit cost	(34,535)	(6,346)	—	—
Nonqualified deferred compensation	(19,508)	(18,003)	(16,476)	(14,831)
Executive share option plan liability	(4,788)	(3,341)	(1,498)	(935)
SERP benefit liability	(2,649)	(2,681)	(2,534)	(2,309)
Executive deferred compensation	(299)	(389)	(447)	(421)
Officer stock-based compensation	(242)	(763)	(1,664)	(1,528)
Capitalized lease liability	(293)	(256)	(15,474)	(14,011)
Stock-based compensation liability (*NFL*)	—	(1,055)	(3,088)	(1,004)
Total financial liabilities	(73,606)	(45,106)	(340,642)	(369,038)
NFL	$ 30,441	$ 62,948	$(295,528)	$(331,923)

Amounts in Thousands; Year Ended	8/29/15	8/27/16	8/26/17	8/25/18
Net sales: Motorized	$ 904,821	$ 881,363	$ 853,360	$ 860,675
Net sales: Towable	71,684	89,412	685,197	1,127,723
Net sales: Other	—	4,451	8,562	28,431
Cost of products sold		(844,921)	(1,291,189)	(1,671,272)
Warranty expense		(16,503)	(31,631)	(42,377)
Advertising expense		(4,900)	(5,700)	(7,400)
Depreciation on capitalized leases		(96)	(113)	(1,658)
SG&A: Selling		(14,923)	(29,968)	(42,450)
SG&A: General and administrative		(33,096)	(55,219)	(75,549)
SG&A: Transaction costs		—	(6,592)	(2,177)
SG&A: Amortization of intangible assets		—	(24,660)	(9,328)
Nonoperating income		457	330	494
Provision for income taxes		(18,968)	(30,132)	(45,939)
NOPAT		$ 42,276	$ 72,244	$ 119,173

Amounts in Thousands; Year Ended	8/29/15	8/27/16	8/26/17	8/25/18
Net periodic postretirement benefit income: Amortization of prior service benefit		$ 7,736	$40,444	$ —
Net periodic postretirement benefit income: Amortization of net actuarial loss		(1,612)	(15,648)	—
Interest expense		(16)	(16,851)	(19,128)
Provision for income taxes		(2,137)	(2,780)	4,954
Financial stock-based compensation expense, net of tax		(685)	(1,753)	1,646
Comprehensive income items:				
Amortization of prior service credit		(4,788)	(25,035)	—
Amortization of net actuarial loss		1,010	9,705	27
Increase in actuarial loss		(674)	(57)	—
Plan amendment		17,701	3,903	—
Change in fair value of interest rate swap		—	(514)	1,947
FEAT		$ 16,533	$ (8,588)	$(10,553)

Chapter Six

Analysis of Enterprise Operations

TAKEAWAYS

When you complete this chapter, you should be able to:

1. Disaggregate profitability of enterprise operations into profit margin and asset turnover.
2. Compute profitability of financial activities.
3. Perform a common-size analysis of *PM* and *ATO*, and compare the results to peer companies.
4. Explain the relation of equity and operating profitability and effects of equity versus debt financing.

In this chapter, we proceed to the third step in the valuation process outlined in Chapter 1. Our goal is to determine the current financial status of a company using its financial statements. The process is often referred to as financial statement analysis. The importance of this step is highlighted by the existence of courses and textbooks bearing this name. The understanding and insights gained will be fundamental to our forecasting and valuation in later chapters.

In their fundamental analysis study, Nissim and Penman (*Review of Accounting Studies*, 2001) described the analysis of historical financial statements as an aid in identifying current ratios. They emphasized the point that "current financial statement ratios are deemed relevant for valuation if they predict future ratios." In order to use ratios in this way, we distinguish "between 'transitory' features of ratios (that bear only on the present) and 'permanent' features (that forecast the future)." (p. 111)

We seek to identify ratios that drive future payoffs. We start by analyzing the return on net operating assets (*RNOA*), which is the ratio of *NOPAT* to the assets that generate the *NOPAT* (i.e., *NOA*). We break *RNOA* into two components, which identify quite different aspects of the operating activities: profitability and resource utilization. The methodology we follow is often referred to as DuPont analysis because the **DuPont Corporation** pioneered its use in the 1920s. Throughout this discussion, we will focus on changes over time in these components of **General Mills**' (GIS) *RNOA*, and we will also compare GIS' *RNOA* to that of its main competitor, **Kellogg** (K). Our goals are to understand the current ratios and to identify the components that are transitory and permanent.

EVALUATING PROFITABILITY OF OPERATIONS

When evaluating an investment opportunity, we often refer to its rate of return. The rate of return considers the amount that will be earned as a portion of the associated investment.

If you are offered the opportunity to undertake an investment with an expected return of \$10,000, you do not have enough information to make a decision as to whether you should accept or reject the offer. Is the required investment \$10,000 or \$1,000,000? The fact that a share of stock is trading at \$10 or at \$70 tells you little if you have no idea of its riskiness and what your expected payoffs would be from buying it. Similarly, an offer of an opportunity to make an investment will

CHAPTER OUTLINE

Analysis of Enterprise Operations

Evaluating Profitability of Operations
- Calculating *RNOA*
- Disaggregating *RNOA*
- Operating Profit Margin
- Operating Asset Turnover

Evaluating Financial Activities
- Calculating *RNFL*

Common-Size Analysis
- Detailed Analysis of *PM*
- Detailed Analysis of *ATO*
- Comparisons to Competitors

Equity Analysis
- Relation of *ROE* and *RNOA*
- Equity versus Debt Financing

not catch your attention unless you understand the expected return. A comparison of the amount earned to the amount invested, however, provides a meaningful metric. *RNOA* provides such a comparison.

The reformulation in Chapters 3 through 5 equipped us to evaluate *RNOA*. We gathered information on *NOPAT* and *NOA*; that is, we learned the amount earned on the amount invested in operating activities. Now we can compare these items to gain a measure of an accounting *ROR*. How profitable (*NOPAT*) was the investment (*NOA*)? By comparing *NOPAT* to *NOA*, we arrive at a measure of *RNOA* that will be examined to determine the current status of the company, used as a central piece of forecasting and employed in our valuation models.

MEASURES OF PROFITABILITY

Many possible measures of return or profitability can be calculated. Common ones are

$$\text{Return on Invested Capital } (ROIC) = \frac{\text{Net Income} - \text{Dividends}}{\text{Invested Capital}}$$

$$\text{Return on Equity } (ROE) = \frac{\text{Net Income}}{\text{Equity}}$$

$$\text{Return on Assets } (ROA) = \frac{\text{Net Income}}{\text{Total Assets}}$$

In each of these measures, issues arise regarding the particulars of computation and measurement. For instance, when calculating *ROIC,* what assets should be included/excluded when calculating invested capital? When computing *ROA*, should we use beginning balance, average balance, or ending balance for assets? And for *ROE*, do we want to look only at common equity or all equity?

By focusing on *RNOA*, we narrow our focus to gaining an understanding of enterprise operations. As was discussed in prior chapters, this allows us to set aside the financial decisions of the company. The goal is a measure of the profitability of the primary business functions, that is, the operations.

It is important to note that *RNOA* is an accounting measure of return on net operating assets and that it likely will differ from the market measure. We will return to this point in Chapter 11, when we compare *RNOA* and the weighted average cost of capital for operations (also known as the unlevered cost of capital).

Calculating Return on Net Operating Assets

The rate of return on operations is reflected in the *RNOA*, defined as follows:

$$RNOA = \frac{NOPAT}{average(NOA)}$$

When analyzing reported (historical) information, we do not know the actual timing of investments and therefore utilize an average balance of *NOA*. The use of the average denominator is common in evaluation of past financial data in order to deal with the fact that the amount of resources employed varied throughout the year.

Ideally, we would know the average amount of resources the company has available each day. Of course, daily financial statements are not available because the cost of creating these would exceed the benefit. Initially, it might appear that we could use quarterly reports to gather more information about the changing amount of resources over the year. Based on differences in financial reporting at interim periods, this would not be wise (see discussion later in this chapter). Thus, we take a rough approximation of the resources used during the year by averaging beginning and ending *NOA*s. Note that, when we form forecasts, we will use beginning-of-period balances rather than averages for the return computation (e.g., *RNOA* = *NOPAT*/*Beginning NOA*); the idea here is that we forecast the *NOPAT* that will be earned on the investment made at the beginning of the period. This use of beginning *NOA* will be possible in a forecasting setting due to the assumed timing of the investments by the debt and equity holders.

Consider a simple example of an investment of $100 on January 1 in an asset with a 10 percent rate of return and a further investment of $100 on July 1. Of course, the rate of return through December 31 is 10 percent, which is equal to $15/[($200 + $100)/2]; that is, the dollar return divided by the average investment. The rate of return through December 31 is obviously not equal to $15/$100, which is the dollar return divided by the investment at the beginning of the year. At the end of the year, however, we would have $200 to invest going forward, and if we use the rate of return for the past year to forecast the expected rate for next year, that rate would be 10 percent, and we would expect to earn $20 in the second year.

ADJUSTING *RNOA* FOR EFFECTS OF 53-WEEK YEARS

GIS' fiscal year-ends on the last Sunday in May. This creates a year that is 53 weeks every fifth or sixth year. As a result, the calculation of *RNOA* shown above, while correct, can, at times, be misleading. The years ending May 2018, 2017, and 2016 were 52 weeks. However, the year ended May 2015 was 53 weeks. If we calculate *RNOA* following the formula each time, we likely will see a higher *RNOA* in 2015 due to the extra week of sales.

For example, assume you earned $1,000 per week in salary and had resources of $100,000 throughout a five-year period. The *RNOA* would be as follows if the middle year had 53 weeks:

	Year 1	Year 2	Year 3	Year 4	Year 5
Weeks in year	52	52	53	52	52
Salary	$ 52,000	$ 52,000	$ 53,000	$ 52,000	$ 52,000
Resources	100,000	100,000	100,000	100,000	100,000
RNOA	52.0%	52.0%	53.0%	52.0%	52.0%

It appears that *RNOA* has increased from 52 to 53 percent in year 3 simply due to having a longer earnings period. Also, in year 4 *RNOA* appears to have decreased from 53 to 52 percent because of the shorter earnings period.

To avoid this issue, we also consider a 52/53-week adjusted *RNOA* year 3, which adjusts *NOPAT* in the years that have an extra week, as follows:

$$RNOA = \frac{NOPAT \times {}^{52}\!/_{53}}{average(NOA)}$$

Using this revised formula for year 3, our example shows an *RNOA* of 52 percent in each of the 5 years. The illusion of growth in profitability in year 3 followed by a subsequent fall off has been removed.

For GIS, we can compute *RNOA* for the year ended May 2018 by dividing its *NOPAT* of $2,316.4 by the average *NOA* of $20,945.6 (average of $25,035.4 in May 2018 and $16,855.9 in May 2017) to get 11.06 percent. Notice that, had we just used beginning *NOA*, we would have estimated 13.74 percent and failed to recognize that there was a large increase in *NOA* during the most recent year. Remember that, before we could do this calculation, we had to reformulate the income statement and the balance sheet to identify the operating and financial components.

Exhibit 6.1 summarizes *RNOA* and its components for the past few years based on the output from our reformulation in Chapters 3 through 5:

EXHIBIT 6.1 GIS' Annual *RNOA*

Amounts in Millions; Year Ended	5/31/2015	5/29/2016	5/28/2017	5/27/2018
NOPAT		1,854.9	1,913.5	2,316.4
NOA	17,463.8	16,493.9	16,855.9	25,035.4
Average *NOA*		16,978.8	16,674.9	20,945.6
RNOA		10.92%	11.48%	11.06%

DISAGGREGATING RETURN ON NET OPERATING ASSETS

LO1: Disaggregate profitability of enterprise operations into profit margin and asset turnover.

Knowing the profitability of the enterprise operations of the firm is helpful but not sufficient to allow us to forecast future operations. Note that, over the last few years, there is not a wide variation in the *RNOA,* as shown in **Exhibit 6.1**. Still, we need additional information to ensure that the firm's profitability is stable and sustainable before we undertake forecasting. Is GIS able to maintain a profitability around 11 percent? 11.5 percent? Are there items in these years that will not continue?

As a part of financial statement analysis, we generally disaggregate *RNOA* into its two components, operating profit margin and asset turnover, to provide further insight into the performance of the enterprise. This disaggregation yields

$$\begin{aligned} RNOA &= \frac{NOPAT}{average(NOA)} \\ &= \frac{NOPAT}{Sales} \times \frac{Sales}{average(NOA)} \\ &= PM \times ATO \end{aligned}$$

where *PM* is profit margin and *ATO* is asset turnover. Thinking of the operating results along these two dimensions is very beneficial and yields insights into the sources of profitability, which will be very helpful in forecasting. The separation into operating profit margin and asset turnover as depicted above is the DuPont method.

Operating Profit Margin

The operating profit margin (*PM*) reveals how much profit the firm earns from each sales dollar. All things equal, a higher *PM* is preferable. *PM* is affected by the level of gross profit (sales revenue minus cost of goods sold) the firm earns on its products, which depends on product prices and manufacturing or purchase costs. *PM* is also affected by the level of operating expenses, which the firm requires to support its products or services. This includes overhead costs, such as wages, marketing, occupancy, and research and development. *PM* is affected by the level of competition (which affects product pricing) and the firm's willingness and ability to control costs.

GIS' *PM* is computed as follows:

$$PM = \frac{NOPAT}{Sales} = \frac{2{,}316.4}{15{,}740.4} = 14.72\%$$

This means that, for each dollar of GIS' sales during the year ended May 2018, the firm earned roughly 14.7 cents of profit after all operating expenses and taxes. As a reference, the median *PM* for publicly traded firms during the past decade is about 6 cents.

PM AND 53-WEEK YEARS

Previously, we considered the required adjustment to the *RNOA* calculation in years that were 53 weeks long. For *PM*, no such adjustment is required. The reason is both the *NOPAT* and sales are measured over 53 weeks, so the length of the year has no effect.

Using the computations of *NOPAT* in Chapter 5 and reported sales, we can also examine the trend of GIS' *PM* over time, as shown in **Exhibit 6.2**.

EXHIBIT 6.2 GIS' Annual Operating *PM*

Amounts in Millions; Year Ended	5/29/2016	5/28/2017	5/27/2018
NOPAT	1,854.9	1,913.5	2,316.4
Sales	16,563.1	15,619.8	15,740.4
Operating *PM*	11.20%	12.25%	14.72%

Clearly, *PM* is not stable for GIS. Further decomposition of the *PM* may yield insight into reasons for the increasing pattern in this ratio over the last 3 years. One issue to consider is the extent to which the changes in the *PM* are being driven by items directly related to sales or by peripheral items (which are still within operating activities).

We could consider looking at a "*PM* from sales" by excluding the earnings from joint ventures, foreign currency translation, and gains/losses on cash flow hedges. Earnings from joint ventures will not change if GIS sells more or less of its products in a particular period. Therefore, it is not included in a computation of *PM* from sales. Additionally, the other two of these items will be assumed to have a zero value in expectation. For instance, although we expect there to be an amount reported for financial statement translation, forecasting a nonzero amount is tantamount to forecasting future changes in foreign currency exchange rates! If we focus on *PM* from sales (as in **Exhibit 6.3**), we see a sharper increase.

EXHIBIT 6.3 GIS' Annual *NOPAT* and *PM* from Sales

Amounts in Millions; Year Ended	5/29/2016	5/28/2017	5/27/2018
Net sales	$16,563.1	$15,619.8	$15,740.4
Cost of sales	(10,728.5)	(10,066.2)	(10,308.8)
Advertising expense	(754.4)	(623.8)	(575.9)
Research expense	(222.1)	(218.2)	(219.1)
Depreciation on capitalized leases	(160.7)	(88.8)	(151.1)
Defined benefit pension plans: Service cost	(134.6)	(119.7)	(102.9)
Other postretirement benefit plans: Service cost	(19.0)	(12.5)	(11.6)
Postemployment benefit plans: Service cost	(7.6)	(8.8)	(8.6)
Defined contribution plan expense	(61.2)	(54.1)	(49.2)
Other selling, general, and administrative expenses	(1,729.2)	(1,730.7)	(1,695.6)
Provision for income taxes	(873.8)	(706.3)	(150.0)
NOPAT from sales	$ 1,871.9	$1,990.7	$2,467.7
PM from sales	11.30%	12.74%	15.68%

This analysis reveals that the operating profitability margin that is directly related to sales of GIS' *PM* has increased even more in recent years than we may have thought from our calculation of *PM* from all operating activities. In fact, the change in the most recent year is an increase of almost 3 percent rather than the 2.5 percent we saw in **Exhibit 6.2**. The identification of *PM* from sales clarifies that a significant element of our forecasting task will be determining whether this increase will be sustained or is transitory. This determination will be necessary to make our value estimate meaningful.

Operating Asset Turnover

Operating asset turnover (*ATO*) measures the productivity of the operating assets. This metric reveals the level of sales the firm realizes from each dollar invested in operating assets. All things equal, a higher *ATO* is preferable. *ATO* can be increased by either increasing sales for a given level of investment in operating assets or by reducing the amount of operating assets necessary to generate a dollar of sales, or both.

Reducing working capital (current operating assets less current operating liabilities) is usually easier than reducing long-term *NOA*. For example, firms can implement strategies to collect their receivables faster, reduce their inventories, and delay payments to their suppliers. All of these actions reduce working capital and thereby increase *ATO*. These strategies must be managed, however, so as not to negatively affect sales or supplier relations. Working capital management is an important part of managing the firm effectively.

It is usually more difficult to reduce the level of long-term *NOA*. The level of property, plant, and equipment required by the firm is determined more by the nature of its products or services than by management action (e.g., firms in the telecommunications industry require more capital investment than do retail stores). Still, managers can take several actions reduce capital investment. Some firms pursue novel approaches, such as corporate alliances, outsourcing, and special purpose entities.

GIS' *ATO* is computed as follows:

$$ATO = \frac{Sales}{average\,(NOA)} = \frac{15{,}740.4}{(25{,}035.4 + 16{,}855.9)/2} = 0.751$$

This means that, for each dollar of operating assets, GIS generated about $0.75 in sales during the year ended May 2018. As a reference, the median *ATO* for publicly traded firms over the past decade was about 1.40.

ATO AND 53-WEEK YEARS

Previously, we considered the required adjustment to the *RNOA* calculation in years that were 53 weeks long. For *ATO*, a similar adjustment is required for the same reasons it was required for *RNOA*. Thus, for years that have an extra week, we calculate *ATO* as follows:

$$ATO = \frac{Sales \times 52/53}{average(NOA)}$$

Using this revised formula avoids the illusion of an increased efficiency in the year with 53 weeks and a subsequent fall in efficiency the following year. These adjustments reflect yet another example of the importance of knowing the business to ensure our analysis, forecasts, and valuation are of the highest possible quality.

Using the computations of *NOA* in Chapter 5 and reported sales, we can examine the trend in GIS' operating *ATO* over time, as shown in **Exhibit 6.4**.

EXHIBIT 6.4 GIS' Annual Operating *ATO*

	Year Ended		
Amounts in Millions	**5/29/2016**	**5/28/2017**	**5/27/2018**
Sales	16,563.1	15,619.8	15,740.4
Beginning *NOA*	17,463.8	16,493.9	16,855.9
Ending *NOA*	16,493.9	16,855.9	25,035.4
Operating *ATO*	0.976	0.937	0.751

As was discussed, *ATO* is generally more stable than *PM* for most firms due to the challenges in altering the assets required to generate sales. This is apparent for GIS. Similar to *PM*, a trend is also apparent for *ATO*. We observe that *ATO* is decreasing and that there has been a large decrease in the most recent year. Further decomposition of the *ATO* may yield insight into this pattern and aid in discovery of its source. We will consider this decomposition later.

CHANGES IN *RNOA*

Studying *RNOA* reveals details of current profitability. Calculating *RNOA*, *PM*, and *ATO* in successive years allows us to see if these values are stable or changing. An alternative approach is a direct analysis of changes in *RNOA*. This analysis can be particularly helpful if the firm is in a growth or decline stage and we believe the changes will recur in the future.

There are some subtleties to an analysis of changes in *RNOA* that must be noted. Consider the following:

$$\begin{aligned} RNOA_t &= PM_t \times ATO_t \\ &= \frac{NOPAT_t}{(NOA_t + NOA_{t-1})/2} \\ &= \frac{NOPAT_t}{Sales_t} \times \frac{Sales_t}{(NOA_t + NOA_{t-1})/2} \\ \Delta RNOA_t &= PM_t \times ATO_t - PM_{t-1} \times ATO_{t-1} \end{aligned}$$

If we subtract and add $PM_t \times ATO_{t-1}$ and then rearrange, we get the following:

$$\begin{aligned} \Delta RNOA_t &= PM_t \times ATO_t - PM_{t-1} \times ATO_{t-1} \\ &= PM_t \times ATO_t + (-PM_t \times ATO_{t-1} + PM_t \times ATO_{t-1}) - PM_{t-1} \times ATO_{t-1} \\ &= (PM_t \times ATO_t - PM_t \times ATO_{t-1}) + (PM_t \times ATO_{t-1} - PM_{t-1} \times ATO_{t-1}) \\ &= \Delta ATO_t \times PM_t + \Delta PM_t \times ATO_{t-1} \end{aligned}$$

Alternatively, if we subtract and add $PM_{t-1} \times ATO_t$ and then rearrange, we get the following:

$$\begin{aligned} \Delta RNOA_t &= PM_t \times ATO_t - PM_{t-1} \times ATO_{t-1} \\ &= PM_t \times ATO_t + (-PM_{t-1} \times ATO_t + PM_{t-1} \times ATO_t) - PM_{t-1} \times ATO_{t-1} \\ &= (PM_t \times ATO_t - PM_{t-1} \times ATO_t) + (PM_{t-1} \times ATO_t - PM_{t-1} \times ATO_{t-1}) \\ &= \Delta PM_t \times ATO_t + \Delta ATO_t \times PM_{t-1} \end{aligned}$$

The decision on which equation to use depends on whether we think operating *PM* or *ATO* is more constant from period to period. The first analysis of the change in *RNOA* uses current *PM* and last year's *ATO* while the second uses current *ATO* and last year's *PM*.

For most companies, the *ATO* is more consistent from year to year and we would choose the first equation for our analysis. That is, the use of lagged *ATO* (implicitly assuming it is near constant) is preferred to using lagged *PM* in the disaggregation of $\Delta RNOA$. Direct examination of changes in *PM* and *ATO* may yield insight helpful to the forecasting of future values and changes.

TRADE-OFF BETWEEN OPERATING PROFIT MARGIN AND ASSET TURNOVER

An infinite number of combinations of operating *PM* and *ATO* could yield a given *RNOA*. **Exhibit 6.5** illustrates this point. The curved line reflects the possible combinations of *PM* and *ATO* that could combine to achieve the median *RNOA* for all publicly traded firms during the most recent decade.

Exhibit 6.5 reveals that some industries, such as communication and utilities, are capital intensive with relatively low *ATO*. Accordingly, for such industries to achieve a required *RNOA* (to be competitive in the overall market), they must attain a higher profit margin. On the other hand, firms such as wholesalers and retailers hold fewer assets and, therefore, can operate on lower *PM* to achieve a sufficient *RNOA*. This is because their *ATO* is far greater.

EXHIBIT 6.5 *PM* and *ATO* by Industry

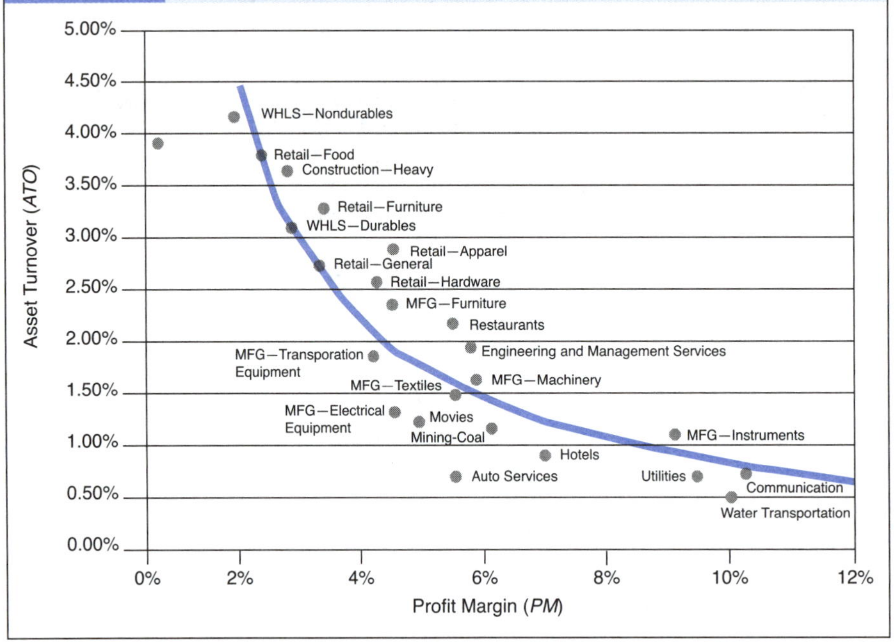

This exhibit warns of the issues encountered if one blindly compares the performance of firms across different industries. For instance, a higher *PM* in the communications industry compared with the retail industry is not necessarily the result of better management. Instead, the communications industry is extremely capital intensive and, thus, to achieve an equivalent *RNOA*, communications firms must earn a higher profit margin to offset their lower *ATO*. Basic economics suggests that all industries must earn an acceptable return on investment if they are to continue to attract investors and survive.

Understanding the relation between operating *PM* and *ATO* is relatively straightforward when comparing firms that operate in one industry (pure-play firms). Analyzing conglomerates, which operate in several industries, may be more challenging. The *PM* and *ATO* of conglomerates are a weighted average of the margins and turnovers for the various industries in which they operate and the various goods/services they offer. For example, Hyatt Hotels (H) represents a blend of a hotel chain renting rooms to travelers and a management company overseeing operations of properties; thus, the margin and turnover benchmarks for Hyatt on a consolidated basis are a weighted average of the margin and turnover of these two different forms of operations.

EVALUATING FINANCIAL ACTIVITIES

LO2: Compute profitability of financial activities.

Although our analysis in this textbook focuses on operating activities, there may be times when we will be interested in an evaluation of financial activities. Before proceeding to further analysis of the operations, we take a moment to introduce the method by which we would evaluate the financial activities. Given our reformulation completed in Chapter 5, we can evaluate financial activities using the return on financial liabilities (*RNFL*), computed using *FEAT* (or *FIAT*) and *NFL*:

$$RNFL = \frac{FEAT}{average(NFL)}$$

In Chapter 9, we will show that this *RNFL* may be helpful as an approximation of the cost of debt capital. **Exhibit 6.6** shows the annual computations of *RNFL* for GIS using the amounts of *FEAT* and *NFL* from our reformulation in Chapter 5:[1]

[1] The negative *RNFL* in the years ended May 2017 and 2018 may seem odd. It arises because of the numerous sources of financial expenses and income, as shown in **Exhibit 5.11**. These yield net financial income despite considerable net financial liabilities (see **Exhibit 5.9**).

EXHIBIT 6.6 GIS' *RNFL*

Amounts in Millions	Year Ended 5/29/2016	5/28/2017	5/27/2018
FEAT (FIAT)	452.9	(323.0)	(364.3)
Beginning *NFL*	12,920.9	12,011.4	12,764.3
Ending *NFL*	12,011.4	12,764.3	18,725.9
RNFL	3.63%	(2.61)%	(2.31)%

CONSIDERING CREDIT RISK

Although we do not focus on financing, in the valuation process, we do need to consider credit risk. The changes over time in *RNFL* may reveal information about changes in the company's ability to borrow. If liquidity (the ability to meet short-term obligations as they become due) or solvency (the ability to meet long-term obligations as they become due) is an issue for a company, it can impact the operations. A growing company that is cash strapped may be limited in its ability to obtain raw materials, pay employees, or acquire equipment. Measures such as "day's receivables outstanding" and "cash conversion cycle" may help with understanding these issues. In our analysis, we focus on the general case where companies are not affected by a liquidity crunch.

DETAILED ANALYSIS OF OPERATING PROFIT MARGIN

LO3: Perform a common-size analysis of *PM* and *ATO*, and compare the results to peer companies.

Having disaggregated *NOA* and *NOPAT* into their many components in Chapter 5, we are ready to undertake a detailed analysis of the two components of *RNOA* (i.e., operating *PM* and *ATO*). Recall from **Exhibit 6.2** that *PM* and *ATO* are is clearly not stable for GIS! As we think about forecasting, we must understand what has caused the *PM* to range from 11.20 to 14.72 percent in the past 4 years. A detailed analysis of the *PM* may yield insight into this lack of discernible pattern.

A simple way of approaching the items that may be affecting the *PM* is common-size analysis. **Exhibit 6.7** shows a common-size income statement where we compute each item of *NOPAT* as a percentage of the sales for the year.

EXHIBIT 6.7 GIS' Common-size Income Statement

Amounts in Millions; Year Ended	5/29/2016	5/28/2017	5/27/2018
Net sales—North America retail	66.03%	65.28%	64.26%
Net sales—Convenience stores and food service	11.61%	11.97%	12.26%
Net sales—Europe and Australia	12.06%	11.68%	12.61%
Net sales—Asia and Latin America	10.29%	11.07%	10.87%
Total sales	100.00%	100.00%	100.00%
Cost of sales	(64.77)%	(64.45)%	(65.49)%
Gross profit	35.23%	35.55%	34.51%
Advertising expense	(4.55)%	(3.99)%	(3.66)%
Research expense	(1.34)%	(1.40)%	(1.39)%
Depreciation on capitalized leases	(0.97)%	(0.57)%	(0.96)%
Defined benefit pension plans: Service cost	(0.81)%	(0.77)%	(0.65)%
Other postretirement benefit plans: Service cost	(0.11)%	(0.08)%	(0.07)%
Postemployment benefit plans: Service cost	(0.05)%	(0.06)%	(0.05)%
Defined contribution plan expense	(0.37)%	(0.35)%	(0.31)%
Other selling, general, and administrative expenses	(10.44)%	(11.08)%	(10.77)%
Divestitures (loss) gain	0.89%	(0.09)%	0.00%
Restructuring, impairment, and other exit costs	(0.91)%	(1.17)%	(1.05)%
Income taxes	(5.28)%	(4.52)%	(0.95)%
After-tax earnings from joint ventures	0.53%	0.54%	0.54%
Foreign currency translation	(0.66)%	0.04%	(0.24)%
Other fair value changes: Hedge derivatives	0.10%	0.34%	(0.32)%
Reclassification to earnings: Hedge derivatives	(0.06)%	(0.16)%	0.11%
Operating *PM*	11.20%	12.25%	14.72%

A review of this information reveals that the primary driver of the fluctuation in GIS' *PM* is the changing income taxes on operations. This item has decreased from 5.28 to 4.52 to 0.95 percent of sales. Looking at the *PM* with income taxes removed over the last 3 years, we find that it would be 16.47, 16.77, and 15.67 percent. We may also consider removing foreign currency translation and fair value changes on hedge derivatives because they will have a zero expectation. With these two items and income taxes removed, the *PM* over the last few years would be 17.03, 16.39, and 16.23 percent in the years ended May 2016, 2017, and 2018, respectively.[2] This smoother series, though still declining, would be more helpful in forecasting future periods than the observed *PM*. Clearly, these items contributed a great deal to the variability recently observed in *PM*.

FURTHER ANALYSES OF OPERATING PROFITABILITY

Additional insight into operations may be gained via additional analysis. One of the primary items to be considered is the gross profit margin:

$$\text{Gross Profit Margin} = \frac{\text{Sales} - \text{Cost of Sales}}{\text{Sales}}$$

This item is of particular interest because it can be thought of as a margin profit to additional dollar of sales. Note that this implies that all cost of sales are variable and all other expenses are fixed in nature. Still, observing that GIS' gross profit margin has decreased from 35.55 to 34.51 percent in the most recent year means there is a smaller benefit to achieving additional sales.

Another option to consider is the profitability of operations before taxes. In doing so, we need to consider whether we want to include items that are not expected to repeat, such as restructuring costs. For GIS, the operating revenues and expenses through other selling, general, and administrative expenses relative to sales in the recent periods are

Year Ended	5/29/2016	5/28/2017	5/27/2018
Recurring profitability before tax.	16.58%	17.27%	16.63%

It appears there was an increase in the year ended May 2017, which coincides with the observed decrease in cost of sales. Analyses such as these will give a stronger understanding of the current profitability that will provide benefits in our forecasting efforts.

The common-size analysis shown above provides a basis that will allow us to forecast each element of *NOPAT* as a percentage of sales, taking into account the business environment, including what we know about the business, its economic environment, and management's future plans.

DETAILED ANALYSIS OF OPERATING ASSET TURNOVER

From the information in **Exhibit 6.4**, it is clear that *ATO* for GIS is decreasing from year to year. Here, the natural question is this: What is causing this decrease? A detailed analysis of the *ATO* may yield insight into this pattern. Remember that it is usually more difficult to adjust the level of long-term *NOA* (i.e., to affect *ATO*) than to change *PM*. For example, retail stores can more easily adjust staffing levels than change their number of stores. Still, managers can take several actions to reduce capital investment. Our goal is to determine what has led to GIS' downward trend in *ATO* and to understand the implications for the future.

When examining operating *ATO*s, it is common to begin with common-size analysis utilizing the inverse of the *ATO* ratio. This shows each item as a percentage of the sales for the year. Using the inverse (i.e., sales as the denominator) allows a common denominator for each item and,

[2] Of course, income taxes are still a reality, but we can consider the numbers with them excluded to determine stability of other elements of *PM*. We know that recent years have seen a drastic change in taxes, which will be explicitly considered in our forecasting of expense items.

more important, negates issues related to small denominators.[3] The common-size analysis for the inverse of *ATO* (utilizing average amounts of the elements of *NOA* in the numerator) for GIS is shown in **Exhibit 6.8**.

EXHIBIT 6.8 GIS' Common-Size Balance Sheet

	Year Ended		
Amounts in Millions	**5/29/2016**	**5/28/2017**	**5/27/2018**
Total sales	$16,563.1	$15,619.8	$15,740.4
OPERATING ASSETS (*OA*)			
Cash and cash equivalents	0.020	0.021	0.020
Receivables: Customers	0.085	0.091	0.101
Receivables: Allowance for doubtful accounts	(0.002)	(0.002)	(0.002)
Inventories: Raw materials and packaging	0.024	0.025	0.025
Inventories: Finished goods	0.073	0.076	0.082
Inventories: Grain	0.005	0.005	0.005
Inventories: Excess of FIFO over LIFO cost	0.000	0.000	0.000
Deferred tax assets: Accrued liabilities	0.006	0.005	0.004
Deferred tax assets: Compensation and employee benefits	0.031	0.029	0.020
Deferred tax assets: Unrealized hedges	0.000	0.000	0.000
Deferred tax assets: Tax credit carryforwards	0.000	0.001	0.001
Deferred tax assets: Capital losses	0.001	0.001	0.001
Deferred tax assets: Net operating losses	0.006	0.007	0.009
Deferred tax assets: Other	0.005	0.005	0.004
Deferred tax assets: Valuation allowance	(0.013)	(0.015)	(0.013)
Prepaid expenses and other current assets: Prepaid expenses	0.010	0.011	0.011
Prepaid expenses and other current assets: Derivative receivables, primarily commodity related	0.004	0.003	0.002
Prepaid expenses and other current assets: Grain contracts	0.000	0.000	0.000
Prepaid expenses and other current assets: Miscellaneous	0.001	0.001	0.001
Land, buildings, and equipment: Land	0.006	0.006	0.005
Land, buildings, and equipment: Buildings	0.136	0.144	0.148
Land, buildings, and equipment: Buildings under capital lease	0.000	0.000	0.000
Land, buildings, and equipment: Equipment	0.363	0.385	0.392
Land, buildings, and equipment: Equipment under capital lease	0.000	0.000	0.000
Land, buildings, and equipment: Capitalized software	0.031	0.034	0.036
Land, buildings, and equipment: Construction in progress	0.040	0.040	0.040
Land, buildings, and equipment: Accumulated depreciation	(0.349)	(0.371)	(0.375)
Capitalized lease asset	0.048	0.058	0.067
Goodwill: North America retail	0.391	0.410	0.407
Goodwill: Pet	0.000	0.000	0.168
Goodwill: Convenience stores and food service	0.056	0.059	0.058
Goodwill: Europe and Australia	0.043	0.045	0.045
Goodwill: Asia and Latin America	0.017	0.019	0.019
Goodwill: Joint ventures	0.024	0.026	0.027
Other intangible assets: Brands and other indefinite-lived intangibles	0.254	0.266	0.349
Other intangible assets: Franchise agreements, customer relationships, and other	0.033	0.034	0.042
Other intangible assets: Accumulated amortization	(0.008)	(0.010)	(0.011)
Other assets: Investments in and advances to joint ventures	0.032	0.033	0.032
Other assets: Life insurance	0.002	0.002	0.002
Other assets: Miscellaneous	0.006	0.007	0.007
	1.379	1.452	1.730

continued

[3] If we looked at an item such as the Deferred tax asset: Accrued liabilities, its average value of $58.6 for the year ended May 2018 would result in a ratio of 268.61 ($15,740.4/$58.6). Values such as these are not helpful in our analysis of the overall *ATO* for GIS, which was 0.751 for the most recent year.

continued from previous page

EXHIBIT 6.8 GIS' Common-Size Balance Sheet

Amounts in Millions	Year Ended 5/29/2016	5/28/2017	5/27/2018
OPERATING LIABILITIES (*OL*)			
Accounts payable	(0.113)	(0.133)	(0.155)
Other current liabilities: Accrued trade and consumer promotions	(0.034)	(0.033)	(0.031)
Other current liabilities: Accrued payroll	(0.023)	(0.023)	(0.021)
Other current liabilities: Accrued taxes	(0.009)	(0.009)	(0.008)
Other current liabilities: Grain contracts	(0.000)	(0.000)	(0.000)
Other current liabilities: Restructuring and other exit costs reserve	(0.006)	(0.005)	(0.005)
Other current liabilities: Derivative payable	(0.005)	(0.002)	(0.001)
Other current liabilities: Miscellaneous	(0.017)	(0.019)	(0.019)
Deferred tax liabilities: Brands	(0.080)	(0.084)	(0.089)
Deferred tax liabilities: Fixed assets	(0.028)	(0.031)	(0.026)
Deferred tax liabilities: Intangible assets	(0.013)	(0.015)	(0.016)
Deferred tax liabilities: Tax lease transactions	(0.003)	(0.003)	(0.002)
Deferred tax liabilities: Inventories	(0.003)	(0.004)	(0.003)
Deferred tax liabilities: Unrealized hedges	(0.001)	(0.002)	(0.002)
Deferred tax liabilities: Other	(0.001)	(0.002)	(0.002)
Other noncurrent liabilities: Accrued taxes	(0.012)	(0.012)	(0.014)
Other noncurrent liabilities: Miscellaneous	(0.007)	(0.008)	(0.006)
	(0.354)	(0.384)	(0.400)
Inverse of operating *ATO*	1.025	1.068	1.331
Operating *ATO*	0.976	0.937	0.751

As might be expected, pinpointing the causes of decreases in ATO between the years ended May 2016 and 2017 is difficult. The change in the most recent year is primarily in goodwill: pet and other intangible assets: brands and other indefinite-lived intangibles. These are driven by the acquisition of Blue Buffalo Pet Products Inc. in fiscal year 2018. If those two items are excluded, the inverse of operating *ATO* only changed by 0.012 in the most recent year! Examination of this detail reassures us that, absent acquisitions, the operations of GIS are very steady in the amount of assets necessary to support sales. Any impact of the Blue Buffalo operations on our forecasted requirements of resources will be considered in the next chapter.

FURTHER ANALYSES OF OPERATING EFFICIENCY

Additional insight into operations may, again, be observed after additional analysis. Several operating items are often examined to determine whether changes are occurring in the operations. A better understanding of the operating efficiency may lead us to discover issues that need to be considered in our forecasting efforts.

The efficient use of working capital is of primary interest but may be obscured by the relative magnitude of property, plant, and equipment when looking at *ATO*. We can examine how quickly cash is collected, inventory is sold, and bills are paid via "days in" types of ratios. Specifically, we can calculate

$$\text{Days Sales Outstanding} = \frac{\text{Average Accounts Receivable} \times 365}{\text{Sales}}$$

$$\text{Days in Inventory on Hand} = \frac{\text{Average Inventory} \times 365}{\text{Cost of Sales}}$$

$$\text{Days in Payables} = \frac{\text{Average Accounts Payable} \times 365}{\text{Cost of Sales}}$$

From these measures, we can examine the company's cash operating cycle as

$$\text{Cash Operating Cycle} = \text{Days in Payables} - (\text{Days in Sales} + \text{Days in Inventory})$$

continued

continued from previous page

Essentially, the cash operating cycle is the period of time it takes a company to pay suppliers less the time required to obtain inventory, sell it, and collect the cash from customers. If the number is positive, no financing of the operations would be necessary. The longer the delay in getting cash from sales, the greater the reliance on financing. Comparing results to those of competitors yields insights into the business environment and risks a company is facing.

Again, a more careful analysis aimed at determining appropriate expectations for future periods will be performed in Chapter 7 as a part of full-information forecasting. The common-size analysis facilitates forecasting of each element of *NOA* as it relates to sales by taking into account the information we know about the business environment, including the business, its economic environment, and management's future plans.

UNDERSTANDING PROFITABILITY BY EXAMINING OTHER COMPANIES

One common method of analyzing operating *PM* and *ATO* is to see how the company is changing over time. This approach, demonstrated above, is referred to as a time-series analysis. Alternatively, or in conjunction, we can also compare GIS with its competitors. The examination of *PM* and *ATO* using comparable companies is referred to as a cross-sectional analysis.

As noted earlier, K is GIS' competitor. From Note 1 of K's most recent Form 10-K, their "fiscal year normally ends on the Saturday closest to December 31 and as a result, a 53rd week is added approximately every sixth year.[4] The Company's 2018, 2017 and 2016 fiscal years each contained 52 weeks and ended on December 29, 2018, December 30, 2017, and December 31, 2016, respectively." GIS' fiscal year ends the last Sunday in May. For our analysis, we will compare the most recent reported full fiscal year of each firm. While we would prefer to match the dates, this difference in year-end does not render our work less useful provided that we keep in mind the difference as we perform our financial statement analysis and the subsequent forecasting.

If we repeat the analysis performed previously on GIS using the financial statements of K as well, we can compare their profitability. In doing so, we will keep in mind the difference in timing of their fiscal years. We also need to consider any major events that have occurred within either company during the year. GIS acquired Blue Buffalo in the most recent year, moving the company into manufacturing food for animals as well as people. Clearly, this change in GIS has affected the May 2018 results as well as comparability with K. This will, in turn, affect future forecasts for the company. **Exhibit 6.9** reports the *RNOA*, *PM*, *ATO*, and *RNFL* of GIS and K.

Looking first at the computations of *RNOA*, we see that GIS has lower profitability than K. GIS' *PM* is almost 3 percent higher than K's, and GIS' *ATO* is much lower. The *PM* could be the result of differences in the cost structures of the companies or in the products they sell and their respective gross profits. The difference in *ATO* could result from inefficiencies or business structure. For instance, if K outsources production, it would not have the same requirement for plant assets, and we might see a related higher cost of products sold.

The next step is to begin digging into the *PM* and *ATO* to determine differences between the companies. In doing so, we are looking for information that helps us with the forecasting of GIS' future operating activities. The information we find may reveal issues on which GIS should focus in an attempt to match the success of competitors or indicate areas where the competitors are simply not comparable. Alternatively, we may find areas where GIS is superior, and we would need to determine whether that competitive advantage currently enjoyed by GIS will continue. Because we found that the *PM* from sales for GIS was very different from current *PM*, we also need to consider whether similar effects are seen with K.

Completing a common-size analysis similar to **Exhibits 6.7** and **6.8** for each competitor can assist in gathering this information. Keep in mind that the numbers for the company and its competitors often will not line up due to different descriptions in the financial statements, levels of

[4] The effects on our analysis of differing year lengths will be discussed shortly. Additional effects will also be seen in subsequent chapters related to forecasting and calculating value.

aggregation of information, and accounting standards employed.[5] Nevertheless, an examination of competitors can be a useful tool that adds to our understanding as we proceed to full-information forecasting.

EXHIBIT 6.9 GIS' and K's *RNOA, PM, ATO,* and *RNFL*

Amounts in Millions		
RNOA	**GIS**	**K**
NOPAT	2,316.4	1,590
Average *NOA*	20,945.6	12,382
RNOA	11.06%	12.84%
PM	**GIS**	**K**
NOPAT	2,316.4	1,590
Sales	15,740.4	13,547
Operating *PM*	14.72%	11.74%
ATO	**GIS**	**K**
Sales	15,740.4	13,547
Average *NOA*	20,945.6	12,382
Operating *ATO*	0.751	1.094
RNFL	**GIS**	**K**
FEAT (*FIAT*)	(364.3)	249
Average *NFL*	15,745.1	10,016.5
RNFL	(2.31)%	2.49%

Next, we step back from our focus on operating activities to consider the relation of *RNOA* to the profitability of the entire company: its return on equity (*ROE*).

ANALYSIS WHEN COMPANIES HAVE DIFFERING YEAR-END DATES

When confronted with differing year-end dates among companies, our goal is to maximize the benefit achieved from the comparison to the other firm. At first thought, several options could exist, including using the information from the most recent annual report of each firm (what we are doing for GIS and K). Another possible option would be to form a pseudo, or "as-if," year for one firm to try to best match reporting periods. For K, this would be a combination of 2017 Q3 and Q4 with 2018 Q1 and Q2. This would nearly match the timing of the information because both firms would then have information covering the period from mid-2017 to mid-2018.

This approach of forming an as-if year by taking the last 12 months for K seems, at first glance, to have solved the problem. Further, it is consistent with the approach of looking at a trailing 12 months (TTM), often seen in finance-oriented approaches or on financial websites. However, forming an as-if year may not be appropriate given the way accounting forms interim reports. Accounting utilizes an integral approach, which views the interim periods as a part of the full year. As a result, combining quarters from different fiscal years may not only be inappropriate, but it may alter the information in important ways.

To see the problem with as-if years, we need to consider the impact of the method by which interim reports are formed. We borrow the following description of the issue from Durtschi and Easton (*Journal of Accounting Research*, 2009):

> U.S. firms follow the integral method of accounting; that is, each quarterly statement is considered an installment in a fiscal year (Accounting Principles Board opinion number 28—APB 28). Under the reporting requirements of APB 28, firms allocate expenses throughout a fiscal year based on forecasted annual figures relating to that particular year (specifically that year's sales).

continued

[5] A company to which GIS might be compared is Nestlé, which files its financial statements using International Financial Reporting Standards (IFRS). This is a more extreme case of differences arising due to accounting standards and requires a more comprehensive understanding of the effects of any differences in the accounting standards.

continued from previous page

> This requirement to estimate costs over interim quarters causes quarter 4 to be intimately connected to the prior three quarters as it is the "settling up" quarter, where estimates made in the first three quarters of the fiscal year are reconciled to the actual outcome in the final/fourth quarter. It follows that "as-if" years, which combine quarterly earnings spanning two integral fiscal years, combine "installments," which have different cost bases and revenue outcomes.

The accounting standard for interim reporting, ASU 270-10-05-2 previously APB 28 paragraph 4, states,

> The determination of the results of operations on a meaningful basis for intervals of less than a full year presents inherent difficulties. The revenues of some entities fluctuate widely among interim periods because of seasonal factors, while in other entities heavy fixed costs incurred in one interim period may benefit other periods. In these situations, financial information for periods of less than a full year may be of limited usefulness. In other situations, costs and expenses related to a full year's activities are incurred at infrequent intervals during the year and need to be allocated to products in process or to other interim periods to avoid distortion of interim financial results. In view of the limited time available to develop complete information, many costs and expenses are estimated in interim periods. For example, it may not be practical to perform extensive reviews of individual inventory items, costs on individual long-term contracts and precise income tax calculations for each interim period. Subsequent refinement or correction of these estimates may distort the results of operations of later interim periods. Similarly, the effects of disposal of a segment of an entity and extraordinary, unusual, or infrequently occurring events and transactions on the results of operations in an interim period will often be more pronounced than they will be on the results for the annual period. Special attention must be given to disclosure of the impact of these items on financial information for interim periods.

Rangan and Sloan (*The Accounting Review*, 1998) amongst others have studied the time-series properties of accounting information. In doing so, they find that time-series of "as-if" years is not the same as that of the reported fiscal years. As further described by Durtschi and Easton (2009), "Because of the integral theory of accounting, a fiscal year is different from a constructed 'as-if' year, and using an 'as-if' year as a benchmark is inappropriate. A second, perhaps more serious, issue is that numbers in interim reports are often restated at the annual audit." Thus, the usefulness for forecasting and valuation of analysis performed on "as-if" years is questionable.

Additional discussion of potential factors that may affect the comparability of an "as-if" year to the fiscal year will arise in our discussions of forecasting and using market multiples for valuation.

THE MAPPING FROM RETURN ON NET OPERATING ASSETS TO RETURN ON EQUITY

LO4: Explain the relation of equity and operating profitability and effects of equity versus debt financing.

Return on equity (*ROE*) is a combination of the returns from operating (*RNOA*) and financial (*RNFL*) activities. *ROE* is the principal summary measure of company performance (rather than just the performance of operating activities) from the perspective of the equity holder. *ROE* may be calculated as follows:

$$ROE = \frac{CI}{average(CSE)}$$

where *CI* is comprehensive income and *CSE* is common shareholders' equity. *ROE* relates earnings to the average investment by shareholders as measured by common stockholders' equity from the balance sheet. Warren Buffett highlights *ROE* as part of his acquisition criteria: "Businesses earning good returns on equity while employing little or no debt." We will examine the components of *ROE* and, in doing so, the point made by Buffett will become clear.

ROE is a company-level measure from the perspective of the equity holder. We break down *ROE* to see how operating and financial activities affect it. There are several steps.

First, we split *CI* into its two components, *NOPAT* and *FEAT*. While the notation *FEAT* implies that the financial activities usually do not show a profit (i.e., they have an expense), for companies that are net lenders (due to excess cash and/or investment securities), *FEAT* is negative, indicating that profit is earned from these financial activities. GIS is in the interesting position in the last

FIRMS WITH NEGATIVE EQUITY

Firms may be in a position where liabilities exceed reported assets. This results in negative equity, which is commonly called an equity deficit. We can still run the numbers in that our spreadsheet and calculations will work. However, interpretation may not be meaningful. Consider a firm that made $10 while reporting a negative $50 in equity. Is the calculated *ROE* of −20 percent really meaningful and helpful in understanding the return you might earn as a shareholder? Generally, no. Firms with negative equity must be carefully reviewed to ensure they have the liquidity to meet short-term obligations and solvency to meet long-term obligations as they come due. If they will not continue to exist, calculating profitability is not useful.

2 years of being a net borrower and having earned a positive amount (i.e., financial income after tax, *FIAT*) on its financial activities:

$$\begin{aligned} ROE &= \frac{CI}{average(CSE)} \\ &= \frac{NOPAT - FEAT}{average(CSE)} \\ &= \frac{NOPAT}{average(CSE)} - \frac{FEAT}{average(CSE)} \end{aligned}$$

Next, we multiply and divide by the net amount of resources related to the operating activities (*NOA*) or financial activities (net financial liabilities, *NFL*).

$$\begin{aligned} ROE &= \frac{NOPAT}{average(CSE)} - \frac{FEAT}{average(CSE)} \\ &= \frac{NOPAT}{average(NOA)} \times \frac{average(NOA)}{average(CSE)} - \frac{FEAT}{average(NFL)} \times \frac{average(NFL)}{average(CSE)} \end{aligned}$$

At this point, we recognize that the first term, *NOPAT/average(NOA)*, is *RNOA* and *FEAT/average(NFL)* is *RNFL*. Finally, notice that *average(NFL)/average(CSE)* is a debt-to-equity ratio, which will be referred to as leverage (*LEV*). This yields

$$\begin{aligned} ROE &= \frac{NOPAT}{average(NOA)} \times \frac{average(NOA)}{average(CSE)} - \frac{FEAT}{average(NFL)} \times \frac{average(NFL)}{average(CSE)} \\ &= RNOA \times \frac{average(NOA)}{average(CSE)} - RNFL \times LEV \end{aligned}$$

We have succeeded in separating *ROE* into an operating component and a financial component. Now we employ the accounting identity, Assets = Liabilities + Equity, in the form *NOA* = *NFL* + *CSE*, Thus, *LEV* emerges again as follows:

$$\begin{aligned} ROE &= RNOA \times \frac{average\ (NOA)}{average\ (CSE)} - RNFL \times LEV \\ &= RNOA \times \frac{average\ (NFL + CSE)}{average\ (CSE)} - RNFL \times LEV \\ &= RNOA \times \left(\frac{average(NFL)}{average(CSE)} + \frac{average(CSE)}{average(CSE)} \right) - RNFL \times LEV \\ &= RNOA \times (LEV + 1) - RNFL \times LEV \end{aligned}$$

One more round of simplifying gets us to the following equation:

$$\begin{aligned} ROE &= RNOA \times (LEV + 1) - RNFL \times LEV \\ &= RNOA \times LEV + RNOA - RNFL \times LEV \\ &= RNOA + LEV \times (RNOA - RNFL) \end{aligned} \quad (6.1)$$

The difference between *RNOA* and *RNFL* is often referred to as the spread. It is the return that can be earned by investing in the operating activities above what will have to be paid on the related debt.

Equation 6.1 shows that *ROE* consists of two returns: (1) the return from the company's operating activities, linked to revenues and expenses from the company's products or services; and (2) an additional return resulting from the company employing leverage to capture the spread between operating and financial returns. Thus, companies can use debt to increase their *ROE*, but this increases the risk to the equity holders because failure to make required debt payments can yield many legal consequences, including bankruptcy. This is one reason why Warren Buffett focuses on companies whose *ROE* is derived primarily from *RNOA* rather than from increased *LEV*.

For GIS, we can compute the *ROE* and its components for the last several years to see the trends, as shown in **Exhibit 6.10**.

EXHIBIT 6.10 GIS' Decomposition of *ROE*

Year Ended	5/29/2016	5/28/2017	5/27/2018
RNOA	10.92%	11.48%	11.06%
RNFL	3.63%	(2.61)%	(2.31)%
LEV	2.762	2.890	3.028
Spread (*RNOA* – *RNFL*)	7.29%	14.08%	13.37%
ROE	31.07%	52.17%	51.55%

Here, we see increasing changes in leverage over time as well as fluctuations in *RNOA* and *RNFL*. These changes combine to drive the observed changes in *ROE*.

Remember that, because we are interested in the profitability of operating activities, *RNOA* is our key metric. This differs from the often cited return on equity (above) or return on assets. Because we have split operating activities from financial activities, we do not have to use a return on equity, which neglects the distinction between these activities.

The use of return on assets fails to recognize that assets arise from both operating and financial activities. It also fails to recognize that there are some liabilities required for operating activities (e.g., accounts payable). Thus, our financial statement analysis centers on the profitability of the operations by focusing the appropriate metric, return on net operating assets.

Combining the DuPont breakdown at the beginning of the chapter with the relation shown in equation 6.1, we show in **Exhibit 6.11** the connections between the elements discussed in this chapter.

The common-size analysis of the income statement and balance sheet compared the components of *NOPAT* and *NOA*, respectively, to sales. This provided a breakdown of operating *PM* and *ATO*. *PM* and *ATO* are the elements of *RNOA*, which is the primary driver of *ROE*. In this chapter, we focused on the level of each item in the figure. We could also examine the change in each item as we attempt to determine how GIS is evolving. The structure in **Exhibit 6.1**, considered both as levels and changes of the items, underlies the forecasting in the next chapter, where the focus will be on determining how the current level of sales, components of *NOPAT*, and components of *NOA* may differ in the future.

Before proceeding to the chapter on full-information forecasting, it is helpful to consider why companies do not take on large amounts of debt if one of their goals is maximizing *ROE*.

EXHIBIT 6.11 Decomposition of *ROE* and Its Elements

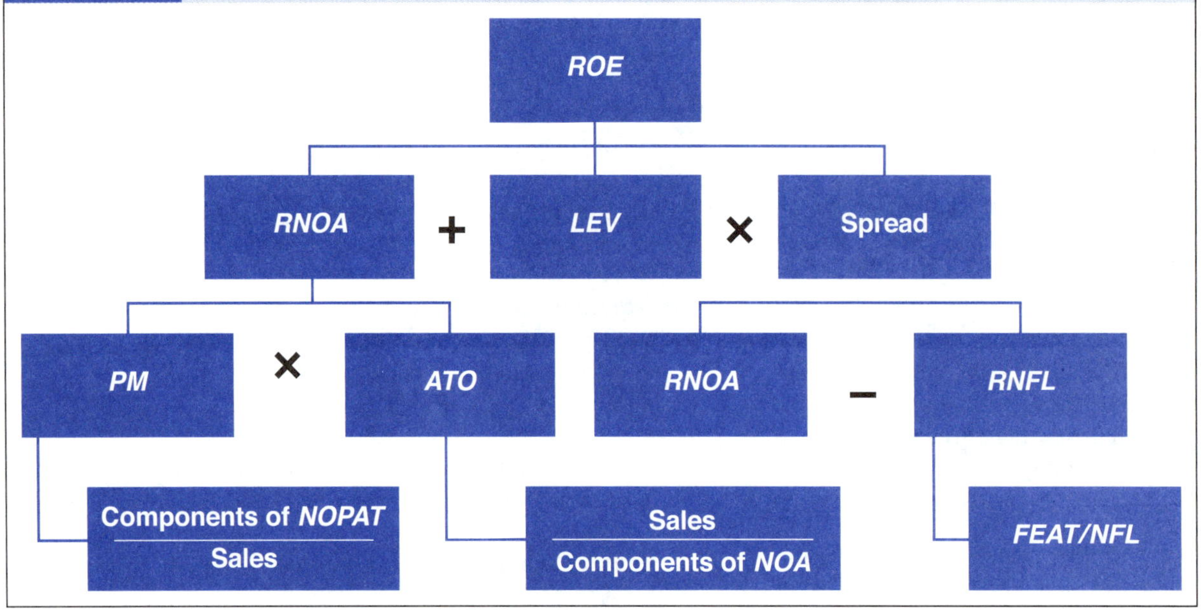

ADVANTAGES AND DISADVANTAGES OF EQUITY VERSUS DEBT FINANCING

If a higher *ROE* is desirable, why don't companies take on large amounts of debt? Because creditors, such as banks and bondholders, charge successively higher interest rates for increasing levels of debt. At some point, the cost of the additional debt exceeds the return on the additional assets acquired from the debt financing. Thereafter, further debt financing does not make economic sense. The debt and equity markets, in essence, place a limit on the level of debt a company can effectively acquire.

In addition, creditors usually require a company to execute a loan agreement that places varying restrictions on the company's activities. These restrictions, called covenants, help safeguard debt holders in the face of increased risk. Covenants exist because debt holders usually do not have a voice on the board of directors like stockholders do. These debt covenants impose a cost on the company beyond that of the interest payments, and these covenants are more stringent as a company increases its reliance on debt financing.

Note that caution should be taken in examining companies based on *ROE*. A high *ROE* can be the result of either profitable operating activities or excessive debt. This is one reason we focus on the analysis of operating activities rather than measures that intermix the operating and financial activities of the company.

SUMMARY

In this chapter, we have seen a systematic process for evaluating profitability both for the company over time and by comparison to similar companies. The breakdown of *ROE* into components of *RNOA*, *LEV*, and spread showed the source of profitability. Through the decomposition of *RNOA* based on the DuPont method, evaluating the effects of operating *PM* and *ATO* separately is possible.

Evaluating *PM* and *ATO* helps identify the drivers of changes or differences in profitability. Through common-size analysis, we are able to compare differing years or companies despite the changing size (measured by sales) of the company and its enterprise operating activities.

In the next chapter, we will see how this detailed evaluation of *PM* and *ATO* is directly tied to full-information forecasting and valuation.

APPENDIX 6A: Informed Ratio Analysis

In this textbook, we have focused on a subset of ratio analysis that helps us understand operating *PM* and *ATO* as elements of *RNOA*. Many other ratios exist that can give additional insights about profitability, liquidity, and solvency. However, a caveat is in order. When performing ratio calculations, make sure to do so in an informed manner.

Your understanding of accounting, financial reporting, and economics risks cannot be set aside in favor of mechanically calculating ratios based on formulas and benchmarks. To illustrate, we provide two examples. The first looks at items included/excluded from a quick ratio, and the second examines at the calculation of daily cash expenditures as part of the defensive interval ratio.

Quick Ratio

The quick ratio is a measure of liquidity that modifies the current ratio to focus on current assets expected to convert into cash quickly. As such, the biggest difference between the current ratio and quick ratio for most firms is the exclusion of inventory. A typical formula for the quick ratio is

$$\text{Quick ratio} = \frac{\text{Cash and cash equivalents} + \text{Short-term marketable securities} + \text{Accounts receivable}}{\text{Current liabilities}}$$

For most firms, the exclusion of inventory is very logical, but that is not always the case.

Consider the effect of blindly following the calculation of the quick ratio above for Dell Technologies (DELL). Using the information from its January 2019 annual report, we find (DELL reported no short-term marketable securities):

$$0.49 = \frac{9{,}676 + 0 + 12{,}371}{44{,}972}$$

This may be an accurate calculation of the formula, but it may miss the desired information. If we calculate DELL's accounts receivable and inventory turnover ratios, we find that the exclusion of inventory may not be a good idea.[6]

$$\text{Accounts Receivable Turnover Ratio} = \frac{\text{Credit sales}}{\text{Average accounts receivable}}$$

$$7.52 = \frac{90{,}621}{(12{,}371 + 11{,}721)/2}$$

$$\text{Inventory Turnover Ratio} = \frac{\text{Cost of goods sold}}{\text{Average inventory}}$$

$$20.73 = \frac{65{,}568}{(3{,}649 + 2{,}678)/2}$$

For DELL, the inventory turnover is higher than the accounts receivable turnover! This raises questions about the appropriateness of including accounts receivable and excluding inventory in trying to understand the ability to convert current assets to cash. Blindly following the formula may yield a different interpretation than we would arrive at if we take the time to think through the ratio calculation in an informed manner. We would be remiss to not recognize that DELL's inventory is moving faster than its receivables.

Daily Cash Expenditures

A defensive interval ratio measures the ability to meet current cash expenditures given current available resources. In doing so, it incorporates a calculation of the daily cash expenditures:

$$\text{Daily Cash Expenditures} = \frac{\text{Cost of goods sold} + \text{Selling, general, and administrative expenses} + \text{Research and development expenses} - \text{Depreciation and amortization expense}}{\text{Number of days in period}}$$

[6] In the calculation of the accounts receivable turnover ratio, we assume that all revenues are on account rather than cash sales. The inventory turnover ratio is computed using total cost of net revenue.

In the numerator of the daily cash expenditure calculation, the depreciation and amortization expense is subtracted to arrive at the portion that is cash expenses. For GIS, this calculation would be appropriate. However, that is not the case for Target (TGT) . Consider Target's 2018 income statement as shown in **Exhibit 6A.1**.

EXHIBIT 6A.1 Target's 2018 Income Statement

Consolidated Statements of Operations (millions, except per share data)	**2018**
Sales	$74,433
Other revenue	923
Total revenue	75,356
Cost of sales	53,299
Selling, general, and administrative expenses	15,723
Depreciation and amortization (exclusive of depreciation included in cost of sales)	2,224
Operating income	4,110
Net interest expense	461
Net other (income)/expense	(27)
Earnings from continuing operations before income taxes	3,676
Provision for income taxes	746
Net earnings from continuing operations	2,930
Discontinued operations, net of tax	7
Net earnings	$ 2,937

Notice that, for TGT, depreciation and amortization expense are separate on the income statement. This means it is not included in cost of sales or selling, general, and administrative expense! Subtracting TGT's depreciation and amortization expense would not yield cash expenditures because it is already segregated from the other expenses. Blindly following the formula (i.e., just plugging in numbers) would yield a correct answer for GIS, but the wrong answer for TGT. We must bring our understanding of accounting to this situation to gather the desired information.

Too often, users of financial statements fall into the trap of not performing informed ratio analysis. Each time, you must consider the question at hand and then seek appropriate information to arrive at an informed decision. Rote calculation of formulas fails to apply your knowledge of accounting, financial reporting, and economics.

QUESTIONS

Q6.1 What two aspects of operating activities are considered in DuPont analysis?

Q6.2 Why is profitability considered via *RNOA* rather than just looking at *NOPAT*?

Q6.3 Why is average *NOA* used as the denominator of *RNOA* in evaluating reported information? Ideally, what would we use?

Q6.4 What is operating *PM*? What does it tell us?

Q6.5 Name two items that might be excluded in computing *PM* from sales.

Q6.6 What is operating *ATO*? What does it tell us?

Q6.7 Which is generally more stable in the short term for most companies, *PM* or *ATO*? Why?

Q6.8 How does step 1 of the valuation process, know the business, relate to DuPont analysis?

Q6.9 Why do we analyze the inverse of *ATO* instead of *ATO*?

Q6.10 What is the difference between time-series and cross-sectional analysis? What are the benefits of each?

Q6.11 What is the relation between the profitability of a company overall and the profitability of its operating activities?

EXERCISES

E6.12 Below is the income statement for Chipotle (CMG) from its 2018 financial statements. What items might be considered as part of *NOPAT* but might be omitted in computing *NOPAT* from sales?

CHIPOTLE MEXICAN GRILL, INC.
Consolidated Statement of Income
(in thousands, except per share data)

	Year Ended December 31,		
	2018	2017	2016
Revenue	$4,864,985	$4,476.412	$3,904,384
Restaurant operating costs (exclusive of depreciation and amortization shown separate below):			
Food, beverage, and packaging	1,600,760	1,535.428	1,365,580
Labor	1,326,079	1,205,992	1,105,001
Occupancy	347,123	327,132	293,636
Other operating costs	680,031	651,644	641,953
General and administrative expenses	375,460	296,388	276,240
Depreciation and amortization	201,979	163,348	146,368
Pre-opening costs	8,546	12,341	17,162
Impairment, closure costs, and asset disposals	66,639	13,345	23,877
Total operating expenses	4,606,617	4,205,618	3,869,817
Income from operations	258,368	270,794	34,567
Interest and other income, net	10,068	4,949	4,172
Income before income taxes	268,436	275,743	38,739
Provision for income taxes	(91,883)	(99,490)	(15,801)
Net income	$ 176,553	$ 176,253	$ 22,938
Earnings per share:			
Basic	$6.35	$6.19	$0.78
Diluted	$6.31	$6.17	$0.77
Weighted-average common shares outstanding:			
Basic	27,823	28,491	29,265
Diluted	27,962	28,561	29,770

Consolidated Statement of Comprehensive Income
(in thousands)

	Year Ended December 31		
	2018	2017	2016
Net income	$176,553	$176,253	$22,938
Other comprehensive income (loss). net of income taxes:			
Foreign currency translation adjustments	(2,736)	4,689	(1,291)
Unrealized gain (loss) on available-for-sale securities	291	(274)	2,251
Tax benefit (expense)	(132)	88	(849)
Other comprehensive income (loss), net of income taxes	(2,577)	4,503	111
Comprehensive income	$173,976	$180,756	$23,049

E6.13 Below is the income statement for Del Taco (TACO) from its 2018 financial statements. What items might be considered as part of *NOPAT* but might be omitted in computing *NOPAT* from Sales?

DEL TACO RESTAURANTS INC.
Consolidated Statements of Comprehensive Income
(In thousands, except share and per share data)

	52 Weeks Ended January 1, 2019	52 Weeks Ended January 2, 2018	53 Weeks Ended January 3, 2017
Revenue:			
Company restaurant sales	$471,193	$452,148	$434,064
Franchise revenue	17,569	16,464	15,676
Franchise advertising contributions	13,300	—	—
Franchise sublease and other income	3,428	2,844	2,343
Total revenue	505,490	471,456	452,083
Operating expenses:			
Restaurant operating expenses:			
Food and paper costs	128,873	125,391	120,116
Labor and related expenses	151,954	145,012	135,725
Occupancy and other operating expenses	97,745	92,825	88,908
General and administrative	43,773	38,154	37,220
Franchise advertising expenses	13,300	—	—
Depreciation and amortization	25,794	23,362	23,129
Occupancy and other—franchise subleases and other	3,167	2,608	2,207
Pre-opening costs	1,584	1,591	731
Impairment of long-lived assets	3,861	—	—
Restaurant closure charges, net	394	191	435
Loss on disposal of assets, net	1,012	1,075	312
Total operating expenses	471,457	430,209	408,783
Income from operations	34,033	41,247	43,300
Other expense (income), net:			
Interest expense	9,075	7,200	6,327
Other income	(660)	—	—
Transaction-related costs	—	—	731
Total other expense, net	8,415	7,200	7,058
Income from operations before provision (benefit) for income taxes	25,618	34,047	36,242
Provision (benefit) for income taxes	6,659	(15,824)	15,329
Net income	18,959	49,871	20,913
Other comprehensive income (loss):			
Change in fair value of interest rate cap, net of tax	122	(162)	172
Reclassification of interest rate cap amortization included in net income, net of tax	44	4	—
Total other comprehensive income (loss), net	166	(158)	172
Comprehensive income	$ 19,125	$ 49,713	$ 21,085

E6.14 Would the removal of the items identified in the prior two questions increase or decrease the comparability of CMG and TACO? That is, would *PM* or *PM* from sales be more comparable?

E6.15 In Chapter 5, we saw that the capitalization of operating leases had a dramatic effect on CMG's *NOA*. The additional asset was almost equal to the total amount of assets reported on the balance sheet! What effect would this adjustment to the accounting have on CMG's *ROE*, *RNOA*, and *ATO*?

E6.16 Littleton Inc. is considering expanding its operations outside of the United States. Littleton has a strong U.S. brand, allowing it to earn to a high *PM*. Littleton's management knows its international *PM* will be significantly lower but believes it can operate more efficiently abroad.

Currently, Littleton has $220 million in *NOA* and $440 million in annual sales, generating a *NOPAT* of $33 million. Littleton's management group believes expanding international would result in incremental sales of $90 million, requiring an investment in additional *NOA*, including supporting working capital of $30 million. Due to a substantial marketing effort, Littleton anticipates its international operating income, after tax, to be $6 million.

Based solely on the above financial consideration, explain whether you would recommend management to expand internationally.

E6.17 Following the passage of the Tax Cut and Jobs Act, Bedford Inc., a small appliance manufacturing firm, is considering adding robotics into its assembly process. With the new tax law, companies can deduct 100 percent of qualified equipment for tax purposes while depreciating on a straight-line basis on their financial statements.

Currently, Bedford has $250.0 million in annual sales, generating a *PM* of 4.5 percent on sales and an *ATO* of 2.5. Bedford's engineering group believes the robotics can be installed and operational within the first few months of the year. Bedford's CFO believes the robotics will reduce operating costs that would pass on to lower sale prices, yielding increased annual sales. The CFO estimates that investing $30 million in the robotics will increase sales by $16.5 million and increase the *PM* to 6.0 percent because fewer workers will be needed.

Based solely on the above financial consideration, explain whether or not you would recommend management consider upgrading automating its assembly process.

E6.18 Moonitz Inc., a consumer products firm, is considering adding a data analytics program in which it can evaluate its customers, shopping transactions and other relevant customer data to craft individualized promotions and recommend additional product offerings.

Currently, Moonitz has $385 million in annual sales, generating a *PM* of 4.0 percent on sales and an *ATO* of 5.0. Moonitz's marketing group believes the data analytics program will increase annual sales by $40 million, with an additional investment in working capital of $4 million to support the increased sales. Costs to run the data analytics program will reduce firm-wide *PM* to 3.9 percent.

Based solely on the above financial consideration, explain whether or not you would recommend management consider adding this new program.

E6.19 From fiscal 2017 to fiscal 2018, Starbucks' (SBUX) *RNOA* increased from 33.7 percent to 76.1. For fiscal 2018, SBUX's *PM* was 16.6 percent, and its *ATO* was 4.60. For fiscal year 2017, the company's *PM* was 11.6 percent and *ATO* was 2.90.

Perform a change in *RNOA* analysis to identify the drivers for the significant increase in SBUX's *RNOA*.

E6.20 From fiscal year 2017 to fiscal year 2018, Bed, Bath and Beyond's (BBY) *RNOA* decreased from 16.6 percent to 10.3. For fiscal year 2018, BBY's *PM* was 3.8 percent and *ATO* was 2.73. For fiscal year 2017, BBY's *PM* was 6.0 percent and *ATO* was 2.75.

Perform a change in *RNOA* analysis to identify the drivers for the significant increase in BBY's *RNOA*.

E6.21 The TJX Companies is a Fortune 100 company with more than 4,300 and 270,000 associates. It is the parent company for the stores TJ Maxx, Marshall's, and HomeGoods. Macy's is one of the nation's premier retailers, operating approximately 680 department stores under the names Macy's and Bloomingdale's as well as 190 specialty stories. Each company applies a different business model.

Following are selected financial data for TJX and Macy's (in millions of dollars).

	2018 Sales	2018 CGS	2018 Net Inc	2018 *NOPAT*	2018 *NOA*	2017 *NOA*	2018 *NFL*	2017 *NFL*	2018 *CSE*	2017 *CSE*
TJX	38,973	27,832	3,060	3,096	4,253	4,115	(796)	(1,033)	5,049	5,148
Macy's	25,739	15,215	1,098	1,031	10,025	10,161	3,589	4,428	6,436	5,733

Calculate the following for TJX and Macy's:

a. Gross margin percentage
b. Profit margin percentage (*PM*)
c. Asset turnover (*ATO*)
d. Return on net operating assets (*RNOA*)
e. Financial leverage (*LEV*)
f. Spread (*RNOA* – *RNFL*)

g. Return on equity (*ROE*)

h. Based on the above analysis, compare the fiscal year 2018 financial performance of both companies.

CONTINUING EXAMPLES

CE6.22 While much of the analysis of **Kellogg's** (K) for the current year was shown in the text, we can perform additional analysis of prior years to complete a time-series analysis. Complete the following for K:

a. Compute *RNOA* for the years 2015–2018.

b, Compute operating *PM* for the years 2015–2018.

c. Compute *NOPAT* from sales and *PM* from sales for the years 2015–2018.

d. Compute operating *ATO* for the years 2015–2018.

e. Compute *RNFL* for the years 2015–2018.

f. Prepare a common-size income statement for the years 2015–2018 to allow for analysis of the *PM*.

g. Prepare a common-size balance sheet for the years 2015–2018 to allow for analysis of the inverse of *ATO*.

h. Verify the decomposition of *ROE* into its components for the years 2015–2018.

CE6.23 Now, consider analyzing **Thor Industries** (THO):

a. Compute *RNOA* for the years 2016–2018. If any reported year has 53 weeks, make the needed adjustment.

b. Compute operating *PM* for the years 2015–2018.

c. Compute *NOPAT* from sales and *PM* from sales for the years 2016–2018.

d. Compute operating *ATO* for the years 2015–2018.

e. Compute *RNFL* for the years 2015–2018.

f. Prepare a common-size income statement for the years 2016–2018 to allow for analysis of the *PM*.

g. Prepare a common-size income statement for the years 2016–2018 to allow for analysis of the *ATO*.

h. Verify the decomposition of Thor Industries' *ROE* into its components for the years 2015–2018.

CE6.24 Now, consider analyzing **Winnebago** (WGO):

a. Compute *RNOA* for the years 2016–2018. If any reported year has 53 weeks, make the needed adjustment.

b. Compute operating *PM* for the years 2015–2018.

c. Compute *NOPAT* from sales and *PM* from sales for the years 2016–2018.

d. Compute operating *ATO* for the years 2015–2018.

e. Compute *RNFL* for the years 2015–2018.

f. Prepare a common-size income statement for the years 2016–2018 to allow for analysis of the *PM*.

g. Prepare a common-size income statement for the years 2016–2018 to allow for analysis of the *ATO*.

h. Verify the decomposition *ROE* into its components for the years 2015–2018.

NOTES

Chapter Seven

Full-Information Forecasting for Valuation

TAKEAWAYS

When you complete this chapter, you should be able to:

1. Explain the roles of sales growth, profit margin, and asset turnover in forecasting.
2. Form parsimonious forecasts for a company and aggregate for an industry.
3. Prepare detailed full-information forecasts of sales via sales growth, *NOPAT* via *PM*, and *NOA* via *ATO*.
4. Evaluate forecasts for reasonableness and potential biases or manipulation.

Forecasting financial performance is central to a variety of business decisions, ranging from investing to managing a firm effectively. We might, for example, wish to value a firm's common stock before purchasing its shares. To that end, we might use one of the valuation models discussed in subsequent chapters, which rely on financial statement forecasts as a crucial input. Or we might be interested in evaluating the creditworthiness of a prospective borrower. In that case, we forecast the same information but choose to focus on the borrower's cash flows to evaluate the borrower's ability to repay obligations. We might also be interested in evaluating alternative strategic investment decisions. In this case, we can use the forecasts to understand the sources of the shareholder value, which the strategic investment alternatives will create. All these decisions require carefully considered and justifiable financial forecasts.

As we continue toward valuation, we make our best effort to capture expectations of future performance. These expectations are summarized in our forecasts of future firm financial information. In this chapter, we illustrate a parsimonious method of forecasting, followed by a more detailed and careful method used to forecast the operating financial information.

OVERVIEW OF THE FORECASTING PROCESS

Before we focus on the mechanics of forecasting, we take a moment to consider some overarching principles that guide us in the forecasting process. We also discuss the central role of forecasts of sales growth, profit margin (*PM*), and asset turnover (*ATO*). In Chapters 3 through 5, we introduced reformulation of current and prior financial statements as a way to identify and understand the sources of operating profitability, which we analyzed in Chapter 6. Once we have isolated the historical operating results, we are ready to forecast future results. To forecast future performance, we create a set of financial statements that focus on those operating items we expect to persist.

First, some cautionary words. You may have heard the argument that we should be conservative in forming financial forecasts in order to minimize the likelihood of making a bad decision. "Be conservative in our forecasts so that we are certain our forecast will be met" is a frequent prelude to the forecasting process. Although this thought might appear reasonable, being conservative in our forecasts may lead to failure to recognize and take advantage of valuable opportunities,

CHAPTER OUTLINE

Full-Information Forecasting for Valuation

Forecasting Operations
- Role of Sales Growth, *PM* and *ATO*
- Parsimonious Forecasting
- Industry Analysis

Full-Information Forecasting
- Sales Growth
- Operating Profit Margin
- Operating Asset Turnover

Preparation for Valuation
- Evaluating Forecasts
- Suspect Accounting

which can amount to a very costly mistake. Instead, our objective is to be neither overly optimistic nor overly conservative. The objective for forecasting is to make our best possible forecast.

Computing forecasts to the nth decimal place is easy today using spreadsheets. This increased precision makes them appear more professional, but does not necessarily make the resulting forecasts more accurate. As we discuss in this chapter, our financial statement forecasts are highly dependent on our revenue forecast. Whether revenues are expected to grow by 2, 3, or 4 percent can have marked effects on profitability and other forecasts. Estimating operating *PM*s or *ATO* to the nth decimal place is meaningless if we have imprecise revenue forecasts. Consequently, borderline decisions that depend on a high level of forecasting precision are probably ill-advised.

The forecasted revenues, *NOPAT*, and *NOA* are linked in the same way as in historical financial statements. The underlying framework of DuPont analysis introduced in Chapter 6 applies in the future periods as well. That is, forecasted revenues, *NOPAT*, and *NOA* must articulate (link within and across time). Following the procedures outlined in this chapter will ensure linkages of the forecasted information such that it articulates between financial statements and across time. We also must ensure that our forecast assumptions are internally consistent. For example, it is, generally, nonsense to forecast large increases in revenues without increases in the related *NOA* or to forecast an increased gross profit margin during an economic recession unless there are contrary compelling arguments.

Analysts commonly perform sensitivity analyses following preparation of their forecasts. This process is similar to the sensitivity analyses related to cost of capital and growth beyond the forecast horizon, which will be discussed in Chapter 13, after the valuation chapters. It entails changing forecast assumptions to identify those that have the greatest effect on our estimate of value; of course, our focus is on those effects that would alter investment or business decisions. Assumptions that are identified as crucial to a decision must be investigated thoroughly to ensure that forecast assumptions are as accurate as possible.

Finally, some professionals assert that forecasting is more art than science. Whatever it is, it must begin with a business analysis, including an assessment of general economic activity and the competitive forces within the broader business environment that we discussed in Chapter 1. Ideally, forecasts would be developed at an individual-product level and consider competitive advantage, trends in manufacturing costs, logistical requirements, necessary marketing support, after-sale customer service, and so forth. The narrower the focus, the more we can focus on the business environment in which the firm operates and the more informed are our forecasts. Unfortunately, as external users of financial statements, we often only have access to general-purpose financial statements, which we adjust as we see fit, given publicly available information and our own assessments. Then, we formulate forecast assumptions that are reasonable and consistent with the economic realities defining the firm.

Knowing the business is especially crucial in times where historical information may not be informative about the future. Situations like this include merger and acquisition (M&A) activity, introductions of new products, fundamental changes in technology, and the like. The effects may also be macroeconomic, such as changing energy prices, interest rates, or inflation. Additional situations that may require adjustment from prior historical trends include shifts to outsourcing, the opening of a new factory, or management changing the focus of operating activities. Each of these requires a very strong understanding of the business and the greater economy to form reasonable forecasts.

Throughout this chapter, our goal is not to arrive at the right answer because our value estimate is driven directly by our assumptions. Nor is the goal to enter into debate about individual assumptions made about line items along the way. Our goal is to demonstrate the process by which forecasting toward valuation can be done and the kinds of information and decisions involved. Having discussed the computation and elements of *RNOA* in the prior chapter, we consider the roles of sales, *PM*, and *ATO* as we forecast future operating income and operating assets.

THE ROLES OF SALES GROWTH, *PM*, AND *ATO*

LO1: Explain the roles of sales growth, profit margin, and asset turnover in forecasting.

In this chapter, we first introduce parsimonious (simple) forecasting. Then we demonstrate detailed full-information forecasting. No matter what level of detail is employed, essentially, we apply the forecasting process in a three-step sequence:

1. Forecast revenues via forecasts of sales growth rates.
2. Forecast *NOPAT* from forecasted sales via forecasts of operating *PM* and components of *PM*.
3. Forecast *NOA* required to generate the forecasted sales via forecasts of operating *ATO* and components of *ATO*.

Notice that forecasting the firm's nonoperating, financial, activities is not necessary. This is because we are valuing the operations and then adjusting for the current value of the net financial liabilities to determine the value of equity (further discussed in subsequent chapters). This allows us to completely disregard the process of forecasting future decisions by management/owners on how the firm will be financed. Estimation of future leverage is avoided.

All forecasts are based on a set of forecasting assumptions. The distinction between parsimonious forecasting and full-information forecasting rests on the level of detail in assumptions and forecasts. Sales growth forecasting can be done at the operations level or in more detail by examining, say, segment, division, or even product information. To forecast *NOPAT*, we must make assumptions about revenue growth and about how expenses will change in relation to changes in revenues (i.e., we make assumptions about components of operating *PM*). Then, to forecast the balance sheet, we make assumptions about the relation between balance sheet accounts and revenues (i.e., we make assumptions about components of operating *ATO*). Consequently, before we make business decisions based on forecasted financial statements, we must understand and agree with the underlying assumptions used to produce them. The quality of our decisions is only as good as the quality of the information on which they are based.

The revenues (sales) forecast is, arguably, the most crucial and difficult estimate in the forecasting process. It is a crucial estimate because all other operating income statement and balance sheet accounts derive, either directly or indirectly, from the revenue forecast. As a result, both *NOPAT* and *NOA* (and components of *NOPAT* and *NOA*) change with changes in revenues. The income statement reflects this growth concurrently. However, different balance sheet accounts reflect revenue growth in different ways. Some balance sheet accounts anticipate (or lead) revenue growth (inventories are one example). Some accounts reflect this growth concurrently (e.g., accounts receivable). And some accounts reflect revenue growth with a lag (e.g., firms usually expand plant assets only after growth is deemed sustainable). Conversely, when revenues decline, *NOPAT* and *NOA* also tend to decline because the firm will take actions such as reducing overhead costs and divestiture of excess assets.

When forecasting operating *PM* and *ATO* we are forecasting the profit generated from expected sales and the resources needed to generate these expected sales. As a result, we can think of these forecasts as a translation of the forecast of sales revenue into the rest of the operations' forecasted financial statements. Therefore, we begin with the forecast of revenues and then move on to the forecasts of *PM* and *ATO*. To illustrate, let us proceed with the formation of a set of parsimonious forecasts for General Mills (GIS).

PARSIMONIOUS FORECASTING

LO2: Form parsimonious forecasts for a company and aggregate for an industry.

The forecasting process generally seeks to use all available information in order to derive accurate forecasts. We can, however, simplify the process if, for instance, time does not permit an extensive search for information. Stock valuation models commonly use more parsimonious methods to compute multiyear forecasts for an initial screening of prospective securities.[1] The forecasts, which we now create, are an example of parsimonious forecasts that could be used in the valuation processes illustrated in subsequent chapters. To understand the source of the assumptions, let us review time-series and cross-sectional information related to GIS that would provide information helpful in determining future sales growth, *PM*, and *ATO*.

In recent years, GIS has experienced varying sales growth rates, as shown in **Exhibit 7.1**. Also, in **Exhibit 7.1**, we provide the same information for GIS' main competitor, Kellogg (K).

EXHIBIT 7.1 GIS' and K's Sales Growth over Time

Amounts in Millions			
GIS Year Ended	**5/29/2016**	**5/28/2017**	**5/27/2018**
Sales	16,563.1	15,619.8	15,740.4
Sales growth	(6.05)%	(5.70)%	0.77%
K Year Ended	**12/31/2016**	**12/30/2017**	**12/29/2018**
Sales	12,965	12,854	13,547
Sales growth	(4.14)%	(0.86)%	5.39%

Note, again, that, because the year-end for GIS is May, the most recent annual financial statement information is as of May 27, 2018. Because the year-end for K is December, its most recently available financial statement information is as of December 29, 2018. As discussed in Chapter 6, we can use this information despite its being misaligned in time. Known issues that may affect comparability must, however, be considered; an example could be a large macroeconomic event, such as a change in energy prices or currency conversion rates occurring during late 2018, which is the non-overlapping period. Internal events such as new product launches or seasonality may also reduce the comparability of the nonoverlapping periods. Although the sales data were available for GIS for the first few quarters of the year ended May 2019, and hence we could have calculated the sales for a GIS year ending February 2019 (by adding the last quarter of 2018 and the first three quarters of the year ended May 2019), we do not. Still, we should be aware of potential effects of this misalignment of the fiscal year-end dates (and therefore misalignment in the data) when using the data as a basis for forecasting.

EFFECT OF ACQUISITIONS ON USE OF HISTORICAL DATA

Clearly, when a company makes a material acquisition, the future sales, *PM*, and *ATO* will be affected. This reduces the ability to rely on the past levels of sales growth, *PM*, *ATO*, and their changes when forecasting.

For large acquisitions, companies' financial statements will often report pro forma information that provides a glimpse into what the combined firm would have looked like. This can be helpful in gaining an understanding of the expected future values but never provides the level of detail that would have been found in historical financial statements.

As a result, we will have to work even more to understand the implications of the acquisition on future sales, costs, and resource requirements. While this may feel, at times, like we are flying blind, so is everyone else! Our advantage continues to be having a structured approach for analysis of information and forecasting, which, when combined with an understanding of the revised business after acquisition, will allow for the best possible forecasts.

Review of the data in **Exhibit 7.1** illustrates how difficult it is to use these data to provide a basis for estimates of the expected sales growth. Recent sales growth for GIS has been much lower than we might expect going forward, especially with negative growth in the years ended May 2016 and 2017. In forecasting what would be expected in the near future, do we focus on the results in 2016 and 2017, suggesting a growth rate around –6 percent, or the results from 2018 of 1 percent, suggesting a small positive growth rate? Do we average the last few years for GIS, suggesting

[1] An extreme example of the use of minimal information for valuation will be the method of multiples discussed in Chapter 8.

approximately −3.7 percent? Do we assume that GIS will trail the rates of K as it has in the periods shown? Do we assume that the increase seen by both companies in the most recent year will continue or that growth will revert to the levels seen in the prior year? Or do we decide that these historic data are not helpful for forecasting and look elsewhere for indications of expected sales growth rates?[2]

USE OF CUMULATIVE ANNUAL GROWTH RATES

Some advocate for the calculation of a cumulative annual growth rate (*CAGR*) for the past few years. They then assume this rate will continue to apply going forward. This approach is a shortcut that fails to use the detailed information available. For instance, the *CAGR* in sales for GIS for the last 4 years would be calculated from the May 2018 and 2014 sales figures as follows:

$$SalesCAGR = \left[\frac{Sales_{2018}}{Sales_{2014}}\right]^{\frac{1}{5}} - 1$$

$$= \left[\frac{15{,}740.4}{17{,}909.6}\right]^{\frac{1}{5}} - 1$$

$$= -2.55\%$$

The problem is that the same *CAGR* would result from the following hypothetical pattern of sales:

	2014	2015	2016	2017	2018
Sales.	17,909.6	13,597.1	14,277.0	14,990.9	15,740.4
Growth in sales.		–24.1%	5.0%	5.0%	5.0%

This is in spite of the last 3 years of this data showing growth of 5.0 percent per year! Clearly, for this hypothetical pattern, an assumption of 5.0 percent growth going forward would be much better than to assume –2.55 percent. Careful consideration of all available data should be used in forecasting at all times.

For the sake of demonstration, we assume that the expected sales growth rate is 1.5 percent per year. This is based partly on a sales growth forecast of 1.8 percent by ValueLine at the beginning of May 2019, which we assume to be a little optimistic. While this seems a straightforward starting point, we also know that we must apply what we know about the business. In April 2018, GIS acquired Blue Buffalo. GIS' Form 10-K noted, "The consolidated results of Blue Buffalo will be reported as our pet operating segment in future periods on a one-month lag. Accordingly, in fiscal 2018, our Consolidated Statements of Earnings do not include Pet operating segment results." Knowing no Blue Buffalo sales are included in the results for the year ended May 2018 is very important. We also must realize the growth rate forecast by ValueLine is after the effects of the Blue Buffalo acquisition are considered.

The base number from which we grow must be the May 2018 sales, including Blue Buffalo. The good news is that the company provides pro forma sales numbers in the years ended May 2017 and 2018. Note 3 of the financial statements provides unaudited pro forma sales estimates as if the acquisition had occurred at the beginning of fiscal 2017. The estimated sales would have been \$16,772.9 and \$17,057.4 in the years ended May 2017 and 2018, respectively. While not perfect, this information is very helpful in getting closer to the results that should be expected in future years. Thus, our estimated growth of 1.5 percent will begin from the pro forma base sales of \$17,057.4.

Our assessment of expected sales growth is tempered by the following Market Realist analysis dated May 23, 2019, that suggests the most recent change from –5.70 to 0.77 percent is not expected to lead to further increases:

[2] We would look at analysts and management forecasts (from MD&A or from conference calls) and use these as a guide, recognizing that these are likely to err toward optimism.

> General Mills' strong financial performance during the last reported quarter and upbeat EPS outlook are expected to support its stock. Higher pricing and a favorable mix will likely drive the company's organic sales and margins.
>
> However, the company faces a tough YoY (year-over-year) comparison in fiscal 2020. General Mills' sales growth is projected to decelerate as it annualizes its Blue Buffalo acquisition. Weakness in organic volumes is also a drag.
>
> General Mills' bottom line is projected to stabilize in fiscal 2020. However, the growth rate will likely be low and could restrict the upside in the stock.[3]

Based on this information, we may think an assumption of sales growth of 1.5 percent is reasonable.

As input to forming forecasts of operating *PM* for GIS, we will focus on recent realizations of *PM* from sales. **Exhibit 7.2** shows the recent *PM* from sales for GIS and K.

EXHIBIT 7.2 GIS' and K's Operating *PM* from Sales over Time

GIS Year Ended	**5/29/2016**	**5/28/2017**	**5/27/2018**
Sales	16,563.1	15,619.8	15,740.4
NOPAT from sales	1,871.9	1,990.7	2,467.7
Operating *PM* from sales	11.30%	12.74%	15.68%
K Year Ended	**12/31/2016**	**12/30/2017**	**12/29/2018**
Sales	12,965	12,854	13,547
NOPAT from sales	1,398	497	1,632
Operating *PM* sales	10.78%	3.87%	12.05%

We use *PM* from sales because the other components of *PM* (i.e., restructuring costs, foreign currency translation, and hedge activities) are expected to be zero on average.[4] For example, the largest item of other comprehensive income for GIS in recent years has been fair value changes in hedge derivatives. Forecasting how much gain or loss GIS will experience in future years is difficult. If we did make a nonzero forecast, we would essentially be implying that GIS can predict changes in the fair value.

Review of GIS' information shows an increasing *PM* from sales. This makes forecasting a challenge because we need to determine whether the increase will continue, the new rate of 15.68 percent will continue, or a return to the prior levels will occur. Looking closer at **Exhibit 7.2**, we see that K has seen a large drop in 2017 and a rebound in 2018 to a level above 2016. When combined with the increases for GIS over recent years, this makes us wonder whether the increased number of 15.68 percent *PM* from sales can continue. What has caused this industry to have these patterns of *PM*? Also, we would need to consider whether pet foods will have a different profitability than items sold in prior years. Our assumption for the parsimonious forecast is that the increased profitability will decline slightly to a *PM* rate of 13.0 percent.

Turning to operating *ATO*, we wish to understand the resources that will be necessary to support the expected sales going forward. This amount also depends on the business model chosen by the firm, the industry in which the firm operates, and many other factors. We first start by examining (see in **Exhibit 7.3**) the recent results for GIS, which we identified as a part of our analysis in Chapter 6, as well as those for K.

From a review of GIS' results over the past few years, we see that *ATO* significantly changed in the most recent year. This is likely due partly to the addition of items included in the Blue Buffalo acquisition near the end of the most recent year (April 24, 2018). To help measure the effect of the acquisition, we may compare the pro forma sales in the year ending May 2018 to the ending *NOA*. Here, we see a ratio of 0.692, which is in line with the recent *ATO* of 0.751. While comparing the pro forma sales to ending *NOA* is not a proper *ATO* calculation, it provides confirmation that a number closer to the 0.751 may be in order.

[3] (https://articles2.marketrealist.com/2019/05/general-mills-analyzing-the-stock-performance-and-outlook/)

[4] Importantly, although we know that some of these items (e.g., the foreign currency translation amount) are likely to be large, our best estimate of the amount is zero (it will be positive some years and negative others) but, on average, it would be expected to be zero. We will return to this point later in the chapter as a part of full-information forecasting.

EXHIBIT 7.3 GIS and K Operating *ATO* over Time

GIS Year Ended	5/29/2016	5/28/2017	5/27/2018
Sales	16,563.1	15,619.8	15,740.4
Beginning *NOA*	17,463.8	16,493.9	16,855.9
Ending *NOA*	16,493.9	16,855.9	25,035.4
Operating *ATO*	0.976	0.937	0.751
K Year Ended	**12/31/2016**	**12/30/2017**	**12/29/2018**
Sales	12,965	12,854	13,547
Beginning *NOA*	11,196	11,080	11,815
Ending *NOA*	11,080	11,815	12,949
Operating *ATO*	1.164	1.123	1.094

Clearly, determining a forecast of *ATO* is tricky. The prior years had shown a decreasing pattern. Also, K displays a decreasing pattern. While this cries out for a more in-depth analysis (especially on the effect of the Blue Buffalo acquisition), we put that on hold for now. Overall, this information justifies our parsimonious forecast of 0.75, which reflects an amount in line with that observed in the most recent year for GIS.

COMPILING PARSIMONIOUS FORECASTS

After review of GIS' financial statements over the years prior to and including May 2018, as well as the financial statements of K as a comparable firm, we arrive at the following assumptions for the foreseeable future using a parsimonious analysis:

Sales growth rate	1.5%
Operating *PM*	13.0%
Operating *ATO*	0.75

Using the above inputs, we can forecast expectations of GIS' future sales, *NOPAT*, and *NOA*. Forecasted numbers for the next 4 years are shown in **Exhibit 7.4**.

EXHIBIT 7.4 GIS' Multiyear Forecasts of Sales, *NOPAT*, and *NOA* ($ millions)

Year Ended	5/27/2018	5/26/2019	5/31/2020	5/30/2021	5/29/2022
Sales	$17,057.4	$17,313.3 ($17,057.4 × 1.0150)	$17,910.9 ($17,313.3 × 1.0153)	$18,179.6 ($17,910.9 × 1.0150)	$18,452.3 ($18,179.6 × 1.0150)
NOPAT		$2,250.7 ($17,313.3 × 13.0%)	$2,328.4 ($17,910.9 × 13.0%)	$2,363.3 ($18,179.6 × 13.0%)	$2,398.8 ($18,452.3 × 13.0%)
NOA	$25,035.4	$23,430.6 ($17,911/0.736)	$24,239.4 ($18,180/0.750)	$24,603.0 ($18,452/0.750)	$24,972.1 ($18,729/0.750)

As was mentioned in Chapter 6, when we form forecasts, we estimate *NOA* using sales of the following period. This is based on the argument that the *NOA* must be in place to generate the sales. Thus, we define forecasted *ATO* as *Sales/Beginning NOA*. Remember that, when analyzing reported (historical) information, we did not know when investments occurred during the year and, therefore, we utilized an average *NOA* in the calculation of historical *RNOA*.

Two major issues must be noted in the creation of the forecasts in **Exhibit 7.4**. First, in the calculation of sales, we do not begin with reported sales. Rather, we begin with a pro forma sales number of $17,057.4 for the year ended May 2018. This allows us to estimate sales for the year ended May 2019 and for subsequent periods, which include Blue Buffalo (the pet segment).

Second, two of the calculations in **Exhibit 7.4** are affected by the fact that the year ended May 31, 2020, and will have 53 weeks rather than the normal 52. As a result, when we forecast sales for that year, we adjust the growth rate (multiplying by 53/52 (1.5% × 53/52 = 1.5288%) to recognize the extra week of sales). Also, for the calculation of required *NOA* at 5/26/2019 (the beginning of the year with 53 weeks), we multiply the forecasted *ATO* by 52/53 ($0.75 \times 52/53 = 0.7358$) to recognize that additional *NOA* is not required simply because we have a longer period over which sales are measured.

In a subsequent chapter, we will use the fact that $FCF = NOPAT - \Delta NOA$ to obtain forecasts of free cash flow from operations.

INTRODUCTION TO INDUSTRY ANALYSIS

In each chapter, our focus is on GIS. If we expanded our efforts to complete the full analysis of K and other competitors, such as **Kraft Heinz** and **Hormel Foods** we would have an industry analysis. We could also add companies from the packaged foods industry, such as **McCormick & Co**, **Campbell Soup**, **JM Smucker**, and others. For a complete industry analysis, we might also review the extent to which companies included may also produce pet food. The more companies within the industry that we include in our analysis, the more complete our view of the business environment becomes. We begin to see the competitive and macroeconomic forces affecting the pricing of products and the cost structure for the company.

One caveat that must be noted is to recognize that few companies today are true pure plays. That is, few companies can be clearly identified as being in only one industry. As we have seen, GIS operates using segments of North America retail, convenience stores and food service, Europe and Australia, Asia and Latin America, and the newly acquired Pet segment. The competitors for these different segments are not always the same companies. For example, Nestlé and JM Smucker have pet foods in their portfolio, but Kraft Heinz does not. Even the disposal of a segment may lead to a reevaluation of which companies are competitors.

Industry analysis is an important element of the valuation exercise. It is often a foundation for the understanding of the business environment, which was our first step. This is why analysts most often cover an industry or a sector rather than a random grouping of companies. The information learned when studying one company creates a spillover to the other firms, leading to refinement of our analysis, forecasts, and valuation.

MOVING FROM PARSIMONIOUS TO FULL-INFORMATION FORECASTING

LO3: Prepare detailed full-information forecasts of sales via sales growth, *NOPAT* via *PM*, and *NOA* via *ATO*.

Our focus in full-information forecasting is on creating a set of forecasted financial statements for the operating activities. We are ultimately forming forecasts of operating income statements and balance sheets, which capture the operating activities for the foreseeable future. Having gathered all available information, adjusted the historical results, and reformulated our adjusted financial statements, we are ready to forecast future results. As a reminder, forecasting financial performance is integral to a variety of business decisions, ranging from investing to managing a company effectively. All these decisions require carefully thought-out and justifiable financial forecasts.

We now undertake the task of forming more detailed forecasts of sales growth, *PM*, and *ATO* by basing the forecasts on all the refined information we have gathered. We will form forecasts bearing in mind the fact that our forecasts of revenues, *NOPAT*, and *NOA* must articulate (i.e., link together within and across time) in the way that they do in historical financial statements. We will ensure that the assumptions, which underpin our forecasts, are internally consistent and reasonable.

Remember that our forecasting must begin with understanding the business, discussed in Chapter 1, including an assessment of general economic activity and the competitive forces within the broader business environment. Additionally, after forecasting and valuing the company, we should perform sensitivity analyses to determine which of our assumptions are the most critical. Assumptions that are identified as crucial to a decision must be investigated thoroughly to ensure that assumptions used in forecasting are meaningful and justified.

Throughout the remainder of this chapter, our goal is to demonstrate the process by which full-information forecasting toward valuation can be done and the kinds of information and decisions involved. Of course, our forecasts are driven by our assumptions, and we may question (or wish to debate) these assumptions. The section will, however, be most helpful if we focus on the process underlying full-information forecasting and on the fact that justifiable assumptions must be made.

No matter what level of detail is employed, parsimonious or full-information, the forecasting process is applied in the same three-step sequence:

1. Forecast revenues via forecasts of sales growth rates.
2. Forecast *NOPAT* via forecasts of operating *PM* and components of *PM*.
3. Forecast *NOA* via forecasts of operating *ATO* and components of *ATO*.

The change from our parsimonious forecasts above is that we are now considering additional information, which allows us to forecast at a much more detailed level. For example, rather than forecasting *PM* for GIS at 13.0 percent, we separately forecast the individual components of *PM* and then sum them to arrive at a composite forecast of *PM*. In doing so, we recognize that the individual components will evolve over time in separate, though sometimes similar, ways. Full-information forecasting will ensure that our forecasting assumptions are consistent with our beliefs and predictions for future growth and key financial relations.

As a reminder, throughout this process, forecasting the company's financial activities is not necessary. This is because we are valuing the operating activities, and then we will adjust for the current value of the net financial liabilities (discussed in a subsequent chapter) to determine the current value of equity. This allows us to disregard the process of forecasting future decisions by management/owners regarding the financing of the company. Forecasting future leverage is avoided.

Full-Information Forecasts of Sales Growth

The revenues (sales) forecast is, arguably, the most crucial and difficult estimate in the forecasting process. To form full-information forecasts of sales, we use all available, relevant information. But deciding what information is relevant and determining how to use the information varies across companies and forecasters. As well, the granularity of the information itself can vary across companies and forecasters. Forecasts that are built from anticipated unit sales and current prices, for example, are generally more informative, and accurate, than those derived from historical dollar sales. Most companies, however, do not provide unit sales data in their Form 10-K. However, if we have access to nonpublic information (e.g., as would a member of the management team) and are developing forecasts as part of the strategic budgeting process for a company, we might have access to data regarding the competitive landscape, consumer trends and disposable income, new product introductions, production and marketing plans, and many other types of inside information. In this case, we can build our revenue forecast from the bottom up with unit sales and unit prices for each product or service sold.

CHALLENGES TO FORECASTING REVENUES

Some circumstances can greatly decrease our confidence in our revenue forecasts. One circumstance is when a company changes its revenue model. For example, consider a company moving from a rental to a subscription model for charging its customers. Essentially, this creates a disconnect between past revenue growth and future growth. Similar issues arise when a company moves to or from a franchising model. In these situations, it may seem that forecasts are baseless and just made up. We must remember that all investors and analysts are facing the same obstacles. Here, our greatest strength will be the strongest possible understanding of the company, its operating environment, and the changes that are occurring.

As an outsider, we usually have much less information available. In this case, we must rely on public statements by management in conference calls and meetings in addition to the information disclosed in the management discussion and analysis (MD&A) section of the Form 10-K and the growth of individual product lines from segment disclosures. We also use publicly available information from competitors, suppliers, and customers for additional insight into broader trends that may affect future revenues. The forecasts of analysts following the company can be examined, not to tell us what to assume, but to inform our interpretation of the available information. Companies often provide "guidance" to outsiders to help refine forecasts. This information may be quite useful because companies have a vested interest in sound forecasting in order to increase the accuracy of the market price of their stock. Generally, managers do not want their company to be underpriced by the market (e.g., this may reduce the value of any stock and share-based compensation), or overpriced (this will lead to a negative reaction by the market when unfavorable information is eventually revealed).

Forecasts are made within the broader context of the general economic environment and the competitive landscape in which the company operates. We must also consider company-specific factors that may affect revenue growth. Consider, for example, the direct effect on sales growth of acquisition of one company by another. The revenues and expenses of the acquired company are consolidated but only from the date of acquisition onward. Acquisitions can greatly affect the acquirer's income statement, especially if the acquisition occurs toward the beginning of the acquirer's fiscal year. **Procter & Gamble**'s (PG) acquisition of **Gillette** in October 2005 provides an example. PG's 2006 sales growth of 20.2 percent [($68,222 sales in 2006/$56,741 sales in 2005) – 1] was driven by this acquisition, and we would have been remiss in forecasting a 20.2 percent increase in sales for 2007. The reported sales for 2006 include Gillette product sales from October 2005 onward (from October 2005 to June 2006); of course, none of Gillette's sales were reported in fiscal 2005.

Understanding the effect of acquisitions on the financial statements is aided in the United States by GAAP's requirement that the acquirer disclose the revenue and net income, which would have been reported had the acquired company been consolidated in recent years; that is, the Form 10-K must include some comparative income statement items, which include the sales and income effects of the acquired company. This what if, disclosure is called a pro forma disclosure. PG's pro forma disclosure in 2006 included information about pro forma results of operations for the years 2006, 2005, and 2004, as if Gillette had been acquired as of the beginning of 2004. Using this disclosure, we would have been able to compute the estimated growth rate in sales for 2006 as 4.5 percent [($71,005 sales in 2006/$67,920 sales in 2005) – 1], and we would have used the pro forma net sales for 2006 as our forecasting base. That is, if we assume continued growth of 4.5 percent, we would have forecasted 2007 net sales as $74,200 (calculated as $71,005 times 1.045). PG was careful to point out, however, that the pro forma earnings estimate must be viewed with caution because "Pro forma results do not include any anticipated cost savings or other effects of the planned integration of Gillette. Accordingly, such amounts are not necessarily indicative of the results if the acquisition had occurred on the dates indicated or that may result in the future."[5] Shortly, we will address GIS' acquisition of Blue Buffalo near the end of the most recent year and its' effects on our forecasts of sales.

For divestitures, companies are required under U.S. GAAP to exclude sales and expenses of discontinued operations from the continuing operations portion of their income statements and to present the net income and gain (loss) on sale of the divested entity, net of tax, below income from continuing operations. The revenues, expenses, and earnings for GIS in each year, as reported in its income statement, *exclude* the revenues, expenses, and earnings from its discontinued operations. The detail relating to the revenues, expenses, and earnings of discontinued operations (and associated gain/loss on sale) is usually reported in a footnote disclosure. This additional information may allow us to better evaluate the drivers of observed growth in revenues and earnings. We would, of course, be remiss if we included the revenues and gains relating to discontinued operations in our forecasts.

PRIOR YEAR'S INFORMATION ON DISCONTINUED OPERATIONS

While the financial statements will contain the information excluding the discontinued operations, this is only for the years presented. Remember, the prior year's financial statements you gather will still contain that information shown as continuing because, during the earlier time period, there was no intent to cease these operations. Recognize that this may reduce the usefulness of the older information in predicting future operations.

In general, we want to determine what drives the sales of the company being examined (step 1: Know the business!). Often, an understanding of the industry is necessary because these drivers may be common across an industry and will be provided in industry-standard language. Examples include airlines reporting revenue per seat mile and hotels reporting revenue per available room. For GIS, as a producer of food and pet products, we find that it discloses detailed information about its business based on designations by segment (in part, determined by U.S. reporting requirements). This information focuses on the components of sales growth, with a particular

[5] Procter & Gamble 2006 Form 10-K.

emphasis on organic net sales growth.[6] Utilizing the North America retail segment as an example, GIS provided the analysis shown in **Exhibit 7.5**.

EXHIBIT 7.5 GIS' MD&A Discussion of North America Retail Segment Sales

NORTH AMERICA RETAIL SEGMENT

Our North America Retail operating segment reflects business with a wide variety of grocery stores, mass merchandisers, membership stores, natural food chains, drug, dollar and discount chains, and e-commerce grocery providers. Our product categories in this business segment are ready-to-eat cereals, refrigerated yogurt, soup, meal kits, refrigerated and frozen dough products, dessert and baking mixes, frozen pizza and pizza snacks, grain, fruit and savory snacks, and a wide variety of organic products including refrigerated yogurt, nutrition bars, meal kits, salty snacks, ready-to-eat cereal, and grain snacks.

North America Retail net sales were as follows:

	Fiscal 2018	Fiscal 2018 vs. 2017 Percentage Change	Fiscal 2017	Fiscal 2017 vs. 2016 Percentage Change	Fiscal 2016
Net sales (in millions)	**$10,115.4**	**(1)%**	$10,196.9	(7)%	$10,936.6
Contributions from volume growth[(a)]		**Flat**		(11)pts	
Net price realization and mix		**(1)pt**		4 pts	
Foreign currency exchange		**Flat**		Flat	

(a) Measured in tons based on the stated weight of our product shipments.

The 1 percent decrease in North America Retail net sales for fiscal 2018 was driven by declines in the U.S. Yogurt operating unit partially offset by growth in the U.S. Snacks and Canada operating units.

The 7 percent decrease in North America Retail net sales for fiscal 2017 was driven by declines in the U.S. Meals & Baking, U.S. Yogurt, U.S. Cereal, and Canada operating units. The decline in net sales also includes the impact of the Green Giant divestiture from the U.S. Meals & Baking and Canada operating units in fiscal 2016.

This disclosure is provided partly as support for and to expand upon the table shown in **Exhibit 7.6**, which reports changes in the details of segment sales.

EXHIBIT 7.6 GIS' MD&A Disclosure of Sales Change Drivers

	Fiscal 2018 vs. 2017 Percentage Change	Fiscal 2017 vs. 2016 Percentage Change
Contributions from organic volume growth[(a)]	Flat	(9)pts
Organic net price realization and mix	(1)pt	4 pts
Organic net sales growth	(1)pt	(5)pts
Foreign currency exchange	Flat	Flat
Acquisitions and divestitures[(b)]	Flat	(2)pts
Net sales growth	(1)pt	(7)pts

(a) Measured in tons based on the stated weight of our product shipments.
(b) Primarily the Green Giant divestiture in fiscal 2016.

From these disclosures in the financial statements of each year, we can arrive at a history of the detailed changes in the sales of the North America retail segment over the previous few years, as shown in **Exhibit 7.7**.

[6] GIS provides the following definition/description of organic net sales growth rates in the MD&A section: "This measure is used in reporting to our executive management and as a component of the Board of Directors' measurement of our performance for incentive compensation purposes. We provide organic net sales growth rates for our consolidated net sales and segment net sales. We believe that organic net sales growth rates provide useful information to investors because they provide transparency to underlying performance in our net sales by excluding the effect that foreign currency exchange rate fluctuations, as well as acquisitions, divestitures, and a 53rd week, when applicable, have on year-to-year comparability."

EXHIBIT 7.7 GIS' North America Retail Segment Sales

Year Ended	5/31/2015	5/29/2016	5/28/2017	5/27/2018
North America Retail Sales	$11,612.1	$10,936.6	$10,196.9	$10,115.4
Contributions from organic volume growth		−2.0%	−9.0%	0.0%
Organic net price realization and mix		1.0%	4.0%	−1.0%
Organic net sales growth		−1.0%	−5.0%	−1.0%
Foreign currency exchange		−1.0%	0.0%	0.0%
Acquisitions and divestitures		−3.0%	−2.0%	0.0%
Other unclassified/rounding		0.2%	0.2%	0.2%
		−4.8%	−6.8%	−0.8%
53rd week impact		−1.0%	0.0%	0.0%
		−5.8%	−6.8%	−0.8%

Based on this analysis and additional information learned from examination of competitors and evaluation of the industry, our goal is to forecast the future revenues of this segment. We choose to assume in forecasting future sales that the items, which are not part of organic sales growth, have no *anticipated* change going forward.[7] As a result, the task becomes forming expectations of the organic sales growth of this segment going forward. This means that, despite realized decreases in sales (negative sales growth) in each of the past 3 years, we see a different pattern of the organic level for the North America retail segment. Based on this information and our understanding of the company, we form the expectations for this segment shown in **Exhibit 7.8**.

EXHIBIT 7.8 GIS' Forecasted Sales for North America Retail Segment

Year Ended	5/26/2019	5/31/2020	5/30/2021
Contributions from organic volume growth	−1.0%	−0.5%	0.0%
Organic net price realization and mix	1.0%	0.8%	0.5%
Organic net sales growth	0.0%	0.3%	0.5%
53rd week impact	0.0%	1.9%	−1.9%
	0.0%	2.2%	−1.4%
Forecasted North America retail segment sales	$10,115.4	$10,340.3	$10,196.9

These forecasts of the revenues for GIS' North America retail segment show the impact in the years ended May 2020 and 2021 of having 53 weeks in the year ended May 2020. This requires an "extra" increase in 2020 because the company will not only grow sales by 0.3 percent but also have one extra week of sales. The following year, we recognize that there will be a return to 52 weeks, which will reduce revenues for the year. The percentage used as the 53rd week impact is computed as 1/52 as we add and then subtract one week.

One way we determine the reasonableness of our forecasts is to consider how they stack up to information either from analysts or management. GIS' MD&A for the year ended May 2018 states, "Our key full-year fiscal 2019 targets include: Organic net sales are expected to be in a range between flat and up 1 percent. Including the impact of the Blue Buffalo acquisition, net sales are expected to increase 9 to 10 percent. Our forecasts reflect this level of organic sales growth continuing for the next couple of years."

For each of GIS' other segments, we could make similar forecasts of GIS' organic net sales growth except for the new segment pet. GIS acquired Blue Buffalo on April 28, 2018. Further, as GIS stated in Note 3 to the financial statements, "The consolidated results of Blue Buffalo will be reported as our Pet operating segment in future periods on a one-month lag. Accordingly, in fiscal 2018, our Consolidated Statements of Earnings do not include Pet operating segment results."

[7] It may be possible in some situations to forecast that the company plans an acquisition or divestiture. These effects would be incorporated into anticipated sales growth and estimates.

There are no sales for Blue Buffalo included in the numbers we analyzed in prior chapters, but, clearly, we must make forecasts for the future.

In Note 3, GIS provided unaudited supplemental pro forma information as if the acquisition had occurred at the beginning of fiscal 2017. While this information was based on management's estimation rather than the sales that occurred, it provides a starting point for our forecasting of the future pet segment sales. From this information, we can determine GIS' estimate of the sales of Blue Buffalo in the most recent 2 years as follows:

Year Ended	5/28/2017	5/27/2018
Pro forma sales	$16,772.9	$17,057.4
Actual reported sales	15,619.8	15,740.4
Implied pet segment sales	$ 1,153.1	$ 1,317.0

Here, we see that the implied pet segment sales increased 14.2 percent in the last year. In our forecast, we assume that this level of increase is not sustainable. We instead forecast growth declining to 6, 5, and then 4 percent for this segment over the next few years. Our forecast of a growth of 6 percent in the pet segment combined with the forecasts of the other segments leads to an overall growth in GIS' sales across all segments of 9.43 percent. This is an amount in line with the company's stated target of 9 to 10 percent growth in sales. Recognize that forecasting sales for a new segment poses more challenges than we normally face because we have no history for GIS operating in this arena.

After summing the segment sales, we have arrived at a much more detailed sales forecast than was formed by merely assuming 1.5 percent growth overall in all future years.[8] This represents a full-information sales forecast where all the information we acquire is used in forming our expectations. The full-information sales forecast for GIS for the next 3 years, formed by adding our detailed forecasts for each segment, is shown in **Exhibit 7.9**.

EXHIBIT 7.9 GIS' Forecasted Sales

Year Ended	2016	2017	2018
Forecasted sales	17,224.4	17,746.9	17,637.8
Sales growth percentage	9.43%	3.03%	–0.62%
Sales growth without 52-/53-week effect	9.43%	1.11%	1.27%

We note the sales growth without the 52-/53-week effect because it will be more indicative of future periods not affected by this issue. From these forecasts, we may be led to choose alternative sales growth forecasts for the periods thereafter. Recognizing that GIS has had negative sales growth before the Blue Buffalo acquisition and our anticipation of a slowdown in the growth of pet sales, we choose to forecast sales growth in 2022 at 1.3 percent, 2023 at 1.25 percent, and thereafter at 1.20 percent. These numbers are significantly more informed than those previously used in our parsimonious valuation because they result from the use of much more detailed information.

USING RECENT FORM 10-QS

Having formed forecasts for the next several years, we must also consider any information reported for the current year. Any quarters for which the company has reported information in the current year can be used to see if our forecasts are reasonable. Of course, remember to be aware of seasonality in sales and expenses. Do not simply assume that each quarter is the same.

[8] It should be noted that the parsimonious forecast started from the $17,057.4 in pro forma sales, implying $17,313.3 in sales in the year ended May 2019. Our full-information forecasting has calculated sales growth of 9.43 percent starting from the reported sales of $15,740.4, implying sales of $17,224.4 in the year ended May 2019. Thus, in this case, our very different approaches led to a similar short-term forecast.

As previously mentioned, our analysis will be driven by the industry and the data that is disclosed. For example, retailers such as Target and Kohl's typically consider revenue growth based on two sources: existing stores (organic growth) and new stores. We would be interested in the breakdown between these two growth sources because the latter is obtained at considerably more cost, and there may be differing persistence of the growth, which each source can provide. Also, retailers typically operate on a 52-/53-week year similar to GIS. Remember that step 1 requires that we must know the business!

SEGMENTING SALES

Similar to the sales from existing stores versus new stores, other natural segments may occur in other industries. For example, the hotel industry may have revenue arising from renting rooms, management fees, and/or sales of time-share properties. In the restaurant industry, some locations may be company owned, and others may be franchises providing only royalty income. Each of these elements may have a different associated sales growth and different implications for costs when we consider forecasting operating *PM*. Clearly, the costs related to a company-owned location will include food and labor, while a franchise location would not.

Full-Information Forecasts of Operating Profit Margin

Our full-information forecasting efforts for sales provided details on the North America retail segment and then reported the results of applying the process to all segments. Similarly, our efforts at forecasting operating *PM* will include some, but not all, key items. In doing so, we will focus on illustrating the thought process and methodology.

While forming a full-information forecast of revenues utilized a great deal of information previously not included in our analysis, the starting point for a full-information forecast of *PM* is the reformulation we completed in Chapter 5 and the common-size analysis shown in Chapter 6. The essence of the task of forming a full-information forecast of *PM* is forecasting each of the components of *PM*. To forecast these components, we may choose among various approaches, including the following:

1. *Steady ratio*: Forecast based on the relation of costs and sales in the most recent years. If that relation (or the time series of the component of *PM*) is somewhat steady, we may believe a similar relation will hold in future periods.
2. *Steady amount*: Forecast a specific dollar amount. An example would be holding a dollar amount constant from year to year going forward.
3. *Follow a trend*: Forecast continuation of a trend of increases or decreases in the relation to sales. Here, we are essentially forecasting a steady rate of change from year to year.
4. *Use other information*: Choose a relation to sales that departs from the historical numbers based on some information and/or expectations. For example, if fuel prices are expected to go down significantly in future years, we may choose a relation to sales that departs from the relation historically observed.
5. *Zero*: Forecast zero revenues or expenses for a particular item. These are items not expected to recur in the future.

Rather than walk through every element of *NOPAT* individually, we illustrate examples where each of these approaches is used. After this, we provide the compiled forecast of future operating *PM* based on the component-level assumptions.

- Steady ratio: For many items, we may conclude that, after looking at the past few years, a constant percent of sales may be assumed to carry forward. For example, GIS' postemployment benefit plans: Service cost has been 0.05 or 0.06 percent of sales in each of the last 3 years. Thus, an assumption of 0.05 percent as a component of *PM* going forward may be reasonable.
- Steady amount: Over the past 4 years, research and development (R&D) has been relatively steady, ranging from \$218.2 to \$222.1. Thus, we may choose to keep R&D expense

relatively steady at $220 per year rather than assuming this amount will grow from year to year with growth in sales. However, because of the addition of Blue Buffalo, this would not be an appropriate assumption for GIS. Determining the level of R&D that will be required in this new segment and the resulting sales in subsequent periods is actually one of the hardest aspects of forecasting, but it must be done!

FIXED VERSES VARIABLE COSTS

Managerial and cost accounting classes (as well as many finance classes) focus on recognition of the nature of costs as either fixed or variable. This mindset is helpful in forecasting for valuation as well. The *Steady Ratio* would represent a pure variable cost where each additional item sold has the same related cost, yielding a steady component level *PM*. The *Steady Amount* would represent a pure fixed cost where there is no expected change in costs dependent on the quantity sold.

Keep in mind that that some fixed costs will increase in discrete jumps. For instance, even if property taxes are a fixed cost, when sales reach the point that a new facility is necessary, then they will increase. Understanding the nature of the items is a key to forecasting future values as the sales of the company change.

- Follow a trend: In recent years, GIS has had advertising costs shrink from 4.55 to 3.66 percent of sales. We may choose to assume that this trend will continue and that this item will be reduced each of the next few years by 0.45 percent of sales. This would yield forecasts of 3.21 percent of sales in 2019, followed by 2.76 percent in 2020. Of course, the appropriateness of forecasting decreasing advertising in a period where sales have been faltering is questionable. Again, we must understand the business we are examining.
- Other information: It is not surprising that a company would state that it intends to manage costs and improve the profitability of operations. GIS described the efforts in its May 2018 MD&A, shown in **Exhibit 7.10**.

EXHIBIT 7.10 GIS' MD&A Disclosures Related to Cost-Reduction Efforts

ITEM 1A Risk Factors

If we are not efficient in our production, our profitability could suffer as a result of the highly competitive environment in which we operate.

Our future success and earnings growth depend in part on our ability to be efficient in the production and manufacture of our products in highly competitive markets. Gaining additional efficiencies may become more difficult over time. Our failure to reduce costs through productivity gains or by eliminating redundant costs resulting from acquisitions or divestitures could adversely affect our profitability and weaken our competitive position. Many productivity initiatives involve complex reorganization of manufacturing facilities and production lines. Such manufacturing realignment may result in the interruption of production, which may negatively impact product volume and margins. We are currently pursuing several multi-year restructuring and cost savings initiatives designed to increase our efficiency and reduce expenses.

ITEM 7 Management's Discussion and Analysis of Financial Condition and Results of Operations

Executive Overview

Fiscal 2018 represented an important step in returning our business to sustainable topline growth. We made significant progress toward competing more effectively, with strong innovation, marketing, and in-store execution driving positive organic sales growth in each of our last three fiscal quarters. We also moved to reshape our portfolio for future growth with the acquisition of Blue Buffalo, a fast-growing, highly profitable pet food business. While our full-year profit results fell short of our initial plans, we finished fiscal 2018, delivering growth in net sales, total segment operating profit, adjusted operating profit margin, and adjusted diluted EPS in the fourth quarter. We maintained a disciplined focus on cash generation, resulting in significant growth in free cash flow this year. We generated substantial Holistic Margin Management (HMM) savings, and we reached our expected annualized savings goal of $700 million in fiscal 2018, compared to the fiscal 2015 base, from recent restructuring actions. However, these results were not enough to offset heightened input cost inflation, increases in other costs impacting cost of sales, and higher merchandising expense. Importantly, we made investments to accelerate our differential growth platforms and expanded our capabilities in e-commerce and Strategic Revenue Management (SRM), which are critical to future growth.

The company provides information about its efforts to reduce and/or maintain costs as outlined in **Exhibit 7.10**. We must consider the company's ongoing efforts at cost management to determine their effects going forward. We also must consider the effects of the recent acquisition of Blue Buffalo on anticipated cost structures. If we believe the company will succeed in maintaining reduced costs as a result of prior efforts, we may choose to make a lower assumption than if we are skeptical. If we believe that Blue Buffalo will have a higher product cost (lower gross profit), we may choose a higher cost assumption than seen historically. Any information we can gather, as well as our understanding of the industry, should inform our cost assumptions.

Our assumption based on the notes above are that cost of sales will continue near 2018 levels in 2019 at 65.5 percent, decrease 0.1 percent in each of the next 2 years, stay at 65.3 percent in 2022, and then stabilize at 65.2 percent thereafter. For other selling, general, and administrative, we anticipate increased costs due to efforts at integrating and dealing with issues related to entering the pet food industry. The recent years have seen a range of 10.44 to 11.08 percent, and we forecast a rise to 11.6 percent in 2019, reduction to 11.55 in the next 2 years, and then 11.5 percent thereafter. This change from observations in 2016 to 2018 seems warranted by our understanding of the business and its intentions.

- Zero: Foreign currency translation has varied from −0.66 percent in the year ended May 2016 to 0.04 percent in 2018. The combination of the items of other comprehensive income included in NOPAT have totaled −0.62, 0.22, and −0.45 in the last 3 years. This variation of more than a half percent from year to year has a substantial effect on observed variation in *PM*. While foreign currency translation is ongoing for a multinational such as GIS and would be expected to recur, the future amounts are not at all predictable, and our best estimate is zero. As a result, we predict foreign currency translation to be zero in forming our forecasts. Most additional components of other comprehensive income are treated in a similar manner. That is, we know they are ongoing. Although we might expect that there will be gains and losses in the future, we have used a forecast of zero because this is the average amount we would expect.

Once we have considered each element of operating *PM*, we can form a full-information forecast by combining (essentially summing) our assumptions to arrive at the *PM* forecast for the year. **Exhibit 7.11** shows the forecasts of operating *PM* we have arrived at for GIS.

EXHIBIT 7.11 GIS' Operating *PM* Forecasts

Year Ended	5/26/2019	5/31/2020	5/30/2021	5/29/2022	Thereafter
Net sales	100.00%	100.00%	100.00%	100.00%	100.00%
Cost of sales	(65.50)%	(65.40)%	(65.30)%	(65.30)%	(65.20)%
Gross profit	34.50%	34.60%	34.70%	34.70%	34.80%
Advertising expense	(3.80)%	(3.90)%	(3.90)%	(3.85)%	(3.85)%
Research expense	(1.40)%	(1.40)%	(1.42)%	(1.45)%	(1.45)%
Depreciation on capitalized leases	(0.60)%	(0.60)%	(0.60)%	(0.60)%	(0.60)%
Defined benefit pension plans: Service cost	(0.65)%	(0.65)%	(0.60)%	(0.60)%	(0.60)%
Other postretirement benefit plans: Service cost	(0.08)%	(0.08)%	(0.08)%	(0.08)%	(0.08)%
Postemployment benefit plans: Service cost	(0.05)%	(0.05)%	(0.05)%	(0.05)%	(0.05)%
Defined contribution plan expense	(0.30)%	(0.30)%	(0.30)%	(0.30)%	(0.30)%
Other selling, general, and administrative expenses	(11.60)%	(11.55)%	(11.55)%	(11.50)%	(11.50)%
Divestitures (loss) gain	0.00%	0.00%	0.00%	0.00%	0.00%
Restructuring, impairment, and other exit costs	(1.10)%	(1.10)%	(1.05)%	(1.05)%	(1.05)%
Income taxes	(3.10)%	(3.15)%	(3.20)%	(3.20)%	(3.20)%
After-tax earnings from joint ventures	0.50%	0.50%	0.50%	0.50%	0.50%
Foreign currency translation	0.00%	0.00%	0.00%	0.00%	0.00%
Other fair value changes: Hedge derivatives	0.00%	0.00%	0.00%	0.00%	0.00%
Reclassification to earnings: Hedge derivatives	0.00%	0.00%	0.00%	0.00%	0.00%
Operating *PM*	12.32%	12.32%	12.45%	12.52%	12.62%

FORECASTING INCOME TAXES

When forming forecasts, most items are thought of as a percent of sales. Taxes should be framed as a percent of profits. Thus, it is important to ensure that we are comfortable with the implied forecasted effective tax rate. For GIS, the implied forecasted effective tax rate is the forecasted *PM* for income taxes (3.1 percent in 2019) divided by the forecasted operating income before income taxes (sum of the items above the income taxes, which was 14.92 percent in 2019). This implies an effective tax rate of 20.77 percent (0.031/0.1492).

Review of the recent financials reveals that the effective tax rate for GIS is reported as:

Year Ended	5/25/2014	5/31/2015	5/29/2016	5/28/2017	5/27/2018
Effective tax rate.	33.3%	33.3%	31.4%	28.8%	2.7%

The striking drop in the most recent year is primarily due to the Tax Cuts and Jobs Act (TCJA). This law lowered the federal maximum statutory rate from 35 to 21 percent. Our expectations for the future periods are that GIS will have taxes hovering near 21 percent.

Clearly, our full-information forecast has provided a markedly different forecast than what was seen in our parsimonious forecast of 13.0 percent for *PM*. In part, this is caused by explicitly starting with the more detailed information contained in the reformulation in Chapter 5. It is also due to removal of items not expected to recur and acceptance of the plans of GIS as documented in the MD&A. Some of these may be ill-advised assumptions, and in seeing the expected ongoing *PM* of 12.62 percent, we could feel that these plans are too optimistic or too pessimistic. A reference point may be the average *PM* realization over the last several years of 12.72 percent. Alternatively, we may look further at competitors for clues as to the role GIS plays in the industry, and we may wish to further consider potential macroeconomic effects.

Full-Information Forecasts of Operating Asset Turnover

In forming our full-information forecast of operating *ATO*, we will use the more-detailed information previously not included in our parsimonious analysis. As we begin to work through the operating assets and liabilities of GIS attempting to forecast the turnovers of each balance sheet item, we seek information about the company's plans regarding the resources necessary to support sales.[9] When undertaking this process, recall that, when forecasting *ATO*, items are considered as an inverse of *ATO* to facilitate the consistent scaling by sales; and we are focusing on the relation between *beginning NOA* and sales (e.g., $ATO_{2022} = \text{Sales}_{2022}/NOA_{2021}$).

The fact that we are comparing sales to beginning *NOA* creates an interesting issue. Above, we have forecasted 2019 sales for GIS, and 2018 ending *NOA* (beginning 2019) is already known. Thus, we have an implied 2019 operating *ATO* at the component level already! This implied 2019 *ATO* therefore becomes another piece of information we can use to assist us in forecasting the subsequent years (i.e., 2020 and beyond). Our forecasts of *ATO* will be based on historical information (calculated using average *NOA*) up to 2018 plus the implied information (calculated using beginning *NOA*) for 2019.

Note that the change from average *NOA* to beginning *NOA* will mechanically cause an increase or decrease in the component *ATO*s. The sign of the change will depend on whether sales are increasing between 2018 and 2019 and whether *NOA* increased or decreased in 2018 (this drives whether average *NOA* for 2017 and 2018 or ending 2018 *NOA* is larger). Because forecasts going forward will be based on beginning *NOA*, we would expect the implied 2019 numbers to be more indicative of the magnitude of future forecasts, while the changes in more recent years may be more helpful in predicting future changes. In short, the implied 2019 forecast is very important as a *starting point* for future forecasts. The historical information from 2018 and earlier is very important in helping understand the *evolution of* the component.

[9] An often very useful source of information on details of line items and future plans is the Investor Relations office at the company.

In reviewing the MD&A disclosures and the notes to the financial statements, we find little information about plans regarding investment in *NOA*. That is, GIS does not appear to have any planned initiatives that would cause a large increase or decrease in *NOA* in the near future. There may be times when a business discloses plans that would significantly alter operating assets and liabilities. An example is implementation of a just-in-time inventory system that would result in a reduction in the inventory on hand. Note that this change may decrease accounts payable as well. Another example is an announcement of planned expansion, or reductions in plant assets. Reasons why this may occur include an increase due to a major plant (building and equipment) investment or a decrease due to outsourcing of production. Absence of planned changes in *NOA* may not be particularly surprising given that altering the resource side of a business is much harder than implementing cost-cutting initiatives.

Similar to our full-information forecasting efforts for sales and *PM*, we will discuss some key items of *ATO* in order to demonstrate the thought process and methodology. Here, again we are forecasting the items in relation to anticipated sales. That is, we are forecasting the amount of the resources necessary to support the sales that we have forecasted. For example, if sales in 2022 are forecasted to be $17,867.1, how much inventory will be necessary as a beginning balance (balance at end of 2021) to support these sales? The assumptions for balance sheet items can take the same forms as those for income statement items. That is, we can forecast a steady ratio, steady amount, follow a trend, use other information, or assume zero.

Items that would most likely be a steady ratio include accounts receivable and inventories because these tie so directly into sales. An account that would be an obvious candidate for a steady amount is land, while assets held for sale would be forecast as zero, unless we know of plans for sales in the near future. We also would consider that construction in progress should not continue but, rather, should become part of buildings (or machinery, depending on the project) upon completion.

EFFECT OF DECREASING SALES

There may be times when future sales are forecasted to decrease. While this does not normally occur for an extended period of time, in periods where economic conditions are changing or an industry is facing changing conditions, it may be found. If this is the case, one must be aware of the effect of this decrease on projected *ATO*. In many cases, companies will be unwilling to undergo significant reductions in operating assets because they want to have them available when sales are expected to rebound. As a result, our forecasts (which use the inverse of asset turnover; that is, the assets divided by sales) will mechanically increase due to the reduced sales number.

Once we have considered each element of the operating assets and liabilities of GIS separately, we can combine these to form a composite forecast of the inverse of operating *ATO*. For GIS, our full-information forecasts that lead to *ATO* are shown in **Exhibit 7.12**.

EXHIBIT 7.12 GIS' Operating *ATO* Forecasts

		Forecasts		
Year Ended	**Implied 5/26/2019**	**5/31/2020**	**5/30/2021**	**Thereafter**
Inverse of *ATO*				
Cash and cash equivalents	0.018	0.020	0.020	0.020
Receivables: Customers	0.099	0.110	0.110	0.120
Receivables: Allowance for doubtful accounts	(0.002)	(0.002)	(0.002)	(0.002)
Inventories: Raw materials and packaging	0.023	0.025	0.025	0.025
Inventories: Finished goods	0.079	0.088	0.090	0.092
Inventories: Grain	0.005	0.006	0.006	0.006
Inventories: Excess of FIFO over LIFO cost	0.000	0.000	0.000	0.000
Deferred tax assets: Accrued liabilities	0.003	0.004	0.004	0.004
Deferred tax assets: Compensation and employee benefits	0.012	0.027	0.026	0.026
Deferred tax assets: Unrealized hedges	0.000	0.000	0.000	0.000
Deferred tax assets: Tax credit carryforwards	0.000	0.001	0.001	0.001
Deferred tax assets: Capital losses	0.001	0.002	0.002	0.002

continued

continued from previous page

EXHIBIT 7.12 GIS' Operating *ATO* Forecasts

Year Ended	Implied 5/26/2019	Forecasts 5/31/2020	5/30/2021	Thereafter
Deferred tax assets: Net operating losses	0.009	0.010	0.010	0.010
Deferred tax assets: Other	0.003	0.006	0.006	0.006
Deferred tax assets: Valuation allowance	(0.010)	(0.010)	(0.010)	(0.010)
Prepaid expenses and other current assets: Prepaid expenses	0.010	0.011	0.012	0.012
Prepaid expenses and other current assets: Derivative receivables, primarily commodity-related	0.002	0.004	0.004	0.004
Prepaid expenses and other current assets: Grain contracts	0.000	0.000	0.000	0.000
Prepaid expenses and other current assets: Miscellaneous	0.001	0.001	0.001	0.001
Land, buildings, and equipment: Land	0.005	0.006	0.006	0.006
Land, buildings, and equipment: Buildings	0.139	0.152	0.154	0.154
Land, buildings, and equipment: Buildings under capital lease	0.000	0.000	0.000	0.000
Land, buildings, and equipment: Equipment	0.362	0.400	0.410	0.420
Land, buildings, and equipment: Equipment under capital lease	0.000	0.000	0.000	0.000
Land, buildings, and equipment: Capitalized software	0.034	0.039	0.039	0.040
Land, buildings, and equipment: Construction in progress	0.040	0.044	0.045	0.045
Land, buildings, and equipment: Accumulated depreciation	(0.346)	(0.375)	(0.380)	(0.380)
Capitalized lease asset	0.065	0.030	0.031	0.031
Goodwill: North America retail	0.372	0.420	0.425	0.430
Goodwill: Pet	0.307	0.340	0.340	0.340
Goodwill: Convenience stores and food service	0.053	0.062	0.064	0.064
Goodwill: Europe and Australia	0.042	0.045	0.045	0.045
Goodwill: Asia and Latin America	0.017	0.021	0.021	0.023
Goodwill: Joint ventures	0.025	0.027	0.027	0.028
Other intangible assets: Brands and other indefinite-lived intangibles	0.396	0.280	0.290	0.295
Other intangible assets: Franchise agreements, customer relationships, and other	0.047	0.034	0.035	0.035
Other intangible assets: Accumulated amortization	(0.011)	(0.010)	(0.010)	(0.010)
Other assets: Investments in and advances to joint ventures	0.029	0.033	0.035	0.035
Other assets: Life insurance	0.002	0.002	0.002	0.002
Other assets: Miscellaneous	0.006	0.007	0.008	0.008
	1.840	1.860	1.892	1.928
Accounts payable	(0.159)	(0.140)	(0.141)	(0.142)
Other current liabilities: Accrued trade and consumer promotions	(0.029)	(0.030)	(0.030)	(0.030)
Other current liabilities: Accrued payroll	(0.020)	(0.020)	(0.020)	(0.020)
Other current liabilities: Accrued taxes	(0.008)	(0.008)	(0.008)	(0.008)
Other current liabilities: Grain contracts	0.000	0.000	0.000	0.000
Other current liabilities: Restructuring and other exit costs reserve	(0.004)	(0.006)	(0.006)	(0.006)
Other current liabilities: Derivative payable	0.000	0.000	0.000	0.000
Other current liabilities: Miscellaneous	(0.018)	(0.020)	(0.021)	(0.021)
Deferred tax liabilities: Brands	(0.087)	(0.086)	(0.086)	(0.088)
Deferred tax liabilities: Fixed assets	(0.019)	(0.031)	(0.031)	(0.031)
Deferred tax liabilities: Intangible assets	(0.015)	(0.015)	(0.015)	(0.015)
Deferred tax liabilities: Tax lease transactions	(0.002)	(0.003)	(0.003)	(0.003)
Deferred tax liabilities: Inventories	(0.002)	(0.004)	(0.004)	(0.004)
Deferred tax liabilities: Unrealized hedges	(0.002)	(0.003)	(0.004)	(0.004)
Deferred tax liabilities: Other	(0.002)	(0.002)	(0.002)	(0.002)
Other noncurrent liabilities: Accrued taxes	(0.015)	(0.011)	(0.011)	(0.011)
Other noncurrent liabilities: Miscellaneous	(0.004)	(0.007)	(0.007)	(0.007)
	(0.387)	(0.386)	(0.389)	(0.392)
Inverse of *operating ATO* (1/*ATO*)	1.453	1.474	1.503	1.536
Implied *operating ATO*	0.688	0.678	0.665	0.651

We have forecast GIS' balance sheet by looking at each element of *NOA* in relation to revenues. Note that, for some items, we forecast no change in dollar amount or may forecast contractual or specified amounts, if desired. The process is to decide what values are desired and then convert them to *ATO* component forecasts. At times, the use of contractual or other specified payment tables to forecast selected balance sheet items may be appropriate.

PREPARING FOR VALUATION

LO4: Evaluate forecasts for reasonableness and potential biases or manipulation.

Now that we have forecasts of future revenues, *PM*, and *ATO* using all available information, adjustments to the accounting, and full-information forecasting, we can assemble our forecasts for use in valuation. The process to estimate value using the full-information forecasts is identical to the process based on parsimonious forecasts. We begin with our detailed full-information forecasts of sales growth, *PM*, and *ATO* that were developed above and forecast numbers for 2019 and beyond, as shown in **Exhibits 7.13** and **7.14**.

EXHIBIT 7.13 GIS' Full-Information Forecast Assumptions

Year Ended	5/26/2019	5/31/2020	5/30/2021	5/29/2022	5/28/2023	Thereafter
Sales growth.	9.43%	3.03%	−0.62%	1.30%	1.25%	1.20%
Profit margin	12.32%	12.32%	12.45%	12.62%	12.62%	12.62%
ATO ratio	0.688	0.678	0.665	0.651	0.651	0.651

Remember that our forecasts for sales growth in the years ended May 2020 and 2021 were affected by having 53 weeks in 2020. When we forecasted *ATO*, we forecasted the resources needed for a normal year; (i.e., 52 weeks). Consider the question of whether additional resources are needed during 2020 just because there will be another week of sales. Most likely not. Thus, we need to compute the amount of *NOA* needed at the beginning of the year after adjusting the sales to reflect what would have happened had the year ended May 2020 had 52 weeks. Thus, that year's calculation is

$$NOA_{2019} = \frac{Sales_{2020} \times \dfrac{52}{53}}{ATO_{2020}}$$

This leads to the forecasted amounts shown in **Exhibit 7.14**.

EXHIBIT 7.14 GIS' Multiyear Full-Information Forecasts of Sales, *NOPAT*, and *NOA*

Year Ended	5/27/2018	5/26/2019	5/31/2020	5/30/2021	5/29/2022	5/28/2023	5/26/2024
Weeks in Year	52	52	53	52	52	52	52
Sales.	$15,740.4	$17,224.4	$17,746.9	$17,637.8	$17,867.1	$18,090.4	$18,307.5
		($15,740.4 × 1.0943)	($17,224.4 × 1.0303)	($17,747.4 × 0.9938)	($17,638.4 × 1.0130)	($17,867.4 × 1.0125)	($18,090.4 × 1.0120)
NOPAT.		$2,122.0	$2,186.4	$2,195.9	$2,254.8	$2,283.0	$2,310.4
		($17,224.4 × 12.32%)	($17,746.9 × 12.32%)	($17,637.8 × 12.45%)	($17,867.1 × 12.62%)	($18,090.4 × 12.62%)	($18,307.5 × 12.62%)
NOA	$25,035.4	$26,291.0	$25,998.1	$26,854.2	$27,786.8	$28,120.3	$28,457.7
		($17,746.9/0.688)	($17,637.8/0.678)	($17,867.1/0.665)	($18,090.4/0.651)	($18,307.5/0.651)	($18,527.2/0.651)

At the end of the forecasting process, we must step back and make sure that the numbers we predict pass the smell test. That is, we need to assess whether our forecasts are reasonable. Do they make economic sense? Do they fit with the underlying relations that drive financial forecasts? For example, if our forecasts depend on increasing selling prices, it is wise to explore the likely consequences of a price increase. Companies generally cannot raise prices without a consequent loss of demand unless the product in question is protected in some way from competitive pressures. Our forecasts must appear reasonable and consistent with basic business economics.

It is important to recognize that *RNOA* exhibits mean reversion over time. That is, if a company has exceptionally high *RNOA* currently, it would be expected to decrease over time as competitors seek to erode any competitive advantages. Alternatively, if *RNOA* is currently very low, it should be apparent that the company would be expected to make changes going forward that will result in an increase. This is necessary as the other option is to go out of business or perhaps be acquired!

Dickinson and Sommers (*Journal of Business, Finance, and Accounting*, 2012) looked at NYSE, AMEX, and NASDAQ firms between 1972 to 2003, calculating *RNOA* for a sample of 65,220 firm-year observations. In each year, they split the observations into quintiles (five groups) and then calculated the average *RNOA* for each group. **Figure 7.1** shows the average *RNOA* across years for each quintile in year 0. The figure also shows how *RNOA* evolved for the groups going forward in each subsequent year. That is, keeping firms in the same group sorted by current performance, the researchers examined subsequent *RNOA* over the next 5 years. As the figure shows, the *RNOA* tended to revert to a mean, with the highest *RNOA* firms seeing a decrease going forward while the lowest firms saw an increase.

FIGURE 7.1 Behavior of *RNOA* over Time—Dickinson and Sommers (2012 *JBFA*)

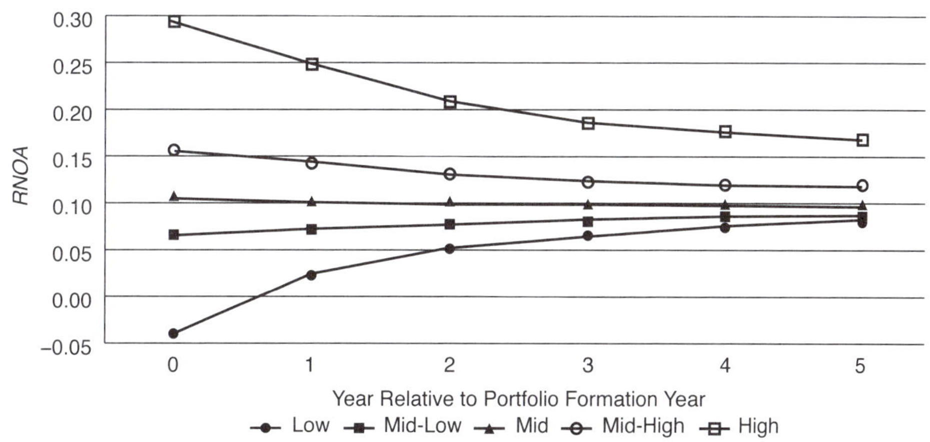

The implication of these analyses is that, after forecasting sales, *PM*, and *ATO*, we should consider the implied *RNOA* and its pattern going forward. The speed and pattern of reversion may differ, but given a long enough horizon, reversion is expected. Remember that optimism often enters forecasting exercises as we assume plans may work or give them the benefit of the doubt. Because our goal is to achieve accurate forecasts, we must scrutinize our forecasts and be assured that they reflect what we think is the most likely outcome.

SUSPECT ACCOUNTING

Despite our efforts to consider all information and make appropriate adjustments in Chapter 5, caution about the accounting numbers must be employed. Given the inherent number of estimates in accounting, there is always the possibility that the information has been manipulated or massaged to influence users. At times, companies may have created hidden reserves, smoothed income, or manipulated assumptions. Our concern is whether these would cause us to have forecasts of the future that are not accurate.

Exhibit 7.15 shows some recent examples of how some managers are alleged to have abused the latitude available in reporting financial results. Whether these were fraudulent is a decision for a court of law, but they definitely influence users' understanding!

EXHIBIT 7.15 Alleged Accounting Abuses

Company	Allegations
Adelphia Communications (ADELQ)	Founding Rigas family collected $3.1 billion in off-balance-sheet loans backed by Adelphia; it overstated results by inflating capital expenses and hiding debt.
American International Group (AIG)	AIG booked loans as revenue, steered clients to insurers with whom AIG had payoff agreements and told traders to inflate AIG stock price, resulting in an approximately $3.9 billion fraud.
Autonomy Corp.	The company engaged in aggressive revenue recognition ("round-trip transactions") where it bought goods from customers and failed to fully record costs; its overstated results allegedly led Hewlett-Packard to overpay when acquiring Autonomy stock.
Enron	Enron created profits and hid debt totaling more than $1 billion by improperly using off-the-books partnerships, manipulated the Texas power market, bribed foreign governments to win contracts abroad, and manipulated the California energy market.
General Electric (GE)	In 2018, it was announced that the Securities and Exchange Commission (SEC) was investigating GE's potentially aggressive accounting practices. The probe was widened in October 2018, when GE took a $22 billion noncash charge related to acquisitions.
Global Crossing (GLBC)	Global Crossing engaged in network capacity "swaps" with other carriers to inflate revenue, and shredded documents related to accounting practices.
Lehman Brothers (LEH)	The company sold $50 billion in toxic assets to Cayman Island banks with the understanding that they would be bought back eventually to create the impression Lehman had $50 billion more cash and $50 billion less in toxic assets.
Time Warner (TWX)	As the ad market faltered and AOL's purchase of Time Warner loomed, AOL inflated sales by booking revenue for barter deals and ads it sold for third parties. These questionable revenues boosted growth rates and sealed the deal. AOL also boosted sales via "round-trip" deals with advertisers and suppliers.
Tyco (TYC)	Ex-CEO L. Dennis Kozlowski was indicted for tax evasion, and Kozlowski and former CFO Mark H. Swartz were convicted of taking unauthorized loans from the company.
Qwest Communications International (Q)	The company inflated revenue using network capacity "swaps" and improper accounting for long-term deals.
WorldCom	WorldCom overstated cash flow by booking $11 billion in operating expenses as capital costs, and loaned founder Bernard Ebbers $400 million off the books.

In 1998, the SEC began an investigation of Microsoft and its deferring of revenues via revenue reserves. It was alleged that "The company would set aside revenue in its more profitable quarters and add them in leaner periods." While it took until 2002, the SEC concluded "that Microsoft recorded reserves, accruals, allowances, and liability accounts relating to marketing expenses, sales, depreciation, inventory obsolescence, valuation of financial assets, interest income, and impairment of manufacturing facilities that did not have properly substantiated bases," which resulted in Microsoft's misstating income by material amounts between July 1, 1994, and June 30, 1998.[10]

Research has shown that for initial public offerings (IPOs), the net income relative to sales (a crude estimate of *PM* without having undergone reformulation to separate operating and financial activities) is extremely high in the year of the IPO. Subsequent years see the ratio decrease. Teoh, Wong, and Rao (*Review of Accounting Studies*, 1998) found that in the year of the IPO, the net income was 4.6 percent of sales, but this decreased in the following 6 years to 2.8, 2.1, 1.6, 1.3, 1.3, and 1.8 percent, respectively. This seems to imply that earnings observed at the time of the

[10] http://money.cnn.com/2002/06/03/technology/microsoft/

IPO are not sustainable. Their study shows this appears to be driven by abnormal (unwarranted?) accruals that later must reverse.

From these examples, it becomes obvious that we must approach the information provided by management with a level of professional skepticism. It must be noted that both cash flow and accounting information can be manipulated, so assuming "cash is king" is not the solution. Companies can offer incentives to customers to speed collections, but this will reduce subsequent years' cash receipts. Remember that if a firm records extra (or not enough) cash or income in a particular period, this must be reversed in a future period. In the absence of fraud, the total of both the cash and the income will be the right amounts in the end.

Generally, a firm's incentives are to show good news as continuing (permanent) and bad news as a one-time event (transitory). Thus, they may tend to take actions such as classifying a gain on disposal as *other income* but a loss as a *discontinued operation*. Of course, there are exceptions where companies defer income for a rainy day. Thus, manipulation is not always done to increase income.

Our best defense against suspect accounting is to increase our knowledge of the business (step 1). To the extent we are current on the events that have affected our business and its industry, we are better equipped to evaluate the information we are provided in the financial statements and related disclosures. Diligence will give us the highest likelihood of noticing when something does not smell right.

Remember that we are forecasting future financial information to use in valuation. Problems in reported information are of concern if they either cause us to forecast values higher or lower than they should be or lead to an assumption that a steady state has been reached when it has not.[11] Whether we focus our valuation on cash flow- or accounting-based models, these concerns remain.

SUMMARY

We have demonstrated how the reformulated financial statements may be used as a basis for a simple analysis that focuses on forecasts of sales growth, *PM*, and *ATO*. These three items are the fundamental building blocks necessary to form both parsimonious and full-information forecasts. In this chapter, we have used the assumptions based on our analysis of past financial statements to create the next few years of future forecasts. The time frame is a choice and could be shortened or lengthened as necessary. Note that, at the end of the explicit forecast period, we will need to estimate a continuing value. This continuing value is generally based *inter alia* on information within the horizon and, often, implicitly, we are expecting our forecast assumptions to continue to hold. Careful consideration of the forecast we see after applying our assumptions may be very revealing. Are we comfortable with the path of future profitability and/or payoffs we are projecting?

After demonstrating parsimonious forecasting, we also demonstrated the process by which we can form detailed, full-information forecasts useful for valuation. If we are seeking a quick approximation, a parsimonious forecast can be used. A more involved approach is to forecast sales revenue growth at the most detailed level possible. For GIS, we found information that allowed us to form segment-level forecasts of sales based on anticipated changes in its organic sales growth. Then, we formed a detailed forecast of operating *PM*, which reflected management's plans for cost cutting and restructuring in future years. Finally, we formed a detailed forecast of GIS' operating *ATO* based on all the sources of information at our disposal.

Armed with these forecasts, we now move to the final step of valuation. Pardon the pun, but this is the payoff to the process we have undertaken. We will start valuation with market-based methods, then discuss estimation of the cost of capital, and conclude with valuation models utilizing cash flows and accounting information.

QUESTIONS

Q7.1 Should forecasts be conservative?

Q7.2 True or false? We can form more accurate forecasts by using spreadsheets. Elaborate.

[11] The concept and definition of steady state will arise in Chapter 10 and be explicitly defined in Chapter 14.

Q7.3 What is the role of sensitivity analysis in forecasting?

Q7.4 In what order do we form forecasts?

Q7.5 Why do we not want to forecast the financial aspects of the company?

Q7.6 What determines the level of detail at which forecasts are formed (e.g., parsimonious or full-information forecasts)?

Q7.7 Why is the forecast of revenue growth so critical?

Q7.8 Why do we analyze the inverse of *ATO* instead of *ATO*?

Q7.9 At the end of the forecasting process, how are expected outcomes evaluated for reasonableness?

Q7.10 What is the best defense to guard against suspect accounting?

EXERCISES

Remember when forecasting that one set of "right" answers does not exist. Rather, the question is whether the assumptions underlying the forecasts are sensible and have considered the appropriate information.

E7.11 For Domino's Pizza (DPZ), the following information on the past 5 years' revenues can be found in the Form 10-K.

(Dollars in Millions, Except per Share Data)	Fiscal Year Ended December 30, 2018	December 31, 2017	January 1, 2017	January 3, 2016	December 28, 2014
Income statement data:					
U.S. company-owned stores	$ 514.8	$ 490.8	$ 439.0	$ 396.9	$ 348.5
U.S. franchise royalties and fees	391.5	351.4	312.3	272.8	230.2
U.S. franchise advertising	358.5	—	—	—	—
U.S. stores	1,264.8	842.2	751.3	669.7	578.7
Supply chain	1,943.3	1,739.0	1,544.3	1,383.2	1,262.5
International franchise royalties and fees	224.7	206.7	177.0	163.6	152.6
Total revenues	$3,432.9	$2,788.0	$2,472.6	$2,216.5	$1,993.8

If this was the only information available, what forecasts of revenue growth in the foreseeable future might be arrived at? What issues immediately arise that might require additional investigation?

E7.12 Below is information for Marriott (MAR) taken from the 2018 Form 10-K. Consider the impact of this disclosure on forecasts of revenues for the firm.

Segment Revenues

The following tables present our revenues disaggregated by major revenue stream as of year-end 2018, year-end 2017, and year-end 2016:

($ millions)	2018 North American Full-Service	North American Limited-Service	Asia Pacific	Other International	Total
Gross fee revenues	$ 1,255	$ 903	$ 479	$ 518	$ 3,155
Contract investment amortization	(33)	(12)	(2)	(11)	(58)
Net fee revenues	1,222	891	477	507	3,097
Owned, leased, and other revenue	593	128	182	668	1,571
Cost reimbursement revenue	11,257	2,198	459	1,091	15,005
Total segment revenue	$13,072	$ 3,217	$ 1,118	$ 2,226	$19,673
Unallocated corporate					1,085
Total revenues					$20,758

($ millions)	2017 North American Full-Service	North American Limited-Service	Asia Pacific	Other International	Total
Gross fee revenues	$ 1,202	$ 842	$ 431	$ 476	$ 2,951
Contract investment amortization	(25)	(11)	(1)	(13)	(50)
Net fee revenues	1,177	831	430	463	2,901
Owned, leased, and other revenue	697	132	191	685	1,705
Cost reimbursement revenue	11,035	2,256	433	1,140	14,864
Total segment revenue	$12,909	$ 3,219	$ 1,054	$ 2,288	$19,470
Unallocated corporate					982
Total revenues					$20,452

($ millions)	2016 North American Full-Service	North American Limited-Service	Asia Pacific	Other International	Total
Gross fee revenues	$ 856	$ 746	$ 231	$ 312	$ 2,145
Contract investment amortization	(21)	(9)	(1)	(9)	(40)
Net fee revenues	835	737	230	303	2,105
Owned, leased, and other revenue	390	119	127	438	1,074
Cost reimbursement revenue	8,199	2,038	274	922	11,433
Total segment revenue	$ 9,424	$ 2,894	$ 631	$ 1,663	$14,612
Unallocated corporate					795
Total revenues					$15,407

Revenues attributed to operations located outside the U.S. were $4,246 million in 2018, $3,830 million in 2017, and $3,187 million in 2016.

E7.13 What impact do the types of operations undertaken by **Marriott** (MAR) have on the forecasting of plant, property, and equipment as a part of estimating *ATO*? The most recent balance sheet information as reported in Note 13 is below.

The following table presents the composition of our property and equipment balances at year-end 2018 and 2017:

($ in millions)	At Year-End 2018	At Year-End 2017
Land	$ 591	$ 601
Buildings and leasehold improvements	1,275	1,052
Furniture and equipment	1,439	1,121
Construction in progress	168	116
	3,473	2,890
Accumulated depreciation	(1,517)	(1,097)
	$1,956	$1,793

E7.14 Occasionally, firms will provide near- and long-term guidance as to their expected financial results. In its 2018 Form10-K, **McDonald's** (MCD) reported the following:

OUTLOOK

2019 Outlook

The following information is provided to assist in forecasting the Company's future results.

- Changes in Systemwide sales are driven by comparable sales, net restaurant until expansion and the potential impacts of hyper-inflation. The Company expects net restaurant additions to add approximately 1 percentage point to 2019 Systemwide sales growth (in constant currencies).

- The Company does not generally provide specific guidance on changes in comparable sales. However, as a perspective, assuming no change in cost structure, a 1 percentage point change in comparable sales for either the U.S. or the new International Operated markets segment would change annual diluted earnings per share by about 6 to 7 cents.
- With about 75% of McDonald's grocery bill comprised of 10 different commodities, a basket of goods approach is the most comprehensive way to look at the Company's commodity costs. For the full year 2019, costs for the total basket of goods are expected to increase about 1% to 2% in the U.S. and about 2% in the Big Five international markets.
- The Company expects full year 2019 selling, general and administrative expenses to decrease about 4% in constant currencies.
- Based on current interest and foreign currency exchange rates, the Company expects interest expense for the full year 2019 to increase about 10% to 12% due primarily to higher average debt balances.
- A significant part of the Company's operating income is generated outside the U.S., and about 40% of its total debt is denominated in foreign currencies. Accordingly, earnings are affected by changes in foreign currency exchange rates, particularly the Euro, British Pound, Australian Dollar and Canadian Dollar. Collectively, these currencies represent approximately 80% of the Company's operating income outside the U.S. If all four of these currencies moved by 10% in the same direction, the Company's annual diluted earning per share would change by about 35 cents.
- The Company expects the effective income tax rate for the full year 2019 to be in the 24% to 26% range. Some volatility may result in a quarterly tax rate outside of the annual range. Primarily due to tax costs associated with new regulations issued in January 2019, the effective income tax rate for the first quarter of 2019 is expected to be in the 28% to 29% range.
- The Company expects capital expenditures for 2019 to be approximately $2.3 billion. About $1.5 billion will be dedicated to our U.S. business, nearly two-thirds of which is allocated to approximately 2,000 EOTF projects. Globally, we expect to open roughly 1,200 restaurants. We will spend approximately $600 million in our wholly owned markets to open 300 restaurants and our developmental licensee and affiliated markets will contribute capital toward the remaining 900 restaurant openings in their respective markets. The Company expects about 750 net restaurant additions in 2019.
- During 2019, the Company expects to return about $9 billion to shareholders, which will complete its cash return to shareholder target of about $25 billion for the 3-year period ending 2019.

<u>Long-Term Outlook</u>

- Over the long-term, the Company expects to achieve the following average annual (constant currency) financial targets:
  - Systemwide sales growth of 3% to 5%;
  - Operating margin in the mid-40% range;
  - Earnings per share growth in the high-single digits; and
  - Return on incremental invested capital in the mid-20% range.

How should company guidance be used in forecasts?

E7.15 Identify which approach (i.e., *steady ratio*, *steady amount*, *follow a trend*, *use other information* and *zero*) to use in forecasting the components of operating *PM* for Cooper Tires (CTB).

Amounts in thousands, Years Ended December 31	2013	2014	2015	2016	2017
Sales—Americas tire	70.65%	73.71%	88.39%	87.17%	83.26%
Sales—international tire	29.35%	26.29%	11.61%	12.83%	16.74%
Cost of products sold:					
Warranty expense	(0.57)%	(0.51)%	(0.31)%	(0.29)%	(0.36)%
Other	(84.75)%	(83.80)%	(80.71)%	(77.00)%	(81.44)%
Gross profit	14.68%	15.70%	18.98%	22.71%	18.20%
Selling, general, and administrative expense:					
Advertising costs	(1.42)%	(1.68)%	(1.78)%	(1.84)%	(1.85)%
Research an development costs	(1.79)%	(1.66)%	(1.74)%	(1.90)%	(2.10)%
Defined contribution plan expense	(0.36)%	(0.37)%	(0.48)%	(0.45)%	(0.49)%
Pension:					
Service cost	(0.29)%	(0.29)%	(0.37)%	(0.33)%	(0.35)%
Amortization of prior service cost	0.01%	0.00%	0.00%	0.00%	0.00%
Service cost	0.00%	(0.07)%	(0.08)%	(0.07)%	(0.07)%
Amortization of prior service cost	0.01%	0.02%	0.02%	0.02%	0.02%

continued

continued from previous page

Amounts in thousands, Years Ended December 31	2013	2014	2015	2016	2017
Depreciation	(0.48)%	(0.53)%	(0.58)%	(0.61)%	(0.63)%
Other	(2.47)%	(2.12)%	(2.11)%	(1.55)%	(1.58)%
Pension settlement charges	0.00%	0.00%	0.00%	(0.42)%	0.00%
Gain on sale of interest subsidiary	0.00%	2.26%	0.00%	0.00%	0.00%
Other nonoperating income (expense)	(0.02)%	(0.08)%	0.04%	0.17%	(0.11)%
Earning from continuing operations before income taxes					
Income taxes on continuing operations	(2.97)%	(3.76)%	(4.18)%	(5.06)%	(5.66)%
Comprehensive income items:					
Financial statement translation	0.54%	(1.60)%	(1.19)%	(1.98)%	1.36%
Financial instruments—change in fair value of derivatives	0.05%	0.16%	(0.08)%	(0.08)%	(0.09)%
Financial instruments—income tax benefit (provision) on derivative instruments	(0.02)%	(0.06)%	0.03%	0.03%	0.03%
Postretirement benefit plans—amortization of prior service costs	(0.02)%	(0.02)%	(0.02)%	(0.02)%	(0.02)%
Operating *PM*	5.74%	5.90%	6.46%	8.63%	6.67%

E7.16 For Starbucks (SBUX), the following table has information for revenues, *PM*, and *ATO* for the past 4 years:

	Fiscal 2014	Fiscal 2015	Fiscal 2016	Fiscal 2017	Fiscal 2018
Sales (millions)	$16,448	$19,163	$21,316	$22,287	$24,720
PM from sales	10.55%	11.36%	11.65%	11.05%	10.59%
PM	10.44%	11.45%	12.39%	11.61%	16.55%
ATO	2.78	2.92	2.80	2.89	4.65

a. Using a parsimonious analysis, prepare the assumptions for foreseeable forecast.
b. Evaluate the reasonableness of the forecasted *RNOA*.

CONTINUING EXAMPLES

For Kellogg (K), we will address the method by which forecasts can be formed while recognizing that one set of "right" answers does not exist. At the end of this section, we provide a set of forecasts that will be used in valuation tasks in subsequent chapters.

CE7.17 Given the analysis of Kellogg (K) performed in Chapter 6, form reasonable parsimonious forecasts for K of sales growth, *PM,* and *ATO*. Use those assumptions to form parsimonious forecasts of sales, *NOPAT,* and *NOA* for 2019–2022.

CE7.18 Gather segment-level sales data for Kellogg (K) for 2015–2018 from the Form 10-Ks. From this information, form analysis of the changes in sales as driven by changes in acquisitions/divestures, shipping day differences, Venezuela operations impact, foreign currency impact, integration and transaction costs, Project K, cost-reduction activities, and organic growth. Then using this information, forecast changes for 2019–2021. After forecasting the segment-level sales, combine them to form a firm-level sales forecast.

CE7.19 Given the common size analysis of Kellogg (K) performed in Chapter 6, form reasonable detailed forecasts for K of *PM* and *ATO* for 2019 to 2021.

For Thor Industries (THO), we will address the method by which forecasts can be formed while recognizing that one set of "right" answers does not exist. At the end of this section, we provide a set of forecasts that will be used in valuation tasks in subsequent chapters.

CE7.20 Given the analysis of Thor Industries (THO) performed in Chapter 6, form reasonable parsimonious forecasts for THO's sales growth, *PM,* and *ATO*. Use those assumptions to form parsimonious forecasts of sales, *NOPAT,* and *NOA* for fiscal years 2019–2022.

CE7.21 Gather segment-level sales data for Thor Industries (THO) for fiscal years 2015–2018 from the Form 10-Ks. From this information, form an analysis of the changes in sales as driven by changes in towable recreational vehicles, motorized recreational vehicles, other and intercompany eliminations. Then, using this information, forecast changes for fiscal years 2019–2021. After forecasting the segment-level sales, combine them to form a firm-level sales forecast.

CE7.22 Given the common size analysis of Thor Industries (THO) performed in Chapter 6, form reasonable detailed forecasts for THO of *PM* and *ATO* for fiscal years 2019–2021.

For Winnebago (WGO), we will address the method by which forecasts can be formed while recognizing that one set of "right" answers does not exist. At the end of this section, we provide a set of forecasts that will be used in valuation tasks in subsequent chapters.

CE7.23 Given the analysis of Winnebago (WGO) performed in Chapter 6, form reasonable parsimonious forecasts for WGO's sales growth, *PM,* and *ATO*. Use those assumptions to form parsimonious forecasts of sales, *NOPAT,* and *NOA* for fiscal years 2019–2022.

CE7.24 Gather segment-level sales data for Winnebago (WGO) for fiscal years 2015–2018 from the Form 10-Ks. From this form an analysis of the changes in sales as driven by changes in motorized, towable, and other. Then, using this information, forecast changes for fiscal years 2019–2021. Additionally, consider the impact of forecasted years with 53 weeks. After forecasting the segment-level sales, combine them to form a firm-level sales forecast.

CE7.25 Given the common size analysis of Winnebago (WGO) performed in Chapter 6, form reasonable detailed forecasts for WGO of *PM* and *ATO* for fiscal years 2019–2021.

The following are the full-information forecasts for Kellogg used in subsequent chapters:

Amounts in Thousands; Years Ending	12/28/2019	1/2/2021	1/1/2022	12/31/2022	12/30/2023	12/28/2024	1/3/2026	1/2/2027	1/1/2028
Weeks in year	52	53	52	52	52	52	53	52	52
Sales growth	0.57%	2.41%	−1.42%	0.50%	0.45%	0.40%	2.32%	−1.49%	0.40%
Profit margin	9.36%	9.58%	10.00%	10.17%	10.55%	10.55%	10.55%	10.55%	10.55%
Asset turnover ratio	1.052	0.974	0.962	0.951	0.951	0.951	0.951	0.951	0.951

The following are the full-information forecasts for Thor Industries used in subsequent chapters:

Amounts in Thousands; Years Ending	7/31/2019	7/31/2020	7/31/2021	7/31/2022	7/31/2023	7/31/2024
Sales growth	5.56%	3.61%	1.61%	1.40%	1.20%	1.00%
Profit margin	5.78%	5.77%	5.40%	5.35%	5.15%	5.15%
Asset turnover ratio	4.815	4.329	4.219	4.098	4.098	4.098

The following are the full-information forecasts for Winnebago used in subsequent chapters:

Amounts in Thousands; Years Ending	8/31/2019	8/29/2020	8/28/2021	8/27/2022	8/26/2023	8/31/2024	8/30/2025	8/29/2026
Weeks in year	53	52	52	52	52	53	52	52
Sales growth	4.56%	0.11%	1.38%	1.30%	1.10%	2.82%	−0.99%	0.90%
Profit margin	6.40%	6.27%	6.20%	6.03%	6.03%	6.03%	6.03%	6.03%
Asset turnover ratio	2.309	2.288	2.294	2.294	2.294	2.294	2.294	2.294

NOTES

Chapter **Eight**

Market Multiple Valuation

TAKEAWAYS

When you complete this chapter, you should be able to:

1. Discuss the prevalence of accounting information in market multiple valuation.
2. Articulate the steps for and issues encountered in implementing market multiple valuation.
3. Compute value estimates using balance sheet, income statement, and multiples of other information.
4. Combine estimates from different calculations, and evaluate the reasonableness of market multiple estimates.

We begin our discussion of valuation in this chapter. We address the most commonly used method for valuation, specifically, the use of market multiples. We will include a discussion of the use of cash flows and accounting information in multiples, the importance of considering debt when valuing using multiples (i.e., the use of equity versus operating multiples), and the inherent limitations to using market multiples as a method of valuation. Valuation based on market multiples is also referred to as the method of comparables. U.S. accounting standards (e.g., Statement of Financial Accounting Standards 142 (ASC 350): *Accounting for Goodwill and Other Intangibles*) refer to this method as the market method.

USE OF ACCOUNTING DATA IN MARKET MULTIPLES

LO1: Discuss the prevalence of accounting information in market multiple valuation.

Market multiples are often used as a first-pass, parsimonious indicator of value; a stock screening device; and/or as a means to create summary metrics for comparison with peer firms. Some who use these market multiples as a basis for valuation argue that they are superior to other methods because they often do not rely on subjective (and sometimes very difficult to obtain) forecasts of future performance. They are viewed as fundamental indicators of the company's value.

We begin by noting that price to earnings (PE), price to book, and price to sales are commonly used multiples. Each of these multiples utilizes a comparison of market price and an accounting fundamental. **Exhibit 8.1** shows a sample screenshot of valuation information for General Mills (GIS) provided by finance.yahoo.com on November 4, 2019.

Notice that three of these ratios refer to accounting earnings (trailing PE, forward PE and price/earnings to growth ratio), but we never see a *P/FCF* multiple used by analysts. Additionally, we see two ratios that specifically reference enterprise (operating) value. The makeup of these ratios and the importance of utilizing operating-based ratios will be discussed throughout this chapter and more fully developed in subsequent chapters.

CHAPTER OUTLINE

Market Multiple Valuation

Introduction to Market Multiples
- Use of Accounting Data
- Steps in Calculation

Implementation
- *NOA* and Book Value Multiples
- *NOPAT* and Net Income Multiples
- Sales, Industry, and Other Common Multiples

Issues in Using Multiples
- Use of *EBITDA* Multiple
- Combining Estimates
- Perspective on Multiples

EXHIBIT 8.1 GIS' Market Multiples from Website

General Mills, Inc. (GIS)
NYSE—NYSE Delayed Price. Currency in USD

51.38 +0.20 (+0.39%)
At close: 4:02PM EST

Valuation Measures	Current
Market Cap (intraday)[5]	31.05B
Enterprise Value[3]	46.02B
Trailing P/E	16.57
Forward P/E[1]	14.98
PEG Ratio (5 yr expected)[1]	2.20
Price/Sales (ttm)	1.85
Price/Book (mrq)	4.20
Enterprise Value/Revenue[3]	2.74
Enterprise Value/EBITDA[6]	12.61

Before proceeding with the measures often seen, we ask why the ratio of price or enterprise (operating) value to *FCF* from operations is rarely considered. *FCF*s are the amount being distributed to (or contributed by) owners of the company whether debt or equity holders. That is, *FCF* is the investment/disinvestment in the company during the period. *FCF* is not an indication of value added or lost. In fact, when *FCF* is **negative** (i.e., there is *FCF* going **to** the operations of the firm) the investment of this *FCF* by the debt and/or equity holders **increases** the value of the firm, but the positive effect on value is not captured until subsequent future *FCF*s from operations occur. Further, note that even in these future periods, the related *FCF*s **out** of the operations are a disinvestment. So, when we use the discounted cash flow valuation model, we value the flows into and out of the operations each period rather than the value created in each period. The goal of multiples should be to capture the creation of value or the amount of value in existence rather than the flow of value into or out of the company. Thus, the ratio of price or operating value to *FCF* is not often observed as a market multiple in practice.

By comparison to *FCF*, *NOA* is the accounting measure of the value of the firm's operations, and *NOPAT* is the accounting measure of value added by the operating activities. Remember that, as discussed in Chapter 2, the relation among *FCF*, *NOPAT*, and *NOA* is captured by Equation 2.2:

$$\begin{aligned} FCF_t &\equiv NOPAT_t + NOA_{t-1} - NOA_t \\ &\equiv NOPAT_t - (NOA_t - NOA_{t-1}) \\ &\equiv NOPAT_t - \Delta NOA_t \end{aligned} \tag{2.2}$$

Importantly, beginning **value** (NOA_{t-1}) plus **value added** ($NOPAT_t$) minus **value distributed** to the owners of the firm from operations (FCF_t) yields **value** at the end of the period (NOA_t). That is, accounting measures value and value added (and, indeed, estimation/measurement of value is the focus of this book), and we use these measures in market multiples as fundamental indicators of value.

CALCULATING MARKET MULTIPLES

LO2: Articulate the steps for and issues encountered in implementing market multiple valuation.

The steps for the method of comparables are (1) select a set of relevant summary fundamental indicators (e.g., earnings, book value, or sales) from the financial statements of the target company we wish to value; (2) identify a company or companies that are comparable to the target company on chosen relevant dimensions (often characteristics such as industry, size, and/or growth are a basis for choosing comparable companies); (3) for the comparable company or companies, compute the ratio of the market value to the selected fundamental indicator—the ratio (or average ratio for comparable companies) is the market multiple; and (4) multiply the fundamental indicator for the target company by the market multiple—that product is the estimated value of the target company.

$$\text{Value} = \text{Fundamental indicator} \times \text{Market multiple}$$

This method does not specify whether the value obtained is the operating value or equity value; nor does it specify whether the fundamental indicator is for the operations or for equity. If we have estimated operating value, we can, as a fifth step, estimate equity value by deducting the value owed to the debt holders from our estimate of operating value.[1]

When using market multiples to estimate value, the choice of fundamental indicator determines whether the output is operating value or equity value. If an operating measure is selected (e.g., *NOPAT* or *NOA*), the output from this method is operating value. If an equity measure is selected (e.g., earnings or book value), the output from this method is equity value.

The more commonly used market multiples are those that may be used to estimate equity value directly because investors are most often interested in equity value and may not be familiar with the methods of identifying operating activities, which we covered beginning in Chapter 2. However, as we shall see in subsequent chapters, when we use market multiples to find equity value directly, we must consider capital structure (i.e., the portion of the operations owned by debt holders versus the portion owned by equity holders) when selecting comparable companies

Steps to Using Market Multiples

To reiterate, there are five steps in estimating value using the market multiple method:

1. Select the fundamental indicator to use as the basis for valuation. Common fundamental indicators are *NOPAT*, *NOA*, earnings, book value, and sales revenue; the method of comparables may be based on current or forecasted fundamental indicators.
2. Select the comparable company or companies.
3. Compute the market multiple from the comparable company's or companies' market values and fundamental indicator. This involves two steps: (a) Compute the ratio of the market value to the fundamental indicator for each comparable, and (b) if a number of companies are used as comparables, combine the individual comparable company multiples into a market multiple by, for example, taking an average. While an average of ratios from comparable companies is com-

[1] The value of the income tax shield should be an adjustment in determining the value of debt when moving from operating value to equity value. However, this is not always done in practice. Often, the book value of debt is used as the difference between the value of operations and equity.

monly used, if a specific comparable company is believed to be more relevant as a benchmark, we may place more weight on its multiple.

4. Compute the value of the target company using its fundamental indicator and the market multiple.
5. If the fundamental indicator is an operating indicator (e.g., *NOPAT* or *NOA*), subtract the value owed to the debt holders, and then divide by shares outstanding to obtain equity value per share. If the fundamental indicator is an equity indicator (e.g., earnings or book value), divide by shares outstanding to get equity value per share. (Of course, if a per-share indicator is used, do not divide by shares outstanding.)

Although the steps are simple, key decisions are made in steps 1, 2 and 3. Additionally, there are many issues confronted in the implementation of multiples. An example is the alignment of dates/information. Notice the trailing PE ratio in **Exhibit 8.1** is labeled "TTM," or trailing twelve months. That is, price is compared to information for the last four quarters reported in the Form 10-Qs/10-Ks. The choice to use this information as compared to the last annual earnings is an implementation decision. This chapter attempts to represent the common implementation of multiples seen in practice. In doing so, we will see how these decisions are made and also discuss difficulties and inherent weaknesses in making these decisions.

First, in step 1, which fundamental indicator is the right one? This question does not have a clear answer because *there is no single correct fundamental*. The value of operations depends on future performance. The previous chapters of the text focusing on financial statement analysis and forecasting showed that no single measure entirely summarizes current period performance, and it is most unlikely that a single measure would provide a sufficient basis for forecasting future company performance. Nevertheless, we could argue that particular fundamental indicators are more suited to and more informative regarding particular companies or industries. For example, *NOA* may be more suitable for companies where reported asset values approximate market values, which is the case with many financial companies (e.g., banks and insurance companies). *NOPAT* may be more suitable for companies that are growing rapidly with relatively little volatility and many assets that are not recorded on the balance sheet (e.g., human capital and brand names). Sales may be more suitable for companies with negative current earnings.[2]

CHOOSING COMPARABLE COMPANIES

Often the choice of comparable companies may seem obvious: **Coca Cola** for **Pepsico**, **UPS** for **FedEx**, and **Kroger** for **Albertsons**. However, when we look more closely, we see that there may be important differences among companies. For example, a considerable portion of Pepsico's operations is in the snack foods industry, reducing comparability! The soft drinks that we think of as the mainstays of Coca Cola and Pepsico are shrinking in popularity, so those companies are expanding into other beverage products, including waters, sports drinks, and energy drinks. Further, finding multiple competitors that have a similar structure or product mix to Pepsico and Coca Cola is impossible.

When trying to choose comparables, we often come away feeling like we want to weld Coke and a snack company (e.g., **Snyder's Lance**) together into a bigger company that is similar to Pepsico. Unfortunately, this lack of comparability is inherent in market multiples because it requires us to ignore many of the unique qualities driving the company's valuation.

Similar issues arise when looking at a company like **Dell** or **Apple**. No other company shares Dell's made-to-order fulfillment process, and no other company matches Apple's brand fanaticism among customers. Having missed qualities like these by using "noncomparable comparables" negates the gains from using such an easy method.

Second, in step 2, what company or companies should we use as comparables? If the comparable companies are under- or overvalued by the market, the computed market multiple will under- or overvalue our target company. We might appeal to market efficiency and claim that the comparable companies are likely fairly priced, but this begs the question of why we are trying to find a value for

[2] In Chapter 11, we will show that, for GIS (and for many firms), *NOA* in itself captures a considerable portion of the value of the operating activities. This amount will serve as the anchor for the residual operating income valuation model (ROIM). And we also have the income statement, which we use in the ROIM to correct for the likelihood that *NOA* understates the value of the operations.

our target company. Should it not also be fairly priced by the market? Even if comparable companies are accurately priced, when they differ in ways that matter for valuation (e.g., on profitability, expected growth, and/or risk), the computed multiple will under- or overvalue our target company.

As you can see, there is an inherent inconsistency in using market multiples to value publicly traded companies. By choosing to value a specific target company using market multiples, the valuer implicitly presumes that the target company is not fairly valued. However, by selecting a comparable company or companies to determine the multiple, the valuer relies on the market to accurately value those companies. How does the valuer know which companies are fairly valued and which are valued with error? Some assert that a group of companies is valued correctly on average. However, if a company deviates from the average, is that a pricing error, a valid variance from the distribution of values, or the result of choosing the wrong summary measure or inadequate comparable companies?

APPROPRIATE SITUATIONS IN WHICH TO RELY ON MARKET MULTIPLES

There are arguments for using market multiples to value companies in some circumstances. As a first example, when valuing a company about to have an initial public offering in an efficient market, multiples for comparable companies that are currently traded may be useful in valuing the initial public offering. This will allow a computation of value of the company based on how the market is viewing other companies. Second, when estimating the intrinsic value of a company where the accounting statements are allegedly fraudulent, market multiples may, reasonably, be applied to the financial statement numbers of the allegedly fraudulent company after the effects of the alleged fraud have been removed. The result is an estimate of the value if the financial statements absent the fraud had been known to the market.

The common thread in both of these instances is that we are not assuming the market has all companies correctly valued except the one we are examining. Rather, we are taking advantage of an opportunity to assume correct valuation of other comparable companies as a way to inform about how the company we are examining would be valued. The need to assume the market is efficient in every case except one is not required.

Third, in step 3, presuming that we are comfortable with the choice of fundamental indicator and choose to use multiple comparable companies, how do we combine the comparable company data to produce a multiple? We could compute the multiple for each company and then use an equally-weighted average or combine the data for all companies and compute a value-weighted average. Or we could use a median of all comparable company ratios or an average after eliminating the highest and lowest observations. Again, there is no correct answer to this question, and others that may arise; this valuation method is ad hoc, and the decisions commonly made in its application are ad hoc as well. Just utilizing a single company as a comparable may remove the need to choose a method of combining the multiples, but the effects of any differences from the target company may be magnified if we do not use several comparable companies.

Fourth, earlier, we mentioned issues relating to dates of available data. We now expand on these issues. Examples include timing issues, such as use of a most recent quarter (MRQ) book value and comparing it to price on the date of the valuation; in our case, where we will be valuing GIS on May 1, 2019, the most recently available book value is for the quarter ending February 24, 2019. This may pose problems because the quarterly book value is not audited, contains very different types of assumptions, and still does not line up to the date of the valuation.

DATE OF VALUATION

In preparing our valuation spreadsheet, as well as the multiples calculations in this chapter, a date must be chosen. All analyses are shown assuming a date of May 1, 2019. In the real world, you would want to use today because that is when you would be considering an investment decision. Then, as time passes, additional information can be incorporated in the analysis, but remember to adjust your assumed valuation date.

Fifth, when we use income measures as the fundamental indicator, should we use operating income (from the income statement, note that this may differ from *NOPAT*), income from continuing operations, net income, or comprehensive income? Again, this chapter will reflect common implementations used in practice while highlighting concerns that may arise.

Despite potential deficiencies in valuing companies, the market multiple method of valuation is commonly applied in practice. The following sections first illustrate the mechanics of using balance sheet and income statement numbers in the method of comparables; we start by estimating company value for GIS using a multiple of *NOA*. Then, we estimate its equity value using a multiple of book value.

IMPLEMENTING THE MULTIPLES METHOD FOR VALUING GENERAL MILLS

LO3: Compute value estimates using balance sheet, income statement, and multiples of other information.

The comparable companies we use in valuing GIS are Kellogg (K), Campbell Soup Company (CPB), and JM Smucker (SJM), all of which are public companies reporting under U.S. GAAP, compete with GIS, and are often considered as comparable companies.[3] Our analyses will be carried out as of May 1, 2019, using data available on that date, which we obtained from the most recently filed Form 10-Qs of these companies. The multiples method requires a market valuation for the comparable companies. Equity market values for each company as of May 1, 2019, are collected from finance.yahoo.com. Operating market values for the comparable companies are computed by adjusting the equity value for the amount of financing (i.e., subtracting the book value of *NFL*).

Review of **Exhibit 8.1** shows that the calculation of many of the multiples, including the trailing PE and price-to-sales ratios for GIS reported on Yahoo! using the TTM approach.[4] References in **Exhibit 8.1** to "mrq" are for the most recent quarter. For each company, we use a combination of reported data combining its most recent year-end information: for GIS (May 27, 2018), K (December 29, 2018), CPB (July 29, 2018), and SJM (April 30, 2018) with year-to-date data through the most recent quarter reported. It should be noted that for K, the TTM is an annual period because the financial statements for the first quarter ended March 30, 2019, were not released until May 3, 2019, and therefore were not available as of our assumed analysis date. Notice that, in this case, we are not able to align dates for computing TTM information across our firms. The issues related to use of data with differing year-end dates were discussed beginning in Chapter 6.

We must consider whether the differing year-end dates impede our use of the multiples method. It would seem that either we introduce a lack of comparability between the company financial data due to the differing dates or may complicate the process by attempting to align dates across companies. As discussed previously, following industry practice, we will align dates by using *NOA* and book value for the comparable companies based on the most recent financial statements available at May 1, 2019.

The most recent TTM period ends at February 24, 2019; December 29, 2018; January 27, 2019; and January 31, 2019 for GIS, K, CPB, and SJM, respectively. For GIS, a TTM period covers March 2018 to February 2019 and is calculated as:

$$(\text{YTD2019Q3}) + (\text{2018K} - \text{YTD2018Q3}) = (\text{2019Q3} + \text{2019Q2} + \text{2019Q1}) + (\text{2018Q4})$$

For CPB, the TTM period covers February 2018 to January 2019 and is calculated as:

$$(\text{YTD2019Q2}) + (\text{2018K} - \text{YTD2018Q2}) = (\text{2019Q2} + \text{2019Q1}) + (\text{2018Q4} + \text{2018Q3})$$

[3] Another company we could have used as a comparable is Nestlé (NSRGY), which reports under IFRS. IFRS sometimes differs considerably from U.S. GAAP. When we choose companies from different accounting regimes as comparables, we need to understand the methods by which the numbers were created and any implications of differences in the fundamental indicators on our valuation. For example, the treatment of development costs, a part of research and development (R&D), differs with IFRS capitalizing them (reporting as assets), while U.S. GAAP expenses them (reporting as current period expense). Another issue with the use of a non-U.S. company as a comparable for GIS is the availability of interim information. NSRGY, as a non-U.S. company, does not report the level of detailed quarterly information seen for U.S. companies. As a result, forming TTM information or making comparisons is difficult. Unfortunately, multiples analysis in practice often fails to incorporate an understanding of differences in accounting method and timing issues and their effects on the reported information.

[4] As discussed in Chapter 6, combining quarterly earnings from different fiscal years may be problematic because accounting practice is based on the integrity of a fiscal year. Despite this, we follow this approach in order to illustrate practice, which is quite common.

Make sure to consider whether you are comfortable with any misalignments in dates. For example, if there was a large macroeconomic or industry-level event in February 2019, its effects would be seen in the financial statements of GIS, but not CPB. This may affect our comfort level with using CPB as a comparable for GIS. Once again, we must do our best to know the business!

Finally, to use Nestlé (NSRGY) as a comparable, we would need to consider the issue of currency. The fact that NSRGY reports in Swiss francs (CHF) would not affect the analysis because the multiples method is based on ratios, which will be the same with or without adjustment for currency differences.

Valuation Using an *NOA* Multiple

For each company shown in **Exhibit 8.2**, *NOA*, book value of equity, amount owed to debt holders, and common shares outstanding are found from the most recent quarter balance sheets using an approach similar to our previous analysis of the balance sheet data. For the comparable companies, the equity value is equal to the closing price per share at May 1, 2019 (the date of our valuation), multiplied by common shares outstanding per the most recent financial statements. Also, for the comparable companies, the operating value is equal to the equity value plus the book value of amounts owed to debt holders per the most recent financial statements.[5]

EXHIBIT 8.2 Data for Valuation Using Balance Sheet Multiples

(in millions)	GIS	K	CPB	SJM
Operating value	$ —	$29,831	$21,099	$20,004
Equity value	$ —	$20,430	$11,534	$13,967
NOA	$22,604	$12,002	$10,834	$14,059
Book value of equity	$ 6,930	$ 2,601	$ 1,269	$ 8,022
NFL (*NFA*)	$15,674	$ 9,401	$ 9,565	$ 6,037
Common shares outstanding	599 shares	344 shares	301 shares	114 shares

We use the data from **Exhibit 8.2** to compute a market multiple based on *NOA* to estimate the value of GIS. We begin by determining the *NOA* market multiple for K, CPB, and SJM, which is computed as the operating value divided by *NOA*. **Exhibit 8.3** shows the results of this computation. For example, K's *NOA* market multiple is 2.49, computed as $29,831/$12,002. We then average the *NOA* market multiples of the comparable companies (i.e., K, CPB, and SJM) to get 1.95, computed as (2.49 + 1.95 + 1.42)/3. This market multiple is used to estimate the operating value of GIS as follows:

Operating value	=	***NOA***	×	***NOA* market multiple**
$44,078	=	**$22,604**	×	**1.95**

In order to obtain GIS' equity value, we subtract the amount owed to debt holders (*NFL*) from its estimated operating value. The equity value is then divided by shares outstanding to yield the per-share value of common equity in GIS, as follows:

Equity value	=	**Operating value**	−	**Amount owed to debt holders (*NFL*)**
$28,404	=	**$44,078**	−	**$15,674**

[5] It is common practice to use the book value of debt from the balance sheet as an estimate of the market value of debt. We follow this practice in our example. Often, the assumption that book value of debt approximates the market value of debt is quite valid. However, in later chapters, we will show that this assumption can sometimes be unreasonable. Because we do not know debt levels at May 1, 2019, the balance per the most recent financial statements is used for the adjustment in this chapter. This is necessary because more recent information is not available.

Then,

$$\textbf{Equity value per share} = \frac{\textbf{Equity value}}{\textbf{Common shares outstanding}}$$

$$\$47.42 = \frac{\$28{,}404}{599\text{ shares}}$$

GIS' stock closed at $51.31 on May 1, 2019, the date of our analysis. Accordingly, this estimate would suggest that GIS was overvalued by about 8 percent on this date! The difference between estimated and observed value for GIS may lead us to question the validity of this estimate. Of course, the estimated value would have been very different had we used K's market multiple alone and different yet again if we had used only one of the other comparable companies. This shows the key roles the choices of comparable companies and the type of market multiple play in estimating value using this method.

EXHIBIT 8.3 Estimating Value Using an *NOA* Multiple

(in millions, except per share)	GIS	K	CPB	SJM
Operating value	$ —	$29,831	$21,099	$20,004
NOA	$22,604	$12,002	$10,834	$14,059
Common shares outstanding	599 shares	344 shares	301 shares	114 shares
NOA market multiple	1.95	2.49	1.95	1.42
Operating value	$44,078			
Equity value	$28,404			
Equity value per share	$47.42			

Valuation Using a Book Value Multiple

We can repeat the analysis above for GIS using the ratio of the market value of equity to the book value of equity as the multiple for estimating the value of the equity ownership of GIS. This multiple is the commonly cited price-to-book ratio, which was included in **Exhibit 8.1** from finance.yahoo.com. The data for this analysis is presented in **Exhibit 8.4**. This ratio relies on different data and, therefore, we will not get the same value computed in the previous section using *NOA*. Specifically, this computation ignores the distinction between the operating and financial activities of the company.

We begin by computing the book value market multiple for the three comparable companies, which is computed as the market value of equity divided by the book value of equity. For example, K's book value market multiple is 7.85, computed as $20,430/$2,601. We then average the book value market multiples of the comparable companies (i.e., K, CPB, and SJM) to get 6.23, computed as (7.85 + 9.09 + 1.74)/3. This market multiple is used to estimate the operating value of GIS as follows:

$$\textbf{Equity value} = \textbf{Book value of equity} \times \textbf{\textit{BV} market multiple}$$

$$\$43{,}176 = \$6{,}930 \times 6.23$$

To obtain GIS' equity value per share, we divide by shares outstanding as follows:

$$\textbf{Equity value per share} = \frac{\textbf{Equity value}}{\textbf{Common shares outstanding}}$$

$$\$72.08 = \frac{\$43{,}176}{599\text{ shares}}$$

The $72.08 stock price estimate using a *BV* multiple shows GIS stock was extremely undervalued (greater than 40 percent!) given its $51.31 closing price for our analysis. This difference would change dramatically if we decided to exclude CPB from our analysis, allowing us to get a value closer to the amount observed in the market. This reinforces the key roles the choice of comparable companies and the type of market multiple plays in determining value under this method.

EXHIBIT 8.4 Estimating Value Using a *BV* Multiple

(in millions, except per share)	GIS	K	CPB	SJM
Equity value	$ —	$20,430	$11,534	$13,967
Book value of equity	$ 6,930	$2,601	$1,269	$8,022
Common shares outstanding	599 shares	344 shares	301 shares	114 shares
BV market multiple	6.23	7.85	9.09	1.74
Equity value	$43,176			
Equity value per share	$72.08			

It is useful for us to compare estimates of GIS' value of equity using the *NOA* multiple vis-à-vis the *BV* multiple. Using the *NOA* multiple, we estimated the value of a share of GIS to be $47.42, while the *BV* market multiple gave an estimate of $72.08. For GIS, the estimates obtained via these two methods are quite different from one another. The large difference between the estimated value based on the BV multiple and the market value suggests that either GIS is undervalued relative to its comparable companies and/or the accounting measure of value in place (in this case, *BV)* is poor or a noncomparable summary fundamental indicator. A shortcoming of the method of comparables is that we cannot determine which of these explanations is more fitting.

How do we assess the quality of the different estimates? To answer this question, let us consider the choice of comparable companies. When choosing comparable companies, we should consider many characteristics other than, say, size and industry. We will look for companies that are similar in terms of profitability, growth, and risk. Arguably, operating risk is similar for companies in the same industry. But, we might have done better by choosing alternative consumer goods companies (potentially NSRGY) with profitability, growth, and financial risk characteristics similar to those of GIS.

Arguably, despite the observed estimates, estimating value based on the *NOA* market multiple is likely more reliable than using *BV*. The reason is that company financial risk does not materially affect the value of *NOA*, but it does affect the value of equity. Thus, differences in capital structures and leverage of GIS, K, CPB, and SJM do not matter when applying *NOA* multiples in valuation. But when using book value multiples (i.e., the price-to-book ratio) are used to estimate value, it is important to select comparable companies with similar capital structures.

Finally, before moving to earnings-based market multiples, we must discuss, again, the natural tendency to compare an estimate to observed market price to determine if the analysis is reasonable. When we considered removing the *BV* estimate of K, we were, in effect, saying we did not like the answer received from this method and changed the estimation process. This is a very dangerous course of action because, essentially, we are computing iteratively until we get the answer we want! What if GIS was not a publicly traded firm and we did not have knowledge of "reasonable" values for multiples?

PRICE-TO-EARNINGS RATIOS OBSERVED IN PRACTICE

Price-to-Earnings (PE) ratios are frequently cited in news articles and analysts' reports and regularly used in stock screens and trading strategies. The intuition in using earnings as the basis for valuing a company is straightforward: Dividends are generated by earnings, and potential dividend payouts are the basis for company value. Accordingly, we should pay more for companies that generate more earnings. Therefore, the most commonly used fundamental indicator for estimating company value with market multiples is earnings.

In **Exhibit 8.1** from finance.yahoo.com, we see three versions of PE comparisons. The trailing PE ratio, utilizes the most recent reported earnings, computed using TTM, as the fundamental indicator to be used in estimating company value. The forward PE ratio, the second version, utilizes the estimated earnings for the upcoming year. While future earnings would be useful because it captures any anticipated changes in the operations of the company and may omit any one-time items that have occurred, the quality of the estimate may differ significantly across sources. (In the last chapter, we observed that the forecasts of future earnings are the outcome of many assumptions.)

The third version is a PEG ratio, which attempts to capture effects of earnings growth because the next year's earnings taken alone may not accurately account for the anticipated growth for the company. A PEG ratio is computed as:

$$PEG_t = \frac{P_t / eps_{t+1}}{[(eps_{t+2} - eps_{t+1})/eps_{t+1}] \times 100}$$

where P_t is the price per share and eps_{t+2} and eps_{t+1} are the forecasted earnings in the next two periods. Here, we are comparing the forward PE ratio of the company, P_t/eps_{t+1}, to the expected short-term earnings growth, $(eps_{t+2} - eps_{t+1})/eps_{t+1}$; hence, the acronym PEG—that is, PE divided by growth.[6] Notice that the expression of this ratio may be simplified as follows:

$$PEG_t = \frac{P_t}{(eps_{t+2} - eps_{t+1}) \times 100}$$

Each of these versions of a PE ratio captures different aspects of the earnings process. Further, in practice, these ratios most often are computed using earnings rather than *NOPAT*. That is, they do not separate the financial activities from the operating activities of the firm. Having understood the methods for separating the operating activities from the financial activities in our earlier chapters, we are in a position to consider PE ratios based on operating activities separated from the financial aspects. Subsequent chapters will address additional reasons why focusing on the operating activities and omitting financial effects is superior. We will begin by focusing on trailing (reported) earnings before utilizing forecasted information to examine forward PE and PEG multiples.

Valuation Using a *NOPAT* Multiple

This section illustrates the mechanics of using *NOPAT* before we illustrate use of net income as the basis for valuation. First, we estimate operating value for GIS using a multiple of TTM *NOPAT*.[7] Next, we will estimate its equity value using a multiple of TTM net income; that is, we compute a trailing PE ratio similar to that shown in **Exhibit 8.1**. Again, we use K, CPB, and SJM as comparable companies. Summary information for all four companies, including computed TTM data for each company, is shown in **Exhibit 8.5**. Again, our task is to estimate the equity value for GIS using information from the comparable companies.

EXHIBIT 8.5 Data for Valuation Using Income Statement Multiples

(in millions)	GIS	K	CPB	SJM
Operating value	$ —	$29,831	$21,099	$20,004
Equity value	$ —	$20,430	$11,534	$13,967
NOPAT	$ 1,866	$ 1,531	$ 156	$ 736
Net income	$ 1,563	$ 1,344	$ (164)	$ 629
NFL (*NFA*)	$15,674	$ 9,401	$ 9,565	$ 6,037
Common shares outstanding	599 shares	344 shares	301 shares	114 shares

We use the data from **Exhibit 8.5** to compute a market multiple based on *NOPAT* to estimate the value of GIS. However, a perusal of the data quickly reveals a potential problem. CPB has a very small $156 TTM *NOPAT*! The *NOPAT* multiplier for CPB is 135.25 ($21,099/$156). Having developed familiarity over time with relative magnitudes of multiples, it is readily apparent that CPB's *NOPAT* multiple is drastically different from normal values and from that observed for the other

[6] The denominator of the PEG ratio has the expected short-term earnings growth multiplied by 100 to convert a percentage to a whole number (e.g., 5 percent becomes 5).

[7] For simplicity, *NOPAT* computations continue to assume a tax rate of 21 percent for the comparable companies in this chapter.

comparable firms.[8] That is, the CPB multiple does not pass the smell test (it stinks!) and should not be used in valuing GIS. This supports an argument for omitting CPB from the analysis.

We begin by determining the *NOPAT* market multiple for K and SJM, which are computed as operating value divided by *NOPAT*. **Exhibit 8.6** reports the results of this computation. For example, K's *NOPAT* market multiple is 19.48, computed as $29,831/$1,531. We then average the *NOPAT* market multiples of the comparable companies to get 23.33, computed as (19.48 + 27.18)/2. This market multiple is used to estimate the operating value of GIS as follows:

$$\textbf{Operating value} = \textbf{\textit{NOPAT}} \times \textbf{\textit{NOPAT}}\ \textbf{market multiple}$$
$$\$43{,}536 = \$1{,}866 \times 23.33$$

To obtain GIS' equity value, we subtract the amount owed to debt holders (*NFL*) from operating value. The equity value is then divided by shares outstanding to yield the per-share value of its common equity as follows:

$$\textbf{Equity value} = \textbf{Operating value} - \textbf{Amount owed to debt holders} (\textbf{\textit{NFL}})$$
$$\$27{,}862 = \$43{,}536 - \$15{,}674$$

Then,

$$\textbf{Equity value per share} = \frac{\textbf{Equity value}}{\textbf{Common shares outstanding}}$$

$$\$46.51 = \frac{\$27{,}862}{599\ \text{shares}}$$

This estimate suggests that GIS was overvalued by about 10 percent by the market with respect to its $51.31 closing price on May 1, 2019. Of course, the estimated value would have been different had we used only K's market multiple alone and different again if we had used SJM's multiple alone, and different yet again if we had computed a weighted average or chosen to include CPB.

EXHIBIT 8.6 Estimating Value Using a *NOPAT* Multiple (CPB Omitted)

(in millions, except per share)	GIS	K	CPB	SJM
Operating value	$ —	$29,831		$20,004
NOPAT	$ 1,866	$ 1,531		$ 736
Common shares outstanding	599 shares	344 shares		114 shares
NOPAT market multiple	23.33	19.48		27.18
Operating value	$43,536			
Equity value	$27,862			
Equity value per share	$46.51			

Another thing that would have changed this estimate drastically would have been the use of *NOPAT* from sales rather than total *NOPAT*. As seen in Chapter 6, realized *NOPAT* for GIS has been volatile in recent years. Using *NOPAT* from sales would have omitted effects of items such as earnings from joint ventures, foreign currency translation, and gains/losses on cash flow hedges. We could consider omitting these items because they all would reasonably be expected to be zero in the future. The *NOPAT* from sales of GIS for the year ended May 2018 was $2,467.7, as computed in **Exhibit 6.3** (recognizing this is not a TTM number), and when used with the 23.33 *NOPAT* market multiple, would yield an equity value per share of $69.94.[9] This would have shown GIS to be drastically undervalued by the market.

[8] Recall that in Chapter 6, we inverted the operating *ATO* in part to have sales as the denominator so that issues with small divisors could be avoided.

[9] For simplicity, we do not adjust the *NOPAT* market multiple from the comparable companies to create a *NOPAT* from sales multiple. In practice, this would have to be considered.

Valuation Using a Net Income Multiple

We can repeat the analysis above using a net income multiple as the basis for valuing the company. Here, we will be using reported (trailing) earnings computed for the TTM, resulting in the commonly cited trailing PE ratio. This approach produces the value of the equity, not of the operations. This method relies on different data and, hence, will yield estimates of value that differ from the estimates obtained in the previous sections.

We begin by computing the market multiples using net income as the fundamental indicator for the comparable companies, which is computed as equity value divided by net income. Again, we immediately see a potential problem. CPB has TTM net income of –$164! A loss! This raises issues on two levels. Mathematically, the net income multiplier for CPB is –70.33 ($11,534/–$164), which, when applied to GIS' positive net income, would yield a negative estimated value. We know that this cannot be correct. Conceptually, we also see that the small negative net income for CPB yields a large magnitude for the multiplier. Either of these is enough to support an argument for omitting CPB from the analysis. Be aware, however, that this may bias our valuation upward because we have removed the poor performing comparable, leaving only the profitable comparables.

Exhibit 8.7 shows the results of the computations using only K and SJM as comparables. K's net income market multiple is 15.20, computed as $20,430/$1,344. We then average the net income market multiples from the comparable companies to get 18.71, computed as (15.20 + 22.21)/2. This net income market multiple is used to estimate the equity value of GIS as follows:

$$\textbf{Equity value} = \textbf{Net income} \times \textbf{\textit{NI} market multiple}$$
$$\$29{,}246 = \$1{,}563 \times 18.71$$

To obtain GIS' equity value per share, we divide by shares outstanding as follows:

$$\textbf{Equity value per share} = \frac{\textbf{Equity value}}{\textbf{Common shares outstanding}}$$
$$\$48.82 = \frac{\$29{,}246}{599 \text{ shares}}$$

EXHIBIT 8.7 Estimating Value Using an *NI* Multiple

(in millions, except per share)	GIS	K	CPB	SJM
Equity value	$ —	$20,430		$13,967
NI	$ 1,563	$ 1,344		$ 629
Common shares outstanding	599 shares	344 shares		114 shares
NI market multiple	18.71	15.20		22.21
Equity value	$29,246			
Equity value per share	$48.82			

The $48.82 value estimate suggests that GIS' stock was overvalued based on a $51.31 closing price. Given the estimates from *NOPAT* and *NI*, we may be feeling pretty confident and just decide to average them for an estimate of $47.67 (average of $46.51 and $48.82) because they are pretty similar. However, we must remember that we already made the choice to exclude CPB to arrive at these numbers. Essentially, we may be just playing with numbers until we like the answer. This, again, illustrates a natural tendency to want to choose comparable companies and metrics that get the answer we desire. Had we obtained an answer around $25 or $80, we might have jumped to the conclusion that the *NI* multiple with comparable companies is not the best choice, but we must realize that this would be a case of justifying our assumptions based on whether we like the outcome. The fact that this is dangerous territory must be kept in mind when applying the method of comparables.

VALUATION USING OTHER MULTIPLES

Having demonstrated how we can compute multiples via the examples of *NOPAT*, *NI*, *NOA*, and *BV*, we will adjust our methods to streamline the remaining calculations contained in this chapter. We will continue to utilize the same comparable companies used thus far (specifically, K, CPB, and SJM). Rather than calculating both measures based on the company and operating activities, we will focus on the measures that eliminate the effects of financial activities. Future chapters on cost of capital and valuation will reinforce the point that the contaminating effects of financial activities should be avoided whenever possible.

We will begin with the operating equivalents of a forward PE ratio and PEG ratio. Then, we will examine other options for multiples-based valuation by examining sales, R&D, and industry-based measures.

Valuation Using Operating Forward Earnings and PEG Multiples

The idea behind use of forecasted future earnings as a fundamental indicator is "P/E ratios are only really valuable when comparing the latest price with expected or forecast earnings rather than last year's earnings because an investor who bought the stock today could not buy last year's earnings."[10] However, while, in subsequent chapters, we will directly relate forecasted earnings to value, it is not quite as simple as this quote from Thomson Reuters implies. From our forecasting efforts for GIS in Chapter 7, we arrived at forecasts of *NOPAT* that included the next 2 years. We could also complete a similar exercise on each of the comparable firms. This would entail a great deal of work, and our concerns about the assumptions pervading each forecast would remain.

An alternative is to estimate *NOPAT* for the comparable firms by adjusting analysts' forecasts of earnings for the expected *FEAT*. We may choose to rely on such forecasts (or use them as a starting point) due to the analysts' industry knowledge and familiarity with the company. For example, the average of the analysts' 2019 earnings forecasts at May 1, 2019, for K is $3.97 per share. Given 344 shares outstanding, this would imply net income of $1,366. Forecasting the amount of expected *FEAT* to allow adjustment to *NOPAT* (because *CI* + *FEAT* = *NOPAT*) is tricky because it requires us to forecast both the amount of *NFL* in the future and the related rate, *RNFL*. One option is to use the current *FEAT* as a proxy for future *FEAT*.[11]

K had TTM *FEAT* excluding other comprehensive income of $235. Thus, we could add its *FEAT* to the *NI* of $1,366 to arrive at a forecasted *NOPAT* of $1,601. The following year, assuming constant *FEAT* and using the average analysts' forecasts of $4.25 per share, we arrive at forecasted *NOPAT* of $1,697, computed as ($4.25 × 344) + $235. Similar computations can be done for CPB and SJM. We continue to assume that the comparable firms are fairly valued (an underlying premise of multiples valuation) and arrive at the information summarized in **Exhibit 8.8**.

EXHIBIT 8.8 Data for Valuation Using Operating Earnings Multiples

(in millions)	GIS	K	CPB	SJM
Operating value	$ —	$29,831	$21,099	$20,004
$NOPAT_{t+1}$	$ 2,330	$ 1,601	$ 1,012	$ 1,112
$NOPAT_{t+2}$	$ 2,426	$ 1,697	$ 1,051	$ 1,144
NFL (*NFA*)	$15,674	$ 9,401	$ 9,565	$ 6,037
Common shares outstanding	599 shares	344 shares	301 shares	114 shares

The operating forward PE for K is 18.63, computed as $29,831/$1,601. Applying the average multiple of 19.16 from the comparable companies to GIS leads to an estimate of operating value of $44,643. This implies an equity value of $28,969 after subtracting *NFL* (computed as $44,643 – $15,674), yielding an estimated price per share of $48.36.

[10] http://glossary.reuters.com/index.php?title=P/E_Ratio

[11] The assumption that the analysts' forecasts of earnings are a forecast of *CI* implies that other *CI* items are expected to be zero in the next year. This is the same assumption made in Chapter 7.

To compute an estimate of value based on the PEG ratio, we begin with a calculation of short-term *NOPAT* growth in dollars for both GIS and its comparables. For K, expected short-term *NOPAT* growth (in dollars) is \$96, computed as \$1,697 – \$1,601. The operating PEG ratio of K is 3.11, computed as \$29,831/(\$96 × 100). We then determine the average operating PEG ratio (i.e., 4.92), calculated from the three comparable companies. In order to apply this multiple to GIS, we first calculate the GIS expected short-term growth in *NOPAT* that also equals \$96, computed as \$2,426 – \$2,330. We then estimate GIS' operating value based on the operating PEG multiple as \$47,232, computed as (\$96 × 100) × 4.92. This implies an equity value of \$31,558 after subtracting *NFL*, computed as \$47,232 – \$15,674, yielding an estimated price per share of \$52.68.

Here, we see that, for estimating the value of GIS, the PEG ratio based on *NOPAT* appears to give a reasonable estimate because it is near the closing price at May 1, 2019, of \$51.31. The forward PE ratio calculated based on *NOPAT* estimates does not provide as reasonable of an estimate of price. Often when estimating value using multiples, an unreasonable estimate may arise from one (or many!) of the methods used. Remember that had we not excluded CPB, our *NOPAT*-based estimate would have been \$162.75! Generally, the analyst will disregard the unreasonable estimates and examine other candidate measures. While this is an understandable approach, it also reflects the fact that this method is shaped by the choices and assumptions made and a certain amount of searching for evidence to back a desired outcome can easily occur. This is, of course, not a reasonable approach.

Valuation Using Other Multiples, including Sales Multiples or Industry-Based Multiples

Of course, there are many multiples, which an analyst may choose as the basis for valuation. Some industries have specific fundamental indicators related to characteristics of the industry that investors and analysts watch closely. For example, in the retail industry, sales per square foot of selling space is a common measure used to understand the sales that each location is able to generate relative to its size. Another example is the airline industry, which focuses on revenues, expenses, or profits per available seat mile (i.e., one aircraft seat flown one mile, whether occupied or not). Companies such as GIS, which engage in R&D, might also use a ratio capturing price less book value (the premium) divided by R&D. To the extent the premium arises from unrecorded assets due to the expensing of R&D, this ratio would be meaningful because it is the premium the market puts on the R&D expenditure. We will illustrate the use of an operating version of this multiple using data for GIS and its comparable companies.

An oft-used multiple is price to sales and the related enterprise (operating) value to revenue, which was shown in **Exhibit 8.1**. We will also illustrate the use of the operating value-to-revenue multiple using GIS as our example.

The data for the calculations of the (Price – Book)/R&D and the price-to-sales multiples are shown in **Exhibit 8.9**. Of our four companies, only CPB reported the amount spent on R&D separately in the Form 10-Q to allow a TTM computation. For GIS, K, and SJM, we have used the most recent fiscal year number assuming no significant change has occurred.

ALL SALES ARE NOT CREATED EQUALLY

When considering any market multiple, you must know the business (step 1). Sales or revenues are no exception to this. For example, sales generated from company-owned locations are very different from franchise fees received. Both the profitability of these sources of sales and their expected future growth may differ, and this may suggest a need for different multiples. The hotel industry provides another example of mixed-revenue sources. There will be variation across hotels based on the proportion of earnings from management fees, accommodations in company-owned hotels, and sales of time shares.

Together, this leads to the caveat that when using sales, remember to consider carefully a company with a similar mix of revenue sources to ensure that the multiple can be applied to the company you are valuing.

EXHIBIT 8.9 Data for Valuation Using Operating Earnings Multiples

(in millions)	GIS	K	CPB	SJM
Operating value	$ —	$29,831	$21,099	$20,004
Sales	$16,594	$13,547	$ 9,751	$ 7,717
R&D expenditures	$ 219	$ 154	$ 103	$ 56
NOA	$22,604	$12,002	$10,834	$14,059
NFL (*NFA*)	$15,674	$ 9,401	$ 9,565	$ 6,037
Common shares outstanding	599 shares	344 shares	301 shares	114 shares

Valuation Using a Sales Multiple

We use the operating value-to-revenue multiple for GIS and its comparables to illustrate the use of a sales multiple to estimate value. Note that the focus on sales should be done with some caution. If, for example, the company we are valuing has a different cost structure than its comparable companies, this will add error to our estimation. Again, note that we use the sales multiple to compute an estimate of operating value rather than equity value. Use of operating value-to-revenue would be expected to be superior to equity value-to-sales because the sales revenues are independent of financial activities. Sales is the driver of value available to both debt and equity holders, so the operating value-to-revenue multiple is more appropriate than the equity value-to-sales ratio, though finance.yahoo.com shows both in **Exhibit 8.1**.

The operating value-to-revenue ratio for K is 2.20, computed as $29,831/$13,547. The average multiple from the three comparable companies is 2.32. Applying this multiple to GIS, we estimate operating value at $38,497. This implies an equity value of $22,823 after subtracting *NFL*, yielding an estimated price per share of $38.10. This stock price estimate suggests that GIS' stock was greatly overvalued by the market based on a $51.31 closing price at May 1, 2019.

Finally, note that, sometimes, the sales multiple is used rather than an income-based multiple when the company being valued (and, perhaps, also the comparable companies) is reporting a loss because a multiple of a loss is meaningless. Such a justification should be viewed with skepticism; the fact that the firm is losing money may in and of itself lead us to question the wisdom of investing in the firm.

Valuation Using the Ratio of (Price – Book) to R&D

To the extent that, for a company with a large amount of R&D, the difference between the market value of equity and the book value of equity may be seen as the market's valuation of R&D, the ratio of (Price – Book)/R&D may be a valid multiple for valuation. In firms where this is possibly so, Price – Book (i.e., P – B) is often viewed as composed primarily of unrecorded assets arising because of the expensing (rather than capitalization) of R&D. If we were examining a firm reporting under IFRS, such as Nestlé, we may need to revisit this assumption because IFRS capitalizes development costs. We illustrate the use of this ratio for GIS.

Because R&D is related to operating activities, the use of price and book value of *equity* appears odd. However, given the common assumption that the book value and market value of *NFL* are equal, this is not a problem. This can be seen as:

$$
\begin{aligned}
V_{Eq} - BV_{Eq} &= (V_{Oper} - V_{NFL}) - (NEA - NFL) \\
&= V_{Oper} - V_{NFL} - NEA + NFL \\
&= (V_{Oper} - NEA) - (V_{NFL} - NFL) \\
&= (V_{Oper} - NEA) - 0 \\
&= V_{Oper} - NEA
\end{aligned}
$$

That is, if the market and book value of *NFL* are equal, the premium is the same for enterprise operations and for equity.[12] Thus, we will calculate the ratio using operating numbers because that

[12] Clearly, the value of the interest tax shield is ignored when this assumption is made.

is our primary focus, but we are reminded that the multiple (P – B)/R&D is unchanged (but the value estimate does change) if the market value and book value of financial activities are equal. If the assumption that the market value and book value of financial activities are equal is not appropriate, that is yet another reason why the calculation should focus on operating value rather than equity value.

To compute an estimate of value based on the (P – B)/R&D ratio, we begin with a calculation of this ratio for K, which is 115.77, computed as ($29,831 – $12,002)/$154. To obtain the estimate of operating value for GIS, we utilize the average multiple for the comparable companies of 107.20 and calculate a value of $46,081, computed as 107.20 × $219 + $22,604. This implies an equity value of $30,407 after subtracting *NFL,* yielding an estimated price per share of $50.76, which nearly matches the observed price of GIS' stock based on a $51.31 closing price.

CONSIDERATION OF *EBITDA* MULTIPLES

The only multiple shown in **Exhibit 8.1** that we have not yet considered is the enterprise (operating) value-to-*EBITDA* multiple. The use, in practice, of a measure of earnings before interest, taxes, depreciation, and amortization in ratio analysis and valuation is widespread. Though *EBITDA* is commonly used, our analysis in prior chapters separating operating activities from financial activities highlights some of the deficiencies in this measure. Omission of interest and the portion of taxes related to financial activities would be appropriate if one is seeking to measure operations, but omitting all taxes from operations is hard to justify. The omission of depreciation and amortization suggests an attempt at capturing a cash-based measure because they are noncash items.

BERKSHIRE HATHAWAY'S (BRK) VIEW ON EBITDA

From Warren Buffet, Chairman and CEO:

> It amazes me how widespread the use of EBITDA has become. People try to dress up financial statements with it.
>
> We won't buy into companies where someone's talking about EBITDA. If you look at all companies, and split them into companies that use EBITDA as a metric and those that don't, I suspect you'll find a lot more fraud in the former group. Look at companies like Wal-Mart, GE and Microsoft—they'll never use EBITDA in their annual report.
>
> People who use EBITDA are either trying to con you or they're conning themselves. Telecoms, for example, spend every dime that's coming in. Interest and taxes are real costs.
>
> BRK Annual Meeting 2002 Tilson Notes

From Buffet and Charlie Munger, Vice Chairman

> *Buffet:*
> People want to send me books with EBITDA and I say fine, as long as you pay cap ex.
>
> There are very few businesses that can spend a lot less than depreciation and maintain the health of the business.
>
> This is nonsense. It couldn't be worse. But a whole generation of investors have been taught this. It's not a non-cash expense—it's a cash expense but you spend it first. It's a delayed recording of a cash expense.
>
> We at Berkshire are going to spend more this year on cap ex than we depreciate.
>
> *Munger added:*
> I think that, every time you saw the word EBITDA [earnings], you should substitute the word "b . . . s . . ." earnings.
>
> BRK Annual Meeting 2003 Tilson Notes

Are the analysts, when utilizing *EBITDA*, seeking a cash number, such as free cash flows from operations? A much cleaner measure of free cash flows was calculated in prior chapters. The calculation of *EBITDA* appears to be, at best, a hybrid of crude measures of *NOPAT* and *FCF*. Given that we can measure each of these directly and use them in multiples, the use of *EBITDA* is not explored. For further consideration of the use of *EBITDA* in valuation, we provide the *Wall Street Journal* article in **Exhibit 8.10**.

EXHIBIT 8.10

Media Frenzy
As reported in the *Wall Street Journal*—February 13, 2004
By Jesse Eisinger, Staff Reporter

Cheerleading for multibillion-dollar media deals seems so early-2000, but the Comcast bid for Disney makes sense despite its supporters' enthusiasm.

Still, Wall Street's justification for the deal demonstrates that muddled thinking about valuations is back. "This is not AOL Time Warner," says investment banker Steven Rattner. "This deal makes sense using old-fashioned numbers."

Uh, no. Comcast's explicit reasoning requires deep faith in EBITDA—and there's nothing stolid and conservative about that measure. But the use of EBITDA is so pervasive that anyone who objects seems faintly ridiculous.

Here is the broken record: EBITDA stands for "earnings before interest, taxes, depreciation and amortization." With the exception of the brief period roughly from June 2002 to October of that year, Wall Street has been addicted to EBITDA as a proxy for operating cash flow since the late 1980s, when it was invented to justify the sale of junk bonds of profitless companies.

The justification is that investors want to measure the actual cash a company throws off. So investors subtract the noncash asset depreciation and goodwill amortization from earnings. Then they subtract taxes and interest, which, though they are real cash payments, supposedly have little to do with the business's underlying cash-generating power.

But EBITDA is a lousy proxy for cash flow from operations, because "most of the fun and games happen in changes in operating assets," says accounting watchdog Howard Schilit. Companies have huge leeway to play with balance-sheet items such as inventory and receivables. "If a company is using it as a metric for operating cash flow . . . it has no value."

Hedge-fund manager Jim Chanos, who has no position in Comcast or Disney, says, "The only case in which you can use EBITDA with absolute certainty is when you know the company doesn't have to reinvest anything in the core business to maintain its competitive position, and there are very few businesses where that is the case."

The EBITDA concept always has snookered cable investors in particular because of the never-ending capital-spending requirements. Indeed, after years of monopolistic safety, the cable industry faces unprecedented threats from the Baby Bells, satellite providers and wireless broadband.

Prudent investors prefer free cash flow, which is typically defined as cash flow from operations (not EBITDA) minus capital expenditure. Even this might overstate the true earnings power of a company. Because technology changes can upend a company's competitive position, a company might be underinvesting in technologies that aren't counted in capital expenditure.

Eschew EBITDA and the result is that Comcast looks overvalued. Thus, the proper way to interpret the Comcast offer is that it is swapping overvalued paper for hard Disney assets (which also are valued using EBITDA, but with slightly more justification). That means if Comcast doesn't win, its investors should worry.

COMBINING ESTIMATES FROM DIFFERING MULTIPLES

LO4: Combine estimates from different calculations, and evaluate the reasonableness of market multiple estimates.

In prior sections, we arrived at a wide variety of estimates of the value of a share of GIS. Rather than attempting to weigh the merits of the different individual estimates, some investors prefer to combine them in the hope that estimation error for a specific multiple is mitigated by other multiples. This combination is typically done using a simple average of the estimates. Consider the example in **Exhibit 8.11**, which first combines all the estimates we previously computed for GIS. In the second column, we repeat the calculation using every other estimate as a random subsample of the values from our prior estimates. Alternatively, we could have made a careful analysis of each estimate to determine its merit. Remember that we must be careful to ensure that we do not choose estimates simply because they support a desired conclusion!

By choosing to compute an estimate using a subset of the different multiples, we get an average estimate of $45.10, which is almost 20 percent lower than the $55.44 estimate of the value of GIS using all our estimates. Worse yet, the full set suggests GIS is undervalued, but the subset suggests

EXHIBIT 8.11 Combining Estimates of Equity Value per Share

Multiple Used	Full Set	Subset
NOA	$47.42	$47.42
BV	$72.08	
Trailing *NOPAT*	$46.51	$46.51
Trailing *NI*	$48.82	
Forward *NOPAT*	$48.36	$48.36
Forward PEG	$52.68	
Sales	$38.10	$38.10
(P – B)/R&D	$50.76	
Average of estimates	$55.44	$45.10

it is overvalued! In other words, our decision to buy, sell, or hold would be the direct result of the decision of which multiples to use rather than a reflection of an underlying reality. It is also clear that choosing to include or exclude the *BV*-based multiple would cause large differences in the estimated value. Before deciding what multiples to use, how we might appropriately weight them, and even which companies should be considered as comparables, we must revisit our concerns about the use of multiples in general.

THE PRODUCT OF A MULTIPLES VALUATION

While we have calculated a wide variety of multiples for GIS, this was done for demonstration purposes. If an analyst or potential investor were undertaking this analysis, the decision of what multiples to utilize would be critical. Remember that multiples should not be chosen based on the outcome of the estimation as that would result in just picking and choosing until we got the answer we desired.

So what likely is most meaningful as a multiple for GIS? Likely GIS' value is more closely aligned with an income measure rather than a book value measure as much of its value comes from its brands and selling them at a premium price. This differs from a firm like a bank, where we would want to look at book value based measures. For GIS, this may lead us to use measures such as Forward *NOPAT*.

We also know that the level of sales of GIS is critical to its value. The increase in 2019 due to the acquisition of Blue Buffalo will directly affect the estimate of value. For a large firm, sales is a critical item, essentially it is the industry measure that drives the value. While R&D may be important going forward, the limited amount of R&D dollars may, in some circumstances, affect the helpfulness of this measure. Clearly, if we were valuing a pharmaceutical firm, the R&D multiple would be crucial to consider.

After choosing two to four multiples of interest, we would combine the estimates they provide to come up with a value estimate. If we were using net income, Forward *NOPAT*, and sales based multiples, these estimates of $48.82, $48.36, and $38.10 would be averaged to arrive at an estimate of $45.09. Based on this estimate, we would be willing to purchase the stock, if available, at a price up to $45.09 and sell the stock at any price above $45.09.

The key to this process is thinking through the choice of multiples to use based on the firm being valued. The better we do the job of choosing a multiple that will be meaningful given the characteristics of the company, the better our estimate of value will be.

PERSPECTIVE ON VALUATION MULTIPLES AND FUNDAMENTAL ANALYSIS

We conclude the discussion of the method of multiples with some perspective on choosing to use valuation multiples to value a target company. This method of market multiples lacks a theoretical foundation. Subsequent chapters will introduce theoretically sound methods of valuing securities—methods based on the sum of discounted free cash flows, residual operating income, and/or abnormal operating income growth. These three methods require explicit forecasts of a company's future performance for valuation. The resulting valuation can contain errors because the forecasts are wrong or the assumed discount rate is wrong, but not because of an inherent problem with the valuation model. This is not so with the method of multiples.

The multiples method does have some intuitive appeal (and it is easy!), but it does not have rigorous theoretical underpinnings. Many errors can arise. For example, the selection of comparable companies might not yield peers that are similar in profitability, growth, and/or risk. Also, the fundamental indicator (e.g., *NOPAT* or *NOA*) might be unstable over time and a poor basis for assessing relative value. In addition, the market might be inefficient, so using prices of comparable companies to infer the value of a target company simply compounds errors. Nonetheless, market multiples are widely used in practice and, if applied with discretion, are sometimes useful for analysis.

If we use market multiples for company valuation, there are at least three steps we should take in implementing this method:

1. Whenever possible, use a forward-looking fundamental indicator to compute the market multiples for comparable companies. Prices are forward-looking and reflect expected future performance of a company, not past performance. Further, use an estimate of the target company's future performance to multiply by the forward-looking market multiple. Forward-looking estimates are especially important for earnings multiples because earnings are more volatile than book values.
2. Select comparable companies with care so as to match them on profitability, growth, and risk profiles with our target company.
3. Use both income statement- and balance sheet-based valuation multiples, and consider industry-based multiples whenever possible. This might induce greater variance in the estimated value of our target company. However, as unsettling as this can be, it requires us to directly consider the reliability of those estimates and the inputs underlying them.

To conclude our discussion of multiples, consider the bold assumption being made in the use of multiples that the fundamental indicator (e.g., earnings in a PE ratio) captures all value-relevant information. Fischer Black, Nobel laureate in economics, argued in the article "The Magic in Earnings" (1980) that investors want an earnings number that they can use to determine value. He provocatively proposed that accountants adopt as their main objective the creation of an earnings number that can be multiplied by a constant (e.g., 10) to yield value. This accounting model would render the balance sheet superfluous to investors. Black suggested that accountants were surprisingly close to producing such a number, as evidenced by the relatively low variance in PE ratios. Whatever your thoughts on the merits of his suggestion, recent actions by the FASB to move from primarily historical cost accounting toward an increasing use of fair value accounting inverts Black's suggestion in that the FASB is trying to move the balance sheet closer to the primary indicator of company value and the income statement toward a less useful status. Still, to think that we will see a fundamental indicator that captures all value-relevant information in a single summary measure remains a bold proposition.

SUMMARY

This chapter demonstrated the method by which the value of equity can be calculated using the market multiples method commonly observed in practice. This method does not have the theoretical underpinnings of a true valuation model. Its appeal lies in the simplicity by which it can be done. If using market multiples to estimate value, you should use a method that estimates operating value rather than equity value directly. This prevents capital structure (leverage) from affecting your estimate. (More on this issue later!)

The market multiple method has five steps: (1) Select the fundamental indicator, (2) select the comparables, (3) compute the market multiple, (4) compute the target company's value by using its fundamental indicator and the market multiple, and (5) adjust for debt if using an operating multiple, and divide by number of shares outstanding if using an equity multiple. Among the most critical are the choices made in steps 1 and 2. Common fundamental indicators are *NOPAT*, *NOA*, earnings, book value, and sales revenue; and remember that the method of comparables may be based on current or forecasted fundamental indicators. Finding one true comparable company is extremely difficult, and finding several is even harder!

In the next chapter, we transition to valuation based on a sound theoretical foundation. We start with the calculation of cost of capital, which will be a very important input to the valuation process. Then, we move to the valuation of cash flows followed by a transition to accounting-based valuation models.

QUESTIONS

Q8.1 What are the biggest concerns when using multiples?

Q8.2 How hard is it to find appropriate comparables?

Q8.3 What is the primary advantage to using an operating-based multiple rather than a company-level multiple?

Q8.4 Why would we use industry-based multiples to estimate value?

Q8.5 When utilizing the multiples method, we assume the market is appropriate valuing the comparable firms. Why might this assumption be a cause for concern?

Q8.6 What are the steps to using market multiples?

Q8.7 What is the primary benefit of combining estimates from different multiples?

Q8.8 A commonly used multiple in practice is *EV/EBITDA* (i.e., enterprise [operating] value to *EBITDA* [earnings before interest, taxes, depreciation, and amortization]) multiple. What are the limitations associated with using *EBITDA*-based multiples?

Q8.9 When is it appropriate to use market multiples for valuation?

Q8.10 When the target company has negative earnings and/or negative equity, can market multiples be used for valuation?

EXERCISES

E8.11 For McDonalds (MCD), which companies might we use as comparable if we are implementing the multiples method? What concerns might we have about the companies chosen?

E8.12 For Hyatt (H) and Marriott (MAR), what is an example of an industry multiple we might employ to estimate firm valuation? What might be a hindrance to using this measure?

E8.13 Beyond Meat (BYND), a plant-based protein company, went public in May 2019. The IPO was priced at $25 per share, but started trading at $46 per share before ending the day at $65.75 per share. Over the next few months, BYND's share price topped $240 with a market capitalization over $15 billion. With less than $100 million in 2018 sales and negative earnings, BYND's market valuation was difficult to support. In August 2019, Bank of America Merrill Lynch published an analyst report with a price objective of $182 per share. Evaluate the implicit assumptions necessary to support a price objective of $182 per share with an operating value-to-sales multiple.

Valuation

Key assumptions to our comparable valuation include: 1) Beyond sales of $1,263mm in FY23, 2) FY23 EBITDA of $194m or a 15.4% EBITDA margin. 2) we assume a 12.0x EV/Sales multiple. These assumptions arrive at a $182 price objective.

Table1: BYND valuation based on EV/sales multiple

BYND Current Valuation	
Share Price	$79.66
Shares Outstanding	60.1
Market Cap	4,789.4
Net Cash	257.4
Enterprise Value	4,531.9
2020 EV/Sales	11.0x

BYND EV/Sales Valuation	FY19E	FY20E	FY21E	FY22E	FY23E
Sales	263.2	411.4	621.3	886.9	1,262.8
Sales Growth		*56.3%*	*51.0%*	*42.8%*	*42.4%*
EBITDA	17.2	43.2	84.1	121.4	194.3
EBITDA Growth		NA	95%	44%	60%
		56.3%	51.0%	42.8%	42.4%

Price Objective	
2023 Sales	1,262.8
2023 EV/Sales	12x
EV	15,154.1
Net Cash	257.4
Market Cap	15,411.6
Share Price	256.3
Years to Discount	4
Discount Rate	9.0%
Price Objective	**$181.59**

Source: BofA Merrill Lynch Global research estimates

E8.14 *Forbes* magazine published the following excerpt a number of years ago:

> *Jim O'Shaugnessy, a money manager in Stamford, Conn., has been using computers for the past 30 years to help him find out what makes the market tick. He originally published "What Works On Wall Street" in 1996 and just put out the book's fourth edition. There is no magic ratio that assures market-beating returns, says O'Shaughnessy, but screens with tried and true value criteria do have a pronounced propensity to turn up winning stocks.*
>
> *In short, if you want the best results over time, go with small cap stocks trading at lower-than-average multiples of earnings, sales and book value–and buy them when they're trending higher. Momentum does matter as history shows that winners tend to keep on winning.*
>
> *As for the merit of one popular measure of value, the price-earnings ratio, O'Shaughnessy's research makes a compelling case for buying low P/E stocks. From January 1, 1964 to December 31, 2009, an investment of $10,000 in the 10% of stocks with the lowest P/E ratios would have grown to $10,202,345.*[13]

If investing is as easy as putting $10,000 into the 10 percent of stocks with the lowest P/E ratios over 35 years and ending up with a portfolio worth more than $10 million, then should everyone be doing this? Explain why an analyst needs to consider doing fundamental research as opposed to relying on stock screens.

E8.15 Barth Co. is a fast-growing company that is considering an initial public offering (IPO) early next year. Barth's expected sales, *NOPAT,* and earnings per share next year are $250 million, $50 million, and $4.00, respectfully. Currently, Barth has $50 million in debt and 10.0 million common shares outstanding.

Barth's CFO identified five public companies that operate in the same industry and gathered estimates of next fiscal year's sales, *NOPAT*, and eps along with the current price, market capitalization, and operating (enterprise) value (*OV*).

	Market Data			Financial Data (FY + 1)		
	Price $/share	Market Cap $M	*OV* $M	Sales $M	*NOPAT* $M	EPS $/share
Paton Corp.	29.45	2,400	2,850	950	190	0.90
Hatfield Ltd.	45.65	6,650	8,000	3,200	640	1.70
Andersen Inc.	29.50	13,200	15,190	4,900	1,600	1.60
Sells Corp.	68.25	9,500	9,990	3,700	800	3.05
Sprague Companies	145.75	10,850	10,120	4,600	600	6.75

For each of the comparable firms, calculate the *OV/Sales*, *OV/NOPAT,* and P/E ratios along with the average and median ratios. What recommendation should the CFO make regarding Barth's equity value?

CONTINUING EXAMPLES

For the examination of Kellogg (K), we will use the same data we used in this chapter for the valuation of General Mills (GIS). However, in this case, we will assume GIS is appropriately valued by the market and use its observed market valuation to estimate the value of K.

CE8.16 Using the data in **Exhibit 8.2** for GIS, CPB, and SJM, estimate the value per share of K using an *NOA* multiple. Additional information for the process is that the operating value and equity value of GIS are $46,409 and $30,735, respectively. Determine whether, based on this estimate, K is over- or underpriced at its May 1, 2019 price of $59.39.

CE8.17 Continue using the data in **Exhibit 8.2** for GIS, CPB, and SJM to estimate the value per share of K using a *BV* multiple. Determine whether, based on this estimate, K is over- or underpriced at its May 1, 2019 price of $59.39. Discuss the validity of the result and what drives your conclusions.

CE8.18 Using the data in **Exhibit 8.5** for GIS, CPB, and SJM, estimate the value per share of K using an *NOPAT* multiple. Additional information for the process is that the operating value and equity value of GIS are $46,409 and $30,735, respectively. Determine whether, based on this estimate, K is over- or underpriced at its May 1, 2019 price of $59.39. Discuss the validity of the result and what drives your conclusions.

[13] https://www.forbes.com/sites/johndobosz/2011/12/13/values-to-hold-dear-when-youre-buying-stocks/#255f29282bbf

CE8.19 Continue using the data in **Exhibit 8.5** for GIS, CPB, and SJM to estimate the value per share of K using a *NI* multiple. Determine whether, based on this estimate, K is over- or underpriced at its May 1, 2019 price of $59.39.

CE8.20 Using the data in **Exhibit 8.8** for GIS, CPB, and SJM to estimate the value per share of K using an operating forward PE multiple. Additional information for the process is that the operating value of GIS is $46,409. Determine whether, based on this estimate, K is over- or underpriced at its May 1, 2019 price of $59.39.

CE8.21 Continue using the data in **Exhibit 8.8** for GIS, CPB, and SJM to estimate the value per share of K using an operating PEG ratio multiple. Determine whether, based on this estimate, K is over- or underpriced at its May 1, 2019 price of $59.39.

CE8.22 Using the data in **Exhibit 8.9** for GIS, CPB, and SJM, estimate the value per share of K using a sales multiple. Additional information for the process is that the operating value of GIS is $46,409. Determine whether, based on this estimate, K is over- or underpriced at its May 1, 2019 price of $59.39.

CE8.23 Continue using the data in **Exhibit 8.9** for GIS, CPB, and SJM to estimate the value per share of K using a ratio of (Price-Book) to R&D multiple. Determine whether, based on this estimate, K is over- or underpriced at its May 1, 2019 price of $59.39. Discuss concerns with the estimation process using this multiple for K.

CE8.24 In reviewing the estimates of price for K based on the multiples method, comment on your confidence in the use of this model.

For the examination of Thor Industries (THO) and Winnebago (WGO), we include two additional companies, Camping World Holdings (CWH) and LCI Industries (LCII). CWH is an outdoor and camping retailer that operates through three segments: consumer services and plans, dealership, and retail. CWH does not build travel trailers, but is impacted by the same industry-related factors. LCII manufactures and supplies components for recreational vehicle manufacturers through its Original Equipment Manufacturers (OEM) segment and operates an Aftermarket segment to retail dealers, wholesale distributors, and service centers.

The table below summarizes the relevant balance sheet metrics as of the latest quarter or year-end prior to the May 1, 2019 measurement date.

(in thousands)	THO	WGO	CWH	LCII
Operating value	$3,382,290	$1,379,042	$3,453,691	$2,474,759
Equity value	$3,563,677	$1,114,599	$1,278,066	$2,181,231
NOA	$1,725,544	$835,109	$2,220,163	$999,783
Book value of equity	$1,906,931	$570,666	$44,538	$706,255
NFL	($181,387)	$264,443	$2,175,625	$293,528
Sales	$7,172,233	$2,024,787	$4,792,017	$2,475,807
$NOPAT_t$	$230,344	$119,185	$148,550	$149,699
$NOPAT_{t+1}$	$290,648	$125,615	$112,855	$148,295
$NOPAT_{t+2}$	$393,065	$141,552	$169.990	$168,683
Net Income	$230,529	$116,336	$10,398	$148,551
Common shares outstanding	55,063 sh.	31,873 sh.	87,900 sh.	24,863 sh.

CE8.25 Using the data above for WGO, CWH, and LCII, estimate the value per share of THO using a *NOA* multiple. Determine whether, based on this estimate, THO is over- or underpriced at its May 1, 2019 price of $64.72. Discuss the validity of the result and what drives your conclusions.

CE8.26 Using the data above for WGO, CWH, and LCII, estimate the value per share of THO using a *BV* multiple. Determine whether, based on this estimate, THO is over- or underpriced at its May 1, 2019 price of $64.72. Discuss the validity of the result and what drives your conclusions.

CE8.27 Using the data above for WGO, CWH, and LCII, estimate the value per share of THO using a *NOPAT* multiple. Determine whether, based on this estimate, THO is over- or underpriced at its May 1, 2019 price of $64.72. Discuss the validity of the result and what drives your conclusions.

CE8.28 Using the data above for WGO, CWH, and LCII, estimate the value per share of THO using a *NI* multiple. Determine whether, based on this estimate, THO is over- or underpriced at its May 1, 2019 price of $64.72. Discuss the validity of the result and what drives your conclusions.

CE8.29 Using the data above for WGO, CWH, and LCII, estimate the value per share of THO using an operating forward PE multiple. Determine whether, based on this estimate, THO is over- or underpriced at its May 1, 2019 price of $64.72. Discuss the validity of the result and what drives your conclusions.

CE8.30 Using the data above for WGO, CWH, and LCII, estimate the value per share of THO using an operating PEG ratio multiple. Determine whether, based on this estimate, THO is over- or underpriced at its May 1, 2019 price of $64.72. Discuss the validity of the result and what drives your conclusions.

CE8.31 Using the data above for WGO, CWH, and LCII, estimate the value per share of THO using a sales multiple. Determine whether, based on this estimate, THO is over- or underpriced at its May 1, 2019 price of $64.72. Discuss the validity of the result and what drives your conclusions.

CE8.32 In reviewing the estimates of price for THO based on the multiples method, comment on your confidence in the use of this model.

CE8.33 Using the data above for THO, CWH, and LCII, estimate the value per share of WGO using a *NOA* multiple. Determine whether, based on this estimate, WGO is over- or underpriced at its May 1, 2019 price of $34.97. Discuss the validity of the result and what drives your conclusions.

CE8.34 Using the data above for THO, CWH, and LCII, estimate the value per share of WGO using a *BV* multiple. Determine whether, based on this estimate, WGO is over- or underpriced at its May 1, 2019 price of $34.97. Discuss the validity of the result and what drives your conclusions.

CE8.35 Using the data above for THO, CWH, and LCII, estimate the value per share of WGO using a *NOPAT* multiple. Determine whether, based on this estimate, WGO is over- or underpriced at its May 1, 2019 price of $34.97. Discuss the validity of the result and what drives your conclusions.

CE8.36 Using the data above for THO, CWH, and LCII, estimate the value per share of WGO using a *NI* multiple. Determine whether, based on this estimate, WGO is over- or underpriced at its May 1, 2019 price of $34.97. Discuss the validity of the result and what drives your conclusions.

CE8.37 Using the data above for THO, CWH, and LCII, estimate the value per share of WGO using an operating forward PE multiple. Determine whether, based on this estimate, WGO is over- or underpriced at its May 1, 2019 price of $34.97. Discuss the validity of the result and what drives your conclusions.

CE8.38 Using the data above for THO, CWH, and LCII, estimate the value per share of WGO using an operating PEG ratio multiple. Determine whether, based on this estimate, WGO is over- or underpriced at its May 1, 2019 price of $34.97. Discuss the validity of the result and what drives your conclusions.

CE8.39 Using the data above for THO, CWH, and LCII, estimate the value per share of WGO using a price-to-sales multiple. Determine whether, based on this estimate, WGO is over- or underpriced at its May 1, 2019 price of $34.97. Discuss the validity of the result and what drives your conclusions.

CE8.40 In reviewing the estimates of price for WGO based on the multiples method, comment on your confidence in the use of this model.

Chapter Nine

Cost of Capital for Operations and Equity

TAKEAWAYS

When you complete this chapter, you should be able to:

1. Explain the difference between the sources of risk and the process of estimation of risk.
2. Estimate the cost of equity capital using the capital asset pricing model and the role of beta (β).
3. Determine an estimate of the cost of debt capital by examining different proxies.
4. Combine the estimated cost of equity capital and debt capital to arrive at the weighted average cost of capital for operations.

In Chapter 8, we considered the use of market multiples as a method for valuation and concluded that, although this is a commonly used method, it has some serious shortcomings. We turn now to sophisticated valuation models. All these models estimate the present (discounted) value of the future streams of payoffs (e.g., free cash flows) from the operations of the firm. In this chapter, we begin with a focus on estimating the discount rate, which we will use in Chapters 10, 11, and 12, to obtain our estimate of value. We maintain the emphasis on valuation of the operating activities but, because the estimation of the discount rate for operations relies on estimates of the value of debt and the value of equity, the relations among the value of operations, the value of debt, and the value of equity become central to our discussion.

We have expressed the accounting relation between the book value of operating assets (*NOA*), the book value of net financial obligations (*NFL*), and the book value of equity (*CSE*) as follows:

$$CSE = NOA - NFL$$

Of course, this relation also holds between the intrinsic value of equity, the intrinsic value of operations, and the intrinsic value of debt, which we estimate in future chapters, as follows:

$$V^{CSE} = V^{NOA} - V^{NFL}$$

Because our main focus is on valuing the operations of the firm, we rewrite this relation as follows:

$$V^{NOA} = V^{CSE} + V^{NFL}$$

That is, the portion of the firm that is owned by the equity holders is V^{CSE}/V^{NOA} and the remainder of the value V^{NFL}/V^{NOA} are attributed to the debt holders. The equity owners expect a rate of return on capital of r_{Eq}, and the cost of the debt is r_D. It follows that the weighted average cost of the capital r_{WACC} that is provided for operations by the equity holders and the debt holders is

$$r_{WACC} = \left(r_{Eq} \times \frac{V^{Eq}}{V^{Oper}}\right) + \left(r_D \times \frac{V^{NFL}}{V^{Oper}}\right) \tag{9.1}$$

CHAPTER OUTLINE

Cost of Capital for Operations and Equity

Estimation of Cost of Operating Capital
- Sources of Risk
- Weighted Average Cost of Capital for Operations

Cost of Equity Capital
- Diversifiable and Non-Diversifiable Risk
- Estimation using Using the Capital Asset Pricing Model
- Multifactor Models

Cost of Debt Capital
- Estimation of Cost of Debt Capital

We discuss this relation and the use of this relation to calculate the rate, which we will use to discount the future expectations of free cash flow to obtain an estimate of the value of operations.

ESTIMATING THE COST OF CAPITAL

LO1: Explain the difference between the sources of risk and the process of estimation of risk.

Investors expect to recover two costs when they provide capital for use in the operations: the time value of money and the compensation for taking the risk of investing in the operating activities. The time value of money can be viewed as the foregone interest from investing in an instrument with future payoffs. The second cost is the investor's compensation for bearing the risk associated with the uncertainty of the future payoffs. These two components make up what we call the risk-adjusted discount rate. It is intuitive that the components of the risk-adjusted discount rate (foregone interest and compensation for risk) equal the return that investors require for investing in an asset. Hence, the risk-adjusted discount rate used in the valuation calculation is exactly equal to the investor's required rate of return or the cost of capital.

When we estimate the cost of capital, we generally rely on some assumptions. First, we assume that current interest rates are a good approximation for expected (future) interest rates. Second, we assume that the current risk of the operating activities is a good approximation of the expected operating risk. We can adjust these assumptions if we expect interest rates to change or a change in the riskiness of investing in the operations. For example, if the firm is entering into an acquisition that will result in a new line of business with a substantially different level of risk compared to current operating activities, we will, of course, adjust our expectation of the riskiness of future operations.

To clarify the relations among a company's cost of capital for operations, cost of debt capital, and cost of equity capital, we must understand the sources of underlying risk and the methods by which the cost of capital is estimated. The most common approach to estimating the cost of capital for operations is to first estimate the cost of debt capital and the cost of equity capital. We do this because debt holders and equity holders provide capital at their respective required rates of return, both being cognizant of the amount of capital provided by the other group (e.g., it the amount of debt increases, equity holders will require a higher rate of return).

Equity ownership is risky because it represents the risk of ownership of the operating activities, the risk of needing to satisfy the obligations to debt holders as they come due, and the tax savings from the interest tax shield. Therefore, the risk of the equity ownership arises from the risks inherent in the operating activities, the cost of debt, and the need to meet the debt obligations. Changes in the riskiness of the operations or cost of debt lead to changes in the riskiness of equity.

To understand this better, consider the cost of capital for operations for General Mills (GIS). The risk of the operating activities in the North America retail or Convenience stores and foodservice segments does not arise because the company has issued stock or because GIS had debt. Those segments are risky because of the operating activities in which they engage independent of whether they are funded by the equity owners of GIS or by borrowed funds. Each segment of the company has a level of risk, which depends on such things as how it is managed, the product market in which GIS competes, and other factors that are independent of the financial choices made by the management of GIS. Whether a particular operating segment is funded by debt or equity holders does not change the level of risk related to the segment and its activities.

Now, consider the cost of equity capital for GIS. The risk of investment in GIS stock is driven by the riskiness of the operating activities in which GIS engages as well as the level and cost of debt. The risk of equity investment in GIS increases with the level and cost of debt because debt holders have first claim on the free cash flows arising from the enterprise operations.

Within reasonable bounds, the riskiness of the operating activities (and therefore the weighted average cost of capital for operations) is not affected by the capital structure of the firm (i.e., the proportion of debt to equity). Nevertheless, as a practical matter, we estimate the weighted average cost of capital for operations from estimates of the cost of debt capital and cost of equity capital.[1] The notion behind this calculation is that equity investors have invested in the operations at their expected rate of return, fully aware of the amount and cost of debt and the riskiness of the operating activities; similarly, debt holders determine their expected rate of return fully aware of the extent of their claims on the assets of the firm. Thus, we calculate the weighted average of the rates at which the two groups of investors (i.e., equity and debt holders) are prepared to contribute capital after they have assessed the riskiness of the operations. That is, proxies for the expected rate of return on equity and the expected cost of debt are weighted to estimate the weighted average cost of capital for operations. **Exhibit 9.1** helps us visualize the relations among riskiness of the operating activities, riskiness of debt, and riskiness of equity investment.

EXHIBIT 9.1 Relations among Risk Elements

Inherent risk in the operations and debt are sources of equity risk,

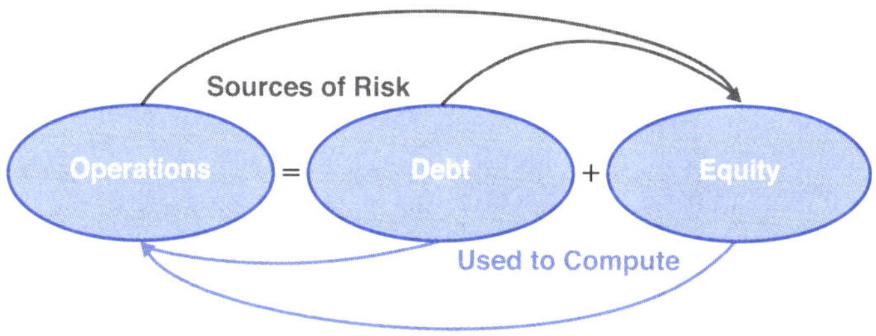

but debt and equity are used to estimate operating risk.

Exhibit 9.1 highlights that the formula in Equation 9.1 reflects how we compute cost of capital estimates. That is, we use the costs of equity and debt capital to calculate the weighted average cost of capital for operations. The sources of risk, as shown in **Exhibit 9.1**, would suggest thinking of the riskiness of equity as a function of the riskiness of the operations and the debt. Rearranging Equation 9.1 yields:

$$r_{Eq} = r_{WACC} + \frac{V^{NFL}}{V^{Eq}} \times (r_{WACC} - r_D)$$

That is, the riskiness of equity is equal to the riskiness of the operations (r_{WACC}) plus the spread ($r_{WACC} - r_D$) times the firm's leverage (V^{NFL}/V^{Eq}).

The relations shown in Exhibit 9.1 hold at any point in time. This also means that when an element (e.g., the riskiness of debt) changes, another element must also change. Understanding of these relations and how they change will drive our estimation of the different cost-of-capital elements.

Calculation of the Weighted Average Cost of Capital for Operations

The weighted average cost of capital for operations, r_{WACC}, is a weighted combination of the cost of equity and the costs of debt, where the weights are the value of equity and the value of debt:

[1] There is a point where further borrowings will subject the company to so much debt that it affects the ability to make payments to creditors in the normal course of business. This would affect the ability to acquire inventory, make payroll, and, in general, run the enterprise operations. We do not consider this situation in our discussion because most firms operate with moderate levels of debt.

$$r_{WACC} = \left(r_{Eq} \times \frac{V^{Eq}}{V^{Oper}} \right) + \left(r_D \times \frac{V^{NFL}}{V^{Oper}} \right) \tag{9.1}$$

Debt is usually the least risky of the three costs of capital because the debt holders' claims on the operating assets of the firm take precedence over the claims of the equity holders. The equity is usually the most risky because it represents two sources of risk: debt and operations. From Equation 9.1, because the weighted average cost of capital for operations is estimated from the cost of capital for debt and the cost of equity capital, it usually falls between the cost of capital for debt and equity. However, if the company is a net lender (*NFA* instead of *NFL*), the relations change. For net lenders, the enterprise operations are usually the most risky, the cost of debt capital is the lowest, and the cost of equity capital falls in between them. This situation may be viewed as the equity holder having two "investments," one in enterprise operations and one in financial assets.

We turn now to the estimation of the components of the weighted average cost of capital for operations; namely, the estimation of the cost of equity capital and the cost of debt capital as inputs to Equation 9.1.

DIVERSIFIABLE AND NON-DIVERSIFIABLE RISK

To explain our use of market data to estimate the cost of equity capital, we first introduce the idea of diversifiable and non-diversifiable risk. The models used to estimate the cost of equity capital assume that investors are only concerned with non-diversifiable risk and willing to accept diversifiable risk without compensation. Diversifiable risk refers to risks that can be diversified away by investors. Diversification is the practice of holding many assets (e.g., stocks and bonds) with different risk exposures in an investment portfolio.

How does diversification affect risk? To answer this question, suppose we invest in just one stock. Our return will depend entirely on the expected movement in the price of that stock. In contrast, if we invest in a number of stocks whose prices are not expected to move up and down with perfect synchronicity, the risk of our investment will be less than the risk of investment in any one of the constituent stocks; the price of some stocks will go up while the price of others will go down, so movement in the value of the portfolio will be less than the movement in the value of individual stocks. Simply put, diversification reflects the wisdom in the saying "Don't put all your eggs in one basket."

An important condition for diversification to reduce risk is that the returns of stocks in a portfolio must be expected to be somewhat independent. If the returns of stocks in our portfolio are correlated, meaning they tend to move in the same direction at the same time, then the effect of diversification on risk is reduced. To illustrate this concept, suppose we have two stocks in our portfolio: PepsiCo (PEP) and Coca-Cola (COKE). For these two stocks, there is the risk that some consumers switch from Coke to Pepsi, or vice versa. Because we hold both stocks, we are not bothered with this risk because the consumer is drinking one of our products. However, there is also the risk that consumers choose to reduce their consumption of sodas in favor of, say, Starbucks coffee. If this happens, then both PEP's and COKE's sales will suffer. Diversification by investing in these two stocks (instead of only one) does not shield us from risk of product substitution. In other words, some risk may be non-diversifiable given the pool of stocks.

Determining whether a particular risk is diversifiable or non-diversifiable is difficult. One way to proceed in this situation is to hold market portfolio, which is to hold all stocks available in the market. The underlying assumption is that, by doing this, we diversify away all the risks that are diversifiable. Hence, the remaining risk in a market portfolio is non-diversifiable. (Of course, holding the market portfolio does not diversify away the risks associated with holding stock as assets rather than some other class of assets, such as land, precious metals, foreign currencies, artwork, baseball cards, or memorabilia.)

By comparing the historical volatility of an individual stock to the historical volatility of the market portfolio, we can estimate the portion of risk that is non-diversifiable in each stock. This is the notion behind the *capital asset pricing model* (CAPM), which is often a core model used as the basis for estimation of the cost of equity capital.

ESTIMATING COST OF EQUITY CAPITAL USING THE CAPITAL ASSET PRICING MODEL

LO2: Estimate the cost of equity capital using the capital asset pricing model and the role of beta (β).

The CAPM expresses the expected return on a particular asset as the sum of three components—the risk-free rate of return, beta risk, and the stock-specific risk. The first two components are used in estimating the cost of equity capital. The third component, the stock-specific risk, is the risk that is diversified away in large portfolios. Thus, stock-specific risk is not included in the cost of equity capital because an investor should not expect to be compensated for risk that can be eliminated through diversification.

In equation form, the CAPM estimation of a company's expected return, or the cost of equity capital (r_{Eq}), is as follows:

$$r_{Eq} = r_{rf} + [\beta \times (r_{Mkt} - r_{rf})] \quad (9.2)$$

The first component of Equation 9.2 is the expected risk-free rate of return, r_{rf}. Due to their lack of default risk, the yields on U.S. Treasury securities are often used as an estimate of r_{rf}. Further, the existence of a yield curve (i.e., differences in the return based on time to maturity) must be considered. We are valuing equity that does not have a maturity, so a longer horizon would be appropriate. The return on long-term (say, 10-, 20-, or even 30-year) U.S. Treasury securities could be used as an estimate of r_{rf}. Some practitioners use rates from the highest-quality corporate bonds as their proxy. We will use monthly Treasury yield curve rates from 10-year constant maturity U.S. Treasury notes as our proxy for r_{rf}. Historically, r_{rf} has fluctuated around 4 to 5 percent, though, in recent years, historically low interest rates have been observed.

The second component of Equation 9.2 is the product of the market risk premium ($r_{Mkt} - r_{rf}$) and the sensitivity (β) of the asset's market return to the overall market return. The market risk premium is the difference between the expected market return (r_{Mkt}) and the expected risk-free rate (r_{rf}). The overall market return, while dependent on the time period, has generally fluctuated between 8 and 13 percent. These figures yield a usual market risk premium of about 5 to 8 percent.[2]

The sensitivity of the firm's market return to the overall market is referred to as the company's market beta (β). Market beta reflects a company's historical stock price volatility relative to the overall market volatility. Market beta is commonly estimated from a regression of the difference between the company's stock returns and the risk-free rate of return (the dependent variable) regressed on the difference between the market index of returns and the risk-free rate of return (the independent variable) over a recent period for which data is available (often, the previous 60 months).[3] The market index of returns represents returns from a portfolio of risky assets; an example of a market index is the S&P 500.

Market beta reflects the risk that cannot be completely diversified away by investing in a portfolio of risky assets (accordingly called systematic risk). In this CAPM framework, the market has a beta of 1.0. (Another way to think of this is that if we had a portfolio consisting of all available stock market assets, the value of our portfolio would, of course, move perfectly with the value of all available stock market assets.) A market beta greater than (less than) 1.0 indicates the company's stock price will change by a larger (smaller) percent with a change in the overall market. For example, in Appendix A, we calculate an estimated beta of 0.643 for GIS, indicating that, if the market index moves by, say, 1 percent up or down, GIS' stock price will be expected to change by 0.643 percent in the same direction.

---

[2] For readings on this topic, see Fama, E.F., and K. R. French, "The Cross-Section of Expected Stock Returns," *Journal of Finance* (June 1992), pp. 427–465; Gebhardt, W., C. Lee, and B. Swaminathan, "Towards an Ex Ante Cost of Capital," *Journal of Accounting Research* (June 2001), pp. 135–176; Claus, J., and J. Thomas, "Equity Premia as Low as Three Percent? Evidence from Analysts' Earnings Forecasts for Domestic and International Stock Markets," *Journal of Finance* (October 2001), pp. 1629–1666; and Easton, P., G. Taylor, P. Shroff, and T. Sougiannis, "Using Forecasts of Earnings to Simultaneously Estimate Growth and the Rate of Return on Equity Investments," *Journal of Accounting Research* (June 2002), pp. 657–676.

[3] Some suggest the use of weekly returns over the last 24 months rather than monthly returns over the last 60 months. While more recent data would be expected to be more predictive, the trade-off is the higher volatility observed in weekly returns as compared to monthly returns. Remember that both sets of data are proxies being used in the process of attempting to forecast expected equity returns.

Appendix A walks through the step-by-step application of the CAPM to GIS. We estimate that an equity investor requires a return of approximately 6.4 percent when investing in GIS' stock. Stated differently, the cost of equity capital for investment in GIS' stock is 6.4 percent. Alternatively, we could have researched a proxy for the risk-free rate, looked at a website to find a β estimate, and made an assumption about the market premium. Similar to the cautions in the last chapter, remember to consider the effect of our assumptions when utilizing the estimates in our valuation process. By altering our assumptions, we can alter our estimate of the cost of equity capital. The process for considering the sensitivity to our estimates is discussed in Chapter 13.

Note that the assumptions made regarding the market risk premium are very important and highly subjective. The assumed market premium of 6.0 percent is our best guess. Our estimated cost of equity capital will change at a rate based on the beta estimate as we alter this assumption. That is, had we assumed a 7.0 percent market risk premium, we would have increased our estimate of the cost of equity capital by 0.643 percent.

Many different values for the expected risk-free rate and market risk premium can be argued and/or supported. A recent study by Green, Hand, and Zhang (*Review of Accounting Studies*, June 2016) found 55 analysts' reports from 2012 and 2013 that detailed their assumptions. The range of expected risk-free rates was 0.2 to 5.0 percent, and the range of market risk premiums was 4.0 to 11.0 percent! These wide-ranging assumptions would obviously greatly impact both our cost of capital estimates and our subsequent valuation. From this discussion, it is clear that estimating a cost of equity capital is a very inexact process. Still, this is the state-of-the-art approach widely used in practice. As a result, we will examine the sensitivity of our value estimates to the cost of capital used in its calculation, a vital task, in Chapter 13.

MARKET BETA

Numerous financial service firms and investor websites provide estimates of a company's market beta. As shown in Appendix A, betas are commonly estimated as the slope coefficient from a linear regression of the difference between the firm's stock returns and the risk-free rate of return (the dependent variable) on the difference between the market index of returns and the risk-free rate of return (the independent variable) over a recent period for which data is available. Of course, these regression-based estimates of beta are just estimates; beta is inevitably measured with error. In addition, these betas are backward looking estimates because they are based on past data, but they are used for decisions about the future. A key assumption in the use of these estimates is that the equity risk does not change substantially. Because beta is estimated from historical information, it likely fails to account for any business changes or industry shifts that alter a company's future risk. Financial service websites can report a wide range of beta estimates. These differences arise due to choices involving the time period for estimation, the frequency of measurement of historical returns (e.g., monthly, weekly, daily) used in the estimation, and the market index, which is used in the estimation. Also, some websites make adjustments to reflect perceptions of the differences between the past and future expectations (Bloomberg, for example, "shrinks" its historical beta toward 1 as follows: adjusted beta equals 2/3 times estimated historic beta plus 1/3). In April 2019, a sampling of several beta estimates from commercial websites found beta estimates for Advanced Auto Parts (AAP) ranging from 0.60 at finance.yahoo.com to 1.29 at etrade.com. Using these differing beta estimates can lead to very different estimates of the cost of equity capital and very different valuations. Changing the assumed beta for AAP from 1.29 to 0.60 in a valuation similar to what we are doing for GIS more than doubles the estimated value per share! Understanding the beta estimate, its source, and the assumptions upon which it is based is, obviously, critical.

Estimating the Cost of Equity Capital Using a Multifactor Model

Given the limitations with the CAPM, researchers have developed other models to compute risk-adjusted returns. These so-called multifactor models share the following basic form:

$$r_{Eq} = r_{rf} + [\beta_1 \times r_1 + \beta_2 \times r_2 + \beta_3 \times r_3 + \ldots]$$

The r_j represents the premium of risk factor j, and β_j captures the sensitivity of the stock to factor j, where j = 1, 2, 3, . . . The CAPM can be viewed as a special case with only one factor: the market risk premium.

In moving to a multifactor model, researchers have attempted to identify the risk factors beyond the market risk premium that should be included. Many of these research studies rely on large-sample data analysis to identify characteristics that vary with, not necessarily cause, differences in cost of capital. For instance, researchers have found that stocks with a high book-to-market ratio (defined as the book value divided by the market value of equity) tend to have higher subsequent stock returns, on average, compared with stocks with a low book-to-market ratio. This result seems to indicate that companies with a high book-to-market ratio are regarded by investors as being more risky, and the excess return simply reflects the compensation for such risk. Other risk factors identified based on similar large-sample analysis are the size of the company and the liquidity of its stock.

Identifying risk factors based on large-sample analysis has a shortcoming: We do not know the reason why such factors matter. Why are small companies more risky than large companies? To answer this question, researchers have tried to identify risk factors based on fundamental analysis. Such risk factors can be classified as follows:

- *Internal:* These include operating leverage, financial leverage, effectiveness of internal control, the management team, and so forth.
- *External:* These include exchange risk, political risk, supply chain risk, industry competition, and so forth.

Research on identifying and measuring risk factors is ongoing. Those factors can be viewed as part of understanding the broader five forces that confront the company and its industry discussed in Chapter 1.

CAPM AND COST OF CAPITAL

A strength of the CAPM is its simplicity. It assumes that the only priced risk factor is the market return (and the effect of this risk factor is referred to as β). When we implement the CAPM, as a practical matter, we assume that the estimate of β for the immediate past is a suitable estimate for future risk. However, these estimates of β may vary considerably over time and are sensitive to the particular model inputs chosen. For example, in **Exhibit 9.2**, ycharts.com provides GIS' beta over the last few years.

EXHIBIT 9.2

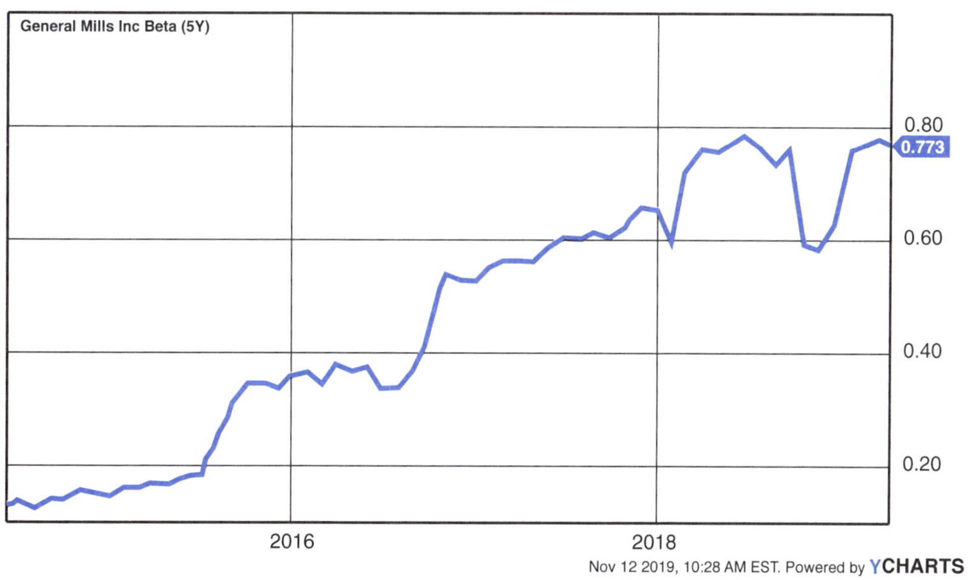

continued

continued from previous page

The estimate of β is clearly not stationary—even when estimated using a consistent set of assumptions! Additionally, in theory, the CAPM is applied using a market index representing all available investments. Using a stock-based index, such as the S&P 500, neglects other investment opportunities. Further, the CAPM attempts to measure covariance with the risk premium of the market, which is arguably time varying, with recent estimates ranging from 2 to 7 percent versus the 5 to 8 percent historical numbers. The CAPM relies on one risk factor and ignores additional risk factors, such as company size. Some argue that inclusion of additional risk factors yields a better cost of capital estimate.

Despite these issues, the CAPM or a multifactor model still is our theoretically-based best option for estimating the cost of equity capital. Remember that our cost of equity capital assumptions will influence our estimate and, therefore, we must carefully consider the sensitivity of our valuation estimates to the inputs and assumptions used.

COST OF DEBT CAPITAL

LO3: Determine an estimate of the cost of debt capital by examining different proxies.

The market interest rate on the debt instruments of a firm is the cost of debt capital. Information that allows for estimation of the cost of debt capital is usually reported in financial statements or can be computed using the stated coupon (interest) rate on the debt instruments along with the fair value of the debt instruments that is either recorded on the balance sheet or disclosed in its footnotes. The reported fair value of the debt instruments normally approximates present (market) value.

A company's borrowing rate depends on its perceived level of risk in the eyes of the lenders. Usual factors considered by lenders include short-term liquidity measures, such as the quick ratio and interest-coverage ratio, and long-term financial stability or solvency measures, such as the debt-to-equity ratio. Several companies, including Moody's Investors Service, Standard and Poor's (S&P), and Fitch, provide rating services for bonds and notes. For instance, those organizations classify debt issuances into the categories shown in **Exhibit 9.3**.

EXHIBIT 9.3 Debt Categories Used by Rating Services

Moody's	S&P	Fitch	Description
Aaa	AAA	AAA	Prime Maximum Safety
Aa1 Aa2 Aa3	AA+ AA AA–	AA+ AA AA–	High Grade, High Quality
A1 A2 A3	A+ A A–	A+ A A–	Upper-Medium Grade
Baa1 Baa2 Baa3	BBB+ BBB BBB–	BBB+ BBB BBB–	Lower-Medium Grade
Ba1 Ba2 Ba3	BB+ BB BB–	BB+ BB BB–	Non-Investment Grade Speculative
B1 B2 B3	B+ B B–	B+ B B–	Highly Speculative
Caa1 Caa2 Caa3	CCC+ CCC CCC–	CCC	Substantial Risk In Poor Standing
Ca			Extremely Speculative
C			May Be in Default
	  D	DDD DD D	Default

The top category is AAA, meaning the bond is very unlikely to experience a default. Bonds with a rating of BBB− (or Baa3) and higher are referred to as investment grade, meaning these bonds are of high quality. Bonds with a rating of BB+ (or Ba1) and lower are referred to as junk bonds, reflecting the higher default risk of those bonds.[4] The cost of debt capital is closely related to the debt rating assigned to a company.

Estimating the Cost of Debt Capital

To arrive at an estimate of the weighted average cost of capital for operations, we have estimated the cost of equity capital as a first step in implementing Equation 9.1. Now, we turn to estimating of the cost of debt capital, r_D. We are seeking an estimate of the cost of capital that a firm must pay on debt before considering the tax effects. Like the cost of capital for operations and the cost of capital for equity, this number is unobservable. Therefore, we must form an estimate. There are multiple methods for obtaining a proxy for the cost of debt capital.

Given our reformulation in Chapters 3 to 5, we can form a proxy for the cost of debt capital as the return on net financial liabilities before consideration of taxes, *RNFL* before tax, computed using *FEAT* and *NFL*:

$$r_D \approx \frac{RNFL}{1-0.21} = \frac{(FEAT)/(1-0.21)}{avg(NFL)}$$

A subtle, but important, issue in this first proxy is where in the process outlined in prior chapters we draw the information for the estimation. For example, our first pass reformulation in Chapter 3 showed a May 27, 2018, *NFL* for GIS of $16,861.9 million, but our calculation after incorporating additional information and adjusting for accounting issues in Chapters 4 and 5 showed an *NFL* of $18,725.9 million on that date. A review of the primary differences (recognition of pension obligation, capitalization of operating lease obligations, and recording of share-based compensation overhang) would lead us to believe that the financial expenses related to the $16,861.9 million of debt reported on the balance sheet would be more representative of the company's borrowing costs than the expenses related to the adjusted *NFL*.

By gathering this information on *FEAT* and *NFL* before the additional information and adjustments (shown in **Exhibit 9.4**), we can examine the trend of this proxy for GIS' borrowing costs over time.

EXHIBIT 9.4 GIS' Annual Borrowing Costs

	5/29/2016	5/28/2017	5/27/2018
FEAT (from Exhibit 3.4)	436.2	(98.4)	80.5
Beginning *NFL*	10,366.4	9,221.0	10,296.5
Ending *NFL* (from Exhibit 3.2)	9,221.0	10,296.5	16,861.9
RNFL	4.45%	−1.01%	0.59%
r_D proxy [*RNFL*/(1 − 0.21)]	6.85%	−1.55%	0.84%

This suggests an assumption of a cost of debt capital of around 0.84 percent would be reasonable at the current time. However, review of the two prior years indicates that this proxy is not stable and may not be our best choice as a cost of debt capital. Further note that, because *FEAT* included the effects of taxes, the tax adjustment to this number was necessary. The contrast to other methods of estimating the cost of debt capital where an adjustment for taxes is not necessary will become apparent shortly.

An alternative proxy estimate of the cost of debt capital is

$$r_D \approx \text{Pretax borrowing rate for debt}$$

[4] Differences in the borrowing rates of high-grade and low-grade bonds are referred to as "credit spreads." In eras of "easy money," credit spreads are low, meaning that investors do not demand much of a risk premium for lending to high-risk entities. In 2007, a sudden shift in investors' appetite for risk led to a marked increase in credit spreads and caused substantial "dislocations" in the market for certain types of high-risk debt.

This estimate of the cost of debt capital requires identification of the pretax (weighted average) borrowing rate for interest-bearing debt. This can be estimated using information available from the most recent financial statement footnotes.

The pretax borrowing rate (also called the average borrowing rate) for interest-bearing debt, including both short- and long-term debt, may be computed as follows:

$$\text{Pretax borrowing rate} = \text{Interest expense/avg(Amount of interest-bearing debt)}$$

We suggest using the unadjusted numbers in this computation just as we did in the first proxy estimated. While it would make sense to include debt from capitalized operating leases and the adjustment to interest from any such capitalized leases, potential estimation error related to the adjustment brings into question whether there is incremental value to using the adjusted numbers. Further, any additional borrowings by the company have a higher likelihood of being similar to the debt shown on the balance sheet than the items we would add from the additional information or adjustments.

BEWARE OF INTEREST CAPITALIZATION

When calculating the pretax borrowing rate, we want the amount of interest cost related to the interest-bearing debt. One subtlety to the accounting is that any capitalized interest must be included in the calculation. When a company is constructing a long-term operating asset, there are interest charges incurred that are related to the construction expenditures. (We borrow money to be able to build the asset and have related interest costs.) These charges are required to be capitalized into the cost of the asset being constructed. That is, a portion of the interest charges may be added to an asset account rather than shown as interest expense on the income statement.

When a company has capitalized interest, the pretax borrowing rate should be estimated as follows:

$$\text{Pretax borrowing rate} = \frac{\text{Interest expense} + \text{Capitalized interest}}{\text{avg(Amount of interest-bearing debt)}}$$

The existence of capitalized interest can often be determined by searching "interest capitalized" or "capitalized interest" in the Form 10-K. For GIS, in note 17 we find that for the year ended May 2018 that they had capitalized interest of $4.1 million. This amount is omitted because it is not material to the calculation of the pretax borrowing rate.

To illustrate this approximation of GIS' cost of debt capital based on pretax borrowing rate, GIS had beginning and ending interest-bearing debt, *Debt due within one year* plus *Long-term debt*, of $9,481.7 and $15,818.6 million, respectively. Utilizing this information with its unadjusted interest expense for the year ended May 2018 of $389.5 million implies a pretax borrowing rate of 3.08 percent. The biggest difference in this proxy for cost of debt capital from the prior estimate is the elimination of the effects of financial assets.

EVALUATING THE COST OF DEBT CAPITAL

When we reformulated the balance sheet in Chapters 3 to 5, we did not focus on the distinction of current versus noncurrent. The ability to meet short-term obligations is often labeled liquidity. Will the company be able to pay the payroll next week? Will it be able to make timely payments for the inventory just acquired? Particularly in times of rapid growth, having sufficient liquidity can become critical for a company. Normally, we would not expect the shorter-term enterprise operations to directly impact the cost of debt capital, but having to borrow to cover these needs may cause an upward shift in the company's cost of debt capital.

The ability to meet long-term obligations is often labeled solvency. Will there be enough cash on hand when the company's bank loans become due or bond maturities occur? Generally, lenders are able to receive additional information beyond the financial statements to allow for a more informed evaluation of solvency. As a result, these solvency risks should be reflected in the rates at which creditors are lending to the company, provided they are able to understand the company's situation.

The company's liquidity and solvency should be considered when evaluating the cost of debt capital estimate. Estimates based on prior results such as *RNFL* may not be appropriate to use as future expectations if the company's risk level is expected to differ going forward.

One more proxy for the cost of debt capital for GIS can be formed based on calculating a weighted average interest rate on long-term debt. To do so, we use the information disclosed in the footnotes about debt outstanding. Using GIS' May 2018 footnotes, we compute this rate to be 3.61 percent. This rate is an alternative to the pretax borrowing rate.

We now have seen three potential proxies for GIS' cost of debt capital estimated as 0.84, 3.08, and 3.61 percent. Evaluation of these proxies to determine the cost of debt capital to utilize in Equation 9.1 includes both consideration of stability over time and their reasonableness. If a particular proxy is fluctuating wildly from year to year, it is probably not a good candidate. Additionally, an estimate that is negative or very near zero clearly would also not be a good candidate. If we think of the risk-free rate as the minimum required return for a debtholder, then estimates below that level should not be used. After reviewing the three proxies for cost of debt capital, it is noteworthy that the middle proxy slightly exceeds the assumed risk-free rate from Treasury bills of 2.52 at May 1, 2019. This is not particularly surprising because GIS is a low-risk borrower (AA rating by Morningstar, indicating "Very Low Default Risk"). Thus, we will choose to assume a cost of debt capital of 3.10, which is justified by the combination of the three estimates of the cost of debt.

Now that we have estimated the cost of equity and debt capital, we can utilize these estimates to estimate the weighted average cost of capital for operations.

COMPUTING THE WEIGHTED AVERAGE COST OF CAPITAL FOR OPERATIONS

LO4: Combine the estimated cost of equity capital and debt capital to arrive at the weighted average cost of capital for operations.

Recall that the weighted average cost of capital is the weighted average of the rate of return expected by the equity holders and the cost of the debt, where the weights are the portion of the value of the operations attributable to the equity holders and the portion attributable to the debt holders. Now that we have computed the cost of equity and debt capital for GIS, we need estimates of the value of equity and the value of debt. We use the market value of equity in lieu of the intrinsic value of equity. The market value of GIS' equity is $30,445.7 million, computed from its May 1, 2019, stock price of $51.31 (per finance.yahoo.com) times its 593,367,848 common shares outstanding.[5]

For computing the value of debt, we need to move from the book value (i.e., *NFL*, which we have computed) to the market value of the debt. If there is a difference between the book value and the market value of debt, companies must disclose the amount by which the fair value of debt differs from its book value in the footnotes. According to GIS' footnotes, at May 27, 2018, the market value of its long-term debt is approximately $14,169.7 million as compared to the book value of $14,268.8 million. This implies a downward adjustment to our computed *NFL* of $18,725.9 million, yielding an estimated fair value of *NFL* of $18,626.8 million ($18,725.9 – $99.1). It is important to note that we must consider a further adjustment in the calculation of value of debt. The ability to deduct interest expense arising from debt creates a tax savings. This is a benefit to the equity holders; remember that we are valuing the firm from their viewpoint. Hence, we must also adjust for the value of the interest tax shield.

The estimation of the value of the interest tax shield is a little trickier because it is not directly disclosed or observable. A common assumption is that the value of the interest tax shield can be computed as pretax interest expense times the tax rate divided by the cost of debt capital. Following this assumption, our estimate of the value of GIS' interest tax shield based on net interest expense of $373.7 million, an assumed future tax rate of 21 percent, and the estimated cost of debt capital of 3.10 percent is:

$$
\begin{aligned}
V^{ITS} &= \frac{ITS}{r_D} \\
&= \frac{\$373.7 \times 0.21}{0.031} \\
&= \$2,531.5
\end{aligned}
$$

[5] The computation of the weighted average cost of capital should be based on intrinsic values (true economic values). However, because intrinsic values are unobservable, we typically use the market value of equity in place of the intrinsic value of equity, and we use the fair value of debt in lieu of the market value of debt. A reiterative estimation of the weighted average cost of capital is possible where, after estimating the value of the debt, interest tax shield, and equity, we then plug those estimates back into Equation 9.1. This yields a revised estimate of the weighted average cost of capital, which can then provide revised estimates of the value of the equity. In most cases, this quickly converges and the weighted average cost of capital stabilizes.

This calculation treats the interest expense as a perpetuity implying that debt levels will be unchanged in the future. Alternative assumptions would, of course, yield different estimates of the value of the interest tax shield.[6]

Taken together, this implies that the value of GIS' net debt (*NFL*) is \$18,626.8 – \$2,531.5 = \$16,095.3, and the intrinsic value of the enterprise operations is the sum of the value of equity and the value of debt (i.e., \$30,445.7 + \$16,095.3 = \$46,541.0). Using this information, we compute GIS' weighted average cost of capital using as follows:

$$r_{WACC} = \left(r_D \times \frac{V^{NFL}}{V^{Oper}}\right) + \left(r_{Eq} \times \frac{V^{Eq}}{V^{Oper}}\right)$$

$$= \left(3.1\% \times \frac{16{,}095.3}{46{,}541.0}\right) + \left(6.4\% \times \frac{30{,}445.7}{46{,}541.0}\right)$$

$$= 5.3\% \text{ (Rounded to the nearest } 0.1\%)$$

VALUING DEBT IN THE COMPUTATION OF THE COST OF CAPITAL FOR OPERATIONS

We have used our calculated value of *NFL* as the value of debt in implementing Equation 9.1. This reflected a refined reformulation separating assets and liabilities into operating and financial activities as well as the adjustments made to the financial statements. The assumption that the book value and the market value of the *NFL* are the same is common and usually reasonable. We have also assumed, prior to our calculations in the following chapters, that the market is properly valuing equity and we can therefore add the value of the debt to the value of equity and subtract the estimated value of the interest tax shield to arrive at an estimated value for enterprise operations.

It should be noted that most financial websites and analyses take a simplified approach rather than going through the steps in Chapters 3 to 5 to calculate *NFL*. Capital IQ, Yahoo's source for data, follows the common process of adding "debt" to the market capitalization of the equity (share price times number of shares outstanding) to arrive at operating value. By examining their description of operating value, we ascertain their approach to computing *NFL*. Capital IQ discloses, "Enterprise (operating) value may be calculated by adding the market value of the company's stock, the balance sheet values of the company's debt, preferred stock and minority equity interests, and then subtracting the amount of cash equivalents that a company has."[7] This means *NFL* is defined by Capital IQ as follows:

NFL = Debt + Preferred stock + Minority interest – Cash equivalents

This clearly is a very simplified reformulation without consideration of additional information or adjustments to the accounting.

As a result of this calculation, the simplifications will alter the calculation of cost of operating capital because it is assumed that debt is reported at market value and the interest tax shield is ignored. Additionally, failing to include the liability related to the stock-based compensation overhang will understate *NFL* and therefore result in a lower weight on the cost of debt capital. The result will be an upwardly biased estimate of the cost of operating capital due to the omission of some "debt."

Given the inherent reliance on so many assumptions in calculating the cost of operating capital, it may seem that this is not a big deal. We should, however, take care to arrive at the best estimate possible rather than cut corners by using a simplified calculation of *NFL*.

When the company has preferred stock, the weighted average cost of capital computation in Equation 9.1 can be expanded to include a third term:

$$r_{WACC} = \left(r_D \times \frac{V^{NFL}}{V^{Oper}}\right) + \left(r_{Eq} \times \frac{V^{Eq}}{V^{Oper}}\right) + \left(r_{PEq} \times \frac{V^{PEq}}{V^{Oper}}\right)$$

[6] As a result of the recent tax reform, starting in 2018, a company can only deduct interest expense of up to 30 percent of its earnings before interest, taxes, depreciation, and amortization. Any amount in interest expense beyond this threshold will no longer be deductible. This will tighten further in 2022, when the deductibility of interest will be capped at 30 percent of earnings before interest and taxes. Most affected will be highly indebted companies that may choose to alter their capital structure as a result of this change. While this will alter the value of the interest tax shield and potentially result in changes in the capital structure, the riskiness of the operations will be unchanged.

[7] Your Guide to S&P Capital IQ™ Stock Reports found at http://www.spcapitaliq.com/stockreportguide/ (2015, p. 9).

This formulation recognizes a separation of equity into common equity and preferred equity. The r_{PEq} is the cost of preferred equity capital, which is usually the dividend payout rate on the preferred stock. The V^{PEq} is the market value of the preferred stock—or book value if market value is difficult to determine. GIS does not have preferred stock, so the weighted average cost of capital is not adjusted for preferred stock.

A final point related to estimating weighted average cost of capital for operations is the treatment of operating leases and stock-based compensation. Similar to preferred stock, adding terms for the financing effects related to these items to the computation of r_{WACC} might be considered if we were using information that had not been adjusted to include these items, as detailed in Chapter 5.

BUT MY ESIMATES DO NOT SEEM TO MAKE SENSE!

When estimating the costs of capital for debt, equity, and operations, it is not uncommon to find information that does not seem to make sense. For example, you may have calculated an implied cost of financial liabilities before tax of 35.99 percent or a cost of equity capital of 1.1 percent. Additionally, you may find that your computed beta differs greatly from that observed on Bloomberg or other financial websites even after verifying every step you have taken. Rather than focusing on mechanically following the steps outlined in this chapter, you need to consider the appropriateness of the information at each step.

As stated earlier, the cost of debt capital generally should be at or above the risk-free rate. The maximum for a cost of debt capital is hard to quantify, but consideration of current yields on junk bonds seems a reasonable approximation. Consider, based on your understanding of the business, how risky loaning money to the company would be.

When evaluating the cost of equity capital, you could examine either the individual inputs, such as beta, the risk-free rate, and the market premium, or you could look at the resulting cost of equity capital estimate. The cost of equity capital estimate also should be greater than the risk-free rate (of course!) and consistent with the risks underlying the industry in which the company operates. Comparisons to other companies in the industry that would likely have similar risk levels may be in order.

If the costs of debt and equity capital seem reasonable, the only remaining factors affecting the cost of operating capital calculation are the estimates of the values of the debt and equity and the effect of the interest tax shield on the value of net debt. For equity, when a company is publicly traded, the value is readily available. Estimation of the value of equity when the company is not publicly traded is extremely hard. After all, our exercise throughout this text is actually to compute this value. It must be noted that this problem exists in all valuations and not just those outlined in this book. (Our methods just happen to shine a light on this issue!)

In the end, it is imperative to always consider the appropriateness of both our assumptions and the estimates they generate. There is no easy answer or quick fix when the numbers do not seem to make sense. All that we can do is attempt to determine the likely source of the issue and consider alternative assumptions or methodologies.

Within Chapter 13, we will revisit cost of capital in the discussion of sensitivity analysis. This will be important as the estimate of 5.3 percent for the weighted average cost of capital still remains just that, an estimate. As you consider the assumptions made to arrive at the weighted average cost of capital, a change at any point would alter the estimate. Using a different proxy for the risk-free rate, assuming a higher or lower market premium, and utilizing a different tax rate in our calculations are just a few examples of things that could alter our estimate. One source of potential change often overlooked is in the choice of beta. Remember that, even when estimating beta directly, as demonstrated in Appendix A to this chapter, as well as when taking an estimate from another source, it is at best an estimate. As a result, a large range of possible values of cost of capital may be justifiable.

SUMMARY

Our goal in this chapter was to establish an understanding of the discount rates that will be used in valuation in the next few chapters. The differences between and relations among the weighted average cost of capital for operations, the cost of equity capital, and the cost of debt capital were discussed. We saw that while the cost of debt capital and cost of equity capital are used to estimate the weighted average cost of capital, they are not the sources of risk for the operating activities. Rather, the risk related to an equity investment arises from operating activities and borrowing (or lending). We also demonstrated the computation of the cost of capital measures and then applied the process to provide our estimate of the cost of capital for GIS.

The next three chapters will introduce the cash-flow-based and accounting-based valuation models and their relations. The calculations in these models will utilize the estimate we found of 5.3 percent for GIS' weighted average cost of capital. Chapter 13 will then discuss directly the issues related to estimating the value of equity and address some loose ends related to dates in estimating value and the process of sensitivity analysis.

APPENDIX 9A: Estimating the Cost of Equity Capital

The estimation of the cost of equity capital using the capital asset pricing model (CAPM) requires a series of steps, which this appendix will illustrate in detail. We will discuss the estimation using GIS as our company of interest, noting that we are seeking an estimate of the cost of capital to be applied to a valuation as at May 1, 2019. For each step, we will detail the information gathered from each source, tools used to estimate, and results obtained. In equation form, the CAPM estimation of the expected return on equity investment, or the cost of equity capital (r_{Eq}), is as follows:

$$r_{Eq} = r_{rf} + [\beta \times (r_{Mkt} - r_{rf})] \tag{9.2}$$

We will first discuss the sources of the information used for r_{Eq}, r_{rf} and r_{Mkt}.

When estimating the cost of equity capital, we use the most recently available observations of rates of return. We demonstrate estimation with 60 months of past returns, but the analyses could be done with other sets of observations (e.g., Bloomberg often uses the past 103 weeks). If 60 months of observations are not available, we may choose to use weekly rates of return or rely on a smaller number of observations.

To obtain equity returns, we can access a website such as finance.yahoo.com that has historical prices. If we start at the Yahoo! Finance home page and request a quote for GIS, we have an option to view historical prices. From the historical prices page, we can request the most recent 60 months of prices, as shown in **Exhibit 9A.1**.

EXHIBIT 9A.1

Time Period: May 14, 2014 - May 14, 2019 ⌄ Show: Historical Prices ⌄ Frequency: Monthly ⌄ **Apply**

The resulting information will contain a link labeled "Download to Spreadsheet" at the top of the output. By clicking on this, we can transfer this information to Excel in spreadsheet format. The first few rows of the spreadsheet we obtain are shown in **Exhibit 9A.2**.

These data provide the prices of GIS' stock at the end of the first trading day of each month. We desire the rate of return for each month. To calculate 60 months of data, we need 61 price points. This allows us to convert the prices to monthly rates of return. Note that, in doing so, we will utilize the "Adj Close" amount in column F rather than the "Close" price in column E because this properly accounts for the dividend payments and stock splits. We compute the rate of return for the month ending June 1, 2014 (the first of our 60 months), as the Adj Close price at June 1, 2014, divided by the Adj Close price at May 1, 2014, less one (i.e., 43.824/45.818 − 1 = −0.0435. This means that, for the month of May 2014, the rate of return for GIS (r_{GIS}) was −4.35 percent. We repeat this calculation for each month to obtain 60 months of r_{GIS}, as shown in **Exhibit 9A.3**.

Similarly, we can obtain a monthly risk-free rate of return, r_{rf}. Arguments can be made for differing potential investments (often debt of varying maturity periods) being used to proxy for a risk-free rate. Some might argue that a very short investment period, such as a 90-day Treasury bill, is essentially risk free. Others might argue for a 30-year Treasury note because the estimated risk-free rate will be applied to the infinite horizon, and short-term rates sometimes differ from long-term expectations. (Use of a longer-term rate is essentially done in lieu of explicit recognition of the yield curve.) Perhaps, as a compromise, the 10-year Treasury note is often used as the proxy for the risk-free rate.

EXHIBIT 9A.2

	A	B	C	D	E	F	G
1	Date	Open	High	Low	Close	Adj Close	Volume
2	5/1/2014	53.220001	54.98	52.450001	54.93	45.818027	45191200
3	6/1/2014	54.869999	55.639999	51.5	52.540001	43.824486	65052400
4	7/1/2014	52.18	53.650002	50.139999	50.150002	41.830944	59323200
5	8/1/2014	50.279999	53.650002	50.240002	53.380001	44.869511	48356700
6	9/1/2014	53.400002	53.84	49.860001	50.450001	42.406651	74338500
7	10/1/2014	49.709999	52	48.32	51.959999	43.675915	65511600
8	11/1/2014	52	53.439999	50.43	52.75	44.705231	52778500
9	12/1/2014	52.529999	54.610001	51.080002	53.330002	45.196774	66498300
10	1/1/2015	53.099998	55.59	51.900002	52.48	44.476402	71590200
11	2/1/2015	52.650002	53.84	51.900002	53.790001	45.941223	51179600
12	3/1/2015	53.610001	57.25	51.43	56.599998	48.341183	77233400
13	4/1/2015	56.389999	57.73	55.110001	55.34	47.265041	53201200
14	5/1/2015	55.509998	57.25	54.939999	56.150002	48.336098	38866200
15	6/1/2015	56.32	57.060001	54.139999	55.720001	47.965935	58554300

EXHIBIT 9A.3

	A	B	C	D	E	F	G	H
1	Date	Open	High	Low	Close	Adj Close	Volume	r_{GIS}
2	5/1/2014	53.220001	54.98	52.450001	54.93	45.818027	45191200	
3	6/1/2014	54.869999	55.639999	51.5	52.540001	43.824486	65052400	−0.04350997
4	7/1/2014	52.18	53.650002	50.139999	50.150002	41.830944	59323200	−0.045489227
5	8/1/2014	50.279999	53.650002	50.240002	53.380001	44.869511	48356700	0.072639217
6	9/1/2014	53.400002	53.84	49.860001	50.450001	42.406651	74338500	−0.054889388
7	10/1/2014	49.709999	52	48.32	51.959999	43.675915	65511600	0.029930777
8	11/1/2014	52	53.439999	50.43	52.75	44.705231	52778500	0.023567131
9	12/1/2014	52.529999	54.610001	51.080002	53.330002	45.196774	66498300	0.010995201
10	1/1/2015	53.099998	55.59	51.900002	52.48	44.476402	71590200	−0.015938571
11	2/1/2015	52.650002	53.84	51.900002	53.790001	45.941223	51179600	0.032934791
12	3/1/2015	53.610001	57.25	51.43	56.599998	48.341183	77233400	0.052239793
13	4/1/2015	56.389999	57.73	55.110001	55.34	47.265041	53201200	−0.022261391
14	5/1/2015	55.509998	57.25	54.939999	56.150002	48.336098	38866200	0.022660659
15	6/1/2015	56.32	57.060001	54.139999	55.720001	47.965935	58554300	−0.007658107

Starting again at finance.yahoo.com to gather our data on the risk-free rate of return, we can get a quote for CBOE Interest Rate 10-Year T-No (^TNX). This is an index of the current yields for the 10-year Treasury notes. The monthly historical prices (yields) can be requested in the same manner that was used to gather GIS' prices, as shown in **Exhibit 9A.1**. Again, we can go to the top of the data and choose the option "Download to Spreadsheet." Be aware that the Adj Close reported in Column F of **Exhibit 9A.4** is an interest rate or yield, not the realized rate of return or price. It is the current expected rate of return for owning the Treasury notes for a 10-year period. However, we do not want to use this amount as the risk-free rate of return for the month. We want the holding period return related to a particular month; this return is due to the change in the price of the note. This change in the price of the note will be caused by the change in the expected rate of return during the month.

EXHIBIT 9A.4

	A	B	C	D	E	F	G
1	Date	Open	High	Low	Close	Adj Close	Volume
2	5/1/2014	2.66	2.7	2.402	2.457	2.457	0
3	6/1/2014	2.5	2.659	2.487	2.516	2.516	0
4	7/1/2014	2.55	2.692	2.448	2.556	2.556	0
5	8/1/2014	2.582	2.591	2.3	2.343	2.343	0
6	9/1/2014	2.393	2.642	2.382	2.508	2.508	0
7	10/1/2014	2.475	2.484	1.868	2.335	2.335	0
8	11/1/2014	2.325	2.407	2.194	2.194	2.194	0
9	12/1/2014	2.157	2.331	2.045	2.17	2.17	0
10	1/1/2015	2.197	2.213	1.651	1.675	1.675	0
11	2/1/2015	1.674	2.152	1.654	2.002	2.002	0
12	3/1/2015	2.014	2.259	1.852	1.934	1.934	0
13	4/1/2015	1.892	2.11	1.843	2.046	2.046	0
14	5/1/2015	2.067	2.335	2.058	2.095	2.095	0
15	6/1/2015	2.125	2.489	2.106	2.335	2.335	0

To compute the holding-period return for the Treasury note, we need to first determine the price at which the note would be trading given the current yield. To do this, we calculate the price of a 10-year $1,000 (assumed) note given the current yield. This calculation can be performed for May 1, 2014, in Excel as [=–PV(E2/100,10,0,1000)], yielding $784.48. When repeated in each month, we get the series of prices shown in **Exhibit 9A.5**. Then, using these prices, we again compute the rate of return for the month of May 2014 as the price at June 1, 2014, divided by the price at May 1, 2014, less one (i.e., 779.98/784.48 – 1= –0.00574). This means that, during May 2014, this proxy for the risk-free rate had a rate of return (r_{rf}) of –0.574 percent. We repeat this calculation for each month to obtain 60 months of r_{rf}, as shown in column I of **Exhibit 9A.5**.

The final piece of required data is a proxy for the rate of return on the market. Theoretically, the market rate of return should be the rate of return from holding all possible investments. This would include international equities, land, baseball cards, gold, and any other possible investment. Clearly, there is not an index that provides a measure of this return. Often, an index of large stocks is used to approximate this rate of return because they represent very liquid investments for which we feel the market has good information. Many financial websites report that the S&P 500 is what they choose to use as their market proxy. An interesting issue arises in estimating the cost of equity capital for GIS in that the company is one of those 500 stocks! Ideally, we would like an index of the other 499 companies, but, given the small influence of a single company on the index, this issue is generally ignored.

Similar to the gathering of the GIS and 10-year Treasury note rate of return data, we gather the historical prices for the S&P 500 (^GSPC). Again, we can go to the top of the data request and choose "Download to Spreadsheet." We then compute the rate of return for the month of May 2014 as the price of the index at June 1, 2014, divided by the price of the index at May 1, 2014, less one (i.e., 1960.23/1923.57 – 1 = 0.01906). This means that, during May 2014, this proxy for the market rate of return (r_{Mkt}) was 1.906 percent. We repeat this calculation for each month to obtain 60 months of r_{Mkt}, as shown in **Exhibit 9A.6**.

EXHIBIT 9A.5

	A	B	C	D	E	F	G	H	I
1	Date	Open	High	Low	Close	Adj Close	Volume	Price	r_{rf}
2	5/1/2014	2.66	2.7	2.402	2.457	2.457	0	$784.48	
3	6/1/2014	2.5	2.659	2.487	2.516	2.516	0	$779.98	−0.005740317
4	7/1/2014	2.55	2.692	2.448	2.556	2.556	0	$776.94	−0.00389347
5	8/1/2014	2.582	2.591	2.3	2.343	2.343	0	$793.27	0.021008372
6	9/1/2014	2.393	2.642	2.382	2.508	2.508	0	$780.59	−0.015980213
7	10/1/2014	2.475	2.484	1.868	2.335	2.335	0	$793.89	0.017034448
8	11/1/2014	2.325	2.407	2.194	2.194	2.194	0	$804.91	0.013883268
9	12/1/2014	2.157	2.331	2.045	2.17	2.17	0	$806.80	0.002351511
10	1/1/2015	2.197	2.213	1.651	1.675	1.675	0	$846.95	0.049765082
11	2/1/2015	1.674	2.152	1.654	2.002	2.002	0	$820.19	−0.031599649
12	3/1/2015	2.014	2.259	1.852	1.934	1.934	0	$825.68	0.006691045
13	4/1/2015	1.892	2.11	1.843	2.046	2.046	0	$816.66	−0.010921394
14	5/1/2015	2.067	2.335	2.058	2.095	2.095	0	$812.75	−0.004789099
15	6/1/2015	2.125	2.489	2.106	2.335	2.335	0	$793.89	−0.023206422

EXHIBIT 9A.6

	A	B	C	D	E	F	G	H
1	Date	Open	High	Low	Close	Adj Close	Volume	r_{Mkt}
2	5/1/2014	1884.39	1924.03	1859.79	1923.57	1923.57	6.36E+10	
3	6/1/2014	1923.87	1968.17	1915.98	1960.23	1960.23	6.33E+10	0.019058332
4	7/1/2014	1962.29	1991.39	1930.67	1930.67	1930.67	6.65E+10	−0.015079831
5	8/1/2014	1929.8	2005.04	1904.78	2003.37	2003.37	5.81E+10	0.037655295
6	9/1/2014	2004.07	2019.26	1964.04	1972.29	1972.29	6.67E+10	−0.015513837
7	10/1/2014	1971.44	2018.19	1820.66	2018.05	2018.05	9.37E+10	0.023201461
8	11/1/2014	2108.64	2075.76	2001.01	2067.56	2067.56	6.36E+10	0.024533589
9	12/1/2014	2065.78	2093.55	1972.56	2058.9	2058.9	8.07E+10	−0.004188588
10	1/1/2015	2058.9	2072.36	1988.12	1994.99	1994.99	7.73E+10	−0.031040806
11	2/1/2015	1996.67	2119.59	1980.9	2104.5	2104.5	6.88E+10	0.054892511
12	3/1/2015	2105.23	2117.52	2039.69	2067.89	2067.89	7.67E+10	−0.017396107
13	4/1/2015	2067.63	2125.92	2048.38	2085.51	2085.51	7.21E+10	0.00852082
14	5/1/2015	2087.38	2134.72	2067.93	2107.39	2107.39	6.52E+10	0.010491382
15	6/1/2015	2108.64	2129.87	2056.32	2063.11	2063.11	7.32E+10	−0.021011672

Now that we have gathered the 60 monthly rates of return for the variables contained in Equation 9.2, we can estimate β. To obtain a statistical estimate of β, we rewrite the equation to highlight the relation between the excess return on our stock (i.e., the premium for investment in GIS vis-à-vis in the risk-free asset) as compared to the excess return on the market (i.e., the premium for investing in the market vis-à-vis the risk-free rate) as follows:

$$(r_{Eq} - r_{rf}) = \beta \times (r_{Mkt} - r_{rf}) \quad (9A.1)$$

These premiums arise due to the risk of GIS and the risk of the market. The estimate of β captures the relation between these two premiums.

The actual estimation of β is accomplished using a regression of these two excess returns. The data we will use is shown in **Exhibit 9A.7**. The sixty observations of premiums contained in columns F and G are the inputs to our estimation. The estimation can easily be computed using Excel add-ins called Analysis ToolPak and Analysis ToolPak—VBA. When these add-ins are installed, choose Data Analysis from the Data menu, and then choose Regression. Then, we use the data we have gathered on excess returns shown in columns F and G of **Exhibit 9A.7** as the Y and X variables, respectively, for the regression shown in **Exhibit 9A.8**. This will create a new worksheet (page) in Excel that contains the regression output shown in **Exhibit 9A.9**.

Our estimate of β, 0.643181324 (rounded to 0.643), is shown in cell B18 of the output. We also learn from the output that the 95 percent confidence interval for β is from 0.372 to 0.915, as shown in cells F18 and G18, respectively. This means our best estimate of β is 0.643, but there is estimation error, and we are 95 percent confident the true value of β lies between 0.372 and 0.915. Often, a calculated β estimate or one from a website is used in the computations as though it has no measurement error and can be relied upon with confidence. The width of the confidence interval for GIS implies a 3.26 percent range of cost of equity capital if we were to assume a 6.0 percent estimate of $r_{Mkt} - r_{rf}$ calculated as ([0.915 – 0.372] × 6.0% = 3.26%).[8] By computing the β and observing the related confidence interval, we are reminded that this is an estimate. Further, had we used a different proxy for the risk-free or market rate of return, we would have obtained a different estimate of β. Additional factors that could have altered our estimate of β are the use of weekly rates of returns or less than 60 observations. In short, we must always remember that β is an estimate. It may be worth checking the reasonableness of the estimated β against estimates of β shown by other sources, such as Bloomberg or financial websites.

EXHIBIT 9A.7

	A	B	C	D	E	F	G
1	Date	r_{GIS}	r_{rf}	r_{Mkt}		$r_{GIS} - r_{rf}$	$r_{Mkt} - r_{rf}$
2	Jun-14	(0.04351)	(0.00574)	0.01906		(0.03777)	0.02480
3	Jul-14	(0.04549)	(0.00389)	(0.01508)		(0.04160)	(0.01119)
4	Aug-14	0.07264	0.02101	0.03766		0.05163	0.01665
5	Sep-14	(0.05489)	(0.01598)	(0.01551)		(0.03891)	0.00047
6	Oct-14	0.02993	0.01703	0.02320		0.01290	0.00617
7	Nov-14	0.02357	0.01388	0.02453		0.00968	0.01065
8	Dec-14	0.01100	0.00235	(0.00419)		0.00864	(0.00654)
9	Jan-15	(0.01594)	0.04977	(0.03104)		(0.06570)	(0.08081)
10	Feb-15	0.03293	(0.03160)	0.05489		0.06453	0.08649
11	Mar-15	0.05224	0.00669	(0.01740)		0.04555	(0.02409)
12	Apr-15	(0.02226)	(0.01092)	0.00852		(0.01134)	0.01944
13	May-14	0.02266	(0.00479)	0.01049		0.02745	0.01528
14	Jun-14	(0.00766)	(0.02321)	(0.02101)		0.01555	0.00219
15	Jul-15	0.04469	0.01279	0.01974		0.03190	0.00695

[8] The assumed market premium is discussed both within the chapter and below.

EXHIBIT 9A.8

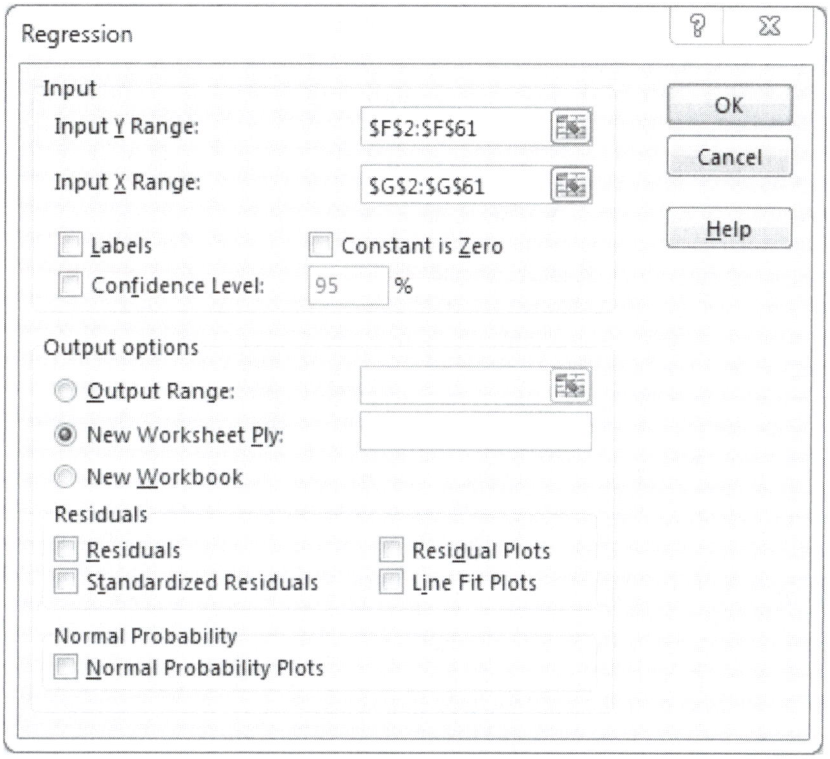

EXHIBIT 9A.9

	A	B	C	D	E	F	G
1	SUMMARY OUTPUT						
2							
3	*Regression Statistics*						
4	Multiple R	0.528534769					
5	R Square	0.279349002					
6	Adjusted R Square	0.266923985					
7	Standard Error	0.044864713					
8	Observations	60					
9							
10	ANOVA						
11		*df*	*SS*	*MS*	*F*	*Significance F*	
12	Regression	1	0.045254307	0.045254307	22.48278592	1.41991E-05	
13	Residual	58	0.116744864	0.002012842			
14	Total	59	0.16199917				
15	alpha	beta					
16		*Coefficients*	*Standard Error*	*t Stat*	*P-value*	*Lower 95%*	*Upper 95%*
17	Intercept	−0.00185737	0.005846691	−0.31767953	0.751868945	−0.013560797	0.009846049
18	X Variable 1	0.643181324	0.135646428	4.74160162	1.41991E-05	0.371655497	0.914707152

One other item to address regarding the output in **Exhibit 9A.9** is the estimate of the intercept contained in cell B17. This is the average monthly rate of return not captured by the relation between the excess return on GIS and the excess return on the market; that is, GIS' rate of return not captured by β. This is referred to as an alpha return (α). Some investors specifically seek out stocks with positive estimates of α believing there is a return available that is not related to risk. We must ask ourselves whether we believe the CAPM appropriately captures risk and α should be zero whether we have missed something. Note that if we feel that α picks up a return not related to risk, this monthly amount shown in the regression output (since monthly data was used in our computation) would need to be annualized when estimating our cost of equity capital. For GIS, the monthly estimate of α of –0.00185737 would equate to an annualized return of –2.206 percent (i.e., $[1 + -0.00185737]^{12} - 1 = -0.02206$). As we feel that the CAPM is an appropriate model to use in estimating the cost of equity capital for GIS, we do not include an α return in our calculation. Also, note that the t-statistic of –0.3177 in cell D17 indicates that the estimate of α is not significantly different from zero.

As an alternative shortcut to the calculation of β, we can forgo the regression and estimate β directly:

$$\beta = \frac{\text{cov}[(r_{GIS} - r_{rf}) \times (r_{Mkt} - r_{rf})]}{\text{var}(r_{Mkt} - r_{rf})}$$

Given the data shown in **Exhibit 9A.6**, this can be calculated in Excel using the command: =SLOPE(F2:F61,G2:G61). The downside to this direct computation approach is that we do not observe the intercept estimate or the confidence intervals. Thus, we may fall into the trap of ignoring the step of considering whether the alpha returns will recur and also may have overconfidence in our estimate of β. Note that this formula for β, which is the formula for the slope coefficient for a simple regression of the GIS premium on the market premium, informs us of the meaning of β; β is the estimate of the co-movement of the stock return with the movement in the market return. If, for example, the estimate of β is 0.8, on average, a 1 percent movement in market prices is expected to be associated with a 0.8 percent movement in the price of the stock.

Now that we have obtained an estimate of β, we can utilize it to form an estimate of the cost of equity capital. To do so, we return to **Equation 9.2**. Calculation of the expected cost of equity capital for GIS requires not just the β, but also the expected risk-free and expected market rates of return. We could utilize the recent yield on the 10-year Treasury note for April 2019 of 3.65 percent shown farther down in column G of **Exhibit 9A.4** as our proxy for the expected risk-free rate of return. While that value may seem appropriate, the prior month's estimate of –0.92 percent would not have been appropriate. We could also average the return over the last 12 months and get an estimate of 0.57 percent. Quickly, we find that we are seeking a number that looks like what we want. Of course, this is always a danger. In the end, we choose the daily market yield on Treasury securities at 10-year constant maturity, per the Federal Reserve on May 1, 2019, drawn from the Federal Reserve website of 2.52 percent as a proxy for r_{rf}.

Rather than forming an expectation of the market rate of return directly, often, we choose to estimate the excess return on the market ($r_{Mkt} - r_{rf}$), which is referred to as the market premium. To get a sense of the historical market premium, finance.yahoo.com has data available to calculate $r_{Mkt} - r_{rf}$ going back to 1962. If we calculate the monthly market premium over the 688 months from January 1962 to April 2019, the average monthly premium is 0.005555191 percent. We can annualize the historical average market premium by compounding as follows:

$$\begin{aligned}\text{Average annual market premium} &= (1 + 0.005555191)^{12} - 1 \\ &= 0.0687\end{aligned}$$

Using our proxies for the risk-free and market rate of return, it would appear that an expected market premium of 6.87 percent would be justifiable based on historical data. If only the last 60 months of realized market premium were used, we would obtain an average annual market premium of 7.29 percent and, for only the last 24 months, the average is 7.35 percent. Here again, we see that the data we use can alter our estimate of the cost of capital. Based on the historical market premiums calculated using the S&P500 and 10-year Treasury notes, we will assume an expected market premium of 6.0 percent going forward.

The computation of an expected cost of equity capital utilizing **Equation 9.2** is as follows:

$$\begin{aligned}r_{Eq} &= r_{rf} + [\beta \times (r_{Mkt} - r_{rf})] \\ &= 2.52\% + 0.643 \times 6.0\% \\ &= 6.378\%\end{aligned} \tag{9.2}$$

The estimate of the cost of equity capital for GIS is rounded to 6.40%, which could now be used within the process outlined in this chapter to estimate the cost of operating capital (r_{WACC}).

Before concluding this tutorial, we offer a couple cautions. The first is that practitioners must become comfortable with expected values on the components of the computation to ensure reasonableness of estimates throughout the process. To illustrate, mathematically, it is possible to calculate a negative β from the regression process shown above. However, assuming a negative β going forward would not make economic sense. We must be aware that, at times, the historical observations may not be predictive of future expectations. Thus, we suggest consulting a website or two to see how similar their estimates of β are to what you obtain.

Similarly, and second, when choosing proxies for r_{Mkt} and r_{rf}, remember that there are many options. A choice to use a different-term Treasury security rather than 10 years would change our estimate. Likewise, using the Russell 2000 instead of the S&P500 would also affect our estimates. And the time period examined can influence our estimates as well. At the end of the day, what we arrive at are exactly what we call them, estimates! Despite these limitations, this appendix provides a useful method and walkthrough of the techniques for estimating cost of equity capital.

QUESTIONS

Q9.1 Which of the following are sources of risk?

a. Enterprise operations

b. Financial borrowings

c. Equity of the firm

Q9.2 Why is the cost of capital related to operations referred to as the weighted average cost of capital? Is this name accurate?

Q9.3 Why must investors be compensated for non-diversifiable risk but not diversifiable risk?

Q9.4 How is the cost of equity capital commonly estimated?

Q9.5 Why would a debt rating from a company such as Standard and Poor's be useful in determining a company's weighted average cost of capital?

Q9.6 What are the three ways for estimating the cost of debt capital?

Q9.7 For the weighted average cost of operating capital (r_{WACC}), how is the interest tax shield calculated?

Q9.8 For calculating the weighted average cost of operating capital (r_{WACC}), what adjustments to net debt (*NFL*) are needed?

Q9.9 Is market beta (β) a reliable metric?

Q9.10 For an unlevered firm, how does a firm's cost of equity capital differ from its cost of capital for operations?

EXERCISES

E9.11 Per ycharts.com, the estimates of beta for **Del Taco** (TACO) and **Chipotle** (CMG) at December 1, 2019, were 0.21 and 0.70, respectively. What does this imply about the riskiness of the equity of these firms?

E9.12 Per ycharts.com, the following is a graphic of beta for **Marriott** (MAR) for the 10 years from 2010 to 2019.

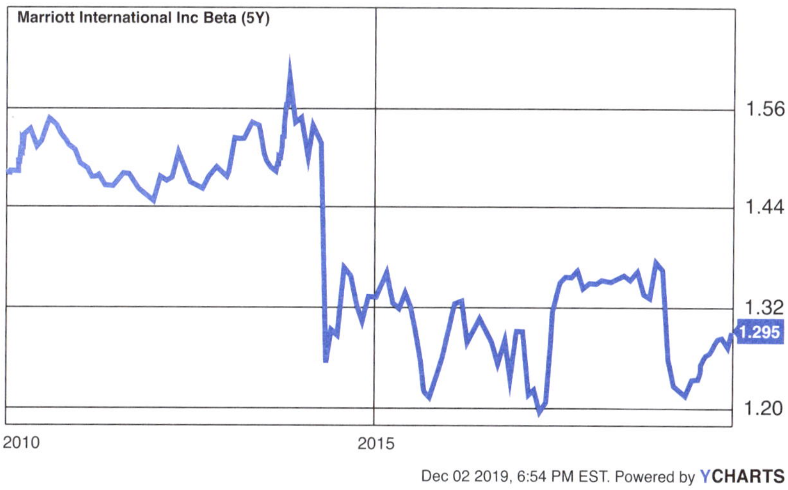

What are the potential implications of this information on our estimation of cost of capital for MAR in particular and other companies in general?

E9.13 Cintas (CTAS), a leading provider of corporate rental uniforms, has significant borrowings and debt. Use the information in CTAS' debt footnote disclosure to estimate its pretax borrowing cost at May 31, 2019.

7. Debt and Derivatives

Cintas' debt is summarized as follows at May 31:

(In thousands)	Interest Rate	Fiscal Year Issued	Fiscal Year Maturity	2019	2018
Debt due within one year					
Commercial paper	2.68%[1]	2019	2020	$ 112,500	$ —
Term loan	3.06%[1]	2019	2020	200,000	—
Debt issuance costs				(236)	—
Total debt due within one year				$ 312,264	$ —
Debt due after one year					
Senior notes	4.30%	2012	2022	$ 250,000	$ 250,000
Senior notes	2.90%	2017	2022	650,000	650,000
Senior notes	3.25%	2013	2023	300,000	300,000
Senior notes[2]	2.78%	2013	2023	51,684	52,119
Senior notes[3]	3.11%	2015	2025	51,973	52,309
Senior notes	3.70%	2017	2027	1,000,000	1,000,000
Senior notes	6.15%	2007	2037	250,000	250,000
Debt issuance costs				(16,150)	(19,119)
Total debt due after one year				$2,537,507	$2,535,309

(1) Variable rate debt instrument. The rate presented is the variable borrowing rate at May 31, 2019.

(2) Cintas assumed these senior notes with the acquisition of G&K in the fourth quarter of fiscal 2017, and they were recorded at fair value. The interest rate shown above is the effective interest rate. The principal amount of these notes is $50.0 million with a stated interest rate of 3.73%.

(3) Cintas assumed these senior notes with the acquisition of G&K in the fourth quarter of fiscal 2017, and they were recorded at fair value. The interest rate shown above is the effective interest rate. The principal amount of these notes is $50.0 million with a stated interest rate of 3.88%.

E9.14 Beresford Corporation, a fast-growing company, has a market beta of 1.25. The expected market return is estimated to be 7.45 percent, and the long-term U.S. Treasury is at 2.75 percent. Calculate Beresford Corporation's cost of equity capital using the capital asset pricing model (CAPM).

E9.15 Use the methodology described in Appendix A and the data below to calculate the 24-month market beta for Salesforce.com (CRM), a provider of customer relationship management software, at May 1, 2019.

Date	CRM Adj Close	10-Yr T-Bond Close	S&P 500 Close
5/1/2017	89.64	2.196	2,411.80
6/1/2017	86.60	2.302	2,423.41
7/1/2017	90.80	2.292	2,470.30
8/1/2017	95.49	2.121	2,471.65
9/1/2017	93.42	2.326	2,519.36
10/1/2017	102.34	2.376	2,575.26
11/1/2017	104.32	2.417	2,584.84
12/1/2017	102.23	2.405	2,673.61
1/1/2018	113.91	2.720	2,823.81
2/1/2018	116.25	2.868	2,713.83
3/1/2018	116.30	2.741	2,640.87
4/1/2018	120.99	2.936	2,648.05
5/1/2018	129.33	2.822	2,705.27

Date	CRM Adj Close	10-Yr T-Bond Close	S&P 500 Close
6/1/2018	136.40	2.849	2,718.37
7/1/2018	137.15	2.964	2,816.29
8/1/2018	152.68	2.853	2,901.52
9/1/2018	159.03	3.056	2,913.98
10/1/2018	137.24	3.159	2,711.74
11/1/2018	142.76	3.013	2,760.17
12/1/2018	136.97	2.686	2,506.85
1/1/2019	151.97	2.635	2,704.10
2/1/2019	163.65	2.711	2,784.49
3/1/2019	158.37	2.414	2,834.40
4/1/2019	165.35	2.509	2,945.83
5/1/2019	151.41	2.142	2,752.06

E9.16 Calculate the cost of capital for operations (r_{WACC}) for Palmrose Inc. The footnotes to Palmrose's financial statements report the long-term debt approximates fair value.

U.S. government long-term bond rate	2.75%
Market risk premium.	5.50%
Equity beta	1.30
Per-share market price.	$100.00
Shares outstanding.	12.5 million
Average long-term debt on balance sheet . . .	$949.0 million
Interest expense.	33.1 million
Statutory tax rate	21.0%

E9.17 Calculate the cost of capital for operations (r_{WACC}) for the Briloff Companies. The Briloff financial statement footnotes report the long-term debt's carry value is $15 million below fair value.

U.S. government long-term bond rate	2.50%
Market risk premium.	6.00%
Equity beta	0.85
Per-share market price.	$65.00
Shares outstanding.	50.0 million
Average *NFL* on balance sheet	$1,350.0 million
FEAT	42.7 million
Interest expense.	41.0 million
Statutory tax rate	21.0%

CONTINUING EXAMPLES

CE9.18 From Bloomberg, Kellogg (K) had an adjusted market beta of 0.699 at May 1, 2019. Find the estimate of the 10-year Treasury yield at that date, and then assume a market risk premium of 6 percent. Using this information, estimate the required cost of equity capital for K at May 1, 2019.

CE9.19 The text offers three approaches to estimating the cost of debt capital. Compute for K at May 1, 2019, the following three estimates, and indicate which might be used as a proxy for the cost of debt capital:

- Pretax *RNFL*
- Pretax borrowing rate for debt
- Weighted average interest rate on long-term debt

CE9.20 Using the methodology described in Appendix A, estimate the cost of equity capital for K as of May 1, 2019. How does this estimate compare to the one formed using the Bloomberg beta above?

CE9.21 Per Chapter 5, the book value of *NFL* for K is $10,348 at May 1, 2019. Additionally, Note 14 to the financials reports the carrying amount of K's long-term debt approximates fair value. Combine this information with the proxies for the cost of equity capital from question CE9.20 and cost of debt capital from question CE9.19 to form an estimate of K's weighted average cost of capital for operations at May 1, 2019.

CE9.22 From Bloomberg, Thor Industries (THO) had an adjusted market beta of 1.477 at May 1, 2019. Find the estimate of the 10-year Treasury yield at that date, and then assume a market risk premium of 6.0 percent. Using this information, estimate the required cost of equity capital for THO at May 1, 2019.

CE9.23 The text offers three approaches to estimating the cost of debt capital. Compute for THO at May 1, 2019, the following three estimates, and indicate which might be used as a proxy for the cost of debt capital:

- Pretax *RNFL*
- Pretax borrowing rate for debt
- Weighted average interest rate on long-term debt

CE9.24 Using the methodology described in Appendix A, estimate the cost of equity capital for THO as of May 1, 2019. How does this estimate compare to the one formed using the Bloomberg beta above?

CE9.25 Per Chapter 5, the book value of *NFL* for THO is $–122,681 at May 1, 2019 (i.e., THO is a net lender with net financial assets). Additionally, in Note 12 to the financials reports that the long-term debt approximate fair value.

Combine this information with the proxies for the cost of equity capital from question CE9.24 and cost of debt capital from question CE9.23 above to form an estimate of THO's weighted average cost of capital for operations at May 1, 2019.

CE9.26 From Bloomberg, Winnebago (WGO) had an adjusted market beta of 1.340 at May 1, 2019. Find the estimate of the 10-year Treasury yield at that date, and then assume a market risk premium of 6.0 percent. Using this information, estimate the required cost of equity capital for WGO at May 1, 2019.

CE9.27 The text offers three approaches to estimating the cost of debt capital. Compute for WGO at May 1, 2019, the following three estimates, and indicate which might be used as a proxy for the cost of debt capital:

- Pretax *RNFL*
- Pretax borrowing rate for debt
- Weighted average interest rate on long-term debt

CE9.28 Using the methodology described in Appendix A, estimate the cost of equity capital for WGO as of May 1, 2019. How does this estimate compare to the one formed using the Bloomberg beta above?

CE9.29 Per Chapter 5, the book value of *NFL* for WGO was $331,923 at August 25, 2018. Additionally, in Note 9 to the financials we find the book value of the debt approximates its fair value. Thus, our estimate of the fair value of the debt of WGO at August 25, 2018. This yields an estimated value for debt $331,923.

Combine this information with the proxies for the cost of equity capital from question CE9.28 and cost of debt capital from question CE9.27 above to form an estimate of WGO's weighted average cost of capital for operations at May 1, 2019.

Chapter Ten

Valuation Using Forecasts of Cash Flows

TAKEAWAYS

When you complete this chapter, you should be able to:

1. Utilize basic time value of money terminology and concepts in a valuation context.
2. Explain the model for valuation of either a finite-life project or a company's operations.
3. Implement free cash flow valuation using multiyear forecasts and continuing value assumptions.
4. Prepare a discounted cash flow valuation spreadsheet for a company's operations.

In this chapter, we introduce the free cash flow (*FCF*) valuation method by which value is estimated based on expected future cash flows from operations. This method is also referred to as the discounted cash flow (DCF) method or model. The notion behind cash flow-based valuation is that value represents the right to receive cash payoffs in the future. With other conditions remaining the same, investment A would, *ceteris paribus*, be more valuable than investment B if it is believed that investment A will provide more benefits (payoffs) in the future than investment B.

Using expected future payoffs (i.e., distributions to the investors) to compute value is very intuitive. But determining the amount, timing, and uncertainty of future payoffs may be very challenging. The care we put into forming our forecasts in Chapter 7 and ensuring we have realistic assumptions must be paired with a correct understanding and implementation of the model. Most often, the analyst community focuses on forecasting the firm's future earnings rather than cash payoffs because earnings are easier to forecast. Nevertheless, the financial statements are a key input to the forecasting process, as we have seen in earlier chapters.

PRACTICAL IMPLEMENTATION OF DCF IS NOT ALWAYS TEXTBOOK

In this model, we will show a process that ensures a calculation of value that is the most accurate possible given our efforts to forecast and estimate the cost of capital. Perhaps, surprisingly, practice does not always follow this route. Green, Hand, and Zhang (June 2016 *Review of Accounting Studies*, p. 598) report that "managing directors who oversee analysts indicated that, in their view, analysts often do not understand key aspects of how to correctly construct and execute a DCF and, at times, embrace economically implausible beliefs about risk-free interest rates or feasible long-run economic rates of return. . . . Analysts also confirmed to us that at times they knowingly diverge from a textbook-perfect approach, particularly with regard to their judgments about key DCF model parameters, in order to support a particular view of the firm they are reporting on." Knowing the proper implementation allows you to construct your own model and ensure proper implementation.

CHAPTER OUTLINE

Valuation Using Forecasts of Cash Flows

Time Value of Money
- Terminology and Concepts

Free Cash Flow Valuation
- Valuing a Finite-Life Project
- The Model (Formula)

Valuation of Operations
- Multiyear Forecasts
- Continuing Values
- Valuing General Mills' Operations

Accounting recognizes the notion that investors are seeking future payoffs and need information to help them project those payoffs. The Conceptual Framework for accounting issued by the Financial Accounting Standards Board states, "Potential users of financial information most directly concerned with a particular business enterprise are generally interested in its ability to generate favorable cash flows because their decisions relate to amounts, timing, and uncertainties of expected cash flows."[1]

It is true that one objective of accounting is to provide information that "may help those who desire to estimate the value of a business enterprise, but financial accounting is not designed to measure directly the value of an enterprise."[2] Stated a different way, *accounting will not tell you how much something is worth but rather provides information that may be very helpful in forming an estimate of value*. Thus, the Conceptual Framework continues by saying that "financial reporting should provide information to help investors, creditors, and others assess the amounts, timing, and uncertainty of prospective net cash inflows to the related enterprise."[3] In this chapter, we revisit the relation of accounting information and the cash flows (cash payoffs) shown in Chapter 2 because these cash flows will be used in discounted cash flow valuation. The next two chapters then introduce alternative valuation models where value is calculated directly from accounting information.

We begin by introducing the concepts behind cash flow-based valuation using an example of an investment in a savings account, and then we move to valuing a finite-life (i.e., limited duration) project. Examination of a finite-life project will provide clarity as to how the valuation model functions. Finally, we apply DCF (i.e., cash flow-based valuation) to General Mills' (GIS) operating activities to see the application to a large, visible, publicly-traded firm. Subsequent chapters follow a similar process as they explore accounting-based valuation models.

To introduce the terminology, concepts, and process of valuation, let us begin with examining a savings account.

VALUATION OF A SAVINGS ACCOUNT AND ILLUSTRATION OF THE CONCEPT OF TIME-VALUE OF MONEY

LO1: Utilize basic time value of money terminology and concepts in a valuation context.

If \$1,000.00 is put into a savings account that will earn 3 percent interest, a year later, \$1,030.00 is expected to be available for withdrawal. That \$1,030.00 represents the future payoff to this investment. The \$1,000.00 invested today is the cost to acquire this investment. The interest rate of 3 percent represents the rate of return on this investment. Of course, this investment has a low rate of return because a savings account has low risk. We can relate the values today and 1 year from today via the following formula, **Equation 10.1**:

$$\begin{gathered} V_0 \times (1+r) = V_1 \\ 1{,}000.00 \times (1+0.03) = 1{,}030.00 \end{gathered} \tag{10.1}$$

[1] SFAC 1: Paragraph 25.

[2] SFAC 1: Paragraph 41.

[3] SFAC 1: Paragraph 37.

V_0, the present value, is the \$1,000.00 invested today (at time zero), r is the rate of return that will be earned on the account, and V_1, the future value at time period one, is the \$1,030.00 that will be available 1 year from today (at time $t = 1$).

Rearranging the terms of Equation 10.1 to create Equation 10.2 allows us to see that today's value is equal to the expected future payoff discounted at the required rate of return:

$$V_0 = \frac{V_1}{1+r} \tag{10.2}$$

We can also rewrite Equation 10.1 to see that the rate of return on the savings account equals the change in value divided by the initial investment:[4]

$$\begin{aligned} V_0 \times (1+r) &= V_1 \\ V_0 + V_0 \times r &= V_1 \\ V_0 \times r &= V_1 - V_0 \\ r &= \frac{V_1 - V_0}{V_0} \end{aligned}$$

We can repeat the process for the subsequent year to see the results we would expect from the investment during year 2. Beginning with the balance at the end of year 1, we would expect the following:

$$\begin{aligned} V_1 \times (1+r) &= V_2 \\ 1{,}030.00 \times (1+0.03) &= 1{,}060.90 \end{aligned}$$

Rearranging the terms in the prior equation yields **Equation 10.3**:

$$V_1 = \frac{V_2}{(1+r)} \tag{10.3}$$

Altering the fact pattern to show a 2-year investment horizon, we can substitute Equation 10.3 into Equation 10.2 to see that the account would grow from \$1,000.00 today to \$1,030.00 at the end of 1 year and then to \$1,060.90 at the end of the 2 years. The formula shows that the value today equals the value at the end of the second year discounted back two periods:

$$\begin{aligned} V_0 &= \frac{V_1}{(1+r)} \\ &= \frac{V_2 / (1+r)}{(1+r)} \\ &= \frac{V_2}{(1+r)^2} \\ &= \frac{1{,}060.90}{(1+0.03)^2} \\ &= 1{,}000.00 \end{aligned}$$

[4] To ensure that terminology is not confused, note that "return" refers to a dollar amount (i.e., $V_1 - V_0$, or \$30), while r, the "rate of return," refers to a percentage [i.e., $(V_1 - V_0)/V_0$ or 3%].

Or more generally,

$$V_0 = \frac{V_T}{(1+r)^T} \tag{10.4}$$

This example illustrates the time value of money; the investor will be indifferent between the opportunity to invest \$1,000, in a savings account paying 3 percent per annum and a lump-sum payment of \$1,060.90 at the end of two years.

CASH FLOW-BASED VALUATION OF A FINITE-LIFE PROJECT

LO2: Explain the model for valuation of either a finite-life project or a company's operations.

Having introduced some terminology and the concept of time value of money, we now turn our attention to valuing a finite-life project. Here, we have an investment with a limited timeframe where the payoff over the entire life can be forecasted. Later, we will move to analysis of the operating activities of a public company; effectively, a public company is comprised of a series of projects where the timeframe is neither entirely observable nor amenable to explicit forecasts.

We have chosen to begin this discussion with cash flow-based valuation rather than accounting-based valuation for two reasons. First, the DCF valuation model is familiar to most people who have an interest in or prior exposure to finance and/or valuation. Second, the accounting-based valuation models that will be explored in subsequent chapters are readily derived from the DCF model. In the next two chapters, we show that the approach of "undoing" or "reversing-out" the accounting accruals to obtain an estimate of the *FCF* from forecasts of earnings, which is often taught in finance classes, is unnecessary. We also see that accounting-based valuation models, which do not require the forecast of cash flows, are based on accounting numbers, which may be taken at face value; accruals do not have to be separately forecasted and then reversed out.

Once we understand the formula used to compute the present value of a savings account (Equation 10.4), where V_0 is the present value, V_t is the future value or future cash flow at a given time *t*, and *r* is the rate of return, we can apply this same approach to valuing any future cash flow stream. By summing the present value of each future cash flow, we can arrive at the present value of a stream of cash flows (e.g., the cash flows from a finite-lived investment or a finite-lived project). This is possible because the value of an investment or project is based on all of the expected future payoffs. Specifically, we determine what we would be willing to pay to acquire the investment or project as the sum of the present values of all future payoffs.

Suppose you are offered the opportunity to invest in a project with the anticipated cash flows at the end of each year shown in **Exhibit 10.1**.

EXHIBIT 10.1 Anticipated Cash Flows of Finite-Life Project

Purchase price		\$1,000.00
Payoffs		
Year 1 cash flow (CF_1)		250.00
Year 2 cash flow (CF_2)		350.00
Year 3 cash flow (CF_3)		320.00
Year 4 cash flows (CF_4)		
Proceeds from sales	\$280.00	
Proceeds from disposition	200.00	
=		480.00
Required rate of return = r_P.		10%

To determine whether investment in this project is worthwhile, one would need to compute the sum of the present value of all the future cash flows and compare this to the purchase price. We can value this project using a four-period cash flow valuation equation as follows:

$$V_0 = \frac{CF_1}{(1+r_P)} + \frac{CF_2}{(1+r_P)^2} + \frac{CF_3}{(1+r_P)^3} + \frac{CF_4}{(1+r_P)^4} = \sum_{t=1}^{4}\left(\frac{CF_t}{(1+r_P)^t}\right) \quad (10.5)$$

V_0 is the intrinsic (or true economic) value of the project, CF_t is the cash flow from the project in period t, and r_P is the required rate of return on the project.[5] Recall that the intuition of the cash flow valuation model is that today's value is driven by the payoffs, which are expected in the future. It follows that the greater the payoffs in the future, the more value today. Further, if those payoffs occur sooner, they are more valuable because they are discounted less.

Substituting the expected cash flows for the project into the formula (10.5), we compute the following present value:

$$\begin{aligned} V_0 &= \frac{250.00}{(1+0.10)^1} + \frac{350.00}{(1+0.10)^2} + \frac{320.00}{(1+0.10)^3} + \frac{480.00}{(1+0.10)^4} \\ &= \frac{250.00}{1.1} + \frac{350.00}{1.21} + \frac{320.00}{1.331} + \frac{480.00}{1.4641} \\ &= 227.27 + 289.26 + 240.42 + 327.85 \\ &= 1{,}084.80 \end{aligned}$$

Then, if we subtract the purchase price, or $1,000, we obtain the net present value of $84.80.

We would conclude that this project is financially viable because the net present value is positive. On the purchase price of $1,000.00, we would expect to make an economic profit of $84.80. Stated in a different way, the investment decision would be to purchase the project at any price of up to $1,084.80 and forgo purchasing the project at any purchase price greater than that.

Shown in tabular format, **Exhibit 10.2** illustrates the valuation of the project using discounted cash flows.

EXHIBIT 10.2 Discounted Cash Flow Model Valuation of Finite-Life Project

	Required rate of return	10.0%				
	Time Period	**0**	**1**	**2**	**3**	**4**
	Net cash from sales		$250.00	$350.00	$320.00	$280.00
+	Proceeds from disposition					200.00
=	Total cash flows		$250.00	$350.00	$320.00	$480.00
÷	Discount factor $(1 + r_P)^t$		1.1	1.21	1.331	1.4641
=	Present value of cash flow		$227.27	$289.26	$240.42	$327.85
	Sum of present value of cash flows	$1,084.80				
=	Value of project	1,084.80				
−	Initial investment	1,000.00				
=	Net present value	$ 84.80				

Having computed the value of the project using forecasted cash flows, we have a benchmark set of analyses to use for comparison when we examine the accounting-based valuation models in upcoming chapters. We know that an alternative valuation model is "working" (and that we have no errors in our calculations) if it also yields a value of $1,084.80 for this project.

[5] This required rate of return for the project is often referred to as the cost of capital. Chapter 9 addressed the concepts behind and computation of cost of capital.

THE FREE CASH FLOW VALUATION MODEL

After purchasing the project discussed above, the project owner would expect to receive the cash flows. Note that the project does not retain any cash; instead, those funds are distributed to the owner of the project.

Similarly, the cash flows generated by the operations of a company (i.e., by the operating activities of the business) become available to either pay the debt holders or be distributed to equity holders who, jointly, are the providers of capital to the company.

Extending our simple project example, the equity investor in the project may decide to borrow money to invest in the project directly. If so, the benefits of ownership and the related cash flows from operations will be used to pay the debt holders as well as the equity investor. In other words, the *FCF*s generated by the project activities are used to pay the debt holders or distributed to equity holders. The most common valuation model computes value by summing the present value of these *FCF*s from the project (the operations) to the capital providers (i.e., the debt and equity holders).

The DCF valuation model as applied to the valuation of operating activities mirrors the process by which we calculated value for the project above. Instead of considering project cash flows, the model uses the cash generated by the operations that is available to either pay debt holders or be distributed to equity holders. Also, instead of a four-period model we assumed for our finite-life project, the firm is expected to be a going concern with a continuing stream of projects and, therefore, it potentially has an infinite stream of future cash flows. Essentially, the firm's operations can be viewed as the sum of all the projects the firm has undertaken or is expected to undertake.

Recognizing these differences between the valuation of a project and the valuation of enterprise operations, yields the following formula mirroring Equation 10.5:

$$\begin{aligned} V_0 &= \frac{FCF_1}{(1+r_{WACC})} + \frac{FCF_2}{(1+r_{WACC})^2} + \frac{FCF_3}{(1+r_{WACC})^3} + \frac{FCF_4}{(1+r_{WACC})^4} + \ldots \\ &= \sum_{t=1}^{\infty}\left(\frac{FCF_t}{(1+r_{WACC})^t}\right) \end{aligned} \tag{10.6}$$

FCF_t is the cash flow generated by the operations that is distributable to debt and equity holders (i.e., the free cash flow from operations at time t), and r_{WACC} is the required rate of return for the operations given its risk as was discussed in Chapter 9.

Valuation of the savings account, the project above, and GIS' operating activities all have the same conceptual underpinnings and can be computed using Equation 10.6.

FORECASTS OF FREE CASH FLOWS FROM OPERATIONS FOR GENERAL MILLS

LO3: Implement free cash flow valuation using multiyear forecasts and continuing value assumptions.

GIS' most recent fiscal year ended on May 27, 2018. In this example, years are fiscal years ending in May. By using GIS' 2018 income statement and balance sheet, after making adjustments in Chapter 5, we found the following information based on the current results:

Sales	$15,750.4
Net operating profit after tax (*NOPAT*)	$ 2,316.4
Net operating assets (*NOA*)	$25,035.4

Prior year (2017) sales for GIS were $15,619.8. As shown in Chapter 6, these results yield the following recent realizations for 2018 sales growth, 2018 profit margin (*PM*, the ratio of *NOPAT* to sales), and 2018 asset turnover (*ATO*, the ratio of sales to average *NOA*):

Sales growth rate	0.77%
Operating *PM*	14.72%
Operating *ATO*	0.751

While understanding what has occurred recently is important, valuation is based on expected future payoffs. Therefore, the motivation to understand what has occurred recently is to glean information from the financial statements and other sources that allows us to form expectations of (i.e., forecasts of) future payoffs.[6]

Forecasts of the stream of future *FCF* from operations may be forecasted directly or inferred from forecasts of the stream of future *NOPAT* and *NOA*. Direct forecasting of *FCF* is usually not done because it can be exceedingly challenging to determine the amount and timing of distributions that will be made to debt and equity holders in the future given that their timing is controlled by management and the cash needs of the continuing operations of the firm. Arriving at an expectation of future *NOPAT* and *NOA* can be more simply achieved by making assumptions regarding future sales growth, *PM*s, and *ATO* ratios. These assumptions allowed us to forecast future *NOPAT* and *NOA* for GIS as shown in Chapter 7.

FORECASTING CASH FLOWS

Forecasting cash flows directly is very challenging. As we saw in Chapter 7, it is much easier to consider sales, profitability (*PM*), and the required resources (*ATO*). From these, we can compute the implied cash flow forecasts. Nissim and Penman (RAST 2001, p. 123) emphasize that "one cannot imagine forecasting free cash flow without first forecasting profitability and the investment in [*NOA*] that drive free cash flow." Trying to determine the amount that the operations will be able to transfer to credit holders and equity holders is nearly impossible unless we directly address how those funds will be generated.

After reviewing GIS' financial statements and those of comparable firms over the years prior to and including 2018 in Chapter 7, we arrived at the assumptions for the foreseeable future shown in **Exhibit 10.3**:

EXHIBIT 10.3 GIS Multiyear Forecasts of Sales Growth, *PM*, and *ATO*

	5/26/2019	5/31/2020	5/30/2021	5/29/2022	5/28/2023	5/26/2024
Sales growth	9.43%	3.03%	−0.62%	1.30%	1.25%	1.20%
Operating *PM*	12.32%	12.32%	12.45%	12.62%	12.62%	12.62%
Operating *ATO*	0.688	0.678	0.665	0.651	0.651	0.651

These assumptions of sales growth, *PM*, and *ATO* are in line with results seen in recent years and appear to reflect reasonable expectations of future outcomes. Further information on the computations supporting these assumptions and the relation to current accounting information were discussed in Chapter 7.

Using the above inputs, we can forecast expectations of GIS' future sales, *NOPAT* and *NOA*. Forecasted sales for each year are the prior year sales multiplied by (one-plus) the expected sales growth rate, or 1.0943 for 2019 sales. *NOPAT* is computed using forecasted sales each year times the forecasted operating *PM*; *NOA* is computed using forecasted sales of the following year divided by the forecasted operating *ATO*. As a reminder, the 2019 *NOA* is the amount of forecasted resources necessary to support the 2020 Sales. Thus, 2019 *NOA* is computed as the 2020 sales

[6] As an example, the 2018 *PM* shown above of 14.72 percent is not considered predictive after looking at its components. This is confirmed by the 2017 and 2016 *PM*s, which were 12.25 and 11.20 percent, respectively. Further analysis found that, although the *PM* appears very unstable, the *PM* resulting directly from sales was higher at 11.30 to 15.68 percent during the last 3 years. This combined with information from competitors led to our assumption of 13.0 percent in Chapter 7 as a parsimonious forecast.

divided by the 2020 *ATO* forecast of 0.678. Forecasted numbers for 2019 through 2024 are shown in **Exhibit 10.4**.

EXHIBIT 10.4 GIS Multiyear Forecasts of Sales, *NOPAT*, and *NOA* ($ millions)

Year Ending	5/27/2018	5/26/2019	5/31/2020	5/30/2021	5/29/2022	5/28/2023	5/26/2024
Weeks in year. . .		52	53	52	52	52	52
Sales.	$15,740.4	$17,224.4 ($15,740.4 × 1.0943)	$17,746.9 ($17,224.4 × 1.0303)	$17,637.8 ($17,747.4 × 0.9938)	$17,867.1 ($17,638.4 × 1.0130)	$18,090.4 ($17,867.4 × 1.0125)	$18,307.5 ($18,090.4 × 1.0120)
NOPAT.		$2,122.0 ($17,224.4 × 12.32%)	$2,186.4 ($17,746.9 × 12.32%)	$2,195.9 ($17,637.8 × 12.45%)	$2,254.8 ($17,867.1 × 12.62%)	$2,283.0 ($18,090.4 × 12.62%)	$2,310.4 ($18,307.5 × 12.62%)
NOA	$25,035.4	$26,291.0 ($17,746.9/0.688) × 52/53	$25,998.1 ($17,637.8/0.678)	$26,854.2 ($17,867.1/0.665)	$27,786.8 ($18,090.4/0.651)	$28,120.3 ($18,307.5/0.651)	$28,457.7 ($18,527.2/0.651)

Note that the computation of *NOA* required at the end of May 2019 to support sales in 2020 includes an adjustment recognizing the 53 weeks in 2020. We explicitly consider that there will be an extra week of sales in 2020 and that additional assets are not necessarily required to support those sales. Thus, we are essentially forecasting based on an average of sales per week.

We can use these forecasts of *NOPAT* and *NOA* to obtain forecasts of *FCF* from operations, which is equal to *NOPAT* minus the change in *NOA*. Note that this is, in fact, the standard calculation seen in most valuation texts where change in *NOA* is broken into several main components, such as change in working capital (i.e., change in inventory, change in accounts receivable, and change in accounts payable), depreciation, and capital expenditure. The calculation of free cash flows would then be as shown in **Exhibit 10.5**.

EXHIBIT 10.5 GIS Multiyear Forecasts of *FCF* ($ millions)

Year ending	5/27/2018	5/26/2019	5/31/2020	5/30/2021	5/29/2022	5/28/2023	5/26/2024
Sales.	$15,740.4	$17,224.4	$17,746.9	$17,637.8	$17,867.1	$18,090.4	$18,307.5
NOPAT.		2,122.0	2,186.4	2,195.9	2,254.8	2,283.0	2,310.4
NOA	25,035.4	26,291.0	25,998.1	26,854.2	27,786.8	28,120.3	28,457.7
Δ*NOA*.		1,255.6	(292.9)	856.1	932.7	333.4	337.4
FCF (*NOPAT*–Δ*NOA*) . . .		866.5	2,479.3	1,339.8	1,322.2	1,949.6	1,973.0

While our analyses have provided forecasts of *FCF* from operations through 2024 (the sixth forecast period), the formula in Equation 10.6 requires expectations of all future cash flows (i.e., including years well beyond 2024). In other words, value arises from all future cash flows expected to be received. Obviously, trying to forecast an infinite stream is impossible whether we forecast *FCF* directly or we compute it indirectly from a stream of *NOPAT* and *NOA*.

We next modify the DCF valuation model to include an estimate of the continuing value (i.e., the forecast of value at the end of the finite forecast horizon, which captures the value of expected payoffs in all periods beyond the horizon).

THE USE OF CONTINUING VALUES IN THE FREE CASH FLOW MODEL

When computing value using the free cash flow model, we partition the future into two separate pieces. The first is the finite-horizon period for which we have formed explicit forecasts (the first 6 years, through 2024, in our GIS example), and the second is the period beyond this horizon (the period from 2025 to infinity). Within the horizon, we have explicit forecasts. A continuing value estimate is made to capture expected payoffs beyond the finite forecast horizon.

Equation 10.6 can be rewritten to emphasize this split into two pieces as follows in **Equation 10.7**:

$$\begin{aligned} V_0 &= \frac{FCF_1}{(1+r_{WACC})} + \frac{FCF_2}{(1+r_{WACC})^2} + \frac{FCF_3}{(1+r_{WACC})^3} + \frac{FCF_4}{(1+r_{WACC})^4} + \frac{FCF_5}{(1+r_{WACC})^5} + \ldots \\ &= \sum_{t=1}^{\infty}\left(\frac{FCF_t}{(1+r_{WACC})^t}\right) \\ &= \sum_{t=1}^{5}\left(\frac{FCF_t}{(1+r_{WACC})^t}\right) + \sum_{t=6}^{\infty}\left(\frac{FCF_t}{(1+r_{WACC})^t}\right) \end{aligned} \quad (10.7)$$

In Equation 10.7, the term capturing the first five periods is referred to as being within the forecast horizon because the contribution of these *FCF*s to value will be calculated using explicit forecasts of *FCF*s for each year. The amount of effort expended to calculate these forecasts within the horizon can vary. Currently, we are working with "full information" forecasts where detailed analysis supported the forecasts. Remember that analysts sometimes spend many hours/weeks working on the forecasts of sales growth alone!

The length of the forecast horizon will be determined by our ability and willingness to gather information for forecasting. We would like to explicitly forecast as far into the future as possible, but we have to recognize that the further into the future we forecast, the less confidence we have in our estimates. Consider estimates of your future earnings. Are you more confident in your estimate of your earnings next year or your estimate of your earnings 20 years from now? How far into the future do you have to go before the estimates become mostly speculation? Similar issues are in play when we form forecasts for firms.

The second term of Equation 10.7 captures the continuing value beyond the explicit forecast period. To help show what is captured by the continuing value, we rewrite the second term of the equation as follows:

$$\begin{aligned} \sum_{t=6}^{\infty}\left(\frac{FCF_t}{(1+r_{WACC})^t}\right) &= \frac{1}{(1+r_{WACC})^5} \times \sum_{t=6}^{\infty}\left(\frac{FCF_t}{(1+r_{WACC})^{t-5}}\right) \\ &= \frac{1}{(1+r_{WACC})^5} \times \left(\frac{FCF_6}{(1+r_{WACC})} + \frac{FCF_7}{(1+r_{WACC})^2} + \frac{FCF_8}{(1+r_{WACC})^3} + \frac{FCF_9}{(1+r_{WACC})^4} + \ldots\right) \end{aligned}$$

Which, based on Equation 10.6, may be expressed as:

$$\begin{aligned} \sum_{t=6}^{\infty}\left(\frac{FCF_t}{(1+r_{WACC})^t}\right) &= \frac{1}{(1+r_{WACC})^5} \times \left(\frac{FCF_6}{(1+r_{WACC})} + \frac{FCF_7}{(1+r_{WACC})^2} + \frac{FCF_8}{(1+r_{WACC})^3} + \frac{FCF_9}{(1+r_{WACC})^4} + \ldots\right) \\ &= \frac{1}{(1+r_{WACC})^5} \times V_5 \end{aligned}$$

That is, in the DCF model, the continuing value equals the expected intrinsic value at the horizon. This creates an interesting problem; in order to determine the value today, we need an estimate of the value of the operating activities several periods in the future. We will return to this issue in future chapters as we discuss alternative valuation methods.

To estimate the value at the horizon, generally, an assumption is made that future payoffs will follow a predictable pattern beyond the horizon. That is, each subsequent payoff is related to the previous payoff in a systematic manner. Usually payoffs are assumed to be related such that they show growth at a constant rate. As a result, the following is assumed to hold:

$$FCF_{t+1} = FCF_t \times (1+g)$$

where g is the rate of growth in FCFs from operations after the forecast horizon. Further, the subsequent payoff (FCF_{t+2}) will reflect two periods of growth such that

$$\begin{aligned} FCF_{t+2} &= FCF_{t+1} \times (1+g) \\ &= [FCF_t \times (1+g)] \times (1+g) \\ &= FCF_t \times (1+g)^2 \end{aligned}$$

The pattern that emerges allows us to continue refining our understanding of the second term of our valuation equation as follows:

$$\begin{aligned} \sum_{t=6}^{\infty}\left(\frac{FCF_t}{(1+r_{WACC})^t}\right) &= \frac{1}{(1+r_{WACC})^5}\times\left(\frac{FCF_6}{(1+r_{WACC})}+\frac{FCF_7}{(1+r_{WACC})^2}+\frac{FCF_8}{(1+r_{WACC})^3}+\ldots\right) \\ &= \frac{1}{(1+r_{WACC})^5}\times\left(\frac{FCF_5\times(1+g)}{(1+r_{WACC})}+\frac{FCF_5\times(1+g)^2}{(1+r_{WACC})^2}+\frac{FCF_5\times(1+g)^3}{(1+r_{WACC})^3}+\ldots\right) \end{aligned}$$

The last portion of the above equation shows a series that will continue to infinity in a very straightforward manner. Each subsequent term has the numerator multiplied by $(1 + g)$ and the denominator multiplied by $(1 + r_{WACC})$. Provided that the discount rate is greater than growth rate ($r_{WACC} > g$) this series may be rewritten as follows:[7]

$$\begin{aligned} \sum_{t=5}^{\infty}\left(\frac{FCF_t}{(1+r_{WACC})^t}\right) &= \frac{1}{(1+r_{WACC})^5}\times\left(\frac{FCF_5\times(1+g)}{(1+r_{WACC})}+\frac{FCF_5\times(1+g)^2}{(1+r_{WACC})^2}+\frac{FCF_5\times(1+g)^3}{(1+r_{WACC})^3}+\ldots\right) \\ &= \frac{1}{(1+r_{WACC})^5}\times\left(\frac{FCF_5\times(1+g)}{r_{WACC}-g}\right) \end{aligned}$$

Combining this with Equation 10.7 yields

$$\begin{aligned} V_0 &= \frac{FCF_1}{(1+r_{WACC})}+\frac{FCF_2}{(1+r_{WACC})^2}+\frac{FCF_3}{(1+r_{WACC})^3}+\frac{FCF_4}{(1+r_{WACC})^4}+\frac{FCF_5}{(1+r_{WACC})^5}+\frac{FCF_6}{(1+r_{WACC})^6}+\ldots \\ &= \sum_{t=1}^{\infty}\left(\frac{FCF_t}{(1+r_{WACC})^t}\right) \\ &= \sum_{t=1}^{5}\left(\frac{FCF_t}{(1+r_{WACC})^t}\right)+\frac{1}{(1+r_{WACC})^5}\times\left(\frac{FCF_5\times(1+g)}{r_{WACC}-g}\right) \end{aligned} \quad (10.8)$$

Note that the growth rate in Equation 10.8 will normally be a positive number because we use nominal payoffs, which include the effect of inflation. However, a constant stream of expected future payoffs can be achieved by setting g equal to zero so that all future payoffs after the horizon are equal to FCF_5. Further, an assumed value between –1 and zero for g will capture an assumption that the payoffs decline over time, exhibiting a pattern of decay.[8] The calculation of a continuing value requires only that we are willing to assume future payoffs after the horizon will follow a pattern that can be captured as $FCF_{t+1} = FCF_t \times (1 + g)$.

[7] The requirement that discount rate is greater than growth rate ($r_{WACC} > g$) serves a mathematical purpose in that it allows the series to converge and be written succinctly as $\left[\frac{FCF_5\cdot(1+g)}{r_{WACC}-g}\right]$. It also serves an economic purpose as well in that if g were greater than r_{WACC}, the growth in the cash flow stream would cause the value of the firm to be infinite.

[8] An assumption that g equals –0.10 means the FCF will decrease 10 percent per year as each subsequent cash flow is equal to the prior cash flow multiplied by 0.90.

Of course, as it is the farthest in the future, our assumption regarding g likely will be the assumption in which we have least confidence. Still, the process outlined in Chapter 7 allows us to arrive at the highest level of confidence possible for a given valuation exercise.

Utilizing Equation 10.8 for valuation requires that the firm has reached a point where we can assume a constant growth rate for future *FCF*s from operations. In other words, Equation 10.8 holds when the growth from year 5 to 6 and all subsequent growth is at g. This is referred to as having reached a steady state. Specifically, we would say that a steady state is reached in period 6 because growth in *FCF* in that year and subsequent years will be at the rate of g. (The concept of and requirements for steady state are discussed in detail in Chapter 14.) Given that the our confidence in our estimates decreases the further into the further we forecast, we would prefer to have a shorter forecast horizon and reach steady state earlier. However, the horizon has to be sufficiently long to allow for an assumption of constant growth to be reasonable.

Now, let us apply Equation 10.8 in the valuation of GIS using the *FCF*s valuation model.

USE OF NOMINAL (RISK-ADJUSTED) VERSUS REAL PAYOFFS

The value of a monetary unit commonly changes over time due to inflation or deflation. Payoffs and discount rates that include the effects of these price-level changes are referred to as nominal or nominal risk-adjusted. If the effects of price-level changes are not included, the payoffs and discount rates are referred to as real. So, should we use nominal or real amounts for valuation? Consider the following example where a nominal payoff of $200 million is expected in 2 years. Assume that there is 3 percent inflation per year expected and the nominal discount rate for this payoff is 10 percent, which implies a real discount rate of 6.8 percent (i.e., $\left[\frac{(1.00+0.10)}{(1.00+0.03)} - 1.00\right]$). We can estimate the value of the expected future payoff using either nominal or real amounts as follows:

Inputs	Payoff	×	Discount Rate	=	Value Today
Nominal:	$200 million	×	$1/1.10^2$	=	$165.3 million
	(nominal)		(nominal—includes inflation)		
Real:	$200 million/1.03^2	×	$1/1.068^2$	=	$165.3 million
	(real)		(real—excludes inflation)		

The computed value of the payoff is unaffected by whether nominal or real inputs are used in the calculation (remember that use of nominal payoffs requires use of nominal discount rates and use of real payoffs requires use of real discount rates). In practice, it is easier to use nominal inputs because analysts generally do not forecast real payoffs or take time to convert nominal rates to real rates. Accordingly, we use nominal inputs for valuations in this book.

FREE CASH FLOW VALUATION OF GENERAL MILLS' ENTERPRISE OPERATIONS

LO4: Prepare a discounted cash flow valuation spreadsheet for a company's operations.

For the valuation of GIS using our detailed forecasts from Chapter 7, we will utilize weighted average cost of capital for operations (r_{WACC}) of 5.3 percent as computed in Chapter 9. In addition to the assumptions in **Exhibit 10.3**, we assume that the sales growth rate will stay at 1.2 percent after 2023. The assumption that the rate of growth in *FCF*s and the rate of growth in sales beyond the horizon are equal reflects that, over time, a firm's growth is driven by its ability to grow sales. If we apply our forecasts going forward, we can see that a steady state where *FCF*s grow at the rate of growth in sales arises. **Exhibit 10.6** shows the forecasts of *FCF*s from operations (essentially **Exhibit 10.5** extended).

Here, we achieve a steady state beginning in 2024 as growth in 2024 and all subsequent years is at a constant rate of 1.2 percent. That is, we see constant growth in *FCF* for 2024 and 2025, and it would continue in all subsequent years as well. The first year in which the continuing constant rate of growth in *FCF* is observed serves as the first year of the continuing value calculation. The years before that are the explicit forecast period. For implementing Equation 10.8, we will use a period of 5 years as our explicit forecast horizon and then use a continuing value to capture periods six and beyond. Using this information and our assumptions of the

EXHIBIT 10.6 GIS Multiyear Assumptions and Forecasts

Year Ending	5/27/2018	5/26/2019	5/31/2020	5/30/2021	5/29/2022	5/28/2023	5/26/2024	5/25/2025
Assumptions:								
Weeks in year . . .		52	53	52	52	52	52	
Sales growth		9.43%	3.03%	−0.62%	1.30%	1.25%	1.20%	
PM.		12.32%	12.32%	12.45%	12.62%	12.62%	12.62%	
ATO.		0.688	0.678	0.665	0.651	0.651	0.651	
Forecasts:								
Sales.	$15,740.4	$17,224.4	$17,746.9	$17,637.8	$17,867.1	$18,090.4	$18,307.5	$18,527.2
NOPAT.		$ 2,122.0	$ 2,186.4	$ 2,195.9	$ 2,254.8	$ 2,283.0	$ 2,310.4	$ 2,338.1
NOA	$25,035.4	$26,291.0	$25,998.1	$26,854.2	$27,786.8	$28,120.3	$28,457.7	$28,799.2
Change in *NOA* . . .		$ 1,255.6	$ (292.9)	$ 856.1	$ 932.7	$ 333.4	$ 337.4	$ 341.5
FCF.		$ 866.5	$ 2,479.3	$ 1,339.8	$ 1,322.2	$ 1,949.6	$ 1,973.0	$ 1,996.6
Growth in *FCF*			186.15%	−45.96%	−1.32%	47.45%	1.20%	1.20%

weighted average cost of capital for operations and the growth rate beyond the horizon in Equation 10.8, we calculate the value of GIS' operations as follows:

$$
\begin{aligned}
V_0 &= \sum_{t=1}^{T}\left(\frac{FCF_t}{(1+r_{WACC})^t}\right)+\frac{1}{(1+r_{WACC})^T}\times\left(\frac{FCF_{T+1}}{r_{WACC}-g}\right)\\
&=\frac{FCF_1}{(1+r_{WACC})}+\frac{FCF_2}{(1+r_{WACC})^2}+\frac{FCF_3}{(1+r_{WACC})^3}+\frac{FCF_4}{(1+r_{WACC})^4}+\frac{FCF_5}{(1+r_{WACC})^5}\\
&\quad+\frac{1}{(1+r_{WACC})^5}\times\left[\frac{FCF_5\times(1+g)}{r_{WACC}-g}\right]\\
&=\frac{866.5}{(1+0.053)}+\frac{2{,}479.3}{(1+0.053)^2}+\frac{1{,}339.8}{(1+0.053)^3}+\frac{1{,}332.2}{(1+0.053)^4}\\
&\quad+\frac{1{,}949.6}{(1+0.053)^5}+\frac{1}{(1+0.053)^5}\times\left[\frac{1{,}949.6\times(1+0.012)}{0.053-0.012}\right]\\
&=\frac{866.5}{1.0530}+\frac{2{,}479.3}{1.1088}+\frac{1{,}339.8}{1.1676}+\frac{1{,}332.2}{1.2295}+\frac{1{,}949.6}{1.2946}+\frac{1}{(1+0.053)^5}\times\left[\frac{1{,}973.0}{0.041}\right]\\
&=\frac{866.5}{1.0530}+\frac{2{,}479.3}{1.1088}+\frac{1{,}339.8}{1.1676}+\frac{1{,}332.2}{1.2295}+\frac{1{,}949.6}{1.2946}+\frac{48{,}121.0}{1.2946}\\
&=822.8+2{,}236.0+1{,}147.5+1{,}075.4+1{,}505.9+37{,}170.0\\
&=43{,}957.7
\end{aligned}
$$

Exhibit 10.7 shows the valuation of GIS's operations using DCF in tabular format.
That is, the estimated intrinsic value of the enterprise operations of GIS is $43,957.7 at May 27, 2018, based on our forecasts and assumptions.

As a preview to the analysis of which valuation method might be preferred, we point out that, in this DCF valuation, the portion of value of the operations captured within the finite forecast horizon is 15.4 percent (i.e., $6,787.7/$43,957.7). If we looked at only the next 4 years because we have a higher confidence in the near term, DCF estimates only capture 12.0 percent of value in the short term. This means almost 90 percent is not captured in the next 4 years, where we are likely to be most confident in our forecasts. The extent to which our valuation models capture value in the early years of the forecast period will vary and be a significant consideration in our evaluation of the differences between the models.

EXHIBIT 10.7 GIS Valuation Using Discounted Cash Flow Model ($ Millions)

Required rate of return (r_{WACC}) 5.30%

Year Ending	5/27/2018	5/26/2019	5/31/2020	5/30/2021	5/29/2022	5/28/2023
Forecasted sales		$17,224.4	$17,746.9	$17,637.8	$17,867.1	$18,090.4
NOPAT (Sales × *PM*)		2,122.0	2,186.4	2,195.9	2,254.8	2,283.0
NOA (Sales/*ATO*)	$25,035.4	26,291.0	25,998.1	26,854.2	27,786.8	28,120.3
ΔNOA		1,255.6	(292.9)	856.1	932.7	333.4
FCF (*NOPAT* – ΔNOA)		866.5	2,479.3	1,339.8	1,322.2	1,949.6
Growth in *FCF*			186.15%	–45.96%	–1.32%	47.45%
Discount factor $(1 + r_{WACC})^t$		1.0530	1.1088	1.1676	1.2295	1.2946
Present value of *FCF* from operations		$ 822.8	$ 2,236.0	$ 1,147.5	$ 1,075.4	$ 1,505.9
Sum of present value of cash flows	6,787.7					
Continuing value						
FCF at horizon						1,973.0
Capitalized						48,121.0
Present value of continuing value	37,170.0					
Operating value	$43,957.7					

CALCULATION OF FREE CASH FLOWS

In Equation 2.2, we showed the following identity:

$$FCF_t \equiv NOPAT_t - \Delta NOA_t$$

This equation represents the definition of *FCF*s from operations sought by investors and others for valuation. We rely on this equation to calculate *FCF*s rather than utilizing the statement of cash flows as our starting point because there may be significant noncash transactions that are omitted from the statement of cash flows.

As an example drawn from PG's experience, we look back to the 2006 acquisition of **Gillette**. In this transaction, PG issued 962,488,000 shares of stock to acquire the assets and liabilities of Gillette. The assets and liabilities acquired were primarily operating in nature. This noncash transaction is not included in the amounts reported as operating, investing, or financing cash flows in PG statement of cash flows. The statement of cash flows shows the following amounts (in millions):

Cash from operating activities	$11,375
Cash used in investing activities	(730)
Cash used in financing activities	(10,578)

We find the Gillette transaction described in a supplemental disclosure to the statement of cash flows as "Gillette acquisition funded by share issuance $53.371 billion." Utilizing the reformulated financials of PG for 2005 and 2006, we can calculate the 2006 *FCF*s as follows:

$$NOPAT_{2006} - [NOA_{2006} - NOA_{2005}] = FCF_{2006}$$

$$\$11,223 - [\$94,550 - \$35,805] = \$(47,522)$$

Note that the effect of the payment for the acquisition of Gillette is included in NOA_{2006} and, hence, it is included in the calculation of FCF_{2006} as it should be. The majority of the negative *FCF* for PG in 2006 arose from the funding by equity holders of the acquisition of Gillette, but this amount is not shown as a cash flow on the statement of cash flows because they did not use cash. The fact that PG used shares as the currency for the purchase of Gillette makes it no more or less a cash outflow than it would had been if PG had used U.S. dollars (i.e., greenbacks).

This example demonstrates the fact that we can and should use the reformulated calculations of *NOPAT* and *NOA* as the basis for our calculation of *FCF* from operations.

SUMMARY

This chapter introduced the terminology and concepts that are necessary for valuation through the examination of a savings account. Valuation was demonstrated using the commonly employed *FCF* valuation, DCF, model. We then demonstrated how to value a firm's operations using our detailed forecasts for GIS, a highly-visible publicly traded firm.

In the next chapters, we will move from valuation based on cash flows to using accounting-based valuation models. To illustrate this, we will continue to focus on an examination of our project and GIS' operations. While DCF is commonly used in practice, this does not mean it is always the best approach. As we explore accounting-based valuation models, we will consider the criteria that should be used to evaluate and decide between models. Also, in Chapter 13, we will consider the direct estimation of value of equity rather than operations.

QUESTIONS

Q10.1 Why would it be natural for cash flows to be used as a basis for the estimation of value?

Q10.2 What characteristics of anticipated cash flows must be determined (or at least estimated) to allow for calculation of value?

Q10.3 What is the difference between these investments?

- A share of stock that can be purchased for $100 that has a related risk of 5 percent
- Depositing $100 in a savings account that promises a return of 5 percent
- Buying a project for $100 that is expected to yield a 5 percent rate of return

Q10.4 To form forecasts of *FCF* from operations, what aspects of enterprise operations must be forecasted?

Q10.5 In cash flow-based valuation, what does the continuing value equal?

Q10.6 What are some disadvantages of using the DCF valuation model?

Q10.7 In a cash-based valuation of a company with forecasted negative *FCF*s (e.g., a high growth company), what are the major challenges?

Q10.8 When has a firm reached a steady state?

Q10.9 What issues arise with estimating *FCF*s from the statement of cash flows?

Q10.10 In evaluating the value of a future payoff, should the analyst use a nominal or real discount rate?

Q10.11 Netflix is a darling of Wall Street. An innovative company that has transformed TV viewing habits for millions of people by successfully utilizing data and predictive analytics in determining TV watching patterns. Its market capitalization of nearly $150 billion is surprising given that it recently became profitable and still has ***negative FCFs***. Analysts suggest that Netflix will incur negative *FCF*s for years to come. Using a cash-based valuation approach, reconcile (in words) Netflix's market valuation to its current financial performance.

EXERCISES

E10.12 If you invested $15,000 today in a fund that earns 8 percent compounded annually, to what amount will the investment grow in 3 years?

E10.13 Assume you will invest $30,000 today and anticipate needing $150,000 in 21 years. What annual interest rate must you earn?

E10.14 Horngren Corporation has $6.5 million in *FCF*s this year and expects *FCF* to increase 6 percent per year indefinitely. What is Horngren's operating value (*OV*) if its r_{WACC} is 10 percent?

E10.15 The Moontiz Group recently reported sales of $20 million on *NOA* of $11 million. Management believes that, over the next 5 years, sales will grow 10 percent with a 15 percent *PM* and *ATO* of 2.0 times. Calculate the expected *FCF* for the next 5 years.

E10.16 Burton Enterprises reported $12.0 million in *FCF*s this year. Analyst consensus forecasts for the next 5 years for Burton's *FCF*s are $13.2 million, $14.5 million, $15.75 million, $17.0 million, and 18.2 million. Calculate Burton's operating value (V^{Oper}) assuming that *FCF* beyond the forecast horizon will continue to grow at 5 percent and Burton has a 9 percent r_{WACC}?

E10.17 On February 2, 2015, the end of Home Depot's (HD) 2014 fiscal year (FY), HD's share price was $104.42.

a. With 1,307 million shares outstanding, what was HD's market capitalization at February 2, 2015?

b. At February 2, 2015, HD's *NFL* was $15,474 million. What was HD's operating value (V^{Oper}) at February 2, 2015?

c. Assuming the market had perfect foresight of HD's future *FCF* for FY 2015–2018, what is the implied growth rate the continuing value (CV) at February 2, 2015? HD's weighted-average cost of capital (r_{WACC}) was 8 percent. The *FCF* (in $ millions) for FY 2015–2018 were

FY 2015	FY 2016	FY 2017	FY 2018
$6,489	$7,777	$9,138	$10,463

d. What is the benefit to the analyst in estimating the implied growth rate for the *FCF* CV?

CONTINUING EXAMPLES

CE10.18 The company has been offered the opportunity to invest in a project expected to yield the following cash flows:

Anticipated Cash Flows of Finite-Life Project	
Purchase price	$2,300
Payoffs:	
Year 1	$600
Year 2	700
Year 3	750
Year 4	625
Year 5	500
Proceeds from disposition	240

In addition, the anticipated risk of the project implies a cost of capital of 10 percent would be appropriate. Using the DCF method, determine the value of the project and whether to make an investment in this project.

CE10.19 Assume that to undergo projects, you have decided to employ a hurdle rate of 15 percent in the evaluation of opportunities. As such, in the evaluation of the project described in CE10.18, utilize a discount rate of 15 percent despite the 10 percent cost of capital. Will you make the investment in the project? What effects does this decision have?

CE10.20 The Hatfield Company evaluates internal projects for their financial viability as part of their overall analysis. One proposed project is to automate a portion of the Hatfield's production process. The additional equipment has an estimated useful life of 6 years. The operations manager provided the expected cost savings from the installation of the robotic equipment. The project is expected to yield the following cash flows:

Anticipated Cash Flows of Finite-Life Project	
Purchase price	$8,500
Payoffs:	
Year 1	$ 700
Year 2	1,900
Year 3	2,900
Year 4	3,500
Year 5	3,000
Year 6	2,700
Proceeds from disposition	400

In addition, Hatfield's management requires a hurdle rate of 16 percent for internally proposed projects, which is greater than the actual project risk. Using the DCF method, determine the financial viability of the project.

CE10.21 Using the following forecast assumptions from Chapter 7 for **Kellogg** (K), the r_{WACC} of 5.2 percent calculated in Chapter 9, and a continuing growth in cash flows beyond the forecast horizon of 0.4 percent, calculate the value of K's operations.

K Multiyear Assumptions	2019E	2020E	2021E	2022E	2023E	2024E	2025E	2026E	2027E
Assumptions:									
Sales growth	0.57%	2.41%	−1.42%	0.50%	0.45%	0.40%	2.32%	−1.49%	0.40%
Operating *PM*	9.36%	9.58%	10.00%	10.17%	10.55%	10.55%	10.55%	10.55%	10.55%
Operating *ATO*	1.052	0.974	0.962	0.951	0.951	0.951	0.951	0.951	0.951

CE10.22 Using the following forecast assumptions from Chapter 7 for **Thor Industries** (THO), the r_{WACC} for operations of 12.60 percent calculated in Chapter 9, and a continuing growth in cash flows beyond the forecast horizon of 1.00 percent, calculate the value of THO's operations.

THO Multiyear Assumptions	FY2019E	FY2020E	FY2021E	FY2022E	FY2023E	FY2024E
Assumptions:						
Sales growth	5.56%	3.61%	1.61%	1.40%	1.20%	1.00%
Operating *PM*	5.78%	5.77%	5.40%	5.35%	5.15%	5.15%
Operating *ATO*	4.815	4.329	4.219	4.098	4.098	4.098

CE10.23 Using the following forecast assumptions from Chapter 7 for **Winnebago** (WGO), the r_{WACC} for operations of 10.60 percent calculated in Chapter 9, and a continuing growth in cash flows beyond the forecast horizon of 0.90 percent, calculate the value of WGO's operations.

WGO Multiyear Assumptions	FY2019E	FY2020E	FY2021E	FY2022E	FY2023E	FY2024E	FY2025E	FY2026E
Assumptions:								
Weeks	53	52	52	52	52	53	52	52
Sales growth	4.56%	0.11%	1.38%	1.10%	2.82%	−0.99%	0.90%	0.90%
Operating *PM*	6.40%	6.27%	6.20%	6.03%	6.03%	6.03%	6.03%	6.03%
Operating *ATO*	2.309	2.288	2.294	2.294	2.294	2.294	2.294	2.294

NOTES

Chapter Eleven

Valuation Using the Residual Operating Income Valuation Model

TAKEAWAYS

When you complete this chapter, you should be able to:

1. Explain that the residual operating income model is mathematically equivalent to the free cash flow model.
2. Compute the value of a finite-life project using the residual operating income model.
3. Understand that the value estimated using the residual operating income model does not change based on accounting methods, choices, or assumptions.
4. Implement residual operating income valuation using multiyear forecasts and continuing value assumptions.
5. Prepare a residual operating income valuation spreadsheet for a company's operations.

Chapter 10 introduced free cash flow valuation and reviewed the relation between cash flows and accounting information from Chapter 2. In this chapter, we continue with the valuation of the project and the operating activities of General Mills (GIS). This time, we move away from cash flow-based valuation and introduce a method by which value may be estimated using forecasted accounting numbers. This method uses accounting data, which are readily available and are the focus of analysts and investors alike. This chapter and the following chapter introduce two valuation models where value is calculated directly from forecasts of accounting data.

We begin by reintroducing the project that will be used as a basis for demonstrating the first accounting-based valuation model, and then we apply this model to valuing our finite-life (i.e., limited duration) project. Examination of the same finite-life project will provide assurance that the model is working and enable us to clarify the steps needed to implement it. Finally, we apply the accounting-based valuation method to the valuation of GIS' operations to see the application for a large, visible publicly-traded firm. Chapter 12 will follow a similar process when we explore another accounting-based valuation model.

MOVING FROM CASH FLOWS TO ACCOUNTING DATA IN VALUING A FINITE-LIFE PROJECT

In Chapter 10, we examined the opportunity to invest in a project with the anticipated cash flows at the end of each year as shown in **Exhibit 11.1**.

CHAPTER OUTLINE

Valuation Using the Residual Operating Income Valuation Model

Residual Operating Income Valuation
- Derivation from Cash Flows Model
- Valuing a Finite-Life Project

Accounting Choices
- Effects of Alternative Depreciation Methods

Valuation of Operations
- Multiyear Forecasts
- Continuing Values
- Valuing General Mills' Operations

EXHIBIT 11.1 Anticipated Cash Flows of Finite-Life Project

Purchase price		$1,000.00
Payoffs		
Year 1 cash flow (CF_1)		250.00
Year 2 cash flow (CF_2)		350.00
Year 3 cash flow (CF_3)		320.00
Year 4 cash flows (CF_4)		
Proceeds from sales	$280.00	
Proceeds from disposition	200.00	
=		480.00
Required rate of return = r_P.		10%

As a reminder, Equation 10.5 showed that we can value a project using cash flows as follows:

$$V_0 = \frac{CF_1}{(1+r_P)} + \frac{CF_2}{(1+r_P)^2} + \frac{CF_3}{(1+r_P)^3} + \frac{CF_4}{(1+r_P)^4}$$
$$= \sum_{t=1}^{4}\left(\frac{CF_t}{(1+r_P)^t}\right) \tag{10.5}$$

When the expected cash flows for the project were entered into the above formula, we computed the following present value:

$$V_0 = \frac{CF_1}{(1+r_P)} + \frac{CF_2}{(1+r_P)^2} + \frac{CF_3}{(1+r_P)^3} + \frac{CF_4}{(1+r_P)^4}$$
$$= \frac{250.00}{(1+0.10)^1} + \frac{350.00}{(1+0.10)^2} + \frac{320.00}{(1+0.10)^3} + \frac{480.00}{(1+0.10)^4}$$
$$= \frac{250.00}{1.1} + \frac{350.00}{1.21} + \frac{320.00}{1.331} + \frac{480.00}{1.4641}$$
$$= 227.27 + 289.26 + 240.42 + 327.85$$
$$= 1{,}084.80$$

Further, Equation 2.2 demonstrated that the free cash flows from a firm's operations, like the distributions from the project, can be measured and stated using accounting numbers as follows:

$$FCF_t \equiv NOPAT_t + NOA_{t-1} \equiv NOA_t$$
$$\equiv NOPAT_t - \Delta NOA_t \tag{2.2}$$

Substituting for the cash flows (using Equation 2.2) into the cash flow valuation for the project in Equation 10.5, we see the following:

$$V_0 = \frac{CF_1}{(1+r_P)} + \frac{CF_2}{(1+r_P)^2} + \frac{CF_3}{(1+r_P)^3} + \frac{CF_4}{(1+r_P)^4}$$

$$= \frac{NOPAT_1 + NOA_0 - NOA_1}{(1+r_P)} + \frac{NOPAT_2 + NOA_1 - NOA_2}{(1+r_P)^2}$$

$$+ \frac{NOPAT_3 + NOA_2 - NOA_3}{(1+r_P)^3} + \frac{NOPAT_4 + NOA_3 - NOA_4}{(1+r_P)^4}$$

$$= \frac{50.00 + 1,000.00 - 800.00}{(1+0.10)} + \frac{150.00 + 800.00 - 600.00}{(1+0.10)^2}$$

$$+ \frac{120.00 + 600.00 - 400.00}{(1+0.10)^3} + \frac{80.00 + 400.00 - 0.00}{(1+0.10)^4}$$

$$= \frac{250.00}{1.10} + \frac{350.00}{1.21} + \frac{320.00}{1.331} + \frac{480.00}{1.4641}$$

$$= 227.27 + 289.26 + 240.42 + 327.85$$

$$= 1,084.80$$

While continuing to find a value of $1,084.80 when computing value using accounting earnings and book values probably appears obvious given the substitution we made, many trained in valuation would not find the fact that we have valued the operations using *only* accounting numbers obvious at all. We now examine the implications for substituting Equation 2.2 into Equation 10.5 as we develop the first of two accounting-based valuation models that are mathematically equivalent to discounted cash flow (DCF) valuation. Later, we will discuss why you may wish to know several valuation models and what factors would determine which model may be used in a particular valuation setting.

DERIVATION OF THE RESIDUAL OPERATING INCOME VALUATION MODEL

LO1: Explain that the residual operating income model is mathematically equivalent to the free cash flow model.

Now that we have seen that we can use forecasted net operating profit after tax (*NOPAT*) and net operating assets (*NOA*) to value the project, we introduce and derive the first valuation model based on these accounting numbers. The derivation is simple and straightforward if we are prepared to pause so that we can carefully understand two unequivocal and indisputable steps. We will first see these steps now in the derivation of the residual operating income valuation model and again in the derivation of the abnormal operating income growth valuation model.

The derivation of the residual operating income valuation model begins with the free cash flow valuation model, which we saw in Chapter 10:

$$V_0 = \frac{FCF_1}{(1+r_{WACC})} + \frac{FCF_2}{(1+r_{WACC})^2} + \frac{FCF_3}{(1+r_{WACC})^3} + \frac{FCF_4}{(1+r_{WACC})^4} + \ldots$$

$$= \sum_{t=1}^{\infty} \left(\frac{FCF_t}{(1+r_{WACC})^t} \right) \quad (10.6)$$

The first step is introduction of *NOA*, which, recall, is the accounting measure of the value of the operating assets. We do so by recognizing the simple mathematical fact that if we add and, at the same time, subtract the present value of each future year's *NOA* in the right side of Equation

10.6, we will not affect the mathematical integrity of the equation. Specifically, we introduce the following zero-sum equality:

$$0 = NOA_0 + \frac{NOA_1 - (1+r_{WACC}) \times NOA_0}{(1+r_{WACC})} + \frac{NOA_2 - (1+r_{WACC}) \times NOA_1}{(1+r_{WACC})^2} + \ldots\ldots \quad (11.1)$$

The fact that we have simply added and subtracted the present value of each year's *NOA* is evident if we rearrange Equation 11.1 as follows:

$$0 = NOA_0 - NOA_0 + \frac{NOA_1}{(1+r_{WACC})} - \frac{NOA_1}{(1+r_{WACC})} + \frac{NOA_2}{(1+r_{WACC})^2} - \frac{NOA_2}{(1+r_{WACC})^2} + \ldots\ldots$$

The second step is to simply add the left hand sides of Equations 10.6 and 11.1 and to add the right sides of Equations 10.6 and 11.1 to obtain the following:

$$V_0 = NOA_0 + \sum_{t=1}^{\infty} \left(\frac{NOA_t + FCF_t - (1+r_{WACC}) \times NOA_{t-1}}{(1+r_{WACC})^t} \right)$$

Recognizing once again the accounting equation $FCF_t \equiv NOPAT_t - \Delta NOA_t$ yields

$$V_0 = NOA_0 + \sum_{t=1}^{\infty} \left(\frac{NOA_t + NOPAT_t - \Delta NOA_t - (1+r_{WACC}) \times NOA_{t-1}}{(1+r_{WACC})^t} \right)$$

Simplifying and rearranging the prior equation yields the residual operating income valuation model:

$$\begin{aligned} V_0 &= NOA_0 + \sum_{t=1}^{\infty} \left(\frac{NOA_t + NOPAT_t - NOA_t + NOA_{t-1} - NOA_{t-1} - r_{WACC} \times NOA_{t-1}}{(1+r_{WACC})^t} \right) \\ &= NOA_0 + \sum_{t=1}^{\infty} \left(\frac{NOPAT_t - r_{WACC} \times NOA_{t-1}}{(1+r_{WACC})^t} \right) \\ &= NOA_0 + \sum_{t=1}^{\infty} \left(\frac{ROPI_t}{(1+r_{WACC})^t} \right) \end{aligned} \quad (11.2)$$

where $ROPI_t = NOPAT_t - r_{WACC} \times NOA_{t-1}$.[1] In Equation 11.2, residual operating income ($ROPI_t$) is equal to $NOPAT_t - r_{WACC} \times NOA_{t-1}$, which is the residual operating income in excess of the expected return on *NOA* (i.e., $r_{WACC} \times NOA_{t-1}$). Notice the effect, if, say, NOA_{t-1} is lower due to an implementation of an accounting rule such as expensing rather than capitalizing reseaerch and development (R&D). Current book value is lower, while the next period *NOPAT* is higher because R&D expenses that are expected to lead to higher sales revenue that are part of this expected *NOPAT* have already been taken. The result is that residual operating income will be higher. Thus, the residual operating income valuation model anchors the valuation on the current book value of *NOA* (NOA_0), and future residual operating income serves as the adjustment to this valuation to counter any effect that accounting rules and procedures have on this valuation starting point.

We saw in Chapter 2 that often, the accruals are helpful in aligning reporting with the underlying economics. Some, including the CFA Institute, suggest review of accruals (particularly reserves and allowances) as part of the use of the residual income valuation model. In making this suggestion, the concern is not with the existence of the reserves but, rather, whether the company is manipulating these accounting estimates. This is an example where the axiom of "know the business" espoused in Chapter 1 becomes central. Many parts of accounting involve estimates,

[1] To emphasize the computations, throughout most of the text, we will write out $NOPAT_t - r_{WACC} \times NOA_{t-1}$ instead of referring to $ROPI_t$.

and unless we are aware of the accounting and the company's business environment, these issues will arise (note, however, that they also arise when we calculate *FCF* from operations based on estimates of *NOPAT* and *NOA*).

We will return to the issue of differences in accounting methods as well as potential for manipulation of accounting. In doing so, we will clarify the potential impacts in residual operating income valuation using several examples.

PROJECT VALUATION USING THE RESIDUAL OPERATING INCOME MODEL

LO2: Compute the value of a finite-life project using the residual operating income model.

The four-period residual operating income valuation model for valuing a project based on Equation 11.2 is

$$\begin{aligned} V_0 &= NOA_0 + \frac{ROPI_1}{(1+r_P)} + \frac{ROPI_2}{(1+r_P)^2} + \frac{ROPI_3}{(1+r_P)^3} + \frac{ROPI_4}{(1+r_P)^4} \\ &= NOA_0 + \frac{NOPAT_1 - r_P \times NOA_0}{(1+r_P)} + \frac{NOPAT_2 - r_P \times NOA_1}{(1+r_P)^2} \\ &\quad + \frac{NOPAT_3 - r_P \times NOA_2}{(1+r_P)^3} + \frac{NOPAT_4 - r_P \times NOA_3}{(1+r_P)^4} \end{aligned}$$

where r_P is the required discount rate for the project.

Recall the accounting information about the project from Chapter 10 shown in **Exhibit 11.2**:

EXHIBIT 11.2 Accounting Income for Finite-Life Project

Time Period	0	1	2	3	4
Net income ($NOPAT_t$)		50.00	150.00	120.00	80.00
Book value of project (NOA_t)	1,000.00	800.00	600.00	400.00	0.00

Inputting the accounting information into the equation above, we can solve for the value of the project as follows:

$$\begin{aligned} V_0 &= NOA_0 + \frac{ROPI_1}{(1+r_P)} + \frac{ROPI_2}{(1+r_P)^2} + \frac{ROPI_3}{(1+r_P)^3} + \frac{ROPI_4}{(1+r_P)^4} \\ &= NOA_0 + \frac{NOPAT_1 - r_P \times NOA_0}{(1+r_P)} + \frac{NOPAT_2 - r_P \times NOA_1}{(1+r_P)^2} \\ &\quad + \frac{NOPAT_3 - r_P \times NOA_2}{(1+r_P)^3} + \frac{NOPAT_4 - r_P \times NOA_3}{(1+r_P)^4} \\ &= 1,000.00 + \frac{50.00 - 0.10 \times 1,000.00}{(1+0.10)^1} + \frac{150.00 - 0.10 \times 800.00}{(1+0.10)^2} \\ &\quad + \frac{120.00 - 0.10 \times 600.00}{(1+0.10)^3} + \frac{80.00 - 0.10 \times 400.00}{(1+0.10)^4} \\ &= 1,000.00 + \frac{50.00 - 100.00}{1.1} + \frac{150.00 - 80.00}{1.21} + \frac{120.00 - 60.00}{1.331} + \frac{80.00 - 40.00}{1.4641} \\ &= 1,000.00 + \frac{-50.00}{1.1} + \frac{70.00}{1.21} + \frac{60.00}{1.331} + \frac{40.00}{1.4641} \\ &= 1,000.00 - 45.45 + 57.85 + 45.08 + 27.32 \\ &= 1,084.80 \end{aligned}$$

Using the residual operating income valuation model to calculate project value, we see that V_0 = $1,084.80, which is the same as the value calculated using the discounted cash flow model in Chapter 10. This must be so because the residual operating income method can be algebraically derived from the free cash flow model and, thus, is equivalent.

Shown in tabular format, the residual operating income valuation model can be demonstrated in **Exhibit 11.3**.

EXHIBIT 11.3 Residual Operating Income Model Valuation of Finite-Life Project

Required rate of return (r_P) 10.0%

	Time Period	0	1	2	3	4
	Revenues		$ 250.00	$350.00	$320.00	$280.00
−	Depreciation		200.00	200.00	200.00	200.00
+	Gain on sale					0.00
=	Net project income ($NOPAT_t$)		50.00	150.00	120.00	80.00
	Beginning book value	$ 0.00	1,000.00	800.00	600.00	400.00
+	Net project income		50.00	150.00	120.00	80.00
−	Distributions	(1,000.00)	250.00	350.00	320.00	480.00
=	Ending book value (NOA_t)	1,000.00	800.00	600.00	400.00	0.00
	Net project income		50.00	150.00	120.00	80.00
−	Expected income given book value ($r_P \times NOA_{t-1}$)		100.00	80.00	60.00	40.00
=	Residual operating income ($ROPI_t$)		(50.00)	70.00	60.00	40.00
÷	Discount factor $(1 + r_P)^t$		1.1	1.21	1.331	1.4641
=	Present value of $ROPI_t$		$ (45.45)	$ 57.85	$ 45.08	$ 27.32
+	Total present value of $ROPI_t$	84.80				
=	Value of project	$1,084.80				

Note that the contribution of funds to purchase the project is shown as a negative free cash flow (i.e., contribution from the owners of the project) in period 0. Also, the distribution in period 4 includes the revenues of the project and the proceeds from the sale of the project. This is, of course, consistent with what was done previously in the free cash flow model.

EFFECTS OF ACCOUNTING CHOICES ON THE RESIDUAL OPERATING INCOME MODEL

LO3: Understand that the value estimated using the residual operating income model does not change based on accounting methods, choices, or assumptions.

Now, let us demonstrate that, in this example, the accountant's choice of the method of depreciation (an example of an accrual) does not affect the valuation of the project. Accounting choices should not affect valuation because the underlying economic transaction has not changed and, so, economic value will be unchanged! An important feature of the accounting-based valuation models is that they continue to give the same answer with alternative accounting methods or if earnings are moved to earlier/later time periods (i.e., there is income shifting due to the choice of accounting method).

In accounting, any effect of taking either excess or too little depreciation is self-corrected by the gain or loss on sale at the end of the project's life. Suppose, for example, in our project example, that the accountant records $200.00 of depreciation at the time the asset is purchased and still records $200.00 in each year thereafter. This will result in a remaining book value of $0.00 at the time of sale. Further, as the project will be fully depreciated by the time it is sold, a gain on sale of $200.00 will be recognized. Although the forecasted project income and the book value of *NOA* will change, the value calculated via the residual operating income model (ROIM) will not change, as we see in the revised chart in **Exhibit 11.4**.

EXHIBIT 11.4 Residual Operating Income Model Valuation of Finite-Life Project with Alternative Depreciation Assumption

	Required rate of return (r_P)	10.0%				
	Time Period	**0**	**1**	**2**	**3**	**4**
	Revenues		\$250.00	\$350.00	\$320.00	\$280.00
−	Depreciation	\$ 200.00	200.00	200.00	200.00	200.00
+	Gain on sale					200.00
=	Net project income ($NOPAT_t$)	(200.00)	50.00	150.00	120.00	280.00
	Beginning book value	0.00	800.00	600.00	400.00	200.00
+	Net project income	(200.00)	50.00	150.00	120.00	280.00
−	Distributions	(1,000.00)	250.00	350.00	320.00	480.00
=	Ending book value (NOA_t)	800.00	600.00	400.00	200.00	0.00
	Net project income		50.00	150.00	120.00	280.00
−	Expected income given book value ($r_P \times NOA_{t-1}$)		80.00	60.00	40.00	20.00
=	Residual operating income ($ROPI_t$)		(30.00)	90.00	80.00	260.00
÷	Discount factor $(1 + r_P)^t$		1.1	1.21	1.331	1.4641
=	Present value of $ROPI_t$		\$ (27.27)	\$ 74.38	\$ 60.11	\$177.58
+	Total present value of $ROPI_t$	284.80				
=	Value of project	\$1,084.80				

This example of changing the choice of depreciation method demonstrates the central role of the self-correcting nature of accounting. In this example, excess depreciation in early years leads to a book value (*NOA*) that is lower. But, once this depreciation has been taken, it cannot be taken again, and future earnings (*NOPAT*) will be higher by exactly the amount of the excess depreciation. Similarly, other accounting choices and rules that lead to lower book values (e.g., expensing rather than capitalizing R&D) will also lead to correspondingly higher future income when R&D expenses that lead to higher future sales have already been taken. Similarly, differing accounting methods between U.S. GAAP and IFRS affect the timing of income but will not change the value calculation using the residual operating income model.

We see in this example that the residual operating income valuation model anchors the valuation on the current book value of net operating assets (NOA_0), which is affected by choice of accounting methods. Future residual operating income is the adjustment to this valuation to counter the effect that accounting rules and procedures have on this valuation anchor. The fact that the value calculated is not being driven by the accounting choices is very important. If a change in accounting methods or reporting choice affected the value calculated, we could not use this model. As it is, because the model is robust to this issue, many of the accusations put forth by proponents of cash flow-based valuation are totally invalid. More discussion of this fact will arise going forward.

Having seen that the residual operating income valuation model produced the same value estimate for our project as the free cash flow model, we proceed to the valuation of GIS' operations based on our detailed forecasts. Here, we will see the implementation of the residual operating income valuation model for a going concern. This situation will include the use of a continuing value similar to that seen in the free cash flow model.

RESIDUAL OPERATING INCOME AS A MANAGEMENT TOOL

Residual operating income, whether calculated as $NOPAT_t - r_{WACC} \times NOA_{t-1}$ or $(RNOA_t - r_{WACC}) \times NOA_{t-1}$, has been adopted by many firms as a management tool. Stern Stewart and Co. introduced the term economic value added (EVA) in the early 1990s and helped firms implement it as a performance measurement. The EVA model was essentially the residual income model with profitability

continued

continued from previous page

being compared to risk for a given level of investment. In doing so, it offered more than 200 adjustments made to financial accounting to improve the measurement.

As seen above when the depreciation method was changed, adjusting the accounting does not change the value calculated, but it does change the amount of *ROPI* (or EVA) in each period. In this text, we focus on valuation, so adjustments are not necessary unless they lead us to differing views of future forecasts (discussed in Chapters 5 and 7). However, if using *ROPI* or EVA as a basis for compensation and/or bonuses, the changes do make a difference. On the project above, when we altered the depreciation, the period 1 *ROPI* changed from –$50 to –$30. Thus, it is important to see that accounting does alter individual period's *ROPI*, but not the total value calculated from the *ROPI*.

Deere & Company discussed a metric called shareholder value added in its 2018 annual report, stating the following on page 21:

> SVA: FOCUSING ON GROWTH AND SUSTAINABLE PERFORMANCE
>
> Shareholder Value Added (SVA)—essentially, the difference between operating profit and the pretax cost of capital—is a metric used by John Deere to evaluate business results and measure sustainable performance. To arrive at SVA, each equipment segment is assessed a pretax cost of assets—generally 12% of average identifiable operating assets with inventory at standard cost (believed to more closely approximate the current cost of inventory and the company's related investment). The financial services segment is assessed a cost of average equity—approximately 15% pretax. The amount of SVA is determined by deducting the asset or equity charge from operating profit.

As you can see, the measure used by Deere & Company is an application of the residual operating income valuation model used by management in measuring the performance of the firm.

DETERMINING VALUE BASED ON THE FORECASTS OF OPERATIONS FOR GENERAL MILLS

LO4: Implement residual operating income valuation using multiyear forecasts and continuing value assumptions.

We will again employ the assumptions in **Exhibit 11.5** for the foreseeable future used to form forecasts of operations for GIS after review of its 2018 financial statements.

EXHIBIT 11.5 GIS Multiyear Forecasts of Sales Growth, *PM*, and *ATO*

	5/26/2019	5/31/2020	5/30/2021	5/29/2022	5/28/2023	5/26/2024
Sales growth.	9.43%	3.03%	–0.62%	1.30%	1.25%	1.20%
Operating *PM*.	12.32%	12.32%	12.45%	12.62%	12.62%	12.62%
Operating *ATO*.	0.688	0.678	0.665	0.651	0.651	0.651

As in Chapters 7 and 10, these assumptions lead to the forecasted numbers shown in **Exhibit 11.6** for 2019 through 2024.

EXHIBIT 11.6 GIS Multiyear Forecasts of Sales, *NOPAT*, and *NOA* ($ millions)

Year Ending	5/27/2018	5/26/2019	5/31/2020	5/30/2021	5/29/2022	5/28/2023	5/26/2024
Weeks in year. . .		52	53	52	52	52	52
Sales.	$15,740.4	$17,224.4 ($15,740.4 × 1.0943)	$17,746.9 ($17,224.4 × 1.0303)	$17,637.8 ($17,747.4 × 0.9938)	$17,867.1 ($17,638.4 × 1.0130)	$18,090.4 ($17,867.4 × 1.0125)	$18,307.5 ($18,090.4 × 1.0120)
NOPAT.		$2,122.0 ($17,224.4 × 12.32%)	$2,186.4 ($17,746.9 × 12.32%)	$2,195.9 ($17,637.8 × 12.45%)	$2,254.8 ($17,867.1 × 12.62%)	$2,283.0 ($18,090.4 × 12.62%)	$2,310.4 ($18,307.5 × 12.62%)
NOA	$25,035.4	$26,291.0 ($17,746.9/0.688) × 52/53	$25,998.1 ($17,637.8/0.678)	$26,854.2 ($17,867.1/0.665)	$27,786.8 ($18,090.4/0.651)	$28,120.3 ($18,307.5/0.651)	$28,457.7 ($18,527.2/0.651)

While we could use these forecasts of *NOPAT* and *NOA* to obtain forecasts of free cash flow from operations (*FCF*) as was done in the previous chapter, this step is not necessary. Based on Equation 11.2, it is clear that value can be computed directly from the accounting information.

While we have forecasts through 2024 (the sixth forecast period), the formula in Equation 11.2 requires the series of all future *NOPAT* and *NOA*. Again, it is obviously impossible to forecast an infinite stream of *NOPAT* and *NOA*. Therefore, we consider the roles of forecasts within an explicit forecast horizon and a forecasted continuing value that captures all periods occurring after the horizon.

THE USE OF CONTINUING VALUES IN THE RESIDUAL OPERATING INCOME VALUATION MODEL

In computing value using the residual operating income valuation model, we again think of the future as containing two separate pieces that are added together just as was done in the *FCF* model. The first is a finite-horizon period for which we have formed explicit forecasts of *ROPI* (the first 5 years through 2023 in our GIS example), and the second is the period beyond this horizon (the period from 2024 to infinity). Within the horizon, we have explicit forecasts where we directly calculate expectations of the forecasts. However, to capture any *ROPI* occurring after the horizon, we must calculate a continuing value, which captures the expectations beyond the horizon. As we will show, this second piece will capture a different proportion of value than was captured in the DCF model.

Equation 11.2 can be rewritten as follows to emphasize this split into two pieces:

$$\begin{aligned} V_0 &= NOA_0 + \sum_{t=1}^{\infty}\left(\frac{NOPAT_t - r_{WACC} \times NOA_{t-1}}{(1+r_{WACC})^t}\right) \\ &= NOA_0 + \sum_{t=1}^{5}\left(\frac{NOPAT_t - r_{WACC} \times NOA_{t-1}}{(1+r_{WACC})^t}\right) + \sum_{t=6}^{\infty}\left(\frac{NOPAT_t - r_{WACC} \times NOA_{t-1}}{(1+r_{WACC})^t}\right) \\ &= NOA_0 + \sum_{t=1}^{5}\left(\frac{ROPI_t}{(1+r_{WACC})^t}\right) + \sum_{t=6}^{\infty}\left(\frac{ROPI_t}{(1+r_{WACC})^t}\right) \end{aligned} \quad (11.3)$$

In Equation 11.3, the term capturing the first five periods is referred to as being within the forecast horizon because it will be computed using forecasts of *NOPAT* and *NOA* for each of the years in the forecast horizon.

The second term of Equation 11.3 captures the continuing value beyond the explicit forecast period. To help show what is captured by the continuing value when using the residual operating income valuation model, we rewrite Equation 11.2 as follows:

$$V_0 = NOA_0 + \sum_{t=1}^{\infty}\left(\frac{NOPAT_t - r_{WACC} \times NOA_{t-1}}{(1+r_{WACC})^t}\right)$$

$$V_0 - NOA_0 = \sum_{t=1}^{\infty}\left(\frac{NOPAT_t - r_{WACC} \times NOA_{t-1}}{(1+r_{WACC})^t}\right)$$

or, more generally, at any point in time *T*:

$$V_T - NOA_T = \sum_{t=1}^{\infty}\left(\frac{NOPAT_{T+t} - r_{WACC} \times NOA_{T+t-1}}{(1+r_{WACC})^t}\right)$$

From this formula, the difference between value and the amount recorded as *NOA* at any point in time *T* is the discounted present value of all future $ROPI_t$ beyond time *T*. This means that Equation 11.3 can be restated as follows:

$$V_0 = NOA_0 + \sum_{t=1}^{5}\left(\frac{NOPAT_t - r_{WACC} \times NOA_{t-1}}{(1+r_{WACC})^t}\right) + \sum_{t=6}^{\infty}\left(\frac{NOPAT_t - r_{WACC} \times NOA_{t-1}}{(1+r_{WACC})^t}\right)$$

$$= NOA_0 + \sum_{t=1}^{5}\left(\frac{NOPAT_t - r_{WACC} \times NOA_{t-1}}{(1+r_{WACC})^t}\right) + \frac{1}{(1+r_{WACC})^5}\sum_{t=6}^{\infty}\left(\frac{NOPAT_t - r_{WACC} \times NOA_{t-1}}{(1+r_{WACC})^{t-5}}\right)$$

$$= NOA_0 + \sum_{t=1}^{5}\left(\frac{NOPAT_t - r_{WACC}\ NOA_{t-1}}{(1+r_{WACC})^t}\right) + \frac{1}{(1+r_{WACC})^5}(V_5 - NOA_5)$$

That is, in the residual operating income valuation model, the continuing value equals the expected difference between intrinsic value and book value of the operations at the horizon. This amount is sometimes referred to as the premium over book value. In the *FCF* model, a problem was that we needed to know the intrinsic value several periods in the future in order to determine the intrinsic value today. Here, we only need to capture the excess of intrinsic value over book value which could even be equal to zero.

To estimate the continuing value at the forecast horizon, we will most often make an assumption that future residual operating income, $NOPAT_t - r_{WACC} \times NOA_{t-1}$, will follow a predictable pattern beyond the horizon. That is, each subsequent amount is related to the previous amount in a systematic manner. Residual operating income can be assumed to show growth that is expected to be constant or fade over time. As a result, we will assume the following holds:

$$NOPAT_{t+1} - r_{WACC} \times NOA_t = (NOPAT_t - r_{WACC} \times NOA_{t-1}) \times (1+g)$$
$$ROPI_{t+1} = ROPI_t \times (1+g)$$

where g is the growth rate in residual operating income after the forecast horizon. Further, the subsequent amount of residual operating income ($NOPAT_{t+2} - r_{WACC} \times NOA_{t+1}$) will reflect two periods of growth such that

$$\begin{aligned} NOPAT_{t+2} - r_{WACC} \times NOA_{t+1} &= (NOPAT_{t+1} - r_{WACC} \times NOA_t) \times (1+g) \\ &= \left[(NOPAT_t - r_{WACC} \times NOA_{t-1}) \times (1+g)\right] \times (1+g) \\ &= (NOPAT_t - r_{WACC} \times NOA_{t-1}) \times (1+g)^2 \\ ROPI_{t+2} &= ROPI_t \times (1+g)^2 \end{aligned}$$

The pattern that emerges allows us to continue refining our understanding of the second term of our valuation equation:

$$\sum_{t=6}^{\infty}\left(\frac{NOPAT_t - r_{WACC} \times NOA_{t-1}}{(1+r_{WACC})^t}\right) = \frac{1}{(1+r_{WACC})^5} \times \left(\begin{array}{l} \dfrac{NOPAT_6 - r_{WACC} \times NOA_5}{(1+r_{WACC})} + \dfrac{NOPAT_7 - r_{WACC} \times NOA_6}{(1+r_{WACC})^2} \\ + \dfrac{NOPAT_8 - r_{WACC}\ NOA_7}{(1+r_{WACC})^3} + \ldots \end{array}\right)$$

$$= \frac{1}{(1+r_{WACC})^5} \times \left(\begin{array}{l} \dfrac{(NOPAT_5 - r_{WACC} \times NOA_4) \times (1+g)}{(1+r_{WACC})} \\ + \dfrac{(NOPAT_5 - r_{WACC} \times NOA_4) \times (1+g)^2}{(1+r_{WACC})^2} \\ + \dfrac{(NOPAT_5 - r_{WACC} \times NOA_4) \times (1+g)^3}{(1+r_{WACC})^3} + \ldots \end{array}\right)$$

$$= \frac{1}{(1+r_{WACC})^5}\left(\frac{ROPI_5\ (1+g)}{(1+r_{WACC})} + \frac{ROPI_5\ (1+g)^2}{(1+r_{WACC})^2} + \frac{ROPI_5\ (1+g)^3}{(1+r_{WACC})^3} + \ldots\right)$$

The last portion of the above equation shows a series that will continue to infinity in a very straightforward manner. Each subsequent term has the numerator multiplied by $(1 + g)$ and the denominator multiplied by $(1 + r_{WACC})$. Provided that the discount rate is greater than the growth rate ($r_{WACC} > g$), this series can be rewritten as follows:

$$\sum_{t=6}^{\infty}\left(\frac{NOPAT_t - r_{WACC}\times NOA_{t-1}}{(1+r_{WACC})^t}\right) = \frac{1}{(1+r_{WACC})^5}\times\left(\begin{array}{l}\dfrac{(NOPAT_5 - r_{WACC}\times NOA_4)\times(1+g)}{(1+r_{WACC})}\\ +\dfrac{(NOPAT_5 - r_{WACC}\times NOA_4)\times(1+g)^2}{(1+r_{WACC})^2}\\ +\dfrac{(NOPAT_5 - r_{WACC}\times NOA_4)\times(1+g)^3}{(1+r_{WACC})^3}+\ldots\end{array}\right)$$

$$= \frac{1}{(1+r_{WACC})^5}\times\left(\frac{(NOPAT_5 - r_{WACC}\times NOA_4)\times(1+g)}{r_{WACC}-g}\right)$$

$$= \frac{1}{(1+r_{WACC})^5}\times\left(\frac{ROPI_5\times(1+g)}{r_{WACC}-g}\right)$$

Combining this with Equation 11.3 yields the following:

$$\begin{aligned} V_0 &= NOA_0 + \frac{NOPAT_1 - r_{WACC}\times NOA_0}{(1+r_{WACC})} + \frac{NOPAT_2 - r_{WACC}\times NOA_1}{(1+r_{WACC})^2} \\ &\quad + \frac{NOPAT_3 - r_{WACC}\times NOA_2}{(1+r_{WACC})^3} + \ldots \\ &= NOA_0 + \sum_{t=1}^{\infty}\left(\frac{NOPAT_t - r_{WACC}\times NOA_{t-1}}{(1+r_{WACC})^t}\right) \\ &= NOA_0 + \sum_{t=1}^{5}\left(\frac{NOPAT_t - r_{WACC}\times NOA_{t-1}}{(1+r_{WACC})^t}\right) \\ &\quad + \frac{1}{(1+r_{WACC})^5}\times\left(\frac{(NOPAT_5 - r_{WACC}\ NOA_4)\times(1+g)}{r_{WACC}-g}\right) \\ &= NOA_0 + \sum_{t=1}^{5}\left(\frac{ROPI_t}{(1+r_{WACC})^t}\right) + \frac{1}{(1+r_{WACC})^5}\times\left(\frac{ROPI_5\times(1+g)}{r_{WACC}-g}\right) \end{aligned} \tag{11.4}$$

Note that the growth rate in Equation 11.4 captures future growth in residual operating income and the growth rate in Equation 10.8 captures future growth in *FCF* from operations. In our examples in this chapter, the growth rate for residual operating income is the same as the growth rate for *FCF*. We will explain the reason for this in Chapter 14. As a reminder, Equation 11.4 holds when the growth rate from year 5 to 6 and all subsequent years is at g.

RESIDUAL OPERATING INCOME VALUATION OF GENERAL MILLS' OPERATIONS

LO5: Prepare a residual operating income valuation spreadsheet for a company's operations.

When valuing GIS' operations using our forecasts formed in Chapter 7, we continue to assume a weighted average cost of capital for operations of 5.3 percent as estimated in Chapter 9. In addition to the assumptions in **Exhibit 11.5**, we assume (as we did in our DCF example) that the sales growth rate stays at 1.2 percent thereafter. We also assume that the growth rate in residual operating income beyond the explicit forecast horizon will be equal to the growth rate in sales of 1.2 percent. The assumption that the growth rates in sales and residual operating income will converge captures the notion that, over time, a firm's growth is driven by its ability to grow sales. If we apply our forecasts going forward, the forecasts of *NOPAT* and *NOA* (essentially **Exhibit 11.6** extended) are as shown in **Exhibit 11.7**.

EXHIBIT 11.7 GIS Multiyear Assumptions and Forecasts

Time Period	5/26/2019	5/31/2020	5/30/2021	5/29/2022	5/28/2023	5/26/2024
Assumptions:						
Sales growth....	9.43%	3.03%	−0.62%	1.30%	1.25%	1.20%
Operating *PM*...	12.32%	12.32%	12.45%	12.62%	12.62%	12.62%
Operating *ATO*..	0.688	0.678	0.665	0.651	0.651	0.651
Forecast (millions):						
Sales..........	$17,224.4	$17,746.9	$17,637.8	$17,867.1	$18,090.4	$18,307.5
NOPAT........	$2,122.0	$2,186.4	$2,195.9	$2,254.8	$2,283.0	$2,310.4
NOA..........	$26,291.0	$25,998.1	$26,854.2	$27,786.8	$28,120.3	$28,457.7

Using this information and our assumptions of the discount rate and growth rate in Equation 11.4, we can calculate the value of GIS' operations. For implementing Equation 11.4, we will use a period of 5 years as our explicit forecast horizon and then use a continuing value to capture period six and beyond. We choose to show the computations in tabular format. The valuation of GIS' operations using residual operating income is illustrated in **Exhibit 11.8**.

EXHIBIT 11.8 Residual Operating Income Model

Required rate of return (r_{WACC}) 5.90%

Time Period	5/27/2018	5/26/2019	5/31/2020	5/30/2021	5/29/2022	5/28/2023
Forecasted sales	$15,740.4	$17,224.4	$17,746.9	$17,637.8	$17,867.1	$18,090.4
NOPAT (Sales × *PM*)...........		2,122.0	2,186.4	2,195.9	2,254.8	2,283.0
NOA (Sales/*ATO*)...............	25,035.4	26,291.0	25,998.1	26,854.2	27,786.8	28,120.3
ROPI ($NOPAT_t - r_{WACC} \times NOA_{t-1}$)...		795.2	793.0	818.0	831.6	810.3
Growth in *ROPI*			−0.27%	3.15%	1.66%	−2.55%
Discount factor $(1 + r_{WACC})^t$........		1.0530	1.1088	1.1676	1.2295	1.2946
Present value of $ROPI_t$...........		755.1	715.2	700.6	676.4	625.9
Sum of present value of $ROPI_t$.....	3,473.2					
Continuing value						
ROPI at horizon...............						820.0
Capitalized						20,000.7
Present value of continuing value...	15,449.1					
Operating value	$43,957.7					

That is, the estimated intrinsic value of the enterprise operations of GIS using the residual operating income valuation model is $43,957.7. Despite using accounting information to estimate value, we arrived at the same result obtained using the well-known free cash flow approach. The fact that we used accounting numbers, which are subject to discretion in choice of accounting methods, did not alter the estimate of value because our assumptions are consistent across the models.

Continuing to preview the decision as to which valuation method might be preferred, we point out that, in this ROIM valuation, the portion of value of the operations captured within the finite forecast horizon is almost 65 percent (i.e., [$25,035.4 + $3,473.2]/$43,957.7). If we looked at only the next 4 years because we have a higher confidence in the near term, the percent of value captured within the short term by the ROIM estimate remains over 63 percent. This means that less than 37 percent is not captured in the next 4 years where we are likely to be most confident in our forecasts. As a reminder, in Chapter 10, almost 90 percent of value was not captured in the next 4 years in the DCF valuation model. Clearly, the anchoring of the value on *NOA* has reduced the portion of the value estimate coming from extended forecasts; importantly, our reliance on the continuing value estimate is diminished.

SUMMARY

This chapter established that accounting information rather than *FCF*s can be used in the valuation of the operations. This is because *FCF* is equal to *NOPAT* adjusted for the change in *NOA*. In this chapter, we derived the residual operating income valuation model and demonstrated its use in valuing a finite-life project. We then demonstrated how to value a firm's operations using our forecasts for GIS, a large, highly-visible, publicly traded firm, using the residual operating income valuation model.

In Chapter 12, we will continue valuation based on accounting information using another accounting-based valuation model. To illustrate this, we will continue to focus on an examination of our project and GIS' enterprise operations. We will also continue to expand on factors to be considered in choosing between valuation models.

QUESTIONS

Q11.1 Explain the role of the equation $FCF = NOPAT - \Delta NOA$ in arriving at the residual operating income valuation formula.

Q11.2 What is the equation for residual operating income?

Q11.3 In words, what is the residual operating income?

Q11.4 What are the three components in ROIM valuation?

Q11.5 What is the role of book value in the ROIM valuation?

Q11.6 In ROIM, what does does the continuing value equal?

Q11.7 What effect does income shifting have on the value calculated using the ROIM?

Q11.8 What is an example of income shifting that is allowable within accounting?

Q11.9 What is an example of income shifting that is not allowed under accounting rules but may arise due to actions taken by managers?

Q11.10 How is the ROIM different from the DCF valuation model?

EXERCISES

E11.11 Beaver Co. completed the year with sales of \$30.0 million and *NOPAT* of \$4.5 million. *NOA* at year end is \$48.5 million. Management estimates for the next 4 years, sales will grow at 6 percent per year with an operating *PM* of 15 percent and operating *ATO* of 0.65 times. Using the ROIM, calculate Beaver's operating value with an 8.0 percent r_{WACC}.

E11.12 Continuing with the data from E11.11, Beaver's management is considering outsourcing some of its production. This will reduce the *NOA* required as well increase Beaver's *ATO* from 0.65 to 0.80 times. However, estimated *PM* will decline from 15 percent to 13 percent. What impact will the outsourcing proposal have on Beaver's operating value?

E11.13 Continuing with the data from E11.11, Beaver's management is considering a promotional opportunity to acquire the naming rights to a prominent sports stadium. This proposal is expected to increase sales growth to 7 percent from 6 percent. However, estimated *PM* will decline from 15 percent to 14 percent. What impact will the stadium naming rights proposal have on Beaver's operating value?

E11.14 At February 2, 2019, Home Depot (HD) had *NOA* of \$25,546 million. Using a r_{WACC} of 8 percent, the present value of the next 4 years (FY2019–FY2022) of the estimated *ROPI* is \$47,462 million.

a. Assume that the $ROPI_{FY2022}$ at the forecast horizon is \$17,300 million. Following the forecast horizon, it is expected that HD's *NOPAT* will equal 8 percent of its *NOA*. That is, the expected *ROPI* beyond the forecast horizon is zero. What is HD's operating value at February 2, 2019, using a ROIM?

b. Assume that the $ROPI_{FY2022}$ at the forecast horizon is \$17,300 million. Following the forecast horizon, it is expected that HD's *ROPI* will remain constant. What is HD's operating value at February 2, 2019, using a ROIM?

c. Assume that the $ROPI_{FY2022}$ at the forecast horizon is \$17,300 million. Following the forecast horizon, it is expected that HD's *ROPI* will grow at 2.0 percent per year. What is HD's operating value at February 2, 2019, using a ROIM?

E11. 15 LKQ Corporation, an automotive specialty part manufacturer, announced a share repurchase program in late 2018. In the company's press release, LKQ's president and CEO stated, "This repurchase program . . . reflects an efficient way to enhance long-term shareholder value."[2]

Do stock buybacks create shareholder value? Explain your answer from a *ROPI* perspective.

LKQ Corporation

LKQ Corporation Announces $500 Million Stock Repurchase Program
October 25, 2018

CHICAGO, Oct. 25, 2018 (GLOBE NEWSWIRE)—LKQ Corporation (Nasdaq:LKQ) today announced that its Board of Directors has authorized a stock repurchase program. Under the program, LKQ Corporation may purchase up to $500 million of its common stock from time to time through October 25, 2021. The timing and the amount of any repurchases of common stock will be determined by LKQ management based on its evaluation of market conditions and other factors. At September 30, 2018, the Company had 318.2 million shares of common stock outstanding.

Dominick Zarcone, President and Chief Executive Officer of LKQ Corporation, stated, "*This repurchase program demonstrates the board's confidence in our future and reflects an efficient way to enhance long-term stockholder value.* Our main priorities are to continue to both invest in the growth of our global business and deleverage the balance sheet. Our strong balance sheet and healthy cash flow position affords us the opportunity to continue investing in our strategic growth drivers while simultaneously utilizing a share repurchase program to maintain a balanced capital allocation strategy."

CONTINUING EXAMPLES

CE11.16 Once again, the company has been offered the opportunity to invest in a project expected to yield the following cash flows. Note that the anticipated risk of the project implies a cost of capital of 10 percent would be appropriate:

Anticipated Cash Flows of Finite-Life Project	
Purchase price	$2,300
Payoffs:	
Year 1	$600
Year 2	700
Year 3	750
Year 4	625
Year 5	500
Proceeds from disposition	240

Assume initially that the company plans to fully depreciate the project using the straight line method over the 5-year period, resulting in $412 in depreciation per period. Using the ROIM, determine the value of the project and whether to make an investment in this project. How does this value compare to the value computed based on cash flows in Chapter 10?

CE11.17 Assume that instead of fully depreciating the project, the company decides to record depreciation of $300 per year. Use the ROIM to value the project. What effect does this change in profits due to altering depreciation have on the value calculation?

CE11.18 Repeat the valuation of the project utilizing the assumption that the company forgot to record any depreciation at all during the project's life. What effect does this change in profits due to altering depreciation have on the value calculation?

CE11.19 The Hatfield Company evaluates internal projects for their financial viability as part of their overall analysis. One proposed project is to automate a portion of Hatfield's production process. The additional equipment has an estimated useful life of 6 years. The operations manager provided the expected cost savings from the installation of the robotic equipment. The project is expected to yield the following cash flows:

[2] https://investor.lkqcorp.com/press-releases/press-releases-details/2018/LKQ-Corporation-Announces-500-Million-Stock-Repurchase-Program/default.aspx

Anticipated Cash Flows of Finite-Life Project	
Purchase price	$8,500
Payoffs:	
Year 1	$700
Year 2	1,900
Year 3	2,900
Year 4	3,500
Year 5	3,000
Year 6	2,700
Proceeds from disposition	400

In addition, Hatfield's management requires a hurdle rate of 16 percent for internally proposed projects, which is greater than the actual project risk. Assume initially that the company plans to fully depreciate the project using the straight-line method over the 6-year period, resulting in $1,350 in depreciation per period. Using the ROIM, determine the value of the project and whether to invest in it. How does this value compare to value computed based on cash flows in Chapter 10?

CE11.20 Using the following forecast assumptions from Chapter 7 for Kellogg (K), the weighted average cost of capital for operations of 5.2 percent calculated in Chapter 9, and a continuing growth in residual operating income beyond the forecast horizon of 0.4 percent, calculate the value of K's operations. How does this estimate of value compare to that arrived at using the cash flow-based valuation method in Chapter 10?

K Multiyear Assumptions	2019E	2020E	2021E	2022E	2023E	2024E	2025E	2026E	2027E
Assumptions:									
Sales growth	0.57%	2.41%	−1.42%	0.50%	0.45%	0.40%	2.32%	−1.49%	0.40%
Operating *PM*	9.36%	9.58%	10.00%	10.17%	10.55%	10.55%	10.55%	10.55%	10.55%
Operating *ATO*	1.052	0.974	0.962	0.951	0.951	0.951	0.951	0.951	0.951

CE11.21 Using the following forecast assumptions from Chapter 7 for Thor Industries (THO), the weighted average cost of capital for operations of 12.60 percent calculated in Chapter 9, and a continuing growth in residual operating income beyond the forecast horizon of 1.00 percent, calculate the value of THO's operations. How does this estimate of value compare to that arrived at using the cash flow-based valuation method in Chapter 10?

THO Multiyear Assumptions	FY2019E	FY2020E	FY2021E	FY2022E	FY2023E	FY2024E
Assumptions:						
Sales growth	5.56%	3.61%	1.61%	1.40%	1.20%	1.00%
Operating *PM*	5.78%	5.77%	5.40%	5.35%	5.15%	5.15%
Operating *ATO*	4.815	4.329	4.219	4.098	4.098	4.098

CE11.22 Using the following forecast assumptions from Chapter 7 for Winnebago (WGO), the weighted average cost of capital for operations of 10.60 percent calculated in Chapter 9, and a continuing growth in residual operating income beyond the forecast horizon of 0.90 percent, calculate the value of WGO's operations. How does this estimate of value compare to that arrived at using the cash flow-based valuation method in Chapter 10?

WGO Multiyear Assumptions	FY2019E	FY2020E	FY2021E	FY2022E	FY2023E	FY2024E	FY2025E	FY2026E
Assumptions:								
Weeks	53	52	52	52	52	53	52	52
Sales growth	4.56%	0.11%	1.38%	1.10%	2.82%	−0.99%	0.90%	0.90%
Operating *PM*	6.40%	6.27%	6.20%	6.03%	6.03%	6.03%	6.03%	6.03%
Operating *ATO*	2.309	2.288	2.294	2.294	2.294	2.294	2.294	2.294

Chapter Twelve

Valuation Using the Abnormal Operating Income Growth Model

TAKEAWAYS

When you complete this chapter, you should be able to:

1. Explain that the abnormal operating income growth model is mathematically equivalent to the free cash flow model.
2. Compute the value of a finite-life project using the abnormal operating income growth model.
3. Understand that the value estimated using the abnormal operating income growth model does not change based on accounting methods, choices, or assumptions.
4. Implement abnormal operating income growth valuation using multiyear forecasts and continuing value assumptions.
5. Prepare an abnormal operating income growth valuation spreadsheet for a company's operations.

Chapters 10 and 11 introduced the free cash flow valuation and residual operating income valuation models. An important prelude to this process was detailing the relation between cash flows and accounting information in Chapter 2. In this chapter, we continue with the valuation of the project and the operations of General Mills (GIS). This time, we continue exploring how value may be estimated using forecasted accounting information by the introduction of the abnormal operating income growth model (AOIGM). This method also uses the accounting information, which is readily available and the focus of analysts and investors alike. A primary difference between AOIGM and the residual operating income model (ROIM), which we discussed in the prior chapter, is the accounting anchor employed. AOIGM anchors the valuation on the capitalized forecast of next-year's net operating profit after tax (*NOPAT*) while the ROIM anchors the valuation on current net operating assets (*NOA*).

We begin by reconsidering the project yet again. We will use the project to demonstrate the second accounting-based valuation model, and then we apply this model to valuing our finite-life (i.e., limited duration) project. Examination of the same finite-life project will provide clarity on whether the model is "working" and clarify the steps in its implementation. Finally, we apply the accounting-based abnormal operating income growth, valuation model to GIS' operations to see the application to this large, visible, publicly-traded firm.

MOVING FROM CASH FLOWS TO ACCOUNTING DATA IN VALUING A FINITE-LIFE PROJECT

Beginning in Chapter 10, we have examined the opportunity to invest in a project with the following anticipated cash flows at the end of each year shown in **Exhibit 12.1**.

CHAPTER OUTLINE

Valuation Using the Abnormal Operating Income Growth Model

Abnormal Operating Income Growth Valuation
- Derivation from Cash Flows Model
- Role of Cum-Free-Cash-Flow Earnings
- Valuing a Finite-Life Project

Accounting Choices
- Effects of Alternative Depreciation Methods

Valuation of Operations
- Multiyear Forecasts
- Continuing Values
- Valuing General Mills' Operations

EXHIBIT 12.1 Anticipated Cash Flows of Finite-Life Project

Purchase price		$1,000.00
Payoffs		
Year 1 cash flow (CF_1)		250.00
Year 2 cash flow (CF_2)		350.00
Year 3 cash flow (CF_3)		320.00
Year 4 cash flows (CF_4)		
Proceeds from sales	$280.00	
Proceeds from disposition	200.00	
		480.00
Required rate of return = r_P.		10%

As a reminder, Equation 10.5 showed that we can value a project using cash flows as follows:

$$V_0 = \frac{CF_1}{(1+r_P)} + \frac{CF_2}{(1+r_P)^2} + \frac{CF_3}{(1+r_P)^3} + \frac{CF_4}{(1+r_P)^4} = \sum_{t=1}^{4}\left(\frac{CF_t}{(1+r_P)^t}\right) \tag{10.5}$$

When the expected cash flows for the project were entered into the above formula, we computed the following present value:

$$\begin{aligned} V_0 &= \frac{CF_1}{(1+r_P)} + \frac{CF_2}{(1+r_P)^2} + \frac{CF_3}{(1+r_P)^3} + \frac{CF_4}{(1+r_P)^4} \\ &= \frac{250.00}{(1+0.10)^1} + \frac{350.00}{(1+0.10)^2} + \frac{320.00}{(1+0.10)^3} + \frac{480.00}{(1+0.10)^4} \\ &= \frac{250.00}{1.1} + \frac{350.00}{1.21} + \frac{320.00}{1.331} + \frac{480.00}{1.4641} \\ &= 227.27 + 289.26 + 240.42 + 327.85 \\ &= 1{,}084.80 \end{aligned}$$

In Chapter 11, we moved from cash flow-based valuation to accounting-based valuation with the aid of the following equation arrived at in Chapter 2:

$$\begin{aligned} FCF_t &= NOPAT_t + NOA_{t-1} - NOA_t \\ &= NOPAT_t - \Delta NOA_t \end{aligned} \tag{2.2}$$

Also in Chapter 11, we utilized a zero-sum equation that anchored on *NOA*. This allowed for the derivation of the residual operating income valuation model. In this chapter, we again utilize a zero-sum equation, but instead of anchoring on *NOA*, we will anchor on capitalized expected net operating profit after tax ($NOPAT/r_{WACC}$).

DERIVATION OF THE ABNORMAL OPERATING INCOME GROWTH VALUATION MODEL

LO1: Explain that the abnormal operating income growth model is mathematically equivalent to the free cash flow model.

The derivation of the *AOIG* valuation model follows the same steps as the derivation of ROIM. The derivation again is simple and straightforward if we are prepared to pause so that we can carefully understand the two unequivocal and indisputable steps. Again, the derivation begins with the discounted *FCF* valuation model:

$$V_0 = \frac{FCF_1}{(1+r_{WACC})} + \frac{FCF_2}{(1+r_{WACC})^2} + \frac{FCF_3}{(1+r_{WACC})^3} + \frac{FCF_4}{(1+r_{WACC})^4} + \ldots = \sum_{t=1}^{\infty}\left(\frac{FCF_t}{(1+r_{WACC})^t}\right) \quad (10.6)$$

The next step is introducing the valuation anchor to be used in this model; that is, capitalized next period *NOPAT* $\left(NOPAT_1/r_{WACC}\right)$. Similar to the derivation of the residual operating income valuation model, we introduce this starting point by recognizing the simple mathematical fact that, if we add and, at the same time, subtract the present value of each future year's capitalized *NOPAT* in the right side of Equation 10.6, we will not affect the mathematical integrity of the equation. Specifically, we introduce the following zero-sum equality:

$$0 = NOPAT_1/r_{WACC} + \frac{NOPAT_2/r_{WACC} - (1+r_{WACC})\,NOPAT_1/r_{WACC}}{(1+r_{WACC})} + \frac{NOPAT_3/r_{WACC} - (1+r_{WACC})\,NOPAT_2/r_{WACC}}{(1+r_{WACC})^2} + \ldots.. \quad (12.1)$$

The fact that we have simply added and subtracted the present value of each future period's capitalized *NOPAT* is more evident if we rearrange Equation 12.1 as follows:

$$0 = NOPAT_1/r_{WACC} - NOPAT_1/r_{WACC} + \frac{NOPAT_2/r_{WACC}}{(1+r_{WACC})} - \frac{NOPAT_2/r_{WACC}}{(1+r_{WACC})} + \frac{NOPAT_3/r_{WACC}}{(1+r_{WACC})^2} - \frac{NOPAT_3/r_{WACC}}{(1+r_{WACC})^2} + \ldots..$$

The next step is to add the left sides of Equations 10.6 and 12.1 and to add the right hand sides to obtain

$$V_0 = NOPAT_1/r_{WACC} + \sum_{t=1}^{\infty}\left(\frac{NOPAT_{t+1}/r_{WACC} + FCF_t - (1+r_{WACC}) \times NOPAT_t/r_{WACC}}{(1+r_{WACC})^t}\right)$$

Simplifying and rearranging the prior equation yields the *AOIG* valuation model:

$$\begin{aligned} V_0 &= \frac{NOPAT_1}{r_{WACC}} + \sum_{t=1}^{\infty}\left(\frac{\frac{NOPAT_{t+1}}{r_{WACC}} + FCF_t - (1+r_{WACC}) \times \frac{NOPAT_t}{r_{WACC}}}{(1+r_{WACC})^t}\right) \\ &= \frac{NOPAT_1}{r_{WACC}} + \sum_{t=1}^{\infty}\left(\frac{NOPAT_{t+1} + r_{WACC} \times FCF_t - (1+r_{WACC}) \times NOPAT_t}{r_{WACC} \times (1+r_{WACC})^t}\right) \\ &= \frac{1}{r_{WACC}} \times \left[NOPAT_1 + \sum_{t=1}^{\infty}\left(\frac{NOPAT_{t+1} + r_{WACC} \times FCF_t - (1+r_{WACC}) \times NOPAT_t}{(1+r_{WACC})^t}\right)\right] \end{aligned} \tag{12.2}$$

The numerator of the last term in Equation 12.2, $[NOPAT_{t+1} + r_{WACC} \times FCF_t - (1 + r_{WACC}) \times NOPAT_t]$, is referred to as abnormal operating income growth, which will be denoted $AOIG_{t+1}$.[1] This allows us to write the formula for the model as follows:

$$\begin{aligned} V_0 &= \frac{1}{r_{WACC}} \times \left[NOPAT_1 + \sum_{t=1}^{\infty}\left(\frac{NOPAT_{t+1} + r_{WACC} \times FCF_t - (1+r_{WACC}) \times NOPAT_t}{(1+r_{WACC})^t}\right)\right] \\ &= \frac{1}{r_{WACC}} \times \left[NOPAT_1 + \sum_{t=1}^{\infty}\left(\frac{AOIG_{t+1}}{(1+r_{WACC})^t}\right)\right] \end{aligned} \tag{12.3}$$

The Role of Cum-Free-Cash-Flow Earnings in the Abnormal Operating Income Growth Valuation Model

Within the discussion of the residual operating income valuation model, it was clear that we were comparing earnings ($NOPAT_t$) to the expected amount of earnings given the level of beginning book value ($r_{WACC} \times NOA_{t-1}$). A similar comparison is occurring in the *AOIG* valuation model, but that fact may not be immediately obvious. Here, we compare cum-free-cash-flow earnings next year ($NOPAT_{t+1} + r_{WACC} \times FCF_t$) to the expected amount of earnings given earnings of the current period $[(1 + r_{WACC}) \times NOPAT_t]$.

The second element of *AOIG*, $[(1 + r_{WACC}) \times NOPAT_t]$, captures the notion that, normally, earnings would be expected to grow at the required rate of return. In our savings account example in Chapter 10, the second period's earnings ($30.90) because 3 percent larger than the first period's earnings ($30.00) as the earnings retained in the account have become part of the investment. Earnings in the future are expected to grow at the required rate of return.

The cum-free-cash-flow earnings, ($NOPAT_{t+1} + r_{WACC} \times FCF_t$), includes an element that serves as an adjustment to earnings expected from the operations ($NOPAT_{t+1}$) by adding $r_{WACC} \times FCF_t$. This adjustment captures earnings that may reasonably be expected to accrue outside of the firm's operations as a result of the reinvestment of the prior year's distribution, FCF_t, which occurred in the prior period. This embodies two important economic principles. First, if a distribution is made, there will be fewer assets remaining in place that can be used to earn in the subsequent period. Second, the party (debt or equity holder) receiving the distribution would be able to invest that distribution elsewhere at an equivalent rate of return. This can best be illustrated by returning to the savings account example.

A small change in the savings account example illustrates the concept behind the reinvestment of the *FCF*. If, at the end of period 1, a withdrawal of $20.00 is made from the savings account, there will only be $1,010.00 left in the bank to earn in the next period. Note that the withdrawal

[1] Throughout most of the text, we will write out $[NOPAT_{t+1} + r_{WACC} \times FCF_t - (1 + r_{WACC}) \times NOPAT_t]$ instead of referring to $AOIG_{t+1}$ to emphasize the computations.

is, in principle, equivalent to a distribution of *FCF*s from a project. Following this withdrawal, the earnings for period 2 would be \$30.30 (i.e., 3% × \$1,010.00). However, the \$20.00 that was withdrawn in period 1 could have been invested at a rate of return equal to that offered by the savings account somewhere else, where it would have earned \$0.60 (i.e., 3% × \$20.00). The total cum-dividend earnings would still be \$30.90, comprised of the amount earned within the account (\$30.30) plus the amount earned outside the account on the money distributed in the prior period (\$0.60). This amount is the same as the expected earnings we would have observed had no distribution occurred (\$30.90 = 3% × \$1,030.00). In other words, cum-free-cash-flow earnings are not affected by the amount distributed in the prior period, while ex-free-cash-flow earnings (i.e., $NOPAT_{t+1}$) are affected.

When computing cum-free-cash-flow earnings, we assume the distribution received was invested in an alternative with equivalent risk. Thus, a distribution from a savings account would be reinvested in an alternative with low risk, a distribution from the project would be reinvested in an alternative with a rate of return equal to r_P, and a distribution from the operations would be reinvested in an alternative with the rate of return equal to r_{WACC}, the weighted average cost of capital for operations.[2]

Now, let us proceed to apply the *AOIG* valuation model to the valuation of the finite-life project.

PROJECT VALUATION USING THE ABNORMAL OPERATING INCOME GROWTH MODEL

LO2: Compute the value of a finite-life project using the abnormal operating income growth model.

The four-period *AOIG* valuation model based on Equation 12.3 is

$$V_0 = \frac{1}{r_P} \times \left[NOPAT_1 + \frac{AOIG_2}{(1+r_P)} + \frac{AOIG_3}{(1+r_P)^2} + \frac{AOIG_4}{(1+r_P)^3} + \frac{AOIG_5}{(1+r_P)^4} \right]$$

where r_P again is the required discount rate for the project.[3] To observe the computation of *AOIG*, we expand the formula as follows:

$$V_0 = \frac{1}{r_P} \times \left[\begin{array}{l} NOPAT_1 + \dfrac{NOPAT_2 + r_P \times FCF_1 - (1+r_P) \times NOPAT_1}{(1+r_P)} \\ + \dfrac{NOPAT_3 + r_P \times FCF_2 - (1+r_P) \times NOPAT_2}{(1+r_P)^2} \\ + \dfrac{NOPAT_4 + r_P \times FCF_3 - (1+r_P) \times NOPAT_3}{(1+r_P)^3} \\ + \dfrac{NOPAT_5 + r_P \times FCF_4 - (1+r_P) \times NOPAT_4}{(1+r_P)^4} \end{array} \right]$$

Recall the following accounting information about the project from Chapter 10 as shown in **Exhibit 12.2**.

[2] The idea here is that, if your chosen investment is a low-risk savings account, this is the risk level at which you are willing to make other investments. Also, note that, if, instead of choosing to reinvest the withdrawn funds from your savings account, you choose to spend these funds on, say, theater tickets, the opportunity cost of this spending is, in this example, 3 percent, and you have foregone earnings in the next period of \$0.60. The notion that an alternative investment with equal risk is available is standard in finance.

[3] Note that $AOIG_1$ does not enter the computation. We notate *AOIG* in such a way that the first term (the *NOPAT*) has the same subscript as *AOIG*.

EXHIBIT 12.2 Accounting Income and Distributions for Finite-Life Project

Time Period	0	1	2	3	4
Net income ($NOPAT_t$)		50.00	150.00	120.00	80.00
Distributions (FCF_t)	(1,000.00)	250.00	350.00	320.00	480.00

Inputting the accounting information into the equation above, we can solve for the value of the project:

$$V_0 = \frac{1}{r_P} \times \left[\begin{array}{l} NOPAT_1 + \dfrac{NOPAT_2 + r_P \times FCF_1 - (1+r_P) \times NOPAT_1}{(1+r_P)} \\ + \dfrac{NOPAT_3 + r_P \times FCF_2 - (1+r_P) \times NOPAT_2}{(1+r_P)^2} \\ + \dfrac{NOPAT_4 + r_P \times FCF_3 - (1+r_P) \times NOPAT_3}{(1+r_P)^3} \\ + \dfrac{NOPAT_5 + r_P \times FCF_4 - (1+r_P) \times NOPAT_4}{(1+r_P)^4} \end{array} \right]$$

$$= \frac{1}{0.10} \times \left[\begin{array}{l} 50.00 + \dfrac{150.00 + 0.10 \times 250.00 - (1+0.10) \times 50.00}{(1+0.10)} \\ + \dfrac{120.00 + 0.10 \times 350.00 - (1+0.10) \times 150.00}{(1+0.10)^2} \\ + \dfrac{80.00 + 0.10 \times 320.00 - (1+0.10) \times 120.00}{(1+0.10)^3} \\ + \dfrac{0.00 + 0.10 \times 480.00 - (1+0.10) \times 80.00}{(1+0.10)^4} \end{array} \right]$$

Note that, in the above equation, $NOPAT_5$ enters into the equation even though the project is only four periods long. This is because, given there were earnings in period 4, we would expect them to grow and even if not earned in the project (since it was completed), the distributed funds (FCF_4) should be expected to generate earnings in period 5. Therefore, expected cum-dividend earnings in period 5 is not zero, and it must be compared to the expected amount given the earnings occurring in period 4.

Continuing to simplify, we see:

$$V_0 = \frac{1}{0.10} \times \left[\begin{array}{l} 50.00 + \dfrac{150.00 + 25.00 - 55.00}{1.1} + \dfrac{120.00 + 35.00 - 165.00}{1.21} \\ + \dfrac{80.00 + 32.00 - 132.00}{1.331} + \dfrac{0.00 + 48.00 - 88.00}{1.4641} \end{array} \right]$$

$$= \frac{1}{0.10} \times \left[50.00 + \frac{120.00}{1.1} + \frac{-10.00}{1.21} + \frac{-20.00}{1.331} + \frac{-40.00}{1.4641} \right]$$

$$= \frac{1}{0.10} \times [50.00 + 109.09 - 8.26 - 15.03 - 27.32]$$

$$= \frac{1}{0.10} \times [108.48]$$

$$= 1{,}084.80$$

Using the *AOIG* valuation model to calculate project value, we again see that $V_0 = \$1{,}084.80$, which matches the value calculated using either the DCF valuation model in Chapter 10 or ROIM in Chapter 11. This reinforces that all three models are mathematically equivalent. This must be so, because the two accounting-based valuation models can be algebraically derived from the DCF model.

Shown in tabular format, the AOIGM valuation can be demonstrated as shown in **Exhibit 12.3**.

EXHIBIT 12.3 Abnormal Operating Income Growth Model Valuation of Finite-Life Project

	Required rate of return (r_P)	10.0%					
	Time period	**0**	**1**	**2**	**3**	**4**	**5**
	Revenues		$250.00	$350.00	$320.00	$280.00	$ 0.00
−	Depreciation		200.00	200.00	200.00	200.00	0.00
+	Gain on sale					0.00	
=	Net project income ($NOPAT_t$)		50.00	150.00	120.00	80.00	0.00
	Revenues		250.00	350.00	320.00	280.00	0.00
+	Proceeds from sale					200.00	
=	Distributions (FCF_t)		250.00	350.00	320.00	480.00	0.00
	Net project income ($NOPAT_t$)		50.00	150.00	120.00	80.00	0.00
+	Earnings from reinvestment of distributions ($r_P \times FCF_{t-1}$)			25.00	35.00	32.00	48.00
=	Cum-*FCF* earnings			175.00	155.00	112.00	48.00
−	Expected income given last period's earnings [$(1 + r_P) \times NOPAT_{t-1}$]			55.00	165.00	132.00	88.00
=	$AOIG_t$			120.00	−10.00	−20.00	−40.00
÷	Discount factor $(1 + r_P)^{t-1}$			1.1	1.21	1.331	1.4641
=	Discounted $AOIG_t$			$109.09	$ −8.26	$−15.03	$−27.32
+	Total discounted $AOIG_t$		58.48				
	Total to be capitalized		$108.48				
	Value of project	$1,084.80					

Note, again, that the calculation using the AOIGM includes a period 5 to recognize the effects of distributions made in period 4. These period 4 distributions include both the revenues of the project and the proceeds from the sale of the project consistent with what was done previously in the DCF and the ROIM valuations.

EFFECTS OF ACCOUNTING CHOICES ON THE ABNORMAL OPERATING INCOME GROWTH MODEL

LO3: Understand that the value estimated using the abnormal operating income growth model does not change based on accounting methods, choices, or assumptions.

Next, let us demonstrate that the accountant's choice of the method of depreciation does not affect the valuation of the project when employing the AOIGM. Accounting choices should not affect valuation using this model because the underlying economic transactions have not changed, so value should be unchanged. Any effect of excess or too little depreciation is taken care of in the gain or loss on sale at the end of the project's life. That is, future earnings will be affected by an offsetting amount. However, because we are capitalizing earnings and changing the timing of earnings recognition, the effect of this accounting choice on the model may not be obvious.

Suppose the accountant records $200.00 of depreciation when the asset is purchased and still records $200.00 in each year thereafter. This will result in a reduction of period 0 income, but this does not appear in our formula. Further, because the project will be fully depreciated by the time it is sold, a gain on sale of $200.00 will need to be recognized, thus increasing period 4 income. Although the forecasted project income will change, the value will not change, as we see in **Exhibit 12.4**.

EXHIBIT 12.4 Abnormal Operating Income Growth Model Valuation of Finite-Life Project with Alternative Depreciation Assumption

Required rate of return (r_P) 10.0%

	Time Period	0	1	2	3	4	5
	Revenues	$ 0.00	$250.00	$350.00	$320.00	$280.00	$ 0.00
−	Depreciation	200.00	200.00	200.00	200.00	200.00	0.00
+	Gain on sale					200.00	
=	Net project income ($NOPAT_t$)	(−200.00)	50.00	150.00	120.00	280.00	0.00
	Revenues		250.00	350.00	320.00	280.00	0.00
+	Proceeds from sale					200.00	
=	Distributions (FCF_t)		250.00	350.00	320.00	480.00	0.00
	Net project income ($NOPAT_t$)		50.00	150.00	120.00	280.00	0.00
+	Earnings from reinvestment of distributions ($r_P \times FCF_{t-1}$)			25.00	35.00	32.00	48.00
=	Cum-*FCF* earnings			175.00	155.00	312.00	48.00
−	Expected income given last period's earnings [$(1 + r_P) \times NOPAT_{t-1}$]			55.00	165.00	132.00	308.00
=	$AOIG_t$			120.00	−10.00	180.00	−260.00
÷	Discount factor $(1 + r_P)^{t-1}$			1.1	1.21	1.331	1.4641
=	Discounted $AOIG_t$			$109.09	$ −8.26	$135.24	$−177.58
+	Total discounted $AOIG_t$		58.48				
	Total to be capitalized		$108.48				
	Value of project	$1,084.80					

The value calculated using the AOIGM remains unchanged.

This example of changing the depreciation method demonstrates the way that the self-correcting nature of accounting is central to AOIGM just as it was to the residual operating income valuation model. In this example, earlier depreciation leads to current (year 0) *NOPAT* that is lower. But, once this depreciation has been taken, it cannot be taken again and future (year 4) *NOPAT* will be higher by exactly the amount of the excess depreciation due to a gain, at the time of sale. Similarly, other accounting choices and rules that lead to lower current earnings (e.g., expensing rather than capitalizing research and development [R&D]) will also lead to correspondingly higher future income when R&D expenses that lead to higher future sales have already been taken.

We see in this example that the *AOIG* valuation model anchors the valuation on capitalized operating income of the next period $\left(NOPAT_1/r_{WACC}\right)$, which is affected by choice of accounting methods. Future *AOIG* will include an adjustment to this valuation to counter the effect that accounting rules and procedures have on this valuation anchor.

Having seen that the AOIGM produced the same value estimate for our project as the DCF model, we proceed to the valuation of GIS' operations based on our detailed forecasts in Chapter 7. Here, we will see the implementation of the *AOIG* valuation model on a going concern. This situation will include the use of a continuing value similar to that seen in the DCF model and ROIM.

DETERMINING VALUE BASED ON THE FORECASTS OF OPERATIONS FOR GENERAL MILLS

LO4: Implement abnormal operating income growth valuation using multiyear forecasts and continuing value assumptions.

We will again employ the assumptions shown in **Exhibit 12.5** for the foreseeable future to form forecasts of operations for GIS after review of its 2018 financial statements:

EXHIBIT 12.5 GIS Multiyear Forecasts of Sales Growth, *PM*, and *ATO*

Year Ending	5/26/2019	5/31/2020	5/30/2021	5/29/2022	5/28/2023	5/26/2024
Sales growth.	9.43%	3.03%	−0.62%	1.30%	1.25%	1.20%
Operating *PM*.	12.32%	12.32%	12.45%	12.62%	12.62%	12.62%
Operating *ATO*.	0.688	0.678	0.665	0.651	0.651	0.651

As in Chapters 7, 10, and 11, these assumptions lead to the forecasted numbers shown in **Exhibit 12.6** for 2019 through 2024.

EXHIBIT 12.6 GIS Multiyear Forecasts of Sales, *NOPAT*, and *NOA* ($ Millions)

Year Ending	5/27/2018	5/26/2019	5/31/2020	5/30/2021	5/29/2022	5/28/2023	5/26/2024
Weeks in year. . .		52	53	52	52	52	52
Sales.	$15,740.4	$17,224.4	$17,746.9	$17,637.8	$17,867.1	$18,090.4	$18,307.5
		($15,740.4 × 1.0943)	($17,224.4 × 1.0303)	($17,747.4 × 0.9938)	($17,638.4 × 1.0130)	($17,867.4 × 1.0125)	($18,090.4 × 1.0120)
NOPAT.		$2,122.0	$2,186.4	$2,195.9	$2,254.8	$2,283.0	$2,310.4
		($17,224.4 × 12.32%)	($17,746.9 × 12.32%)	($17,637.8 × 12.45%)	($17,867.1 × 12.62%)	($18,090.4 × 12.62%)	($18,307.5 × 12.62%)
NOA	$25,035.4	$26,291.0	$25,998.1	$26,854.2	$27,786.8	$28,120.3	$28,457.7
		($17,746.9/0.688) × 52/53	($17,637.8/0.678)	($17,867.1/0.665)	($18,090.4/0.651)	($18,307.5/0.651)	($18,527.2/0.651)

We can use these forecasts of *NOPAT* and *NOA* to obtain the forecasts of *FCF*, which is equal to *NOPAT* minus the change in *NOA*. The calculation of *FCF*s from operations utilized in the AOIGM and the *AOIG* would then be as shown in **Exhibit 12.7**.

EXHIBIT 12.7 GIS Multiyear Forecasts of *AOIG* ($ Millions)

Year Ending	5/26/2019	5/31/2020	5/30/2021	5/29/2022	5/28/2023	5/26/2024
Sales.	$17,224.4	$17,746.9	$17,637.8	$17,867.1	$18,090.4	$18,307.5
NOPAT.	2,122.0	2,186.4	2,195.9	2,254.8	2,283.0	2,310.4
NOA	26,291.0	25,998.1	26,854.2	27,786.8	28,120.3	28,457.7
Δ*NOA*.	1,255.6	(292.9)	856.1	932.7	333.4	337.4
FCF (*NOPAT* − Δ*NOA*) . . .	866.5	2,479.3	1,339.8	1,322.2	1,949.6	1,973.0
AOIG.		−2.2	25.0	13.5	−21.2	9.7

Thus, we have forecasts of *NOPAT* and *FCF* to allow us to utilize the AOIGM for GIS. While we have forecasts through 2024 (the sixth forecast period), the formula in Equation 12.3 requires the series of all future *AOIG*. Again, it is obviously impossible to forecast an infinite stream of *NOPAT* and *FCF* for computing *AOIG*. Therefore, we consider the roles of forecasts within an explicit forecast horizon and a forecasted continuing value that captures all periods occurring after the horizon.

THE USE OF CONTINUING VALUES IN THE ABNORMAL OPERATING INCOME GROWTH VALUATION MODEL

In computing value using the *AOIG* valuation model, we need to think of the future as containing two separate pieces that are added together just as we did in the DCF model and ROIM. The first is a finite-horizon period for which we will form explicit forecasts of *AOIG* (the first five realizations of *AOIG* through 2024 in our GIS example), and the second is the period beyond this horizon (the period from 2025 to infinity).[4] Within the horizon, we have explicit forecasts where we directly calculate expectations of the forecasts. However, to capture any *AOIG* occurring after the horizon, we must calculate a continuing value that captures the expectations for that period. As we will show, this second piece is different from that captured in the DCF model or in ROIM.

Equation 12.3 can be rewritten to emphasize this split into two pieces:

$$V_0 = \frac{1}{r_{WACC}} \times \left[NOPAT_1 + \sum_{t=1}^{\infty} \left(\frac{NOPAT_{t+1} + r_{WACC} \times FCF_t - (1+r_{WACC}) \times NOPAT_t}{(1+r_{WACC})^t} \right) \right]$$

$$= \frac{1}{r_{WACC}} \times \left[\begin{array}{l} NOPAT_1 + \sum_{t=1}^{5} \left(\frac{NOPAT_{t+1} + r_{WACC} \times FCF_t - (1+r_{WACC}) \times NOPAT_t}{(1+r_{WACC})^t} \right) \\ + \sum_{t=6}^{\infty} \left(\frac{NOPAT_{t+1} + r_{WACC} \times FCF_t - (1+r_{WACC}) \times NOPAT_t}{(1+r_{WACC})^t} \right) \end{array} \right] \quad (12.4)$$

$$= \frac{1}{r_{WACC}} \left[NOPAT_1 + \sum_{t=1}^{5} \left(\frac{AOIG_{t+1}}{(1+r_{WACC})^t} \right) + \sum_{t=6}^{\infty} \left(\frac{AOIG_{t+1}}{(1+r_{WACC})^t} \right) \right]$$

In Equation 12.4, the term capturing the first five *AOIG* forecasts is referred to as being within the horizon because it will be computed using forecasts of each year's *NOPAT* and *FCF*. The length of the horizon period will be determined based on our ability and willingness to gather information for forecasting. We would like to explicitly forecast as far into the future as possible, but we have to recognize that the farther into the future we forecast, the less confidence we have in our point estimates.

The second term of Equation 12.4 captures the continuing value beyond the explicit forecast period. To help show what is captured by the continuing value when using the *AOIG* valuation model, we rewrite Equation 12.4 as follows:

$$V_0 = \frac{1}{r_{WACC}} \times \left[NOPAT_1 + \sum_{t=1}^{\infty} \left(\frac{NOPAT_{t+1} + r_{WACC} \times FCF_t - (1+r_{WACC}) \times NOPAT_t}{(1+r_{WACC})^t} \right) \right]$$

$$V_0 = \frac{NOPAT_1}{r_{WACC}} + \frac{1}{r_{WACC}} \times \left[\sum_{t=1}^{\infty} \left(\frac{NOPAT_{t+1} + r_{WACC} \times FCF_t - (1+r_{WACC}) \times NOPAT_t}{(1+r_{WACC})^t} \right) \right]$$

$$V_0 - \frac{NOPAT_1}{r_{WACC}} = \frac{1}{r_{WACC}} \times \left[\sum_{t=1}^{\infty} \left(\frac{NOPAT_{t+1} + r_{WACC} \times FCF_t - (1+r_{WACC}) \times NOPAT_t}{(1+r_{WACC})^t} \right) \right]$$

or, more generally, at any point in time *T*:

$$V_T - \frac{NOPAT_{T+1}}{r_{WACC}} = \frac{1}{r_{WACC}} \times \left[\sum_{t=1}^{\infty} \left(\frac{NOPAT_{T+t+1} + r_{WACC} \times FCF_{T+t} - (1+r_{WACC}) \times NOPAT_{T+t}}{(1+r_{WACC})^t} \right) \right]$$

[4] Note that, when using AOIGM, *AOIG* reaches steady-state a year later than either *FCF* or *ROPI*. This is because the calculation of cum-dividend earnings is based on lagged *FCF*, which is, in turn, based on (further) lagged *NOA*, so that it takes one more year for *AOIG* to be growing at the steady-state growth rate.

From this formula, the difference at any point in time T between value and the amount represented by capitalized next period's *NOPAT* is the discounted present value of all future $AOIG_t$. This means that Equation 12.4 can be restated as follows:

$$V_0 = \frac{1}{r_{WACC}} \times \left[\begin{array}{l} NOPAT_1 + \sum_{t=1}^{5} \left(\frac{NOPAT_{t+1} + r_{WACC} \times FCF_t - (1 + r_{WACC}) \times NOPAT_t}{(1 + r_{WACC})^t} \right) \\ + \sum_{t=6}^{\infty} \left(\frac{NOPAT_{t+1} + r_{WACC} \times FCF_t - (1 + r_{WACC}) \times NOPAT_t}{(1 + r_{WACC})^t} \right) \end{array} \right]$$

$$= \frac{1}{r_{WACC}} \times \left[\begin{array}{l} NOPAT_1 + \sum_{t=1}^{5} \left(\frac{NOPAT_{t+1} + r_{WACC} \times FCF_t - (1 + r_{WACC}) \times NOPAT_t}{(1 + r_{WACC})^t} \right) \\ + \frac{1}{(1 + r_{WACC})^5} \times \sum_{t=6}^{\infty} \left(\frac{NOPAT_{t+1} + r_{WACC} \times FCF_t - (1 + r_{WACC}) \times NOPAT_t}{(1 + r_{WACC})^{t-5}} \right) \end{array} \right]$$

$$= \frac{1}{r_{WACC}} \times \left[\begin{array}{l} NOPAT_1 + \sum_{t=1}^{5} \left(\frac{NOPAT_{t+1} + r_{WACC} \times FCF_t - (1 + r_{WACC}) \times NOPAT_t}{(1 + r_{WACC})^t} \right) \\ + \frac{1}{(1 + r_{WACC})^5} \times \left(V_5 - \frac{NOPAT_6}{r_{WACC}} \right) \end{array} \right]$$

That is, in the *AOIG* valuation model, the continuing value equals the expected difference between intrinsic value and capitalized earnings from operations (i.e., *NOPAT*) at the horizon. In the DCF model, the problem was that we needed to know the value several periods in the future to determine the value today. Here, similar to ROIM, where we needed the excess of intrinsic value over book value (the anchor), we only need to capture excess of intrinsic value over capitalized earnings (the anchor), which could even be equal to zero.

To estimate the continuing value at the horizon, again, we will most often make an assumption that future *AOIG*, $[NOPAT_{t+1} + r_{WACC} \times FCF_t - (1 + r_{WACC}) \times NOPAT_t]$, will follow a predictable pattern after reaching the horizon. That is, each subsequent amount is related to the previous amount in a systematic manner. *AOIG* can be assumed to show growth, be constant, or fade over time. As a result, we will assume the following holds:

$$NOPAT_{t+2} + r_{WACC} \times FCF_{t+1} - (1 + r_{WACC}) \times NOPAT_{t+1} = \left[NOPAT_{t+1} + r_{WACC} \times FCF_t - (1 + r_{WACC}) \times NOPAT_t \right] \times (1 + g)$$
$$AOIG_{t+2} = AOIG_{t+1} \times (1 + g)$$

where g is the growth rate in *AOIG* after the forecast horizon. Further, the subsequent amount of *AOIG* $[NOPAT_{t+3} + r_{WACC} \times FCF_{t+2} - (1 + r_{WACC}) \times NOPAT_{t+2}]$ will reflect two periods of growth such that:

$$\begin{aligned} NOPAT_{t+3} + r_{WACC} \times FCF_{t+2} - (1 + r_{WACC}) \times NOPAT_{t+2} &= \left[NOPAT_{t+2} + r_{WACC} \times FCF_{t+1} - (1 + r_{WACC}) \times NOPAT_{t+1} \right] \times (1 + g) \\ &= \left\{ \left[NOPAT_{t+1} + r_{WACC} \times FCF_t - (1 + r_{WACC}) \times NOPAT_t \right] \times (1 + g) \right\} \times (1 + g) \\ &= \left[NOPAT_{t+1} + r_{WACC} \times FCF_t - (1 + r_{WACC}) \times NOPAT_t \right] \times (1 + g)^2 \\ AOIG_{t+3} &= AOIG_{t+1} \times (1 + g)^2 \end{aligned}$$

The pattern that emerges allows us to continue refining our understanding of the second term of our valuation equation as follows:

$$\sum_{6}^{\infty}\left[\frac{NOPAT_{t+1}+r_{WACC}\times FCF_t-(1+r_{WACC})\times NOPAT_t}{(1+r_{WACC})^t}\right]=\frac{1}{(1+r_{WACC})^5}\times\left[\begin{array}{l}\frac{NOPAT_7+r_{WACC}\times FCF_6-(1+r_{WACC})\times NOPAT_6}{(1+r_{WACC})}\\+\frac{NOPAT_8+r_{WACC}\times FCF_7-(1+r_{WACC})\times NOPAT_7}{(1+r_{WACC})^2}\\+\frac{NOPAT_9+r_{WACC}\times FCF_8-(1+r_{WACC})\times NOPAT_8}{(1+r_{WACC})^3}+\ldots\end{array}\right]$$

$$=\frac{1}{(1+r_{WACC})^5}\times\left[\begin{array}{l}\frac{[NOPAT_6+r_{WACC}\times FCF_5-(1+r_{WACC})\times NOPAT_5]\times(1+g)}{(1+r_{WACC})}\\+\frac{[NOPAT_6+r_{WACC}\times FCF_5-(1+r_{WACC})\times NOPAT_5]\times(1+g)^2}{(1+r_{WACC})^2}\\+\frac{[NOPAT_6+r_{WACC}\times FCF_5-(1+r_{WACC})\times NOPAT_5]\times(1+g)^3}{(1+r_{WACC})^3}+\ldots\end{array}\right]$$

$$=\frac{1}{(1+r_{WACC})^5}\times\left[\frac{AOIG_6\times(1+g)}{(1+r_{WACC})}+\frac{AOIG_6\times(1+g)^2}{(1+r_{WACC})^2}+\frac{AOIG_6\times(1+g)^3}{(1+r_{WACC})^3}+\ldots\right]$$

The last portion of the above equation shows a series that will continue to infinity in a very straightforward manner. Each subsequent term has the numerator multiplied by $(1 + g)$ and the denominator multiplied by $(1 + r_{WACC})$. Provided that the discount rate is greater than the growth rate (i.e., $r_{WACC} > g$), this series can be rewritten as follows:

$$\sum_{6}^{\infty}\left[\frac{NOPAT_{t+1}+r_{WACC}\times FCF_t-(1+r_{WACC})\times NOPAT_t}{(1+r_{WACC})^t}\right]=\frac{1}{(1+r_{WACC})^5}\times\left[\begin{array}{l}\frac{[NOPAT_6+r_{WACC}\times FCF_5-(1+r_{WACC})\times NOPAT_5]\times(1+g)}{(1+r_{WACC})}\\+\frac{[NOPAT_6+r_{WACC}\times FCF_5-(1+r_{WACC})\times NOPAT_5]\times(1+g)^2}{(1+r_{WACC})^2}\\+\frac{[NOPAT_6+r_{WACC}\times FCF_5-(1+r_{WACC})\times NOPAT_5]\times(1+g)^3}{(1+r_{WACC})^3}+\ldots\end{array}\right]$$

$$=\frac{1}{(1+r_{WACC})^5}\times\frac{[NOPAT_6+r_{WACC}\times FCF_5-(1+r_{WACC})\times NOPAT_5]\times(1+g)}{r_{WACC}-g}$$

$$=\frac{1}{(1+r_{WACC})^5}\times\frac{AOIG_6\times(1+g)}{r_{WACC}-g}$$

Combining this with Equation 12.4 yields

$$V_0=\frac{1}{r_{WACC}}\times\left[\begin{array}{l}NOPAT_1+\frac{NOPAT_2+r_{WACC}\times FCF_1-(1+r_{WACC})\times NOPAT_1}{(1+r_{WACC})}\\+\frac{NOPAT_3+r_{WACC}\times FCF_2-(1+r_{WACC})\times NOPAT_2}{(1+r_{WACC})^2}\\+\frac{NOPAT_4+r_{WACC}\times FCF_3-(1+r_{WACC})\times NOPAT_3}{(1+r_{WACC})^3}+\ldots\end{array}\right]$$

$$=\frac{1}{r_{WACC}}\times\left[NOPAT_1+\sum_{t=1}^{\infty}\left[\frac{NOPAT_{t+1}+r_{WACC}\times FCF_t-(1+r_{WACC})\times NOPAT_t}{(1+r_{WACC})^t}\right]\right] \quad (12.5)$$

$$=\frac{1}{r_{WACC}}\times\left[\begin{array}{l}NOPAT_1+\sum_{t=1}^{5}\left[\frac{NOPAT_{t+1}+r_{WACC}\times FCF_t-(1+r_{WACC})\times NOPAT_t}{(1+r_{WACC})^t}\right]\\+\frac{1}{(1+r_{WACC})^5}\times\left(\frac{[NOPAT_6+r_{WACC}\times FCF_5-(1+r_{WACC})\times NOPAT_5]\times(1+g)}{r_{WACC}-g}\right)\end{array}\right]$$

$$=\frac{1}{r_{WACC}}\times\left[NOPAT_1+\sum_{t=1}^{5}\left[\frac{AOIG_{t+1}}{(1+r_{WACC})^t}\right]+\frac{1}{(1+r_{WACC})^5}\times\left[\frac{AOIG_6\times(1+g)}{r_{WACC}-g}\right]\right]$$

Note that the growth rate in Equation 12.5 captures future growth in *AOIG* and the other formulas we have seen capture future growths in *FCF* in Equation 10.8 and in residual operating income in Equation 11.4, respectively. The change in *AOIG* will often be a positive number, in part, due to the conservative nature of accounting, which causes *NOPAT* to generally be lower, which causes capitalized earnings to understate value. As a reminder, Equation 12.5 holds when the growth rate from year 6 to 7, year 7 to 8, and all subsequent growth is at *g*.

ABNORMAL OPERATING INCOME GROWTH VALUATION OF GENERAL MILLS' OPERATIONS USING FORECASTS

LO5: Prepare an abnormal operating income growth valuation spreadsheet for a company's operations.

For valuing GIS' operations using our forecasts, we continue to assume a weighted average cost of capital for operations of 5.3 percent, as estimated in Chapter 9. In addition to the assumptions in **Exhibit 12.5**, we assume that the sales growth rate will stay at 1.2 percent after 2023. We also assume that the rate of growth in *AOIG*, essentially the rate of sales growth, beyond the explicit forecast horizon will be 1.2 percent. The assumption that the rate of growth in *AOIG* and the rate of growth in sales beyond the horizon are equal reflects that, over time, a firm's growth is driven by its ability to grow sales. If we apply our forecasts going forward, we can see that a steady state where *AOIG* changes at the rate of growth in sales arises. The forecasts of *AOIG* (essentially **Exhibit 12.6** extended) are shown in **Exhibit 12.8**.

Using this information and our assumptions of the discount rate and growth rate in Equation 12.5, we calculate the value of GIS' operations. When implementing Equation 12.5, we will use a period of 6 years as our explicit forecast horizon and then use a continuing value to capture period 7 and beyond. One more year of explicit forecasts is needed for this model than for DCF or ROIM. This is the same issue we saw with the project where a fifth period was required to evaluate a four-period project. The reason for this will become clearer when, shortly, we more closely examine the relation between *AOIG* and *ROPI*. We choose to show the computations in tabular format, the valuation of GIS' enterprise operations using *AOIG*, as illustrated in **Exhibit 12.9**.

EXHIBIT 12.8 GIS Multiyear Assumptions and Forecasts ($ Millions)

	5/26/2019	5/31/2020	5/30/2021	5/29/2022	5/28/2023	5/26/2024
Assumptions:						
Sales growth	9.43%	3.03%	−0.62%	1.30%	1.25%	1.20%
Operating *PM*	12.32%	12.32%	12.45%	12.62%	12.62%	12.62%
Operating *ATO*	0.688	0.678	0.665	0.651	0.651	0.651
Forecast (millions):						
Sales	$17,224.4	$17,746.9	$17,637.8	$17,867.1	$18,090.4	$18,307.5
NOPAT	2,122.0	2,186.4	2,195.9	2,254.8	2,283.0	2,310.4
NOA	26,291.0	25,998.1	26,854.2	27,786.8	28,120.3	28,457.7
Δ*NOA*	1,255.6	(292.9)	856.1	932.7	333.4	337.4
FCF (*NOPAT* − Δ*NOA*)	866.5	2,479.3	1,339.8	1,322.2	1,949.6	1,973.0
AOIG		−2.2	25.0	13.5	−21.2	9.7

That is, the estimated intrinsic value of the enterprise operations of GIS using the *AOIG* valuation model is $43,957.7 million. Despite using accounting information to estimate value, we arrived at the same result as using the highly-touted *FCF*-based approach. Again, we emphasize that the fact that we used accounting numbers, which are subject to discretion in choice of accounting methods, did not alter the estimate of value because our assumptions are consistent across the models.

EXHIBIT 12.9 Abnormal Operating Income Growth Model ($ Millions)

Required rate of return (r_{WACC})	5.30%						
Time Period	**5/27/2018**	**5/26/2019**	**5/31/2020**	**5/30/2021**	**5/29/2022**	**5/28/2023**	**5/26/2024**
Forecasted sales	$15,740.4	$17,224.4	$17,746.9	$17,637.8	$17,867.1	$18,090.4	$18,307.5
NOPAT		2,122.0	2,186.4	2,195.9	2,254.8	2,283.0	2,310.4
NOA	25,035.4	26,291.0	25,998.1	26,854.2	27,786.8	28,120.3	28,457.7
Δ*NOA*		1,255.6	−292.9	856.1	932.7	333.4	337.4
FCF (*NOPAT* − Δ*NOA*)		866.5	2,479.3	1,339.8	1,322.2	1,949.6	1,973.0
$NOPAT_t$		2,122.0	2,186.4	2,195.9	2,254.8	2,283.0	2,310.4
$AOIG_t$ $[NOPAT_t + r_{WACC} \times FCF_{t-1} - (1 + r_{WACC}) \times NOPAT_{t-1}]$			−2.2	25.0	13.5	−21.2	9.7
Growth in *AOIG*				−1,253.97%	−45.83%	−256.84%	−145.77%
Discount factor $(1 + r_{WACC})^{t-1}$			1.0530	1.1088	1.1676	1.2295	1.2946
Present value of $AOIG_t$			−2.1	22.6	11.6	−17.3	7.5
Sum of present value of $AOIG_t$		22.3					
Continuing value							
AOIG at horizon							9.8
Capitalized							240.0
Present value of continuing value		185.4					
Total to be capitalized		2,329.8					
Operating value	$43,957.7						

In this AOIGM valuation, the portion of value of the operations captured within the finite forecast horizon is over 92.0 percent ($40,458.5/$43,957.7)! Because over 90 percent of the value is coming from the forecasts for the next 4 years, we would potentially have higher confidence in this forecast. This is because we have a higher confidence in the near-term forecasts. Clearly, the anchoring of the value on *NOPAT* has greatly reduced the portion of the value estimate coming from extended forecasts; specifically, our reliance on the continuing value estimate is minimized.

SUMMARY

This chapter added another accounting-based valuation model to our arsenal. It also continued to demonstrate that accounting information can be used in lieu of *FCF* to value enterprise operations. Both the AOIGM and the ROIM are driven by *FCF* being equal to *NOPAT* adjusted for the change in *NOA*. They use different accounting-based anchors in the valuation.

In this chapter, we derived the abnormal operating income growth valuation model and demonstrated its use in valuing the finite-life project. We then demonstrated how to value a firm's operations using forecasts for GIS, a large, highly-visible, publicly traded firm using the abnormal operating income growth valuation model as well.

In Chapter 13, we will discuss the calculation of equity value. In doing so, we will explore not only the relation to enterprise operating value, but also reconsider cost of capital and how issues related to leverage affect our calculations. Then, in the final chapter, we will examine the decision to use a particular valuation model and the relation of the choice to the issue of steady state.

QUESTIONS

Q12.1 What is abnormal operating income growth AOIG (i.e., the equation)? What are the two pieces, and what do they represent?

Q12.2 What is *AOIG* in words?

Q12.3 What is the role of earnings in the *AOIG* valuation model?

Q12.4 In the AOIGM, what does the continuing value equal?

Q12.5 The *AOIG* valuation model requires an extra period relative to the DCF model or ROIM. Explain why this is necessary.

Q12.6 What are cum-free-cash-flow earnings?

Q12.7 Does accounting policy choice impact the *AOIG* valuation model?

Q12.8 Under what conditions is the AOIGM equivalent to the DCF model?

Q12.9 Can a firm grow its earnings and not impact the firm's operating value?

Q12.10 What is the difference between *AOIG* and the change in *ROPI*?

EXERCISES

Q12.11 Baxter Inc. forecasts (in $ thousands) its future sales, *NOPAT*, and *NOA* for the next 4 years as follows:

	2019A	2020E	2021E	2022E	2023E
Sales.	7,000	7,500	8,300	9,100	10,000
NOPAT.	900	1,100	1,350	1,700	2,200
NOA	12,500	13,400	14,250	15,000	15,900

Baxter's r_{WACC} is 10 percent. Calculate Baxter's *FCF*, *AOIG*, and *AOIG* growth rate for 2020–2023.

Q12.12 Trueblood Enterprises is expected to earn the following *NOPAT* next year followed by *AOIG* for the following 4 years.

	Year 0	Year 1	Year 2	Year 3	Year 4	Year 5
NOPAT.		$5,000,000				
AOIG.			$75,000	$85,000	$92,250	$94,000

Calculate Trueblood's operating value assuming that the *AOIG* will continue to grow at 1.90 percent following the forecast horizon. Trueblood's r_{WACC} is 8 percent.

Q12.13 Wyatt Corporation is considering a project requiring a $15 million initial investment. The expected project income and distributions are

($ thousand)	Year 1	Year 2	Year 3	Year 4	Year 5
Net project income (*NOPAT*)	2,500	3,900	4,300	4,100	2,700
Distributions (*FCF*)	3,200	4,500	5,300	4,700	3,600

Using the AOIGM, determine whether the project is financially feasible assuming the project rate of return is 12 percent.

Q12.14 Finney Inc. is a construction company specializing in commercial real estate projects. Finney has contracted with the Perry Companies to build an office building for $20 million. Finney estimates the construction costs will be about $16 million, with the construction taking over 2 years to complete. Due to the uncertainties with such a project, Finney requires a 14 percent return. The expected net operating income on a percentage of completion basis and distributions over the next 3 years are

($ thousand)	Year 0	Year 1	Year 2	Year 3
Net project income (*NOPAT*)	—	1,500	2,100	2,400
Distributions (*FCF*)	—	1,500	2,100	2,400

a. Assume, Finney uses the percentage of completion method for recognizing revenue (i.e., revenue is recognized each period as it earned), determine the value of the project with AOIGM.

b. Assuming Finney uses the completed contract method for recognizing revenue (i.e., all profit recognized in the final period), determine the value of the project with AOIGM.

c. Explain whether the choice of the accounting revenue recognition policy impacts the project's value.

CONTINUING EXAMPLES

CE12.15 Once again, the company has been offered the opportunity to invest in a project expected to yield the following cash flows. Note that the anticipated risk of the project implies a cost of capital of 10 percent would be appropriate:

Anticipated Cash Flows of Finite-Life Project	
Purchase price	$2,300
Payoffs:	
Year 1	$600
Year 2	700
Year 3	750
Year 4	625
Year 5	500
Proceeds from disposition	240

Assume, initially, that the company plans to fully depreciate the project using the straight-line method over the 5-year period, resulting in $412 in depreciation per period. Using the *AOIG* valuation method, determine the value of the project and whether to invest in it. How does this value compare to value computed based on cash flows in Chapter 10 and residual operating income in Chapter 11?

CE12.16 Assume that instead of fully depreciating the project, the company decides to record depreciation of $300 per year. Use the *AOIG* valuation model to value the project. What effect does this change in profits due to altering depreciation have on the value calculation?

CE12.17 Repeat the valuation of the project one more time utilizing the assumption that the company forgot to record any depreciation during the project's life. What effect does this change in profits due to altering depreciation have on the value calculation?

CE12.18 The Hatfield Company evaluates internal projects for their financial viability as part of an overall analysis. One proposed project is to automate a portion of Hatfield's production process. The additional equipment has an estimated useful life of 6 years. The operations manager provided the expected cost savings from the installation of the robotic equipment. The project is expected to yield the following cash flows:

Anticipated Cash Flows of Finite-Life Project	
Purchase price	$8,500
Payoffs:	
Year 1	$ 700
Year 2	1,900
Year 3	2,900
Year 4	3,500
Year 5	3,000
Year 6	2,700
Proceeds from disposition	400

In addition, Hatfield's management requires a hurdle rate of 16 percent for internally proposed projects, which is greater than the actual project risk. Assume, initially, that the company plans to fully depreciate the project using the straight-line method over the 6-year period, resulting in $1,350 in depreciation per period. Using the AOIGM, determine the value of the project and whether the company should invest in it. How does this value compare to the value computed based on cash flows in Chapter 10?

CE12.19 Using the following forecast assumptions from Chapter 7 for Kellogg (K), the weighted average cost of capital for operations of 5.2 percent calculated in Chapter 9, and a continuing growth in *AOIG* beyond the forecast horizon of 0.4 percent, calculate the value of K's operations. How does this estimate of value compare to that arrived at using the cash flow-based valuation method in Chapter 10 or ROIM in Chapter 11?

K's Multiyear Assumptions	2019E	2020E	2021E	2022E	2023E	2024E	2025E	2026E	2027E
Assumptions:									
Sales growth	0.57%	2.41%	−1.42%	0.50%	0.45%	0.40%	2.32%	−1.49%	0.40%
Operating *PM*	9.36%	9.58%	10.00%	10.17%	10.55%	10.55%	10.55%	10.55%	10.55%
Operating *ATO* . . .	1.052	0.974	0.962	0.951	0.951	0.951	0.951	0.951	0.951

CE12.20 Using the following forecast assumptions from Chapter 7 for Thor Industries (THO), the weighted average cost of capital for operations of 12.60 percent calculated in Chapter 9, and a continuing growth in *AOIG* beyond the forecast horizon of 1.00 percent, calculate the value of THO's operations. How does this estimate of value compare to that arrived at using the cash flow-based valuation method in Chapter 10 or ROIM in Chapter 11?

THO's Multiyear Assumptions	FY2019E	FY2020E	FY2021E	FY2022E	FY2023E	FY2024E
Assumptions:						
Sales growth	5.56%	3.61%	1.61%	1.40%	1.20%	1.00%
Operating *PM*	5.78%	5.77%	5.40%	5.35%	5.15%	5.15%
Operating *ATO*	4.815	4.329	4.219	4.098	4.098	4.098

CE12.21 Using the following forecast assumptions from Chapter 7 for Winnebago (WGO), the weighted average cost of capital for operations of 10.60 percent calculated in Chapter 9, and a continuing growth in *AOIG* beyond the forecast horizon of 0.90 percent, calculate the value of WGO's operations. How does this estimate of value compare to that arrived at using the cash flow-based valuation method in Chapter 10 or ROIM in Chapter 11?

WGO's Multiyear Assumptions	FY2019E	FY2020E	FY2021E	FY2022E	FY2023E	FY2024E	FY2025E	FY2026E
Assumptions:								
Weeks	53	52	52	52	52	53	52	52
Sales growth	4.56%	0.11%	1.38%	1.10%	2.82%	−0.99%	0.90%	0.90%
Operating *PM*	6.40%	6.27%	6.20%	6.03%	6.03%	6.03%	6.03%	6.03%
Operating *ATO* . . .	2.309	2.288	2.294	2.294	2.294	2.294	2.294	2.294

Chapter Thirteen

Valuation of Equity

TAKEAWAYS

When you complete this chapter, you should be able to:

1. Adjust the estimate of the value of operations by net financial liabilities to obtain an estimate of the value of equity.
2. Understand the relation between models that value operations and models that value equity and why valuation of operations is preferable.
3. Explain issues with steady state that are encountered when using analysts' forecasts in equity valuation.
4. Correctly adjust forecasts to midyear and align dates in valuation calculations.
5. Perform sensitivity analyses on key variables to determine areas of concern and/or focus.

In prior chapters, we focused on the valuation of the enterprise operating activities. In this chapter, we apply similar concepts to the valuation of equity. We also show how equity may be valued directly. Thus far, we have focused on what is owned by both debt and equity holders. At times, as current or potential investors, we may be interested in the portion owned by just the equity holders.

We will begin by showing how to convert the value of operations calculated in Chapters 10, 11, or 12 to a value of equity. Then, we will show and discuss the methods by which equity value can be calculated directly. We conclude this chapter with brief coverage of two outstanding related issues: (1) the misalignment of the date on which we wish to determine value and the end of the fiscal period for which financial statements are prepared and financial accounting data are forecasted and (2) the analysis of the sensitivity of our valuations to key assumptions.

CALCULATING THE VALUE OF EQUITY FROM THE VALUE OF OPERATIONS

LO1: Adjust the estimate of the value of operations by net financial liabilities to obtain an estimate of the value of equity.

The enterprise operating activities that we have valued thus far belong to both debt and equity holders. In order to determine the value of the equity ownership, we subtract the value of debt. This process is often relatively straightforward because debt is often shown in the company's balance sheet at an amount approximating market value. For example, if the company has a $100,000 loan from the bank, that most often appears on the books as a $100,000 liability and has a fair value of $100,000. When the debt is not shown on the balance sheet at an amount equal to fair value, information to adjust the carrying value to fair value is provided within the financial statement footnotes. These disclosures are required under U.S. GAAP as a part of disclosure requirements for financial instruments.[1]

[1] ASC 825-10-50-10 requires firms to report "the fair value of financial instruments for which it is practicable to estimate that value." This includes a firm's debt.

CHAPTER OUTLINE

Valuation of Equity

Equity Value
- Adjusting Operating Value to Equity Value

Equity Valuation Models
- Dividend Discount, Residual Earnings, and Abnormal Earnings Growth Models
- Choosing Operations or Equity to Value
- Use of Analysts' Net Income Forecasts to Value Operations

Details of Estimating Equity Share Price
- Midyear Adjustment
- Valuation Date Adjustments
- Sensitivity Analysis

In addition to adjusting to the fair value, we also need to adjust the value of debt for the interest tax shield. This is because, for an equity holder (the view we are now taking), the existence of debt will cause a reduction in taxes when the interest expense is deducted. As discussed in Chapter 9 when computing cost of capital, a common assumption is that the value of the interest tax shield can be computed as pretax interest expense times the tax rate divided by the cost of debt capital. This calculation treats the interest expense as a perpetuity, implying that debt levels will not change in the future.[2]

ADJUSTMENT FOR NET DEBT (CONSIDERING THE INTEREST TAX SHIELD)

Throughout the text, we have consistently treated the interest tax shield as a financial effect. That is, we have viewed the net value of debt as including the value of the interest tax shield.

Pointing out the details of the methodology is important because finance textbooks often present two methods that differ slightly; these are labeled the discounted cash flow (DCF) and adjusted present value (APV) methods. In their presentation of the APV method, Berk and DeMarzo (*Corporate Finance*, fourth edition, 2017) describe the approach as "an alternative valuation method in which we determine the levered value V^L of an investment by first calculating its *unlevered value* V^U, which is its value without any leverage, and then adding the value of the interest tax shield." (p. 648) The implementation in this text of discounted cash flows shown in Chapter 10 and the computation of weighted average cost of operating capital, in Chapter 9 mirror the APV approach.

Beginning in Chapter 2, our reformulation has sought to isolate enterprise operations from all effects of financing. That is, we have worked to determine the unlevered value of the operations. The value estimate for operations in the model described as DCF in finance texts and the related cost of capital both will change with changes in the value of the interest tax shield. That is, they depend on the firm's leverage! Similar to our reformulation, our calculation of the weighted average cost of capital for operations in Chapter 9 was a calculation of the unlevered cost of capital as we considered explicitly the value of the interest tax shield in our valuation of net debt rather than as a part of the value of operations.

To see the difference between the approaches of the DCF and APV methods as presented in finance textbooks consider the following:

$$\text{DCF: } V^{Eq} = \underbrace{(V^{Oper} + V^{ITS})}_{\text{Levered Operations}} - V^{NFL}$$

$$\text{APV: } V^{Eq} = \underbrace{V^{Oper}}_{\text{Unlevered Operations}} + \underbrace{V^{ITS} - V^{NFL}}_{\text{Net Debt}}$$

The difference between the approaches is subtle, but very important. Further, if properly implemented, there should be no change in the estimated value of equity, V^{Eq}. It must be noted that the discount rate used to value operations will differ between the DCF and APV methods. Finance textbooks refer to the discount rate for levered operations as the weighted average cost of capital and the discount rate for unlevered operations as the unlevered cost of capital.

continued

[2] Despite our attempts to focus our attention on valuation of operations and avoid issues of leverage, leverage does come into play when adjusting to equity value. This is unavoidable because the amount of debt a company chooses to take on in the future will affect the value of the tax shield.

continued from previous page

Most important, in the DCF method, the changing relative values of operations and the income tax shield cause the weighted average cost of capital to change from period to period. This is not an issue in the APV method as it relies on a discount rate that only reflects the risk of unlevered operations.

In each step up to now, we have sought to focus on valuing operations (V^{Oper}) without any effects of financing activities. That is, we have followed an approach mirroring the APV method. This allows the cost of capital, which we calculated, to be used in each future period without need to consider adjustments as the level of debt (and therefore the value of the interest tax shield) adjusts. Because we valued operations only, we now proceed to adjust for net debt to arrive at equity value.

Let us examine how the value of equity in General Mills (GIS) is determined after we have estimated the value of GIS' operating activities. In prior chapters, we calculated the operating value of $43,957.7 million. This amount represents the total value for all of the capital providers (i.e., both the debt and equity holders' interests in the operations). Therefore, to compute the value of the equity holders' interest separately, we simply need to subtract the value of the debt from the operating value. Throughout this chapter, we will continue to assume, as we did in prior chapters, that we are estimating value at May 1, 2019. Thus, we need to adjust for the amount of debt at that time.

We don't know the amount of debt at May 1, 2019, but, we can obtain an approximation using the reformulated balance sheet and disclosures in the Form 10-Q for the third quarter ended February 24, 2019. In Chapter 5, we reformulated GIS' May 2018 balance sheet and can use this reformulated balance sheet to identify net financial liabilities (*NFL*) as was shown in Exhibit 5.11. **Exhibit 13.1** repeats the information for GIS in May 2018 and includes some items that we can

EXHIBIT 13.1 GIS Computation of *NFL*

Amounts in Millions	5/27/2018
Financial Assets (*FA*)	
Cash and cash equivalents	$ 84.2
Deferred tax assets: Pension	57.1
Deferred tax assets: Stock, partnership, and miscellaneous investments	147.9
Deferred tax assets: Stock-based compensation	0.0
Prepaid expenses and other current assets: Other receivables	174.4
Other assets: Exchangeable note with related party	0.0
Defined benefit pension plans: Plan assets	6,177.4
Other postretirement benefit plans: Plan assets	726.1
	7,367.1
Financial Liabilities (*FL*)	
Accounts payable	
Current portion of long-term debt	(1,600.1)
Notes payable: U.S. commercial paper	(1,213.5)
Notes payable: Financial institutions	(336.3)
Other current liabilities: Dividend payable	(17.5)
Other current liabilities: Accrued interest, including interest rate swaps	(107.7)
Long-term debt	(12,668.7)
Deferred tax liabilities: Stock, partnership, and miscellaneous investments	(317.1)
Other noncurrent liabilities: Accrued compensation and benefits, including pensions	(178.5)
Defined benefit pension plans: Benefit obligation	(6,416.0)
Other postretirement benefit plans: Benefit obligation	(871.8)
Postemployment benefit plans: Benefit obligation	(126.7)
Capitalized lease liability	(1,111.6)
Stock-based compensation liability	0.0
Redeemable interest	(776.2)
Noncontrolling interests	(351.3)
	(26,093.0)
Net financial liabilities (*NFL*)	$(18,725.9)

update from the February 2019 Form 10-Q. While many items are still shown at the May 2018 book values, updating where we can makes sense.

Remember that the *Redeemable interest* and the *Noncontrolling interest* are included as part of the computation of debt because they are amounts owed to parties other than common equity holders. These are amounts not available to the common equity holders.

In updating the value of debt to May 1, 2019, we can split the items shown above into three groups: those we leave unchanged, those we update to the February 2019 (most recent) balance, and those we update to the February 2019 fair value reported in the Form 10-Q. As we have mentioned, the book value of most items in *NFL* will rarely differ materially from their fair values. In cases where they do differ, disclosure will be made that can assist us in making an adjustment. In addition, there are some items such as investments where using an updated value as of the most recent quarter would seem a logical assumption. In **Exhibit 13.2**, we break up the *NFL* based on how we arrive at an estimated value on May 1, 2019.

EXHIBIT 13.2 Updating GIS' *NFL* to May 1, 2019

Amounts in Millions	5/27/18	Assumed Unchanged	2/24/19 Form 10-Q Balance	2/24/19 Form 10-Q Fair Value
Financial Assets (*FA*)				
Cash and cash equivalents	$ 84.2	$ 84.2		
Deferred tax assets: Pension	57.1	57.1		
Deferred tax assets: Stock, partnership, and miscellaneous investments	147.9	147.9		
Prepaid expenses and other current assets: Other receivables	174.4	174.4		
Defined benefit pension plans: Plan assets	6,177.4	6,177.4		
Other postretirement benefit plans: Plan assets	726.1	726.1		
Financial Liabilities (*FL*)				
Current portion of long-term debt	(1,600.1)		$ (1,407.2)	
Notes payable: U.S. commercial paper	(1,213.5)		(1,804.9)	
Notes payable: Financial institutions	(336.3)		(166.4)	
Other current liabilities: Dividend payable	(17.5)	(17.5)		
Other current liabilities: Accrued interest, including interest rate swaps	(107.7)	(107.7)		
Long-term debt	(12,668.7)		(11,642.6)	
Long-term debt fair value adjustment (Note 5)	—			$89.0
Deferred tax liabilities: Stock, partnership, and miscellaneous investments	(317.1)	(317.1)		
Other noncurrent liabilities: Accrued compensation and benefits, including pensions	(178.5)	(178.5)		
Defined benefit pension plans: Benefit obligation	(6,416.0)	(6,416.0)		
Other postretirement benefit plans: Benefit obligation	(871.8)	(871.8)		
Postemployment benefit plans: Benefit obligation	(126.7)	(126.7)		
Capitalized lease liability	(1,111.6)	(1,111.6)		
Redeemable interest	(776.2)		(548.9)	
Noncontrolling interests	(351.3)		(319.0)	
		(1,779.8)	(15,889.0)	89.0
Net Financial Liabilities (*NFL*)	$(18,725.9)		$(17,579.8)	

The items in the unchanged column of **Exhibit 13.2** are those that we generally would not necessarily be able to update as of February 2019 given the information in the Form 10-Q. An exception is cash and cash equivalents. While we have an updated value, how much of it is operating as compared to financial would be difficult to determine. As such, we assume the amount that is financial is unchanged from May 2018. If GIS had investments, we would assume that the February 2019 balance as reported on the Form 10-Q is more useful than the older balance in determining the current value of the *NFL*.

For long-term debt, GIS' financial statements provide information indicating an adjustment to fair value is necessary. Note 7 to the May 2018 financial statements stated that the fair value of long-term debt was $14,169.7 million. Even more recent information is available from the February 2019 Form 10-Q: Note 7 shows that, at the end of this most recently reported quarter, the fair value of GIS' long-term debt (including the current portion) was $12,960.8 million while the book value was $13,049.8 million. This implies that a fair value adjustment to the reported numbers of $89.0 million is necessary, decreasing the amount of *NFL*.

To complete our estimate of the value of the *NFL* as of May 1, 2019, we need to include the interest tax shield. In Chapter 9, our estimate of the value of GIS' interest tax shield was based on net interest expense of $373.7 million. Using the adjusted interest expense after consideration of operating leases, we had adjusted a net interest of $416.1 million. With net interest expense of $416.1 million, an assumed tax rate of 21 percent, and the estimated cost of debt capital of 3.1 percent, the value of the interest tax shield is:

$$\begin{aligned} V^{ITS} &= \frac{ITS}{r_D} \\ &= \frac{\$416.1 \times 0.21}{0.031} \\ &= \$2,819.0 \end{aligned}$$

Again, this calculation treats the interest expense as a perpetuity, implying that debt levels will be unchanged in the future. Ideally, we would seek to avoid an assumption regarding management's financial plans in the future. (This is why we have focused on enterprise operations throughout the entire process.) Still, to recognize that the ability to deduct interest payments creates a benefit to the equity holders, the value of the tax shield must be incorporated when moving from operating value to equity value.

After examining the February 24, 2019, Form 10-Q, our best estimate of the adjusted fair value of *NFL*, debt, at May 1, 2019, is $14,760.8 million ($17,579.8 million from **Exhibit 13.2** less the interest tax shield of $2,819.0 million). While we would like to do further adjustments, the information does not permit a more detailed examination.

The difference between the value of operations and the value of equity is the value of the firm's financing activities. After reformulating the financial statements, the calculation of equity value is quite straightforward: We subtract the estimate of the fair value of *NFL* of $14,760.8 million from our estimate of the value of operations ($43,957.7 million) to obtain an estimate of the value of equity of $29,196.9 million. Further adjustments to this estimate are necessary due to issues related to the dates of the valuation, but before examining these adjustments later in this chapter, let us consider the direct valuation of equity based on the valuation models shown in Chapters 10, 11, and 12.

VALUATION FORMULAS FOR EQUITY

LO2: Understand the relation between models that value operations and models that value equity and why valuation of operations is preferable.

Beginning in Chapter 10, we focused on the cash flows to the debt and equity holders. Some refer to these as *FCF*s of the firm to distinguish them from the *FCF*s to equity, which is the portion of *FCF*s that will go to the equity holders. The *FCF*s to equity are the payoffs the equity holders receive. More commonly, we refer to the payoffs to equity holders as dividends.

In Chapter 10, we valued the operations based on the payoffs expected to be made to the debt and equity holders. We now show the formula that may be used to value the firm based on expected payoffs to the equity holders. That is, we show the formula based on dividends to equity holders:

$$V_0^{Eq} = \frac{div_1}{(1+r_{Eq})} + \frac{div_2}{(1+r_{Eq})^2} + \frac{div_3}{(1+r_{Eq})^3} + \frac{div_4}{(1+r_{Eq})^4} + \ldots$$
$$= \sum_{t=1}^{\infty}\left(\frac{div_t}{(1+r_{Eq})^t}\right) \tag{13.1}$$

where div_t is the net dividend to the equity holders, which can be negative if funds are provided to the company, and r_{Eq} is the cost of capital for equity. Remember that the notion of dividends in Equation 13.1 captures the net distributions made to the equity holders of the firm (i.e., cash dividends, payments to the equity holders for repurchased shares, and receipts of cash from the equity holders who purchase newly issued shares). That is, the dividends are the *FCF*s to equity holders, FCF^{Eq}. Going forward, we will switch our notation from *div* to FCF^{Eq}. The parallel between this dividend (i.e., *FCF* to equity holders) discount model, as it relates to valuing equity, and the DCF model, as it relates to valuing the operations (i.e., *FCF*s to debt and equity holders), is now readily apparent.

Our transition from cash flow-based valuation to accounting-based valuation was rooted in Equation 2.2:

$$FCF_t \equiv NOPAT_t + NOA_{t-1} - NOA_t$$
$$\equiv NOPAT_t - \Delta NOA_t \tag{2.2}$$

This equation linked *FCF*s from operations to the earnings (*NOPAT*) and to the book value of the net operating assets (*NOA*). A similar relation holds for equity. The *FCF*s to the equity holders are equal to the earnings available to equity holders minus the change in book value of equity.

The relation between dividends (i.e., the *FCF*s to equity holders), comprehensive income, and book value of common equity is as follows:

$$FCF_t^{Eq} = CI_t + CSE_{t-1} - CSE_t$$
$$= CI_t - \Delta CSE_t \tag{13.2}$$

where CI_t is the comprehensive income for period t and CSE_t is the book value of common stockholders' equity at time t.

Specifically, for this equation to hold, earnings must be comprehensive. Comprehensive income is the net income from the income statement plus any income items flowing directly to equity. Comprehensive income is most often shown on the statement of stockholders' equity or in a separate statement of comprehensive income as is the case for GIS. In our reformulation of the financial statements in Chapter 3, we used comprehensive income rather than just net income.

Just as we used Equation 2.2 and the DCF model to derive the residual operating income model (ROIM), we can use Equation 13.2 and the dividend discount model (Equation 13.1) to derive the residual earnings model (REM) as follows:

$$V_0^{Eq} = CSE_0 + \sum_{t=1}^{\infty}\left(\frac{CI_t - r_{Eq} \times CSE_{t-1}}{(1+r_{Eq})^t}\right)$$
$$= CSE_0 + \sum_{t=1}^{\infty}\left(\frac{RE_t}{(1+r_{Eq})^t}\right) \tag{13.3}$$

where RE_t is residual earnings in period t. The parallel between the REM as it relates to valuing equity and ROIM as it relates to valuing the operations is readily apparent.

Finally, just as we derived the abnormal operating income growth model (AOIGM) by using the next period capitalized operating earnings (*NOPAT*) as an anchor, we can use the next period earnings available to equity holders to derive the abnormal earnings growth model (AEGM) by using Equations 13.1 and 13.2 as follows:

$$
\begin{aligned}
V_0^{Eq} &= \frac{1}{r_{Eq}}\left[CI_1 + \sum_{t=1}^{\infty}\left(\frac{CI_{t+1} + r_{Eq} \times FCF_t^{Eq} - (1+r_{Eq}) \times CI_t}{(1+r_{Eq})^t}\right)\right] \\
&= \frac{1}{r_{Eq}}\left[CI_1 + \sum_{t=1}^{\infty}\left(\frac{AEG_{t+1}}{(1+r_{Eq})^t}\right)\right]
\end{aligned} \tag{13.4}
$$

where AEG_{t+1} is the abnormal earnings growth in period $t + 1$. The parallel between AEGM, as it relates to valuing equity and the AOIGM, as it relates to valuing the operations is readily apparent.

A point to note in using Equation 13.3 or 13.4 is that often the items of other comprehensive income included in comprehensive income that are not included in net income will be expected to be zero in future periods. For instance, GIS' largest item in recent years has been net actuarial loss. Our best estimate of the net actuarial loss amount for any future period is zero because forecasting any other amount would be equivalent to saying GIS can anticipate changes to actuarial rates. This point was discussed in Chapter 7.

CHOOSING BETWEEN AN OPERATIONS OR EQUITY VALUATION MODEL

Although we have shown that the value of equity can be calculated directly via Equation 13.1, 13.3 or 13.4, we have chosen throughout the text to focus on valuation of the operating activities. The reason for this is rooted in a concept discussed in Chapter 9. When we estimate cost of capital, we assume stability of risk going forward so we can assume a constant cost of capital in the future. When we value the operating activities, we use the weighted average cost of capital for operations (r_{WACC}), which would not be expected to change from period to period unless the risk of the operating activities is expected to change. To utilize an equity valuation model would require an assumption that equity risk will be constant in future periods.

Assuming the cost of equity capital will be constant going forward is a much less tenable assumption than assuming a constant weighted average cost of capital for operations. To see this, let us return to how we estimate the weighted average cost of capital for operations. To estimate r_{WACC}, we use the weighted average cost of capital formula, which can be written as follows:

$$r_{WACC} = \left(r_D \times \frac{V^{NFL}}{V^{Oper}}\right) + \left(r_{Eq} \times \frac{V^{Eq}}{V^{Oper}}\right)$$

Rearranging this relation yields

$$r_{WACC} \times V^{Oper} = r_D \times V^{NFL} + r_{Eq} \times V^{Eq}$$

which emphasizes the structure shown in **Exhibit 9.1** of Chapter 9. Recognizing that $V^{Oper} = V^{NFL} + V^{Eq}$, we can rearrange and solve for r_{Eq} to yield

$$
\begin{aligned}
r_{Eq} \times V^{Eq} &= r_{WACC} \times V^{Oper} - r_D \times V^{NFL} \\
r_{Eq} \times V^{Eq} &= r_{WACC} \times (V^{Eq} + V^{NFL}) - r_D \times V^{NFL} \\
r_{Eq} \times V^{Eq} &= r_{WACC} \times V^{Eq} + r_{WACC} \times V_D - r_D \times V^{NFL} \\
r_{Eq} \times V^{Eq} &= r_{WACC} \times V^{Eq} + V^{NFL} \times (r_{WACC} - r_D) \\
r_{Eq} &= r_{WACC} + \frac{V^{NFL}}{V^{Eq}} \times (r_{WACC} - r_D)
\end{aligned}
\tag{13.5}
$$

Equation 13.5 emphasizes that the risk of equity arises as a result of risk of the operations and the leverage that the debt offers to the equity holders. The effect of this leverage depends on the ratio of the value of debt to the value of equity and the difference (i.e., the spread) between the expected return on the operations of the firm and the expected interest rate on debt.

Notice in Equation 13.5 that the cost of capital of equity depends on the leverage of the firm. Unless we are willing to assume that the leverage will be constant in the future, we cannot assume a constant cost of equity going forward. Assuming that leverage will be constant would be a heroic assumption. Trying to forecast leverage to generate annual estimates of the cost of equity capital indefinitely would be impossible because we do not know whether management will choose to use debt or equity as funding at each point in the future.

USING ANALYSTS' FORECASTS AS A SHORTCUT TO VALUATION

LO3: Explain issues with steady state, which are encountered when using analysts' forecasts in equity valuation.

Despite having explained why valuation of the operating activities should be the focus of our efforts, there are times when a ballpark number might be calculated using a shortcut to valuation. We may, for example, attempt to get an indication of value from analysts' forecasts of earnings and dividends. The extent to which the estimate obtained from this shortcut differs from our estimated per-share equity value of $48.76 ($29,196.9 million from above divided by 598,790,681 common shares outstanding per February 24, 2019 Form 10-Q) will provide a sense of the extent to which this indication of value is likely to be meaningful.

Professional analysts tend to forecast dividends and earnings.[3] For a large company like GIS, these forecasts are available from a variety of sources. For example, **Exhibit 13.3** shows forecasts ValueLine provided for GIS in October 2019.

EXHIBIT 13.3 ValueLine Forecasts for GIS as of October 18, 2019

Earnings per share 2019	$ 3.22
Earnings per share 2020	$ 3.33
Earnings per share 2022–2024	$ 3.80
Dividends declared per share 2019	$ 1.96
Dividends declared per share 2020	$ 1.98
Dividends declared per share 2022–2024	$ 2.28
Book value per share 2018	$10.35

We assume that the 2022–2024 forecasts reflect a point estimate for 2023 and then compute the annual rate of growth that ValueLine is implicitly forecasting. For earnings to grow from $3.33 in 2020 to $3.80 in 2023 would require a 4.499 percent growth rate $\left[\sqrt[3]{1+\frac{3.80-3.33}{3.33}}-1\right]$. For dividends, to grow from $1.98 in 2020 to $2.28 in 2023 would require a 4.815 percent growth rate $\left[\sqrt[3]{1+\frac{2.28-1.98}{1.98}}-1\right]$. This yields the annual forecasts for GIS based on ValueLine shown in **Exhibit 13.4**.

[3] Analysts have more recently been forecasting cash flow numbers, which must be used cautiously because they are likely not *FCF* from operations as defined in Chapter 2.

EXHIBIT 13.4 ValueLine Implied Forecasts for GIS

Year Ended May	2019	2020	2021	2022	2023	2024
Earnings per share	3.22	3.33	3.48 (\$3.33 × 1.04499)	3.64 (\$3.48 × 1.04499)	3.80 (\$3.64 × 1.04499)	3.97 (\$3.80 × 1.04499)
Dividends per share	1.96	1.98	2.08 (\$1.98 × 1.04815)	2.18 (\$2.08 × 1.04815)	2.28 (\$2.18 × 1.04815)	2.39 (\$2.28 × 1.04815)
Book value per share . . .	11.61	12.96	14.36	15.83	17.35	18.93

To demonstrate the use of these analysts' forecasts as a shortcut to valuation, let us begin by implementing the dividend discount model and then proceed to the REM. Our assumed cost of equity capital will be 6.4 percent, as calculated in Chapter 9.

To implement the dividend discount model, the remaining issue is estimation of the continuing value. We know from Chapters 10, 11, and 12 that a continuing value can be estimated by assuming a growth rate at the forecast horizon. Given that dividends are forecast to grow at 4.815 percent within the horizon, we might, for example, consider using this rate beyond the horizon. Be aware that, often, the growth within the horizon may be nearly equal to or exceed our assumed cost of equity capital. Rather than try to arbitrarily pick a dividend growth percentage after the horizon, we can instead use the projected future price, sometimes called target price. ValueLine projects a target price range of \$46 to \$69 per share, with a midpoint of \$58, which we will use; this is a forecast of the amount the investor would get if he or she liquidated the investment at the forecast horizon. This would yield the following per-share value estimate for GIS using the dividend discount model in Equation 13.1:

$$
\begin{aligned}
V_0^{Eq} &= \frac{div_1}{(1+r_{Eq})} + \frac{div_2}{(1+r_{Eq})^2} + \frac{div_3}{(1+r_{Eq})^3} + \frac{div_4}{(1+r_{Eq})^4} + \frac{div_5}{(1+r_{Eq})^5} + \frac{div_6}{(1+r_{Eq})^6} + \frac{CV_6}{(1+r_{Eq})^6} \\
&= \frac{1.96}{(1+0.064)} + \frac{1.98}{(1+0.064)^2} + \frac{2.08}{(1+0.064)^3} + \frac{2.18}{(1+0.064)^4} + \frac{2.28}{(1+0.064)^5} + \frac{2.39}{(1+0.064)^6} + \frac{58.00}{(1+0.064)^6} \\
&= \frac{1.96}{1.064} + \frac{1.98}{1.1321} + \frac{2.08}{1.2046} + \frac{2.18}{1.2816} + \frac{2.28}{1.3637} + \frac{2.39}{1.4509} + \frac{58.00}{1.4509} \\
&= 1.84 + 1.75 + 1.72 + 1.70 + 1.67 + 1.65 + 39.97 \\
&= 50.30
\end{aligned}
$$

That is, ValueLine's forecasts of dividends and terminal price, and our estimate of the cost of equity capital, suggest that the market price of GIS should be \$50.30 per share. Before commenting on this estimate, let us first estimate the value using the REM.

To utilize the REM with analysts' forecasts, we again need an assumption of a continuing value. One approach would be to check whether the firm has reached steady state within the horizon by examining the growth in *RE* up to 2024.[4] **Exhibit 13.5** shows residual income based on ValueLine's forecasts.

EXHIBIT 13.5 ValueLine Implied Forecasts for GIS

Year Ended May	2019	2020	2021	2022	2023	2024
Residual earnings ($RE_t = NI_t - r_{Eq} \times BV_{t-1}$). . . .	\$2.56	\$2.59	\$2.65	\$2.72	\$2.79	\$2.86
Growth in *RE*		1.15%	2.45%	2.52%	2.58%	2.64%

Here, we see a growth rate during the horizon that is growing each year. While this rate may stabilize if we went another 10 to 15 years out, we know the farther into the future we forecast, the less confidence we have in our estimates. Because we must assume a number for growth, let us pick 3 percent seemingly at random for the purposes of computation. This would yield the following per-share value estimate for GIS using the *RE* model in Equation 13.3:

[4] The issue of steady state and its relation to the continuing growth rate will be fully developed and discussed in Chapter 14.

$$
\begin{aligned}
V_0^{Eq} &= CSE_0 + \frac{RE_1}{(1+r_{Eq})} + \frac{RE_2}{(1+r_{Eq})^2} + \frac{RE_3}{(1+r_{Eq})^3} + \frac{RE_4}{(1+r_{Eq})^4} \\
&\quad + \frac{RE_5}{(1+r_{Eq})^5} + \frac{RE_6}{(1+r_{Eq})^6} + \frac{1}{(1+r_{Eq})^6} \times \frac{RE_6 \times (1+g)}{r_{Eq} - g} \\
&= 10.35 + \frac{2.56}{(1+0.064)} + \frac{2.59}{(1+0.064)^2} + \frac{2.65}{(1+0.064)^3} + \frac{2.72}{(1+0.064)^4} \\
&\quad + \frac{2.79}{(1+0.064)^5} + \frac{2.86}{(1+0.064)^6} + \frac{1}{(1+0.064)^6} \times \frac{2.86 \times (1.03)}{0.064 - 0.03} \\
&= 10.35 + \frac{2.56}{1.064} + \frac{2.59}{1.1321} + \frac{2.65}{1.2046} + \frac{2.72}{1.2816} + \frac{2.79}{1.3637} + \frac{1}{1.4509} \times \frac{2.95}{0.034} \\
&= 10.35 + 2.40 + 2.29 + 2.20 + 2.12 + 2.04 + 1.97 + 59.73 \\
&= 83.11
\end{aligned}
$$

That is, ValueLine's forecasts of earnings and dividends, our estimate of the cost of equity capital, and our assumption of the growth in *RE* beyond the horizon suggest that the market price of GIS should be \$83.11 per share.

Two observations immediately arise from this effort to use analysts' forecasts. First, if we use the analysts' forecasts for GIS, the firm is clearly not stable (i.e., in steady state) at the horizon. This is evidenced by computing different value estimates from the dividend discount model (\$50.30) and the REM (\$83.11). Second, we must consider that the known optimistic bias in analysts' forecasts may lead to inflated estimates of equity value.[5] The REM estimate using analysts' forecasts is markedly different from the estimate based on our detailed forecasts and also GIS' market value. We conclude that these are, at best, very rough ways to use analyst forecast data to obtain an indication of value.

Having discussed the valuation of equity and the potential use of analysts' forecasts, we now turn to two remaining issues in valuation: (1) the misalignment of the date on which we wish to determine value and the end of the fiscal period for which financial statements are prepared and financial accounting data are forecasted and (2) the analysis of the sensitivity of our valuations to key assumptions.

ANALYSTS' FORECASTS OF A TARGET PRICE LOWER THAN TRADING PRICE

We would expect that a firm's share price should increase at the cost of equity capital if prices accurately reflect the market's expectations. As a result, when we see analysts forecasting a target price lower than the current trading price, it implies that analysts think prices will decrease. This means the analysts' expectations of future earnings must be lower than the market's expectations.

As an example, consider the following information from Thompson Reuters on **AutoNation** (AN) as of December 1, 2019:

PRICE TARGET

The chart indicates where analysts predict the stock price will be within the next 12 months compared to the current price.

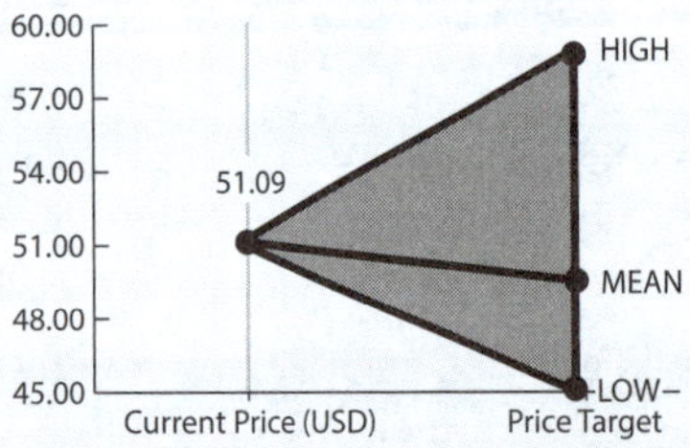

12-Month Price Target	
Mean (USD)	49.60
High	59.00
Low.	45.00
Target versus current	–2.9%
Number of analysts.	9

continued

[5] Optimistic bias in analysts' earnings forecasts is well-established in the academic literature; see, for example, O'Brien (1988); Mendenhall (1991); Brown (1993); Dugar and Nathan (1995); Das, Levine, and Sivaramakrishnan (1998); and Easton and Sommers (2007). Forecasts made well in advance tend to be much more optimistic than those made closer to the earnings announcement; see Richardson, Teoh, and Wysocki (2004).

continued from previous page

A price decrease from the current price of $51.09 to the average target price of $49.60 would mean the market is expected to revise down its expectations over the next year. Our job would be to determine whether our forecasts agree more with the market's or the analysts' expectations. This would determine whether we think the current price is warranted (i.e., agree with market expectations) or a price decrease is coming (i.e., agree with analyst expectations).

MIDYEAR ADJUSTMENT

LO4: Correctly adjust forecasts to midyear and align dates in valuation calculations.

An issue that has not been considered is the timing of the payoffs. Within each valuation model, payoffs are assumed in the formula to occur at year-end and discounted for the entire year. An alternative is to assume that payoffs occur evenly during the year. A common adjustment is to multiply the estimated value by a midyear adjustment factor defined as $(1 + r_{WACC})^{0.5}$. Another common approximation of the adjustment factor is $(1 + [r_{WACC} / 2])$. For GIS, our r_{WACC} estimate of 5.3 percent would yield an adjustment factor of 1.026158 ($1.053^{0.5}$), which increases the estimate of operating valuation to \$45,107.5 million (i.e., \$43,957.7 × 1.026158).

ADJUSTING VALUATION TO THE VALUATION DATE

Thus far, we have implicitly estimated the value of the operations as of the balance sheet date using available accounting numbers and forecasts of cash flows or future *NOPAT* and *NOA*. However, most often, we want to know the value on a date that differs from the date of the last balance sheet. For our GIS example, we are not interested in the value of the operations at May 27, 2018, but at May 1, 2019.

This issue is exacerbated by the fact that we often use information beyond the last balance sheet in forming our forecasts of sales, profit margins (*PM*s), and asset turnover (*ATO*). For example, if we know a new product has been launched subsequent to the last financial statement date and is showing great initial sales, we would want to revise future expected sales rather than ignore this information. In other words, our value calculation is as of the balance sheet date, but our forecasts normally contain newer (current) information.

We must understand the effect of the newer information contained in our forecasts on the value estimate. For discussion of this issue, let us focus on the ROIM from Equation 11.4, although the issue relates to any valuation model:

$$V_0 = NOA_0 + \sum_{t=1}^{T}\left(\frac{NOPAT_t - r_{WACC} \times NOA_{t-1}}{(1+r_{WACC})^t}\right) + \frac{1}{(1+r_{WACC})^T}\left(\frac{(NOPAT_T - r_{WACC} \times NOA_{T-1}) \times (1+g)}{(r_{WACC} - g)}\right) \tag{11.4}$$

When we used this equation to estimate the value of GIS' operating activities, we arrived at a value of \$45,107.5 million (after midyear adjustment) as of May 27, 2018. But let us suppose that the estimates of *NOPAT* and *NOA* are based on information at the valuation date and that the valuation date is May 1, 2019. Of course, in forming these forecasts, we will use information that was not known at May 27, 2018. So, how do we interpret the estimate of value of \$45,107.5 million? It is best described as *the estimate of the operating value that would have been observed on May 27, 2018 had the knowledge available through May 1, 2019 already been known.* This is an odd thought. The good news is that this issue of misalignment of dates can be easily addressed.

If all the information learned between May 27, 2018 and May 1, 2019, had, instead, been known at May 27, 2018, the only change in the value of the operations between those dates would be what was expected at May 27, 2018. That is, the value of the operating activities would be expected to increase at r_{WACC} (because no new information arrives to further affect future expectations of *NOPAT* and *NOA*). This means that, in order to change an estimate of value at May 27, 2018, which reflects information through May 1, 2019, to an estimate of value at May 1, 2019, we simply have roll the value estimate forward at r_{WACC}. We would multiply the May 27, 2018, estimate of $45,107.5 million by 1 plus r_{WACC} of 5.3 percent for an 11-month period (i.e., we compound it forward) to arrive at a May 1, 2019, estimate of $47,294.2 million (i.e., [$\$45,107.5 \times (1 + 0.053)^{11/12}$]). The fraction 11/12 represents that approximately 11 months have passed since the balance sheet date.

Having estimated the value of GIS' operating activities at $47,294.2 million at May 1, 2019, we can use this estimate in making buy/sell/hold decisions as a potential or existing equity holder. Ensuring the alignment of information and value estimates is an often overlooked element of valuation that should be carefully considered.

MIDYEAR AND TIMING ADJUSTMENTS IN PRACTICE

The midyear adjustment and adjustment for the valuation date are appropriate and will increase the accuracy of our valuation. However, these steps, are not always seen in practice. Green, Hand, and Zhang (2016 *RAST*) found the midyear adjustment was omitted in 83 percent of the reports studied and the timing adjustment was omitted in 93 percent of reports.

Despite these adjustments rarely being seen in practice, they are appropriate to consider in valuation. Omission of these adjustments would reduce the accuracy of our calculation and also bias our estimate of value downward. The end result may be a failure to purchase a stock or undertake a project that would be profitable.

DEMONSTRATION OF STEPS FOR COMPARISON OF VALUE ESTIMATE TO MARKET PRICE

Again, we assume that we are using the estimated value of GIS to compare to the observed market price at May 1, 2019 (11 months after the balance sheet date). We have indicated that several steps are necessary before we can make a comparison.

1. Adjust for a midyear payoff: We will adjust for the fact that payoffs are assumed in the valuation model to occur at year-end rather than spread throughout the year.
2. Adjust the valuation date: We will adjust for the fact that we have estimated a value at May 27, 2018, but are presuming that, in doing so, we have used information available until May 1, 2019.
3. Adjust for the value of debt: We will adjust for an estimate of the fair value of debt to move from the value of operations to the value of equity.
4. Estimate the per-share value: We will divide the estimated value of equity by current shares outstanding to achieve an estimate of value per share.

We begin with the estimation of the value of the operations arrived at in Chapters 10 to 12 using one of the valuation models and our detailed forecasts formed in Chapter 7. This estimate of $43,957.7 million is not the number we would use to compare to the market price observed at May 1, 2019. By following the steps outlined above, we can maintain the integrity of our estimation process and ensure the most accurate estimate of value for comparing to the observed market price.

Step 1: As discussed earlier in this chapter, the value estimate of $43,957.7 million assumes that payoffs (*FCF*s from operations, *ROPI*, or *AOIG*) will occur at the end of the period. An alternative is to assume that the payoffs happen evenly throughout the period. This assumption is equivalent to having the payoffs at the midpoint of the year. To accomplish this, we grow the value estimate for a half-year period at r_{WACC}, yielding a value of $45,107.5 million [$\$43,957.7 \times (1 + 0.053)^{6/12}$].

Step 2: Before adjustment, the estimate of value reflects information available through to the date of the valuation (assumed to be May 1, 2019) but is calculated as of May 27, 2018. In other words, we have calculated a value at May 27, 2018, that uses information we would not yet know on that date. Further, what we really seek is an estimate of value at

May 1, 2019, that includes the information that is known as of May 1, 2019, so we can compare the estimated value to the observed market price.

We recognize that the value of the operating activities will grow at r_{WACC} during the next 11 months. To reflect this, we grow the value estimate from step 1 for 11 months (i.e., May 27, 2018 to May 1, 2019), yielding a value of $47,294.2 million [$45,107.5 × $(1 + 0.053)^{11/12}$].

Step 3: To arrive at a value for equity, the adjustment for the value of debt demonstrated at the beginning of this chapter was straightforward. However, in reality, we want the fair value of the financing activities at May 1, 2019. A review of the last few years' calculations of *NFL* and the most recent Form 10-Q reveals that there has not been a large variation in the amount of debt. As a result, using the May 2018 *NFL* of $18,725.9 million continues to be a good starting place for many items. After adjusting investments, debt levels, and equity accounts to the most recent quarter, the only other refinements we make to the *NFL* estimate is to adjust the long-term debt to the most recent fair value and adjust for the interest tax shield.

GIS had filed its third quarter Form 10-Q of GIS with the Securities and Exchange Commission (SEC), making the form available for our May 1, 2019, adjustment. As shown in **Exhibit 13.2**, with this information and updates to current values on other items, we arrive at an adjusted value of $17,579.8 million as of May 1, 2019. By then subtracting the estimated value of the interest tax shield of $2,819.0 million, we arrive at an estimated fair value of debt of $14,760.7 million. Utilizing this value for debt, we have an estimated value of equity at May 1, 2019, of $32,533.5 million ($47,294.2 – $14,760.7).

Step 4: To find a per-share value from our estimated value of equity of $32,533.5 million, we divide by the current number of shares outstanding. The most recent Form 10-Q reveals that 598,790,681 shares were outstanding at February 24, 2019. Therefore, our estimate of the per-share value of equity is $54.33. This estimate reflects our understanding of the business, the reformulation we performed to separate operating and financial activities, the information gleaned from examining competitors, our estimate of cost of capital, and the full-information forecasts we prepared.

ESTIMATION AT THE FIRM OR SHARE LEVEL

Throughout this text, we have worked toward an estimate of equity value for GIS ($32,533.5 million above). Another approach sometimes used is to work on estimating the value per share directly. This is most often seen in implementations of the multiples approach discussed in Chapter 8. For example, the price-to-earnings (PE) ratio may be viewed as price per share divided by earnings per share.

We have chosen to focus on firm-level estimation because share effects can muddy the calculation. When looking at a trailing PE ratio calculated using per-share inputs, should we use basic earnings per share or diluted earnings per share? Other options are to calculate net income or comprehensive income per share outstanding at year-end. Additionally, shares outstanding can change due to share buybacks (purchases of treasury stock) or stock issuances.

Rather than attempt to deal with all these issues, it is cleaner to estimate value at the firm level and then adjust for the number of shares outstanding as demonstrated above in step 4.

DETERMINING NUMBER OF SHARES OUTSTANDING

The easiest way to determine the number of shares outstanding is to look at the front page of the Form 10-K or 10-Q. At the bottom of that page, the company will disclose the number as of the filing date. For GIS, the February 24, 2019, Form 10-Q states, "Number of shares of Common Stock outstanding as of March 11, 2019: 598,790,681 (excluding 155,822,647 shares held in the treasury)." From this, we can utilize the 598,790,681 in adjusting our estimate of value to a per-share estimate. (Note that we have estimated the value of equity in millions.)

The May 1, 2019, observed closing price for GIS was \$51.31. Our estimated value of \$54.33 would imply that the company was undervalued by about 5.9 percent. Having approached our valuation in a systematic manner by beginning with the valuation formulas, we can consider the source of this difference. Essentially, either our expectations of future payoffs are higher than the market's (a numerator difference) or our expectation of the risk of GIS is lower than the market's (a denominator difference). From this, we can circle back and take another pass through our work thus far to ensure we are comfortable with our assumptions. If we confirm the estimate of \$54.33, then our action would be to buy shares of GIS because we think the market has underpriced them.

SENSITIVITY ANALYSIS AND VALUATION

LO5: Perform sensitivity analyses on key variables to determine areas of concern and/or focus.

The GIS example we have worked with throughout Chapters 7 and beyond has used only one set of assumptions and derived only one estimate of value. We can perform sensitivity analyses to help us further understand our valuation. For example, the GIS illustration uses 5.3 percent for r_{WACC}, which is our best estimate of the company's risk level. We might consider using a larger and/or a smaller cost of capital with all other forecasts unchanged to gauge how sensitive our valuation is to changes in the discount rate. Extending this idea, we commonly derive a worst-case stock valuation by simultaneously applying the lowest reasonable assumptions for sales growth, *PM*, and *ATO*, and the highest reasonable assumption for cost of capital. We also commonly derive the best-case scenario by applying the highest reasonable assumptions for sales growth, *PM*, and *ATO*, and the lowest reasonable assumption for cost of capital. This provides a range of reasonable stock values and gives us more information and confidence about potential outcomes.

Make sure in valuation to be mindful that cost of capital is a very imprecise estimate. Beta is often the biggest driver of changes in our value estimate! Given the number of assumptions made and the confidence interval on our estimate of cost of capital, assuming a high level of confidence in the dollar amount estimated would be foolish. We have made our best effort by applying a systematic process to valuation, but at the end of the day, it is subject to error.

SPREADSHEETS AID SENSITIVITY ANALYSIS

The building of our valuation spreadsheet aids our ability to do what-if analysis, or sensitivity analysis. As seen on the spreadsheet page labeled "13 Sensitivity," it is common to examine changes in the forecasts of revenue growth, *PM*, *ATO*, and cost of capital. To understand the way the table works and successfully implement its use in Excel, heed the following guidance on two important issues:

Flow of information:

The flow of information must be from the forecasts pages to the sensitivity page to the valuation page. Working backward, this means that the last year's forecast at cell H7 on "10-12 Valuation" references cell B7 on "13 Sensitivity," which references cell L4 on "7 F-Rev." Similar trails exist for cells F8, F9, and C11 on "10-12 Valuation."

Setup for table function:

For the table calculation on "13 Sensitivity," cell E14 is a link to the final valuation estimate at "13 Final." Cells F14.J14 and E15.E19 must be values. This means if you try to copy the information from F12.J12 to F14.J14, you must paste **values** rather than use the normal paste function.

The table function for cells F15.J19 is set up by highlighting cells E14.J19 (notice the top and side rows are included!) and then choosing from the menu Data, What If, Data Table. For row input cells, put in the item referenced across the top of the table, and for column input cells, put in the item referenced across the side of the table. (This may feel backward!) Repeat for the second table.

From the tables on "13 Sensitivity," we see that the two biggest drivers of the valuation of GIS are the discount rate and the *ATO*. An incremental change in either r_{WACC} or *ATO* causes the per-share estimate to change by approximately \$4. Stated in a different way, the change in assumption alters our computed value estimate by more than 7 percent!

continued

continued from previous page

Now, we bring our understanding of the business (step 1) and our knowledge of where the company is (step 3) to bear. GIS has had a pretty consistent *ATO* until the addition of Blue Buffalo. We should think very carefully about whether the most recent value would be expected to be the new norm or whether there will be a change in the level of resources employed in the near future. At this point, while the value estimate is sensitive to *ATO*, we are pretty confident in our value. This would lead us to understand that, for GIS, the discount rate is the primary issue we should focus on to gain additional confidence going forward.

Another use of sensitivity analysis is to create a what-if analysis. Currently, many cities and states are considering the idea of raising the minimum wage to $15 per hour. If you were examining a company such as McDonald's, it would be advisable to consider forecasting this potential scenario. Immediately obvious would be to consider the effect on labor costs. However, that is not the only effect that would need to be considered. What effect would there be on the materials costs and, most important, sales? Similar issues arise in other industries where a commodity plays a key role (e.g., fuel prices for a transportation company). Our knowledge of the business should drive our thoughts as we seek to identify key issues.

SUMMARY

This chapter demonstrated that the value of equity can be estimated by subtracting the value of the debt holders' ownership from the calculated value of operating activities. This is useful because debt is generally shown in the financial statements at market value. At times when the debt is not at market value, accounting's required disclosures provide an adjustment to assist in the calculation.

We also showed the formulas for the dividend discount model, the residual earnings model, and the abnormal earnings growth models, which are equity equivalents to the models introduced in Chapters 10, 11, and 12. However, using these models to value equity directly is discouraged because they require a very strong assumption that leverage will be constant in the future.

The shortcut approach to valuation by relying on analysts' forecasts was considered despite the fact that it also requires the assumption of constant leverage. In using analysts' forecasts, we saw that the issue of leverage actually was dwarfed by issues related to achieving stability in growth within the forecast horizon and the effect of analysts' bias in their forecasts.

Issues related to the dates involved in computing the value estimate and potential use of a mid-year adjustment were also addressed in this chapter. While we compute our best estimate of value, the process of sensitivity analysis is a useful tool for determining the effects of our assumptions on our estimate of value. We can use this technique to evaluate the confidence we have in our estimate.

Green, Hand, and Zhang (2016 *RAST*) note that analysts "typically use DCF to support a multiples-based valuation, rather than to originate a target price." (p. 624) One of the analysts they interviewed stated that "the DCF model is often there because it forces us to think about our business assumptions about the firm we're covering and, through discussing those assumptions and views in the report, enables us to engage with our clients in intelligent conversation and debate about their assumptions." As we have seen in this text, DCF is superior to the multiples approach because it is theoretically sound. Further, in most cases ROIM or AOIGM would outperform DCF because more value will be captured within a shorter-horizon than DCF. Given our diminishing confidence as we forecast at longer horizons, this is a high priority.

QUESTIONS

Q13.1 We have focused on valuing operating activities. What is necessary for moving to an estimate of equity value?

Q13.2 Can we assume debt is at fair value?

Q13.3 Describe how the valuation using DCF in Chapter 10 is related to the valuation of dividends shown in this chapter.

Q13.4 How does the REM differ from the ROIM?

Q13.5 Explain the implication of $r_{Eq} = r_{WACC} + \frac{V^{NFL}}{V^{Eq}} \times (r_{WACC} - r_D)$ on the choice between using a model that values operating activities or equity.

Q13.6 What assumptions must be made in using analysts' forecasts for estimating value?

Q13.7 Do dates matter in valuation?

Q13.8 What two adjustments are used to adjust the firm's operating value from its year-end balance sheet date to the valuation date?

Q13.9 What are the implications for determining an equity value per share for publicly traded companies?

Q13.10 What role does sensitivity analysis play?

Q13.11 *The End of Accounting* (Wiley, 2016) is a book that is critical of current GAAP and the related financial statements. The book notes the widening differences between book value per share (BVPS) and market value per share. That is, the book-to-market ratio is increasing over time as business has changed over time. The book states that intangible assets (e.g., patents, brands, information technology) are the "prime value creators of businesses." Of course, internally created intangible assets are not reflected on the firm's balance sheet. For example, Disney's Mickey Mouse, Google's algorithms, and Facebook's data mining abilities are not reflected on their balance sheet.

Is the *RE* model effective for valuing companies with substantial amounts of internally created intangible assets not reflected in its book value?

EXERCISES

E13.12 The following forecasts of earnings per share (EPS) and dividend per share (DPS) were made at the end of 2019 for Haskins Inc. with a BVPS of $25.00:

	2020E	2021E	2022E	2023E	2024E
EPS	3.50	3.85	4.24	4.66	5.12
DPS	1.00	1.00	1.00	1.00	1.00

Haskins has an equity cost of capital of 10 percent.

a. Calculate BVPS for 2020–2024.

b. Calculate the *RE* per share for 2020–2024.

c. Calculate the year over year (YOY) forecasted EPS growth rates *and RE* growth rates for the period 2020–2024.

d. Review the EPS and *RE* growth rate trends over the forecast horizon. Explain why the EPS is *not the same* as the *RE* growth rate.

E13.13 Bank of America (BofA) provides equity research on publicly traded firms. On June 27, 2019, BofA issued a research report on Nike (NKE).

In the report, BofA lowered its expectations of NKE to underperform with a 12-month price target of $70. NKE's share price at the date of the report was $83.66. Additionally, BofA provided its estimates of future EPS and DPS for NKE's FY2020–2022.

Estimates (May) (US$)	2018A	2019A	2020E	2021E	2022E
EPS	2.39	2.49	2.95	3.50	4.00
GAAP EPS	1.17	2.49	2.95	3.50	4.00
EPS Change (YoY)	–4.8%	4.2%	18.5%	18.6%	14.3%
Consensus EPS (Bloomberg)			3.01	3.51	NA
DPS	0.75	0.85	0.93	1.02	1.12

NKE's BVPS at May 31 is $5.77. Assume NKE's equity cost of capital is 9.0 percent.

a. Calculate NKE's expected *RE* for the forecast horizon (FY2020–2022)?

b. Assuming the *RE* estimate at the forecast horizon (FY2022) will continue to grow at a constant rate into the future, calculate the implied growth rate, *g*, in the market share price of $83.66 at June 27, 2019?

c. Assuming the *RE* estimate at the forecast horizon (FY2022) will continue to grow at a constant rate into the future, calculate the implied growth rate, *g*, in the BofA price objective of $70.00 at June 27, 2019?

d. What is the benefit of determining the implied growth rates in a *RE* valuation model.

E13.14 On August 31, an analyst evaluating Zeff Co. has estimated operating value (V^{Oper}) at $1,250 million as of December 31, its year-end date. The *NFL* at December 31 were estimated to be $300 million.

a. Prepare a midyear adjustment to Zeff's estimated operating value assuming cost of capital for operations is 8.0 percent.

b. Prepare the adjustment to Zeff's estimated operating value from (a) above to August 31.

c. Based on Zeff's latest Form 10-Q, the fair market value of its *NFL* is $35 million lower than at December 31. Calculate the estimated value of Zeff's equity at August 31.

d. At December 31, Zeff reported 25 million common shares outstanding. By August 31, the latest Form 10-Q reported 22.5 million common shares outstanding. What is the analyst's estimated per-share price for Zeff at August 31?

CONTINUING EXAMPLES

CE13.15 Before the adjustments for dates and fair value of financial liabilities detailed in the chapter, what is the first pass estimated value of **Kellogg** (K) equity based on our estimates of the value of operating activities in Chapters 10 to 12 and the *NFL* calculated in Chapter 5?

CE13.16 Why is a midyear adjustment needed for K? What is the estimated value of operating activities after performing a midyear adjustment?

CE13.17 Our calculations of cost of capital and our forecasting for K have utilized information available through May 1, 2019. This has been applied to information drawn from the 2018 financial statements. What issues does this create, and what is the estimate of value of enterprise operating activities for K as of May 1, 2019, after addressing this issue?

CE13.18 The first quarter 10-Q for K was filed with the SEC on May 3, 2019. Thus, it was not available on May 1, 2019. Consequently, given the estimated *NFL* at December 2018 along with the estimate of the value of operating activities at May 1, 2019, what is the estimated value of equity of K as of May 1, 2019?

CE13.19 Now, as a final step to the valuation process, compute the value per share of K at May 1, 2019, using the number of shares outstanding shown in the December 2018 Form 10-K. How does this amount compare to the closing price of K on that day?

CE13.20 Reflecting on the valuation exercise, which of the following assumptions for K do you have the most concerns about relying on?

- Continuing growth in sales of 0.40 percent
- Ongoing operating *PM* of 10.55 percent
- Weighted average cost of capital for operations of 5.20 percent

Examine the sensitivity to altering each of these assumptions up or down by 0.2 percent. Which appears to be most critical, and how would this affect the valuation effort?

CE13.21 Before the adjustments for dates and fair value of financial liabilities detailed in the chapter, what is the first pass estimated value of **Thor Industries** (THO) equity based on our estimates of the value of operating activities in Chapters 10 to 12 and the *NFL* calculated in Chapter 5?

CE13.22 Why is a midyear adjustment needed for THO? What is the estimated value of operating activities after performing a midyear adjustment?

CE13.23 Our calculations of cost of capital and our forecasting for THO have utilized information available through May 1, 2019. This has been applied to information drawn from the 2018 financial statements. What issues does this create, and what is the estimate of value of operating activities for THO as of May 1, 2019, after addressing this issue?

CE13.24 Below is the balance sheet from THO's Form 10-Q dated January 31, 2019:

	Jan. 31, 2019
Assets	
Current assets:	
Cash and cash equivalents	$ 305,833
Accounts receivable, trade, net	325,783
Accounts receivable, other, net	18,999
Inventories, net	561,842
Prepaid income taxes, expenses, and other	35,699
Total current assets	1,248,156
Property, plant, and equipment, net	550,471
Other assets:	
Goodwill	377,693
Amortizable intangible assets, net	363,231
Deferred income taxes, net	80,205
Equity investment in joint venture	48,264
Other	62,178
Total other assets	931,571
Total assets	$2,730,198
Liabilities and Stockholders' Equity	
Current liabilities:	
Accounts payable	$ 219,881
Accrued liabilities:	
Compensation and related items	59,183
Product warranties	257,869
Income and other taxes	16,285
Promotions and rebates	72,945
Product, property, and related liabilities	13,092
Foreign currency forward contract liability	73,707
Other	37,681
Total current liabilities	750,643
Unrecognized tax benefits	10,562
Other liabilities	62,062
Total long-term liabilities	72,624
Contingent liabilities and commitments	—
Stockholders' equity:	
Preferred stock—authorized 1,000,000 shares; none outstanding	—
Common stock—par value of $.10 per share; authorized 250,000,000 shares; issued 62,933,415 and 62,765,824 shares, respectively	6,293
Additional paid-in capital	263,899
Retained earnings	1,984,885
Less treasury shares of 10,126,434 and 10,070,459, respectively, at cost	(348,146)
Total stockholders' equity	1,906,931
Total liabilities and stockholders' equity	$2,730,198

The second quarter Form 10-Q for THO was filed with the SEC on March 6, 2019. Using this information, our estimated *NFL* at July 31, 2018, and our estimate of the value of operating activities at May 1, 2019, what is the estimated value of equity of THO as of May 1, 2019?

CE13.25 Now, as a final step to the valuation process, compute the value per share of THO at May 1, 2019, using the number of shares outstanding shown in the 2019 Form 10-Q for the second quarter. How does this amount compare to THO's closing price on that day?

CE13.26 Reflecting on the valuation exercise, which of the following assumptions for THO do you have the most concerns about relying on?

- Continuing growth in sales of 1.00 percent
- Ongoing operating *PM* of 5.15 percent
- Weighted average cost of capital for operations of 12.60 percent

Examine the sensitivity to altering each of these assumptions up or down by 0.2 percent. Which appears to be most critical, and how would this affect the valuation effort?

CE13.27 Before the adjustments for dates and fair value of financial liabilities detailed in the chapter, what is the first pass estimated value of Winnebago (WGO) equity based on our estimates of the value of operating activities in Chapters 10 to 12 and the *NFL* calculated in Chapter 5?

CE13.28 Why is a midyear adjustment needed for WGO? What is the estimated value of operating activities after performing a midyear adjustment?

CE13.29 Our calculations of cost of capital and our forecasting for WGO have utilized information available through May 1, 2019. This has been applied to information drawn from the FY2018 financial statements. What issues does this create, and what is the estimate of value of operating activities for WGO as of May 1, 2019, after addressing this issue?

CE13.30 Below is is the balance sheet from WGO's Form 10-Q dated February 23, 2019:

(in Thousands, Except Per-Share Data)	Feb. 23, 2019
Asset	
Current assets:	
Cash and cash equivalents	$ 3,017
Receivables, less allowance for doubtful accounts ($163 and $197, respectively)	179,940
Inventories, net	189,611
Prepaid expenses and other assets	15,217
Total current assets	387,785
Property, plant, and equipment, net	117,761
Other assets:	
Goodwill	275,072
Other intangible assets, net	260,791
Investment in life insurance	26,963
Other assets	9,764
Total assets	$1,078,136
Liabilities and Stockholders' Equity	
Current liabilities:	
Accounts payable	$ 92,592
Income taxes payable	472
Accrued expenses:	
Accrued compensation	25,112
Product warranties	40,305
Self-insurance	14,488
Promotional	21,333
Accrued interest	3,002
Other	12,463
Current maturities of long-term debt	2,750
Total current liabilities	212,517
Noncurrent liabilities:	
Long-term debt, less current maturities	274,168
Deferred income taxes	4,595
Unrecognized tax benefits	1,712
Deferred compensation benefits, net of current portion	14,228
Other	250
Total noncurrent liabilities	294,953

continued

continued from previous page

(in Thousands, Except Per-Share Data)	Feb. 23, 2019
Stockholders' equity:	
Preferred stock, par value $0.01: Authorized—10,000 shares; Issued—none	—
Common stock, par value $0.50: Authorized—60,000 shares; Issued—51,776 shares	25,888
Additional paid-in capital	89,682
Retained earnings	805,851
Accumulated other comprehensive income	252
Treasury stock, at cost: 20,292 and 20,243 shares, respectively	(351,007)
Total stockholders' equity	570,666
Total liabilities and stockholders' equity	$1,078,136

The second quarter Form 10-Q for WGO was filed with the SEC on March 26, 2019. Using this information, our estimated *NFL* at August 25, 2018, and our estimate of the value of operating activities at May 1, 2019, what is the estimated value of equity of WGO as of May 1, 2019?

CE13.31 Now, as a final step to the valuation process, compute the value per share of WGO at May 1, 2019, using the number of shares outstanding shown in the 2019 Form 10-Q for the second quarter. How does this amount compare to WGO's closing price on that day?

CE13.32 Reflecting on the valuation exercise, which of the following assumptions for WGO do you have the most concerns about relying on?

- Continuing growth in sales of 0.90 percent
- Ongoing operating *PM* of 6.03 percent
- Weighted average cost of capital for operations of 10.60 percent

Examine the sensitivity to altering each of these assumptions up or down by 0.2 percent. Which appears to be most critical, and how would this affect the valuation effort?

NOTES

Chapter Fourteen

Steady State and Forecast Horizon

TAKEAWAYS

When you complete this chapter, you should be able to:

1. Clearly articulate the necessary requirements for a firm's future operations to be in steady state.
2. Explain why a shorter forecast horizon is desired provided steady state is achieved.
3. Choose a steady state growth rate that is appropriate for valuing a firm's operations.
4. Relate market multiples to valuation models and understand requirements for them to be useful in valuation.

Chapters 10, 11, and 12 introduced three mathematically equivalent valuation models: free cash flow (*FCF*), residual operating income (*ROPI*), and abnormal operating income growth (*AOIG*). We saw that the mathematical equivalence of these models is maintained in our valuations based on forecasts for **General Mills'** (GIS) operating activities if we forecast sufficiently far into the future to ensure that steady state growth rate is reached. We begin this chapter with a clarification of the meaning of steady state and a discussion of the point in time when steady state is reached. Then, we show that, although forecasting to steady state will lead to valuations that are identical across the three models, the portion of the value that is captured within the short-term future differs considerably across the models; of course, we are much more confident about our short-term forecasts, and this likely will influence our choice of valuation model. Finally, we suggest a straightforward method for dealing with the often-seen situation where our forecasted sales revenues are relatively high in the short term and this growth rate is not sustainable in the very long run; although steady state may not be reached for many years into the future, this does not significantly affect the complexity of our valuation analyses.

DEFINING STEADY STATE

We must remember that the models will yield the same value for operations ($43,957.7 million for GIS) if steady state is reached. What is steady state? How does steady state affect the implementation of each of the valuation models?

LO1: Clearly articulate the necessary requirements for a firm's future operations to be in steady state.

Steady state is reached when all of the following occur:

1. Sales are growing at a constant rate.
2. The net operating profit after tax (*NOPAT*) from each dollar of sales is constant (i.e., operating profit margin [*PM*], which is equal to $NOPAT_t/Sales_t$, is constant).
3. The net operating assets (*NOA*) required for each dollar of sales is constant (i.e., operating asset turnover [*ATO*], which is equal to $Sales_t/NOA_{t-1}$, is constant).

CHAPTER OUTLINE

Steady State and Forecast Horizon

Steady State
- Definition of Steady State
- Timing of Steady State

Implementing Valuation Models
- Evaluation of Models
- Steady State Growth Rate

Revisiting Market Multiples
- Connection between Valuation Models and Market Multiples

That is, steady state is reached when everything (profitability and resources) is growing at the sales growth rate. Until this point, steady state has not been reached.

A subtle but important issue in the implementation of the three valuation models relates to the point in time when a constant rate of growth in *FCF*, *ROPI*, and *AOIG* is reached. This point in time differs across the models.

Notice that, because constant *ATO* means constant $Sales_t/NOA_{t-1}$, *NOA* will grow at a constant rate a year before sales grow at a constant rate. And, because FCF_t equals $NOPAT_t$ less change in NOA_t (which is NOA_t less NOA_{t-1}) and $ROPI_t$ equals $NOPAT_t$ less $r_{WACC} \times NOA_{t-1}$, both FCF_t and $ROPI_t$ will grow at a constant rate in the year that steady state is reached.

AOIG reaches a constant growth rate 1 year later than *FCF* and *ROPI* because the calculation is based on two prior estimates of *NOA*. The FCF_{t-1}, which is part of the calculation of $AOIG_t$ equals $NOPAT_{t-1}$ less change in NOA_{t-1} (which is NOA_{t-1} less NOA_{t-2}). This becomes clear when we recognize the fact that *AOIG* equals the change in *ROPI*.

Consider the point in time, *T*, when *AOIG* reaches a constant growth rate. We can write $AOIG_T$ as follows:

$$\begin{aligned} AOIG_T &= NOPAT_T + r_{WACC} \times FCF_{T-1} - (1 + r_{WACC}) \times NOPAT_{T-1} \\ &= NOPAT_T + r_{WACC} \times FCF_{T-1} - NOPAT_{T-1} - r_{WACC} \times NOPAT_{T-1} \\ &= NOPAT_T - NOPAT_{T-1} + r_{WACC} \times FCF_{T-1} - r_{WACC} \times NOPAT_{T-1} \\ &= NOPAT_T - NOPAT_{T-1} + r_{WACC} \times (FCF_{T-1} - NOPAT_{T-1}) \end{aligned}$$

We also know from Equation 2.2 that

$$\begin{aligned} FCF_{T-1} &= NOPAT_{T-1} - \quad NOA_{T-1} \\ FCF_{T-1} &= NOPAT_{T-1} - NOA_{T-1} + NOA_{T-2} \\ FCF_{T-1} - NOPAT_{T-1} &= -NOA_{T-1} + NOA_{T-2} \end{aligned}$$

Substituting for $FCF_{T-1} - NOPAT_{T-1}$ in the equation for $AOIG_T$ yields the following:

$$\begin{aligned} AOIG_T &= NOPAT_T - NOPAT_{T-1} - r_{WACC} \times (FCF_{T-1} - NOPAT_{T-1}) \\ &= NOPAT_T - NOPAT_{T-1} + r_{WACC} \times (-NOA_{T-1} + NOA_{T-2}) \\ &= NOPAT_T - NOPAT_{T-1} - r_{WACC} \times NOA_{T-1} + r_{WACC} \times NOA_{T-2} \\ &= NOPAT_T - r_{WACC} \times NOA_{T-1} - NOPAT_{T-1} + r_{WACC} \times NOA_{T-2} \\ &= (NOPAT_T - r_{WACC} \times NOA_{T-1}) - (NOPAT_{T-1} - r_{WACC} \times NOA_{T-2}) \\ &= ROPI_T - ROPI_{T-1} \end{aligned}$$

This mathematical exercise demonstrates that *AOIG* equals the change in *ROPI*. As a result, obtaining a constant growth rate in *AOIG* requires 2 years of *NOA* growing at the sales growth rate and 1 year of *NOPAT* growing at the sales growth rate. *ROPI* is already at a constant growth rate (as is *FCF*) in year *T* – 1, while *AOIG* reaches a constant growth rate in year *T*.

Now that we have defined steady state and its implications for the timing of a constant rate of growth in *FCF*, *ROPI*, and *AOIG*, let us examine how it was implemented in Chapters 10 to 12 to ensure we do not misapply each model. After that, we can consider what would happen to the models if we failed to properly implement steady state.

IMPLEMENTATION OF STEADY STATE

Because the models are mathematically equivalent, the critical issue in the valuation exercise is not choice of model but whether the forecasting horizon is sufficient to reach steady state. Unless we have reached steady state, we are unable to calculate a reliable continuing value, and the value estimate will appear to differ across models. To see this, let us return to the forecasts from Chapter 7 to verify the conditions of steady state are satisfied. Then, we will see the effect on the forecasts of the *FCF*, *ROPI*, and *AOIG* numbers used in calculating continuing value.

In Chapter 7, we arrived at the forecasts shown in **Exhibit 14.1**:

EXHIBIT 14.1 GIS Multiyear Forecasts

Year Ended	5/26/2019	5/31/2020	5/30/2021	5/29/2022	5/28/2023	5/26/2024
Sales growth.	9.43%	3.03%	–0.62%	1.30%	1.25%	1.20%
Operating *PM*	12.32%	12.32%	12.45%	12.62%	12.62%	12.62%
Operating *ATO*	0.688	0.678	0.665	0.651	0.651	0.651

We also assumed that, going forward from 2024 (i.e., 2025 and each year thereafter), GIS' sales growth would continue at 1.20 percent, *PM* would remain at 12.62 percent, and *ATO* would remain at 0.651. These assumptions imply that steady state has been reached and we can calculate a continuing value for 2024 and beyond.

To be clear, the first requirement of steady state is that sales are growing at a constant rate. This is not the case until 2024 because the prior year they grew by 1.25 percent. However, beginning in 2024, we have the same rate each year (1.20 percent), so this condition of steady state is satisfied. The second requirement is that the *NOPAT* from each dollar of sales, *PM*, is constant. This is reached beginning in 2022 because both 2022 and 2023 (and all subsequent years) show forecasted *PM* of 12.62 percent. Additionally, the third requirement that the *NOA* required for each dollar of sales, *ATO*, is constant is also satisfied beginning in 2022. Note that even though two of the three requirements are met beginning in 2022, we have not reached steady state until all three conditions are satisfied.

Now, let us examine the forecasted payoffs, which we used in the different valuation models. **Exhibit 14.2** shows the *FCF*, *ROPI*, and *AOIG* forecasts used in the valuations in Chapters 10 to 12. Also included in the exhibit are the year-to-year growth rates in the forecasted values.

EXHIBIT 14.2 GIS Forecasted Valuation Model Payoffs

Year Ended	5/26/2019	5/31/2020	5/30/2021	5/29/2022	5/28/2023	5/26/2024	5/25/2025
FCF.	$866.5	$2,479.3	$1,339.8	$1,322.2	$1,949.6	$1,973.0	$1,996.6
Growth in *FCF*		186.15%	–45.96%	–1.32%	47.45%	1.20%	1.20%
ROPI.	$795.2	$ 793.0	$ 818.0	$ 831.6	$ 810.3	$ 820.0	$ 829.9
Growth in *ROPI* . . .		–0.27%	3.15%	1.66%	–2.55%	1.20%	1.20%
AOIG.		$ –2.2	$ 25.0	$ 13.5	$ –21.2	$ 9.7	$ 9.8
Growth in *AOIG* . . .			–1253.97%	–45.83%	-256.84%	–145.77%	1.20%

In order to calculate the terminal (continuing) value, we must have a constant growth beyond the horizon in the variable that is the basis of our valuation model, whether it be *FCF*, *ROPI*, or *AOIG*. The calculation of a continuing value requires constant growth from that point forward; otherwise, we are unable to capture the continuing value as either $\frac{FCF}{r_{WACC}-g}$, $\frac{ROPI}{r_{WACC}-g}$, or $\frac{AOIG}{r_{WACC}-g}$.

From **Exhibit 14.2**, *FCF* has not been forecast to grow constantly until 2024. Between 2019 and 2023, it is forecasted to grow from year to year by rates varying from −45.96 to 186.15 percent. It is not until 2024 that we see constant growth at 1.20 percent in that year and beyond. Thus, at that point, we can use the forecasted *FCF* of $1,973.0 in 2024 to calculate the continuing value for the discounted cash flow (DCF) model.

DCF VALUATION USING THE MULTIPLES APPROACH TO CONTINUING VALUE

As a hybrid, in implementing the DCF valuation model, a multiples approach is sometimes suggested for calculating continuing value. In Chapter 10, the continuing value of the DCF model was shown to equal the expected intrinsic value. Substituting an estimate of the continuing value based on a multiples model is an option sometimes observed.

The most common multiple used in practice is an estimate of *EBITDA*. By using *EBITDA* at the horizon multiplied by an *EBITDA* multiple, a continuing value estimate can be calculated. This amount is then added to the DCFs from the forecast horizon. The result is a modified version of Equation 10.7 as follows:

$$V_0 = \frac{FCF_1}{(1+r_{WACC})} + \frac{FCF_2}{(1+r_{WACC})^2} + \frac{FCF_3}{(1+r_{WACC})^3} + \frac{FCF_4}{(1+r_{WACC})^4} + \frac{FCF_5}{(1+r_{WACC})^5} + \ldots$$

$$= \sum_{t=1}^{\infty} \frac{FCF_t}{(1+r_{WACC})^t}$$

$$= \sum_{t=1}^{T} \frac{FCF_t}{(1+r_{WACC})^t} + \frac{1}{(1+r_{WACC})^T} \times EBITDA_T \times EBITDAMultiple$$

This approach is done in practice in part because of the variability of *FCF* forecasts. However, note that all the issues raised in Chapter 8 related to the use of multiples continue to apply here. Further, finding a multiple today is hard, so why would we be confident in our multiple several years from now? Observed current multiples for competitor firms are influenced by many factors, such as growth that may have changed over time, or they may not apply to the subject firm compounding the issues in estimation of an appropriate multiple at the forecast horizon. Also, bear in mind the shortcomings of using *EBITDA* multiples raised in earlier chapters.

ROPI in **Exhibit 14.2** is more stable than *FCF* from year to year, having growth rates ranging from −2.55 to 3.15 percent between 2019 and 2023. Nevertheless, it, too, does not reach a constant growth rate of 1.20 percent until 2024. Thus, we use the $820.0 forecasted *ROPI* in 2024 to calculate the continuing value for the residual operating income model (ROIM).

In the prior section, we showed that AOIGM requires one more period to reach a constant growth. This becomes clear in **Exhibit 14.2**. While the other two models had the same growth rate in both 2024 and 2025, AOIGM does not have a constant growth rate until 2025 and beyond. Also, notice that, within the horizon, the growth rate on *AOIG* is the most variable, ranging from −1253.97 to −45.83 percent during 2020 to 2024.

EVALUATING VALUATION MODELS

LO2: Explain why a shorter forecast horizon is desired provided steady state is achieved.

Now that we have introduced three valuation models and discussed the relation between steady state and constant growth in *FCF*, *ROPI* and *AOIG*, the question naturally arises as to how one would choose between the three models in practice. Although we have shown that, mathematically, the models are equivalent, this does not mean that they will have similar ease of use in all situations. Evaluation of the models centers on the idea that the farther into the future, we forecast the less confidence we have in our estimates. That is, we would prefer to capture more of value within a shorter horizon.

Predicting the short term is not easy. It is, however, usually significantly easier than predicting the long term. Consider trying to answer these questions: How much will you earn next year, and how much 10 years from now? In most cases, there is very little confidence in an estimate 10 years from now because so much may change between now and then. The same is true for our forecasts for a company, even when our forecasts are systematically determined using our best information, as was done in Chapter 7. When we forecast the change in sales volume in the North America retail segment for GIS, for example, it may seem that we are simply guessing even in the first couple years. This serves as a reminder that, while we may make our best efforts to forecast as accurately as possible, our forecasts are still associated with considerable uncertainty. Our degree of uncertainty will be far greater regarding forecasts 15 years from now!

Thus, we would prefer a model that has more value captured in the short-term future; in other words, we would prefer less reliance on the forecast of growth at the horizon. Even within the horizon, the sooner the value is captured, the better!

Exhibit 14.3 compares values calculated using the DCF model, ROIM, and AOIGM based on our forecasts in Chapter 7 for GIS. We break each value estimate into the portion based on our explicit forecasts within the horizon (through 2024/2025 for GIS depending on model) and the portion arising from the continuing value calculation.

EXHIBIT 14.3 Breakdown of GIS Value Estimate Based on Horizon

	Discounted Cash Flow Model		Residual Operating Income Model		Abnormal Operating Income Growth Model	
	Amount	Percent	Amount	Percent	Amount	Percent
No forecast necessary	$ —	0.0%	$25,035.4	57.0%	$ —	0.0%
Based on forecasts within horizon	6,787.7	15.4%	3,473.2	7.9%	40,459.8	92.0%
Based on continuing value	37,170.0	84.6%	15,449.1	35.1%	3,497.9	8.0%
Total estimated value	$43,957.7	100.0%	$43,957.7	100.0%	$43,957.7	100.0%

In this case, we see that, for GIS, the DCF model has almost 85 percent of the value estimate coming from the periods beyond the forecast horizon; that is, almost 85 percent of the value estimate is the continuing value. Recall the discussion in Chapter 10 where we learned that the continuing value for the DCF model is the estimate of value at the horizon—we see that very little of our value estimate results from the explicit forecasts within the horizon but, instead, almost all of the estimate results from our forecast of the operating value at the horizon. If we don't know the value of the operations today, we are likely to have very little confidence in our forecasted value at the horizon. Of course!

For the ROIM, anchoring on current *NOA*, which is known because it is available from GIS' balance sheet, provides 57 percent of our value estimate before we begin to use our forecasts. As a result, we do not rely as much on the forecast of the continuing value because it provides just under 45 percent of our value estimate (still a large number, but better).

When using AOIGM, we see that the portion of the estimated value coming from the periods beyond the explicitly forecasted horizon is only 8 percent. This is, by far, the lowest reliance on the continuing value. The degree to which the capitalized earnings (an element based on forecasts within the horizon) captures value in AOIGM will vary depending on the extent to which the forecasted earnings will be recurring rather than transitory.

To demonstrate the reliance on our forecasts, **Figure 14.1** shows how much of the total value estimate of $43,957.7 million for GIS' operations is captured as we add each year of the forecast period. This chart depicts the portion of value captured during the earlier years, when our confidence in the forecasts is high, and the later years when our confidence is low.

For GIS, as long as we are willing to forecast earnings 1 year ahead, we have already captured over 90 percent of value. Thus, if we are willing to forecast only 1 year ahead, it would appear that AOIGM is the model we would choose. Using only 1 year of forecasts provides less than 2 percent of the value for the DCF model! Note that ROIM, by anchoring on *NOA*, provides a considerable portion of value (for GIS, 57 percent) before we even begin to forecast.

FIGURE 13.1 Percent of Value Captured with Additional Forecasted Years for GIS

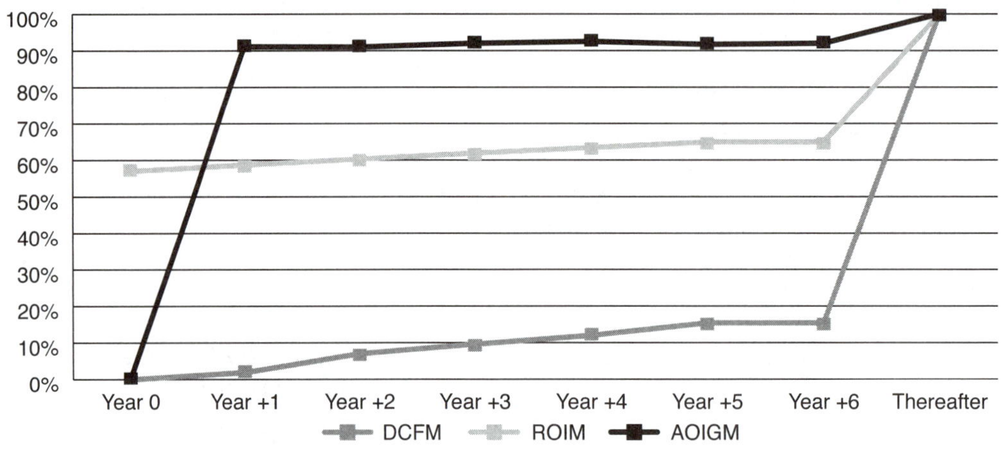

The takeaway is that, if we are unsure of our short-term earnings estimates, have concerns about the weighted average cost of capital for operations used, or are valuing a company for which it will take a long time to reach steady state, the accounting models clearly outperform the DCF model. From our examination of the various models in Chapters 10, 11, and 12, we saw the following related to the anchors for valuation:

1. DCF model does not have an anchor.
2. ROIM anchors on book value (NOA_0) and often the subsequent forecasts within horizon earnings capture a lot of value.
3. AOIGM anchors on capitalized earnings ($NOPAT_1/r_{WACC}$), which generally captures a lot of value.

These insights stem from the fact that *NOA* is the accounting measure of value and *NOPAT* is the accounting measure of value earned in the period. The practical choice of a valuation model requires one to question the confidence in the estimate obtained. In most cases, the answer to this question remains that we will be more confident within the horizon (i.e., before steady state is reached) than beyond it (i.e., after steady state is reached).

When discussing models, one must also consider sources of information. Generally, firms, analysts, and investors first consider the earnings of a company and, from these, obtain forecasts of *FCF*s. It is unclear if and when someone would directly forecast *FCF*s and then use them to determine implied earnings. Additionally, when users are intent on using the DCF model, where *FCF* forecasts may, indeed, all be negative during the horizon (e.g., in a growing firm), they, essentially, will have to know the value at the horizon multiple years in the future to value the stock today.

CHOICE OF STEADY STATE GROWTH

LO3: Choose a steady state growth rate that is appropriate for valuing a firm's operations.

The steady state growth rate is one of the most important choices in forecasting and implementing a value calculation. To make an intelligent choice, one must understand what it represents and its tie to the overall economy. Green, Hand, and Zhang (2016 *RAST*) found that 24 of 37 analyst reports, which explicitly stated their continuing (steady state) growth assumption, had a rate greater than 10 percent. Because this rate is unlikely to exceed the long-term growth in the economy, these forecasted rates are unachievable, yielding a value estimate that will be overly optimistic.

In Chapter 10, we introduced an assumption related to the continuing value by stating, "The assumption that the rate of growth in *FCF* and the rate of growth in sales beyond the horizon are equal reflects that, over time, a firm's growth is driven by its ability to grow sales." The same point can be made with respect to growth in *ROPI* and growth in *AOIG*.

In this section, we underscore the point that, if implementation of the models is not done correctly and if steady state is not reached, the estimate of operating value will differ.[1] The common instructions to take the last explicit forecast, grow it, and then capitalize it are only appropriate if steady state has been reached. Essentially, when forecasting, we must forecast to a horizon that is sufficiently far in the future to ensure that we are comfortable with the assumption that the forecasted growth rate is sustainable in the very long run. A frequently made assumption is that, eventually, the steady state growth rate will be equal to an assumed long-term economic growth rate.

LEGAL GUIDANCE ON APPROPRIATE TERMINAL GROWTH RATES

The precedent decision by Chancellor Bouchard in *Owen v. Cannon* in the Court of Chancery of the state of Delaware provides authoritative support and guidance on reasonable terminal growth rate assumptions. Given this court's role as the foremost U.S. valuation court, its linking of the rate to expected inflation is notable. Quoted excerpts from the decision memorandum show the following:

> In a typical DCF valuation, the terminal growth rate 'attempt[s] to capture the future growth prospects of the firm while recognizing that over time firms cannot continue to grow at a rate that is materially in excess of the real growth of the economy.' (p. 60)
>
> Although calculating the appropriate terminal growth rate is one of several challenging estimations for a law-trained judge tasked with determining a corporation's fair value, two well-reasoned principles guide my analysis. In *Merion Capital, L.P. v. 3M Cogent, Inc.*, the Court observed that, in most cases, "a terminal growth rate should not be greater than the nominal growth rate for the United States economy, because '[i]f a company is assumed to grow at a higher rate indefinitely, its cash flow would eventually exceed America's [gross national product].'" (p. 61)
>
> Conversely, as the Court noted in *Global GT LP v. Golden Telecom, Inc.*, "the rate of inflation is the floor for a terminal value estimate for a solidly profitable company that does not have an identifiable risk of insolvency." Because the 2013 Projections contemplate that ESG would remain profitable even after taking into account increasing competitive pressures as of the Merger, I find that it is appropriate under *Golden Telecom* to calculate the terminal growth rate as a premium to inflation. In my judgment, Jacobs's 3% rate strikes the appropriate balance. Indeed, a 3% rate is very close to the 2.5% rate utilized in the Grant Thornton Valuation contemporaneous with the Merger. (p. 62)

Additionally, in directly addressing the transition from growth rates within the horizon to the terminal rate, the memorandum stated,

> Courts have acknowledged that a non-trivial spread in the growth rate for the discrete forecast period and the terminal growth rate is common. Thus, the 3% difference between the revenue growth rate in the final year of the 2013 Projections (6.0% for 2017) and the terminal growth rate I adopt (3%) should not be controversial. There also is considerable precedent in Delaware for adopting a terminal growth rate that is a premium, such as 100 basis points, over inflation. (p. 62)

Thus, it is necessary to recognize that the terminal growth rate choice must consider the anticipated long-term economic growth.

During the beginning of this century, Starbucks (SBUX) was growing revenues at a very high rate. From the time Starbucks went public in 1992, the firm's sales growth was greater than 20 percent until 2008! However, if we were looking at the company in the late 1990s or early 2000s, the assumption that the short-term growth in revenues (often exceeding 30 percent per year) would continue indefinitely would have been inappropriate. To value SBUX, like any firm, requires a sufficiently long forecast horizon to arrive at steady state. That is, forecasts for SBUX would need to extend far enough into the future that things have leveled off and the company is growing in line with economic growth.

In our forecasting for GIS outlined in Chapter 7, arriving at a forecast mirroring economic growth after 5 years did not appear to be too strong of an assumption, but to do so for a growing company like SBUX would have been inappropriate.

[1] This reminds us of the reason why additional information was included in Chapter 4 and adjustments were made in Chapter 5. We wanted to ensure that we did not mistakenly think we had reached steady state when we had not, and we wanted to ensure that the forecasted values going forward were not incorrect due to misunderstanding current information.

Consider SBUX during its period of growth prior to the 2008 economic downturn. Assume we are in 2002 and making explicit full-information forecasts for 2003 to 2007. By looking at its actual results for the years ending in September 2003 to 2007, we can see that perfect-foresight forecasts would be the estimates of sales growth, *PM*, and *ATO* shown in **Exhibit 14.4**:

EXHIBIT 14.4 Starbucks Estimates of Sales Growth, *PM*, and *ATO*

Year Ended September	2003	2004	2005	2006	2007
Sales growth	23.9%	29.9%	20.3%	22.3%	20.9%
Operating *PM*	7.3%	8.3%	8.8%	8.6%	8.3%
Operating *ATO*	2.54	2.66	2.99	3.23	3.16

This information might lead us to suggest stable forecasted rates of 22 percent for sales growth, 8.5 percent for *PM*, and 3.1 for *ATO* as our ongoing parsimonious assumptions. However, these assumptions are not a steady state because there is no way a sales growth rate of 22 percent can be maintained indefinitely (otherwise, our oceans would eventually be filled with coffee!). Instead, we would need to extend the horizon to a point where steady state is reached.

The extension of the horizon is normally implemented by assuming a fade pattern after the explicit forecasting horizon. For SBUX, we might reasonably assume that *PM* and *ATO* are sustainable, and we focus our efforts on determining the sales growth. We must determine how many years we believe are necessary before we reach a steady state growth in sales mirroring economic growth and also the pattern necessary to reach it. If we thought 3 percent was an appropriate long-term growth rate in sales, we could make the 19 percent adjustment from 22 percent to 3 percent over a particular chosen period. Options would include, for example, a 1.9 percent fade per year for 10 years or even a 1 percent fade per year for 19 years. The point is that we must reach a sustainable growth rate to have reached steady state.

Although for the SBUX data in **Exhibit 14.4** we may think *PM* and *ATO* are sustainable, these also may need an adjustment period prior to reaching steady state. If they were believed to need adjustment, perhaps due to anticipated erosion of competitive advantages, we first choose a target value, then the pattern of adjustment over time. Often, a median value for the industry is used as a target based on the assumption that deviations will be driven away by competition and changes made by the firm.

Assume the 1.9 percent fade in the sales growth rate for the following 10 years and constant values for *PM* and *ATO* would yield the forecasts for SBUX shown in **Exhibit 14.5**.

EXHIBIT 14.5 Starbucks Forecasts

	Sales Growth	*PM*	*ATO*
2008	22.0%	8.5%	3.1
2009	20.1%	8.5%	3.1
2010	18.2%	8.5%	3.1
2011	16.3%	8.5%	3.1
2012	14.4%	8.5%	3.1
2013	12.5%	8.5%	3.1
2014	10.6%	8.5%	3.1
2015	8.7%	8.5%	3.1
2016	6.8%	8.5%	3.1
2017	4.9%	8.5%	3.1
2018	3.0%	8.5%	3.1
Thereafter	3.0%	8.5%	3.1

With the forecasts extended to a point at which steady state is reached, a calculation of operating value for SBUX would now be possible.

In short, the forecast horizon must be long enough that assuming sales growth equivalent to the economic growth, constant *PM*, and constant *ATO* are reasonable. This will ensure that steady state has been reached and the horizon growth rate is appropriate for valuation.

TYING MARKET MULTIPLES TO VALUATION MODELS

LO4: Relate market multiples to valuation models and understand requirements for them to be useful in valuation.

Before completing our discussion on choosing a valuation model, we return to the use of multiples as presented in Chapter 8. Multiples used in valuation can be split into two groups: those that are restricted forms of the models in Chapters 10 to 12 and those that are ad hoc. For multiples that are restricted forms of theoretically sound valuation models, we can evaluate the restrictions to determine our comfort with the necessary assumptions. For those that do not tie to valuation models, we must consider why a payoff based valuation model would not be used. In practice, the earnings-based approaches are probably the most commonly observed. When relying on earnings, many would argue for using forecasted information because value is related to future payoffs, and use of forecasts may avoid issues of temporary changes in reported earnings due to one-time events.

THE EFFECT OF REVENUE FORECASTS ON CHOOSING STEADY-STATE GROWTH

With SBUX, we saw that the sales growth rate will need to reach an economic growth rate before the company reaches steady state. Sometimes, the struggle in forecasting results from current operations needing to stabilize. **Deere & Company** (DE) has reported the following revenues over a recent 5-year period:

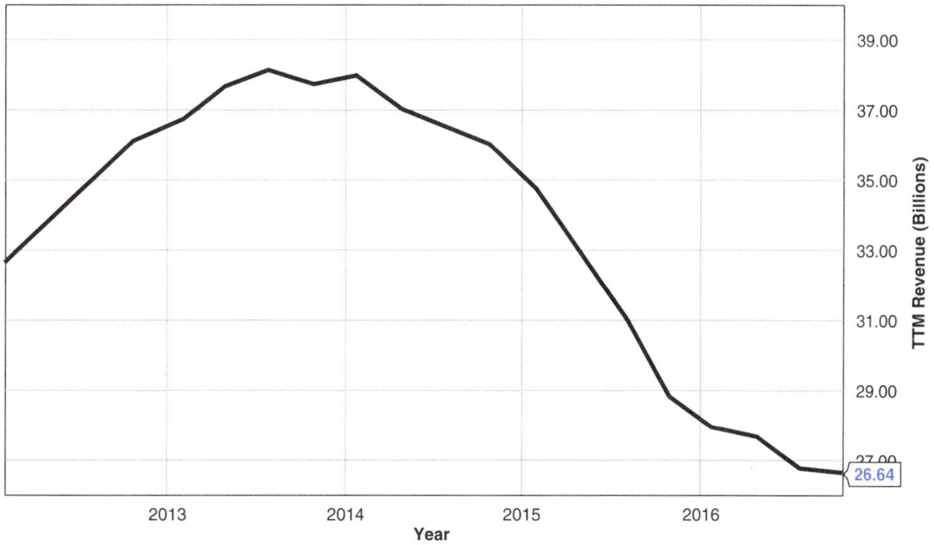

In trying to determine the steady-state growth rate, we would need to determine whether the downturn in revenues will reverse, stabilize, or continue. The choice of forecast horizon length is directly tied to this issue because we must go far enough into the future to achieve a sustainable and steady growth forecast. As would be expected, choices made in forecasting revenues will be the predominant driver of our valuation of DE. Thus, to estimate value, one would need to take steps to ensure that all relevant information about future revenues is gathered and processed in an unbiased manner. The valuation result depends on it!

The forward PE ratio, where price is compared to next period forecasted earnings, can be considered a special case of AOIGM. Starting with Equation 12.3, if we assume the sum of all future *AOIG* equals zero, we arrive at the following:

$$V_0 = \frac{1}{r_{WACC}} \times \left[NOPAT_1\right]$$

A simple rearrangement isolates the forward price-to-earnings (PE) ratio on the left side:

$$\frac{V_0}{NOPAT_1} = \frac{1}{r_{WACC}}$$

This is very insightful because it shows that a sort on forward PE captures the inverse of risk.

Another ratio often used is the PEG ratio. Proponents argue that this ratio implicitly takes into account growth in earnings beyond the next year. Again, starting with Equation 12.3, assumptions that long-term growth and FCF_1 are both equal to zero will yield the following:

$$V_0 = \frac{1}{r_{WACC}} \times \left[NOPAT_1 + \left(\frac{NOPAT_2 - (1 + r_{WACC}) \times NOPAT_1}{r_{WACC}}\right)\right]$$

$$= \frac{1}{r_{WACC}} \times \left(NOPAT_1 + \frac{NOPAT_2}{r_{WACC}} - \frac{NOPAT_1}{r_{WACC}} - NOPAT_1\right)$$

$$= \frac{1}{r_{WACC}} \times \left(\frac{NOPAT_2 - NOPAT_1}{r_{WACC}}\right)$$

$$= \frac{NOPAT_2 - NOPAT_1}{r_{WACC}^2}$$

A simple rearrangement isolates the PEG ratio:

$$\frac{V_0}{NOPAT_2 - NOPAT_1} = \frac{V_0 / NOPAT_1}{NOPAT_2 - NOPAT_1 / NOPAT_1} = \frac{ForwardPE}{EarningsGrowth} = \frac{1}{r_{WACC}^2}$$

That is, when we form the PEG ratio, the forward PE divided by short-term earnings growth, we again capture the inverse of risk!

Grounding our valuation on sound theoretical models permits an analysis of the implicit assumptions in the use of the multiples model. Adding seemingly ad hoc assumptions to the uncertainty already contained in forecasting future operating activities and estimations of cost of capital likely would hurt, rather than help, our accuracy.

SUMMARY

In this chapter, we examined the assumptions behind steady state and its implications for valuation. For Chapters 10 to 12, the estimate of GIS' value was the same because we forecast to a steady state and calculated continuing values after constant growth was achieved. When choosing a valuation model in practice, factors such as the portion of value captured within the forecasting horizon may be considered. This will almost always lead to using an accounting-based model. Still, the most important issue is choosing a forecasting horizon such that steady state is reached.

In this textbook, we have presented and guided you through a five-step process:

1. Know the company's environment—understanding the business environment.
2. Isolate the company's enterprise operations—reformulation of the financial statements.
3. Determine the current status of the company—financial statement analysis.
4. Formalize expectations of where the company is going—forecasting future payoffs.
5. Calculate the company's worth—valuation.

We applied each step to GIS, a large, publicly traded company. The steps above have been explicitly linked based on our desire to focus on valuation of the company's operating activities (i.e., valuation of enterprise operations) while providing full coverage of both cash flow- and accounting-based methods of valuation.

With the tools learned, you are equipped to value public companies, private companies, divisions, projects, or any other items. The structure and issues surrounding estimation of expected future payoffs and the related risks captured within valuation models are universal across valuation exercises.

QUESTIONS

Q14.1 What are the requirements for steady state?

Q14.2 In which period does each valuation model have constant growth when the steady state is reached?

Q14.3 If sales begin to grow at a constant rate in 2024, *PM* becomes constant in 2024, and *ATO* becomes constant in 2024, what is the first year's payoff that can be used to calculate the continuing value in each of our three valuation models?

Q14.4 Which is more critical to successful estimation of value, choice of model or having achieved steady state?

Q14.5 When choosing a steady state growth rate to calculate continuing values, what constrains the choice of reasonable values? What is the implication for forecasts and calculations of value?

Q14.6 In the DCF model, typically, the final *FCF* in the forecast horizon is used to determine the continuing value. What alternative metric can be used for the continuing value in this model?

Q14.7 In evaluating valuation models, what attribute is preferred?

Q14.8 What are the accountant's measure of value and value earned in a period?

Q14.9 For a company with a high sales growth rate, what technique is used to extend the forecast horizon to the steady state?

Q14.10 What are the five steps to valuing a company?

EXERCISES

E14.11 The following are the sales, in millions, reported by Tesla Inc. (TSLA) for each of the past 7 years. Given the sales growth realizations, what might be a reasonable parsimonious steady state growth assumption? Is a fade or adjustment period needed between now and the achievement of that growth assumption and, if yes, what path might you consider?

	2012	2013	2014	2015	2016	2017	2018
Sales. . .	$413.2	$2,103.5	$3,198.4	$4,046.0	$7,000.1	$11,758,7	$21,461.3

E14.12 Evaluate the forecasts of Benson's sales growth, operating *PM*, and operating *ATO* as to whether the steady state is achieved and, if so, in which year.

a.

	Year 1	Year 2	Year 3	Year 4	Year 5	Year 6	Year 7
Sales growth.	15.0%	12.0%	10.0%	5.0%	3.0%	3.0%	3.0%
Operating *PM*.	20.0%	21.0%	17.0%	14.0%	11.0%	11.0%	11.0%
Operating *ATO*.	0.85	0.91	0.88	0.85	0.80	0.80	0.80

b.

	Year 1	Year 2	Year 3	Year 4	Year 5	Year 6	Year 7
Sales growth.	15.0%	12.0%	10.0%	5.0%	3.0%	3.0%	3.0%
Operating *PM*.	20.0%	21.0%	18.0%	16.0%	15.0%	12.0%	12.0%
Operating *ATO*.	0.85	0.91	0.88	0.85	0.80	0.80	0.80

c.

	Year 1	Year 2	Year 3	Year 4	Year 5	Year 6	Year 7
Sales growth.	15.0%	12.0%	10.0%	9.0%	7.0%	6.0%	6.0%
Operating *PM*.	20.0%	21.0%	17.0%	14.0%	11.0%	11.0%	11.0%
Operating *ATO*.	0.85	0.91	0.88	0.85	0.80	0.80	0.80

E14.13 The following forecasts were developed for Burns LLC based on a NOA_0 of $215,000 and sales of $500,000.

$NOPAT_1$ = $58,850
Sum of present value of forecasted *FCF* = $208,027
Sum of present value of forecasted *ROPI* = $155,410
Sum of present value of forecasted *AOIG* to period 1 = $6,608
Present value of *FCF* continuing value = $541,276
Present value of *ROPI* continuing value = 378,893
Present value of *AOIG* continuing value to period 1 = $9,472

a. Determine the estimated value for Burns using the *FCF* model, ROIM, and AOIGM, assuming a 10.0 percent operating cost of capital.

b. Prepare a breakdown of each valuation model by estimated value in dollars and percentage by (1) no forecast necessary, (2) based on forecasts within the horizon, and (3) based on estimated value.

E14.14 The forward PE ratio for Edwards Inc. and Bell Corp. is 20 and 10, respectively. Assuming all future *AOIG* is zero, which company has the lower risk (i.e., the lower r_{WACC})?

CONTINUING EXAMPLES

CE14.15 Compare the breakdown of the value estimates for Kellogg (K) based on the horizon by completing the following chart. What do you learn from this exercise?

Breakdown of Kellogg's Value Estimate Based on Horizon

	Discounted Cash Flow Model		Residual Operating Income Model		Abnormal Operating Income Growth Model	
	Amount	Percent	Amount	Percent	Amount	Percent
No forecast necessary						
Based on forecasts within horizon						
Based on continuing value	_____	_____	_____	_____	_____	_____
Total estimated value	=====	=====	=====	=====	=====	=====

CE14.16 Compare the breakdown of the value estimates for Thor Industries (THO) based on the horizon by completing the following chart. What do you learn from this exercise?

Breakdown of THO Value Estimate Based on Horizon

	Discounted Cash Flow Model		Residual Operating Income Model		Abnormal Operating Income Growth Model	
	Amount	Percent	Amount	Percent	Amount	Percent
No forecast necessary						
Based on forecasts within horizon						
Based on continuing value	_____	_____	_____	_____	_____	_____
Total estimated value	=====	=====	=====	=====	=====	=====

CE14.17 Compare the breakdown of the value estimates for Winnebago (WGO) based on the horizon by completing the following chart. What do you learn from this exercise?

Breakdown of WGO Value Estimate Based on Horizon						
	Discounted Cash Flow Model		Residual Operating Income Model		Abnormal Operating Income Growth Model	
	Amount	Percent	Amount	Percent	Amount	Percent
No forecast necessary						
Based on forecasts within horizon						
Based on continuing value						
Total estimated value						

INDEX

The letters "e" and "n" following page number(s) refer to exhibit and footnote respectively.

The letters "e" and "n" following page number(s) refer to exhibit and footnote respectively.

The letters "e" and "n" following page number(s) refer to exhibit and footnote respectively.

Quick Reference Guide

CHAPTER 1

1.7	Five-step process: 1. Understand the Business Environment 2. Reformulate the Financial Statements 3. Financial Statement Analysis 4. Forecast Future Payoffs 5. Valuation
1.10	Porter's Value-Chain Model 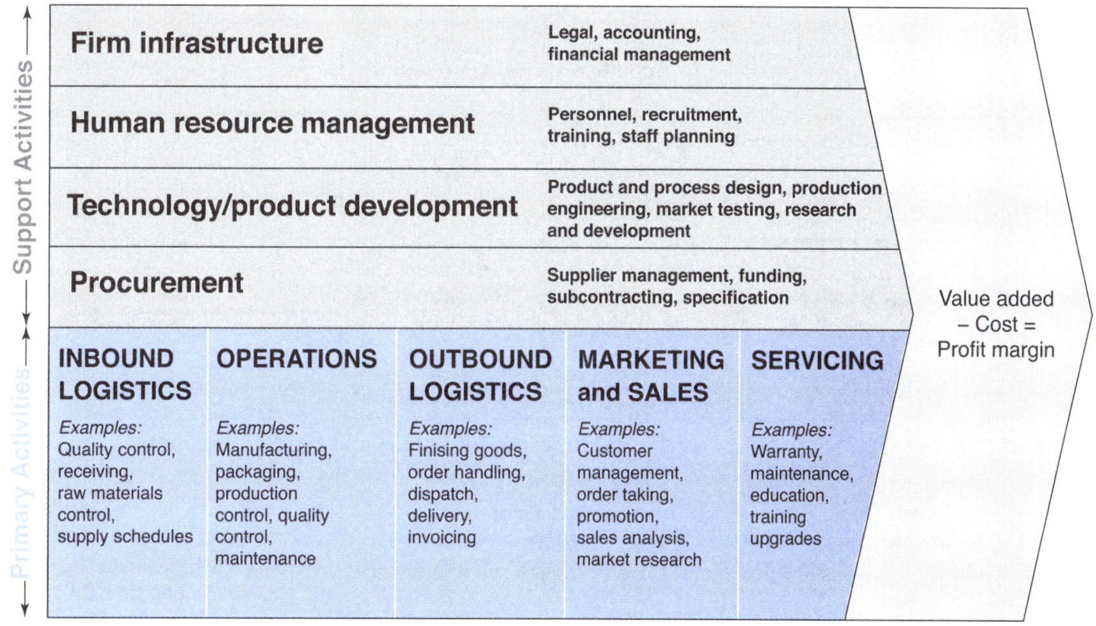
1.11	Strengths, Weaknesses, Opportunities, and Threats Framework 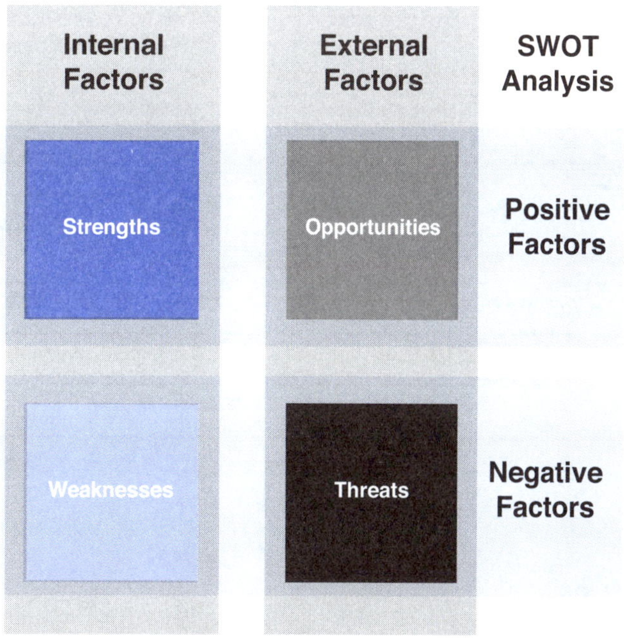

1.12 Dickinson's (2011) Life Cycle Stages

Cash Flow Type	Introduction	Growth	Mature	Shake-Out	Decline
Operating	Negative	Positive	Positive	Either	Negative
Investing	Negative	Negative	Negative	Either	Positive
Financing	Positive	Positive	Negative	Either	Either

CHAPTER 2

2.5 Relation between Operating and Financial Activities

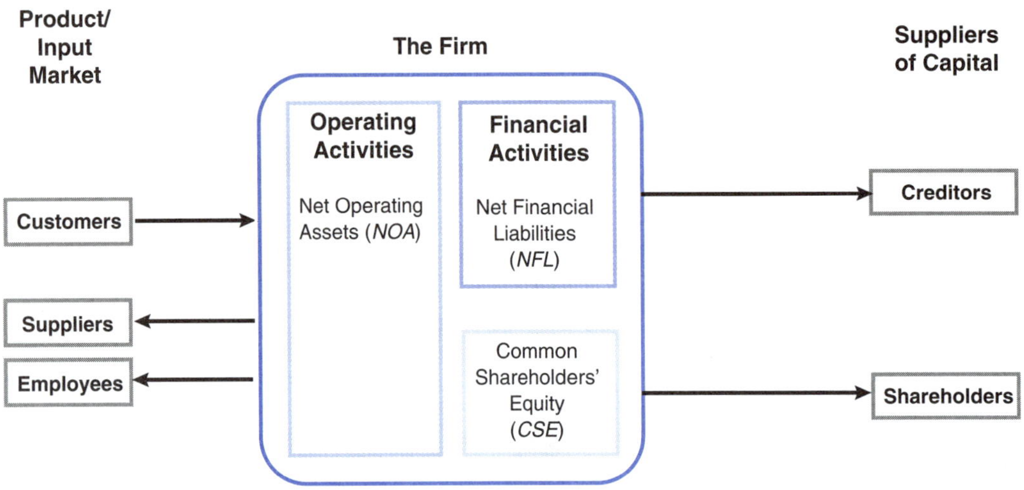

2.6 Interactions of Operating and Financial Activities with Markets and Capital Suppliers

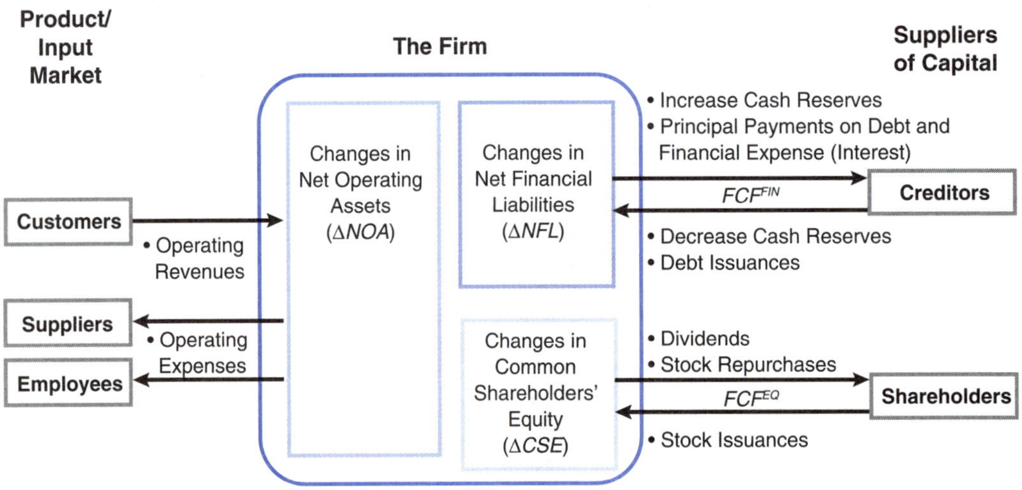

2.6	$FCF = FCF^{FIN} + FCF^{EQ}$ (2.1)	**2.9**	$FCF_t \equiv NOPAT_t - \Delta NOA_t$ (2.2)
2.9	$RE_{t-1} + NI_t - div_t = RE_t$	**2.9**	$NOA_{t-1} + NOPAT_t - FCF_t = NOA_t$
2.9	$NFL_{t-1} + FEAT_t - FCF_t^{FIN} = NFL_t$	**2.10**	$CSE_{t-1} + CI_t - FCF_t^{EQ} = CSE_t$

2.14 Relation between Financial Statements

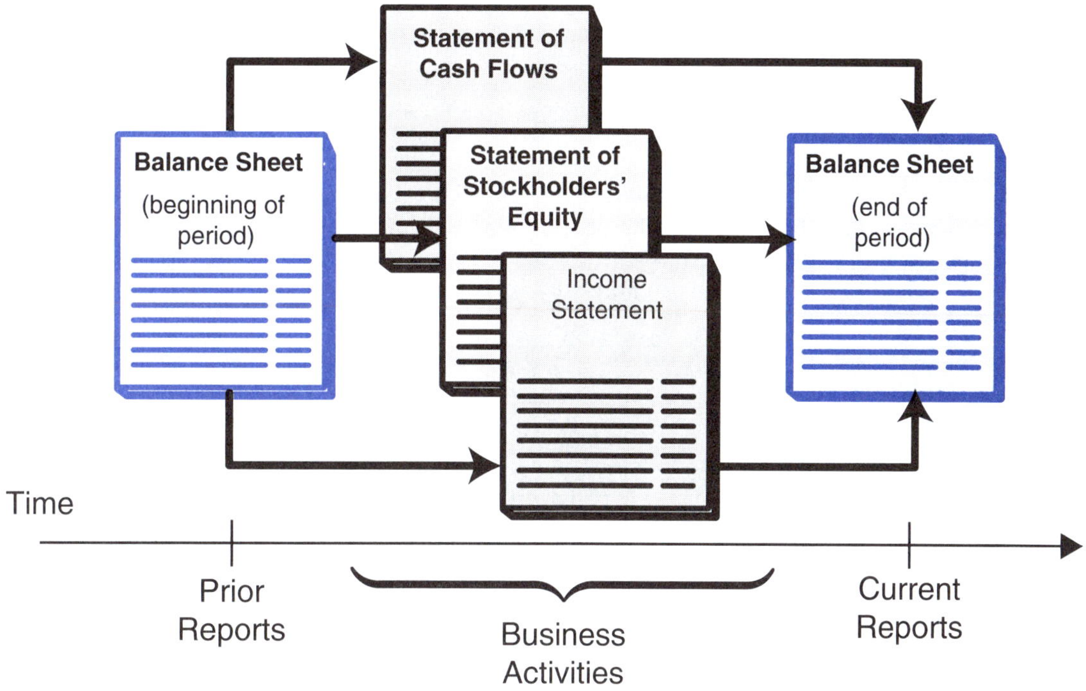

CHAPTER 3

3.1	The operating activities are the business/production activities undertaken by the company (i.e., what the company does). The financial activities are the borrowing/lending activities undertaken by the company (i.e., where the company gets the money).
3.4	The components of *NOA* reported on the balance sheet generate the components of *NOPAT* reported on the income statement.
3.10	Since our goal is to value the common equity of the company, we treat preferred equity and noncontrolling interests as additional financial liabilities, based on the logic that, from the common shareholder's viewpoint, they represent claims on the firm's net assets by another party.
3.15	We would like to know the marginal tax rate on financial activities to allow us to determine the extent to which taxes are reduced due to the deduction of the net interest expense for tax purposes (this amount is called the interest tax shield). We assume, for the sake of simplicity for this calculation the federal statutory rate.
3.19	Summary of reformulation 1. Begin reformulation with a focus on the balance sheet. The goal is to determine what *NOA*s are available/required in operating activities. 2. Classification of an item as financial will exclude it from the calculation of cost of operating capital and the valuation of enterprise operations. It also assumes that either the amount shown is at fair value or that the fair value is readily available/determinable through other sources. 3. When moving to the elements of comprehensive income, think about what assets/liabilities would be related to these elements. Whenever possible, the classification of an item of revenue/expense as either operating or financial in nature should mirror the classification of the related assets/liabilities.

CHAPTER 4

4.1	Our goals when gathering additional information are (1) to focus more clearly on identification of operating activities and financial activities and (2) to use the data to facilitate improved forecasting.
4.6	Whenever adding information from sources beyond the balance sheet and income statement, you must ensure total balances are unchanged.
4.9	Our ideal outcome in separating operating and financial profitability for valuation is to estimate the amount of tax that would have been paid had the firm not had any financial expense; that is, the tax rate for the interest tax shield. Stated a different way, we want to know what the tax would have been on the operating activities if the firm had been funded entirely by equity and, therefore, would have had no financial income or expense.

CHAPTER 5

<table>
<tr><td>5.3</td><td>If past accounting data are used as the basis for forecasting, income shifting or differing accounting method choices may lead to less comparability or create an appearance of comparability where it does not actually exist. Appropriate assumptions for forecasted sales growth, profit margins, and asset turnovers may depend, to some extent, on observed values of past sales growth, NOPAT, NOA, and their components for the company as well as for comparable companies.</td></tr>
<tr><td>5.3</td><td>An adjustment should be considered even if all companies being compared use LIFO. Valuation of the inventory of both companies using FIFO is necessary to ensure comparability.</td></tr>
<tr><td>5.6</td><td>Classifying leases as operating rather than capital has differing financial reporting consequences for the lessee under the old and new financial reporting standards.</td></tr>
<tr><td>5.7</td><td>Despite the financial reporting differences, choosing to account for a lease as capital or operating does not change the fact that the company has acquired the use of an asset and has agreed to make payments as a result. For this reason, analysts and users of financial information often adjust the accounting in a process called constructive capitalization, which attempts to reconstruct the financial ratios to what they would have been had the operating leases been capital leases. This process not only allows us to see the full amount of resources (the operating asset) and the related obligation (the financial liability), it also recognizes that a portion of the payment is financial in nature (effectively interest expense).</td></tr>
<tr><td>5.8</td><td>Lease constructive capitalization process:
<table>
<tr><th></th><th>Old Standard</th><th>New Standard</th></tr>
<tr><td>1.</td><td>Determine the discount rate.</td><td>Same.</td></tr>
<tr><td>2.</td><td>Compute the present value of future lease payments this year and last.</td><td>Not required.</td></tr>
<tr><td>3.</td><td>Adjust the balance sheet to include the present value from step 2 as a lease liability, and include the related asset.</td><td>Not required because the right-of-use asset and related liability are already recognized.</td></tr>
<tr><td>4.</td><td>Adjust the income statement to include depreciation and interest in lieu of the rent (lease) expense.</td><td>Same.</td></tr>
</table></td></tr>
<tr><td>5.17</td><td>Implications of Special-Purpose Entities for analyses:
<ul>
<li>Cost of debt capital: SPEs reduce business risk and bankruptcy risk for their lenders. Consequently, the sponsoring company is able to obtain capital at a lower cost.</li>
<li>Liquidity: SPEs provide financial reporting benefits by having assets and their related debt moved off the balance sheet. Thus, the sponsoring company enjoys an improved asset-turnover ratio (i.e., assets are typically less in the denominator of the turnover ratio) and an improved financial leverage ratio (i.e., liabilities are less in the numerator of the debt-to-equity ratio).</li>
</ul></td></tr>
</table>

5.18	Accounting fails to recognize the liability existing due to outstanding prior commitments to employees arising from share-based compensation (SBC). The implied transfer to employees as share price increases over time is also omitted from the financial statements.
5.19	Three types of SBC that are most easily distinguished based on the related disclosures. • The first category is stock options, and they are distinguished by the disclosures that include information on both outstanding and exercisable options. • The second and third categories are comprised of restricted stock, restricted stock units, and share units (often, either performance or time based), which may be classified as either equity or a liability. These two categories have a different set of disclosures. The classification as either equity-classified or liability-classified share-unit items depends on the settlement mechanism or restrictions placed on the award.
5.23	Summary of adjustments for SBC:

	Stock Options	Equity-Classified Share Units	Liability-Classified Share Units
Add beginning liability with offset to deferred tax and equity	Yes	Yes	No
Change in liability (and deferred tax) shown as expense and tax effect	Yes	Yes	No
Infer compensation from excess tax benefit disclosure if possible (done net of tax pre-change or gross post-change in accounting standards)	Yes	Yes	Yes

CHAPTER 6

6.2 Rate of return on operations for historical information:

$$RNOA = \frac{NOPAT}{average(NOA)}$$

6.3 Rate of return on operations when forecasting information:

$$RNOA = \frac{NOPAT}{beginningNOA}$$

6.4 DuPont analysis (disaggregating *RNOA*):

$$RNOA = \frac{NOPAT}{average(NOA)} = \frac{NOPAT}{Sales} \times \frac{Sales}{average(NOA)} = PM \times ATO$$

6.8 Rate of return on financial liabilities:

$$RNFL = \frac{FEAT}{average(NFL)}$$

6.10 When examining operating *ATO*s, begin with the inverse of the *ATO* ratio; that is, show each item as a percentage of the sales for the year.

6.15 Rate of return on equity:

$$ROE = \frac{CI}{average(CSE)}$$

6.16

$$ROE = RNOA \times LEV \times (RNOA - RNFL) \qquad (6.1)$$

CHAPTER 7

7.3	Forecasting is a three-step sequence: 1. Forecast revenues via forecasts of sales growth rates. 2. Forecast *NOPAT* from forecasted sales via forecasts of operating *PM* and components of *PM*. 3. Forecast *NOA* required to generate the forecasted sales via forecasts of operating *ATO* and components of *ATO*.
7.3	Forecasting the firm's nonoperating, financial, activities is not necessary. This is because we are valuing the operations and then adjusting for the current value of the net financial liabilities to determine the value of equity.
7.7	When we form forecasts, we estimate *NOA* using sales of the following period. This is based on the argument that the *NOA* must be in place to generate the sales. Thus, we define forecasted *ATO* as *Sales/Beginning NOA*. Remember that, when analyzing reported (historical) information, we did not know when investments occurred during the year and, therefore, we utilized an average *NOA* in the calculation of historical *RNOA*.
7.8	We are ultimately forming forecasts of operating income statements and balance sheets, which capture the operating activities for the foreseeable future.
7.9	In moving from parsimonious (simple) forecasts to full-information forecasts, we consider all available information. This allows us to forecast at a much more detailed level. For example, we separately forecast the individual components of *PM* and then sum them to arrive at a composite forecast of *PM*. In doing so, we recognize that the individual components will evolve over time in separate, though sometimes similar, ways. Full-information forecasting will ensure that our forecasting assumptions are consistent with our beliefs and predictions for future growth and key financial relations.
7.9	The revenues (sales) forecast is the most crucial and difficult estimate in the forecasting process. The full-information forecasts of sales are built from anticipated unit sales and prices.
7.14	Forecasting approaches for components of *PM* and *ATO* include: 1. Steady ratio: Forecast based on the relation in the most recent years. 2. Steady amount: Forecast a specific dollar amount. 3. Follow a trend: Forecast continuation of a trend of increases or decreases in the relation to sales. 4. Use other information: Choose a relation to sales that departs from the historical numbers based on some information and/or expectations. 5. Zero: Forecast zero as the future amount for a particular item.
7.17	Taxes should be framed as a percent of profits. Thus, it is important to ensure that we are comfortable with the implied forecasted effective tax rate.
7.20	At the end of the forecasting process, we must assess whether the numbers we predict are reasonable. Do they make economic sense? Do they fit with the underlying relations that drive financial forecasts?
7.23	Approach the information provided by management with a level of professional skepticism. It must be noted that both cash flow and accounting information can be manipulated, so assuming "cash is king" is not the solution.

CHAPTER 8

8.3	Steps in estimating value using the market multiple method: 1. Select the fundamental indicator to use as the basis for valuation. Common fundamental indicators are *NOPAT*, *NOA*, earnings, book value, and sales revenue; the method of comparables may be based on current or forecasted fundamental indicators. 2. Select the comparable company or companies.

	3. Compute the market multiple from the comparable company's or companies' market values and fundamental indicator. Two steps: (a) Compute the ratio of the market value to the fundamental indicator for each comparable, and (b) if a number of companies are used as comparables, combine the individual comparable company multiples into a market multiple. 4. Compute the value of the target company using its fundamental indicator and the market multiple. 5. If the fundamental indicator is an operating indicator, subtract the value owed to the debt holders, and then divide by shares outstanding to obtain equity value per share. If the fundamental indicator is an equity indicator, divide by shares outstanding to get equity value per share.
8.4	Key decisions: • Which fundamental indicator is the right one? • What company or companies should we use as comparables? • How do we combine the comparable company data to produce a multiple?
8.9	The trailing PE ratio utilizes the most recent reported earnings, computed using trailing twelve months (TTM), as the fundamental indicator to be used in estimating company value. The forward PE ratio utilizes the estimated earnings for the upcoming year.
8.10	PEG ratio attempts to capture effects of earnings growth because the next year's earnings taken alone may not accurately account for the anticipated growth for the company. $$PEG_t = \frac{P_t}{(eps_{t+2} - eps_{t+1}) \times 100}$$
8.14	Some industries have specific fundamental indicators related to characteristics of the industry that investors and analysts watch closely.
8.17	Be careful to ensure that we do not choose estimates simply because they support a desired conclusion!
8.19	If we use market multiples for company valuation, there are at least three steps we should take in implementing this method: 1. Whenever possible, use a forward-looking fundamental indicator to compute the market multiples for comparable companies. 2. Select comparable companies with care so as to match them on profitability, growth, and risk profiles with our target company. 3. Use both income statement- and balance sheet-based valuation multiples, and consider industry-based multiples whenever possible.

CHAPTER 9

9.1	$$r_{WACC} = \left(r_{Eq} \times \frac{V^{Eq}}{V^{Oper}}\right) + \left(r_D \times \frac{V^{NFL}}{V^{Oper}}\right) \quad (9.1)$$
9.2	Investors expect to recover both the time value of money, the foregone interest from investing in an instrument with future payoffs, and the compensation for taking the risk of investing in the operating activities due to the uncertainty of the future payoffs.
9.2	Assumptions when estimating cost of capital: 1) current interest rates are a good approximation for expected (future) interest rates and 2) current risk of the operating activities is a good approximation of the expected operating risk.

9.3

EXHIBIT 9.1 Relations among Risk Elements

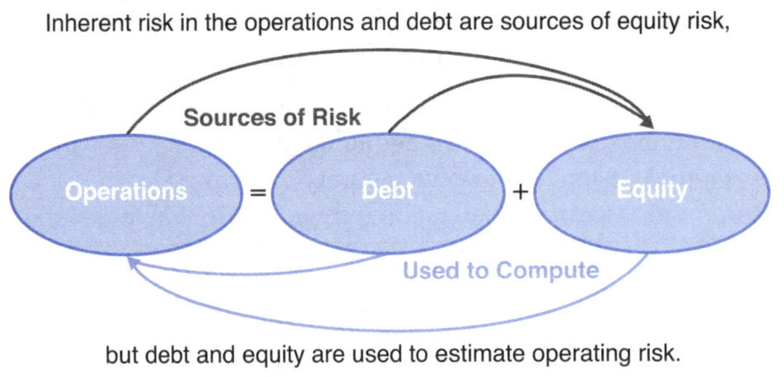

9.3

$$r_{Eq} = r_{WACC} + \frac{V^{NFL}}{V^{Eq}} \times (r_{WACC} - r_D)$$

9.4 Capital Asset Pricing Model:

$$r_{Eq} = r_{rf} + [\beta \times (r_{Mkt} - r_{rf})] \qquad (9.2)$$

Market beta reflects the risk that cannot be completely diversified away by investing in a portfolio of risky assets (systematic risk).

9.6 Differences arise in beta estimates due to choices involving the time period for estimation, the frequency of measurement of historical returns (e.g., monthly, weekly, daily) used in the estimation, and the market index, which is used in the estimation. Also, some suggest adjustments to reflect perceptions of the differences between the past and future expectations. Understanding the beta estimate, its source, and the assumptions upon which it is based is, obviously, critical.

9.9 Cost of Debt Capital proxies:

- $r_D \approx \dfrac{RNFL}{1-TaxRate} = \dfrac{\dfrac{FEAT}{(1-TaxRate)}}{avg(NFL)}$
- $r_D \approx$ Pretax borrowing rate for debt
  = Interest expense/avg (Amount of interest-bearing debt)
- Weighted average interest rate on long-term debt based on footnote information

9.11

$$V^{ITS} = \frac{ITS}{r_D} = \frac{InterestExpense \times TaxRate}{r_D}$$

9.13 When estimating the costs of capital for debt, equity, and operations, it is imperative to always consider the appropriateness of both our assumptions and the estimates they generate. Attempt to determine the likely source of the issue and consider alternative assumptions or methodologies.

CHAPTER 10

10.2 Accounting will not tell you how much something is worth but rather provides information that may be very helpful in forming an estimate of value.

10.6

$$V_0 = \frac{FCF_1}{(1+r_{WACC})} + \frac{FCF_2}{(1+r_{WACC})^2} + \frac{FCF_3}{(1+r_{WACC})^3} + \frac{FCF_4}{(1+r_{WACC})^4} + \ldots$$

$$= \sum_{t=1}^{\infty} \left(\frac{FCF_t}{(1+r_{WACC})^t} \right) \qquad (10.6)$$

10.7 Forecasts of the stream of future *FCF* from operations may be forecasted directly or inferred from forecasts of the stream of future *NOPAT* and *NOA*. Direct forecasting of *FCF* is usually not done because it can be exceedingly challenging to determine the amount and timing of distributions that will be made to debt and equity holders in the future given that their timing is controlled by management and the cash needs of the continuing operations of the firm. Arriving at an expectation of future *NOPAT* and *NOA* can be more simply achieved by making assumptions regarding future sales growth, *PM*s, and *ATO* ratios.

10.9 The length of the forecast horizon will be determined by our ability and willingness to gather information for forecasting. We would like to explicitly forecast as far into the future as possible, but we have to recognize that the further into the future we forecast, the less confidence we have in our estimates.

10.9 In the DCF model, the continuing value equals the expected intrinsic value at the horizon.

10.10

$$V_0 = \frac{FCF_1}{(1+r_{WACC})} + \frac{FCF_2}{(1+r_{WACC})^2} + \frac{FCF_3}{(1+r_{WACC})^3} + \frac{FCF_4}{(1+r_{WACC})^4} + \ldots$$

$$= \sum_{t=1}^{\infty}\left(\frac{FCF_t}{(1+r_{WACC})^t}\right)$$

$$= \sum_{t=1}^{5}\left(\frac{FCF_t}{(1+r_{WACC})^t}\right) + \frac{1}{(1+r_{WACC})^5} \times \left(\frac{FCF_5 \times (1+g)}{r_{WACC} - g}\right) \quad (10.8)$$

In Equation 10.8, the term capturing the first five periods is referred to as being within the forecast horizon because the contribution of these *FCF*s to value will be calculated using explicit forecasts of *FCF*s for each year.

10.11 The computed value of the payoff is unaffected by whether nominal or real inputs are used in the calculation (remember that use of nominal payoffs requires use of nominal discount rates and use of real payoffs requires use of real discount rates). In practice, it is easier to use nominal inputs because analysts generally do not forecast real payoffs or take time to convert nominal rates to real rates.

10.12

EXHIBIT 10.7 GIS Valuation Using Discounted Cash Flow Model ($ Millions)

Required rate of return (r_{WACC}) 5.30%

Year Ending	5/27/2018	5/26/2019	5/31/2020	5/30/2021	5/29/2022	5/28/2023
Forecasted sales		$17,224.4	$17,746.9	$17,637.8	$17,867.1	$18,090.4
NOPAT (Sales × *PM*)		2,122.0	2,186.4	2,195.9	2,254.8	2,283.0
NOA (Sales/*ATO*)	$25,035.4	26,291.0	25,998.1	26,854.2	27,786.8	28,120.3
Δ*NOA*		1,255.6	(292.9)	856.1	932.7	333.4
FCF (*NOPAT* − Δ*NOA*)		866.5	2,479.3	1,339.8	1,322.2	1,949.6
Growth in *FCF*			186.15%	−45.96%	−1.32%	47.45%
Discount factor $(1 + r_{WACC})^t$		1.0530	1.1088	1.1676	1.2295	1.2946
Present value of *FCF* from operations		$ 822.8	$ 2,236.0	$ 1,147.5	$ 1,075.4	$ 1,505.9
Sum of present value of cash flows	6,787.7					
Continuing value						
FCF at horizon						1,973.0
Capitalized						48,121.0
Present value of continuing value	37,170.0					
Operating value	$43,957.7					

CHAPTER 11

11.3 Derivation of the ROIM begins with the DCF model to which we add and, at the same time, subtract the present value of each future year's *NOA*. The anchor in this model is current *NOA* (NOA_0) .

11.4

$$V_0 = NOA_0 + \sum_{t=1}^{\infty}\left(\frac{NOPAT_t - r_{WACC} \times NOA_{t-1}}{(1+r_{WACC})^t}\right)$$

$$= NOA_0 + \sum_{t=1}^{\infty}\left(\frac{ROPI_t}{(1+r_{WACC})^t}\right) \quad (11.2)$$

11.6 Accounting choices should not affect valuation because the underlying economic transaction has not changed and, so, economic value will be unchanged! An important feature of the accounting-based valuation models is that they continue to give the same answer with alternative accounting methods or if earnings are moved to earlier/later time periods (i.e., there is income shifting due to the choice of accounting method).

11.7 ROIM anchors the valuation on the current book value of net operating assets (NOA_0), which is affected by choice of accounting methods. Future *ROPI* is the adjustment to this valuation to counter the effect that accounting rules and procedures have on this valuation anchor.

11.10 In ROIM, the continuing value equals the expected difference between intrinsic value and book value of the operations at the horizon; the premium over book value.

11.11

$$V_0 = NOA_0 + \sum_{t=1}^{\infty}\left(\frac{NOPAT_t - r_{WACC} \times NOA_{t-1}}{(1+r_{WACC})^t}\right)$$

$$= NOA_0 + \sum_{t=1}^{5}\left(\frac{ROPI_t}{(1+r_{WACC})^t}\right) + \frac{1}{(1+r_{WACC})^5} \times \left(\frac{ROPI_5 \times (1+g)}{r_{WACC} - g}\right) \quad (11.4)$$

In Equation 11.4, the term capturing the first five periods is referred to as being within the forecast horizon because the contribution of these *ROPI*s to value will be calculated using explicit forecasts of *ROPI*s for each year.

11.12

EXHIBIT 11.8 Residual Operating Income Model

Required rate of return (r_{WACC}) 5.90%

Time Period	5/27/2018	5/26/2019	5/31/2020	5/30/2021	5/29/2022	5/28/2023
Forecasted sales	$15,740.4	$17,224.4	$17,746.9	$17,637.8	$17,867.1	$18,090.4
NOPAT (Sales × *PM*)		2,122.0	2,186.4	2,195.9	2,254.8	2,283.0
NOA (Sales/*ATO*)	25,035.4	26,291.0	25,998.1	26,854.2	27,786.8	28,120.3
ROPI ($NOPAT_t - r_{WACC} \times NOA_{t-1}$)		795.2	793.0	818.0	831.6	810.3
Growth in *ROPI*			−0.27%	3.15%	1.66%	−2.55%
Discount factor $(1 + r_{WACC})^t$		1.0530	1.1088	1.1676	1.2295	1.2946
Present value of $ROPI_t$		755.1	715.2	700.6	676.4	625.9
Sum of present value of $ROPI_t$	3,473.2					
Continuing value						
ROPI at horizon						820.0
Capitalized						20,000.7
Present value of continuing value	15,449.1					
Operating value	$43,957.7					

CHAPTER 12

12.3 Derivation of the AOIGM begins with the DCF model to which we add and, at the same time, subtract the present value of each future year's capitalized *NOPAT*. The anchor in this model is capitalized next period *NOPAT* $\left(NOPAT_1 / r_{WACC}\right)$.

12.4

$$V_0 = \frac{NOPAT_1}{r_{WACC}} + \sum_{t=1}^{\infty}\left(\frac{\frac{NOPAT_{t+1}}{r_{WACC}} + FCF_t - (1+r_{WACC}) \times \frac{NOPAT_t}{r_{WACC}}}{(1+r_{WACC})^t}\right)$$

$$= \frac{1}{r_{WACC}} \times \left[NOPAT_1 + \sum_{t=1}^{\infty}\left(\frac{NOPAT_{t+1} + r_{WACC} \times FCF_t - (1+r_{WACC}) \times NOPAT_t}{(1+r_{WACC})^t}\right)\right] \quad (12.2)$$

12.4 Cum-free-cash-flow earnings: $NOPAT_{t+1} + r_{WACC} \times FCF_t$
Expected amount of earnings next period given current earnings: $(1 + r_{WACC}) \times NOPAT_t$

12.4 Adding $r_{WACC} \times FCF_t$ captures earnings that may reasonably be expected to accrue outside of the firm's operations as a result of the reinvestment of the prior year's distribution. This occurs because if a distribution is made, there will be fewer assets remaining in place that can be used to earn in the subsequent period and the party (debt or equity holder) receiving the distribution would be able to invest that distribution elsewhere at an equivalent rate of return.

12.7 Accounting choices should not affect valuation because the underlying economic transaction has not changed and, so, economic value will be unchanged! An important feature of the accounting-based valuation models is that they continue to give the same answer with alternative accounting methods or if earnings are moved to earlier/later time periods (i.e., there is income shifting due to the choice of accounting method).

12.8 AOIGM anchors the valuation on capitalized operating income of the next period $\left(\frac{NOPAT_1}{r_{WACC}}\right)$, which is affected by choice of accounting methods. Future *AOIG* is the adjustment to this valuation to counter the effect that accounting rules and procedures have on this valuation anchor.

12.11 In AOIGM, the continuing value equals the expected difference between intrinsic value and capitalized earnings from operations (*NOPAT*) at the horizon.

12.12

$$V_0 = \frac{1}{r_{WACC}} \times \left[NOPAT_1 + \sum_{t=1}^{\infty}\left(\frac{NOPAT_{t+1} + r_{WACC} \times FCF_t - (1+r_{WACC}) \times NOPAT_t}{(1+r_{WACC})^t}\right)\right]$$

$$= \frac{1}{r_{WACC}} \times \left[NOPAT_1 + \sum_{t=1}^{5}\left(\frac{AOIG_{t+1}}{(1+r_{WACC})^t}\right) + \frac{1}{(1+r_{WACC})^5} \times \left(\frac{AOIG_6 \times (1+g)}{r_{WACC} - g}\right)\right] \quad (12.5)$$

In Equation 12.5, the term capturing the first five realizations of *AOIG* (through period 6) is referred to as being within the forecast horizon because the contribution of these *AOIG*s to value will be calculated using explicit forecasts of *AIOG*s for each year.

12.14

EXHIBIT 12.9 Abnormal Operating Income Growth Model ($ Millions)

Required rate of return (r_{WACC}) 5.30%

Time Period	5/27/2018	5/26/2019	5/31/2020	5/30/2021	5/29/2022	5/28/2023	5/26/2024
Forecasted sales	$15,740.4	$17,224.4	$17,746.9	$17,637.8	$17,867.1	$18,090.4	$18,307.5
NOPAT		2,122.0	2,186.4	2,195.9	2,254.8	2,283.0	2,310.4
NOA	25,035.4	26,291.0	25,998.1	26,854.2	27,786.8	28,120.3	28,457.7
ΔNOA		1,255.6	−292.9	856.1	932.7	333.4	337.4
FCF (*NOPAT* − Δ*NOA*)		866.5	2,479.3	1,339.8	1,322.2	1,949.6	1,973.0
$NOPAT_t$		2,122.0	2,186.4	2,195.9	2,254.8	2,283.0	2,310.4
$AOIG_t$ $[NOPAT_t + r_{WACC} \times FCF_{t-1} - (1 + r_{WACC}) \times NOPAT_{t-1}]$			−2.2	25.0	13.5	−21.2	9.7
Growth in *AOIG*				−1,253.97%	−45.83%	−256.84%	−145.77%
Discount factor $(1 + r_{WACC})^{t-1}$			1.0530	1.1088	1.1676	1.2295	1.2946
Present value of $AOIG_t$			−2.1	22.6	11.6	−17.3	7.5
Sum of present value of $AOIG_t$		22.3					
Continuing value							
AOIG at horizon							9.8
Capitalized							240.0
Present value of continuing value		185.4					
Total to be capitalized		2,329.8					
Operating value	$43,957.7						

CHAPTER 13

13.1	In order to determine the value of the equity ownership, we subtract the value of debt. This is often straightforward because debt is often shown in the balance sheet at an amount approximating market value. When the debt is not shown at fair value, information to adjust the carrying value to fair value is provided within the financial statement footnotes.
13.2	We need to adjust the value of debt for the interest tax shield because, for an equity holder, the existence of debt will cause a reduction in taxes when the interest expense is deducted.
13.2	We treat the interest tax shield as a financial effect; viewing the net value of debt as including the value of the interest tax shield. Most finance textbooks refer to this approach as the adjusted present value (APV) method. We determine the unlevered value of the operations to avoid changes in operating value with changes in the value of the interest tax shield. Our weighted average cost of capital for operations is the unlevered cost of capital.
13.6	Dividend discount model: $$V_0^{Eq} = \frac{FCF_1^{Eq}}{(1+r_{Eq})} + \frac{FCF_2^{Eq}}{(1+r_{Eq})^2} + \frac{FCF_3^{Eq}}{(1+r_{Eq})^3} + \frac{FCF_4^{Eq}}{(1+r_{Eq})^4} + \ldots = \sum_{t=1}^{\infty}\left(\frac{FCF_t^{Eq}}{(1+r_{Eq})^t}\right) \quad (13.1)$$
13.6	$$FCF_t^{Eq} = CI_t + CSE_{t-1} - CSE_t = CI_t - \Delta CSE_t \quad (13.2)$$
13.6	Residual earnings model (REM): $$V_0^{Eq} = CSE_0 + \sum_{t=1}^{\infty}\left(\frac{CI_t - r_{Eq} \times CSE_{t-1}}{(1+r_{Eq})^t}\right) = CSE_0 + \sum_{t=1}^{\infty}\left(\frac{RE_t}{(1+r_{Eq})^t}\right) \quad (13.3)$$
13.7	Abnormal earnings growth model (AEGM): $$V_0^{Eq} = \frac{1}{r_{Eq}} \times \left[CI_1 + \sum_{t=1}^{\infty}\left(\frac{CI_{t+1} + r_{Eq} \times FCF_t^{Eq} - (1+r_{Eq}) \times CI_t}{(1+r_{Eq})^t}\right)\right] = \frac{1}{r_{Eq}} \times \left[CI_1 + \sum_{t=1}^{\infty}\left(\frac{AEG_{t+1}}{(1+r_{Eq})^t}\right)\right] \quad (13.4)$$
13.7	When we value the operating activities, we use the weighted average cost of capital for operations (r_{WACC}), which would not be expected to change from period to period unless the risk of the operating activities is expected to change. To utilize an equity valuation model would require an assumption that equity risk will be constant in future periods. $$r_{Eq} = r_{WACC} + \frac{V^{NFL}}{V^{Eq}} \times (r_{WACC} - r_D) \quad (13.5)$$ In Equation 13.5, the cost of capital of equity depends on the leverage of the firm. Unless we are willing to assume that the leverage will be constant in the future, we cannot assume a constant cost of equity going forward.

13.10	If using analysts' forecasts, recognize that the firm is usually not stable (i.e., in steady state) at the horizon. Also, consider that the known optimistic bias in analysts' forecasts may lead to inflated estimates of equity value.
13.11	Midyear adjustment – Assume that payoffs occur evenly during the year by multiplying the estimated value by a midyear adjustment factor defined as $(1 + r_{WACC})^{0.5}$.
13.12	Adjusting date of valuation – Assume no other new information would arrive by multiplying the estimated value at the balance sheet date by $(1 + r_{WACC})$ for the time elapsed [e.g., if 11 months $(1 + r_{WACC})^{11/12}$].
13.12	Final steps in valuation: 1. Adjust for a midyear payoff 2. Adjust the valuation date 3. Adjust for the value of debt (including interest tax shield) 4. Estimate the per-share value: divide the estimated value of equity by current shares outstanding
13.14	Sensitivity analysis is the process of altering different assumptions to determine effect on the value estimate. (We usually focus on sales growth, *PM*, *ATO*, and cost of capital.)

CHAPTER 14

14.1	Steady state is reached when all of the following occur: 1. Sales are growing at a constant rate. 2. The net operating profit after tax (*NOPAT*) from each dollar of sales is constant (i.e., operating profit margin [*PM*], which is equal to $NOPAT_t/Sales_t$, is constant). 3. The net operating assets (*NOA*) required for each dollar of sales is constant (i.e., operating asset turnover [*ATO*], which is equal to $Sales_t/NOA_{t-1}$, is constant). That is, steady state is reached when everything (profitability and resources) is growing at the sales growth rate.
14.2	*AOIG* reaches a constant growth rate 1 year later than *FCF* and *ROPI* because the calculation of $AOIG_t$ is based on two prior estimates of *NOA* because FCF_{t-1}, which is part of the calculation of $AOIG_t$ equals $NOPAT_{t-1}$ less change in NOA_{t-1} (which is NOA_{t-1} less NOA_{t-2}). This becomes clear when we recognize the fact that *AOIG* equals the change in *ROPI*. $$AOIG_T = ROPI_T - ROPI_{T-1}$$
14.4	As a hybrid, in implementing the DCF valuation model, a multiples approach is sometimes suggested for calculating continuing value via an *EBITDA* multiple.
14.4	Although we have shown that, mathematically, the models are equivalent, this does not mean that they will have similar ease of use in all situations. Evaluation of the models centers on the idea that the farther into the future, we forecast the less confidence we have in our estimates. That is, we would prefer less reliance on the forecast of growth at the horizon.
14.6	Anchors for valuation: 1. DCF does not have an anchor. 2. ROIM anchors on book value (NOA_0) and often the subsequent forecasts within horizon earnings capture a lot of value. 3. AOIGM anchors on capitalized earnings ($NOPAT_1/r_{WACC}$), which generally captures a lot of value.
14.7	If implementation of the models is not done correctly and if steady state is not reached, the estimate of operating value will differ. The common instructions to take the last explicit forecast, grow it, and then capitalize it are only appropriate if steady state has been reached. Essentially, when forecasting, we must forecast to a horizon that is sufficiently far in the future to ensure that we are comfortable with the assumption that the forecasted growth rate is sustainable in the very long run. A frequently made assumption is that, eventually, the steady state growth rate will be equal to an assumed long-term economic growth rate.

14.8	The extension of the horizon is normally implemented by assuming a fade pattern after the explicit forecasting horizon.
14.9	Market multiples can be split into two groups: those that are restricted forms of the models and those that are ad hoc. For multiples that are restricted forms of theoretically sound valuation models, we can evaluate the restrictions to determine our comfort with the necessary assumptions. For those that do not tie to valuation models, we must consider why a payoff based valuation model would not be used.
14.9	Assuming the sum of all future *AOIG* equals zero, we find that sorting on the forward price-to-earnings (PE) ratio captures the inverse of risk: $$\frac{V_0}{NOPAT_1} = \frac{1}{r_{WACC}}$$
14.10	Assuming long-term growth and FCF_1 are both equal to zero, we find that sorting on the PE divided by short-term earnings growth (PEG) ratio also captures the inverse of risk: $$\frac{V_0}{NOPAT_2 - NOPAT_1} = \frac{V_0 / NOPAT_1}{NOPAT_2 - NOPAT_1 / NOPAT_1} = \frac{ForwardPE}{EarningsGrowth} = \frac{1}{r_{WACC}^2}$$

NOTES